os Ordnance Survey

C000022737

STREET ATLAS
Staffordshire

Contents

III Key to map symbols

IV Key to map pages

VI Administrative and post code boundaries

1 Street maps

282 Extra-large-scale maps of town centres

282 Hanley   284 Newcastle-under-Lyme
283 Longton

285 Town maps

285 Congleton   286 Chesterfield
285 Macclesfield   287 Derby
286 Buxton   287 Matlock

288 Index of hospitals, railway stations, schools, shopping centres, street names and universities

PHILIP'S

First edition published 1995
First colour edition published 1998
Reprinted in 2000 by

George Philip Ltd, a division of
Octopus Publishing Group Ltd
2-4 Heron Quays
London E14 4JP

ISBN 0-540-07549-3 (hardback)
ISBN 0-540-07550-7 (spiral)

To the best of the Publishers' knowledge, the information in this atlas
was correct at the time of going to press. No responsibility can be
accepted for any errors or their consequences.

The representation in this atlas of a road, track or path is no evidence
of the existence of a right of way.

**The mapping between pages 1 and 287 (inclusive) in this atlas is
derived from Ordnance Survey® Large Scale and Landranger®
mapping, and revised using Land-line® data.**

Ordnance Survey, Land-line and Landranger are registered trade marks
of Ordnance Survey, the national mapping agency of Great Britain.

Printed and bound in Spain by Cayfosa

Digital Data

The exceptionally high-quality mapping
found in this book is available as digital
data in TIFF format, which is easily
convertible to other bit-mapped (raster)
image formats.

The index is also available in digital form
as a standard database table. It contains
all the details found in the printed index
together with the National Grid reference
for the map square in which each entry
is named and feature codes for places
of interest in eight categories such as
education and health.

For further information and to discuss
your requirements, please contact
Philip's on 0171 531 8440 or
george.philip@philips-maps.co.uk

III

Motorway (with junction number)	
Primary route (dual carriageway and single)	
A road (dual carriageway and single)	
B road (dual carriageway and single)	
Minor road (dual carriageway and single)	
Other minor road	
Road under construction	
Pedestrianised area	
County and Unitary Authority boundaries	
Railway	
Tramway, miniature railway	
Rural track, private road or narrow road in urban area	
Gate or obstruction to traffic (restrictions may not apply at all times or to all vehicles)	
Path, bridleway, byway open to all traffic, road used as a public path	

The representation in this atlas of a road, track or path is no evidence of the existence of a right of way

170

52

Adjoining page indicators

267

The map area within the pink band is shown at a larger scale on the page indicated by the red block and arrow

Acad	**Academy**	Mon	**Monument**
Cemy	**Cemetery**	Mus	**Museum**
C Ctr	**Civic Centre**	Obsy	**Observatory**
CH	**Club House**	Pal	**Royal Palace**
Coll	**College**	PH	**Public House**
Ent	**Enterprise**	Recn Gd	**Recreation Ground**
Ex H	**Exhibition Hall**	Resr	**Reservoir**
Ind Est	**Industrial Estate**	Ret Pk	**Retail Park**
Inst	**Institute**	Sch	**School**
Ct	**Law Court**	Sh Ctr	**Shopping Centre**
L Ctr	**Leisure Centre**	Sta	**Station**
LC	**Level Crossing**	TH	**Town Hall/House**
Liby	**Library**	Trad Est	**Trading Estate**
Mkt	**Market**	Univ	**University**
Meml	**Memorial**	YH	**Youth Hostel**

British Rail station	
Metrolink station	
Underground station	
Docklands Light Railway station	
Tyne and Wear Metro	
Private railway station	
Bus, coach station	
Ambulance station	
Coastguard station	
Fire station	
Police station	
Accident and Emergency entrance to hospital	
Hospital	
Church, place of worship	
Information centre (open all year)	
Parking, Park and Ride	
Post Office	
Important buildings, schools, colleges, universities and hospitals	Prim Sch
Water name	River Medway
Stream	
River or canal (minor and major)	
Water	
Tidal water	
Woods	
Houses	
Non-Roman antiquity	House
Roman antiquity	VILLA

■ The dark grey border on the inside edge of some pages indicates that the mapping does not continue onto the adjacent page

■ The small numbers around the edges of the maps identify the 1 kilometre National Grid lines

The scale of the maps is 5.52 cm to 1 km (3½ inches to 1 mile)

0	¼	½	¾	1 mile
0	250m	500m	750m	1 kilometre

The scale of the map on pages numbered in red is 11.04 cm to 1 km (7 inches to 1 mile)

0	220 yards	440 yards	660 yards	½ mile
0	125m	250m	375m	½ kilometre

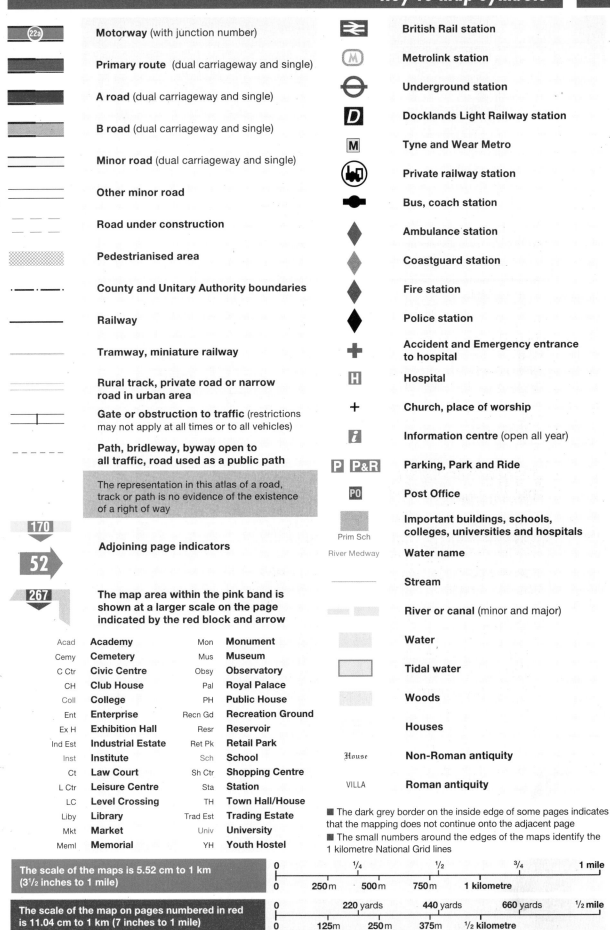

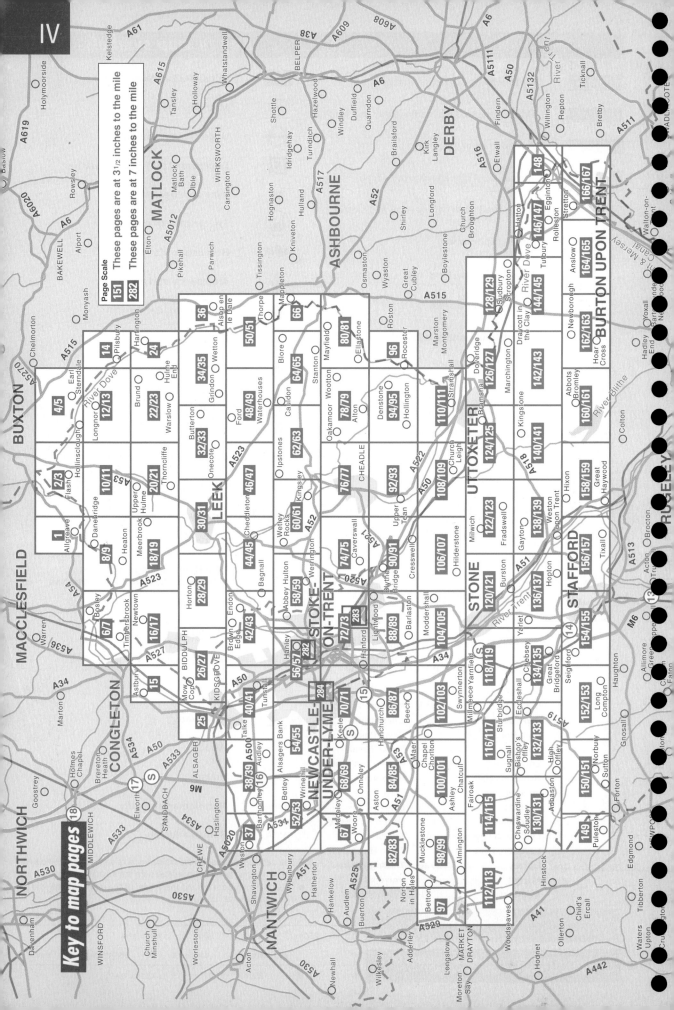

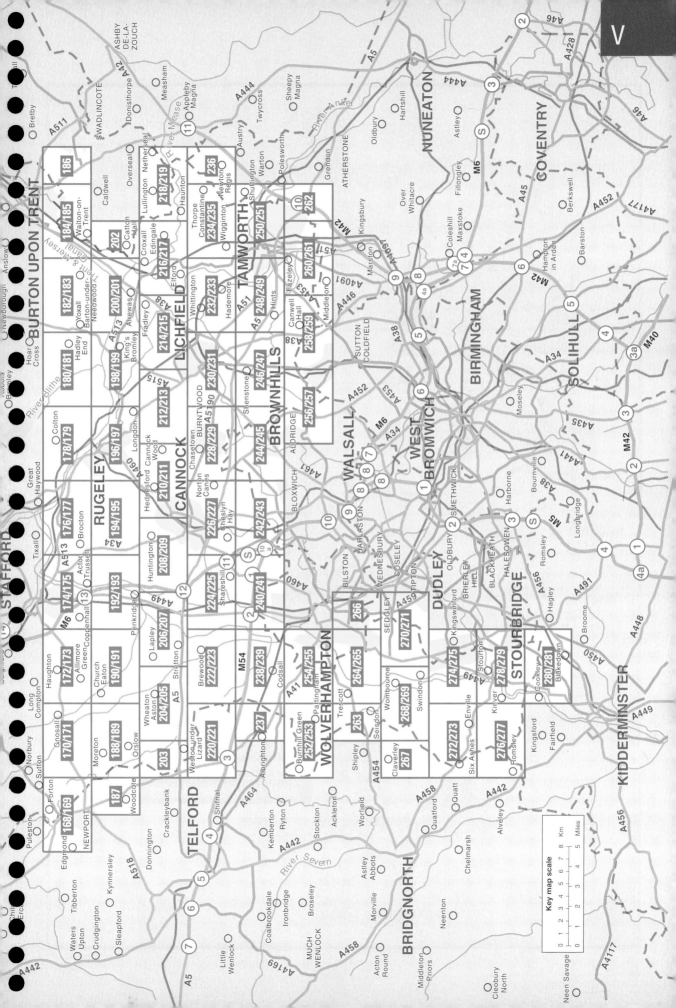

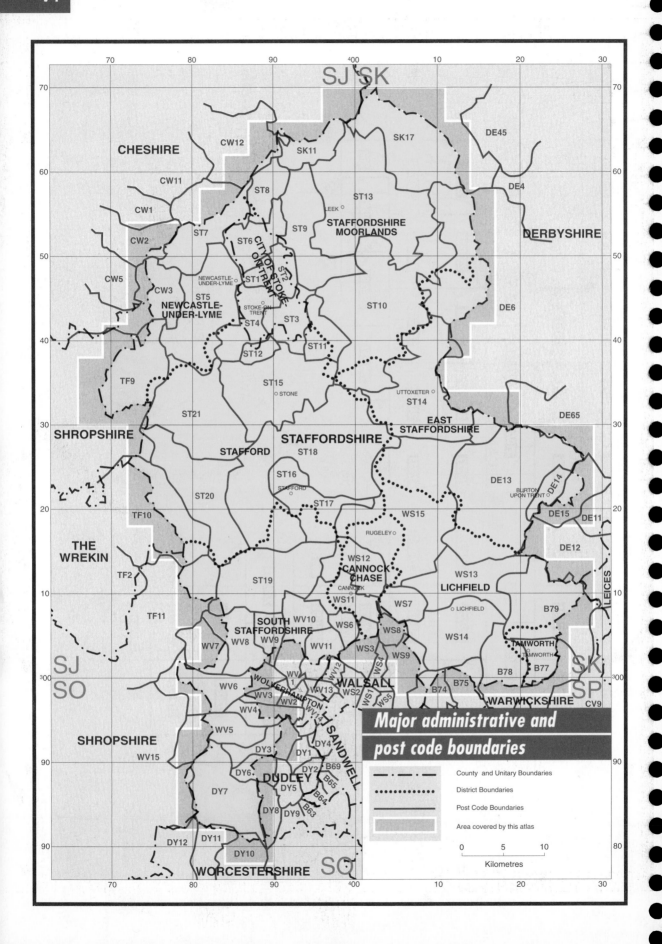

Major administrative and post code boundaries

	County and Unitary Boundaries
	District Boundaries
	Post Code Boundaries
	Area covered by this atlas

0   5   10
Kilometres

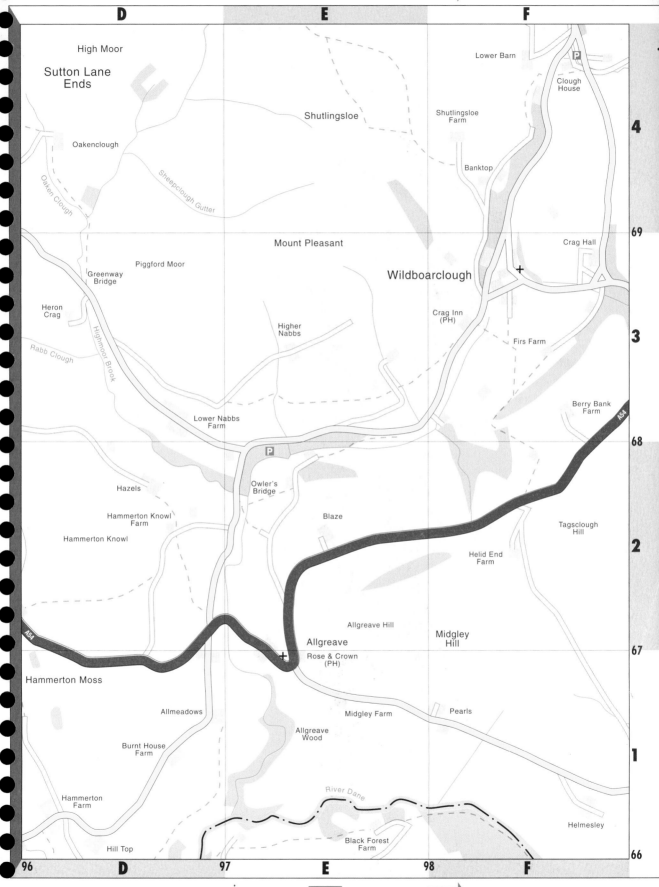

2 →

D E F

High Moor

Sutton Lane
Ends

Lower Barn

Clough
House

Shutlingsloe

Shutlingsloe
Farm

4

Oakenclough

Banktop

Sheepclough Gutter

69

Oaken Clough

Mount Pleasant

Crag Hall

Piggford Moor

Wildboarclough

Greenway
Bridge

Crag Inn
(PH)

3

Heron
Crag

Higher
Nabbs

Firs Farm

Rabb Clough

Highmoor Brook

Berry Bank
Farm

Lower Nabbs
Farm

A54

68

Hazels

Owler's
Bridge

Blaze

Tagsclough
Hill

Hammerton Knowl
Farm

Helid End
Farm

2

Hammerton Knowl

Allgreave Hill

Midgley
Hill

67

A54

Allgreave

Rose & Crown
(PH)

Hammerton Moss

Allmeadows

Midgley Farm

Pearls

Allgreave
Wood

Burnt House
Farm

1

Hammerton
Farm

River Dane

Helmesley

Hill Top

Black Forest
Farm

66

96 D 97 E 98 F

↓ 9

2 →

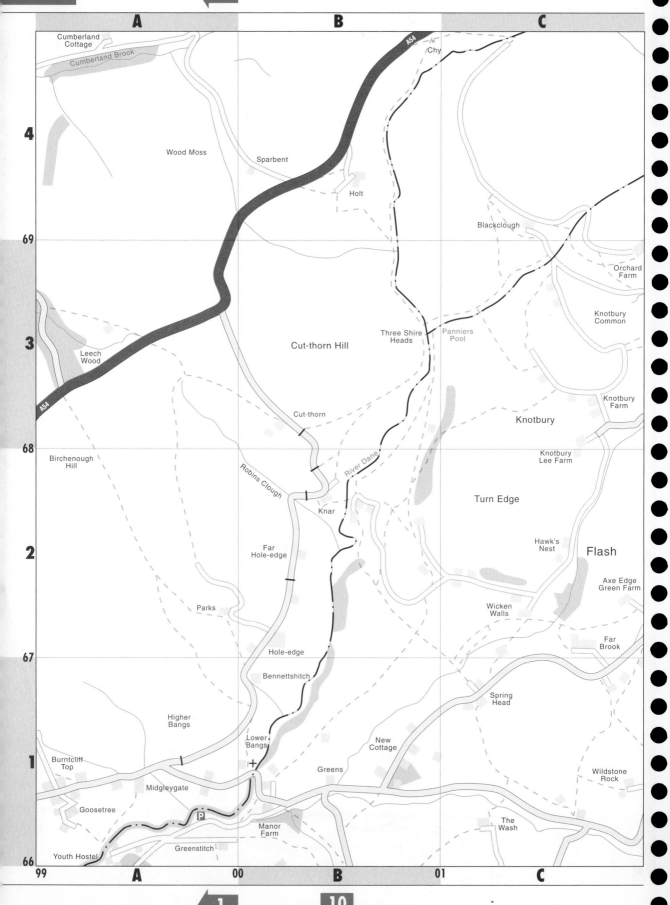

A   B   C

4

69

3

68

2

67

1

66

99   A   00   B   01   C

Cumberland
Cottage
Cumberland Brook

Wood Moss

Sparbent

A54

Chy

Holt

Blackclough

Orchard
Farm

Knotbury
Common

Leech
Wood

Cut-thorn Hill

Three Shire
Heads

Panniers
Pool

Knotbury
Farm

A54

Cut-thorn

Knotbury

Birchenough
Hill

Robins Clough

River Dane

Knotbury
Lee Farm

Knar

Turn Edge

Far
Hole-edge

Hawk's
Nest

Flash

Axe Edge
Green Farm

Parks

Wicken
Walls

Far
Brook

Hole-edge

Bennettshitch

Spring
Head

Higher
Bangs

Lower
Bangs

New
Cottage

Wildstone
Rock

Burntcliff
Top

Midgleygate

Greens

P

Goosetree

The
Wash

Manor
Farm

Youth Hostel

Greenstitch

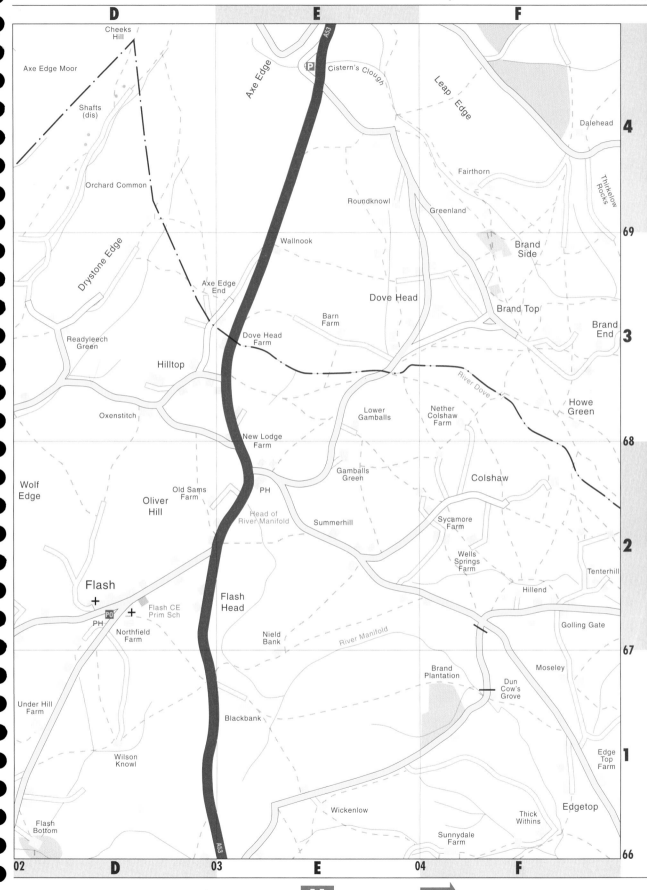

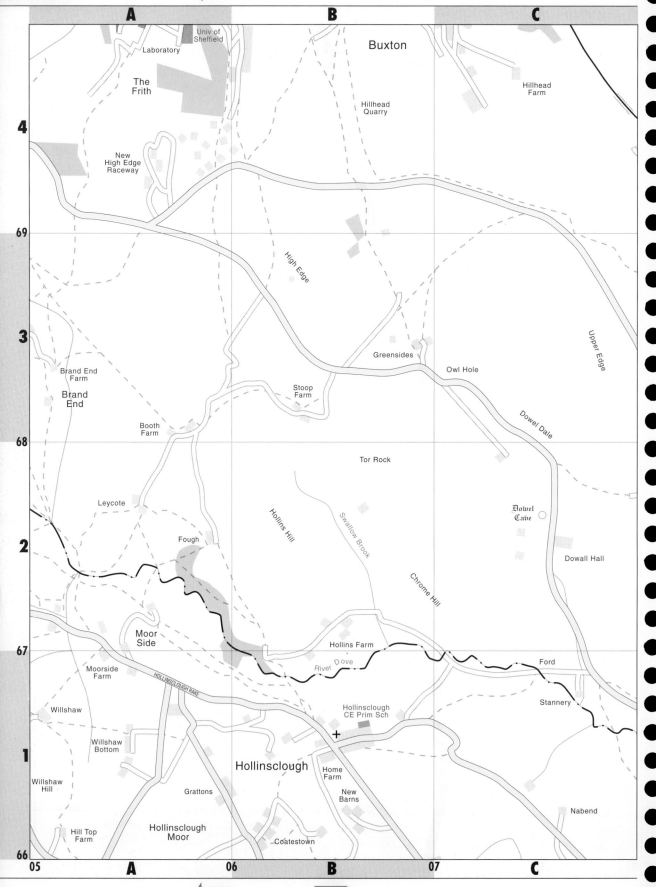

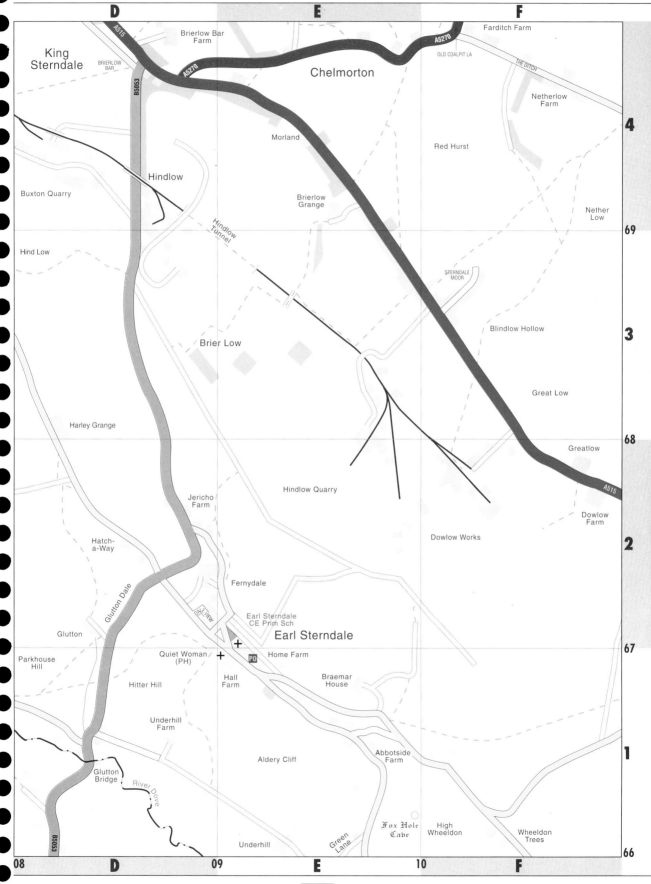

King Sterndale

Brierlow Bar Farm

A515

BRIERLOW BAR

B5053

A5270

Chelmorton

Farditch Farm

OLD COALPIT LA

THE DITCH

Netherlow Farm

Hindlow

Morland

Red Hurst

Buxton Quarry

Brierlow Grange

Nether Low

Hindlow Tunnel

Hind Low

Brier Low

STERNDALE MOOR

Blindlow Hollow

Harley Grange

Great Low

Greatlow

A515

Jericho Farm

Hindlow Quarry

Dowlow Farm

Hatch-a-Way

Dowlow Works

Glutton Dale

Fernydale

DALE VIEW

Earl Sterndale CE Prim Sch

Earl Sterndale

Glutton

Quiet Woman (PH)

PO

Home Farm

Parkhouse Hill

Hitter Hill

Hall Farm

Braemar House

Underhill Farm

Aldery Cliff

Abbotside Farm

Glutton Bridge

River Dove

Green Lane

Underhill

Fox Hole Cave

High Wheeldon

Wheeldon Trees

B5053

4

69

3

68

2

67

1

66

08 D 09 E 10 F

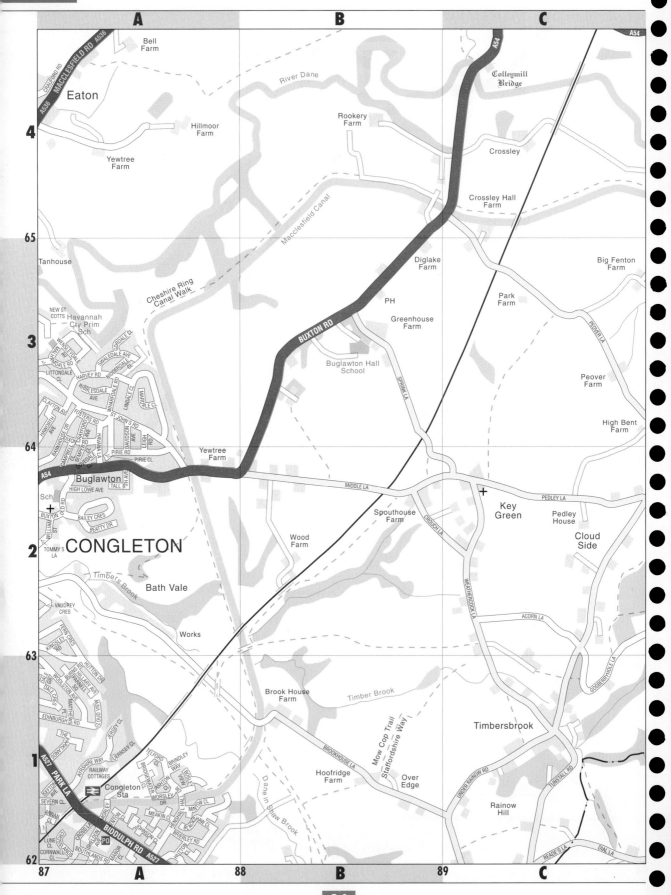

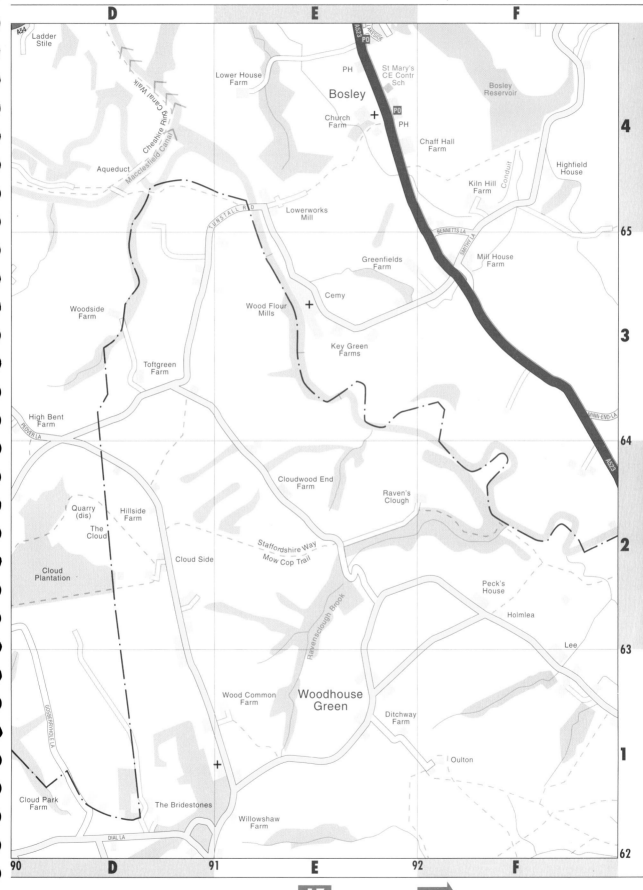

7

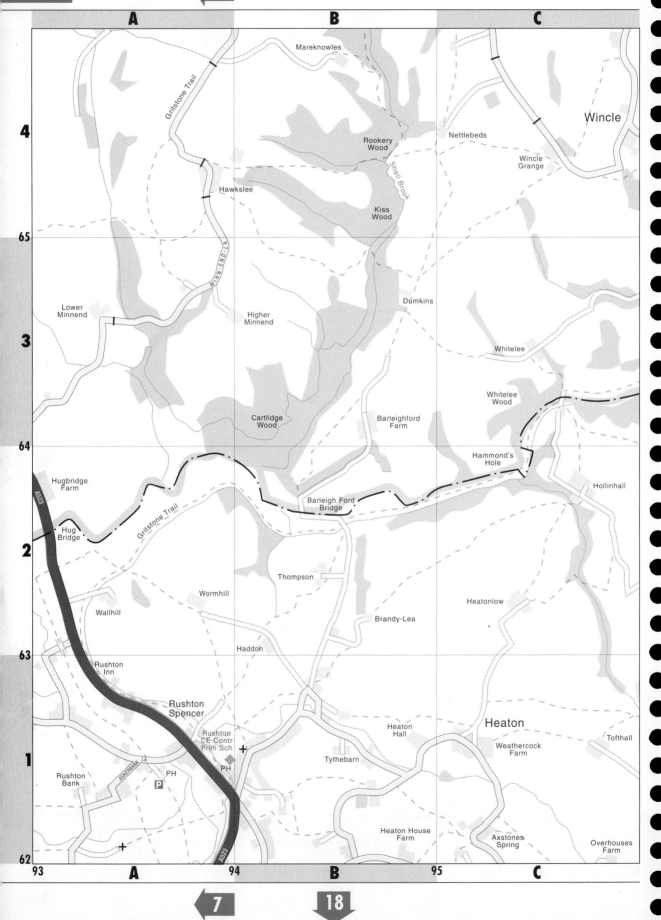

7
18

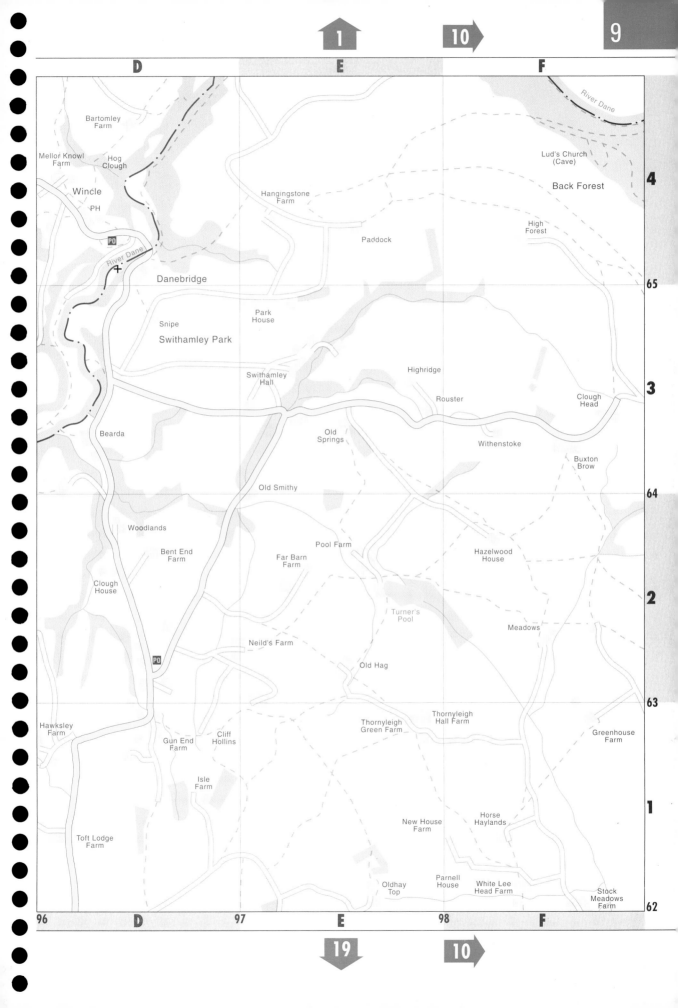

A **B** **C**

Gradbach

Bradley Howel

Middle Edge

Green Gutter Head

Sniddles

Gradbach Hill

Little Hillend

4

Gradbach Wood

Sniddles Head Farm

Cloughead

65

Black Brook

Moss Top

Black Forest

Moss End Farm

Gib Torr Rocks

Goldsitch Moss

3

Roach End

Goldsitch House

Blackbank

64

Bald Stone

Newstone Farm

Brownsett

Shaw Bottom

Hazel Barrow

2

Shawside

Shaw House

Shafts (dis)

Roche Grange

Shawtop

63

Harpersend

Five Clouds

The Roaches

Roach Side Farm

Blue Hills

Newsett Farm

1

Summerhill

Pheasants Clough

Ramshaw Rocks

Roach House

P

Rockhall

Well Farm

A53

62

99 **A** 00 **B** 01 **C**

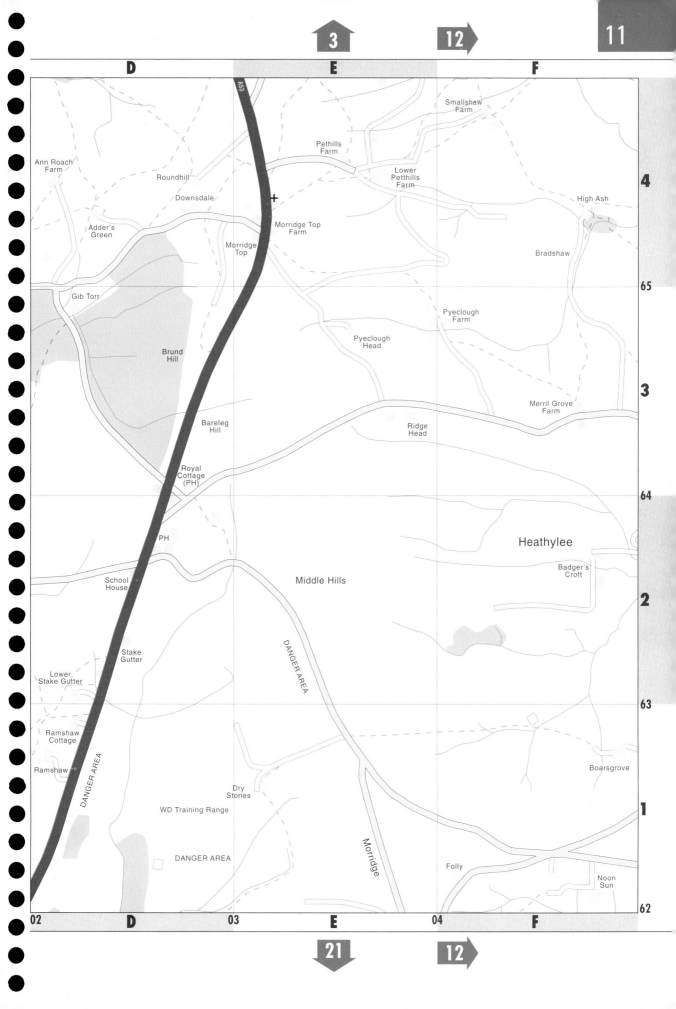

D E F

Smallshaw Farm

Ann Roach Farm

Roundhill

Downsdale

Pethills Farm

Lower Petthills Farm

4

High Ash

Adder's Green

Morridge Top Farm

Morridge Top

Bradshaw

Gib Torr

65

Pyeclough Farm

Brund Hill

Pyeclough Head

3

Bareleg Hill

Ridge Head

Merril Grove Farm

Royal Cottage (PH)

64

PH

Heathylee

Badger's Croft

School House

Middle Hills

2

Stake Gutter

Lower Stake Gutter

DANGER AREA

63

Ramshaw Cottage

Boarsgrove

Ramshaw

DANGER AREA

Dry Stones

1

WD Training Range

Morridge

Folly

Noon Sun

DANGER AREA

A53

62

02 D 03 E 04 F

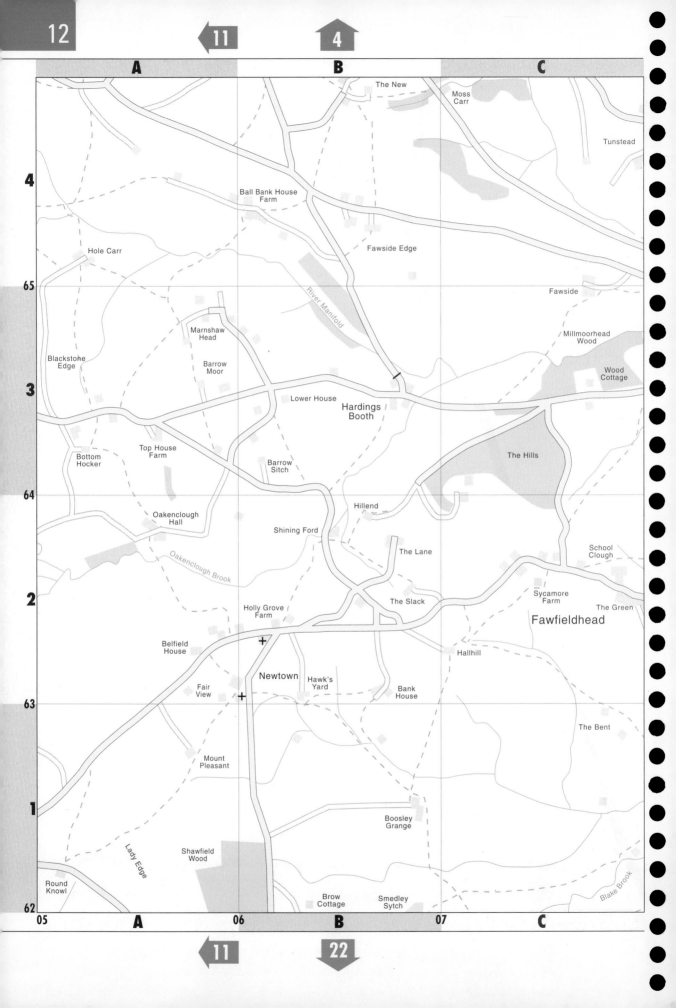

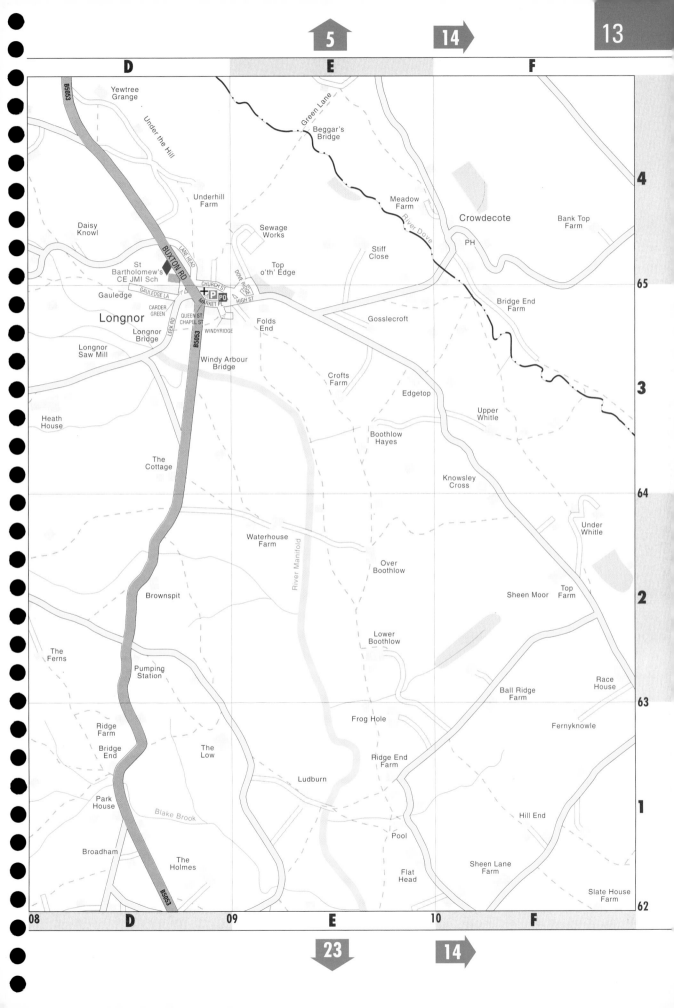

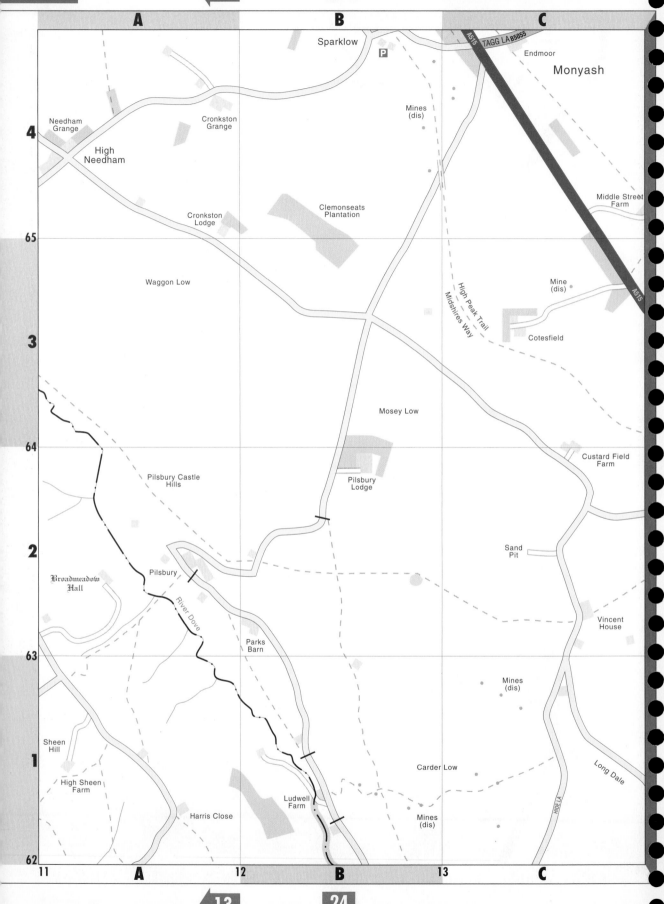

A　　　　　　B　　　　　　C

Sparklow

🅿

A515 TAGG LA B5055

Endmoor

Monyash

Mines
(dis)

Needham
Grange

Cronkston
Grange

4

High
Needham

Clemonseats
Plantation

Middle Street
Farm

Cronkston
Lodge

65

Waggon Low

Mine
(dis)

High Peak Trail
Midshires Way

Cotesfield

A515

3

Mosey Low

Custard Field
Farm

64

Pilsbury Castle
Hills

Pilsbury
Lodge

2

Broadmeadow
Hall

Pilsbury

Sand
Pit

Vincent
House

River Dove

Parks
Barn

63

Mines
(dis)

Sheen
Hill

1

Carder Low

Long Dale

High Sheen
Farm

Ludwell
Farm

HIDE LA

Harris Close

Mines
(dis)

62

11　　　　　A　　　　12　　　　B　　　　13　　　　C

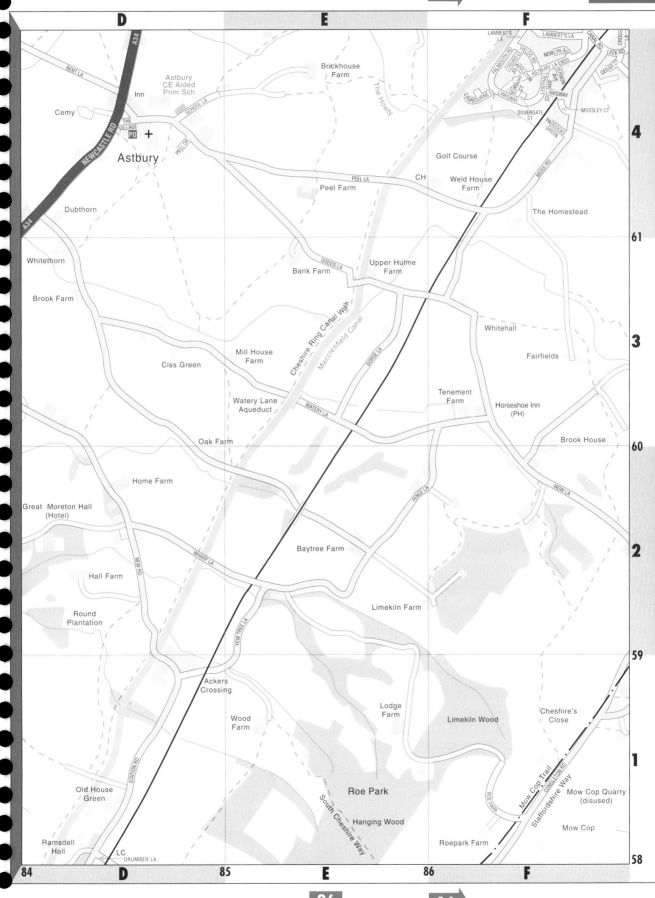

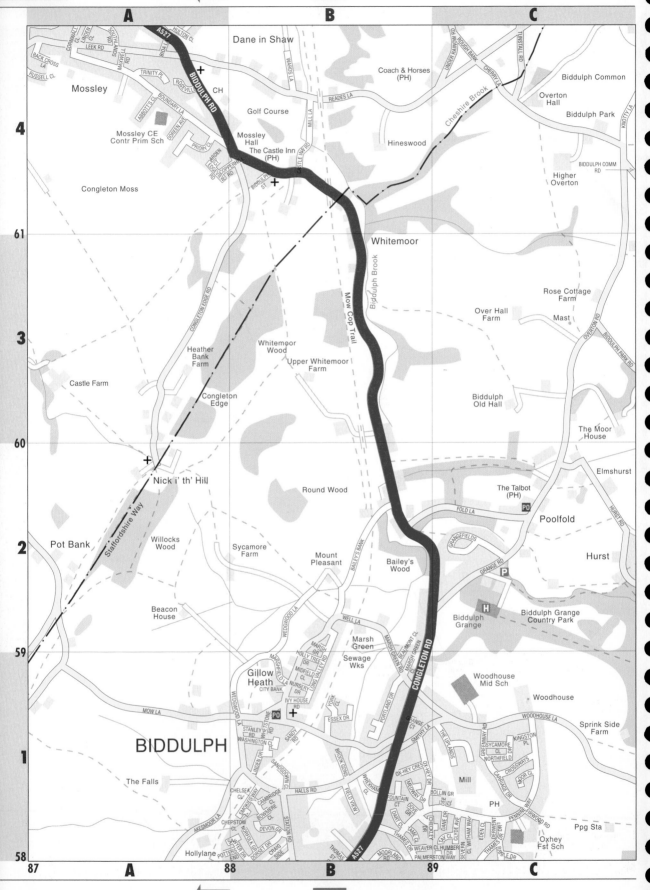

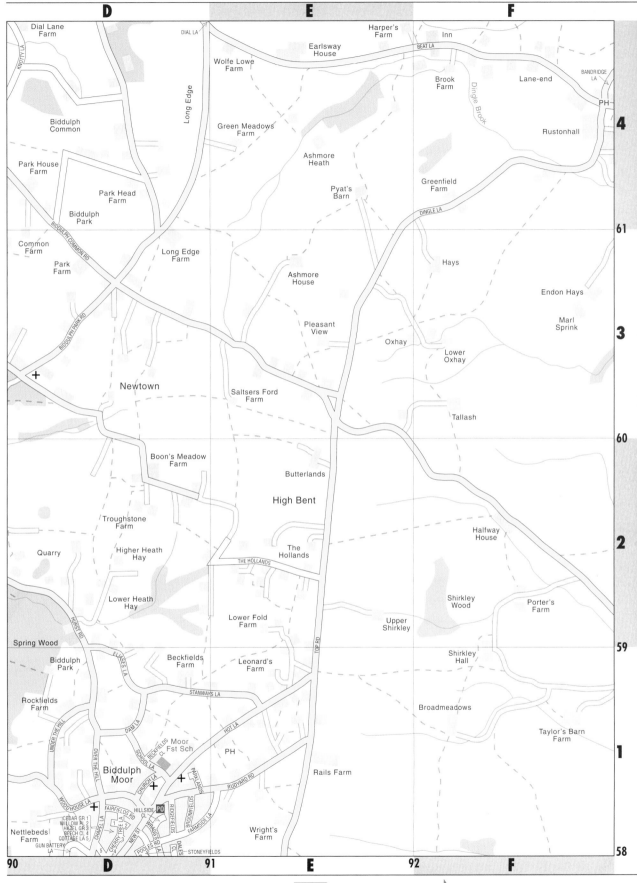

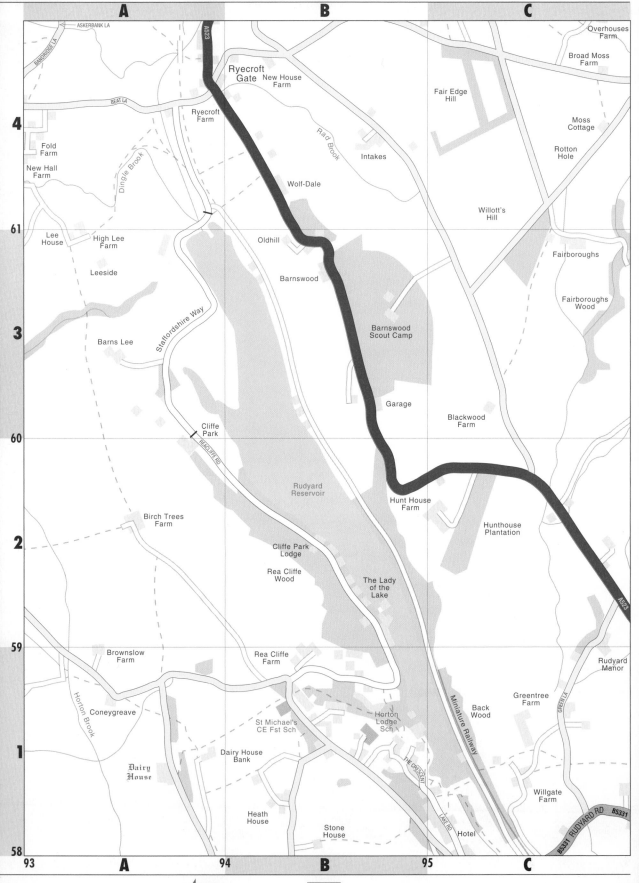

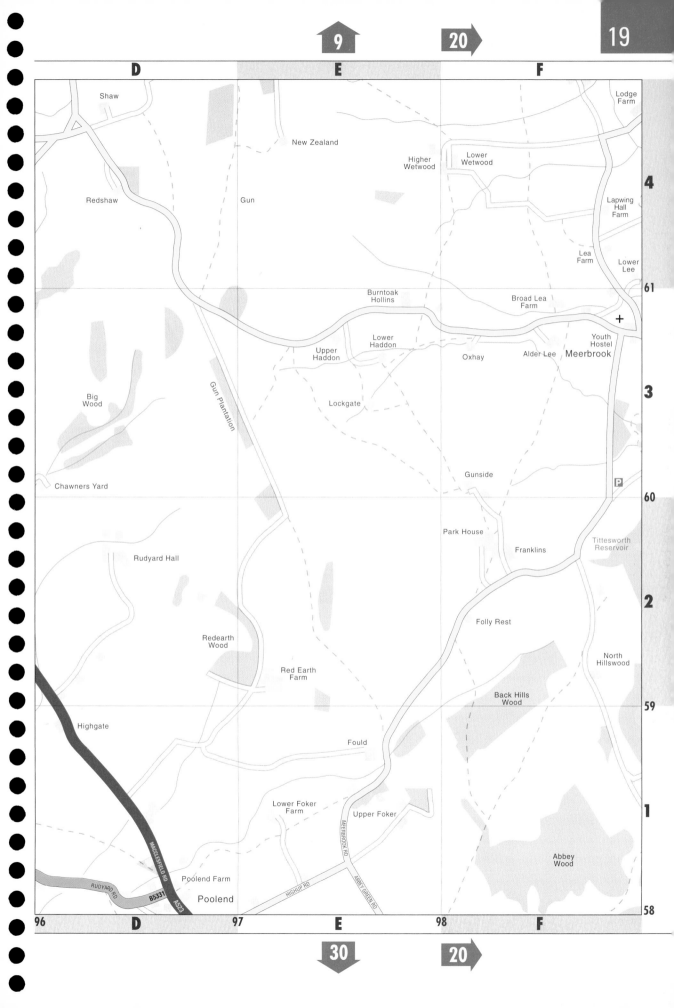

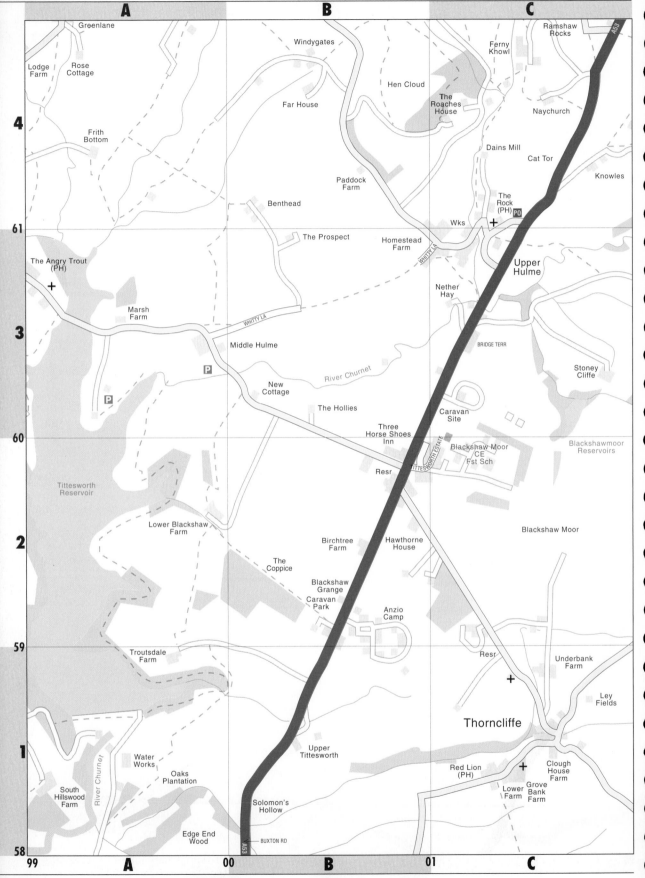

A   B   C

Greenlane

Lodge
Farm

Rose
Cottage

Windygates

Hen Cloud

Ferny
Khowl

Ramshaw
Rocks

A53

4

Far House

The
Roaches
House

Naychurch

Frith
Bottom

Paddock
Farm

Dains Mill

Cat Tor

Knowles

Benthead

The Rock
(PH)

PO

61

The Prospect

Homestead
Farm

Wks

WHITTY LA

The Angry Trout
(PH)

Upper
Hulme

Marsh
Farm

Nether
Hay

3

Middle Hulme

WHITTY LA

BRIDGE TERR

P

River Churnet

Stoney
Cliffe

New
Cottage

P

The Hollies

Caravan
Site

60

Three
Horse Shoes
Inn

Blackshaw Moor
CE
Fst Sch

Blackshawmoor
Reservoirs

Resr

TITTESWORTH ESTATE

Tittesworth
Reservoir

Lower Blackshaw
Farm

Birchtree
Farm

Hawthorne
House

Blackshaw Moor

2

The
Coppice

Blackshaw
Grange
Caravan
Park

Anzio
Camp

Troutsdale
Farm

Resr

Underbank
Farm

59

Thorncliffe

Ley
Fields

1

Water
Works

Upper
Tittesworth

Red Lion
(PH)

Clough
House
Farm

River Churnet

Oaks
Plantation

Lower
Farm

Grove
Bank
Farm

South
Hillswood
Farm

Solomon's
Hollow

Edge End
Wood

A53

BUXTON RD

58

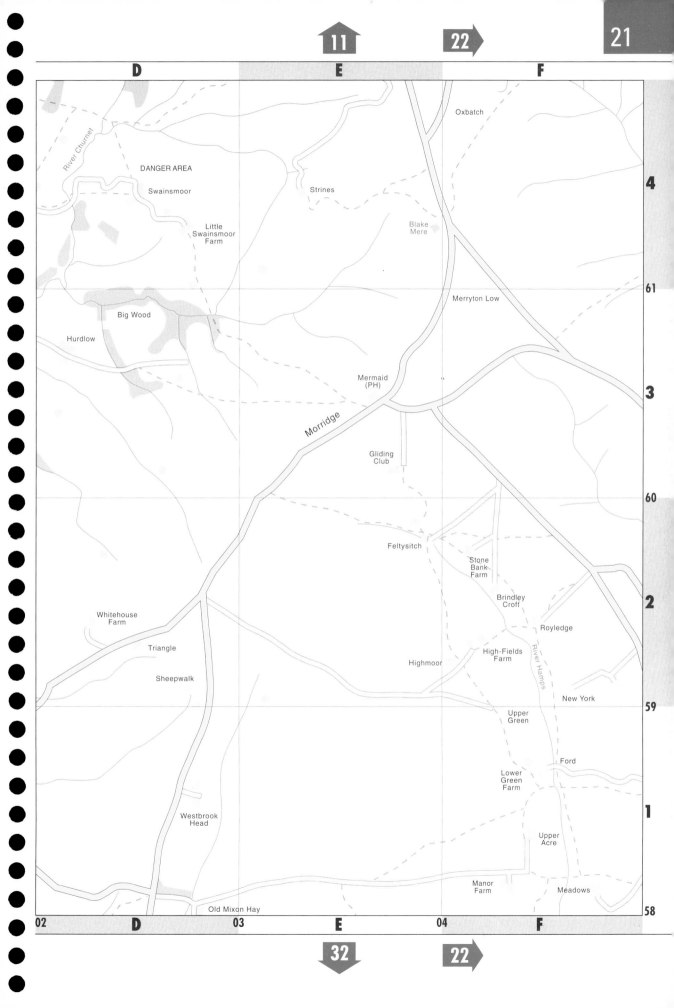

D E F

4

61

3

60

2

59

1

58

02 D 03 E 04 F

River Churnet

DANGER AREA

Swainsmoor

Oxbatch

Strines

Little
Swainsmoor
Farm

Blake
Mere

Merryton Low

Big Wood

Hurdlow

Mermaid
(PH)

Morridge

Gliding
Club

Feltysitch

Stone
Bank
Farm

Brindley
Croft

Whitehouse
Farm

Royledge

Triangle

High-Fields
Farm

River Hamps

Sheepwalk

Highmoor

New York

Upper
Green

Ford

Westbrook
Head

Lower
Green
Farm

Upper
Acre

Manor
Farm

Meadows

Old Mixon Hay

21
12

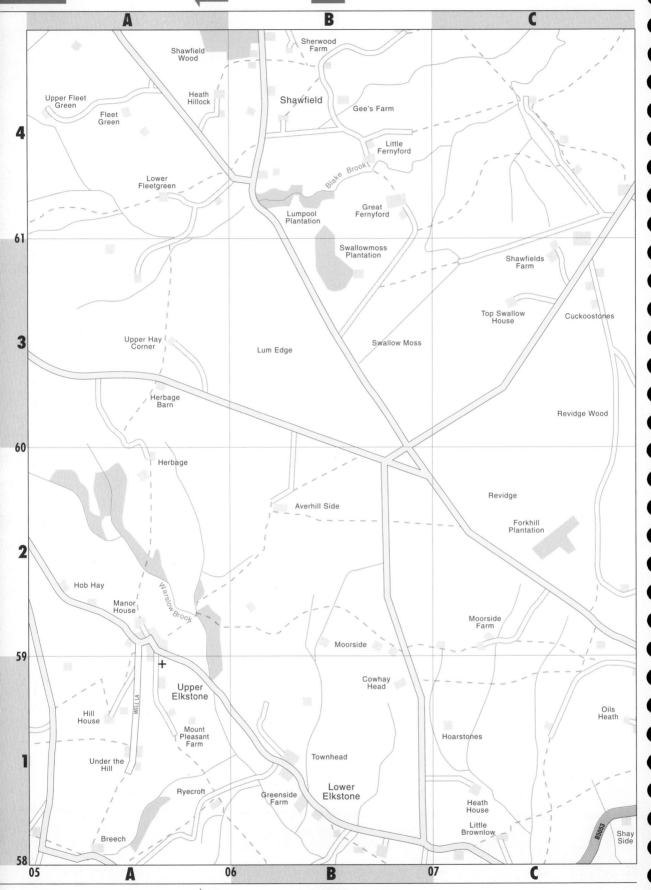

21
33

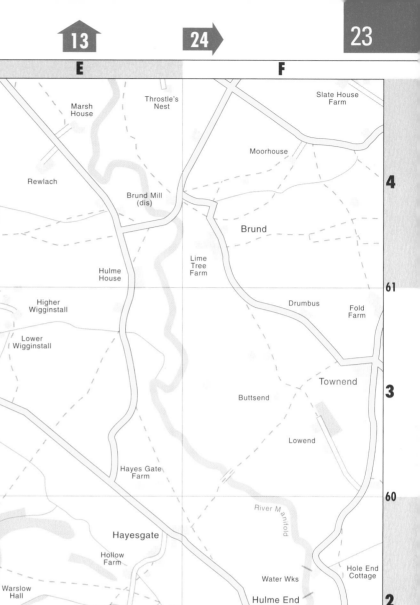

D E F

Moorside
Farm

Reaps Moor
Butcher's Arms
(PH)

Knowle
Farm

B5053

Marsh
House

Throstle's
Nest

Slate House
Farm

Moorhouse

Rewlach

Brund Mill
(dis)

Brund

4

Field
Farm

New
Road

Kirkham Yard
Farm

Hulme
House

Lime
Tree
Farm

61

Spout
Farm

Higher
Wigginstall

Drumbus

Fold
Farm

Lower
Wigginstall

Townend

3

Hayes Farm

Buttsend

Lowend

Hayes Gate
Farm

60

Hayeshead

River Manifold

Hayesgate

Hayes
Cottage

Hollow
Farm

Water Wks

Hole End
Cottage

Steps

Warslow
Hall

Hulme End

2

B5054

Upper
Brownhill

Clough
Head

Cowlow

P

Sycamore
Farm

Light
Railway
Hotel
(PH)

Manifold
CE Prim
Sch

B5054

Cliff
House

COWLOW LA

Copse
Field

59

Greyhound
Hotel
(PH)

Gap
Farm

STACEY CL

Westside
Mill

Endon
Cottage

Ind
Est

PO

CHURCH
TERR

BUTTS LA

Dale
Cottage

Manifold Way

THE DALE

Hobcroft
Farm

Ecton

1

Warslow

Dale
Bridge

Vicarage

Ivy
House
Farm

East Ecton

Villa Farm

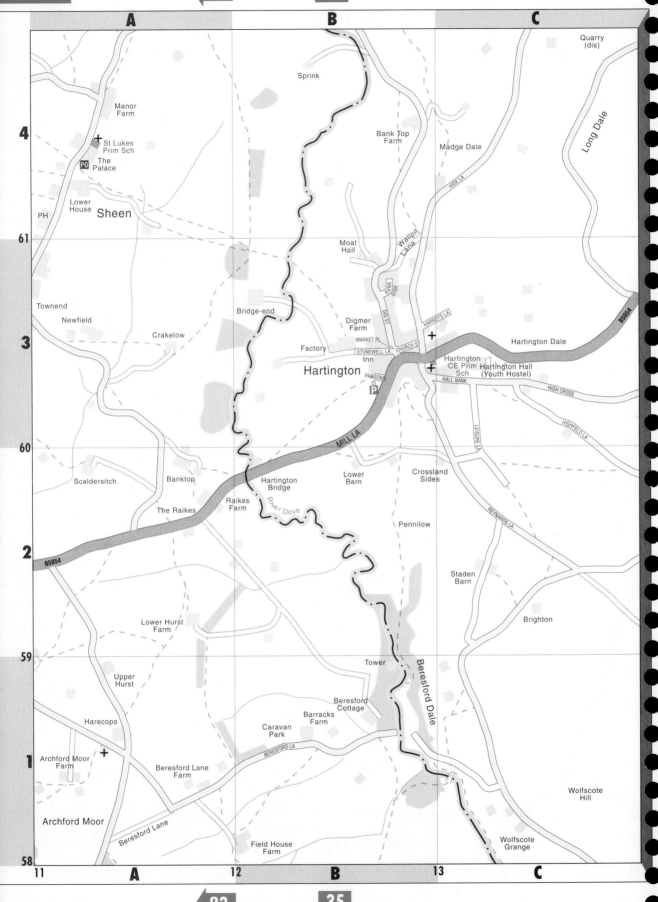

A B C

4
Manor Farm
St Lukes Prim Sch
PO The Palace
Lower House
Sheen
PH

Sprink

Bank Top Farm

Madge Dale

Long Dale

Quarry (dis)

HIDE LA

61
Townend
Newfield
Crakelow

Bridge-end

Moat Hall

Wallpit Lane

BANK SIDE

3
Factory
Hartington
Inn

Digmer Farm
MARKET PL
STONEWELL LA
CHURCH ST
DIG ST

HARROTS LA

Hartington Dale

B5054

Hartington CE Prim Sch
Hartington Hall (Youth Hostel)
PARSONS CL
P

HIGH CROSS
HALL BANK

60
Scaldersitch
Banktop
The Raikes
Raikes Farm
Hartington Bridge
River Dove

MILL LA

Lower Barn

Crossland Sides

LEISURE LA

HIGHFIELD LA

2
B5054

Pennilow

Staden Barn

REYNARDS LA

Brighton

59
Lower Hurst Farm

Upper Hurst

Tower

Beresford Cottage

Beresford Dale

1
Harecops
Archford Moor Farm
Beresford Lane Farm
Caravan Park
Barracks Farm
BERESFORD LA

Wolfscote Hill

Archford Moor
Beresford Lane
Field House Farm

Wolfscote Grange

58

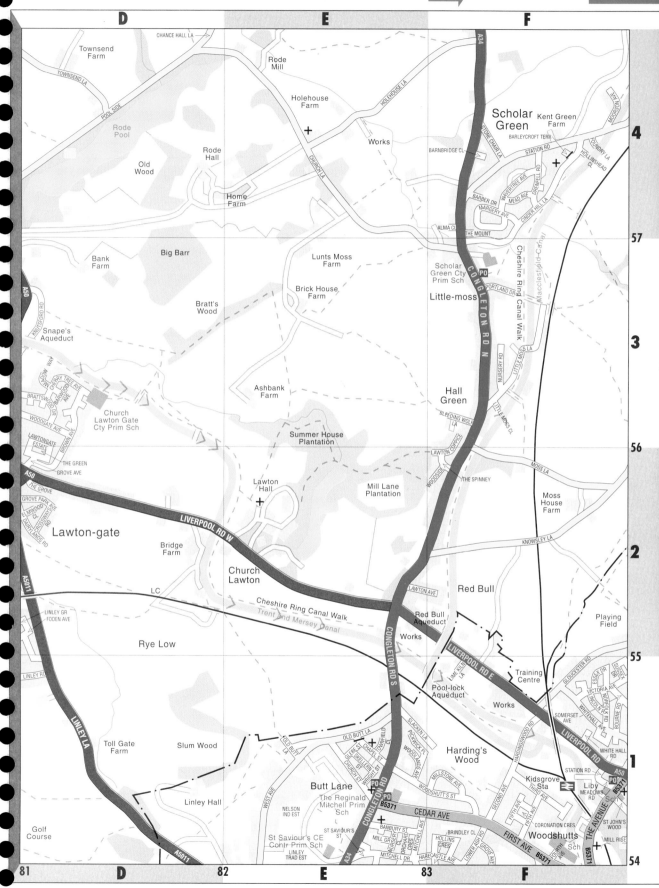

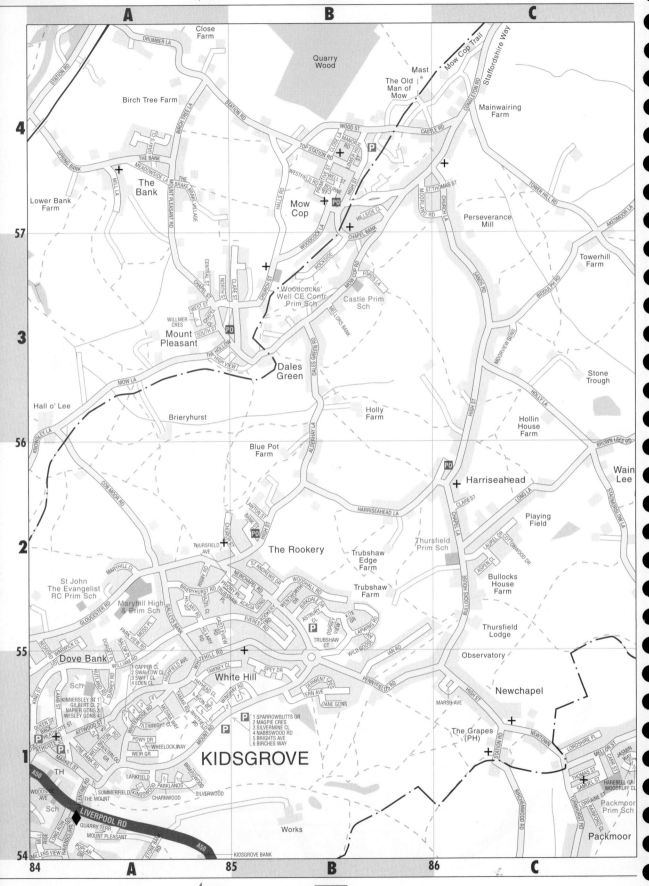

KIDSGROVE

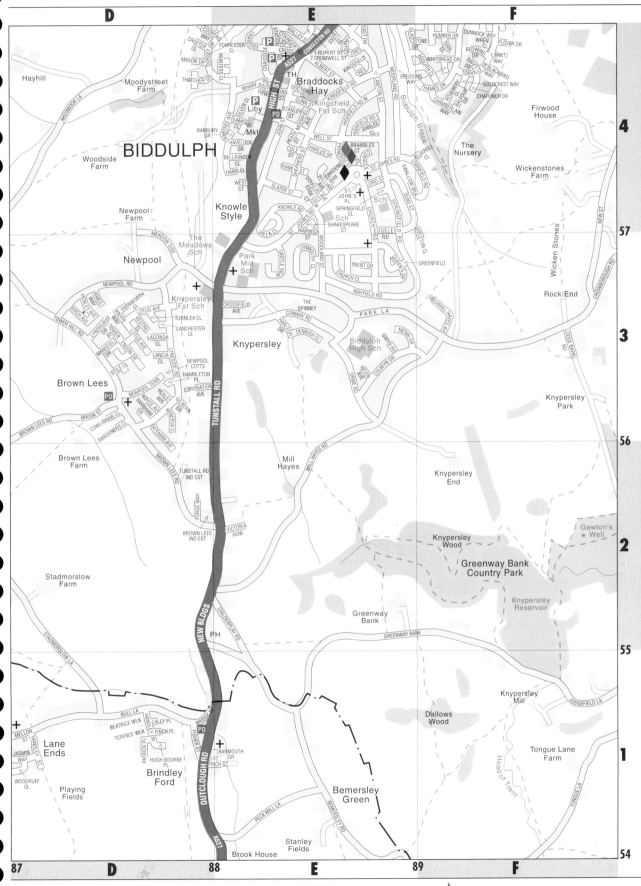

D · E · F

4

57

3

56

2

55

1

54

87 · D · 88 · E · 89 · F

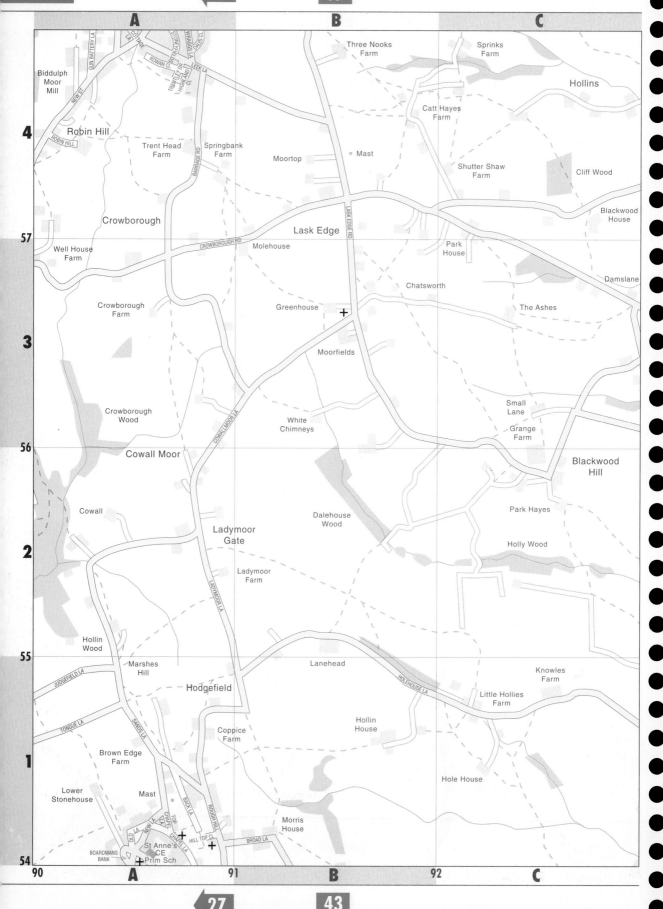

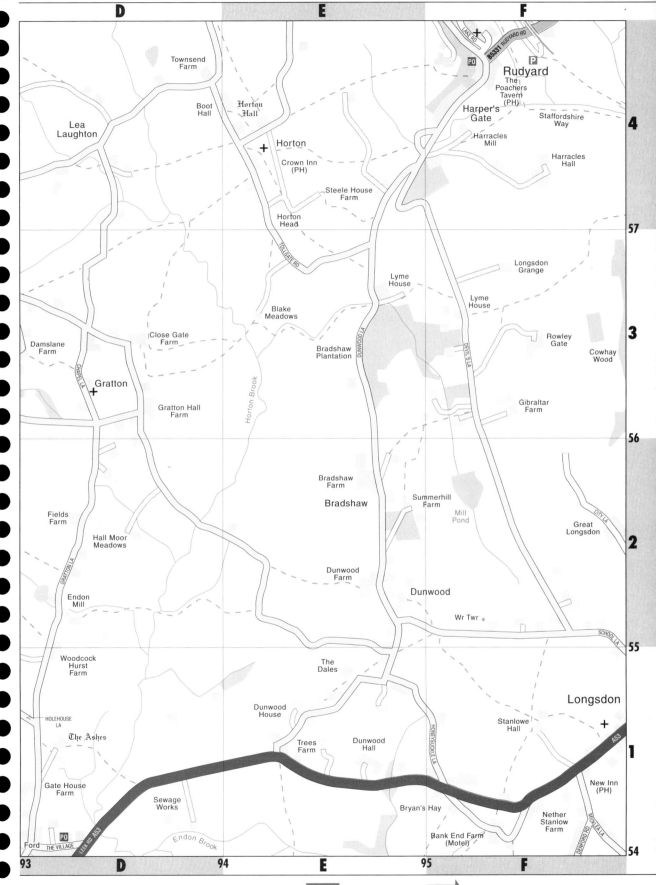

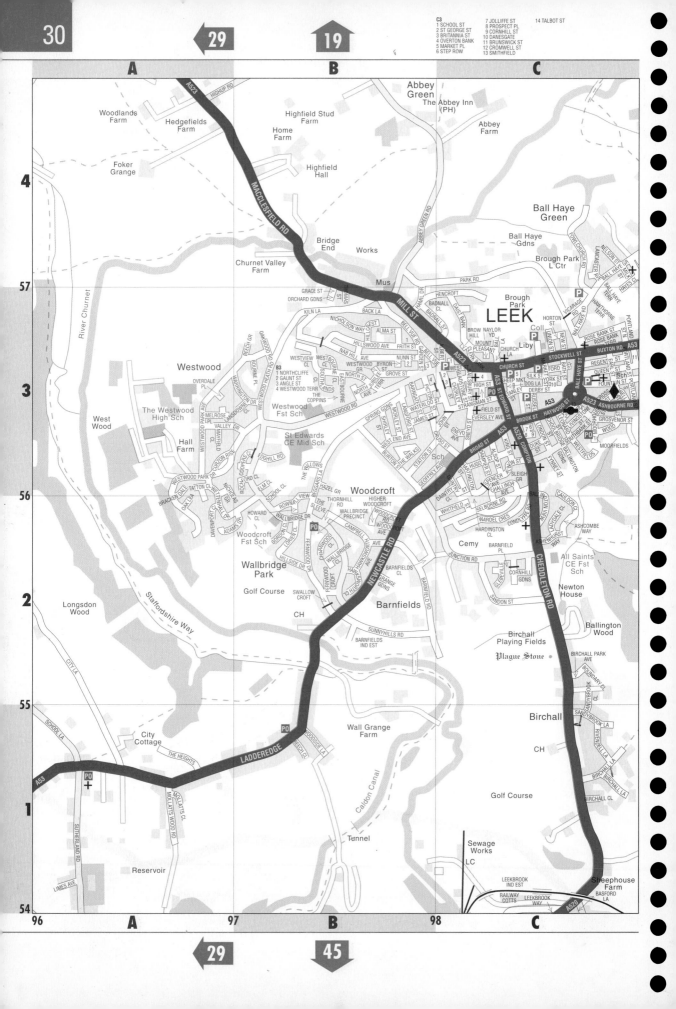

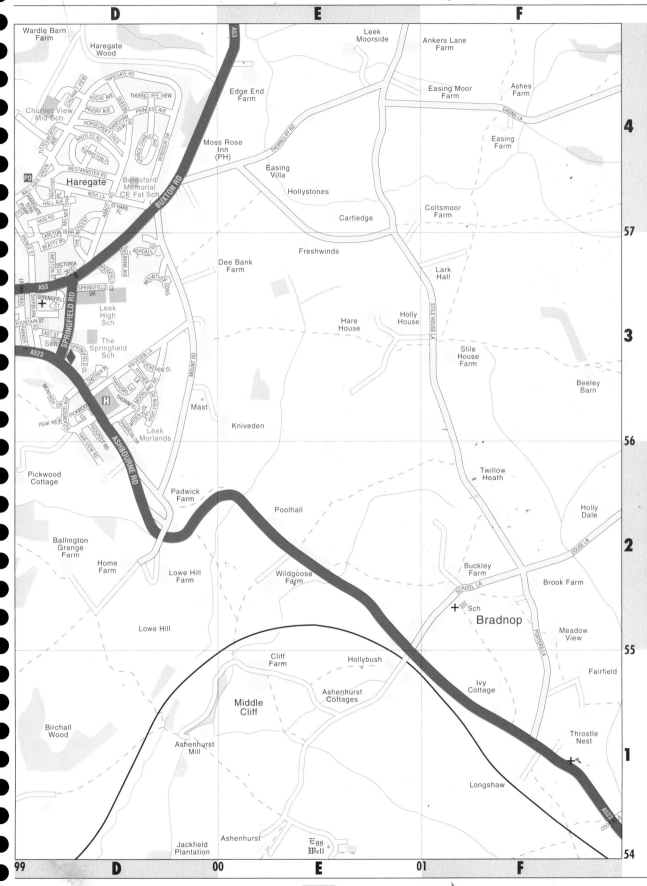

D   E   F

Wardle Barn Farm

Haregate Wood

Churnet View Mid Sch

Haregate

Beresford Memorial CE Fst Sch

Edge End Farm

Moss Rose Inn (PH)

Easing Villa

Hollystones

Cartledge

Freshwinds

Leek Moorside

Ankers Lane Farm

Easing Moor Farm

Ashes Farm

EASING LA

Easing Farm

Coltsmoor Farm

4

57

Dee Bank Farm

Hare House

Holly House

Lark Hall

STILE HOUSE LA

Stile House Farm

Beeley Barn

3

Leek High Sch

The Springfield Sch

Kniveden

Mast

Leek Morlands

Pickwood Cottage

Ballington Grange Farm

Home Farm

Lowe Hill Farm

Lowe Hill

Padwick Farm

Poolhall

Wildgoose Farm

Twillow Heath

Holly Dale

Buckley Farm

SCHOOL LA

Sch

Bradnop

Brook Farm

PORTERS LA

Meadow View

DOUSE LA

2

56

55

Birchall Wood

Cliff Farm

Middle Cliff

Ashenhurst Mill

Ashenhurst

Jackfield Plantation

Hollybush

Ashenhurst Cottages

Egg Well

Ivy Cottage

Longshaw

Fairfield

Throstle Nest

A523

COOK LA

1

54

A

B

C

EASING LA

Old Mixon
Hay

Cave

4

Westbrook

New Mixon
Hay

Mixon
Grange

Mixon
Mines

Mixon

Dunlea
Farm

57

Wormlow
Farm

Dale
House

Newhouse
Farm

River Hamps

Morridge

Harvey
Gate

3

White Lea
Farm

Wellington
Farm

Rue Hayes
Farm

56

Waterhouse

High
Cross

Onecote Lane
Head

DOUSE LA

Cemy

Onecote
Grange

2

Intake
Farm

Onecote Lane
End

Onecote

+

55

Newhouse
Farm

Moor
Top

Vicarage

Willowmeadow

Upper
Moorside

Lower Moorside
Farm

B5053

WETLEY LA

Cliffhead

Weatherworth
Farm

Hopping
Head

Moorside

Morridge
Side

Garstones

Slate
House

New
Farm

1

COOKS LA

Town Field
Farm

A523

Lane-end

Astonsitch

Hobmeadows

B5053

54

02

A

03

B

04

C

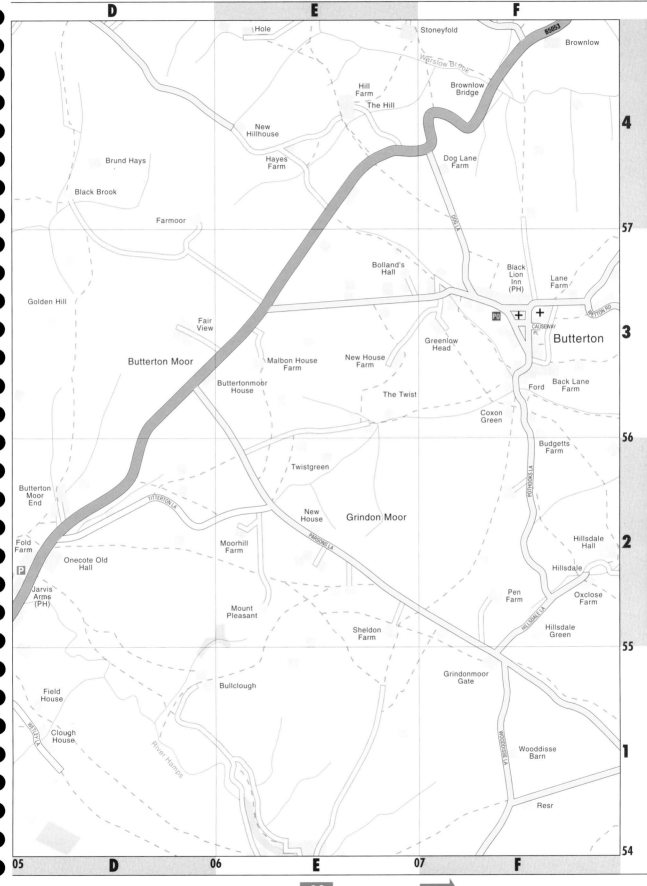

D

E

F

Hole

Stoneyfold

B5053

Brownlow

Warslow Brook

Hill Farm

Brownlow Bridge

The Hill

4

New Hillhouse

Dog Lane Farm

Brund Hays

Hayes Farm

Black Brook

Farmoor

57

DOG LA

Bolland's Hall

Black Lion Inn (PH)

Lane Farm

Golden Hill

Fair View

Greenlow Head

PO

✛

✛

Butterton

CAUSEWAY PL

3

Butterton Moor

Malbon House Farm

New House Farm

Back Lane Farm

Buttertonmoor House

The Twist

Ford

Coxon Green

56

Budgetts Farm

Twistgreen

POTHOOKS LA

Butterton Moor End

TITTERTON LA

New House

Grindon Moor

Hillsdale Hall

Moorhill Farm

Fold Farm

PARSONS LA

Hillsdale

2

Onecote Old Hall

P

Pen Farm

Oxclose Farm

Jarvis Arms (PH)

Mount Pleasant

HILLSDALE LA

Hillsdale Green

Sheldon Farm

55

Grindonmoor Gate

Field House

Bullclough

WETLEY LA

Clough House

WOODDISSE LA

Wooddisse Barn

1

River Hamps

Resr

05

D

06

E

07

F

54

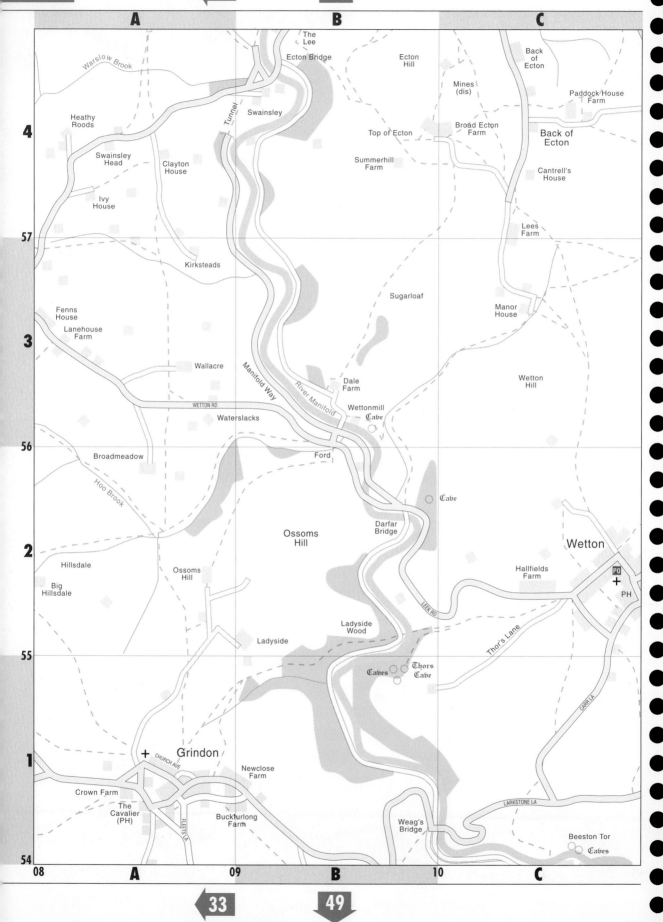

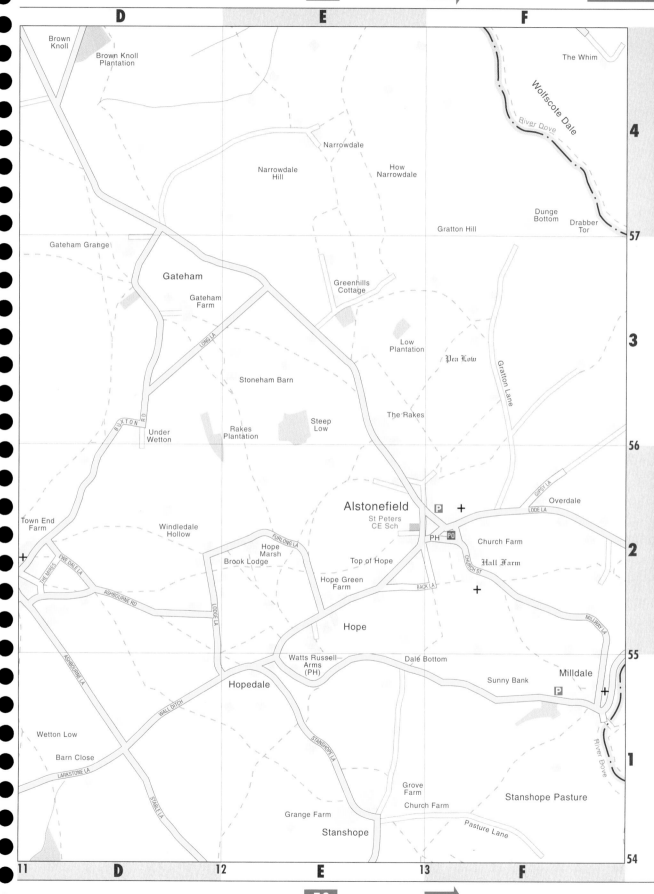

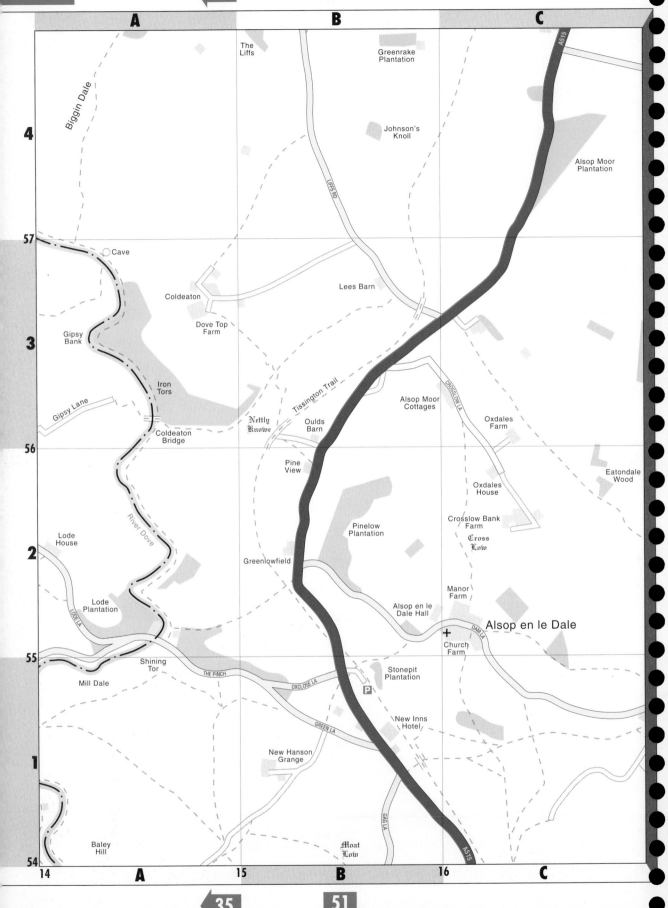

A   B   C

4

Biggin Dale

The Liffs

Greenrake Plantation

Johnson's Knoll

Alsop Moor Plantation

A515

57

Cave

Coldeaton

Lees Barn

LIFFS RD

Dove Top Farm

3

Gipsy Bank

Iron Tors

Gipsy Lane

Tissington Trail

Alsop Moor Cottages

CROSSLOW LA

Oxdales Farm

Nettly Knowe

 Oulds Barn

Coldeaton Bridge

56

Pine View

Oxdales House

Eatondale Wood

River Dove

Pinelow Plantation

Crosslow Bank Farm

Cross Low

Lode House

2

Greenlowfield

Manor Farm

Alsop en le Dale Hall

Alsop en le Dale

Lode Plantation

LODE LA

DAM LA

Church Farm

55

Shining Tor

THE PINCH

Stonepit Plantation

Mill Dale

OXCLOSE LA

P

GREEN LA

New Inns Hotel

1

New Hanson Grange

GAG LA

Baley Hill

Moat Low

A515

54

14   A   15   B   16   C

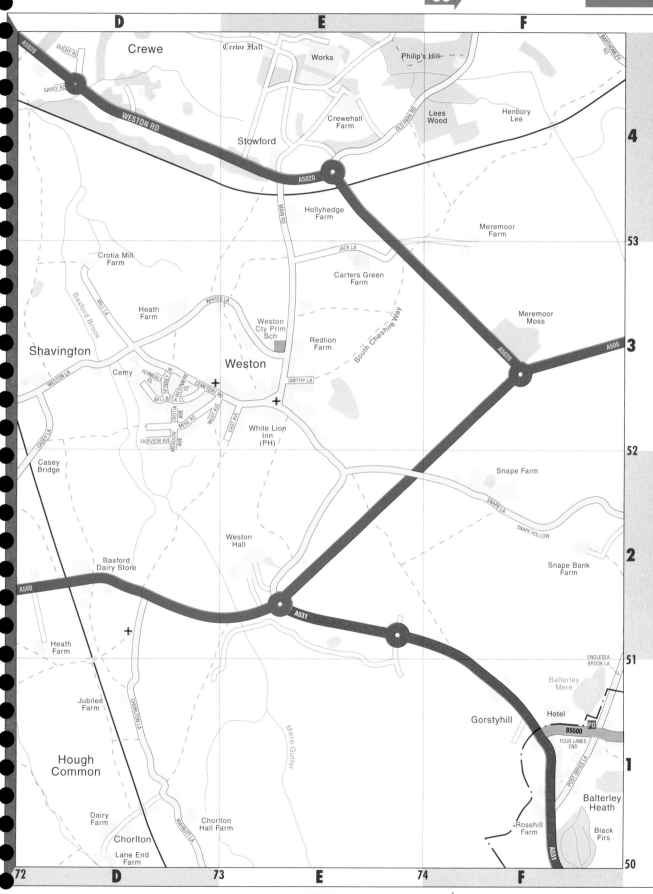

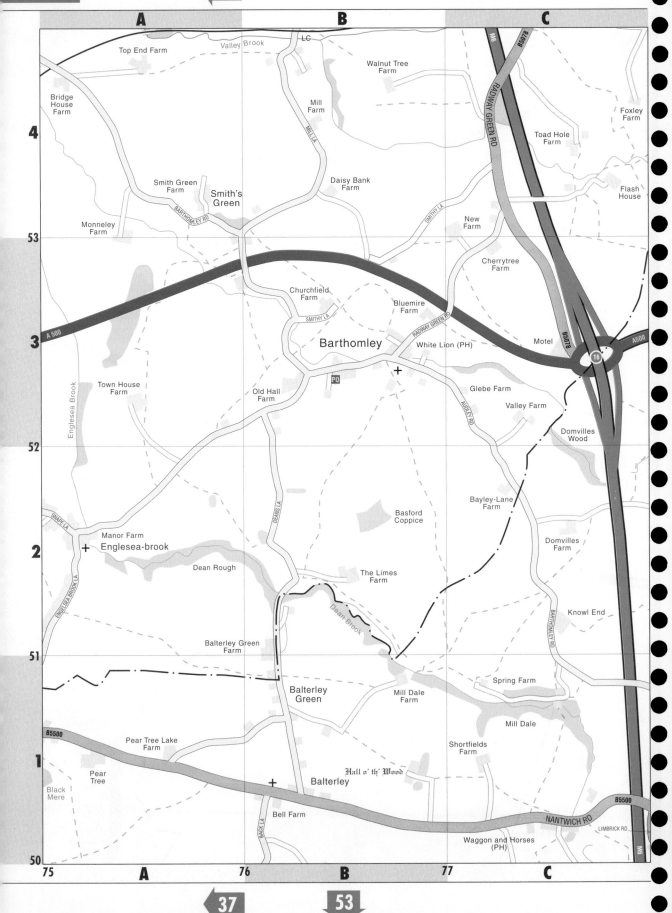

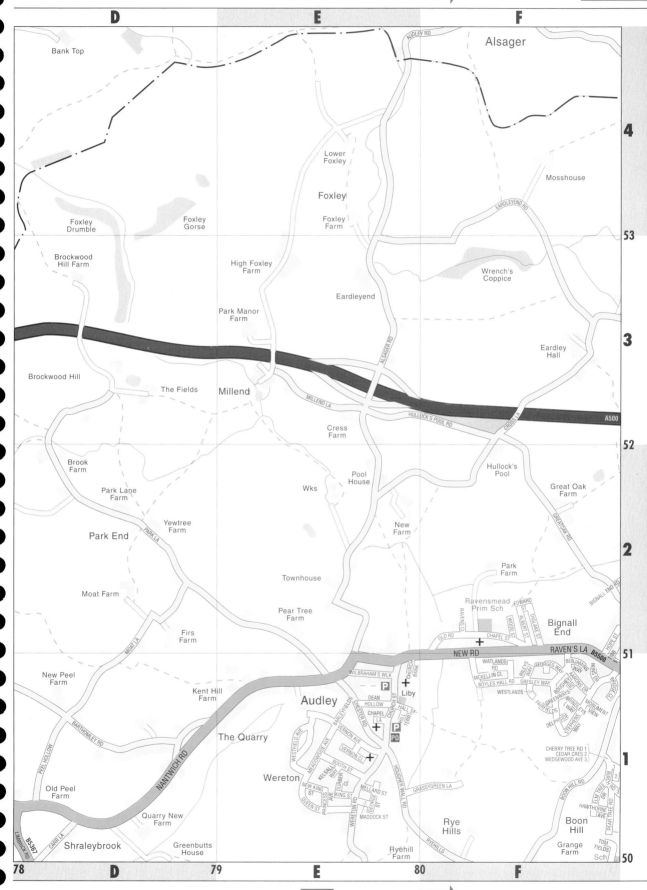

D E F

4

53

3

A500

52

2

51

1

50

78 D 79 E 80 F

Alsager

AUDLEY RD

Bank Top

Lower
Foxley

Mosshouse

Foxley

EARDLEYEND RD

Foxley
Farm

Foxley
Drumble

Foxley
Gorse

Wrench's
Coppice

High Foxley
Farm

Brockwood
Hill Farm

Eardleyend

Park Manor
Farm

ALSAGER RD

Eardley
Hall

Brockwood Hill

The Fields

Millend

MILLEND LA

HULLOCK'S POOL RD

CROSS LA

Cress
Farm

Brook
Farm

Pool
House

Hullock's
Pool

Great Oak
Farm

Park Lane
Farm

Wks

GREAT OAK RD

Yewtree
Farm

PARK LA

Park End

New
Farm

Park
Farm

BIGNALL END RD

Moat Farm

Townhouse

Ravensmead
Prim Sch

EDWARD
ST

Bignall
End

RAVENS CL

WOODS ST

ALBERT ST

DOUGLAS ST

HOPE ST

Firs
Farm

MOAT LA

Pear Tree
Farm

OLD RD

CHAPEL ST

RAVEN'S LA B5500

KINS DR

OLD PEEL RD

New Peel
Farm

WATLANDS
RD

GEORGES WAY

RILEYS WAY

BENJAMINS
WAY

AARONS DR

NEW RD

WILBRAHAM'S WLK

P

MCKELLIN CL

BOYLES HALL RD

GRESLEY WAY

WESTLANDS

ROUGHS WAY

GREENWAYS

BRINTLEY'S WAY

MONUMENT

Kent Hill
Farm

DEAN
HOLLOW

Liby

CHURCH
BANK

FAIRFIELDS

GREENWAYS

DELPHSIDE

STEPHENS
WAY

Audley

BAILEY FIELDS

CHESTER RD

CHAPEL
LA

P

CHURCH ST

HALL ST

FERR

PD

CHERRY TREE RD 1
CEDAR CRES 2
WEDGEWOOD AVE 3

BARTHOMLEY RD

NANTWICH RD

The Quarry

WESTFIELD AVE

MEADOWSIDE AVE

KEL SALL
WAY

VERNON AVE

VERNON CL

BOOTH ST

HOUGHER HALL RD

1
2
3

ELM TREE DR

BOON HILL RD

Wereton

PRINCESS AVE

KING ST

DURBER
CL

GEORGE
ST

MELLARD ST

GRASSYGREEN LA

HAWTHORNE
AVE

PEAR TREE RD

PEEL HOLLOW

Old Peel
Farm

NEW KING
ST

WERE TON RD

MADDOCK ST

Rye
Hills

Boon
Hill

B5367

CABR LA

QUEEN ST

Grange
Farm

TOM
FIELDS
Sch

LIMBRICK RD

Shraleybrook

Quarry New
Farm

Greenbutts
House

Ryehill
Farm

RYEHILLS

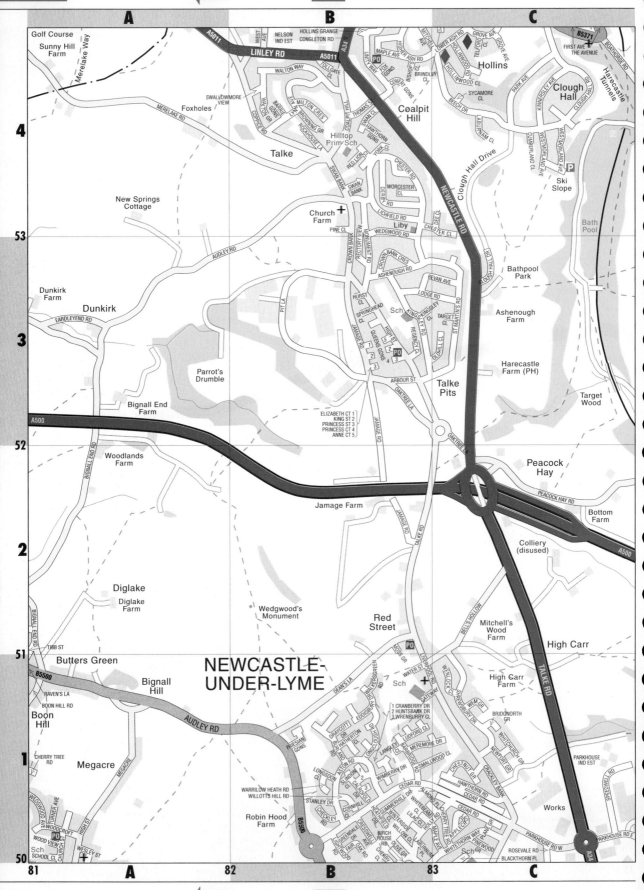

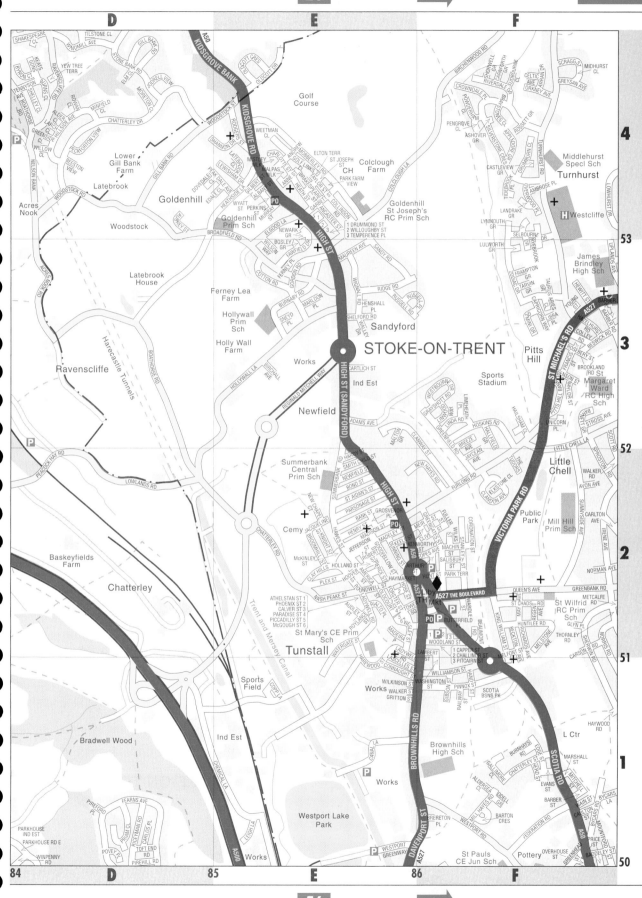

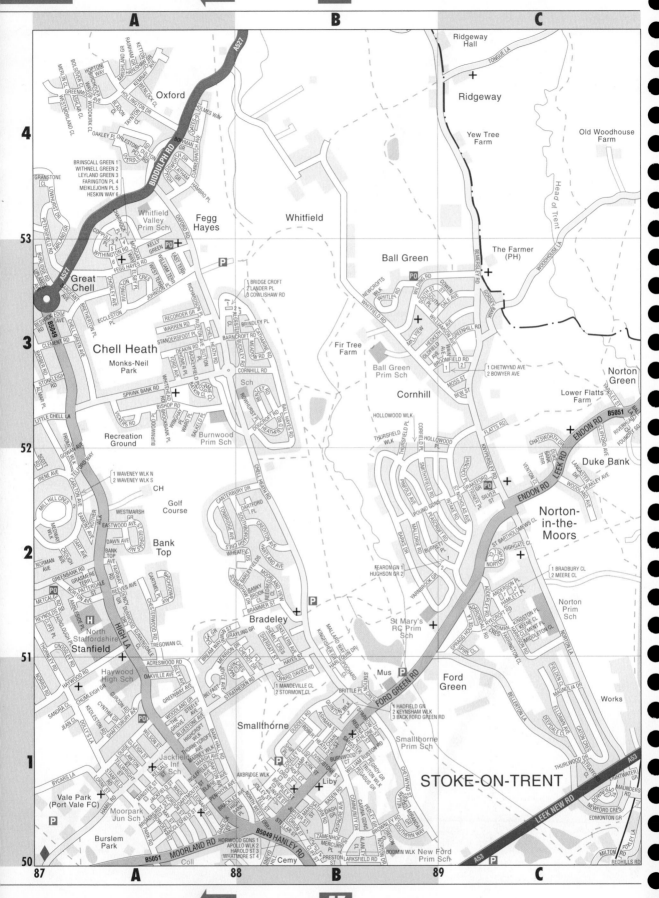

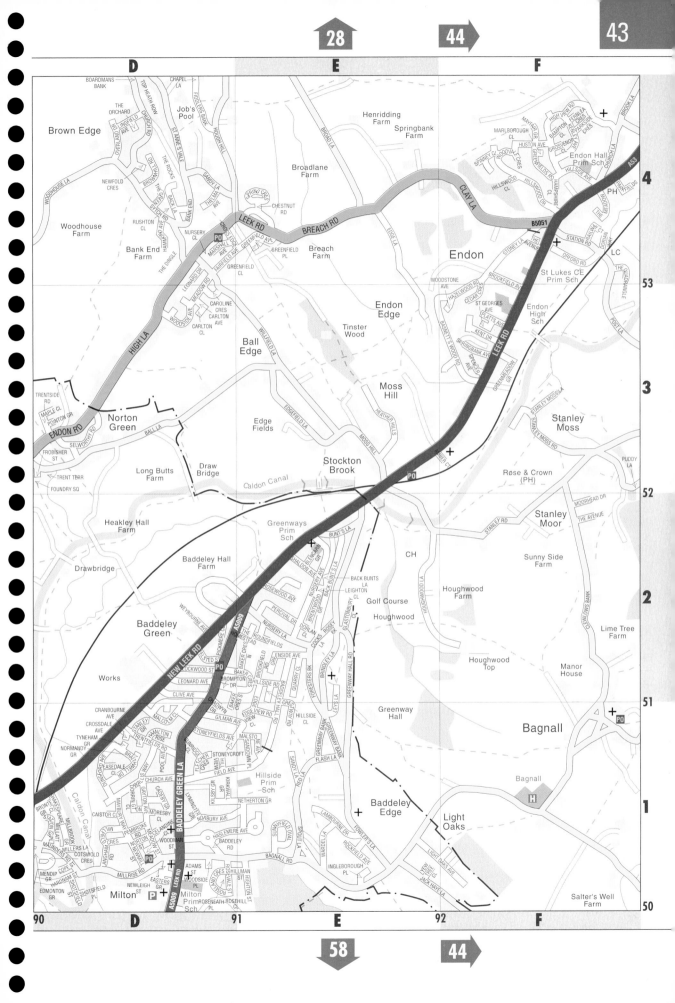

A   **B**   **C**

1 BROOK CL
2 FORGE SIDE
3 EMBERS WAY
4 THE MEADOWS

BROOKSIDE DR

BROOK LA

LEEK RD

A53

Railway (disused)

Denford

MICKLEA LA

Caldon Canal

DENFORD RD

SANDY LA

Manor Farm

Hazelhurst Aqueduct

HOLLY BUSH COTTAGES

Holly Bush (PH)

Denford Farm

Hayes Farm

PARK LA

Lawn Farm

Little Hollinhurst

Hollinhurst

Hazelhurst

Cumberledge Park

HUNTLEY RD

4

53

Reynolds Hay Farm

Cats Edge

Ladygreen

3

POST LA

Travellers Rest (PH)

STANLEY BANK

Acres Barn

Moss House

Lee House

Dogcroft Farm

PUDDY LA

Newhouse

Clough House

BLACK BANK RD

Stanley

Whistonshaw

52

Stanley Head Outdoor Education Centre

TOMKIN RD

Rose Bank Farm

Coal Pit Ford Farm

P

Stanley Pool

Wood Lane Farm

COALPITFORD LA

Ford Farm

BRUND LA

2

Cliff Wood

Tompkin

KNOWSLEY RD

Bigwood

Big Susan's Wood

Bagnall Grange

OLD MILL LA

P

Knowsley Farm

Old Mill Lane

Pool Meadows

51

OLD MILL LA

Moor Hall

SPRINGS BANK

Bagnall

Ford

Westwood Manor (Cicely Haughton Sch)

1

Spring Bank

THORNYEDGE RD

Little Lawn Farm

Birch Wood

Far Rownall Farm

THORNYEDGE RD

Rownall Cottage Farm

Newhouse Farm

Thornyedge

Rownall Farm

Bramhouse Farm

50

93   **A**   94   **B**   95   **C**

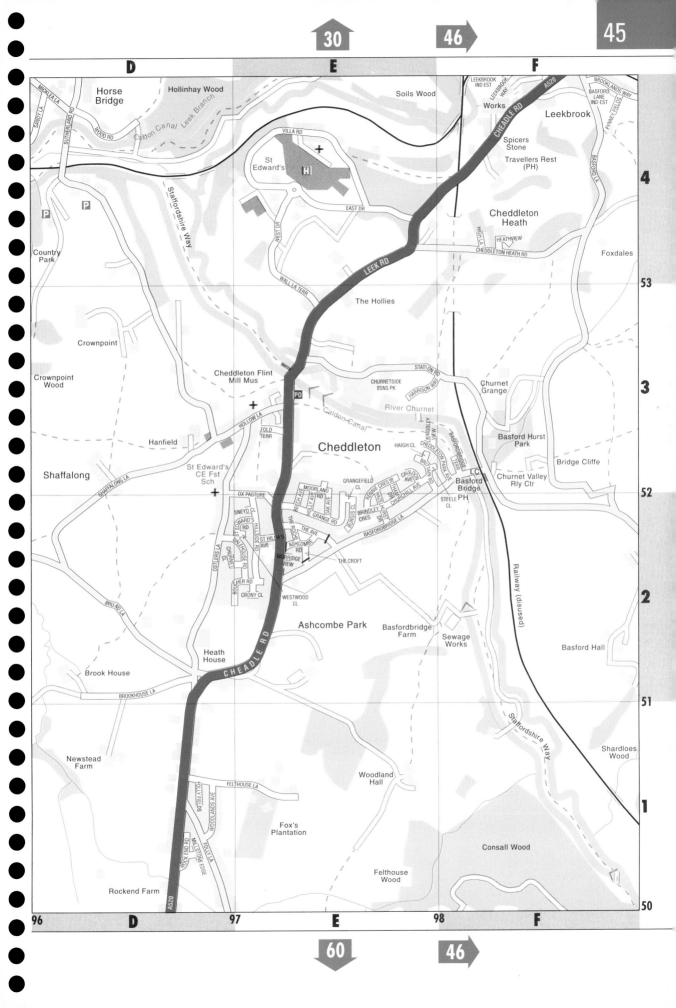

A | B | C

45
31

BROOKLANDS WAY

Fynneylane Farm

Roost Hill

Revedge

4

Yew Tree Farm

Ballfields

Apesford

Sixoaks Farm

Crowholt

Roughstone Hole

53

Ringehay

Nature Reserve

Sixoaks Wood

Barnfield

Ferny Hill

Cloughmeadow Cottage

Oldfield

Combes Brook

Padwick

Padwick Wood

3

The Combes

Spiritholes Wood

Upper Fernyhill Farm

Blackhill Wood

Lower House Farm

Sharpcliffe Hall

Home Farm

Basford Grange

52

Sneyd Arms Farm

Low Wood

Whitehough Wood

Little Rocks Plantation

The Ridge

Basford Green

Mill Wood

Crab Tree Farm

Whitehough

2

Mosslee Mill Farm

Brockholes

Mosslee Barn

51

Collyhole

The Clough

Hills Farm

Blackbank Wood

Coltstone

Mosslee Hall Farm

Stakebank Wood

Collyhole Brook

Middle Farm

1

CHURCH LA

Railway (disused)

Turner's Knipe

Intake

Stocks Green

CHURCHFIELD CT

CHURCH MEADOW

Rough Intake

Oddo Hall

River Churnet

50

99 | A | 00 | B | 01 | C

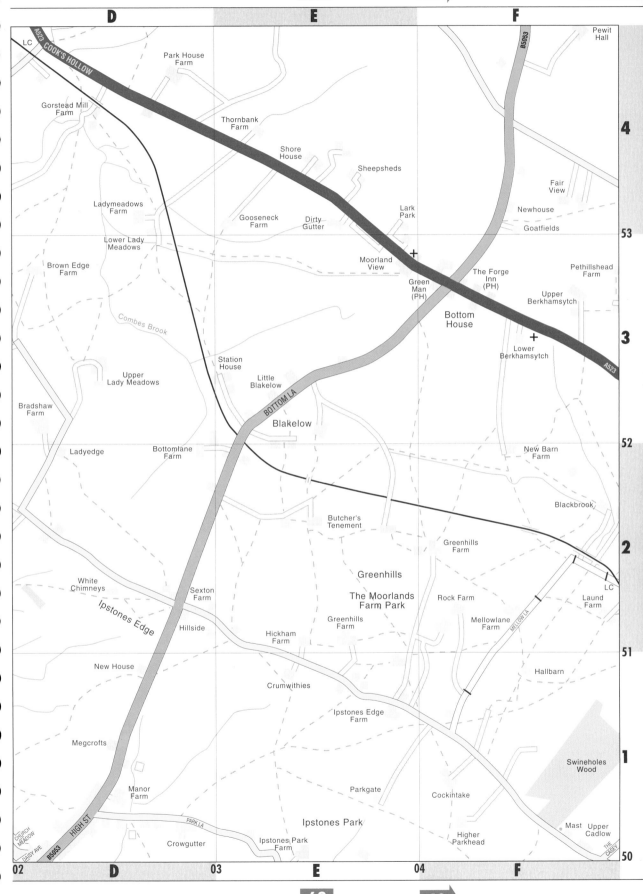

LC

A523 COOK'S HOLLOW

B5053

Pewit Hall

Park House Farm

Gorstead Mill Farm

Thornbank Farm

Shore House

Sheepsheds

Fair View

Newhouse

Goatfields

4

Ladymeadows Farm

Gooseneck Farm

Dirty Gutter

Lark Park

53

Lower Lady Meadows

Brown Edge Farm

Moorland View

Green Man (PH)

The Forge Inn (PH)

Pethillshead Farm

Upper Berkhamsytch

Combes Brook

Bottom House

Upper Lady Meadows

Station House

Little Blakelow

Lower Berkhamsytch

3

A523

Bradshaw Farm

BOTTOM LA

Blakelow

Ladyedge

Bottomlane Farm

New Barn Farm

52

Blackbrook

Butcher's Tenement

Greenhills Farm

2

LC

White Chimneys

Sexton Farm

Greenhills

The Moorlands Farm Park

Rock Farm

Mellowlane Farm

MELLOW LA

Laund Farm

Ipstones Edge

Hillside

Hickham Farm

Greenhills Farm

New House

Crumwithies

Hallbarn

51

Megcrofts

Ipstones Edge Farm

Swineholes Wood

1

Manor Farm

HIGH ST

PARK LA

Parkgate

Cockintake

Mast Upper Cadlow

CHURCH MEADOW

DAISY AVE

B5053

Crowgutter

Ipstones Park Farm

Ipstones Park

Higher Parkhead

THE CASEY

50

47
33

A
B
C

4

Ford

Dairy House

Ford Farm

Ford Wetley

Ryebrook

Ten Acre Barn

Ford Grange

Sycamore Lodge

Felthouse

Bingham

53

Stonyslack

Pethills Bank Cottage

Martin's Low

Grub Low

Pethillshead

3

Backlane

Martinslow Farm

Moorside

Lawnfield

A523

Pethills

Gibgreen

Old Hall Farm

Newstreet

Ironpits

52

MARTINSLOW LA

Newstreet Farm

Winkhillbank

Croftshead

Bank Farm

Coate's Cottage

Bank Flatts

Blackbrook World of Birds

River Hamps

BROMLEYHEDGE LA

Waterfall Cross

Waterfall Common

Common Side

Green Farm

2

Black Brook

Moorland View

WATERFALL LA

Blackbrook Bridge

CROSS LA

LC's

Woodbine Cottage

Winkhill

BENTYGRANGE LA

LIME GR

51

Gutter Farm

Stonylow Farm

BREECH CL

Benty Grange

Waterhouses CE Prim Sch

WATERFALL LA

Station House

California

Paper Mill Farm

PORTLAND PL

THE CASEY

Dulce Domun

Cotton Grange

Willow House

Redmoorlee Farm

CROWTREES FARM IND EST

HAMPS VALLEY RD

1

Swineholes Wood

ELLASTONE RD

A523

Casey Head Farm

Crowtrees

Moorland View

DUKE'S LA

Steps Cottage

Birch Head

Broomyshaw

New House Farm

Lee Brook

50

05
A
06
B
07
C

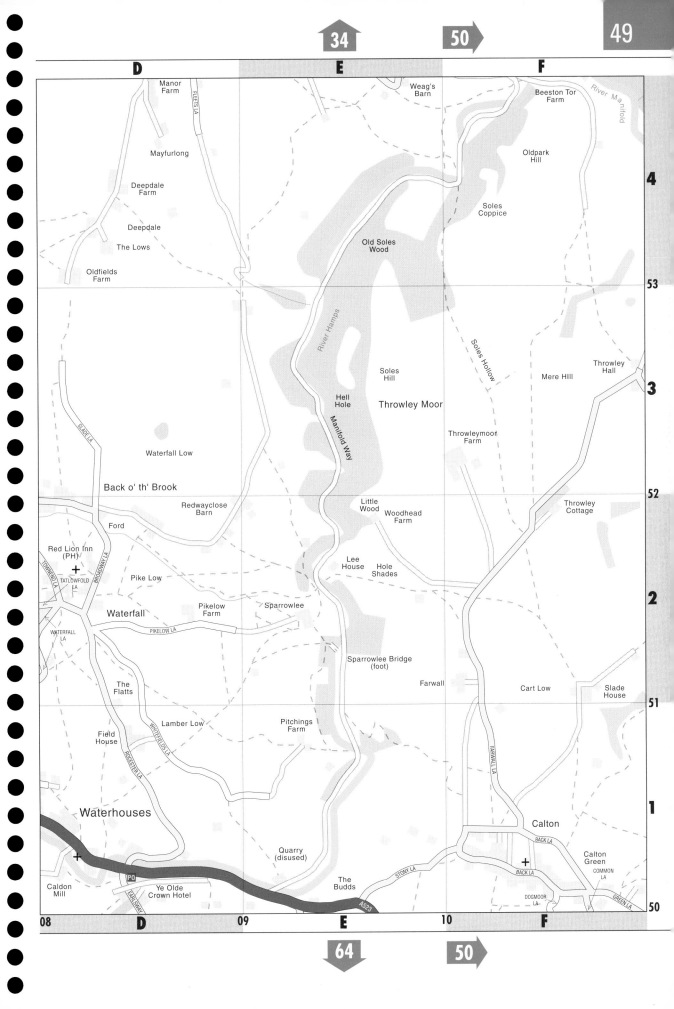

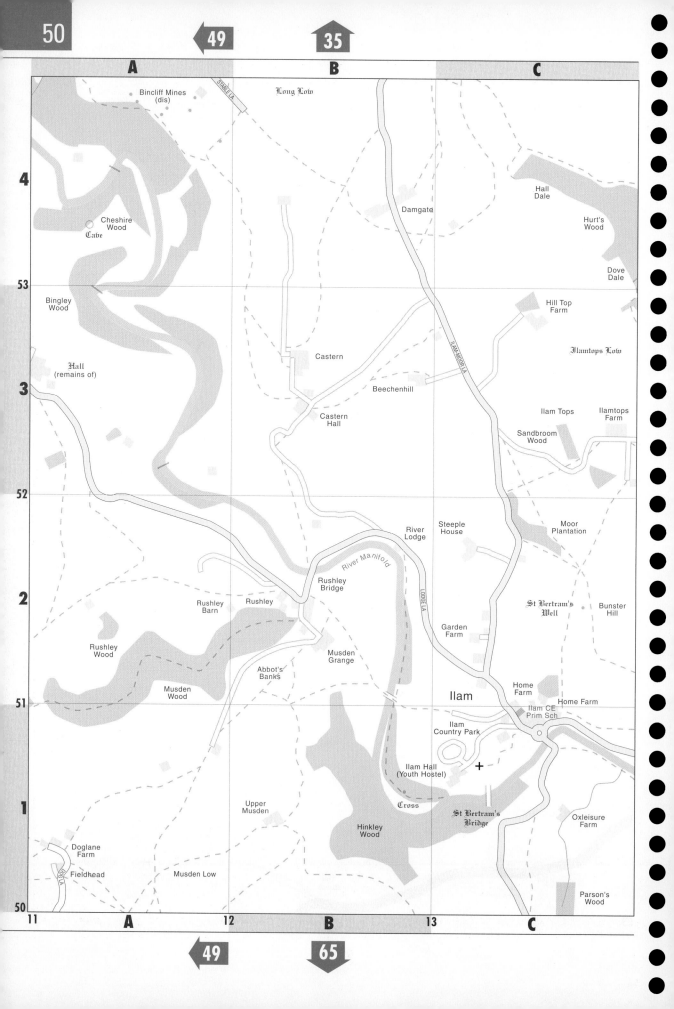

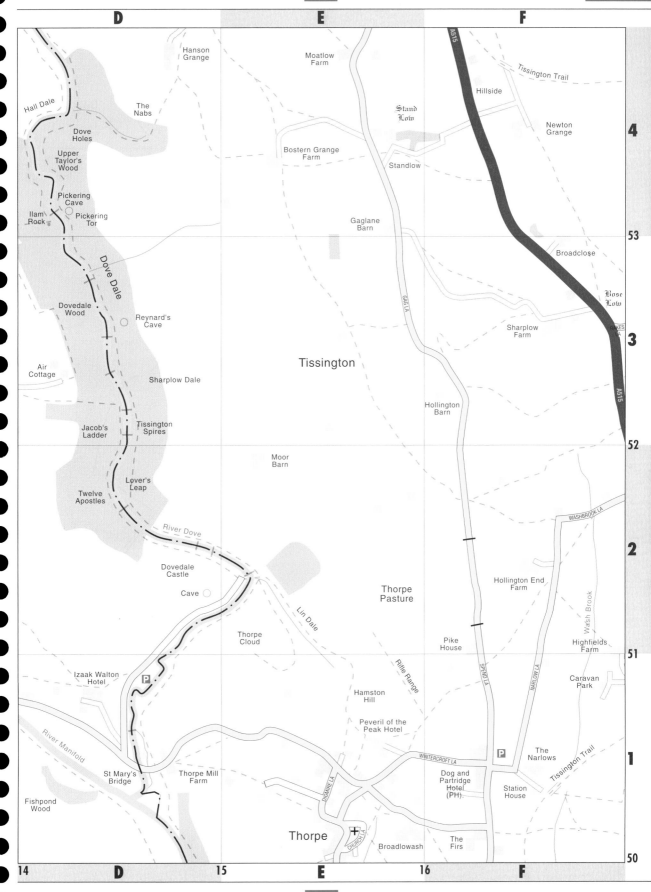

D

Hall Dale

The Nabs

Hanson Grange

Moatlow Farm

Stand Low

Hillside

Tissington Trail

Newton Grange

4

Dove Holes

Upper Taylor's Wood

Bostern Grange Farm

Standlow

Pickering Cave

Ilam Rock

Pickering Tor

Gaglane Barn

Broadclose

53

Dove Dale

Dovedale Wood

Reynard's Cave

Tissington

Sharplow Farm

Rose Low

3

Air Cottage

Sharplow Dale

Hollington Barn

Jacob's Ladder

Tissington Spires

52

Moor Barn

Twelve Apostles

Lover's Leap

River Dove

Dovedale Castle

Cave

Lin Dale

Thorpe Pasture

Washbrook La

Hollington End Farm

Wash Brook

2

Thorpe Cloud

Pike House

Highfields Farm

51

Izaak Walton Hotel

P

Hamston Hill

Rifle Range

Caravan Park

River Manifold

Peveril of the Peak Hotel

Wintercroft La

Spend La

Narlow La

The Narlows

Tissington Trail

1

St Mary's Bridge

Thorpe Mill Farm

Digmire La

Dog and Partridge Hotel (PH)

P

Station House

Fishpond Wood

Thorpe

Church La

Broadlowash

The Firs

50

14

D

15

E

16

F

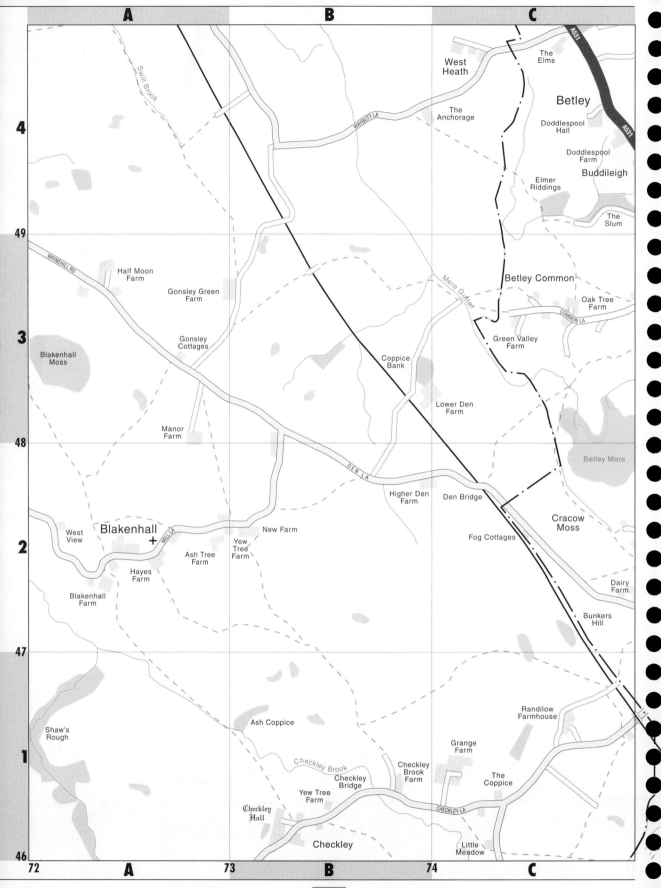

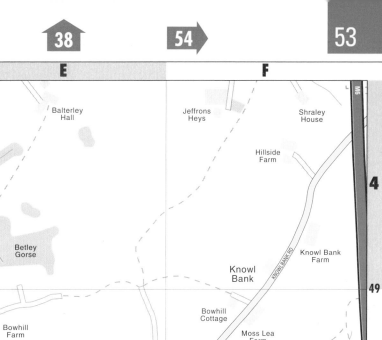

53
39

A **B** **C**

Rising Sun
Inn
(PH)

KNOWL BANK RD

LIMBRICK RD

B5367

Shraleybrook

Wynbrook

Dean Brook

WERETON RD

Wynbank
Farm

RYEHILLS

MILES GREEN RD

PEGGY'S BANK

TOMFIELDS

APEDALE
Sch RD

Miles Green
Farm

Miles
Green

4

Golden Hay
Farm

Hollins
Farm

STATION RD

WYNBANK CL

HEATHCOTE RD

VICTORIA AVE

Burgess's
Wood

Yewtree

SHRALEYBROOK RD

Halmerend
Hall

Chapel
Farm

P

STATION WLK

HOLDING CRES

Halmer
End

Sir Thomas
Boughey
High Sch

PH

WESLEY PL

HARRISON CL

HAYESWOOD LA

YANSEY CL

Church
Farm

Mast

49

Minnie
Farm

PH

HIGH ST

PODMORE LA

Heathcote
Prim Sch
Gresley
Arms
(PH)

HILL CRES

PODMORE AVE

THE DRIVE

ROBERTS CL

Alsagers
Bank

Hayes

PO

3

Pheasant
Hall

RED HALL LA

M6

Industrial
Estate

Hayes
Wood

SCOT HAY RD

B5367 HIGH LA

Waste
Farm

48

Red Hall
Farm

Opencast
Mine

Scot Hay

LEYCETT RD

CHURCH VIEW

BANKFIELD GR

2

Bullthorns
Wood

CRACKLEY LA

Pool End
Farm

SCOT HAY RD

DROITWICH CL

HARROGATE RD

MOFFAT WAY

REDES RD

BATH RD

WOODHALL PL

47

The
Gladings

Walton's
Wood

Lane
Farm

LEYCETT LA

Leycett

Banktop
Farm

STRETTON RD

BIRKDALE

CHELTENHAM GR

BATH RD

CHEDDAR DR

ILKLEY PL

MALVERN AVE

REDHEATH CL

Haying Wood

Finney
Green

M6

A531

Sunnybank

AGGER HILL

Upper
Farm

Lower
Farm

Agger Hill
Farm

HOLLYWOOD LA

PEPPER ST

B5044

Wks

Tunnel

QUARRY BANK RD

Quarry
Bank

Redheath
Plantation

UNDERWOOD RD

1

46

78 **A** 79 **B** 80 **C**

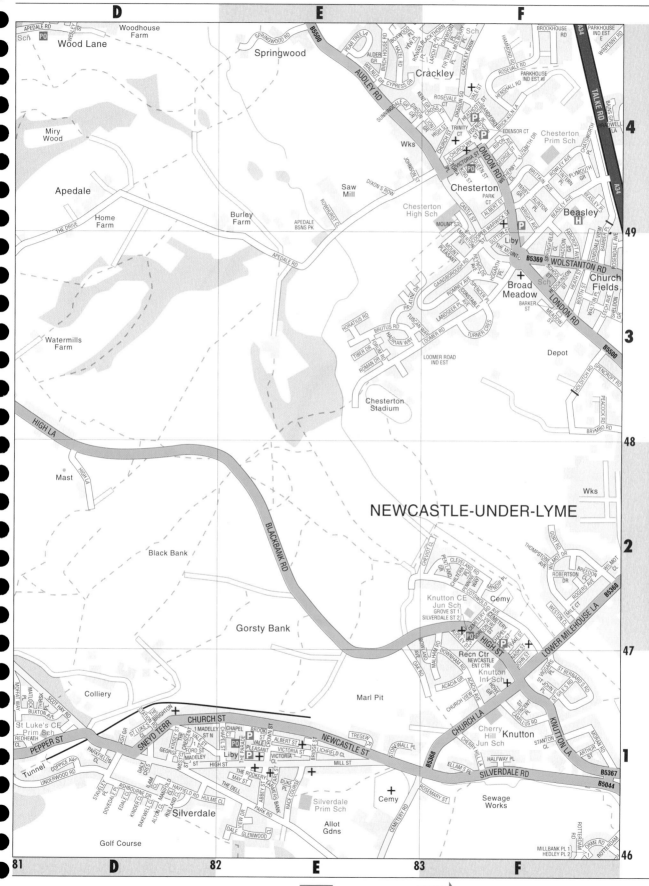

Longport Bradwell Wood Bradwell Hall Bradwell Prim Sch Bradwell Longport Sta Middleport Burslem Grange Park Porthill Park Porthill Wolstanton NEWCASTLE-UNDER-LYME Dimsdale Golf Course Cross Heath Merryfields Sch Hempstalls Prim Sch May Bank Wolstanton High Sch St Margaret's CE Jun Sch Wolstanton Retail Park Works Stoke Ski Ctr Etruria Marina Basford The Brampton St John Fisher RC High Sch Knutton La Ryecroft Etruria Sta Cliff Vale Trent and Mersey Canal Festival Way

For full street detail of the highlighted area see page 284.

D4
1 HAMIL RD
2 JACKSON ST
3 OWEN GR
4 DOULTON ST
5 REGINALD ST
6 MAYER BANK
7 HOLECROFT ST
8 STIRLING ST
9 BAPTIST ST
10 BOURNES BK
11 LOWER ST
12 SWAINSLEY CL
13 BRONANT WLK
14 WARBURTON ST
15 CAMOYS CT
16 BLEAK PL
17 GILCHRIST PL
18 RUSHTON GR

42
58
57

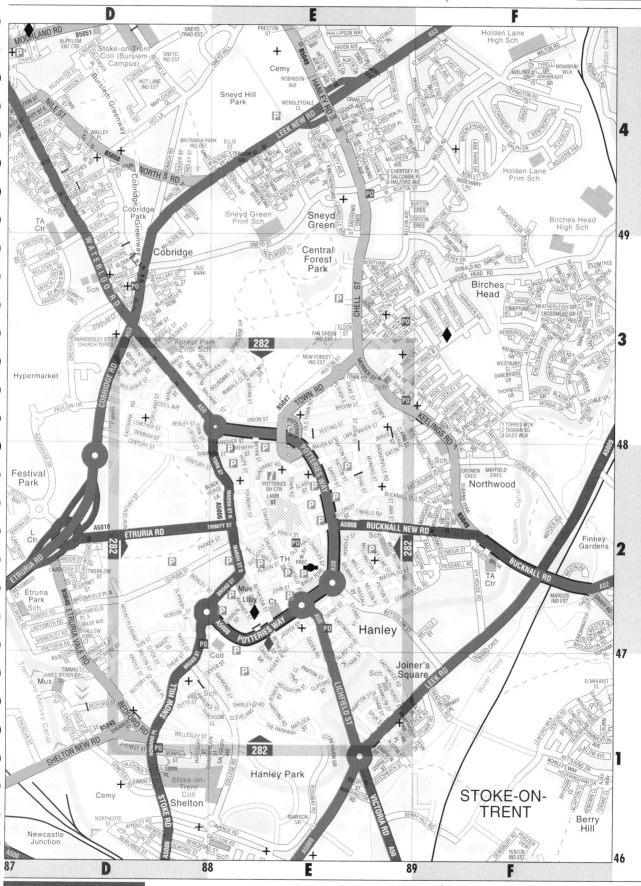

STOKE-ON-TRENT

For full street detail of the highlighted area see page 282.

72
58

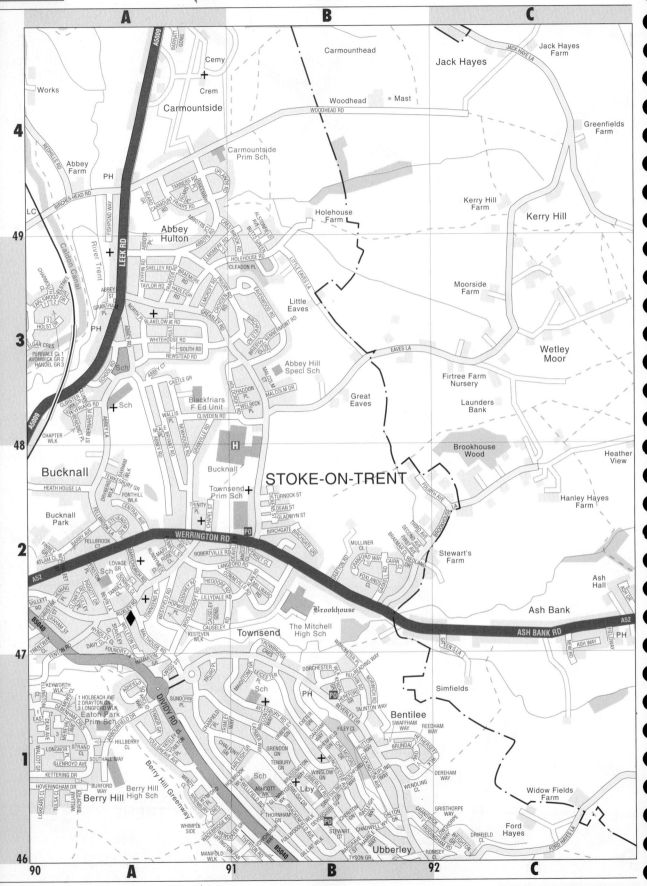

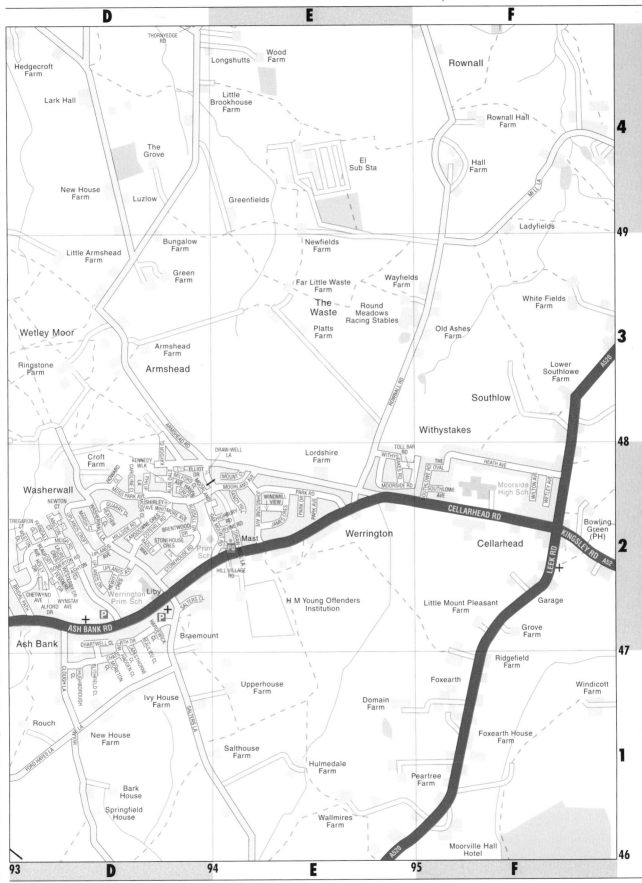

A **B** **C**

4

Barns Farm

Park House

Consall Wood

CHEADLE RD

A520

Rock View Farm

Powys Arms (PH)

St John's CE Prim Sch

MILL LA

Smithy Pool

MAIN RD

A522

Wetley Rocks

Spout House

Smithy Sprink

THE BUNTING

PLOUGH BANK

Plough Inn (PH)

PO

Long Meadows

Old Hall Farm

A522

49

OAKLANDS CT

CELLARHEAD RD

MEADOW AVE

Knowle Bank Farm

Consall Hall

Platt Newhouse Farm

LEEK RD

Park House

RANDLES LA

ABBEY RD

Lower Farm

Consall

Middle Farm

Keeper's Lodge Farm

Darleyshire

A520

Tunnel Farm

3

New Farm

Upper Farm

Lodge Spinney

Highfields Farm

Blackbank Plantation

Upper Ladypark Wood

Wetley Abbey

Wetley Abbey Farm

Ivy House Farm

48

Consall Wood

Gate House

Windyhouse Wood

Out Wood

Rangemoor Farm

Broadoak Wood

2

A52

New Park Farm

New Farm

Blakeley Farm

Little Broadoak Farm

Broadoak Farm

A522

Overmoor

Richmoorhill Farm

Blakeley Lane

Youngsgreen Farm

Brough's Wood

47

Abovepark Farm

Greenhead

Mount Pleasant

DAIRYHOUSE LA

Little Abovepark

Greenhead Farm

Moor Farm

A52

1

Waggon and Horses Inn (PH)

A522

Kingsley Moor

TICKHILL LA

Little Bank Top Farm

Bank Top Farm

Dairy House Farm

Lower Above Park

46

96 **A** **97** **B** **98** **C**

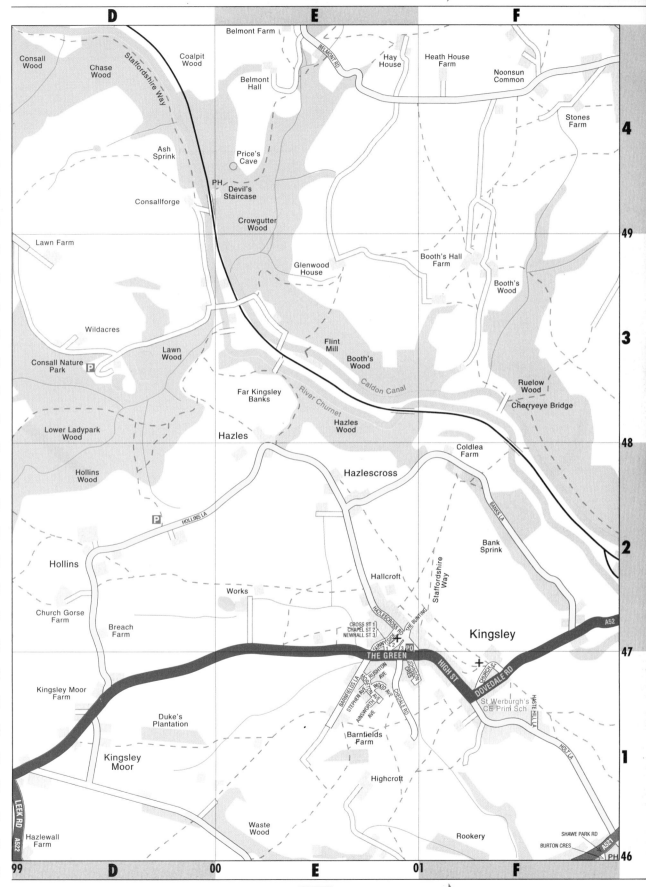

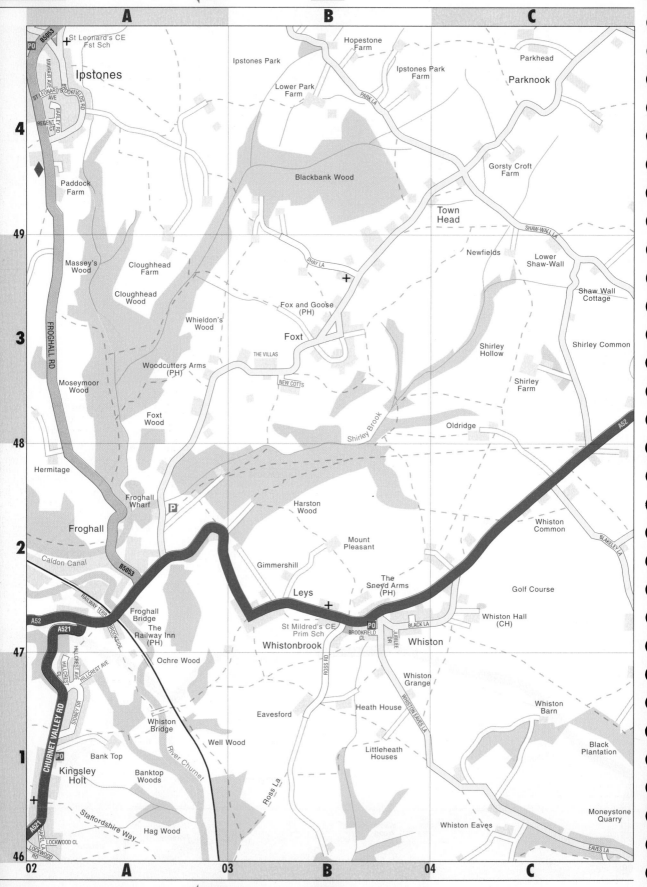

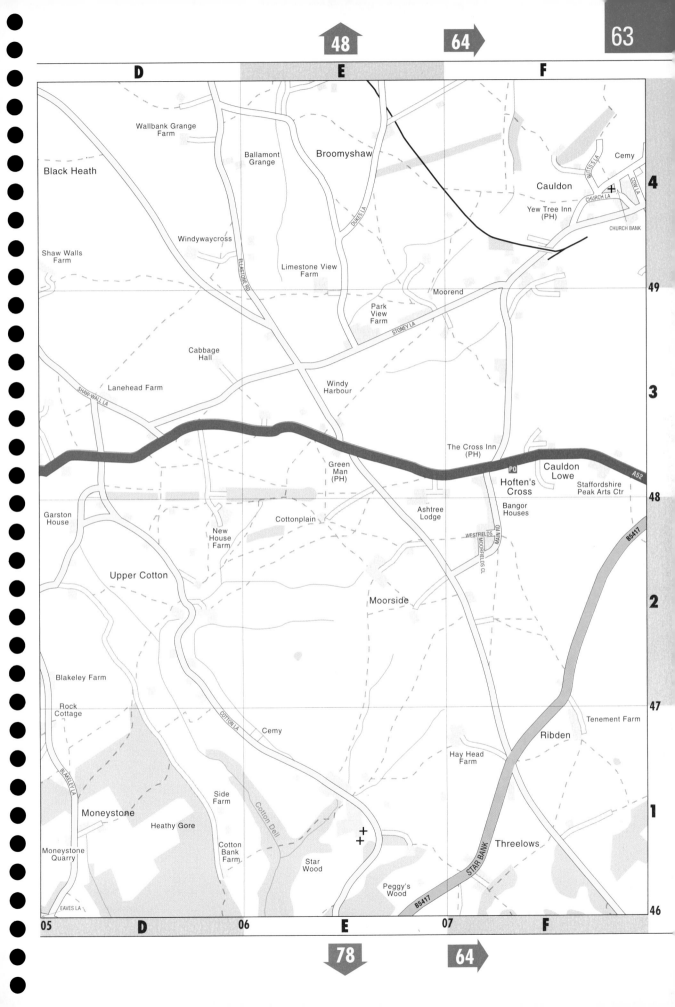

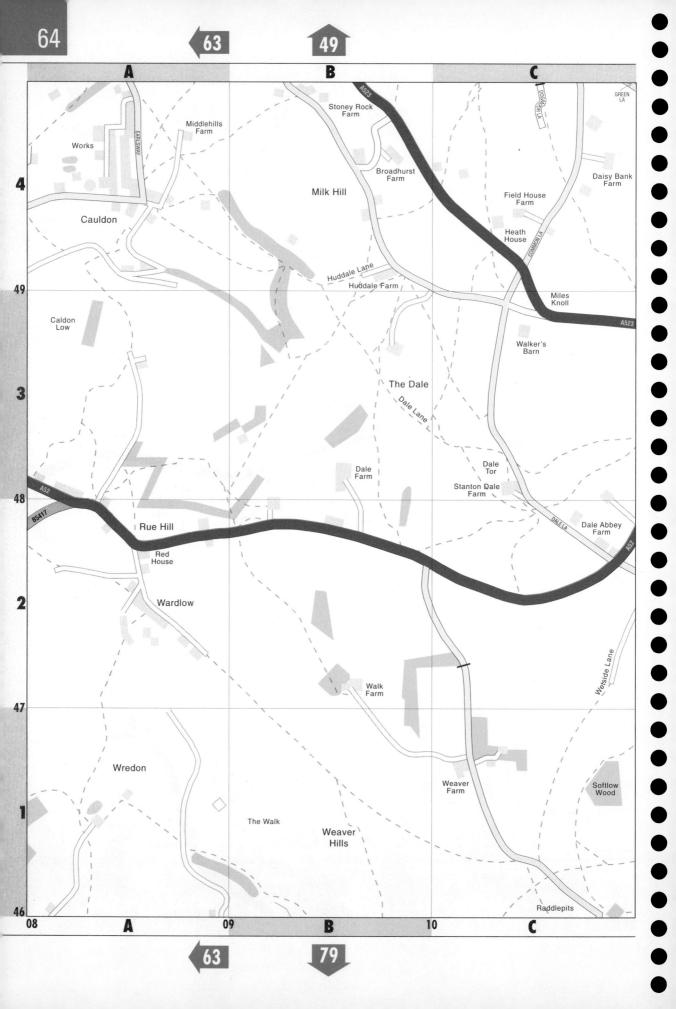

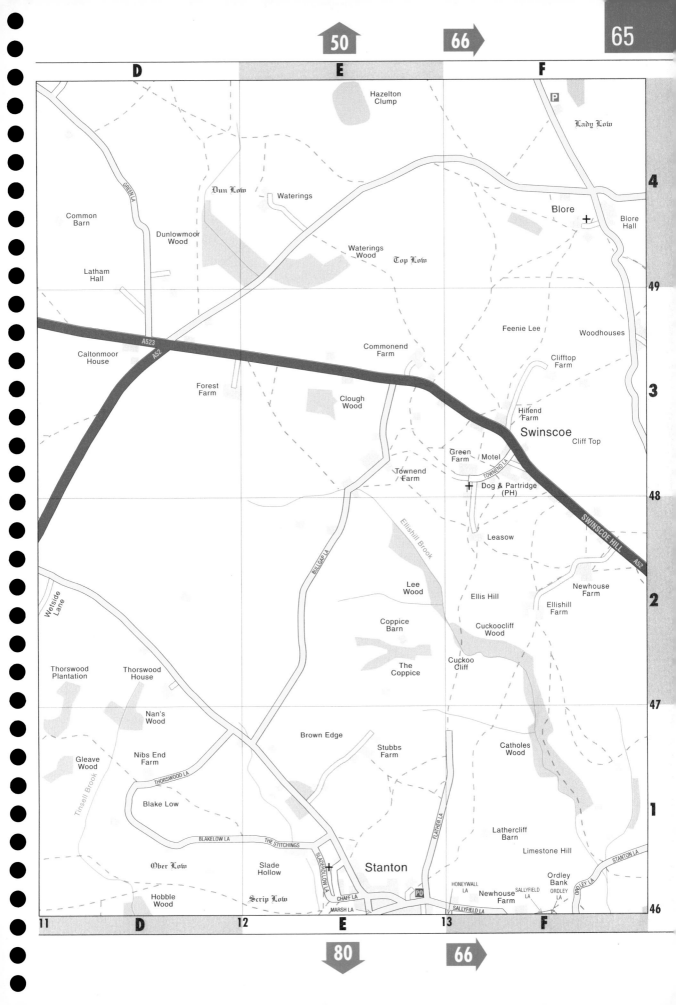

A   B   C

Coldwall
Bridge

4

Coldwall

Little
Peg's
Wood

Tissington Trail

Spendlane
Farm

SPEND LA

49

Littlepark

Hinchley
Wood

Lees House
Farm

Yerley
Farm

Kendar
Wood

Hinchleywood

3

Swinscoe

YERLEY HILL

Cowclose
Wood

Okeover
Hall

Mill

Bank
Farm

Okeover
Bridge

Okeover
Arms
(PH)

Mappleton

Martin
Hill

48

Marten
Hill

Okeover
Park

River Dove

Lower
Grounds
Farm

Smythe's
Plantation

Manor
House

Callowend
Farm

A52

2

The
Orchards

Cornpark

BIRDSGROVE LA

Callow
Hall

47

Snelsdale

Snelsdale
Wood

STANTON LA

Throstle
Nest

Butler's
Holme

Lordspiece

Birdsgrove
Farm

Bentley Brook

Ashbourne

1

SWINSCOE HILL

The
Cliffs

Harlow
Farm

Big
Quarry
Wood

Birdsgrove
House

Sewage
Works

Upper
Mayfield

GALLOWSTREE LA

HOLLOW LA

Buckholme

Cemy

PICCADILLY LA

A52

WATERY LA

SLACK LA

46

14   A   15   B   16   C

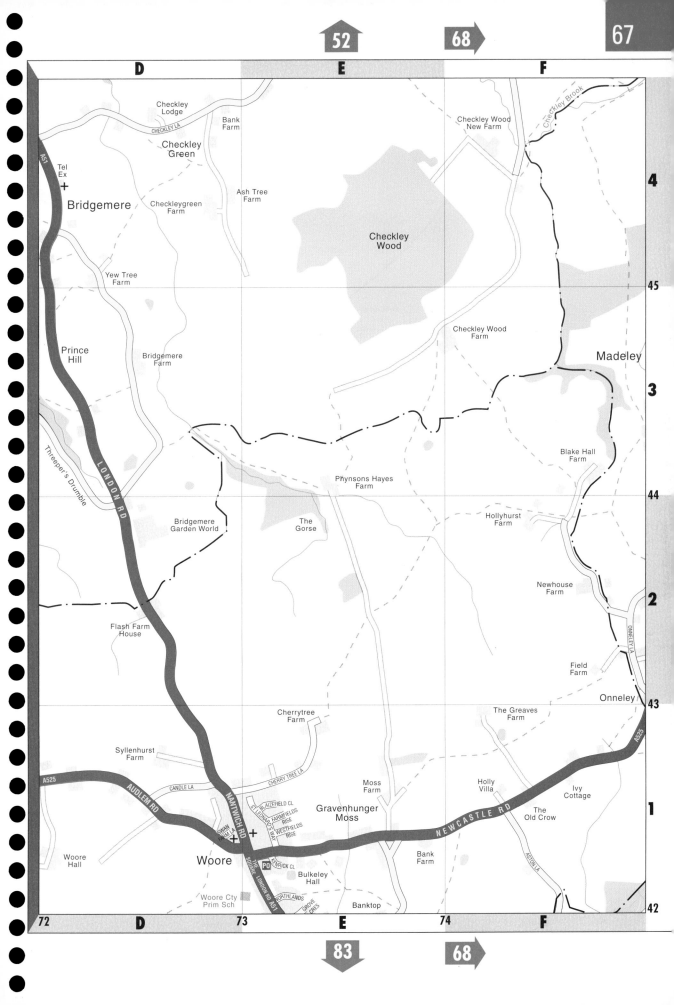

A   B   C

4

Wrinehill Hall

River Lea

Higher Thornhill

Madeley Manor

Manor Park Farm

Little Madeley

Park House

Windy Arbour

Grafton's Wood

The Lum

Lowermill House

WOODLANDS HILLS
HIDDEN HILLS
BONSEY WOOD RD
HEIGHLEY CASTLE WAY
PARK CL
COLLEGE CL
THORNHILL DR
HOLLY OAK DR
GARNERS WAY
HERON CL
BECK RD KINGFISHER CL
WOODSIDE GREEN
ARBOUR CL MEADOWS RD
BEECH CROFT
SALISBURY WAY
NEWCASTLE RD
PO
BEVAN PL
MIDDOWS LA

A525

M6

Middle Madeley

45

Wrinehill Wood

Bowerend

Moss House Farm

Beechfields

APESCROFT
HEATHER BLADE
FERN DRIVE
THE PEAR TREE
THE BRIDLE PATH
PRIMROSE
DELL COTTON
CHARLES
PLOVER FIELD
FIELD DR
THE CLOSE
RIVER LEA MEWS
MERLIN GREEN
CHERRY
BRAMBLE LEA
GRAYLING
WILLOWS
WATERSIDE CL
BIRCH DALE
LAVEROCK GR
MORNINGSIDE
JOHN OFFLEY RD
BOWER END LA
MOSS LA
POOLSIDE
Madeley High Sch
PH

Madeley

3

Wood Farm

Beech Wood

Moor Hall Farm

Barhill Wood

Sir John Offley CE Prim Sch

IZAAC WALTON WAY
VICARAGE LA
PASTORAL CL
KNIGHTLEY
HUNGERFORD LA
PO
CASTLE LA
POST OFFICE SQ
BIRCH MEWS
NETHERSET HEY LA
STATION RD

Birches Farm

44

ONNELEY LA

Yewtree Farm

Field House

Sandfield House

Monument

Works

2

Golf Course

Bar Hill

Bar Hill House Farm

Red Lane

Cemy

Hey House

Bar Hill Farm

BAR HILL

Wheatsheaf Inn (PH)

CH

MANOR RD

River Lea

43

A525

Onneley

STATION RD

Peak's Farm

Upper Bitterns Wood

Manor Farm

1

Onneley Hall Farm

New Terrace

Lower Bitterns Wood

42

Lea Head Manor

Aston Cliff

Old Madeley Manor (rems of)

75   A   76   B   77   C

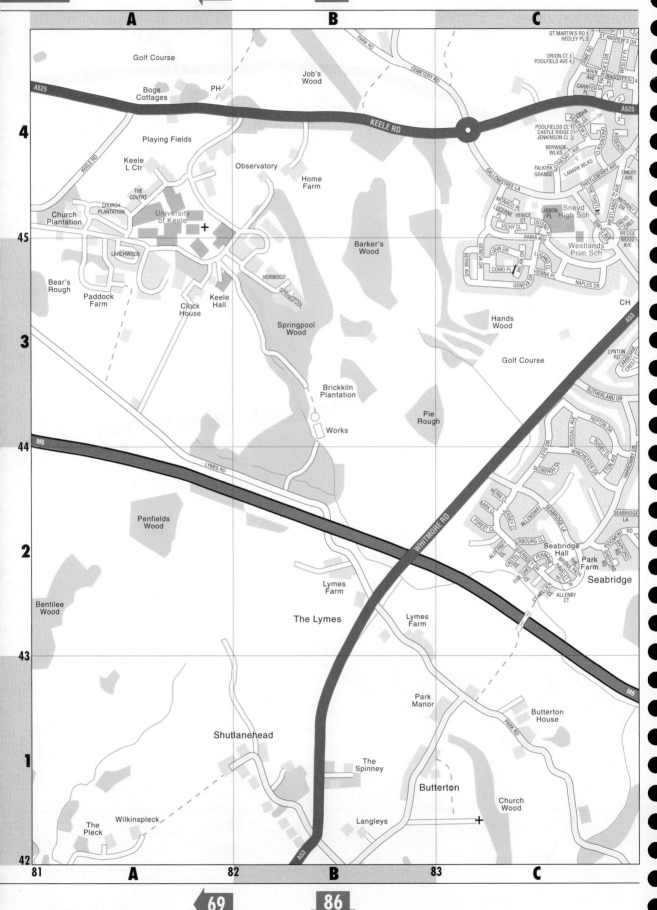

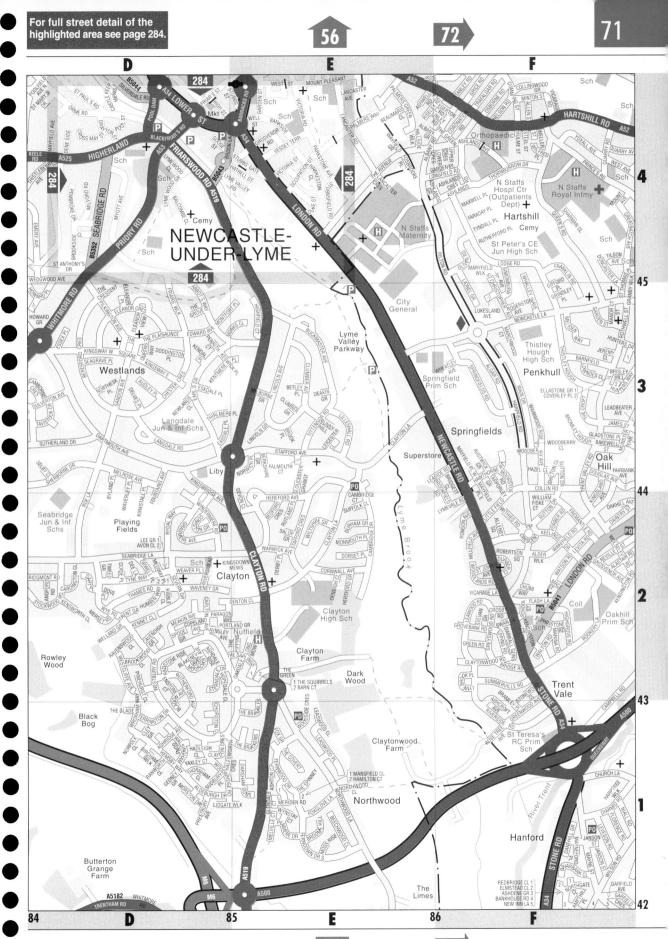

For full street detail of the highlighted area see page 284.

56

72

71

NEWCASTLE-UNDER-LYME

Westlands

Penkhull

Hartshill

Springfields

Oak Hill

Clayton

Northwood

Trent Vale

Hanford

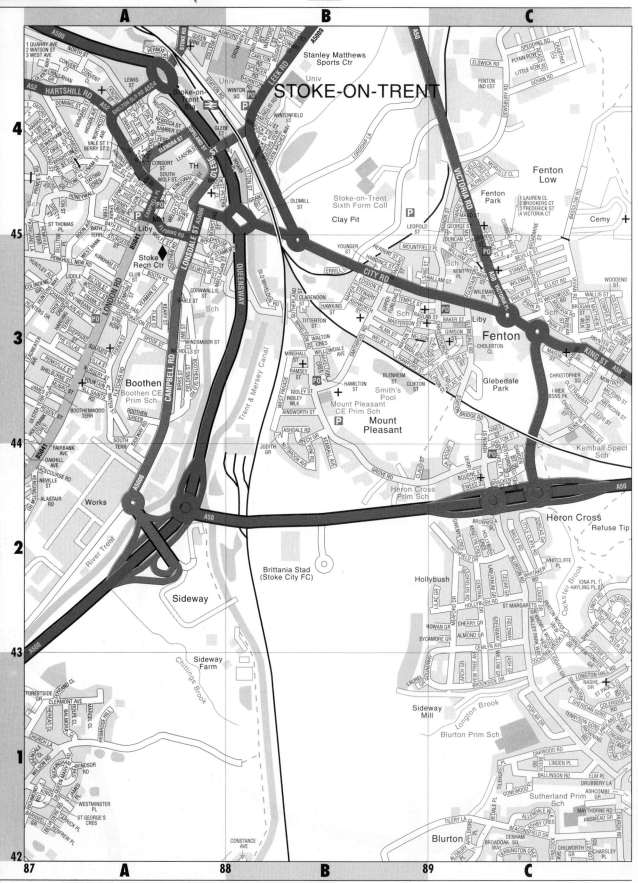

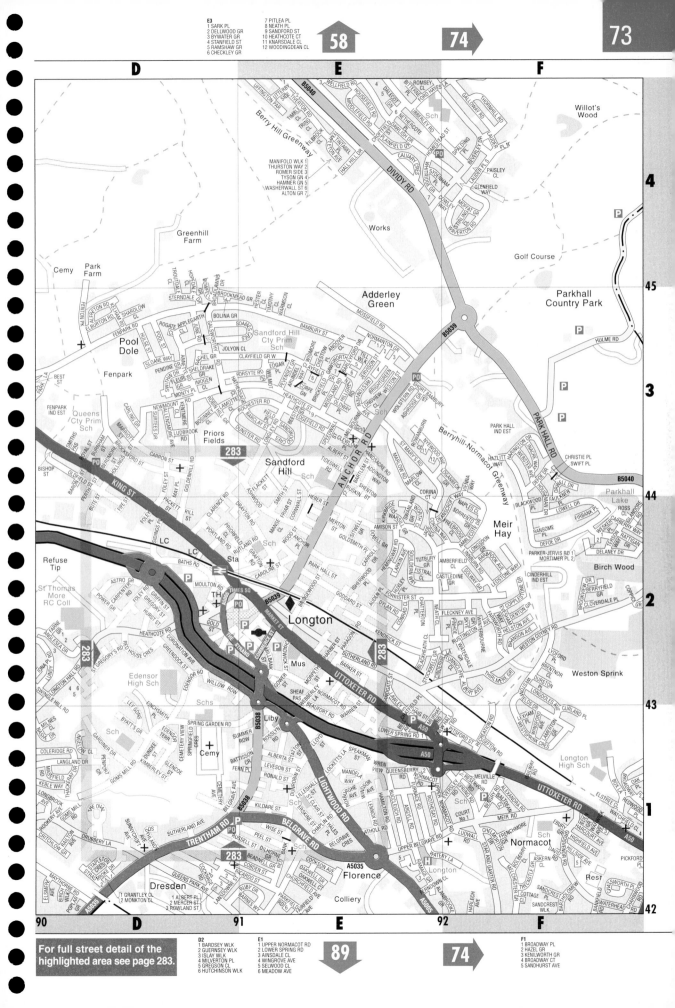

A B C

4

HULME LA
Stonehouse Farm
Hulme
The Candlesticks (PH)
Hall Farm
Winterfield Farm
HULME RD
WINTERFIELD LA
MALTHOUSE LA
SALTERS LA
Malthouse Farm
Captain's Barn
Smallbrook Farm
LEEK RD
A520
Creswell's Piece

45

Blythe Lea
Ford
Sheepwash Farm
Sheepwash
Ward Hill Farm

3

P
Parkhall Ctry Pk
Boltongate Farm
Roughcote
Caverswall Common
Hardiwick Farm
Tickhill Farm
ASTER CL
CARNATION CL
DAHLIA CL
EAST ST
LYNN ST
SELBY ST
P
COALVILLE PL
FERNLEA GR
COUPE DR
BATH ST
CROSS ST
FOXGLOVE
IRIS CL
LILAC CL
LIME CL
MAIN ST
GATE ST
FLINT ST
DIMMELOW
LAVENDER CL
WEST ST
River Blithe
ROUGHCOTE LA
TICKHILL LA

44

Weston Coyney
PARK HALL RD
B5040
HORTON DR
ENGLESEA AVE
EDWARD
PARK AVE
OSWALL AVE
THE CLOSE
HEATHCOTE RISE
WELDON AVE
MANN ST
HEYSHAM CL
HOLYHEAD CRES
STRANFAER
Sch
Cocking Farm
HANDLEY BANKS
Intakes Farm

2

Weston Sprink
GLADSTONE RD
PARK HALL RD
MINARD GR
MANNIN GR
ROSS CL
TAME WLK
IBSEN CL
GEOFFREY
CABBERLY WAY
RATTIGAN DR
WESTON COYNEY RD
PARKHEAD GR
PARTON GR
RADWORTH GR
COYNEY GR
SPRINKWOOD GR
NEW KINGSWAY
QUEENS WLK
PRINCESS
FIELD VIEW
THE MOAT
HALL DR
FITZGERALD CL
PALADIN AVE
HAYNER GR
CAVERSWALL RD
AVON CRES
DALE VIEW
YORK RD
DAWN VIEW
TERRY CL
MICHAEL CL
BRINDON CL
VALLEY RD
Weston Coyney Jun Sch
Cookshill
THE GREEN
LONG ROW
HALLDEARN AVE
NATHAM CL
MILL CL
Green Farm
Yewtree Farm
WESTON RD
Tunstall Sytch

43

MACDONALD CRES
TILLEE GREEN
LANSBURY GR
GLYNNS
MYRTLE AVE
BIRD RD
GOODWIN RD
MAXTON WAY
ODGER SNOWDEN LA
TAWNEY CRES
WHITCOMBE RD
THE GRANGE
BROOKHOUSE
LEASON RD
BURNS
BONDFIELD WAY
TREVOR DR
VICARAGE RD
HIGH ST
THE HOLLOW
DILHORNE LA
Cookshill Hall
The Red House PH
Caverswall
St Peter's CE Prim Sch
THE DAMS
Castle
St Filumena's RC Prim Sch
CHURCH TERR
STOKE-ON-TRENT

1

OAK PL
BROADWAY
CHERRY HILL AVE
DENEHURST CL
BROWNFIELD RD
WESTWOOD RD
WOODVILLE RD
WOODVILLE
MEIR VIEW
YARNFIELD PL
THE SQUARE
MAPLE
MEADOW
BRIARWOOD PL
HARVEY CT
BLATCHFORD
WOOD PL
STANSMORE RD
MONTGOMERY
PENNINGTON
BEVERIDGE LA
DEWAR
THE WALK
THE WOOD
DENWOOD DR
PINEWOOD CRES
Pinewood Prim Sch
Wood House Farm
Caverswall Park
SCHOOL LA
BLYTHE BRIDGE RD

PICKFORD PL
LOMBARDY
GIBSON RD
BRIGHT ST
REDWOOD
EAST GR
QUEENSWAY
A50
P
Meir
Liby
P
UTTOXETER RD
A520
SANDON RD
SARAGH
GRANGEWOOD RD
CHARTHILL
HARDWICK
MOLLISON
George Ave
Road under construction
Meir Prim Sch
WILLOWOOD GR
CAVERSWALL LA
LC
APPLEWOOD CRES
DENHURST AVE
Foxfield Steam Railway
1 CHATSWORTH PL
2 CROSSLAND PL
3 WCOBHAM PL

42

93 A 94 B 95 C

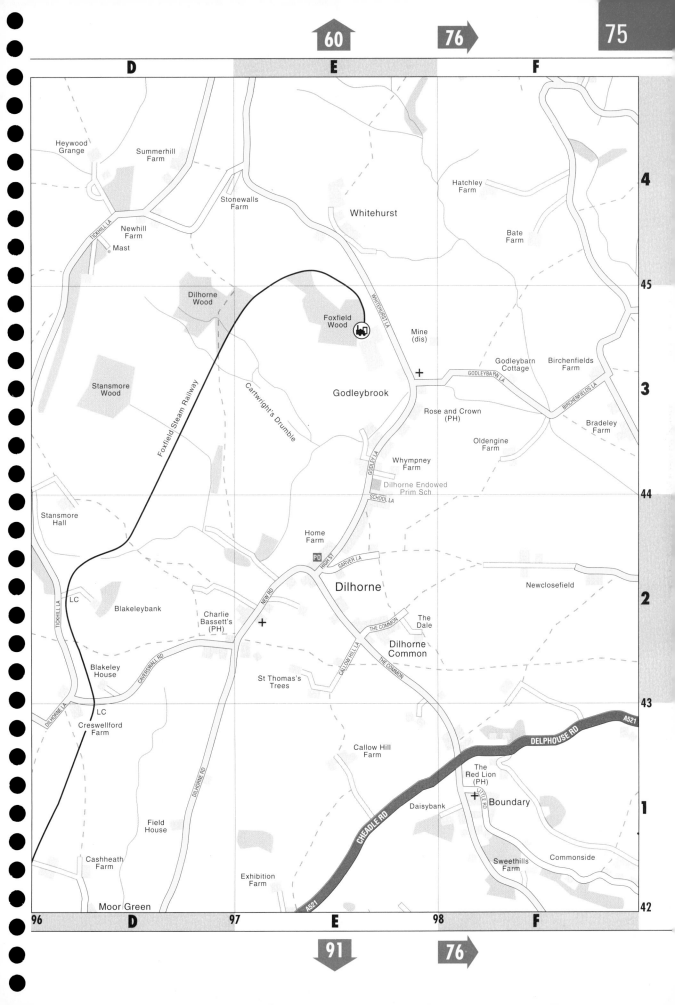

D
E
F

Heywood Grange
Summerhill Farm
Stonewalls Farm
Whitehurst
Hatchley Farm
Bate Farm

TICKHILL LA
Newhill Farm
Mast

4

Dilhorne Wood
Foxfield Wood
Mine (dis)
WHITEHURST LA

45

Foxfield Steam Railway
Cartwright's Drumble
Stansmore Wood
Godleybrook
Godleybarn Cottage
Birchenfields Farm
GODLEYBARN LA
BIRCHENFIELDS LA

3

Rose and Crown (PH)
Bradeley Farm

GODLEY LA
Whympney Farm
Oldengine Farm

Stansmore Hall
Dilhorne Endowed Prim. Sch

44

SCHOOL LA
Home Farm
PO
HIGH ST
SARVER LA
Newclosefield

TICKHILL LA
LC
Blakeleybank
Charlie Bassett's (PH)
NEW RD
Dilhorne
The Dale

2

Blakeley House
CAVERSWALL RD
THE COMMON
Dilhorne Common
CALLOW HILL LA
THE COMMON

St Thomas's Trees

43

DILHORNE LA
LC
Creswellford Farm
DILHORNE RD
Callow Hill Farm
DELPHOUSE RD
A521
The Red Lion (PH)
STILE RD
Boundary

1

Field House
CHEADLE RD
Daisybank
Commonside

Cashheath Farm
Exhibition Farm
A521
Sweethills Farm

42

Moor Green

96
D
97
E
98
F

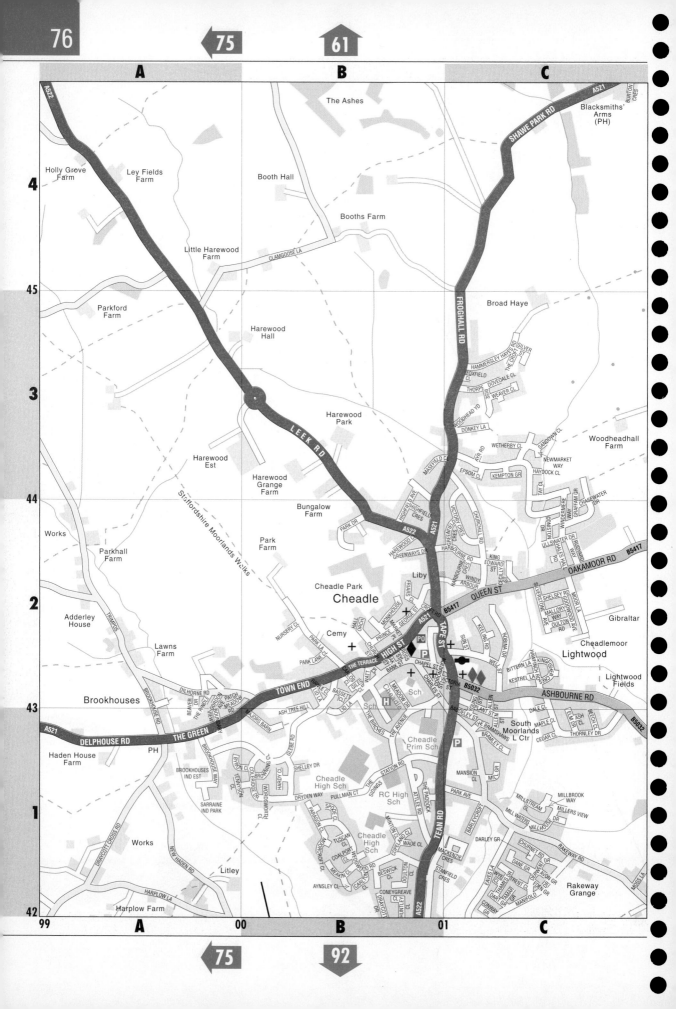

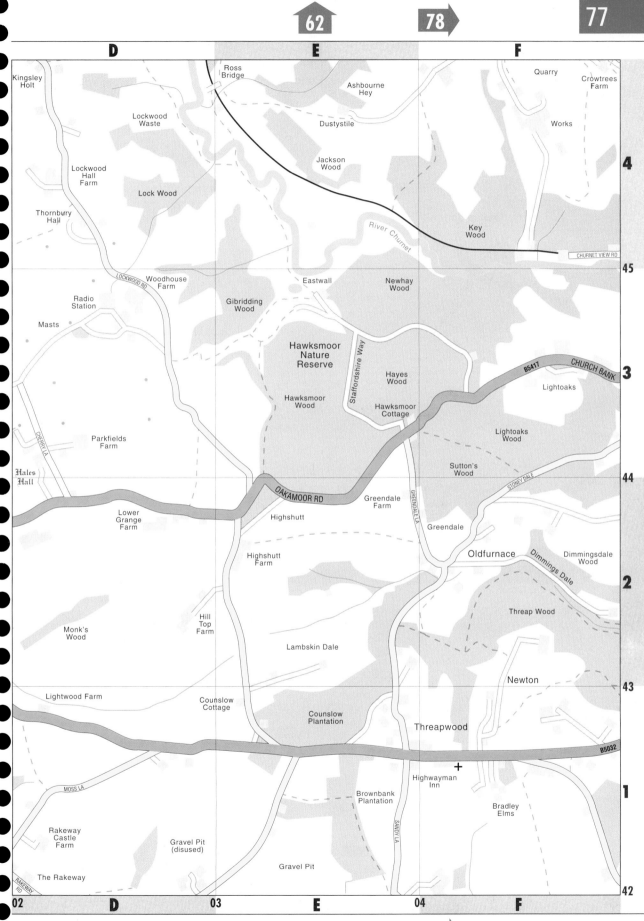

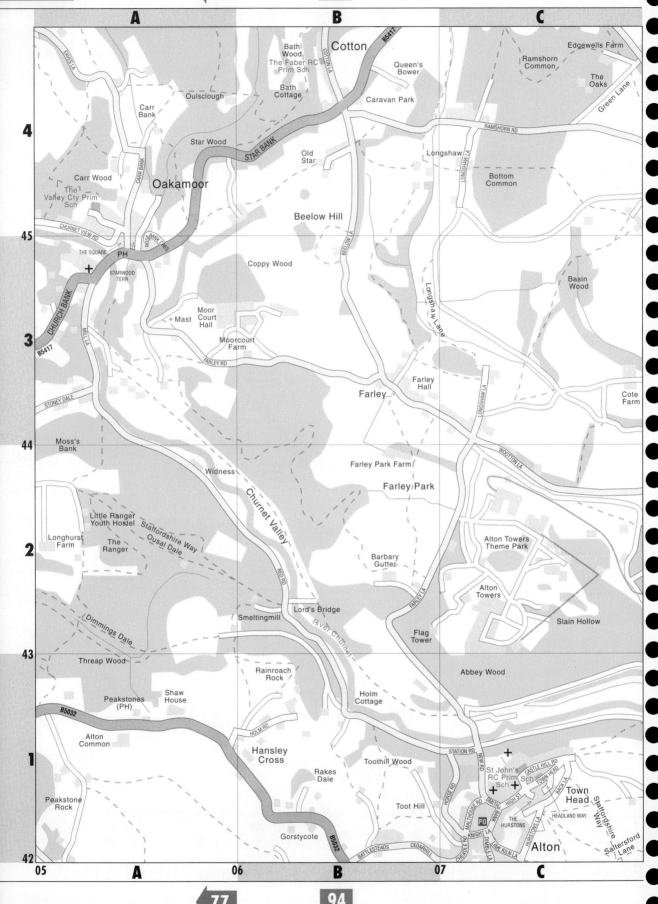

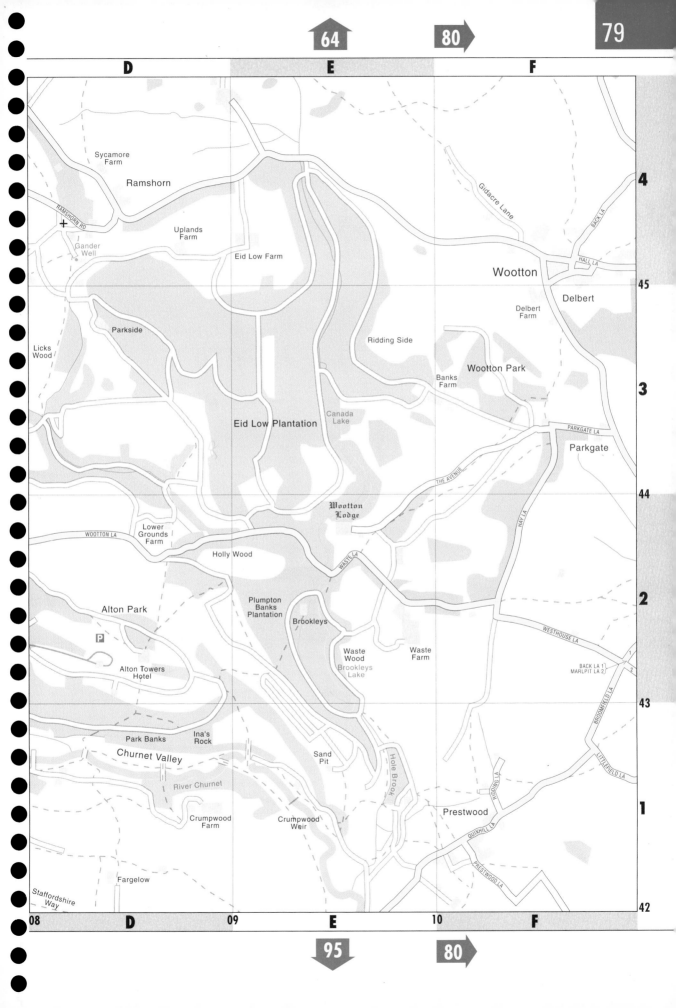

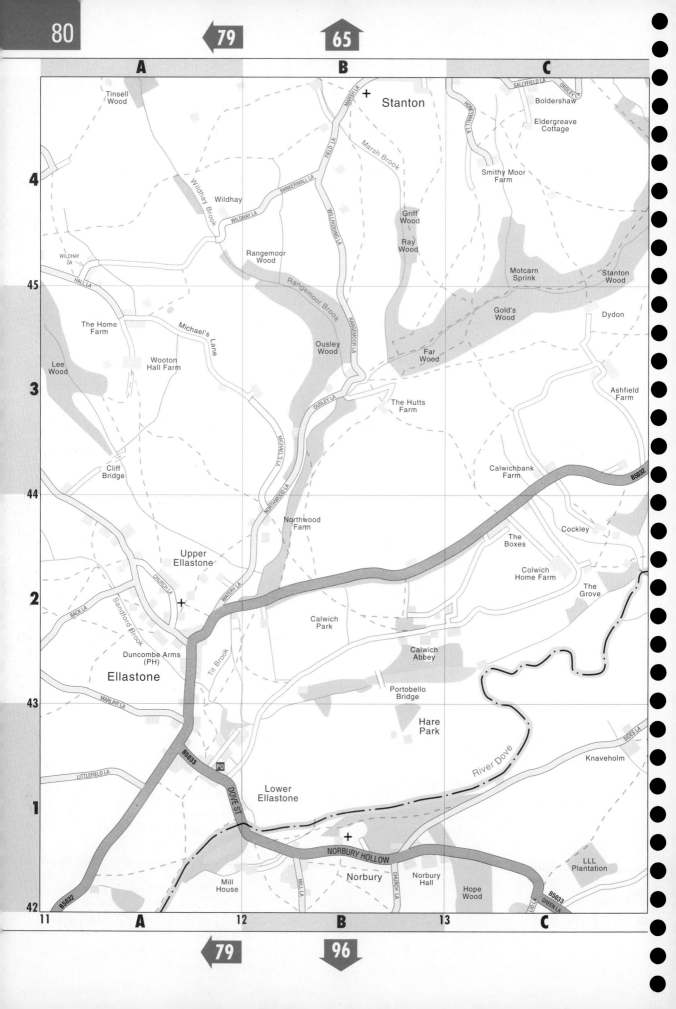

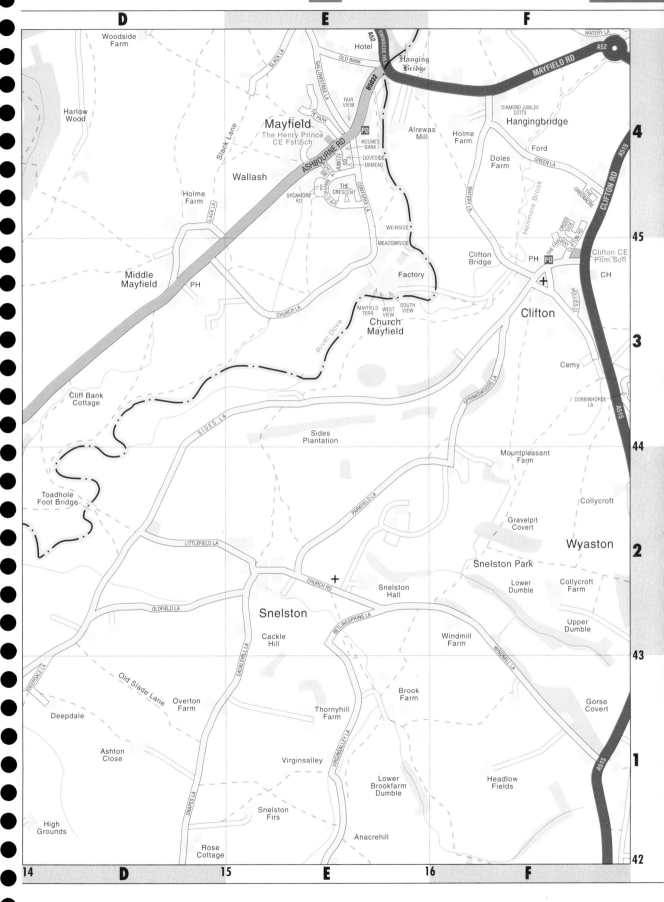

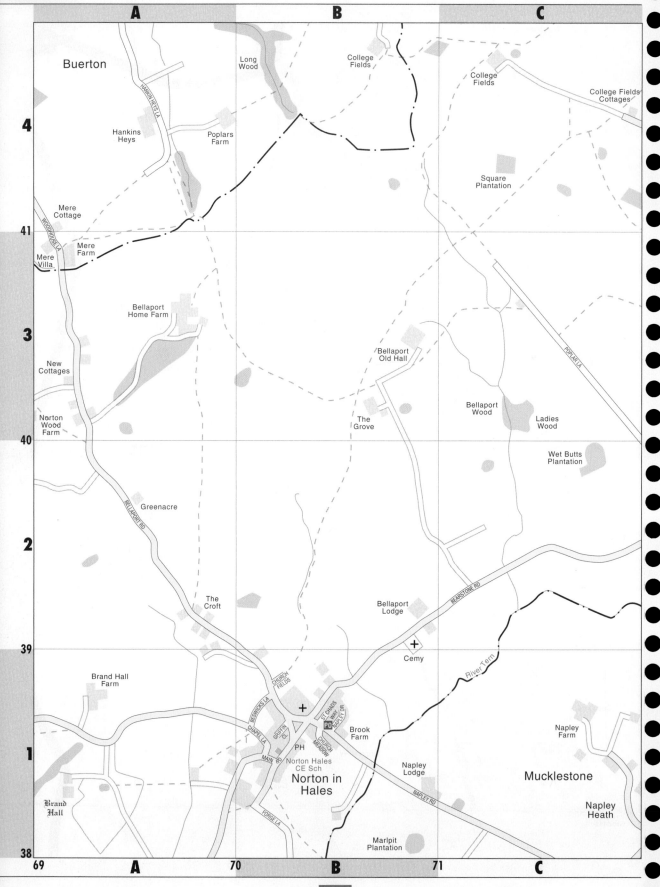

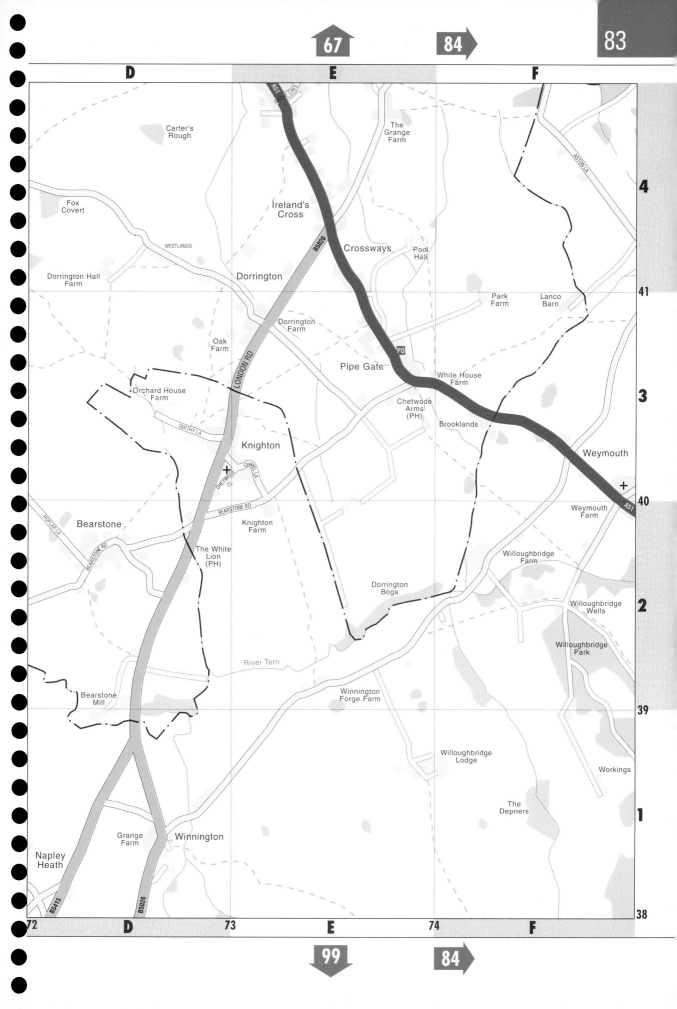

A **B** **C**

4

Radwood
Copse

Rock House
Farm

Lunts
Farm

Radwood Hall
Farm

Aston

ASTON LA

SCHOOL LA

41

Yew Tree
Farm

HOLLOWAY LA

Radwood
Farm

CAMP HILL

3

Minnbank

Bank
Farm

Holloway
Pit Holes

Holloway
Farm

Holloway Lane
Farm

Mast

Minnbank
Farm

MAERWAY LA

Maerway Lane
Farm

Camp Wood

Greenfields

Willoughbridge

40

A51

The Dorothy
Clive Garden

Sidway Hall
Farm

Maer Hills

Sidway

2

BADGER LA

Willoughbridge
Bogs

Sidway
Mill

+

A53

39

THE CROFT

River Tern

Blackbrook

A51

Park House

White
Farm

Swan with
Two Necks
(PH)

A53

The Bogs

1

Lower Bogs
Plantation

WHARMADINE LA

Maer Moss
Farm

MOSS LA

Workings

Hungersheath
Farm

NEWCASTLE RD

PARK LA

The
Wellings

A53 ROCK W

38

75 **A** **76** **B** **77** **C**

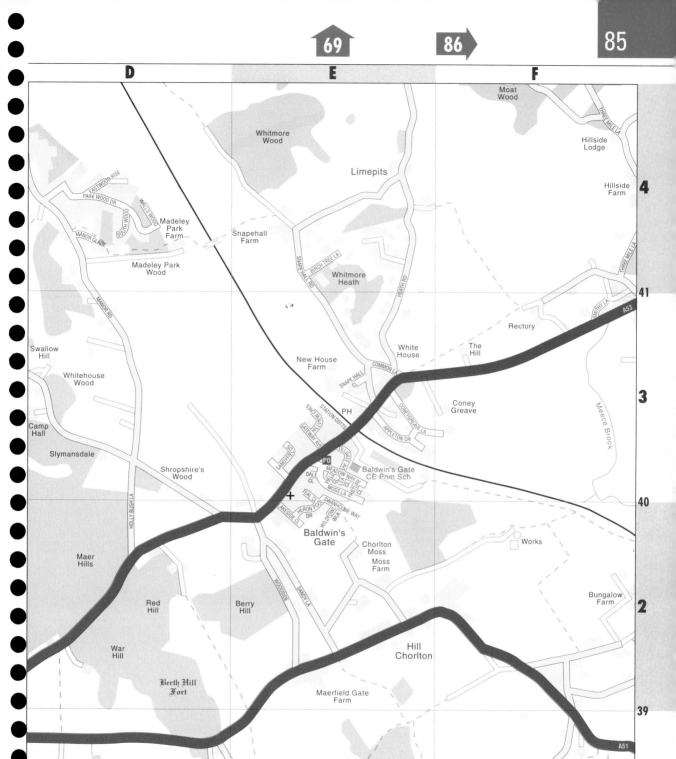

D E F

4

41

3

40

2

39

1

38

Moat Wood
Hillside Lodge
Hillside Farm
THREE MILE LA

Whitmore Wood
Limepits

Eastwood Rise
PARK WOOD DR
WALL'S WOOD
SOUTH WOOD
Madeley Park Farm
MANOR GLADE
Madeley Park Wood

Snapehall Farm
Whitmore Heath
SNAPE HALL RD
BIRCH TREE LA
HEATH RD

Rectory
SMITHY LA
A53

New House Farm
White House
The Hill
Coney Greave
Meece Brook

Swallow Hill
Whitehouse Wood
MANOR RD
Camp Hall
Slymansdale
Shropshire's Wood
HOLLY BUSH LA

Snape Hall CL
COMMON LA
CONGREAVE LA
APPLETON DR
PH
STATION COTTS
GATEWAY AVE
MILL CASTLE CRES
SANDYFIELDS
PO
COLLEGE AVE
MEADOW WAY
DALE CL
MOSS LA
Baldwin's Gate CE Prim Sch
THE PASTURE
TEAL CL
SWANHOLME WAY
HERON POOL DR
LAKESIDE CL
WILDFOWL WALK
Baldwin's Gate
Chorlton Moss
Moss Farm
Works

Maer Hills
Red Hill
Berry Hill
WOODSIDE
SANDY LA
War Hill
Berth Hill Fort
Hill Chorlton
Maerfield Gate Farm
Bungalow Farm

MOSS LA
The Ridding
Maer Pool
Maer Hall
Maer
Bates Farm
A51
Coombesdale
COOMBESDALE
Coombe's Rough
Little Lane
HADDON LA
Broughton Plantation
The Old Rectory

78 D 79 E 80 F

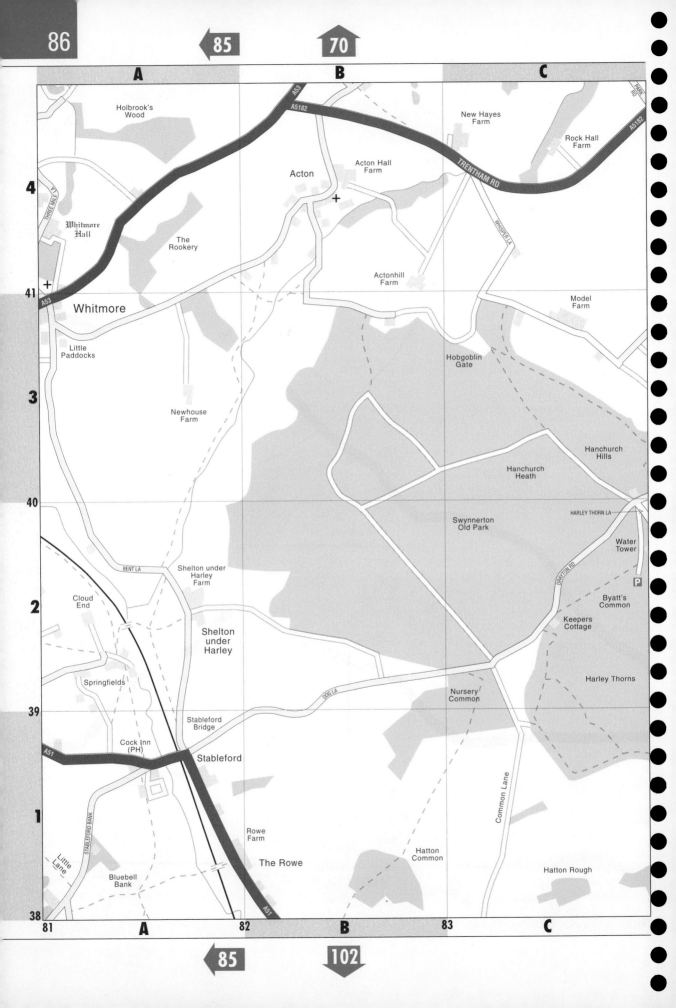

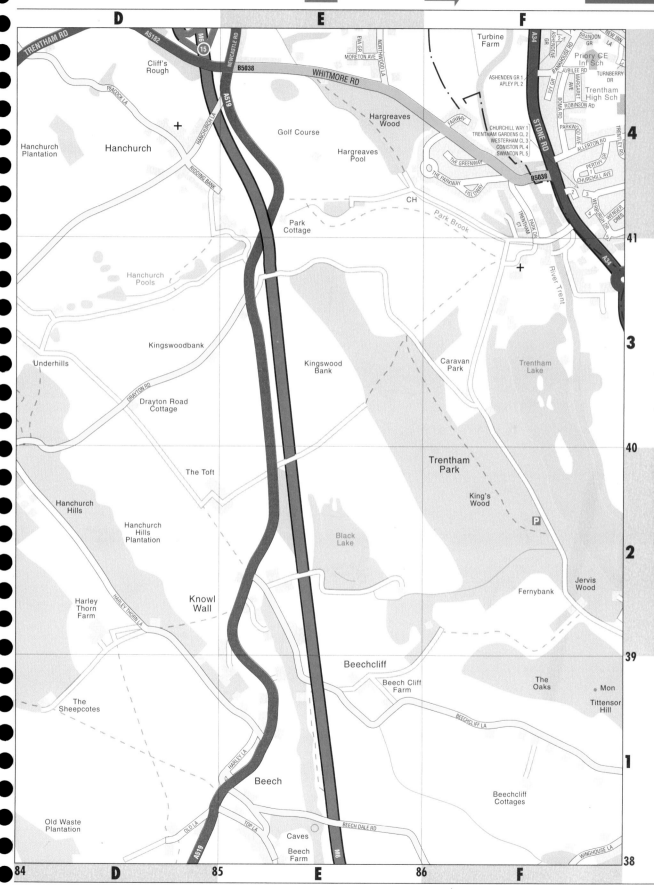

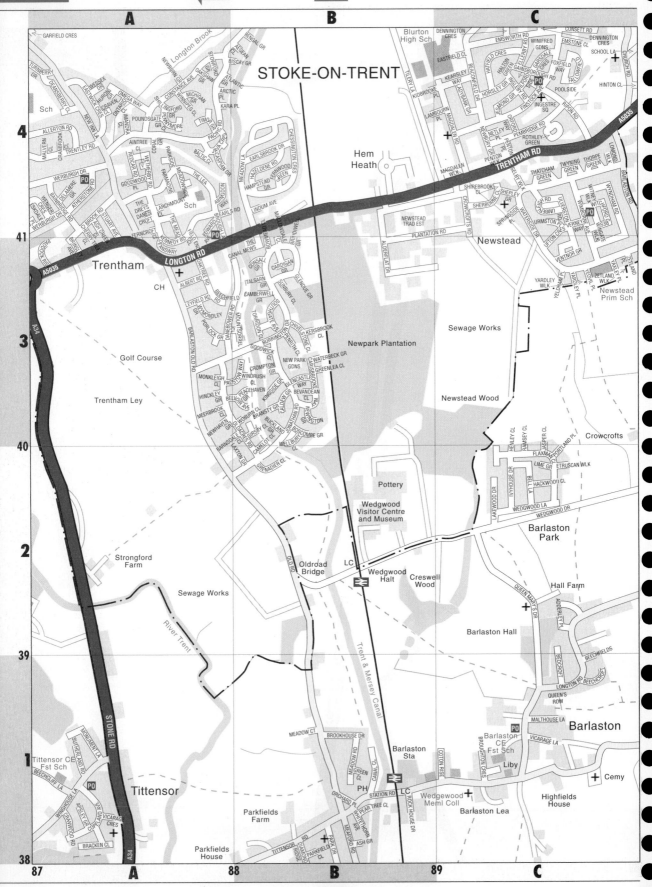

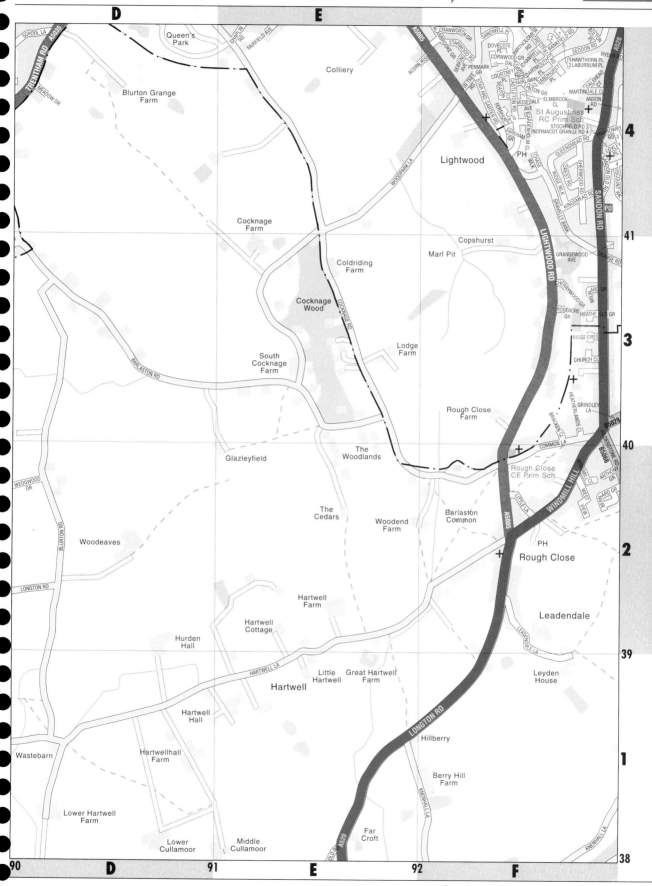

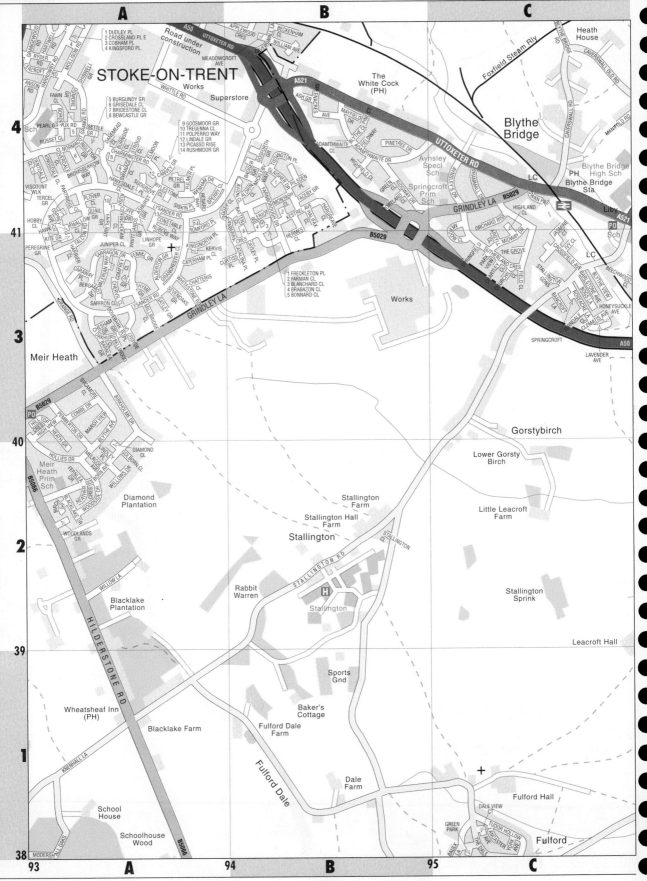

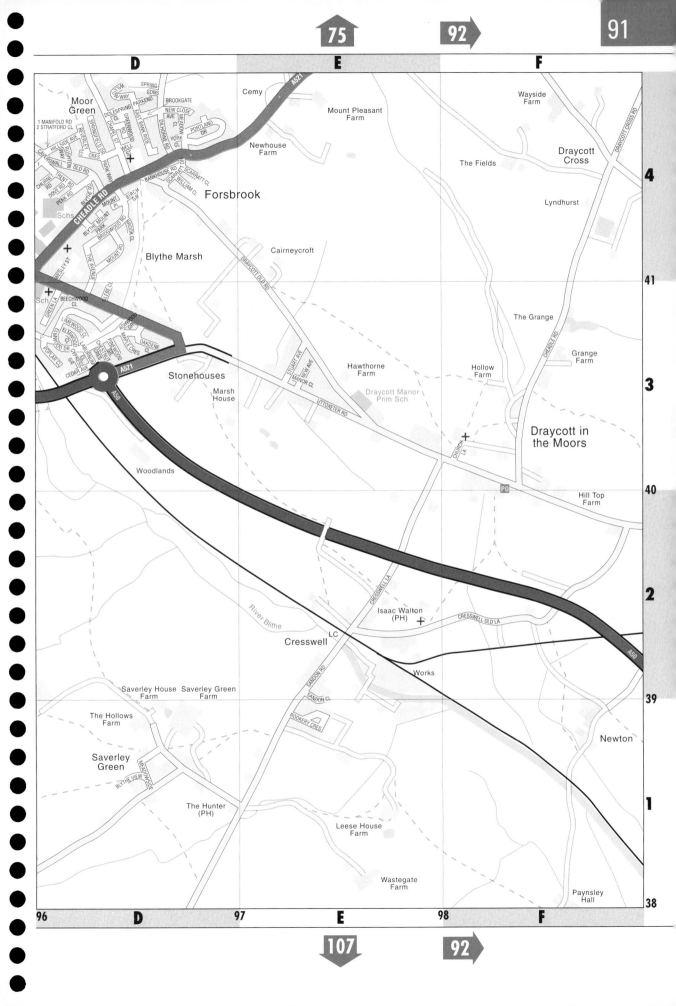

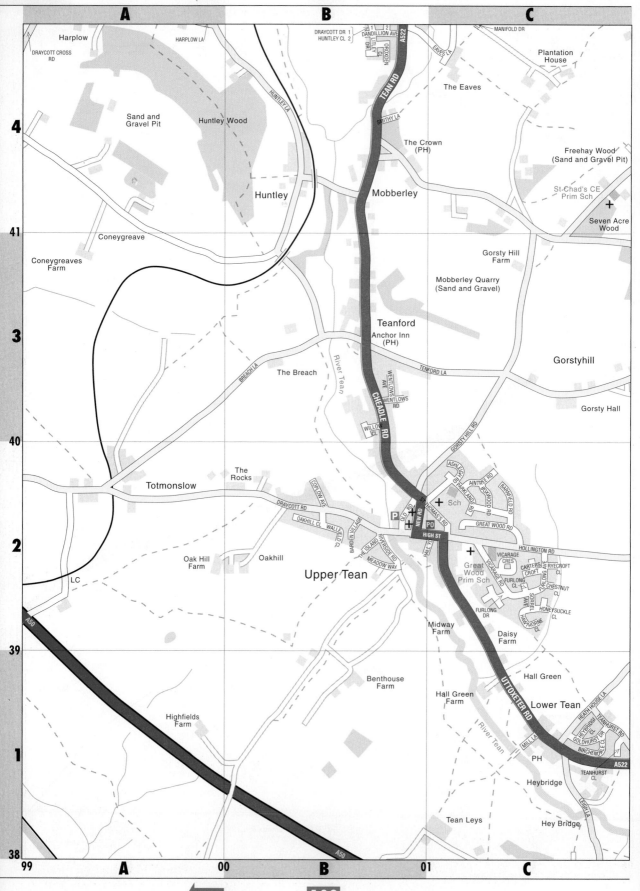

D   E   F

4

41

3

40

2

39

1

38

Rakeway

RAKEWAY RD

Queen's Arms (PH)

Brown Bank Farm

Sand and Gravel Pit

Cheadle Common

Freehay

Beech Farm

Coneydale Farm

SANDY LA

Lightoaks Farm

Coneydale Farm

Dale Bank Farm

Lord's Coppice

Spring Farm

Winnothdale

Pad Plantation

Temple Wood

North Plantation

The Temple

Paradise Cottage

Lodgedale Farm

HOLLINGTON RD

Goldhurst

Hollybush

Broadview

Common End

HEATH HOUSE LA

Heath House

Broadgate Hall

Highridges

Broadgatehall Drumble

TEANHURST RD

Checkleyfields Cottage

Checkleyfields Farm

Fourtrees

UTTOXETER RD

CRANBERRY AVE

A522

BADGERS HOLLOW

Overton

Overton Farm

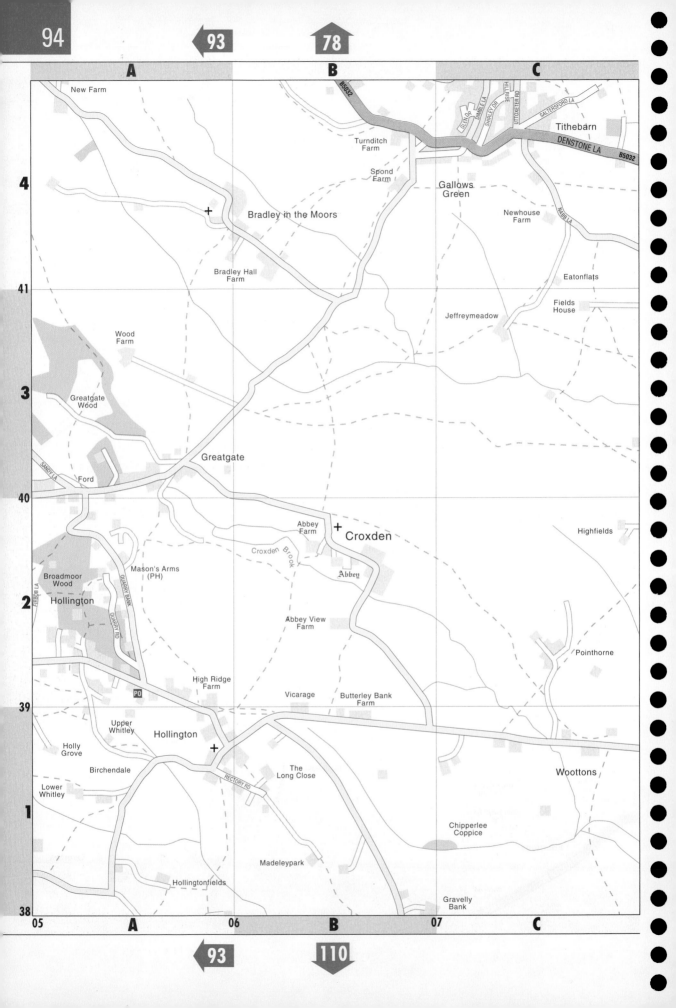

A   B   C

New Farm

B5032

GLEN DR
DIMBLE LA
SHIRLEY DR
HILLRISE
UTTOXETER RD
SALTERSFORD LA

Tithebarn

DENSTONE LA   B5032

Turnditch
Farm

Spond
Farm

Gallows
Green

Newhouse
Farm

NABB LA

4

+

Bradley in the Moors

Eatonflats

Bradley Hall
Farm

41

Jeffreymeadow

Fields
House

Wood
Farm

SANDY LA

3

Greatgate
Wood

Greatgate

Ford

40

Abbey
Farm

+ Croxden

Highfields

Croxden Brook

Mason's Arms
(PH)

Abbey

NABB LA

Broadmoor
Wood

QUARRY BANK

QUARRY RD

2

Hollington

Abbey View
Farm

Pointhorne

High Ridge
Farm

PO

Vicarage

Butterley Bank
Farm

39

Upper
Whitley

Hollington

+

Holly
Grove

Birchendale

RECTORY RD

The
Long Close

Woottons

Lower
Whitley

1

Chipperlee
Coppice

Madeleypark

Hollingtonfields

Gravelly
Bank

38

05   A   06   B   07   C

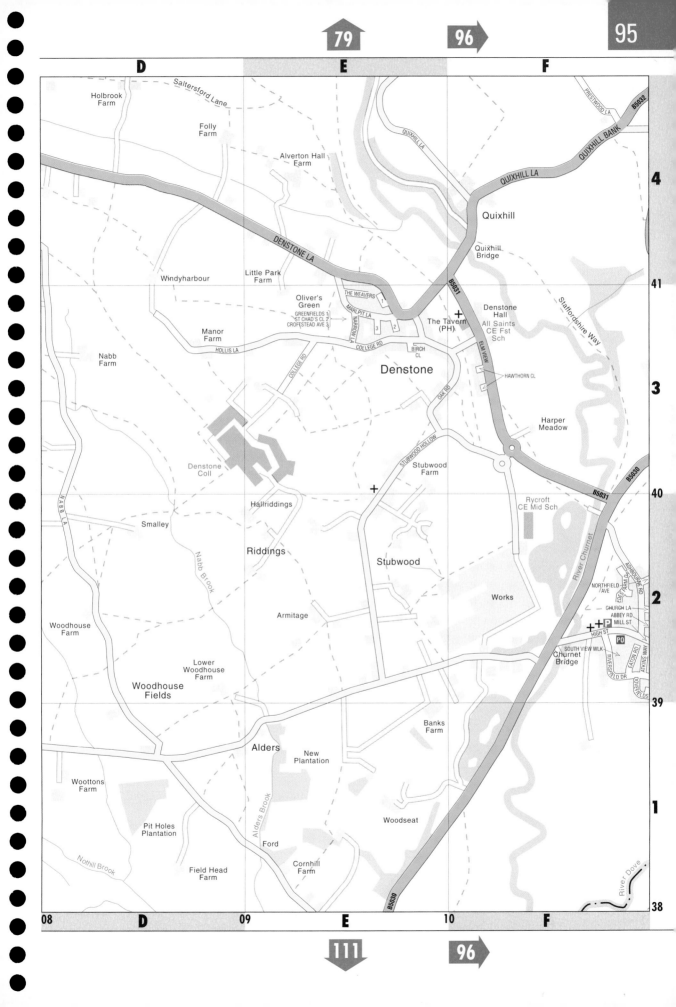

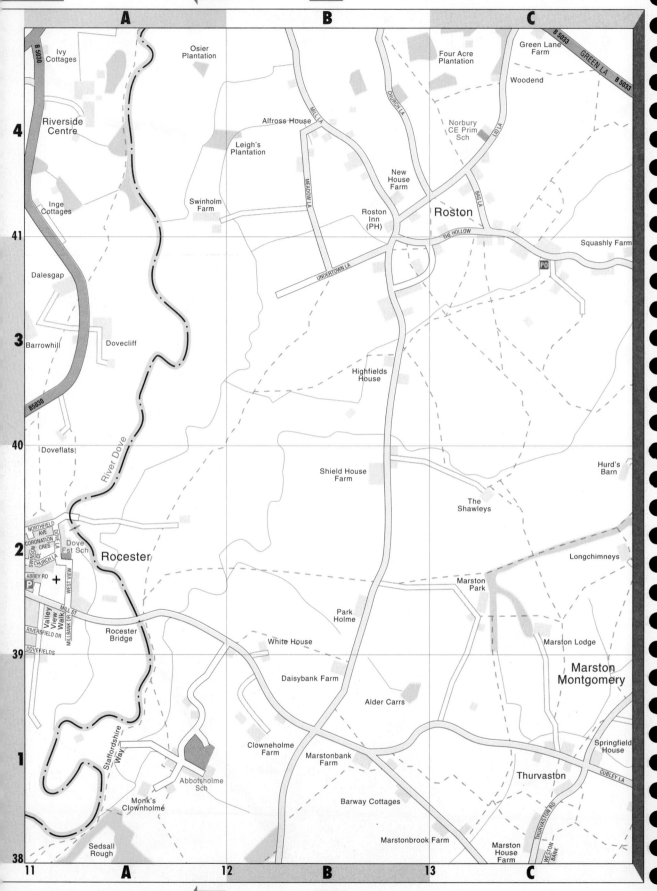

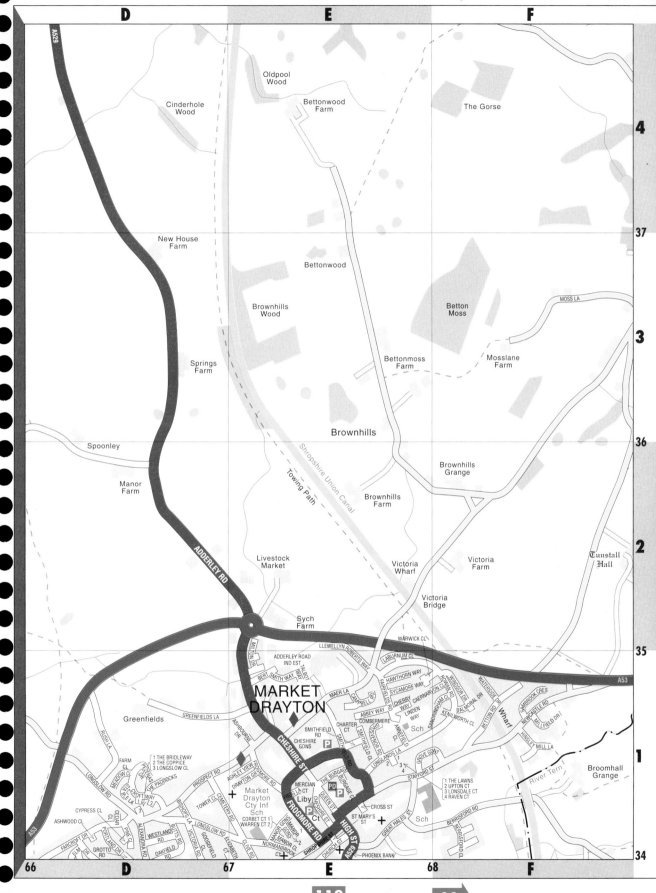

D   E   F

A529

Oldpool
Wood

Cinderhole
Wood

Bettonwood
Farm

The Gorse

4

New House
Farm

Bettonwood

37

MOSS LA

Brownhills
Wood

Betton
Moss

3

Springs
Farm

Bettonmoss
Farm

Mosslane
Farm

Shropshire Union Canal

Brownhills

36

Spoonley

Towing Path

Brownhills
Grange

Manor
Farm

Brownhills
Farm

ADDERLEY RD

Livestock
Market

Victoria
Wharf

Victoria
Farm

Tunstall
Hall

2

Victoria
Bridge

Sych
Farm

WARWICK CL

35

LLEWELLYN ROBERTS WAY

LABURNUM CL

A53

MILTON DR

ADDERLEY ROAD
IND EST

BERT SMITH WAY

TALBOT WAY

HAWTHORN WAY

SYCAMORE WAY

WINDSOR DR

ROWAN RD

WATERSIDE DR

BALMORAL DR

SEABROOK CAES

MARKET
DRAYTON

MAER LA

CAMPBELL ST

FAIRFIELDS RD

CHERRY WAY

CAERNARVON CL

KENILWORTH CL

BETTON RD

NEWCASTLE RD

MILLFIELD DR

Greenfields

GREENFIELDS LA

ABBEY WAY

LINDEN WAY

COMBERMERE

Sch

HINSLEY RD

MILL LA

CHARTER CT

ANNEFIELD CL

Wharf

ASHBOURNE DR

SMITHFIELD
RD

CHESHIRE
GDNS

P

SMITHFIELD RD

LONGLANDS LA

GROVE GDNS

River Tern

Broomhall
Grange

RUSH LA

1 THE BRIDLEWAY
2 THE COPPICE
3 LONGSLOW CL

PROSPECT RD

ASHLEY VIEW

DRAYTON DR

FROGMORE RD

CHESHIRE ST

THE BURGAGE

1 2

3 4

STAFFORD ST

1 THE LAWNS
2 UPTON CT
3 LONSDALE CT
4 RAVEN CT

1

MEADOW CL

FARM CL

PICKSTOCK CL

THE PADDOCKS

TOWER LA

Market
Drayton
Cty Inf
Sch

MERCIAN CT

FROG LA CT

Liby

Ct

P

QUEEN ST

P

P

CROSS ST

GREAT HALES ST

ST MARY'S ST

Sch

BERRISFORD RD

BERRISFORD CL

CYPRESS CL

LONGSLOW RD

BISHOPS LA

CEMETERY RD

CORBET CT 1
WARREN CT 2

ELIZABETH

FROGMORE RD

CHURCH ST

ASHWOOD CL

FARCROFT DR

CEDAR CL

PINE CL

ALEXANDRA RD

PORTLAND DR

GROTTO RD

ELM CL

WESTLAND RD

BUTTS RD

VICTORIA RD

OAKFIELD RD

LONGSLOW RD

GOOSEFIELD

MANOR CL

NORMANBROOK

MANOR GR

HIGH ST

A529

SHROPSHIRE ST

Phoenix Bank

66   D   67   E   68   F

34

112

98 ➤

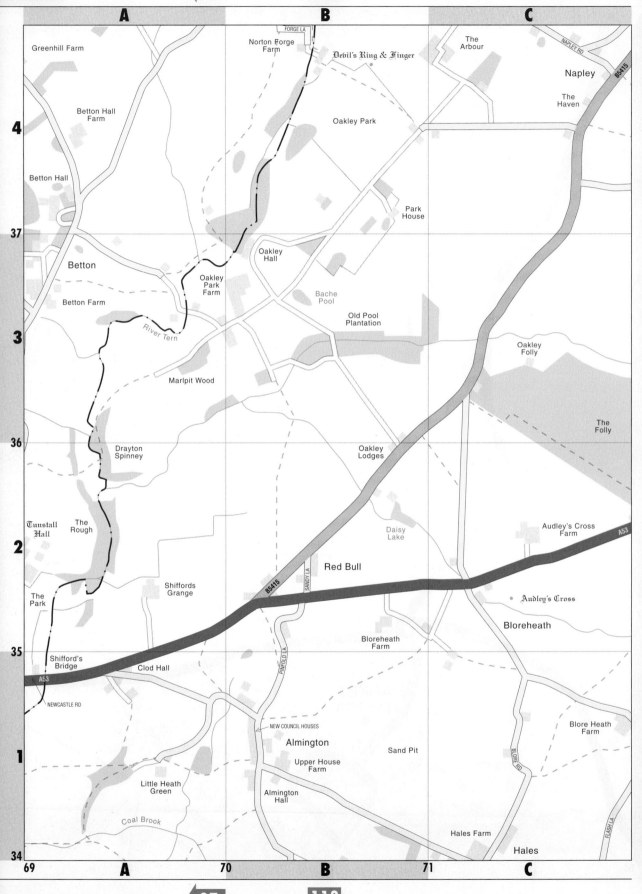

A

B

C

FORGE LA

Greenhill Farm

Norton Forge
Farm

Devil's Ring & Finger

The
Arbour

NAPLEY RD

Napley

B5415

Betton Hall
Farm

4

Oakley Park

The
Haven

Park
House

Betton Hall

37

Betton

Oakley
Hall

Oakley
Park Farm

Bache
Pool

Old Pool
Plantation

Oakley
Folly

Betton Farm

River Tern

3

Marlpit Wood

The
Folly

36

Drayton
Spinney

Oakley
Lodges

Tunstall
Hall

The Rough

Daisy
Lake

Audley's Cross
Farm

A53

2

The
Park

Shiffords
Grange

B5415

SANDY LA

Red Bull

Audley's Cross

Bloreheath

Shifford's
Bridge

Clod Hall

PINFOLD LA

Bloreheath
Farm

BLORE RD

35

A53

NEWCASTLE RD

NEW COUNCIL HOUSES

Almington

Sand Pit

Blore Heath
Farm

1

Upper House
Farm

RASH LA

Little Heath
Green

Almington
Hall

Coal Brook

Hales Farm

Hales

34

69

A

70

B

71

C

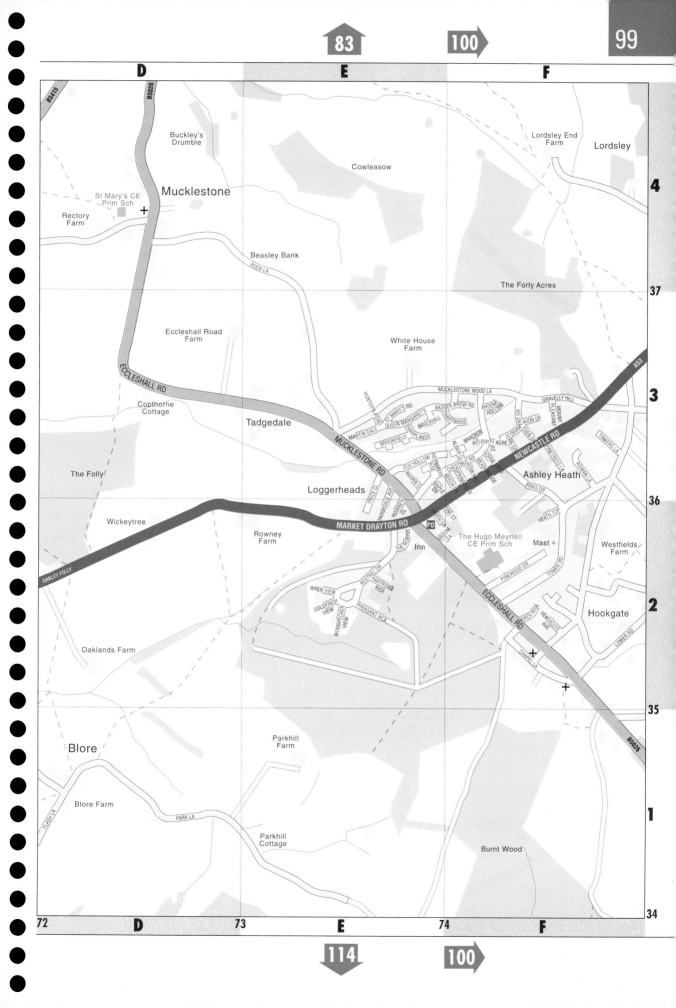

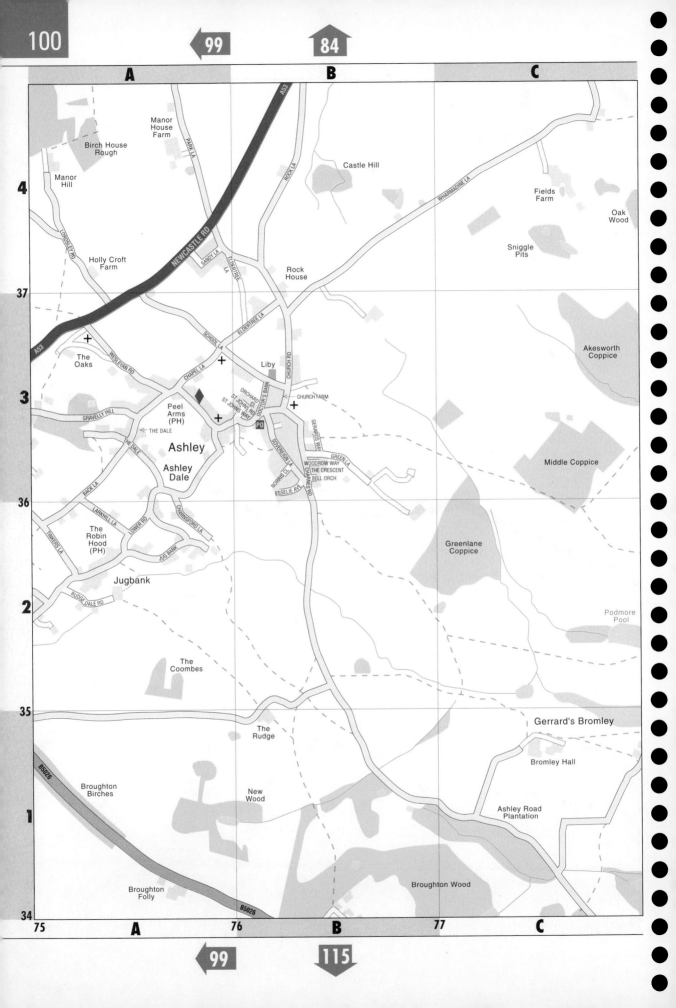

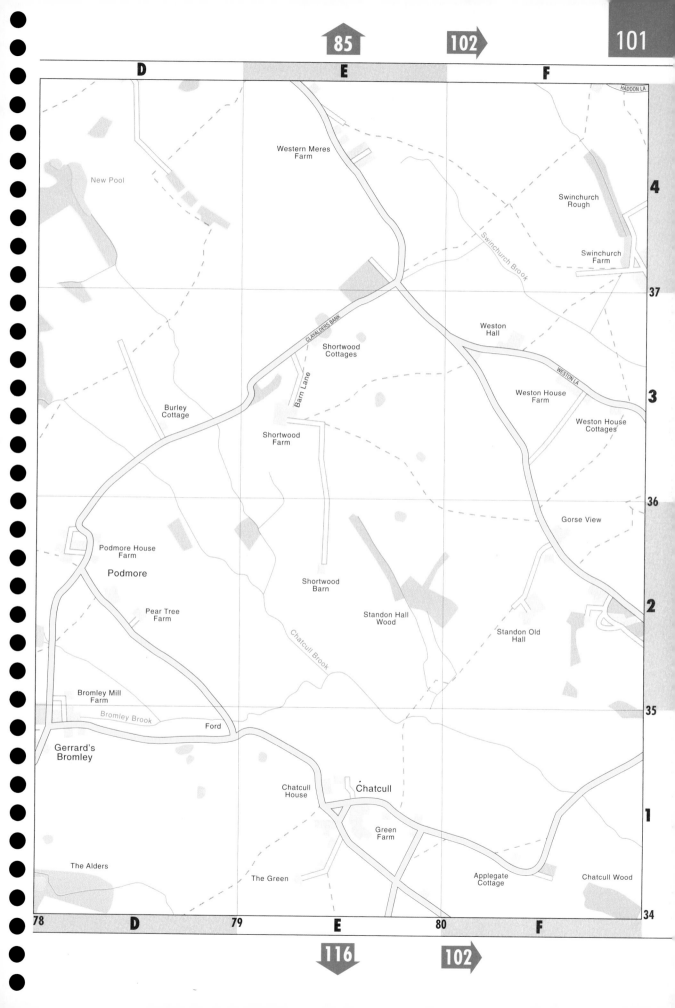

HADDON LA

4

Western Meres
Farm

New Pool

Swinchurch
Rough

Swinchurch
Brook

Swinchurch
Farm

37

CLAYALDERS BANK

Shortwood
Cottages

Weston
Hall

Weston LA

Burley
Cottage

Barn Lane

Weston House
Farm

3

Shortwood
Farm

Weston House
Cottages

36

Gorse View

Podmore House
Farm

Podmore

Shortwood
Barn

Chatcull Brook

Standon Hall
Wood

Standon Old
Hall

2

Pear Tree
Farm

Bromley Mill
Farm

Bromley Brook

Ford

35

Gerrard's
Bromley

Chatcull
House

Chatcull

1

Green
Farm

The Alders

The Green

Applegate
Cottage

Chatcull Wood

34

A | B | C

A51

Chapel Chorlton

4

Dimmock's Farm

Hatton Waterworks Cotts

Upper Hatton

Clifford's Wood

Hatton Bogs

Black Bank

37

Hatton Mill

Lodgebarn

A51

Clifford's Wood Cottages

Swinchurch Brook

Lower Hatton

A519

3

Butt House

BUTTHOUSE LA

Meere Brook

Marlpit Plantation

The Gorse Covert

GORSEY LA

Beech Hill

BACK LA

The Red Lion (PH)

School Farm

36

Cranberry

Outdoor Activities Centre

Bowers Hall Farm

Cotes Heath Bank

Bowers

Bowers Bent

WESTON LA

SANDY BANK

SANDY LA

Cotes Lodge

Moorfields

MOORFIELDS IND EST

2

CHURCH LA

Bowers Farm

Cotes Heath

Staun Wood

Osier Beds

Westfield House

Standon House

All Saints Fst Sch

Mill

Cotes Hall

35

MILL LA

CHESTNUT CT

ST JAMES GREEN

BRIAR WAY

The Old Rectory

PO

NELSON CRES

Standon

Little Standon Farm

The Beeches

Ashlyn

1

A519

Chatcull Brook

Broadacres

34

81 | 82 | 83
A | B | C

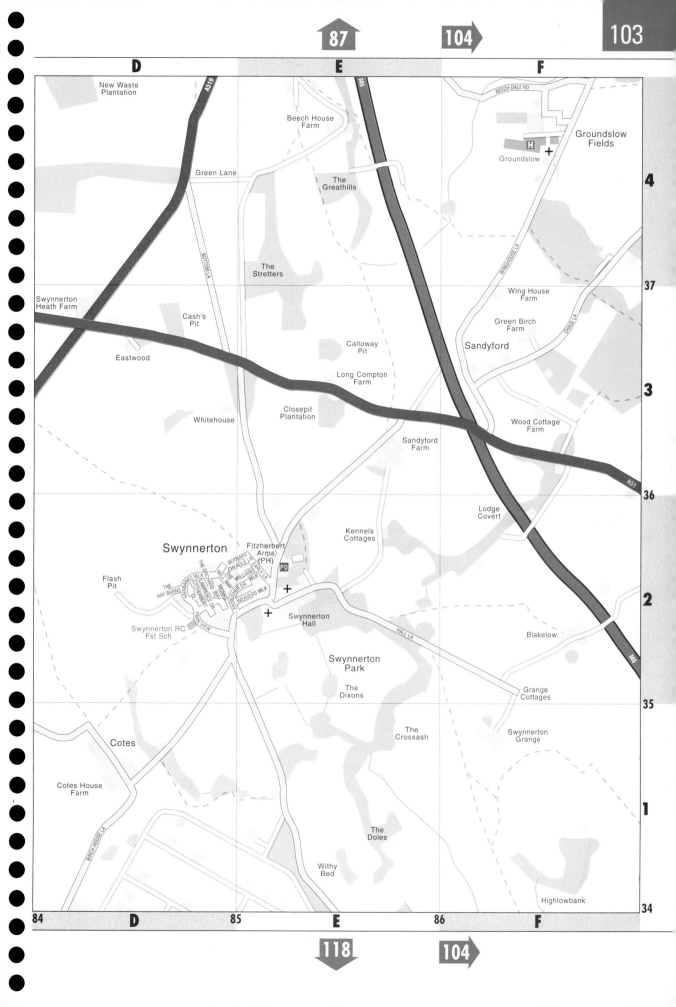

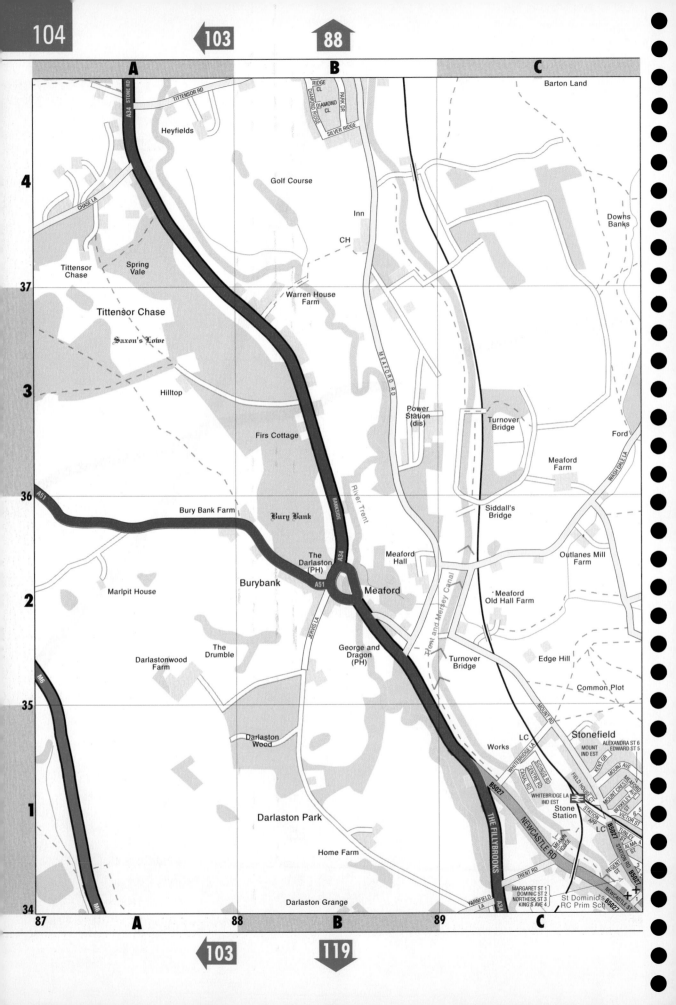

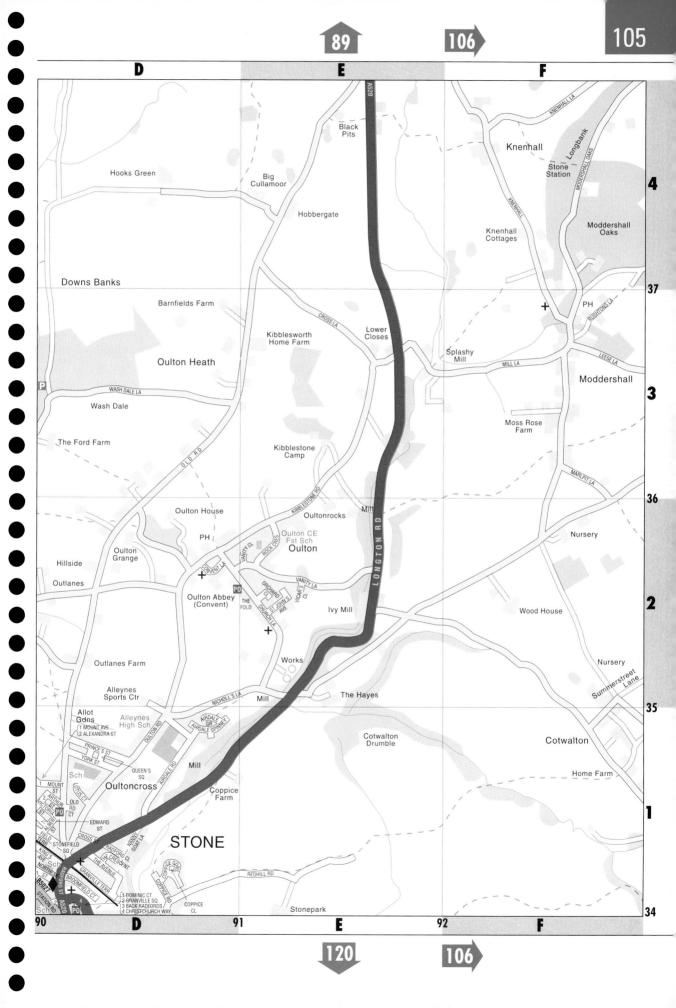

D   E   F

4

37

3

36

2

35

1

34

Black
Pits

Knenhall

Longbank

Stone
Station

Moddershall
Oaks

Hooks Green

Big
Cullamoor

Knenhall
Cottages

Hobbergate

Downs Banks

PH

Barnfields Farm

CROSS LA

Lower
Closes

RUSHTONS LA

KNENHALL

Kibblesworth
Home Farm

Splashy
Mill

LEESE LA

Oulton Heath

MILL LA

Moddershall

WASH DALE LA

Wash Dale

Moss Rose
Farm

The Ford Farm

OLD RD

Kibblestone
Camp

MARLPIT LA

KIBBLESTONE RD

Oulton House

Outlonrocks

Mill

Nursery

PH

Oulton CE
Fst Sch

VANITY CL

ROCK CRES

Oulton

LONGTON RD

Oulton
Grange

Hillside

CONVENT LA

VANITY LA

VICARS CL

Outlanes

Oulton Abbey
(Convent)

PO

THE
FOLD

ORCHARD
CT

ST JOHN'S
AVE

Ivy Mill

Wood House

CHURCH LA

Outlanes Farm

Works

Nursery

Alleynes
Sports Ctr

The Hayes

Summerstreet
Lane

Allot
Gdns

Alleynes
High Sch

NICHOLL'S LA

Mill

Cotwalton
Drumble

1 MOUNT AVE
2 ALEXANDRA ST

AIRDALE
GR

AIPDALE SPINNEY

Cotwalton

OULTON RD

PRINCE'S ST

Mill

YORK ST

AIRDALE RD

QUEEN'S
SQ

Home Farm

Sch

LOTUS CT

Oultoncross

1 MOUNT
ST

ARTHUR
ST

VICTORIA
ST

OLD
RD
CT

STONE

EDWARD
ST

PO

FIELD
TERR

STONEFIELD
SQ

NIXON
CROFT LA

Coppice
Farm

CROSS ST

RADFORD CL
CRESCENT

King's
AVE

RADFORD ST

THE AVENUE

BROOMFIELD CT

GRANVILLE TERR

COPPICE
GDNS

REDHILL RD

NORTHES

B5027

Sch

STATION RD

A520

PO

1 DOMINIC CT
2 GRANVILLE SQ
3 BACK RADFORDS
4 CHRISTCHURCH WAY

COPPICE
RD

COPPICE
CL

Stonepark

105
90

A **B** **C**

Moddershall Grange

Fulford

CHERRY CL

BAULK LA

KINGFISHER CRES

HOLLOW RD

TOWNEND

HILLSIDE CL

MEADOW LA

SAVERLEY GREEN RD

HILLSIDE CL

Townend

Idlerocks Farm

Stallington Heath

Broom's Farm

FULFORD RD

Fulford Cty Prim Sch

PO

Longlane Head Farm

4

Idlerocks

Spot Acre

Crossgate

Greensitch Farm

Idlerocks

Spot Acre Spinney

Mossgate

37

Nurseries

Flats

Spotgate Inn (PH)

Mosslane

LEES LA

BALAAM'S LA

MOSS LA

Nursery

Rushlade

3

Farthings

The Spot

HILDERSTONE RD

The Leasows

Spot Farm

Bird in Hand (PH)

36

Spot Grange

The Hurstage

High Elms

2

Home Farm

CRESSWELL RD

Manor House Farm

HALL LA

35

Sewage Works

Hilderstone Hall

Crossgate Barn

BARNES CROFT

BRAMPTON CROFT

THE MEADOWS

Newfields

FARM LEA 1

FARM VIEW 2

Hall Wood

1

Hilderstone

SANDON RD

Roebuck Inn (PH)

Hall Farm

Peakshill Wood

EASTHOLME

Wooliscroft

WHITESYTCH LA

B5066

34

B5066

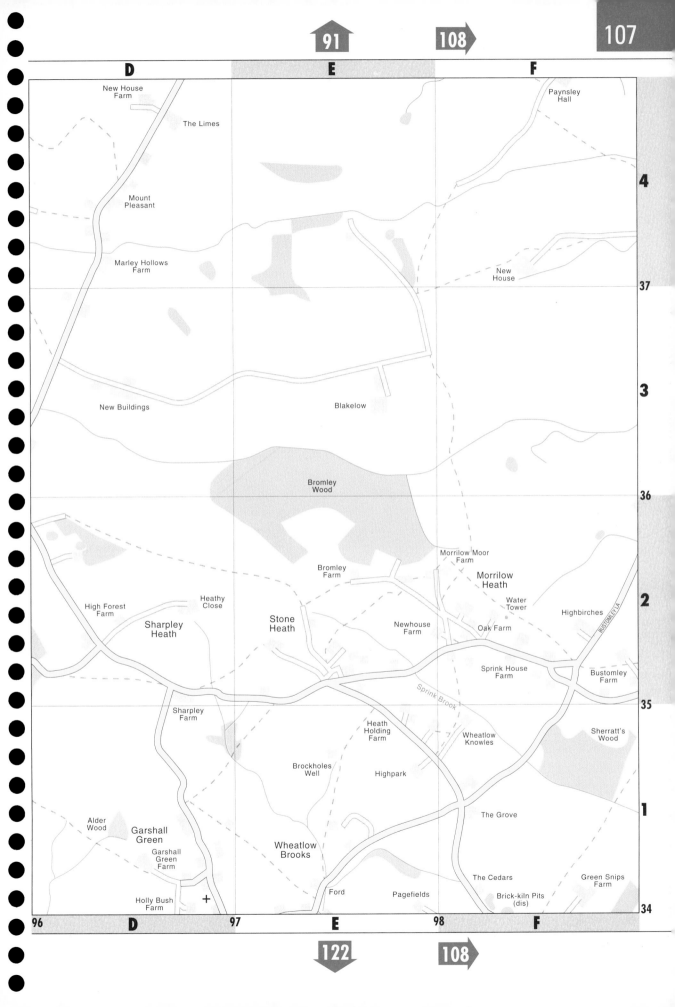

D
E
F

New House Farm

The Limes

Paynsley Hall

4

Mount Pleasant

Marley Hollows Farm

New House

37

New Buildings

Blakelow

3

Bromley Wood

36

Morrilow Moor Farm

Bromley Farm

Morrilow Heath

High Forest Farm

Heathy Close

Water Tower

Highbirches

2

Sharpley Heath

Stone Heath

Newhouse Farm

Oak Farm

BUSTOMLEY LA

Sprink House Farm

Bustomley Farm

35

Sharpley Farm

Heath Holding Farm

Wheatlow Knowles

Sherratt's Wood

Sprink Brook

Brockholes Well

Highpark

Alder Wood

Garshall Green

The Grove

1

Wheatlow Brooks

Garshall Green Farm

Holly Bush Farm

Ford

Pagefields

The Cedars

Brick-kiln Pits (dis)

Green Snips Farm

34

A   B   C

4

Blythe
House

Far
Teanleys

A50

The
Wing
Drumble

Shortwoods

Leighbank
Farm

LEIGH BANK

Leigh
Lane
Farm

Leighbank
Gorse

37

River Blithe

Dairy
House
Farm

Yew Tree
Farm

BROOK LA

Blythe Gate
Farm

HEN LA

3

Bitternsdale

Blythe
House

Moor
Farm

Manor
House

LEIGH LA

Upper
Leigh

Ivy
House

Bridge
Farm

LC

MOOR LA

RUSTOMLEY LA

36

Fields
Farm

Heempit
Gorse

Brook
Farm

Lower
Leigh

LC

INTAKES LA

2

Middleton
Green
Farm

HILL LA

Rose
Cottage

Middleton
Green

Wood
Leasow
farm

Dodsley
Fields

35

Windy
Fields

Manor
Farm

Dods
Leigh

White's
Wood

Top House
Farm

LEES LA

1

Sprink Brook

Lees Lane

Dodsley
Cottage
Farm

Bear's Brook

Godstone

Black
Plantation

Birchwood
Park

New
Plantation

34

99   A   00   B   01   C

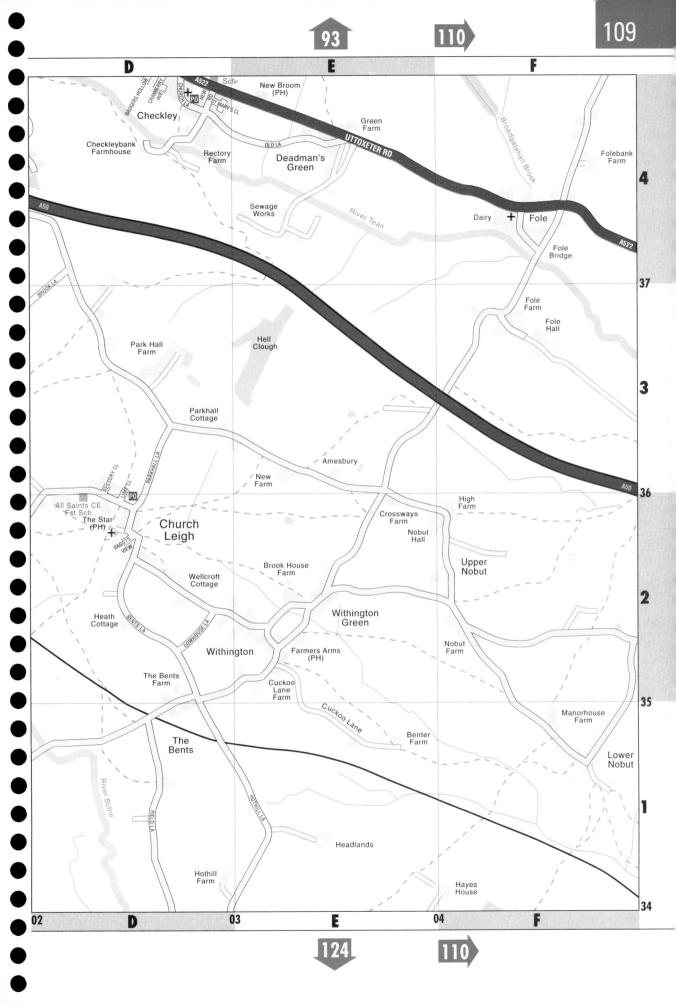

D
E
F

4
37
3
36
2
35
1
34

Checkley
New Broom (PH)
Green Farm
Folebank Farm
Checkleybank Farmhouse
Rectory Farm
Deadman's Green
Dairy
Fole
Fole Bridge
Sewage Works
River Tean
Fole Farm
Fole Hall
A50
A522
UTTOXETER RD
Broadgatehall Brook

BADGERS HOLLOW
CRANBERRY AVE
CHURCH LA
A522
NEW RD
ST MARY'S CL
Sch
OLD LA
PO

Park Hall Farm
Hell Clough
Parkhall Cottage
Amesbury
New Farm
High Farm
Crossways Farm
Nobut Hall
Upper Nobut
BROOK LA
PARKHALL LA

All Saints CE Fst Sch
The Star (PH)
Church Leigh
Wellcroft Cottage
Brook House Farm
Withington Green
Nobut Farm
Manorhouse Farm
RECTORY CL
LIME CL
PO
BAGOTS VIEW

Heath Cottage
Withington
Farmers Arms (PH)
Lower Nobut
BENTS LA
COWHOUSE LA
The Bents Farm
Cuckoo Lane Farm
Cuckoo Lane
Benter Farm
The Bents
River Blithe
FIELD LA
HOTHILL LA
Headlands
Hothill Farm
Hayes House

A   B   C

4

Oldwood

Hollywood
Farm

Nothill
Wood

Cotton's
Wood

Nothill Farm

Old
Turnpike

Pale
Flatts
Farm

37

A522

Madeley
Farm

High
Farm

Dove
House

The Alders

Lawn
Farm

Creighton
Park

Townend
Farm

Beamhursthall
Farm

New
House
Farm

3

Beamhurst

Oldwood

Overfole

Beamhurst
Hall

PH

Spar Flat
Farm

Flashes
Farm

Newhouse

HOLLINGTON LA

36

A50

River Tean

Mount
Pleasant

CEDAR DR 1
CHURCH FARM 2

Beamhurst
Bridge

Mill
Farm

Springfields

ST MICHAEL'S RD

Beamhurst
Lane

Waterloo
Farm

POPPIT'S LA

VICARAGE DR

2

Deggs
Leasow

Park
View

Broadoak
Farm

35

Lightwoodfields

PIGEONHAY LA

Parks' Farm

The Parks

TORRANCE DR

TUNNICLIFFE WAY

A522

A50

1

Dagdale
Farm

Banktop

ELMWOOD GR

KIMBERLEY DR

PENNYCROFT
RD

Dagdale

Moss
Beds

Sch

Yew Tree
Farm

LIGHTFOOT DR

34

05   A   06   B   07   C

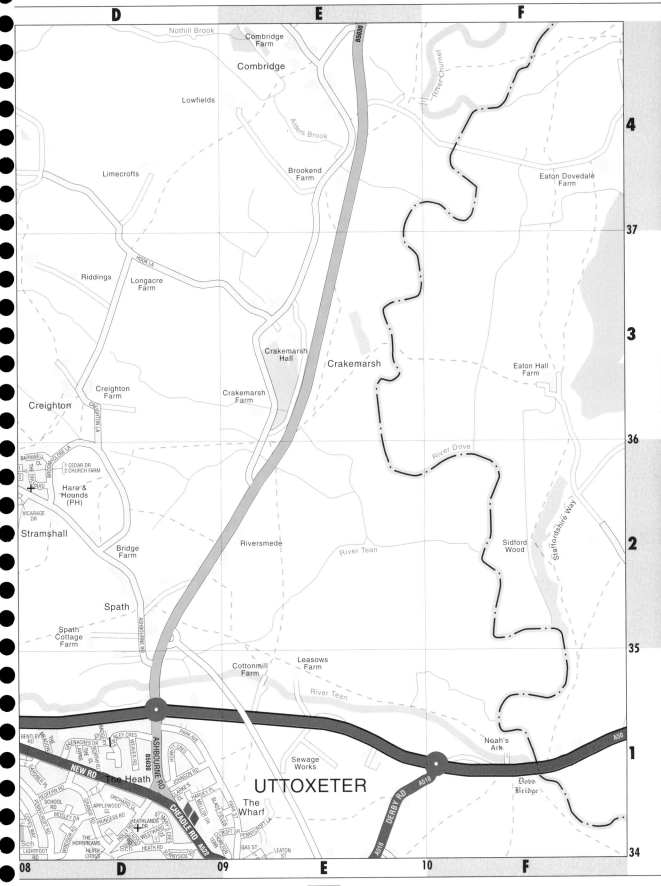

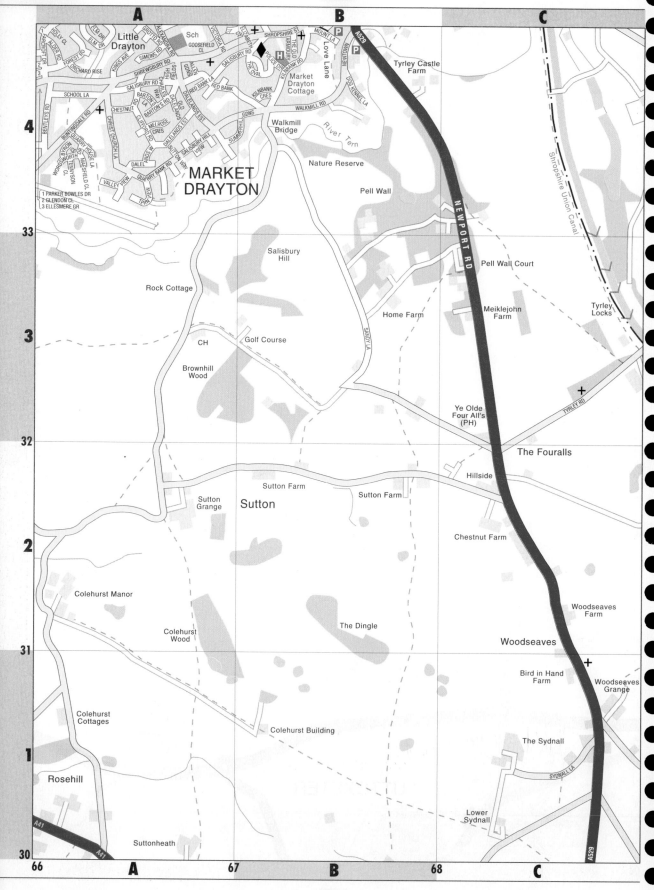

Little Drayton

Sch
GOOSEFIELD CL

Shropshire St

Tyrley Castle Farm

Love Lane

Market Drayton Cottage

Walkmill Bridge

WALKMILL RD

River Tern

Nature Reserve

MARKET DRAYTON

Pell Wall

1 PARKER BOWLES DR
2 GLENDON CL
3 ELLESMERE GR

Salisbury Hill

Rock Cottage

NEWPORT RD

Pell Wall Court

Home Farm

Meiklejohn Farm

Tyrley Locks

CH

Golf Course

SANDY LA

Brownhill Wood

Ye Olde Four All's (PH)

TYRLEY RD

The Fouralls

Hillside

Sutton Farm

Sutton Farm

Sutton Grange

Sutton

Chestnut Farm

Colehurst Manor

Woodseaves Farm

Colehurst Wood

The Dingle

Woodseaves

Bird in Hand Farm

Woodseaves Grange

Colehurst Cottages

Colehurst Building

The Sydnall

SYDNALL LA

Rosehill

Lower Sydnall

A41

Suttonheath

A529

D   E   F

The Hills

Home Farm

Peatswood
Hall

The Brodder

BLORE RD
Hales Hall

Hales

FLASH LA

Home
Farm

4

Coal Brook

The
Lloyd

33

Old Springs
Farm

Dairy
House

Wood
Farm

Stoneyford

Johnson's Wood
Farm

3

Tyrley Wharf

Saw Pit
Wood

Old Springs
Hall

Tyrley
Farm

32

Chipnall Wood

Shropshire Union Canal Main Line

Bridlands Wood

The
Lodge

2

Cheswardine Park
Farm

TAG LA

31

Haywood
Drumble

Lawn
Drumble

Woodseaves Manor
Farm

1

Haywood Farm

Cheswardine
Road
Bridge

HAYWOOD LA

LAWN LA

30

69   D   70   E   71   F

113
99

A B C

4

Park Springs

Burnt Wood

Burntwood Farm

Lloyd Drumble

Keeper's Lodge

Smith's Rough

Bishop's Wood

Park Springs Farm

Knowleswood

The Lloyd Farm

33

The Nook Farm

Glass Houses

Goldenhill Farm

Dales Wood

The Lees

3

Coal Brook

Chipnall Lees

Heatherdale Farm

Chipnall Mill Farm

32

Lipley Heath Farm

Rushymoss Wood

Chipnallhall Farm

Chipnall Farm

Lipley Farm

2

Lipley

TAG LA

Chipnall

MOSS LA

Bishop's Wood

Moss Lane Farm

31

Cheswardine Hall

Sycamore Cottage

Lipley Cottages

1

Lipley Hall Farm

Lipley Villa

Greaves Plantation

Marsh House

30

72 A 73 B 74 C

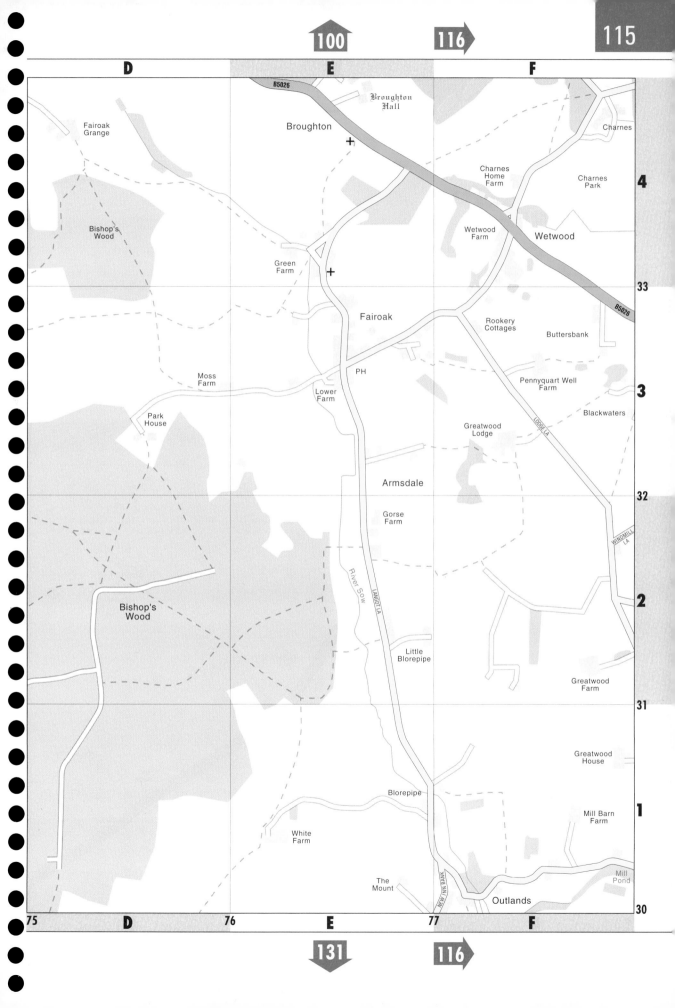

D   E   F

B5026

Broughton
Hall

Broughton

Fairoak
Grange

Charnes

Charnes
Home
Farm

Charnes
Park

4

Bishop's
Wood

Wetwood
Farm

Wetwood

Green
Farm

33

Fairoak

Rookery
Cottages

Buttersbank

B5026

Moss
Farm

PH

Pennyquart Well
Farm

3

Lower
Farm

Blackwaters

Park
House

Greatwood
Lodge

LODGE LA

Armsdale

32

Gorse
Farm

WINDMILL LA

Bishop's
Wood

River Sow

LANGOT LA

2

Little
Blorepipe

Greatwood
Farm

31

Greatwood
House

Blorepipe

Greatwood
House

1

Mill Barn
Farm

White
Farm

NEW INN BANK

Mill
Pond

The
Mount

Outlands

30

75   D   76   E   77   F

A

B

C

Charnes
Old Hall

Brooklyn
Farm

Whittington

Chatcull
Wood

Whittington
Farm

Brockton Brook

Foxley

4

Fir
Grove

Midley
Pits

33

SHUT LA

Newhouse
Farm

B5026

Villa
Farm

PH

Highlanes
Corner
Farm

Highlanes

CHURCH LA

Croxtonbank

Highlanes
Farm

3

THE HIGHFIELDS

Arnhill
Cottage

Twr

PO

Croxton

32

WINDMILL LA

Cutleyhorn Lane

Holts
Farm

Windmill

The
Cedars

Little
Sugnall

Woodwall
Green

Villa
Farm

Top
Farm

Little
Sugnall
Farm

2

GINGER LA

Russia Tree
Farm

Sugnall
Hall

Marsh
Farm

31

Redgreet

Sugnall

Redgreet
Farm

Home
Farm

The
Cottage

Woodlands
Farm

1

Big
Wood

Sugnall
Park

Offleybrook

Broughton
Pool

Jackson's
Coppice

B5026

30

78

A

79

B

80

C

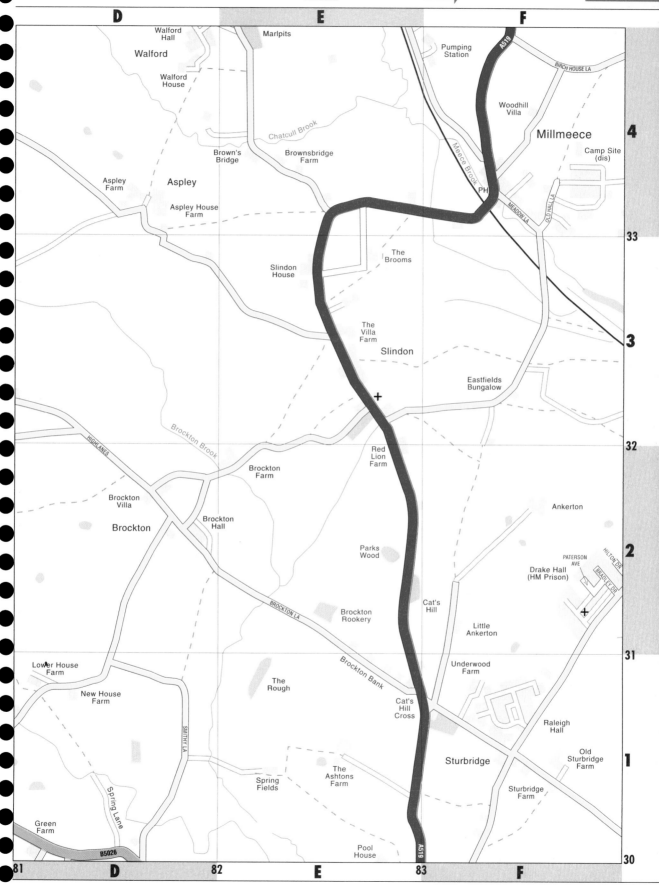

D | E | F

Walford Hall
Marlpits
Walford
Walford House
Pumping Station
A519
BIRCH HOUSE LA
Woodhill Villa
Millmeece
4
Chatcull Brook
Brown's Bridge
Brownsbridge Farm
Aspley Farm
Aspley
Camp Site (dis)
Aspley House Farm
Meece Brook
PH
MEADOW LA
OLD HALL LA
33
The Brooms
Slindon House
The Villa Farm
3
Slindon
Eastfields Bungalow
Brockton Brook
+
HIGHLANES
Red Lion Farm
32
Brockton Farm
Brockton Villa
Ankerton
Brockton
Brockton Hall
HILTON DR
PATERSON AVE
Drake Hall (HM Prison)
BRADLEY DR
2
Parks Wood
+
BROCKTON LA
Cat's Hill
Little Ankerton
Brockton Rookery
Lower House Farm
Underwood Farm
31
New House Farm
The Rough
Brockton Bank
Cat's Hill Cross
Raleigh Hall
Old Sturbridge Farm
SMITHY LA
Sturbridge
1
Spring Lane
Spring Fields
The Ashtons Farm
Sturbridge Farm
A519
Green Farm
B5026
Pool House
30

81 | D | 82 | E | 83 | F

A B C

4

33

3

32

2

31

1

30

84 A 85 B 86 C

New Birch House

BIRCH HOUSE LA

Pilstones Wood

The Highlows

Mast

Beatty Hall

British Telecom Technical College

Swynnerton Training Area

Howard Hall

High Lows Lane

SUMMERFIELDS

FIELDSIDE

MILKTONVIEW

FORD DR

HIGH LOWS LA

TIMBERFIELDS

HOLLY FIELDS

Springfields Cty Fst Sch

Yarnfield

THE WILLOWS

POTTERS

Meece House

COLLEGE FIELDS

YARNFIELD LA

THE PADDOCKS

CALVELEY CL

SOPWITH CL

ASHDALE PARK

Works

STATION RD

SOUTH RD

MEECE RD

Coldmeece

PO

OLD MEECE RD

BRIAR GR

GREENSIDE

MAPLE CL

THE FURLONG

BATTEN WLK

MITCHELL RISE

COBHAM CL

DE HAVILLAND DR

ASH LA

Eastfields

Post Office Technical Training College

The Broom

Hill Farm

Baden Hall Lodge

The Rookery

Middle Heamies

Upper Heamies Cottages

HILTON DR

2

Baden Hall Cottages

Drake Hall (HM Prison)

Baden Hall

Meece Brook

Upper Heamies

Lower Heamies

B5026

Pool Plantation

Lower Heamies Wood

Magpie Wood

Hilcote Cottages

Oxleasows

Norton Bridge

STATION RD

Hilcote Farm

B5026

SCAMNELL LA

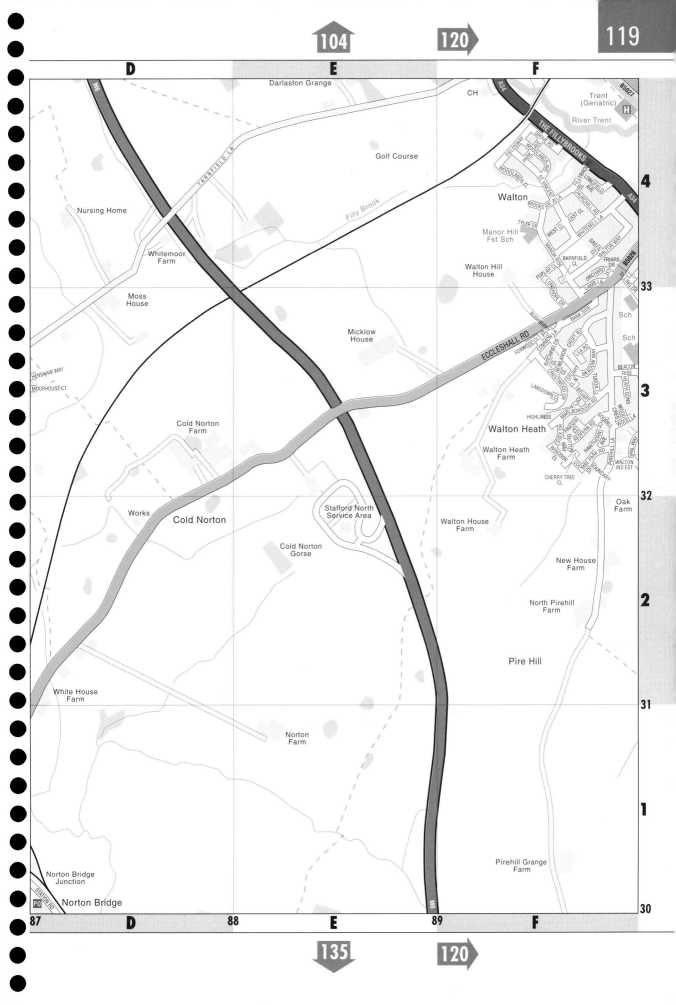

119
105

A   B   C

STONE

NEWCASTLE ST
Liby
MILL ST
HIGH ST
CHERRY RD
REDHILL
REDHILL GDNS
CROWN ST
ALLIANCE WORKS IND EST
CHURCH CL
CHURCH ST
ST MICHAELS
ST GEORGE'S
STAFFORD RD
A520
A34
B5026
A520
B5027
CLAREMONT CL
ABBEY ST
OLD RECTORY
CEDAR PK
JORDAN WAY
LC

1 WULFAD CT
2 RUFFIN CT
3 KINGSLAND CT
4 ASHFORD GR
5 RIDGEMONT CL
6 FERNHURST CL
7 SHEPLEY CL
8 MILLWALK AVE

Astonlodge Farm

Lodge Plantation

Sports Ctr
PO
Walton Bridge

SYCAMORE RD
OAK RD
ASH RD
BEECH CL
PINGLE LA
CHERRY RD
KINGSLAND RD
HOLT RD
PEARSON
NEWMAN
ASTON CHASE
AMBLESIDE CL
ULLSWATER DR
DERWENT AVE
CONISTON CL
STUBBS DR
LANDER CL
PHILLIPS CL

B5027
UTTOXETER RD

LICHFIELD RD
PARK HOUSE DR
GRANGE RD
MERCER AVE
STANES CT
BOWERS CT
COOPER CL
SADDLER CL
LEACROFT
GEORGE LA
BLACKIES LA

4

33

Andre Mills Bridge

1 THE GLEN
2 ASHDALE CL

1 ERNALD GDNS
2 CLINTON GDNS

St Michael's CE Fst Sch

THE REDLANDS
CHASE CL
ST MICHAELS MOUNT
BROOKFIELD CT
Little Stoke
LC
B5027
MOUNT PLEASANT CL

1 ROWAN CL
2 BROOMFIELD CL
3 AVON GR
4 MALLORY CL
5 THE WILLOWS
6 LARCHFIELDS

Sch

WALTON IND EST

STAFFORD RD

HILL CRES
HILL DR
BEACON CL
BEACON RD
SPRING GDNS

BALMORAL GR
VALLEY RD
GREENWAY
KINGSTON
REDWOOD RD
MOORLAND CL
CEDARS DR
THE LINDENS

SHARDLOW CL
WATERSMEET CT
WESLEY DR
FERNIE CL
OLDFIELD
McKAIN
MEADOWBROOK CT

1 HAWLEY CL
2 BOSTOCK CL

The Orange Hayes

3

Sewage Works

Hotel
Cemy

DIAMOND WAY
A51
BROOMS RD
STONE ENT CTR
EMERALD WAY
OPAL WAY

HOLYRHOOD
MELROSE
CAERNARVON
KENSINGTON
HIGHGROVE
GLAMIS DR

Forge Farm
Aston Bridge

B5027

Trent and Mersey Canal
River Trent

32

Redhouse Farm

STONE BSNS PK

Aston Hall

Aston-By-Stone

Carr House Bridge

Carr House

2

THE GROVE
WILLOW DALE
BOWERS LA
Aston Hall Farm
ASTON LA

BUTTERHILL BANK A51

Field House Farm
PH

Pirehill House (Fire and Rescue HQ)
Mast

Crown Inn La

Iron Bridge

31

Pirehill Cottages

Astonhill Farm

1

A34

ENSON LA

Wood Farm

Birch Farm

30

90   A   91   B   92   C

119
136

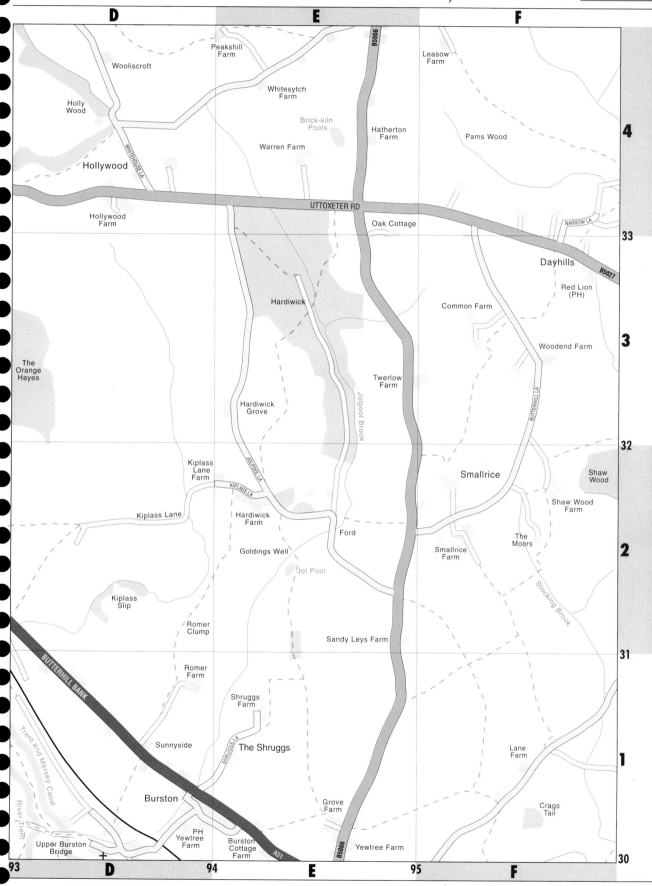

121
107

A   **B**   **C**

FOUR LANE ENDS

Garshall Green

Garshall House

4

Dayhills Farm

Oulton House

Grange Farm

Castle Farm

Birch Rough

Wheatlow Brook

Summerhill

Withysitch Lane

Withysitch Farm

Calloway Farm

33

B5027

Grimblebrook Farm

Darley Lane

Coton Hayes

Coton Hill

B5027

3

Burleypool Bridge

Salt's Bridge

THE ALLWAYS

ALL WAYS

ALLWAYS

Milwich

UTTOXETER RD

CROSSHILL BANK

Burley Pool Farm

Green Man Inn (PH)

Milwich Hall

Coton Cottage

SANDON LA

Wheatsheaf Inn (PH)

Coton

32

Vic +

Shaw Wood

Coton Green Farm

Park Farm

MILL LA

Green Lea Fst Sch

2

Cromer Hill

Oxclose Wood

Coton Mill Farm

Mill Lane

WALBROOK RD

Fradswell Hall Farm

Beacon Bank Farm

31

Lander's Wood Farm

Lander's Wood

Beacon Bank

Model Farm

HAWKINS LA

Kendrick's Barn Farm

Fox's Wood Farm

Old Gayton Gorse

The Doglands

1

Sandon Wood Farm

Gayton Brook

DOGLANDS RD

30

96   **A**   97   **B**   98   **C**

Kendrick's Wood

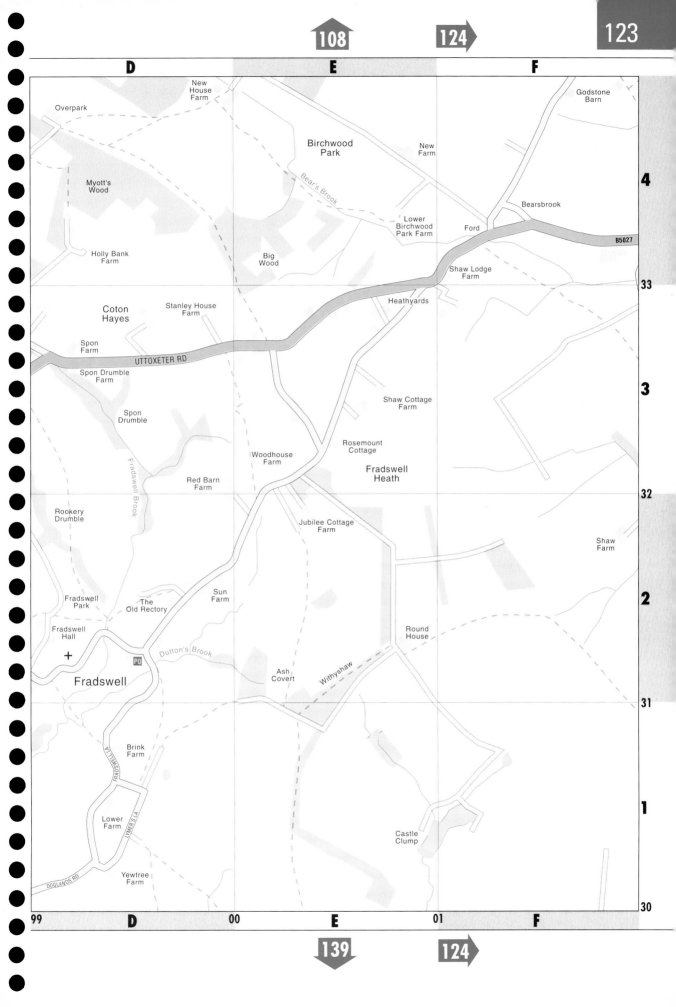

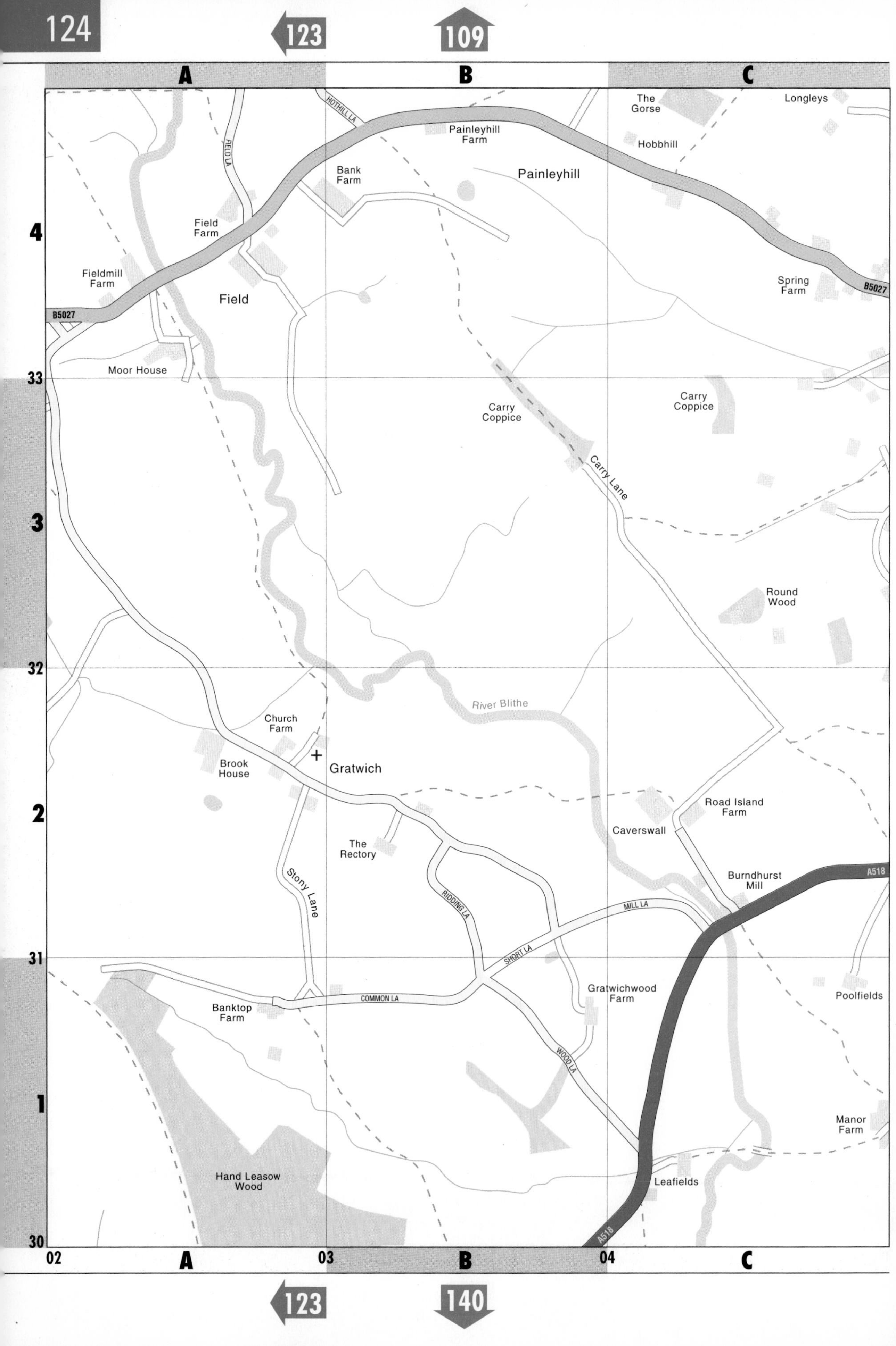

A   **B**   **C**

The Gorse

Longleys

HOTHILL LA

Painleyhill Farm

Painleyhill

Hobbhill

Bank Farm

FIELD LA

Field Farm

Fieldmill Farm

4

Spring Farm

B5027

Field

B5027

Moor House

33

Carry Coppice

Carry Coppice

Carry Lane

Round Wood

3

32

River Blithe

Church Farm

Brook House

+ Gratwich

Road Island Farm

Caverswall

2

The Rectory

Stony Lane

RIDDING LA

Burndhurst Mill

A518

MILL LA

SHORT LA

31

Gratwichwood Farm

Poolfields

Banktop Farm

COMMON LA

WOOD LA

Manor Farm

1

Leafields

Hand Leasow Wood

A518

30

02   **A**   03   **B**   04   **C**

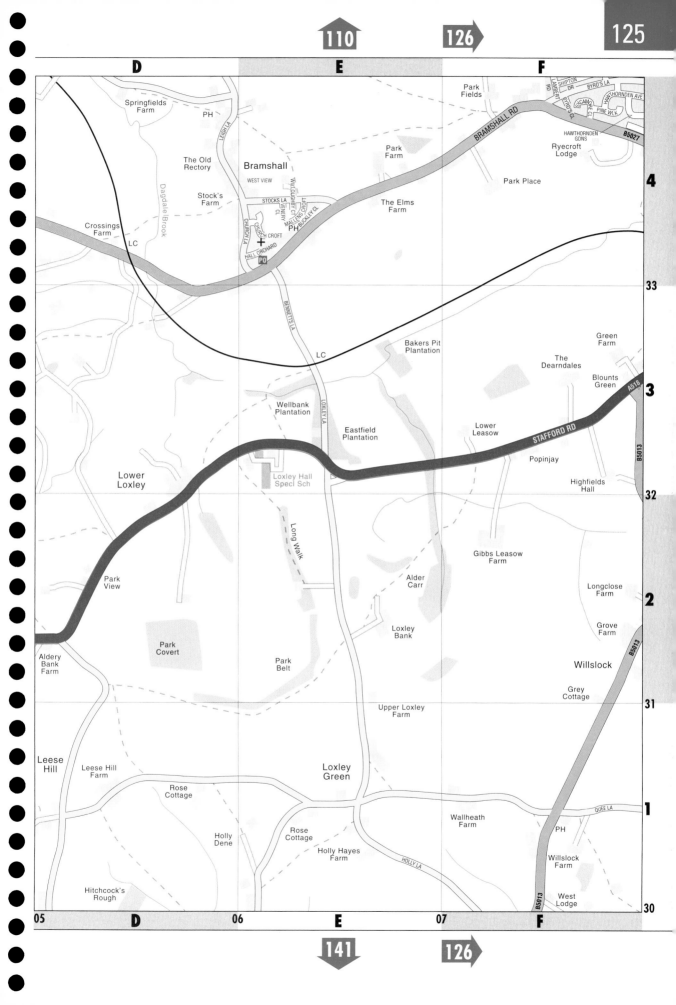

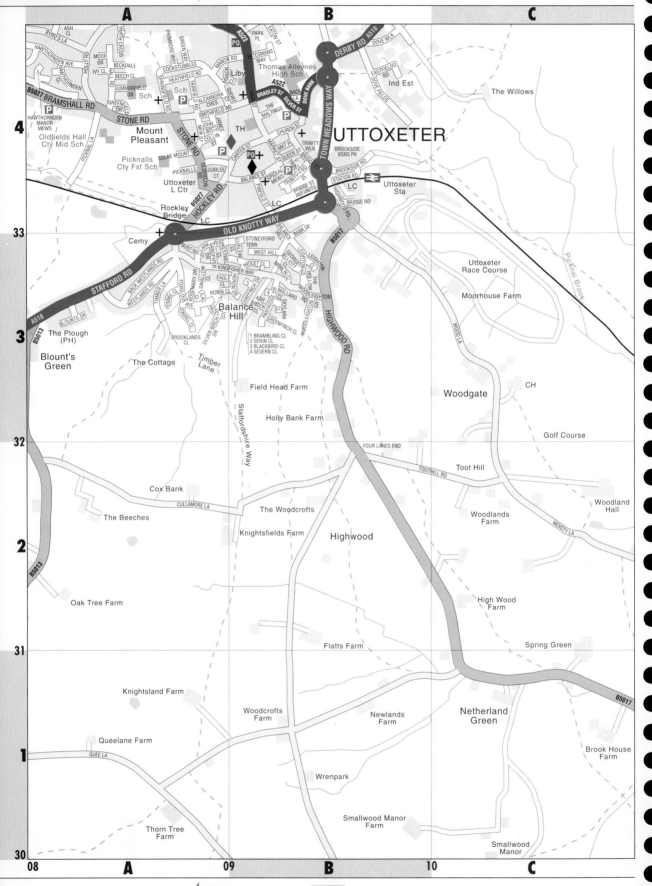

125
111

UTTOXETER

A522
PARK PL
EATIN ST
DERBY RD A518
DOVE WLK
PO
BYRD'S LA
ASH CL
HEATH CROSS
HAWTHORNDEN AVE
HOLLY RD
MOOR GR
IVY CL
BEECKDALE
BATESMANS WAY
Thomas Alleynes High Sch
EASTFIELDS RD
DOVE FIELDS
Ind Est
The Willows
HAWTHORNDEN
HALL RD
SUMMERFIELD DR
Sch
PRIMROSE WAY
GREEN WAY
COCKSTUBBLES
MANOR RD
Liby
A522
BRADLEY ST
SILVER ST
DOVE BANK
B5027 BRAMSHALL RD
STONE RD
SPRINGFIELD RD
HEATHFIELD RD
FAIRFIELD RD
Sch
The MALTINGS
BROOKSIDE BSNS PK
P
Hawthornden Manor Mews
Oldfields Hall Cty Mid Sch
Mount Pleasant
STONE RD
ALEXANDRA CRES
SMITHFIELD RD
JOHN ST
COLLIN
TH
CARTER ST
MKT ST
CHURCH ST
TRINITY WLK
Brookside BSNS PK
BROOKSIDE RD
Picknalls Cty Fst Sch
PICKNALLS
COLNE MOUNT
JUBILEE CT
BALANCE ST
PO
QUEEN ST
STATION RD
LC
Uttoxeter Sta
Uttoxeter L Ctr
HOCKLEY RD
B5027
PINFOLD ST
SPICEAL MEWS
BRIDGE ST IND UNITS
TRINITY RD
P
BRIDGE RD
HIGHWOOD RD
Hockley Bridge
LC
LC
OLD KNOTTY WAY
Cemy
BANK CR
BANK
B5017
Uttoxeter Race Course
Pickhal Brook
Stoneyford Terr
WEST HILL
STAFFORD RD
BACK WESTLANDS RD
WESTLANDS RD
TIMBER LA
FOXGLOVE
FENNEL CL
ROSEMARY DR
BUNTING DR
CURLEW
SANDPIPER
WREN
SWALLOW
EAGLE CL
HERON DR
CHAFFINCH DR
ROBIN CL
KINGFISHER WAY
NOCET CL
MERLIN CL
GEORGE
LEIGHTON CL
LEIGHTON
HOLLOW
MALLARD
ASH BROOK
SKYLARK
WOODLEIGHTON
Moorhouse Farm
Woodgate
CH
A518
B5013
The Plough (PH)
BLOUNTS DR
BROOKLANDS CL
SILVER BIRCH DR
SORREL CL
Balance Hill
GREENFINCH CL
HIGHWOOD RD
WOOD LA
Golf Course
1 BRAMBLING CL
2 SERIN CL
3 BLACKBIRD CL
4 SEVERN CL
Blount's Green
The Cottage
Timber Lane
Field Head Farm
Holly Bank Farm
Woodland Hall
MOISTY LA
Staffordshire Way
Cox Bank
CULLAMORE LA
The Woodcrofts
FOUR LANES END
TOOTHILL RD
Toot Hill
Woodlands Farm
The Beeches
Knightsfields Farm
Highwood
High Wood Farm
B5013
Oak Tree Farm
Spring Green
B5017
Knightsland Farm
Flatts Farm
Woodcrofts Farm
Newlands Farm
Netherland Green
Brook House Farm
Queelane Farm
QUEE LA
Wrenpark
Thorn Tree Farm
Smallwood Manor Farm
Smallwood Manor

125
142

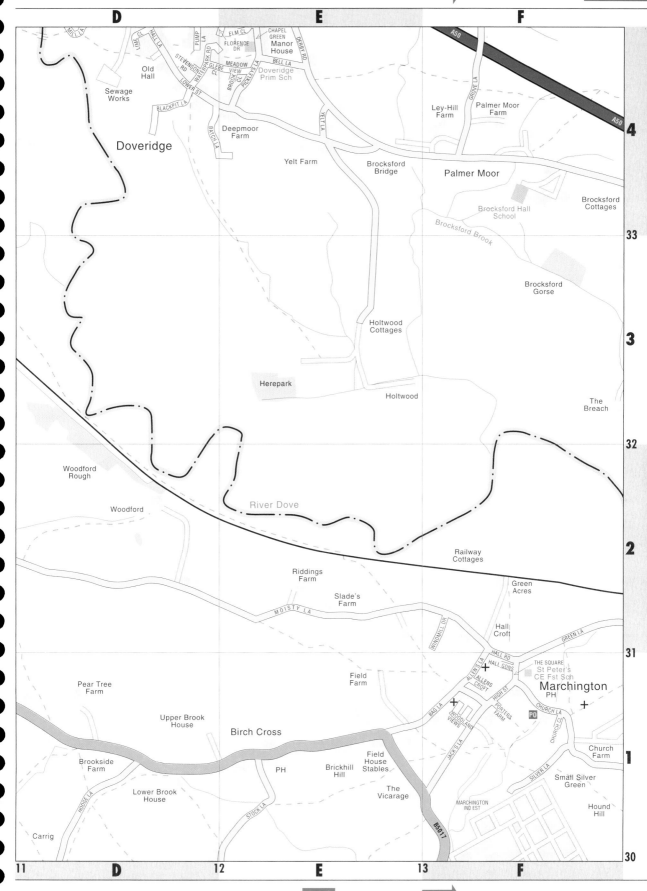

127

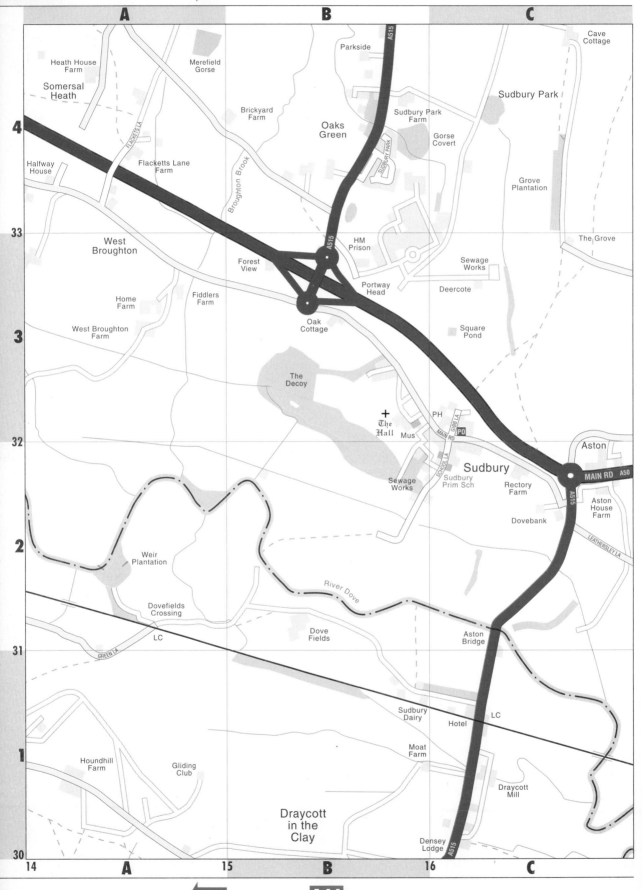

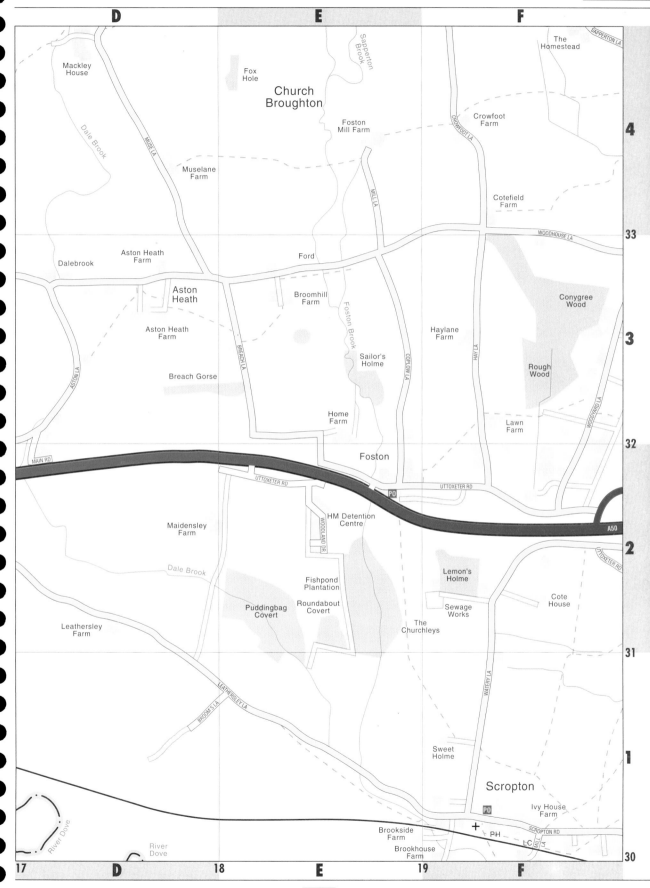

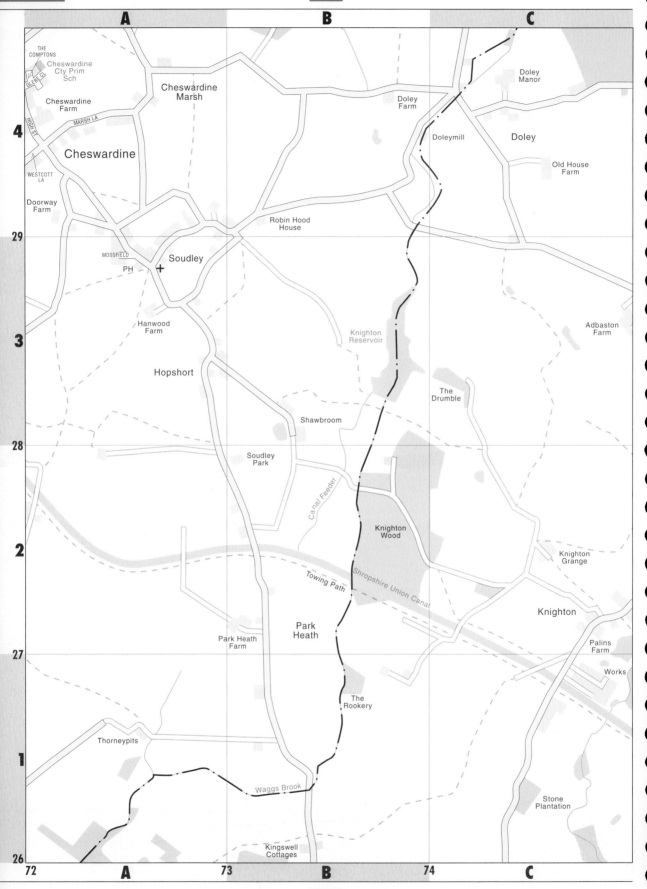

THE COMPTONS
Cheswardine Cty Prim Sch
GLEBE CL
Cheswardine Farm
HIGH ST
Cheswardine Marsh
MARSH LA
4
Cheswardine
WESTCOTT LA
Doorway Farm
Doley Manor
Doley Farm
Doleymill
Doley
Old House Farm
Robin Hood House
29
MOSSFIELD
PH
+
Soudley
Hanwood Farm
Knighton Reservoir
Adbaston Farm
3
Hopshort
The Drumble
Shawbroom
28
Soudley Park
Canal Feeder
Knighton Wood
Knighton Grange
2
Towing Path
Shropshire Union Canal
Knighton
Park Heath Farm
Park Heath
Palins Farm
27
Works
The Rookery
1
Thorneypits
Waggs Brook
Stone Plantation
Kingswell Cottages
26
72   A   73   B   74   C

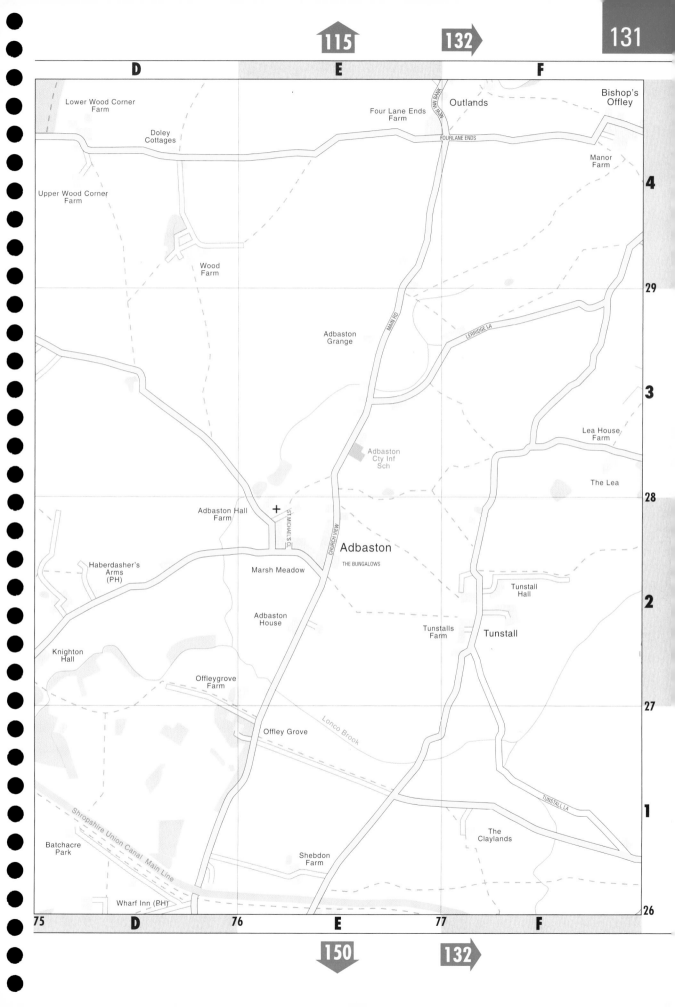

D
E
F

Lower Wood Corner Farm

Doley Cottages

Four Lane Ends Farm

Outlands

Bishop's Offley

FOURLANE ENDS

Manor Farm

Upper Wood Corner Farm

4

Wood Farm

Adbaston Grange

MAIN RD

LERRIDGE LA

29

3

Adbaston Cty Inf Sch

Lea House Farm

The Lea

28

Adbaston Hall Farm

ST MICHAEL'S CL

CHURCH VIEW

Adbaston

THE BUNGALOWS

Haberdasher's Arms (PH)

Marsh Meadow

Tunstall Hall

2

Adbaston House

Tunstalls Farm

Tunstall

Knighton Hall

Offleygrove Farm

27

Offley Grove

Lonco Brook

Shropshire Union Canal Main Line

1

Batchacre Park

Shebdon Farm

The Claylands

TUNSTALL LA

Wharf Inn (PH)

26

75
D
76
E
77
F

131
116

A   **B**   **C**

Walk Mill

Offleybrook

PH

Walk Mill

Cop Mere

Pershall Pool

Bishop's Offley

Offleyrock

Offleyhay

PO

PH

Villa Farm

Copmere End

White House Farm

MERE RISE

4

SANDY LA

Offleymarsh

Marsh House

29

Brann Farm

The Drumble

Rufford

Peafield Covert

Lea Knowl

Windsend

3

The Manor

Little Horsley

Villa Farm

HORSLEY LA

Kempsage Farm

28

Kempsage Lane

Shop House Farm

Horsley Farm

Lonco Brook

Old House Farm

Rue Barn Farm

CASH LA

Villa Farm

2

Park Mill

27

1

Parkfields

Park Hall Farm

PARK LA

High Offley

Knightly Eaves Farm

PH

PEGGS LA

26

78   **A**   79   **B**   80   **C**

131
151

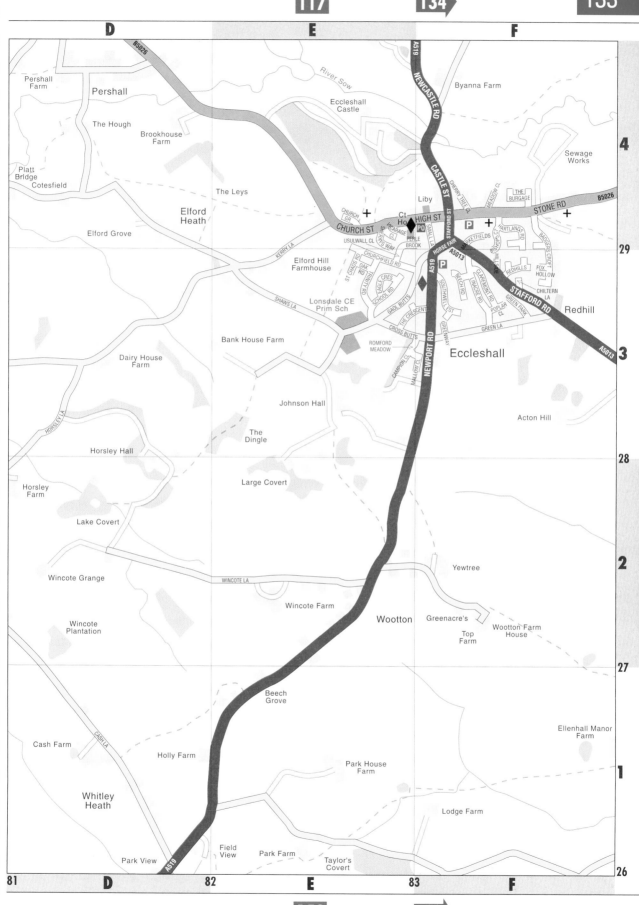

133
118

A   B   C

4

B5026

Scamnel
Farm

Smallwood
Pit

Hillcote
Hall

Hillcote
Wood

The
Leas

STONE RD

Rodgeley
Lodge

SCAMNEL LA

B5026

Bridge
Farm

29

The Vicarage

Fieldhouse
Farm

Drumble Wood

Mill
Farm

THE GREEN

The
Dingle

River Sow

MILL FARM CT

Chebsey

Riverside Farm

3

STAFFORD RD A5013

FOUR LANE
ENDS

Walton Hall
Specl Sch

Walton
Gorse

Pyebirch
Manor

PYEBIRCH LA

28

Round
Covert

Long Covert

Walton
Farm

Walton

Waltonbank
Wood

A5013

WALTONHURST LA

Walton
Grove

Waltonbank

2

Spurleybrook
Farm

27

Waltonhurst

Oncote
Covert

Brook
Covert

Gamesley Brook

1

Ellenhall
Manor
Farm

Seggersley Farm
House

Ladfordfield

B5405

LADFORDFIELDS
IND EST

Ellenhall

The
Marsh

Cocktails
Gorse

GRANGE CL

MARSH LA

BRIDLE LA

LADFORD COVERT
IND PK

B5405

26

84   A   85   B   86   C

133
153

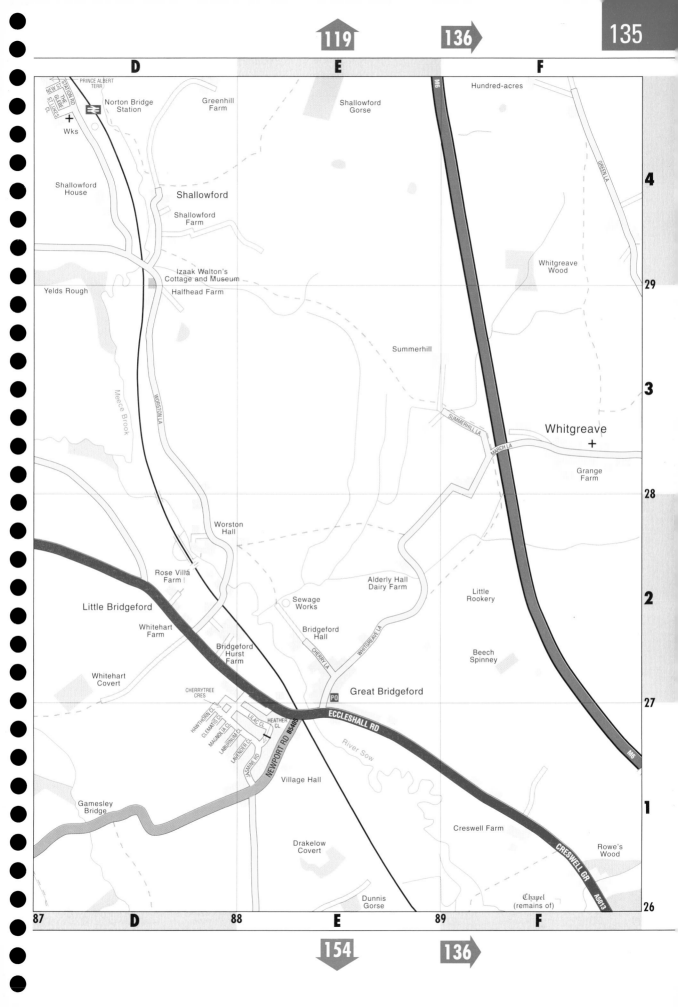

135
120

A **B** **C**

Peasley Bank

Newhouse Farm

Spring Farm

Far Enson Farm

Elmhurst

4

New Plantation

Yarlet Bank Farm

Yarlet Hall

Yarlet Hall Prep Sch

Yarlet Hall Farm

ENSON LA

Yarlet Hill

29

Meadow Farm

Grove Farm

Ensonmoor Farm

Greenwood

Greyhound Inn (PH)

GREEN LA

3

Yarlet

Black Plantation

Whitgreave

Top Farm

Park Farm

YARLET LA

Manor Farm

New Farm

28

WHITGREAVE LA

Upper Farm

Grange Farm

Marston

Woodhill Farm

Church Farm

Whitgreave Manor

MARSTON LA

2

Marston Farm

Brook Farm

Newbuildings Cottage

27

STONE RD

Redhill Farm

Newbuildings Farm

Marstongate Farm

M6

Little Gorse

Marston Brook

1

New Plantation

1 CHAULDEN RD
2 BUCKLAND RD
3 ASHRIDGE WLK
4 MARSWORTH WAY

RAF Stafford

Creswell Grove

BEACONSIDE

Stafford Common

M6

A513

A34

ALDERSHAW

AMBLEFIELD WAY

PARKSIDE AVE

ALDBURY CL

FELDEN CL

Stafford Common

CHURCH RD

A513

26

LAWNSFIELD WLK

PARKSIDE AVE

PITSTONE CL

90 **A** **91** **B** **92** **C**

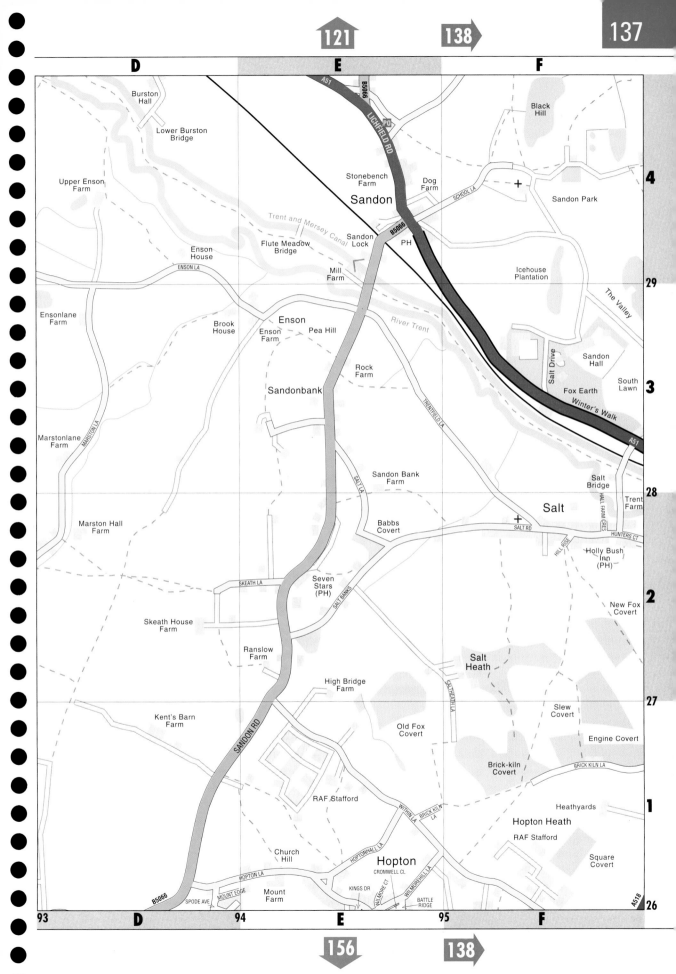

121
138

D E F

4

29

3

28

2

27

1

26

Burston Hall

Lower Burston Bridge

Upper Enson Farm

Enson House

Ensonlane Farm

Trent and Mersey Canal

Flute Meadow Bridge

ENSON LA

Brook House

Enson

Enson Farm

Pea Hill

Sandonbank

Rock Farm

Marstonlane Farm

MARSTON LA

Marston Hall Farm

SKEATH LA

Skeath House Farm

Ranslow Farm

Kent's Barn Farm

SALT LA

SALT BANKS

Sandon Bank Farm

Babbs Covert

Seven Stars (PH)

High Bridge Farm

SANDON RD

Church Hill

Mount Farm

MOUNT EDGE

SPODE AVE

HOPTON LA

B5066

A51

B5066

PO

LICHFIELD RD

Stonebench Farm

Sandon

Dog Farm

SCHOOL LA

Sandon Lock

PH

B5066

Mill Farm

River Trent

TRENTFIELD LA

Black Hill

Sandon Park

Icehouse Plantation

The Valley

Salt Drive

Sandon Hall

South Lawn

Fox Earth

Winter's Walk

A51

Salt Bridge

HALL FARM CRES

Trent Farm

Salt

SALT RD

HUNTERS CT

HILL RISE

Holly Bush Inn (PH)

New Fox Covert

Salt Heath

SALTHEATH LA

Slew Covert

Engine Covert

Old Fox Covert

Brick-kiln Covert

BRICK KILN LA

RAF Stafford

WITHIN LA

BRICK KILN LA

Heathyards

Hopton Heath

RAF Stafford

Square Covert

Hopton

CROMWELL CL

HOPTONHALL LA

KINGS DR

WILLMORE CT

WILMOREHILL LA

BATTLE RIDGE

A518

93 94 95

D E F

156
138

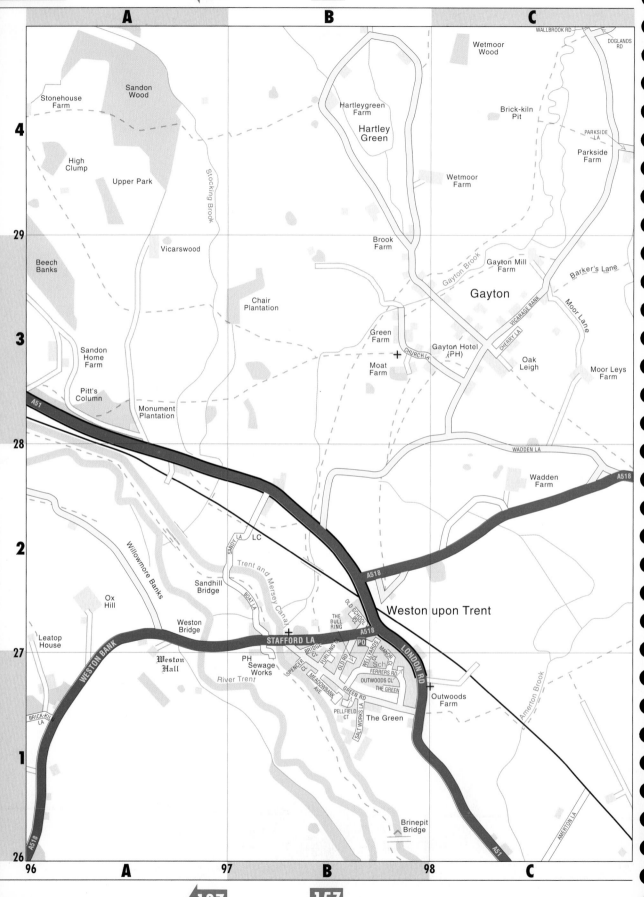

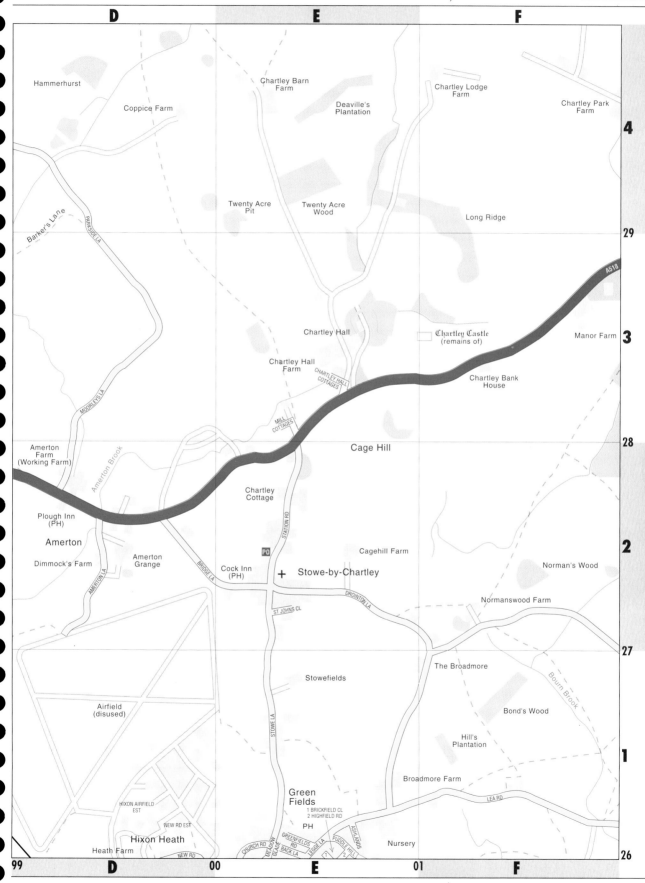

D
E
F

Hammerhurst

Coppice Farm

Chartley Barn
Farm

Deaville's
Plantation

Chartley Lodge
Farm

Chartley Park
Farm

4

Barker's Lane

PARKSIDE LA

Twenty Acre
Pit

Twenty Acre
Wood

Long Ridge

29

A518

MOORLEYS LA

Chartley Hall

Chartley Castle
(remains of)

Manor Farm

3

Chartley Hall
Farm

CHARTLEY HALL
COTTAGES

Chartley Bank
House

MILL
COTTAGES

Amerton
Farm
(Working Farm)

Amerton Brook

Cage Hill

28

Chartley
Cottage

STATION RD

Plough Inn
(PH)

Amerton

Dimmock's Farm

AMERTON LA

Amerton
Grange

BRIDGE LA

PO

Cock Inn
(PH)

+ Stowe-by-Chartley

Cagehill Farm

Norman's Wood

2

Normanswood Farm

DROINTON LA

ST JOHNS CL

27

The Broadmore

Bourn Brook

Airfield
(disused)

STOWE LA

Stowefields

Bond's Wood

Hill's
Plantation

1

Broadmore Farm

LEA RD

HIXON AIRFIELD
EST

NEW RD EST

Hixon Heath

Heath Farm

NEW RD

Green
Fields

1 BRICKFIELD CL
2 HIGHFIELD RD

PH

CHURCH RD

MEADOW
GLADE

GREENFIELDS
RD

BACK LA

LEGGE LA

PUDDLE HILL

ASHLANDS

Nursery

26

139
124

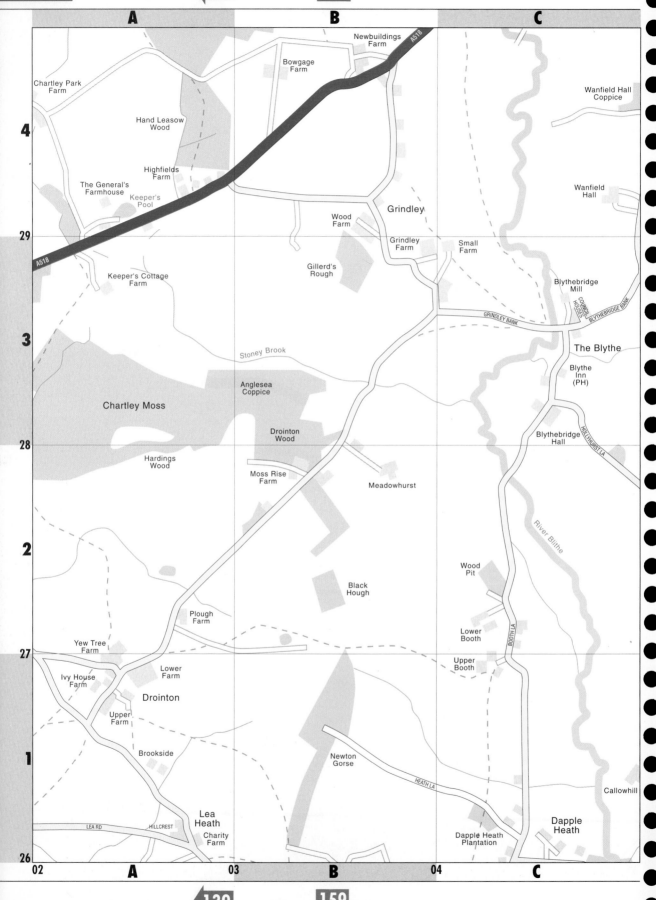

A   B   C

Chartley Park Farm

Hand Leasow Wood

Highfields Farm

The General's Farmhouse

Keeper's Pool

Bowgage Farm

Newbuildings Farm

A518

Wanfield Hall Coppice

Wanfield Hall

Grindley

Wood Farm

Grindley Farm

Small Farm

Blythebridge Mill

COUNCIL HOUSES

BLYTHEBRIDGE BANK

A518

Keeper's Cottage Farm

Gillerd's Rough

GRINDLEY BANK

The Blythe

Blythe Inn (PH)

Stoney Brook

Anglesea Coppice

Chartley Moss

Drointon Wood

Blythebridge Hall

HOLLThURST LA

Hardings Wood

Moss Rise Farm

Meadowhurst

River Blithe

Wood Pit

Black Hough

Plough Farm

Lower Booth

BOOTH LA

Yew Tree Farm

Lower Farm

Upper Booth

Ivy House Farm

Drointon

Upper Farm

Brookside

Newton Gorse

Callowhill

HEATH LA

Dapple Heath

Lea Heath

LEA RD

HILLCREST

Charity Farm

Dapple Heath Plantation

02   A   03   B   04   C

4

29

3

28

2

27

1

26

139
159

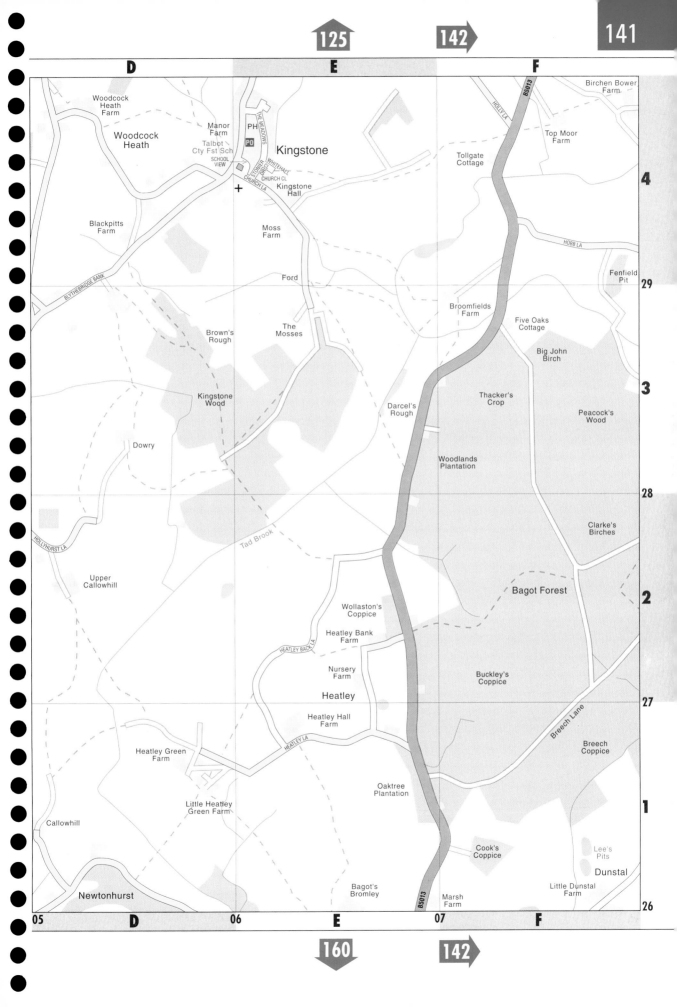

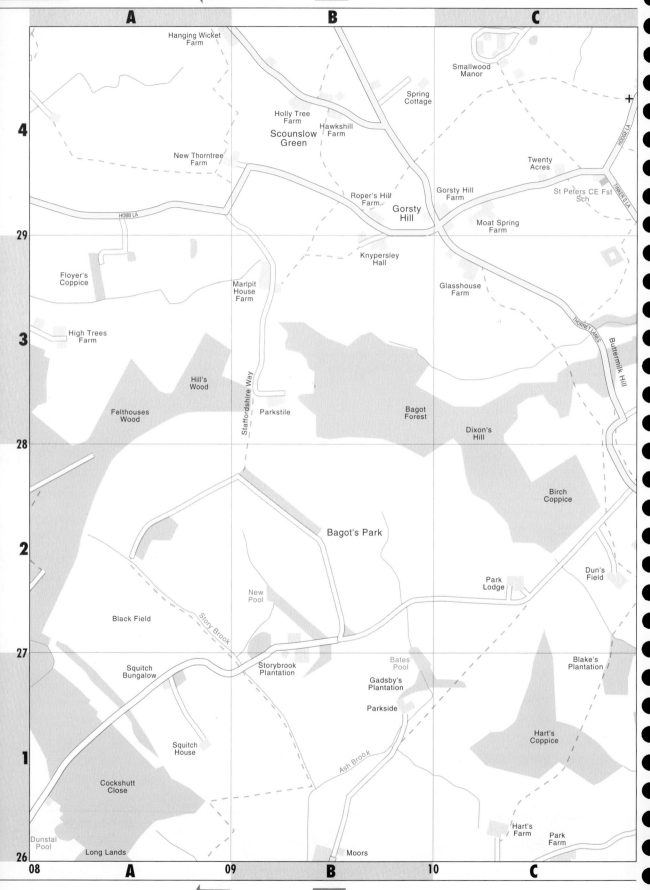

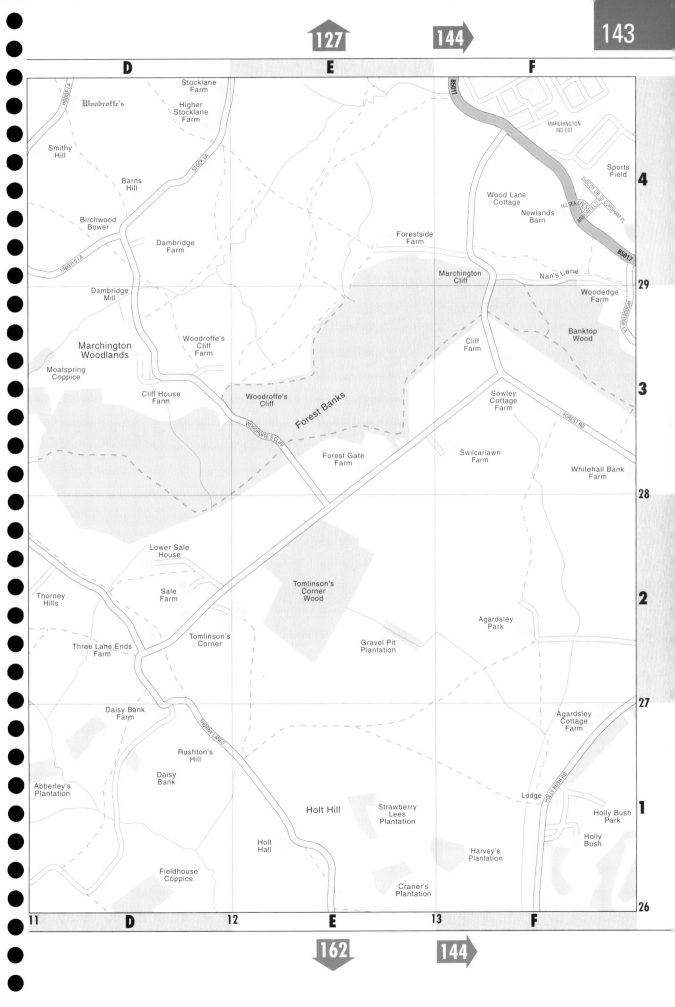

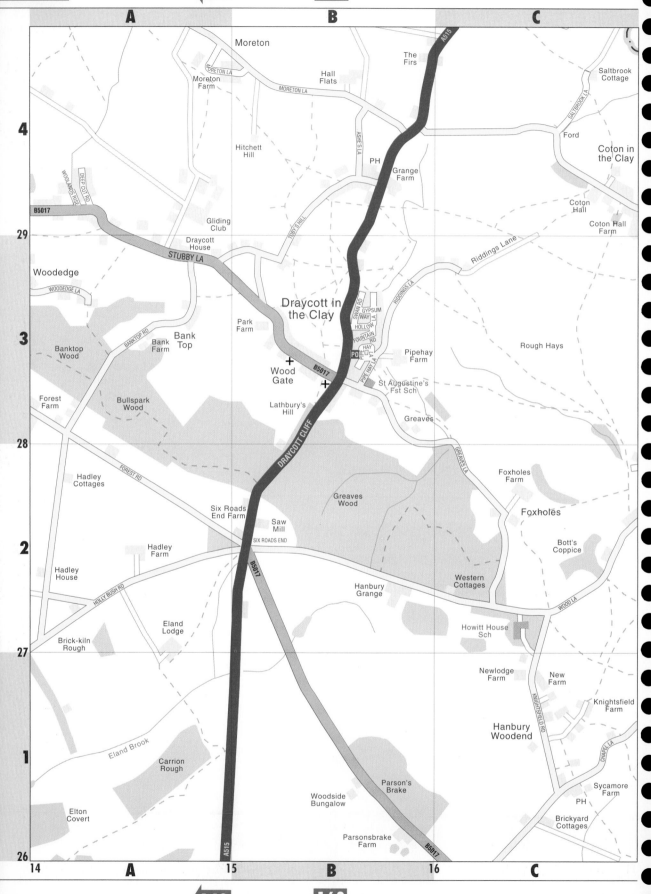

A   B   C

Moreton

The Firs

Saltbrook
Cottage

Moreton Farm
MORETON LA

Hall
Flats

MORETON LA

Ford

Coton in
the Clay

4

Hitchett
Hill

ASHES LA

PH

Grange
Farm

A515

SALTBROOK LA

Coton
Hall

Coton Hall
Farm

29

B5017

WOOLANDS RISE
DEEP CUT RD

Gliding
Club

TOB'S HILL

Draycott
House

STUBBY LA

Riddings Lane

RIDDINGS LA

Woodedge

WOODEDGE LA

Bank
Farm

BANKTOP RD

Bank
Top

Park
Farm

Draycott in
the Clay

SWAN RD
GYPSUM
WAY
HOLLOW

FOUNTAIN

Rough Hays

3

Banktop
Wood

Bullspark
Wood

Wood
Gate

B5017

HAY
RD
PO

PIPEHAY LA

Pipehay
Farm

Forest
Farm

Lathbury's
Hill

St Augustine's
Fst Sch

28

Hadley
Cottages

FOREST RD

Six Roads
End Farm

Greaves

Greaves
Wood

GREAVES LA

Foxholes
Farm

Foxholes

2

Hadley
House

HOLLY BUSH RD

Hadley
Farm

Saw
Mill

SIX ROADS END

B5017

Hanbury
Grange

Western
Cottages

WOOD LA

Bott's
Coppice

Brick-kiln
Rough

Eland
Lodge

Howitt House
Sch

27

Newlodge
Farm

New
Farm

KNIGHTSFIELD RD

Knightsfield
Farm

1

Eland Brook

Carrion
Rough

A515

Woodside
Bungalow

Parson's
Brake

Hanbury
Woodend

CHAPEL LA

Sycamore
Farm

Elton
Covert

Parsonsbrake
Farm

B5017

PH

Brickyard
Cottages

26

14   A   15   B   16   C

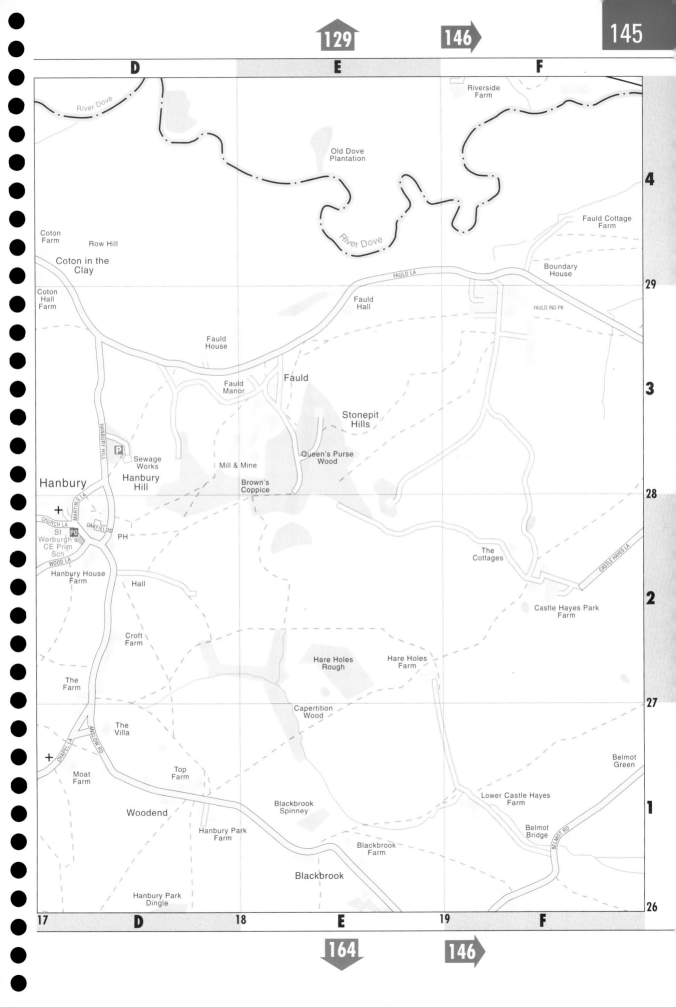

145

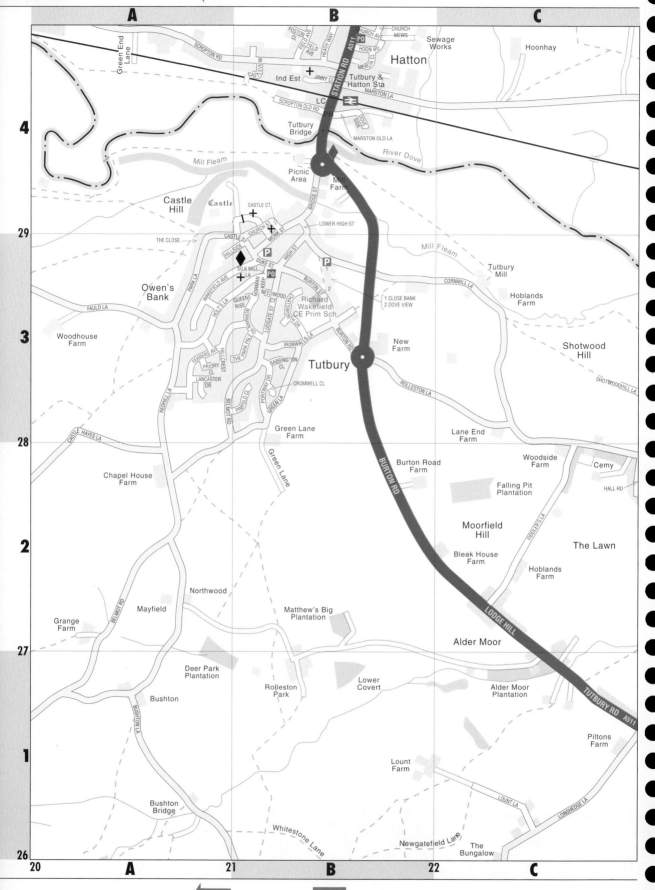

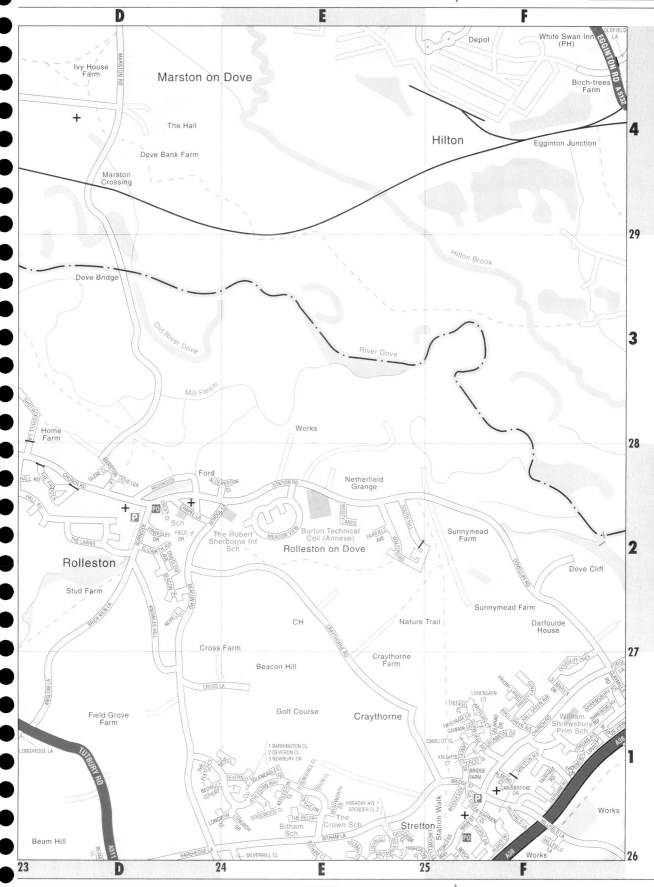

D   E   F

OLDFIELD LA

Depot

White Swan Inn (PH)

EGGINTON RD A5132

Birch-trees Farm

Ivy House Farm

Marston on Dove

The Hall

4

Hilton

Dove Bank Farm

Egginton Junction

Marston Crossing

MARSTON RD

29

Hilton Brook

Dove Bridge

Old River Dove

River Dove

3

Mill Fleam

Works

28

Home Farm

Ford

Netherfield Grange

Hall RD

THE PADDOCK

CHURCH RD

HALL RD

GLEBE CL

MARSTON DOVE LEA

BROOKSIDE

ALDERBROOK CL

STATION RD

TWENTY LANDS

SOUTH HILL

Sunnymead Farm

CROFT CL

CHAPEL LA

SCHOOL LA

MEADOW VIEW

Burton Technical Coll (Annexe)

FAIRFIELD AVE

WINGFORD

Dove Cliff

PO

Sch

FIELD DR

The Robert Sherborne Inf Sch

Rolleston on Dove

2

Rolleston

HAWKSLEY DR

ELIZABETH AVE

KEDLESTON AVE

BEACON DR

BEACON RD

Sunnymead Farm

Darfoulde House

Stud Farm

NEVILLE CL

CH

CRAYTHORNE RD

Nature Trail

DOVECLIFF RD

BRICK KILN LA

KNOWLES HILL

Cross Farm

Craythorne Farm

27

ANSLOW LA

Beacon Hill

CROSS LA

Golf Course

Craythorne

DOVECLIFF CRES

FORGE LA

PRIORY LANDS

PRIORY CT

ST MARYS DR

SHREWSBURY RD

CRANHILL

Field Grove Farm

LOHENGRIN CT

SONVIL

HALL GREEN AVE

HALL GREEN RD

CHURCH RD

William Shrewsbury Prim Sch

SHREWSBURY RD

LONGHEDGE LA

TINTAGEL CL

TRISTRAM GR

ARTHUR'S CL

GAWAIN DR

GUINEVERE CL

CALAHAD

GRUBMORE DR

JORDAN AVE

PEN VIEW

A38

TUTBURY RD A511

1

1 BARRINGTON CL
2 DEVERON CL
3 NEWBURY DR

CAMELOT CL

KNIGHTS CT

GUINEVERE CL

CREST CL

ALMOND

GRETTON AVE

FAIRHAM

FAIRHAM RD

THORNEYW

LOVATT

THE FLETCHES

NENE CL

SEVERN CL

GLENEAGLES

ATHLESTAN WAY

DUNSDALE CL

TROON CL

WENTWORTH DR

FARADAY AVE 1
SPENCER CL 2

BRIDGE FARM

BRIDGE ST

THE GREEN

CARISBROOKE DR

BEOWULF COVERT

KEDLESTON CL

CHEVIN

The Crown Sch

Station Walk

BRIDGESIDE

P

WARREN

LONGBOW CL

LONGBOW GR

GOODWOOD CL

THE BELFRY

Bitham Sch

BITHAM LA

Stretton

MAIN ST

HURST DR

HILLFIELD LA

Works

Beam Hill

BEAM CL

HAREHEDGE LA

SILVERHILL CL

BITHAM CT

KELMAR CL

ELWYN CL

BRITANNIA

GATCOMBE CL

HIGH GROVE CL

PRINCESS WAY

LADYWELL CL

LUKIN

HURST

BEECH

PO

HILLFIELD LA

A38

Works

26

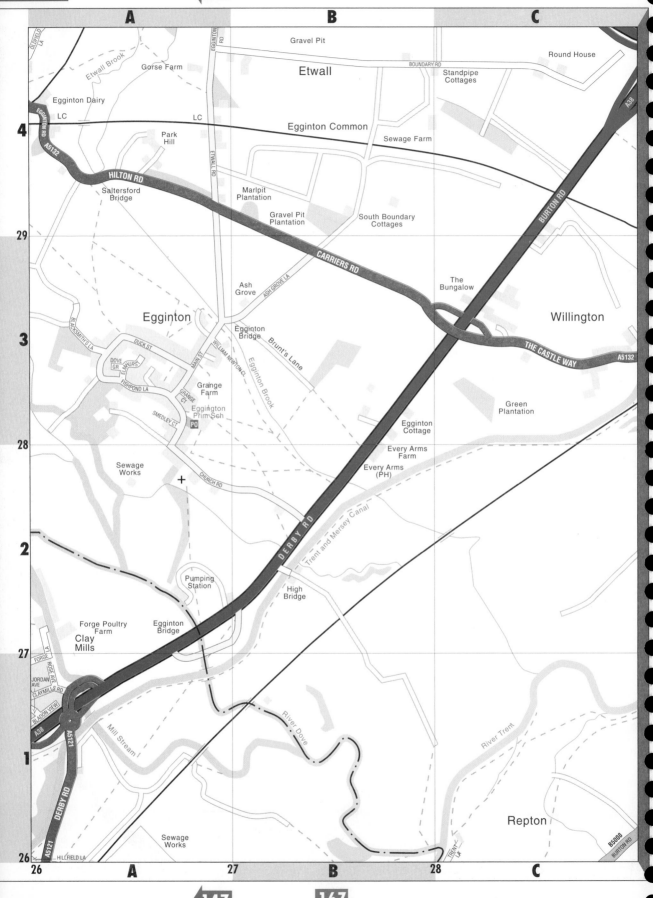

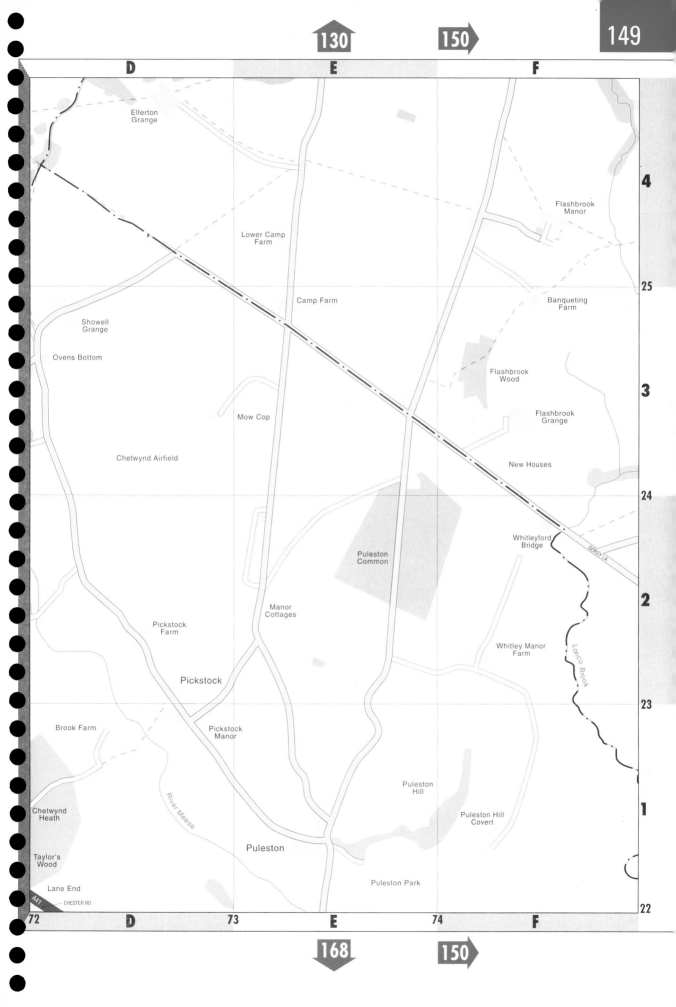

D
E
F

4

Ellerton
Grange

Flashbrook
Manor

Lower Camp
Farm

25

Camp Farm

Banqueting
Farm

Showell
Grange

Ovens Bottom

Flashbrook
Wood

3

Flashbrook
Grange

Mow Cop

Chetwynd Airfield

New Houses

24

Whitleyford
Bridge

GORSY LA

Puleston
Common

2

Manor
Cottages

Whitley Manor
Farm

Lonco Brook

Pickstock
Farm

Pickstock

23

Brook Farm

Pickstock
Manor

Puleston
Hill

River Meese

Chetwynd
Heath

1

Puleston Hill
Covert

Taylor's
Wood

Lane End

Puleston

A41
CHESTER RD

Puleston Park

22

A   **B**   **C**

Forge
Farm

Shebdon

Old Lea

Peggs
Farm

Chapel
Farm

PEGGS LA

Shropshire Union Canal

4

Batchacre
Hall

Anchor Inn
(PH)

Kemsey
Cottage

Oldershaws

OLDERSHAWS LA

25

The Leawoods

Kemsey
Manor

Leawood
Farm

GREGORY LA

THE STREET

Loynton
Farm

3

Lonco Brook

Loynton
Hall

Loynton

Weston Jones
Farm

Weston Jones

Deansbridge
Covert

24

Weston Jones
Mill

Bank
Farm

BAKER'S LA

WELL LA

A519

Pool House

2

GORSY LA

SHAY LA

Heybridge
Farm

23

Whitley
Ford

Warton
Grange

Warton

Fernhill

BLACK LA

1

GREEN LA

CLIFFS LA

Top
Farm

Sutton

A519

GUILD LA

22

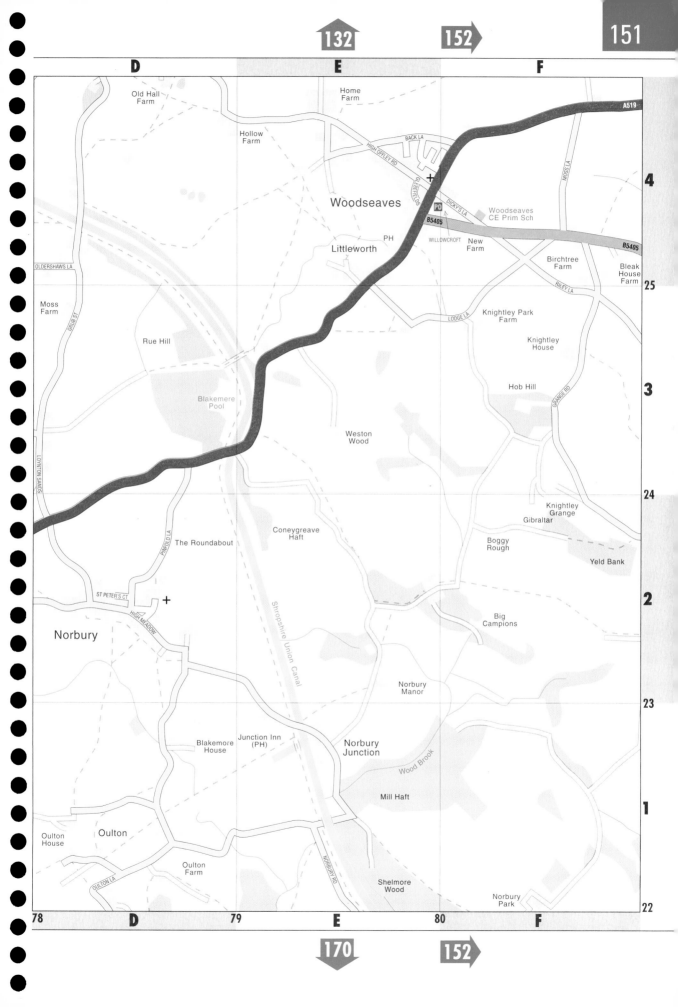

151   133

A   B   C

A519

A519

4

Gorse
Farm

Gorse
Covert

Taylor's
Covert

Bond's
Covert

Walton's
Rough

+

B5405

25

Yewtree
Farm

Hilltop
Farm

Lawnhead

Woodhill
Farm

Addison's
Covert

Depot

B5405

Knightley

The
Triangle

Common
Belt

3

RILEY LA

Rose Tree
Farm

Ashwoodhead
Farm

Ash
Wood

Wavell Lane

Ranton
Abbey

Old
Farm

LOWER RD

Green
Farm

24

Humphrey's
Wood

Lower
Knightley

Yeld
Bank
Farm

GRANGE RD

Simpkin's
Covert

Woise
Lane

2

Knightley
Green

GNOSALL RD

Knightley
Dale

New
Covert

Big
Wood

Woodside

Knightley
Hall

Yewtree
Farm

Hollies Brook

Hollybank
Farm

Prospect
Hill

23

Bellingham's
Covert

Ash's
Covert

Brough
Hall

1

Nut
Wood

KNIGHTLEY RD

Moor End
Farm

Hell
Hole

Hollies
Common

22

81   A   82   B   83   C

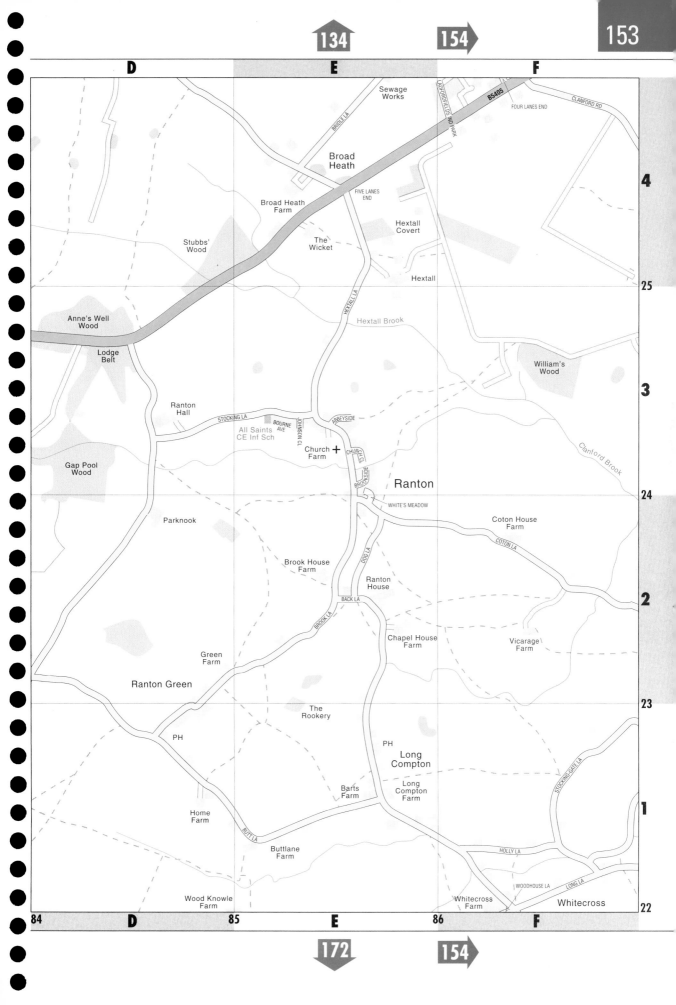

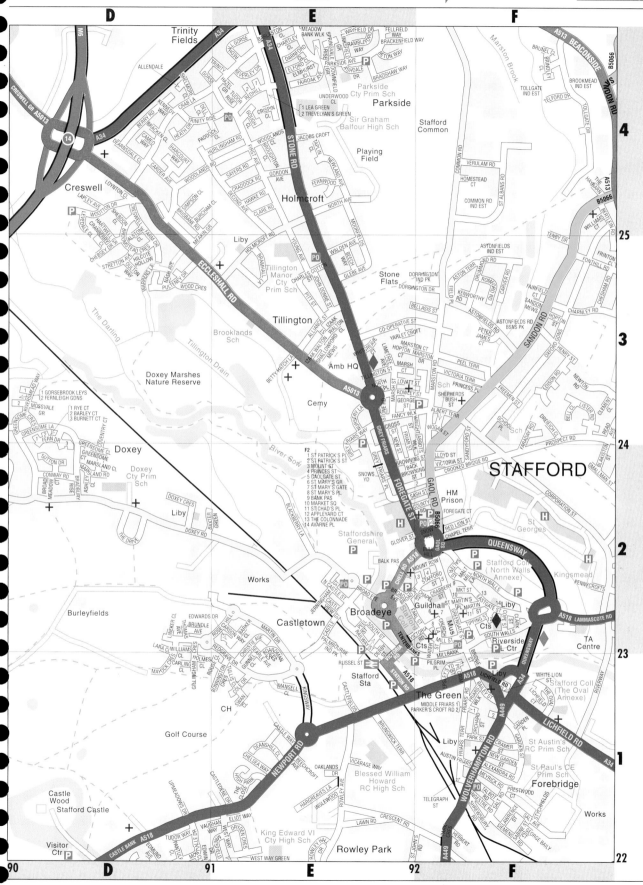

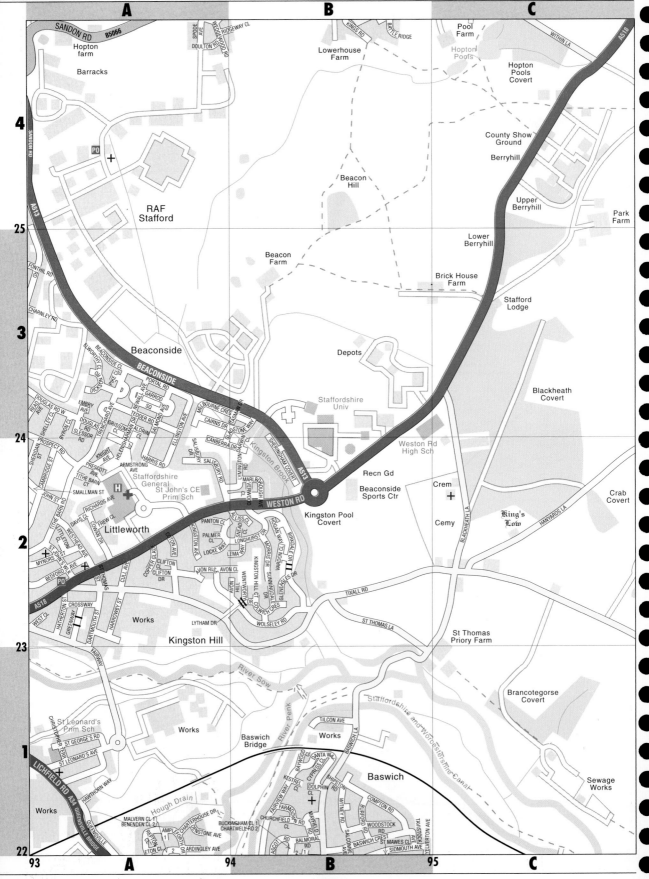

A **B** **C**

SANDON RD B5066

Hopton farm

Barracks

PO

4

RAF Stafford

25

FONTHILL RD

CHARNLEY RD

3

Beaconside

BEACONSIDE

Littleworth

Staffordshire General

St John's CE Prim Sch

WESTON RD

Kingston Brook

Staffordshire Univ

Kingston Pool Covert

Recn Gd

Beaconside Sports Ctr

2

A518

PO

WEST CL

Works

Kingston Hill

23

River Sow

River Penk

St Leonard's Prim Sch

Works

Baswich Bridge

Works

1

LICHFIELD RD A34

QUEENSVILLE BRIDGE

Hough Drain

Works

22

Lowerhouse Farm

KINGS RD

BATTLE RIDGE

Beacon Hill

Beacon Farm

Depots

Brick House Farm

Weston Rd High Sch

TIXALL RD

ST THOMAS LA

Baswich

Staffordshire and Worcestershire Canal

TILCON AVE

BASWICH LA

Pool Farm

Hopton Pools

Hopton Pools Covert

County Show Ground

Berryhill

Upper Berryhill

Park Farm

Lower Berryhill

Stafford Lodge

Blackheath Covert

Crem

Cemy

Crab Covert

King's Low

HANYARDS LA

St Thomas Priory Farm

Brancotegorse Covert

Sewage Works

WITHIN LA

A518

93 A 94 B 95 C

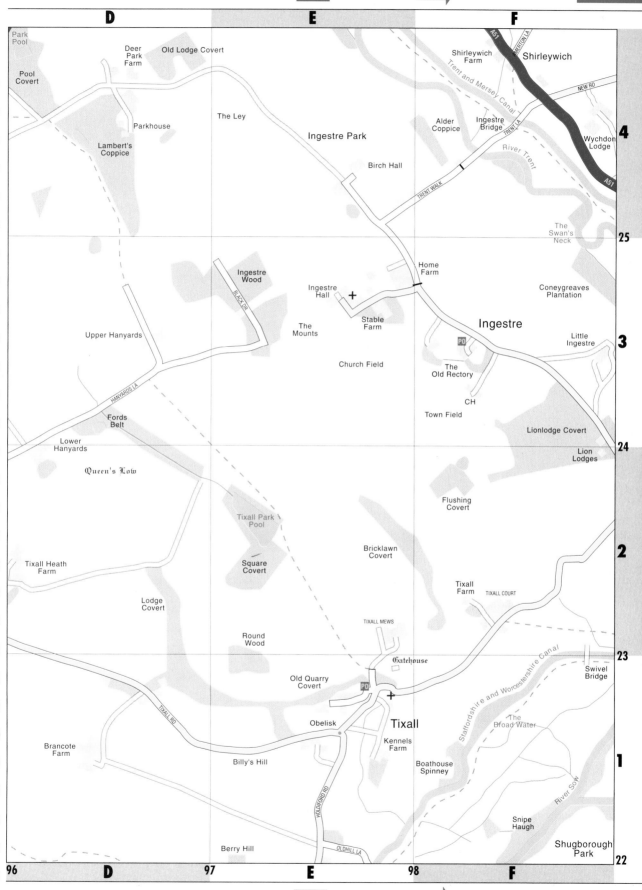

A   **B**   **C**

NEW RD

LC

Knowle Farm

Walledge Barn

CHURCH RD
MEADOW GLADE
WAL NUT CL
HIGHFIELD RD
BRICKFIELD CL

NEW RD
SNOW HILL
FEATHERBED LA
RIDGEWAY

ELM CRES
MARTINS WAY
THE CROFT
PO
SMITHY LA

VINE CL
SYCAMORE DR
BATHS LA
IVY CT CL

THE CROFT
HAMMONDS CL

Hixon

4

St Peters
CE Prim Sch

Grange Farm

EGG LA

Red Barn

Common Farm

White Barn

HIXON IND EST

A51

25

Pasturefields
Motel

PASTUREFIELDS LA

Factory

Yoxley Plantation

PASTUREFIELDS IND PK

Sewage Works

3

Little Ingestre

Farley Bridge

Swansmoor

Ginders Covert

Farley Farm

Lower Swansmoor Farm

Hoo Mill Lock

Farley Cottage

Gorse House

HOOMILL LA

24

Hoo Mill

Farley Lane

Tolldish

River Trent

MORETON LA

Trent and Mersey Canal

TOLLDISH LA

2

Little Covert

Tithebarn Covert

Tithebarn Farm

Oldfields Lane

MILL LA
MILL CROFT
ABBEYFIELDS
OLDFIELDS CL
ESSEX DR
LEASAWE
OLDFIELDS
CROFT

23

ESSEX COVERT CL

Jewstrump Covert

Haywood Mill

THE STABLES
LEASAWE CL
THE CROFT

ELM CL
MANOR CL
BREWERY LA
SCHOOL LA
THE SQUARE
PO
TRENT LA
St John's Sch
HAZELDENE
THE UPLANDS
MARLBOROUGH CL
LITTLE TIXALL LA

Oaklands Farm

Coley

Essex Bridge

Anson
CE Prim Sch

Great Haywood

Higher Coley Farm

Far Coley Farm

Shugborough
House & Gardens

TILLEDGE CRES
MORETON DR
ROCK CL
OAK CL
CLIFF RD
CLIFF LA
LICHFIELD DR

1

Shugborough Park

Staffordshire Way

COLEY LA

A51

Kilnhurst Covert

THE RING

BILLINGTON AVE

22

99   **A**   **00**   **B**   **01**   **C**

159 **141**

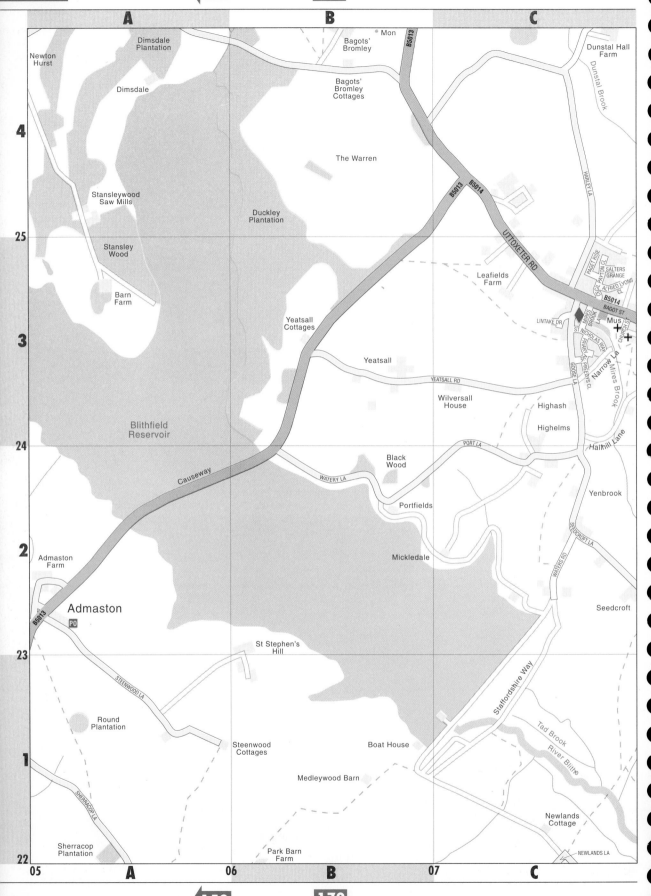

159 **179**

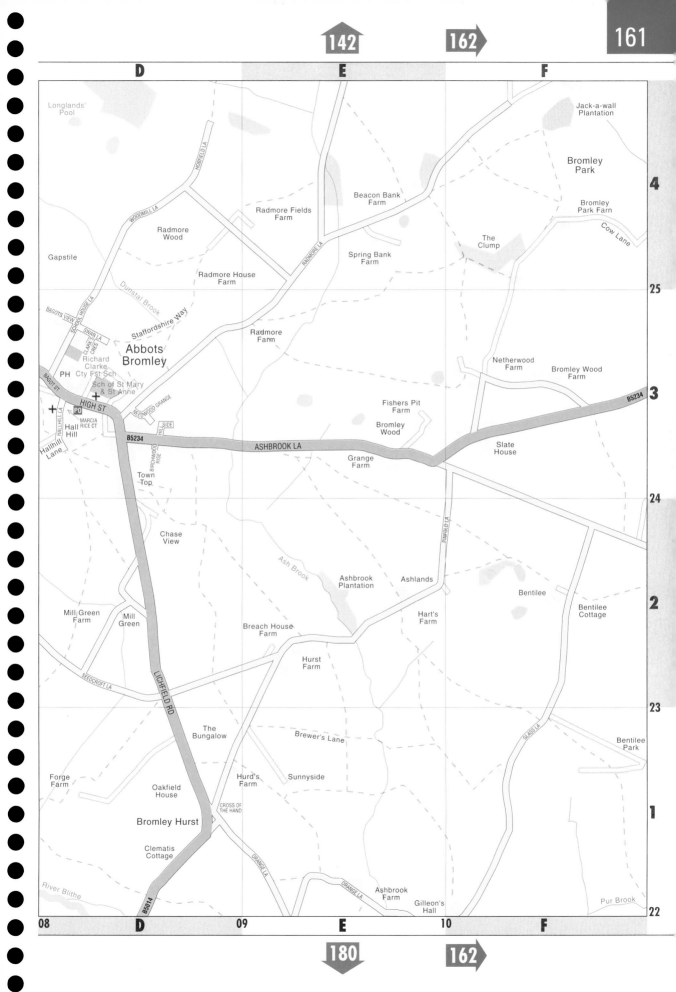

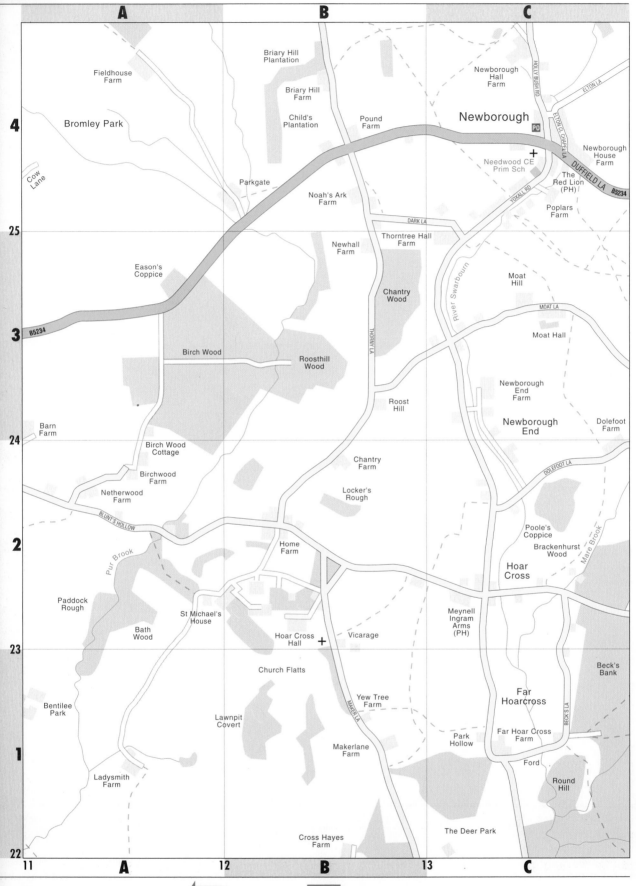

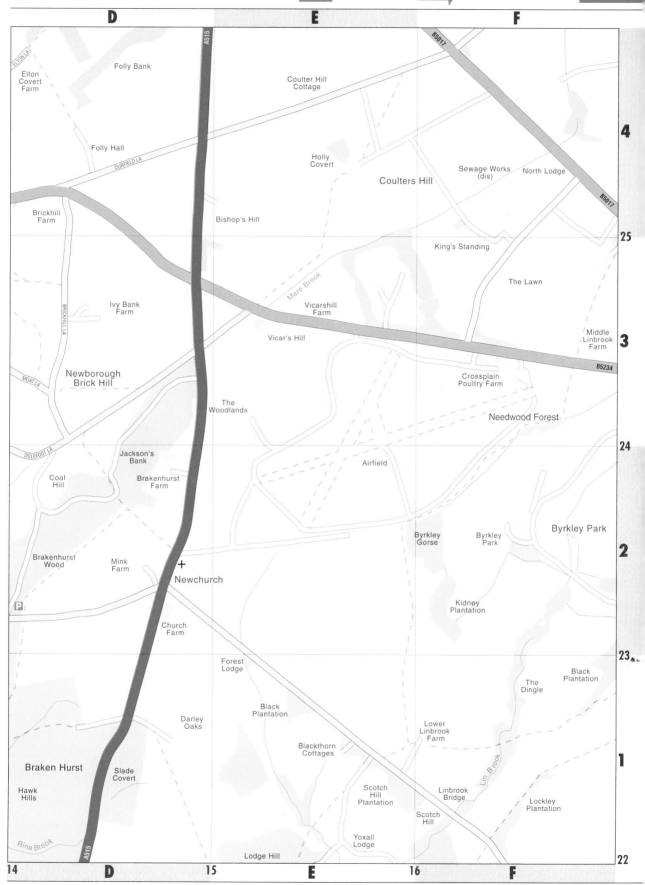

Elton La

Folly Bank

Coulter Hill
Cottage

B5017

Elton Covert
Farm

4

Folly Hall

Durfield La

Holly
Covert

Sewage Works
(dis)

North Lodge

B5017

Brickhill
Farm

Bishop's Hill

Coulters Hill

King's Standing

25

Brickhill La

Mare Brook

Ivy Bank
Farm

Vicarshill
Farm

The Lawn

Moat La

Vicar's Hill

Middle
Linbrook
Farm

3

B5234

Newborough
Brick Hill

Crossplain
Poultry Farm

The
Woodlands

Needwood Forest

Dolefoot La

24

Jackson's
Bank

Airfield

Coal
Hill

Brakenhurst
Farm

Byrkley Park

Byrkley
Gorse

Byrkley
Park

2

Brakenhurst
Wood

Mink
Farm

Kidney
Plantation

P

Newchurch

Church
Farm

Forest
Lodge

23

The
Dingle

Black
Plantation

Black
Plantation

Darley
Oaks

Lower
Linbrook
Farm

Blackthorn
Cottages

Lin Brook

1

Braken Hurst

Slade
Covert

Scotch
Hill
Plantation

Linbrook
Bridge

Lockley
Plantation

Hawk
Hills

Scotch
Hill

Rine Brook

A515

Yoxall
Lodge

Lodge Hill

22

163 145

A　　　B　　　C

Hanbury Park

Carvel Wood

Belmot Farm

Blackbrook Farm

Hanbury Park Coppice

Ivy Cottage

Forest Farm

Hanbury Park Gate

Needwood House Farm

SAND RD

Fishpond Plantation

Anslow Gate

Gate Farm

Needwood House

Church Farm

B5017

Upper Linbrook Cottages

Bell House Farm

Bell House

New Inn Plantation

East Lodge

North Lodge

Home Farm

Works

B5234

Needwood

BELLHOUSE LA

B5234

Paradise Farm

Barley Fields

New Inn (PH)

New Inn Farm

Nettlebeds

Byrkley Park

Oaks Farm

Gorse Covert Farm

Lin Brook

Callingwood Gate Farm

B5017

Stud Wood

Knightley Farm House

Stud Farm

Brickley Wood

Holly Bank

Knightley Park Cottage

CALLINGWOOD LA

Byrkley Park Ctr

Gable Lodge Farm

Callingwood Hall Farm

Black Plantation

Knightley Park

Forest Gate Farm

CHAPEL LA

PO

Rangemore

Vicarage Plantation

TATENHILL LA

All Saints CE Prim Sch

Dingle Farm

Linthurst Farm

Needwood Manor

Cuckoo Cage Farm

Hill Farm

TATENHILL COMM

Rangemore Hall

Rangemore Dingle

Higg's Hill

The Belt

CUCKOO CAGE LA

Tatenhill Common

Farm Plantation

Home Farm

Sewage Works

Rangemore Park

17　　A　　18　　B　　19　　C

163 183

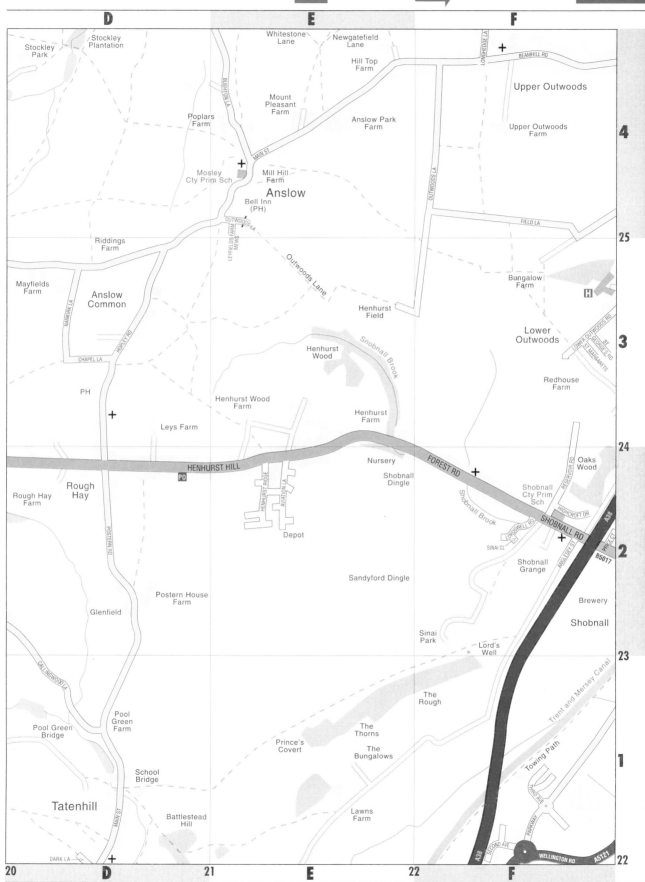

D | E | F

Stockley
Park
Stockley
Plantation

Whitestone
Lane
Newgatefield
Lane

Hill Top
Farm

LONGHEDGE LA
BEAMHILL RD

Upper Outwoods

BUSHTON LA

Poplars
Farm

Mount
Pleasant
Farm

Anslow Park
Farm

Upper Outwoods
Farm

OUTWOODS LA

4

MAIN ST

Mosley
Cty Prim Sch

Mill Hill
Farm

FIELD LA

Anslow

Bell Inn
(PH)

25

OUTWOODS LA

Riddings
Farm

LEYFIELDS FARM MEWS

Outwoods Lane

Bungalow
Farm

LOWER OUTWOODS RD
LOWER ST GEORGES RD
ST MARGARETS

H

Mayfields
Farm

NANKIRK LA

Anslow
Common

HOPLEY RD

Henhurst
Field

Lower
Outwoods

Redhouse
Farm

3

CHAPEL LA

Henhurst
Wood

Snobnall Brook

PH

Henhurst Wood
Farm

Henhurst
Farm

RESERVOIR RD

Oaks
Wood

Leys Farm

FOREST RD

Nursery

HIGHCROFT DR

24

HENHURST HILL

PO

HENHURST RIDGE
AVIATION LA

Shobnall
Dingle

Shobnall Brook

Shobnall
Cty Prim
Sch

A38

Rough Hay
Farm

Rough
Hay

Depot

SINAI CL
CROSSNELL RD
ANGLESEY ST

SHOBNALL RD

PRICE CT
B5017

2

POSTERN RD

Postern House
Farm

Sandyford Dingle

Shobnall
Grange

Brewery

Glenfield

Shobnall

CALLINGWOOD LA

Sinai
Park

Lord's
Well

The
Rough

23

Trent and Mersey Canal

Pool
Green
Farm

Prince's
Covert

The
Thorns

The
Bungalows

Towing Path

THIRD AVE

1

Pool Green
Bridge

Pool Green
Farm

School
Bridge

MAIN ST

Tatenhill

Battlestead
Hill

Lawns
Farm

PARKWAY

SECOND AVE

A38

WELLINGTON RD
A5121

22

DARK LA

20 | 21 | 22

D | E | F

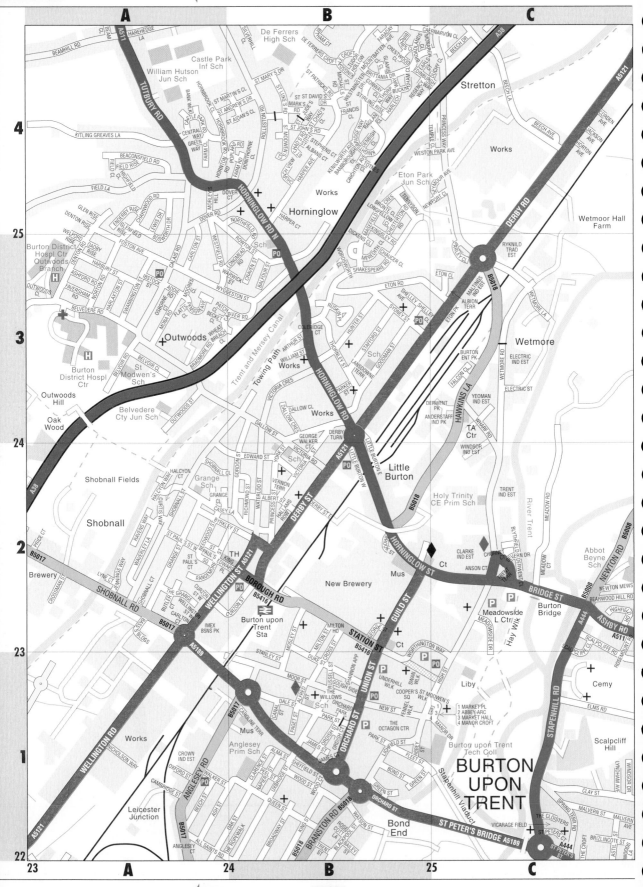

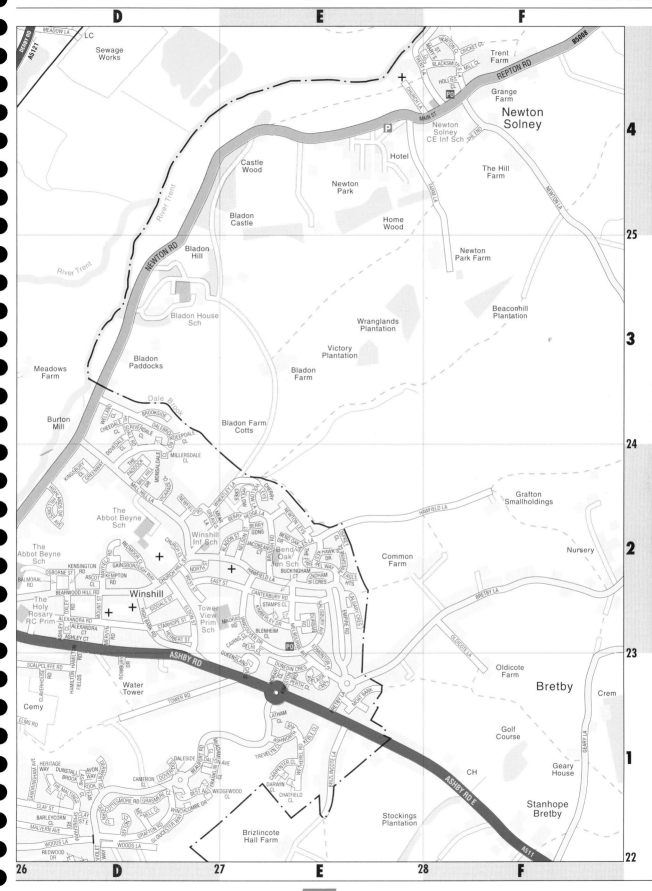

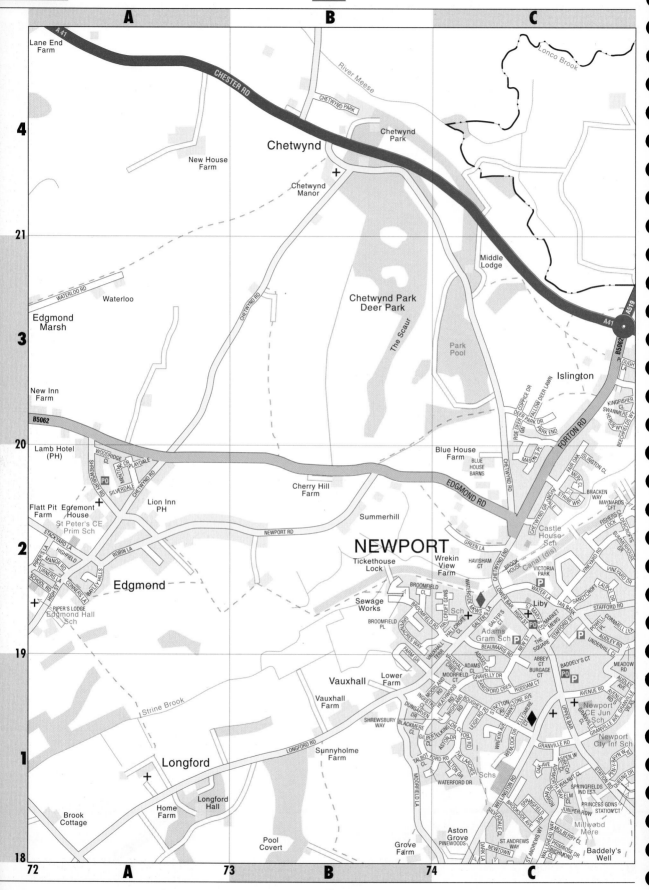

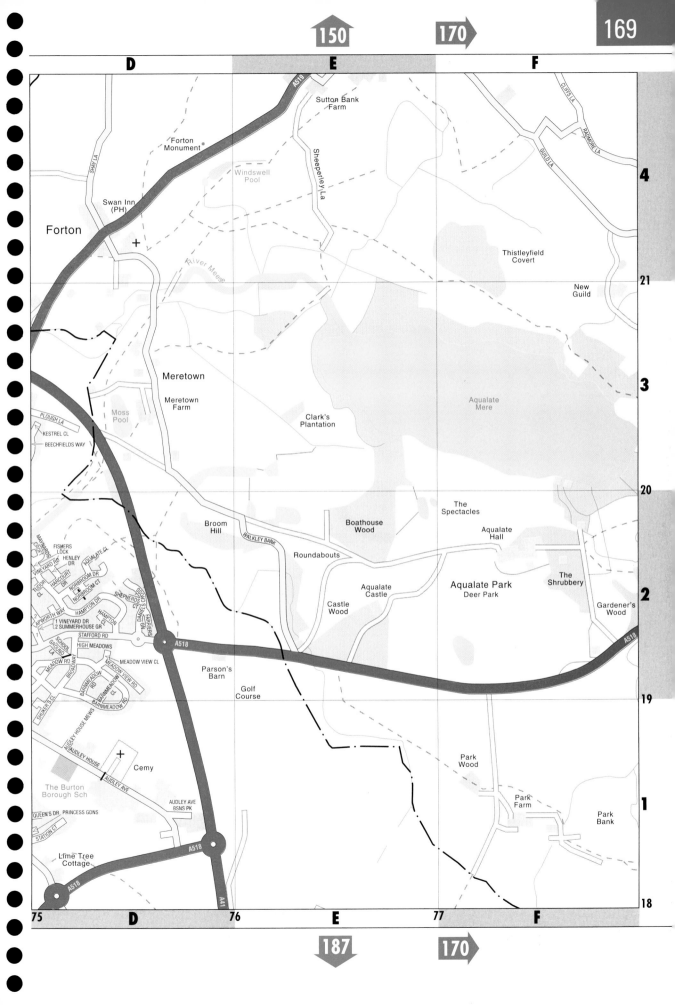

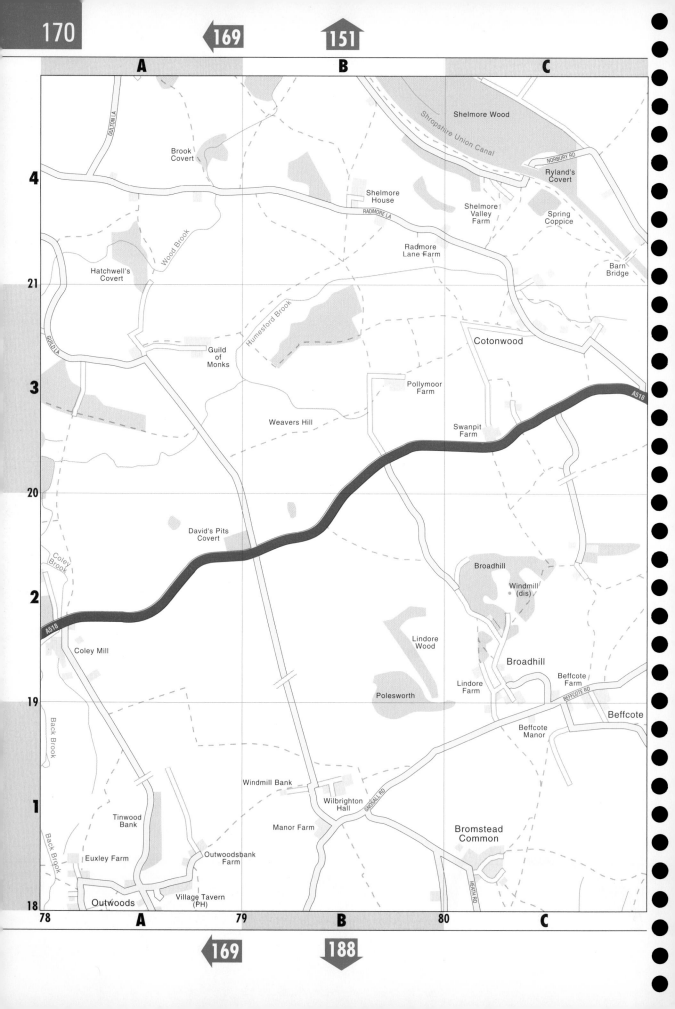

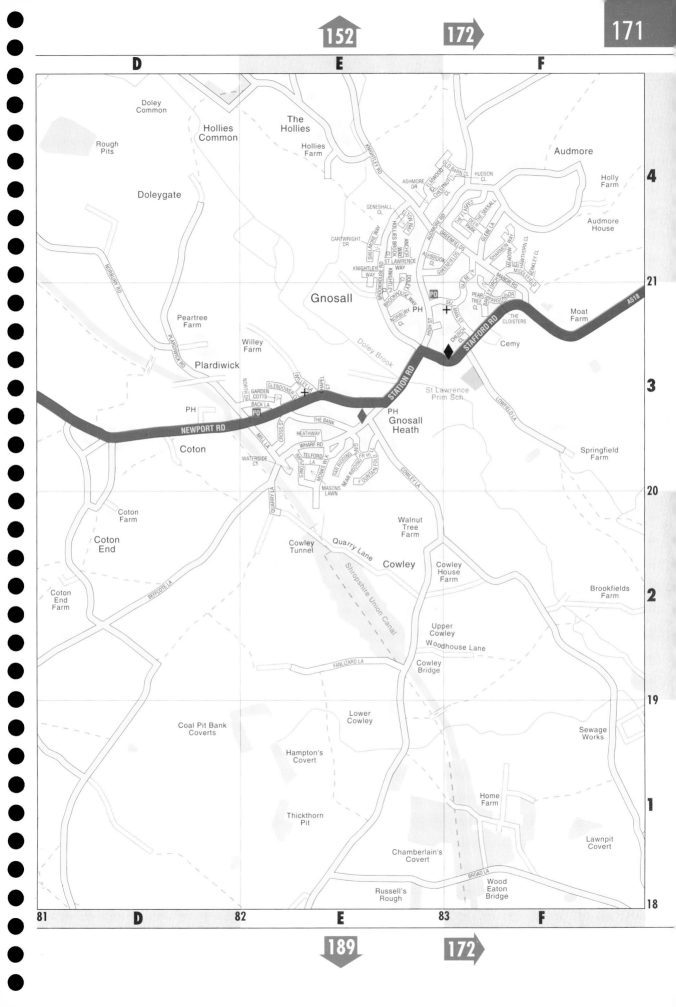

171

153

A   **B**   **C**

The Sheppy Farm

Bleak House Farm

Whitecross

Shutt Heath Farm

Shut Heath

Brazenhill

WOODHOUSE LA

SHIPPY LA

SHAMMANS LA

STATION RD

BRAZENHILL LA

Woodhouse Farm

Brazenhill Farm

4

Ivy House Farm

Hurst Farm

Leasows Farm

Parkhead House

Mayo Farm

21

A518

Pear Tree Bank Farm

HAWTHORNE CL

Old Park House

Shropshire Inn (PH)

New Park House

MEADOW DR

MOAT HOUSE DR

POPLAR CL

BROYDS CL

ST GILES GR

BROOK END

CHURCH CL

Grassy La

Haughton CE Prim Sch

Upper Reule Farm

The Old Hall

Haughton Farm

PO

RECTORY LA

PARK LA

OAK RD

BIRCH CL

PRINCE AVE

ASH DR

BACK LA

3

Reule Covert

Haughton

JOLT LA

Middle Covert

20

Ox Leasow Covert

Booden Farm

Black Hough

Allimore Brook

WATERY LA

Lower Reule Farm

Birches Gorse

Hough Farm

The Black Hough Farm

Hanging Pits Farm

2

Wheatcroft Covert

Reulemill Pools

Apeton Bank Covert

Allimore Green

19

Church Eaton Brook

Alstone Hall Farm

Lower Alstone

ALSTONE LA

Alstone Farm

Apeton Slang

Apeton Brook

1

Apeton

Alstone Cottages

Ford

Upper Barton

18

84   **A**   85   **B**   86   **C**

171

190

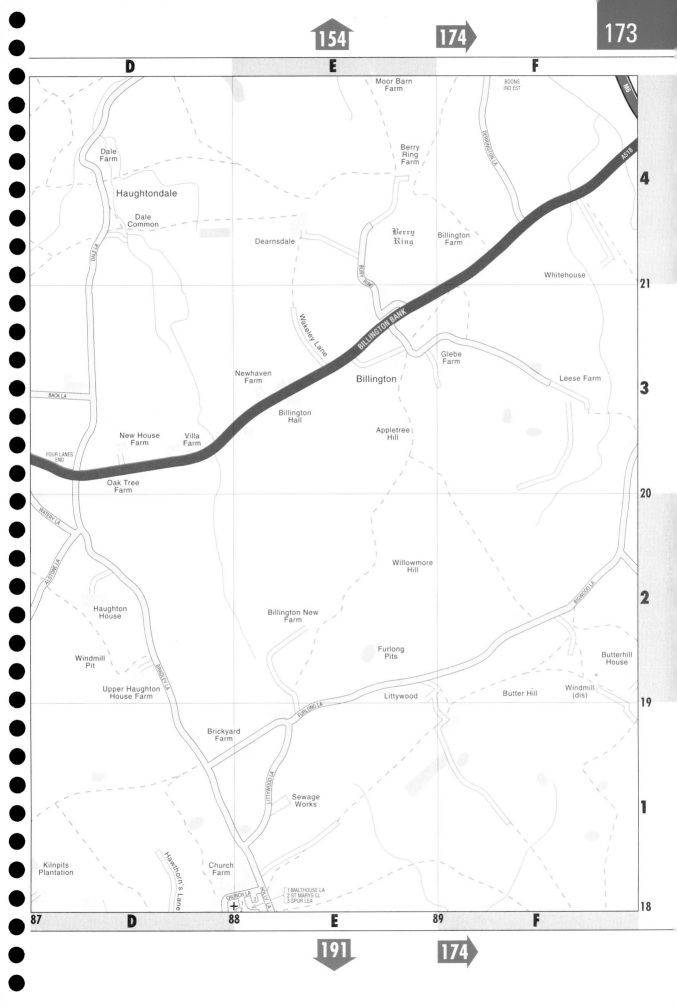

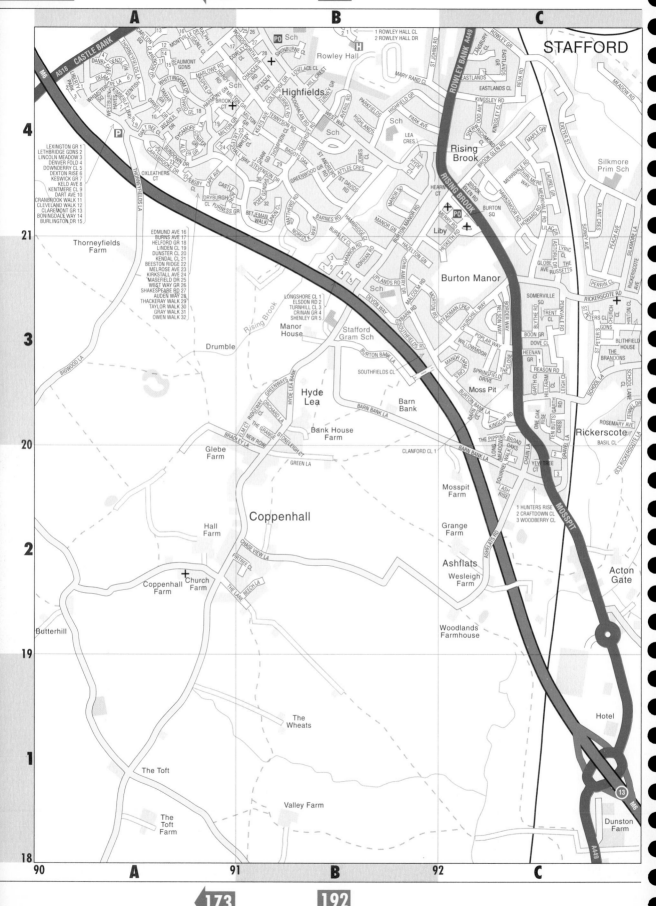

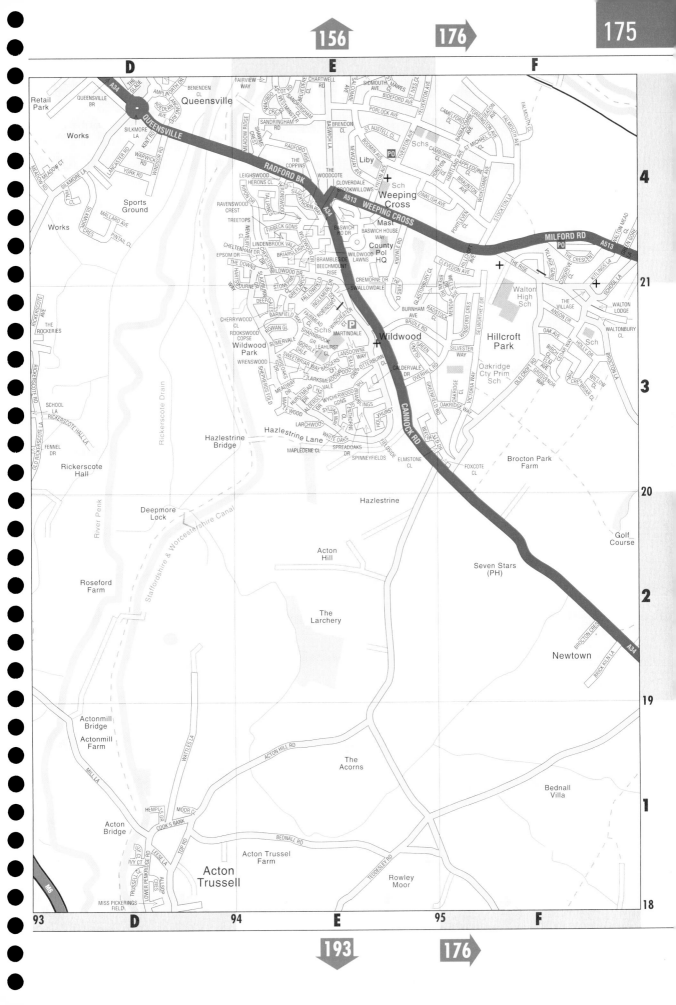

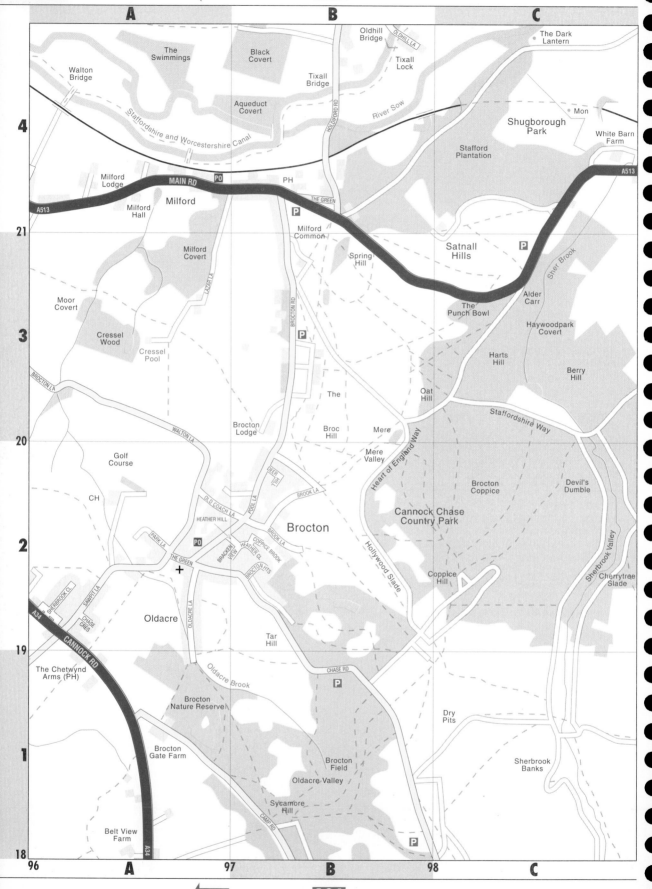

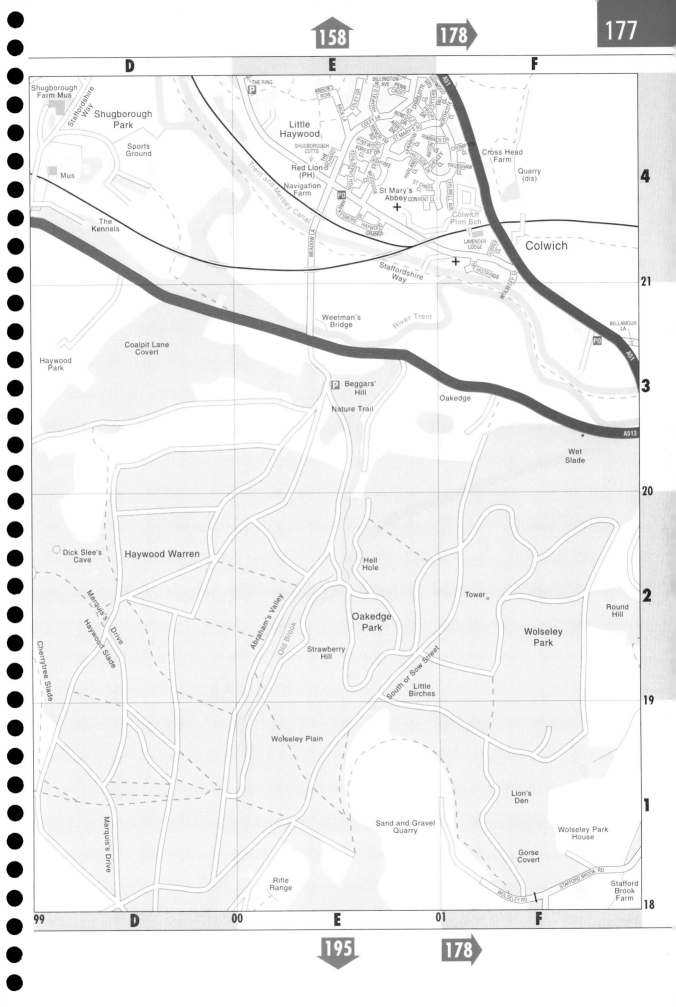

A B C

4

Bishton Farm

Lount Farm

Moreton Lane

Hamley Cottage Farm

Hamleyheath

MOOR LA

B5013

Bishton Lane Farm

Bellamour

21

Wilmour Farm

Bishton
Bishton Hall
St Bedes Sch

Boughey Hall Farm

SCHOOL LA WAY

Taft Farm

Taft Bridge

BELLAMOUR LA

St Mary's CE Prim Sch

BELLAMOUR LA WAY

3

BISHTON LA

A51

Trent and Mersey Canal

Staffordshire Way

Colwich Lodge

Bellamour Lodge Farm

A513

PH

Wolseley Garden Park

Wharf Cottage

20

River Trent

COLTON RD

Rydal Farm

Long Covert

Chapel Hill

Sewage Works

RUGELEY

Rugeley Trent Valley Sta

Stafford Brook

Pumping Station

TRENT VALLEY TRAD EST

2

The Beeches

The Beeches

ALBANY DR

BRINDLEY BANK RD

Bower House

Highland Way

ALLEN BIRT WLK

OLD EATON RD

19

Trent Farm

TRENT VALLEY TRAD EST

COLTON RD

Sch Chapelside

Arthur Wood Pl

Playing Field

WOLSELEY RD

STATION RD

Pump Lane

Sch

PO

A51

WESTERN SPRINGS RD

Chancel Cty Inf Sch

Etchinghill

1

Etching Hill Grange

Sch

Aelfgar Sixth Form Ctr

TA Cen

Liby

18

PENKRIDGE BANK

02 A 03 B 04 C

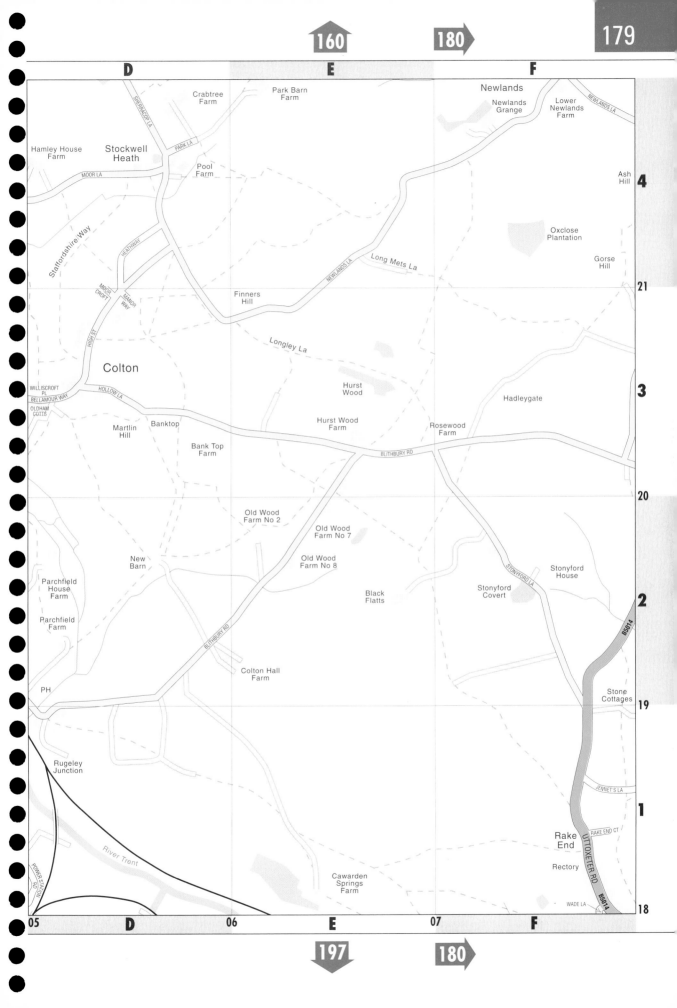

D
E
F

Crabtree
Farm

Park Barn
Farm

Newlands

Newlands
Grange

Lower
Newlands
Farm

NEWLANDS LA

Hamley House
Farm

SHERRACROFT LA

Stockwell
Heath

PARK LA

Ash
Hill

4

MOOR LA

Pool
Farm

Staffordshire Way

HEATHWAY

Oxclose
Plantation

Gorse
Hill

NEWLANDS LA

Long Mets La

MOOR CROFT

MANOR WAY

Finners
Hill

21

HIGH ST

Longley La

Colton

Hurst
Wood

Hadleygate

3

WILLISCROFT PL

HOLLOW LA

BELLAMOUR WAY

OLDHAM COTTS

Martlin
Hill

Banktop

Hurst Wood
Farm

Rosewood
Farm

BLITHBURY RD

Bank Top
Farm

20

Old Wood
Farm No 2

Old Wood
Farm No 7

New
Barn

Old Wood
Farm No 8

STONYFORD LA

Stonyford
House

2

Parchfield
House
Farm

Black
Flatts

Stonyford
Covert

B5014

Parchfield
Farm

BLITHBURY RD

Stone
Cottages

PH

Colton Hall
Farm

19

Rugeley
Junction

JENNET S LA

RAKE END CT

1

River Trent

Rake
End

UTTOXETER RD

POWER STATION RD

Rectory

B5014

Cawarden
Springs
Farm

WADE LA

18

A | **B** | **C**

Blithford Farm

Mount Pleasant

Rookery Farm

ORANGE LA

NEWLANDS LA

B5014

Poplar Farm

Old Lane

Ash Hill

The Willows

4

Little Blithe

The Hurst

Porter's Hill

21

NUNS LA

Priory Farm

Old Lane

Bank House Farm

PEARTREE LA

UTTOXETER RD

Blithbury Farm

3

Braddocks Barn

Manor Farm

River Blithe

Pur Brook

BLITHBURY RD

Blithbury

Longacres

Hayend Wood

20

New House Farm

Hayend

PIPE WOOD LA

Westwood Sch

B5014

Pipewood Cottage

Pipe Wood

Town End Farm

Hamstall Hall

2

BLITHBURY RD

Coatfield

Hamstall Ridware

Bentley Farm

19

Goldhayfields

Shoulder of Mutton (PH)

PO

JENNIES LA

Woodhouse Farm

Hunger Hill

Cowley Hill

BLYTHE VIEW

LICHFIELD RD

1

Cowley Hill

Quintin's Orchard

Blythe House Farm

CHADWICK CRES

OAKLANDS CL

18

08 | **A** | 09 | **B** | 10 | **C**

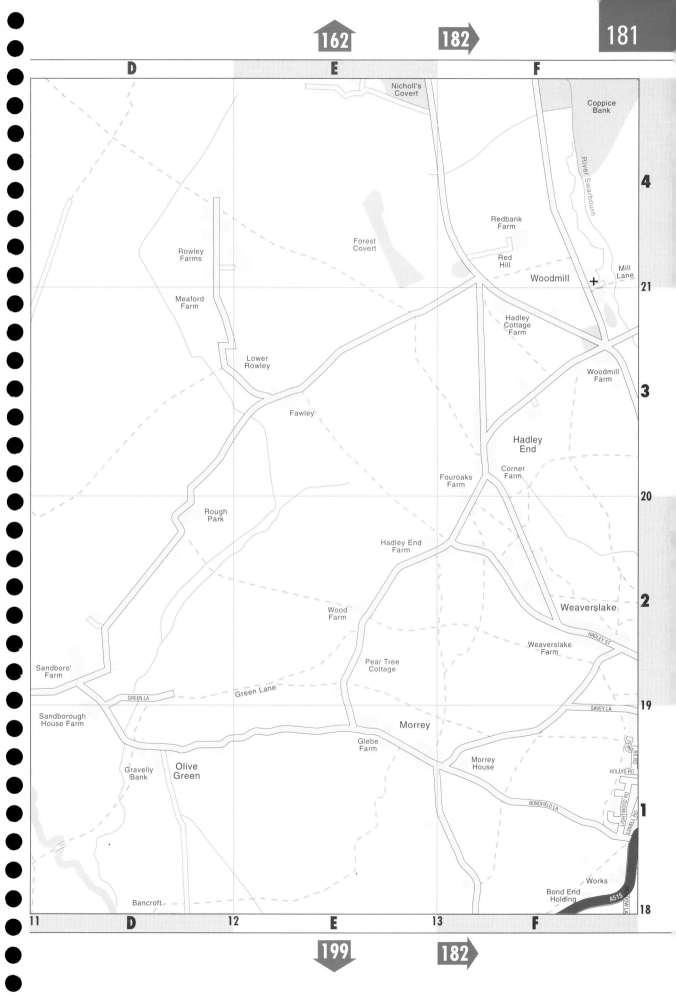

D E F

4

21

3

20

2

19

1

18

11 D 12 E 13 F

Nicholl's Covert

Coppice Bank

River Swarbourn

Redbank Farm

Red Hill

Woodmill

Mill Lane

Rowley Farms

Forest Covert

Meaford Farm

Hadley Cottage Farm

Woodmill Farm

Lower Rowley

Fawley

Hadley End

Fouroaks Farm

Corner Farm

Rough Park

Hadley End Farm

Weaverslake

Wood Farm

HADLEY ST

Weaverslake Farm

Sandboro' Farm

Pear Tree Cottage

Green Lane

SAVEY LA

GREEN LA

Sandborough House Farm

Morrey

FERRERS RD

HOLLYS RD.

Gravelly Bank

Olive Green

Glebe Farm

Morrey House

LOVELL RD

BONDFIELD LA

Bancroft

Works

Bond End Holding

A515

MEADOW LA

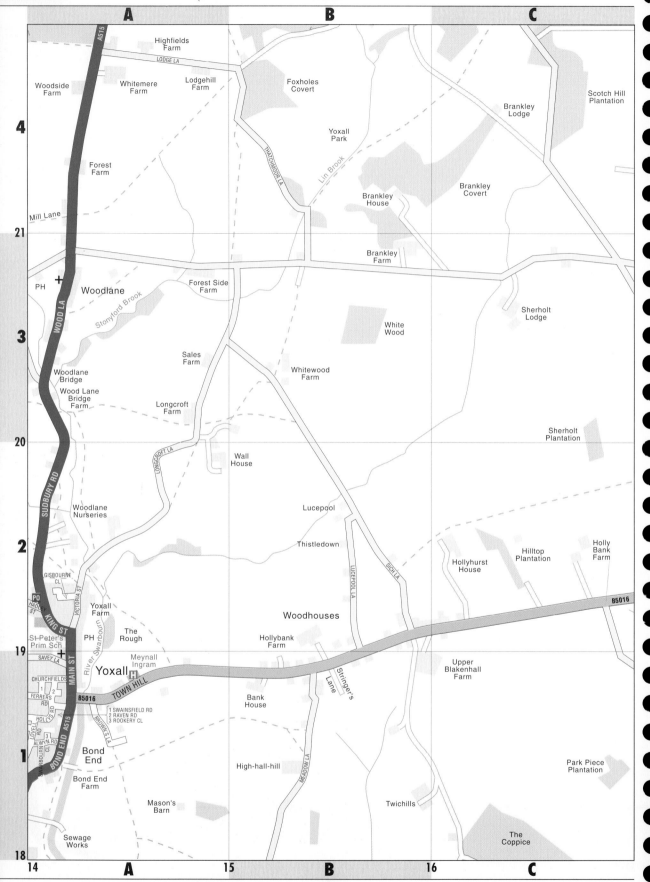

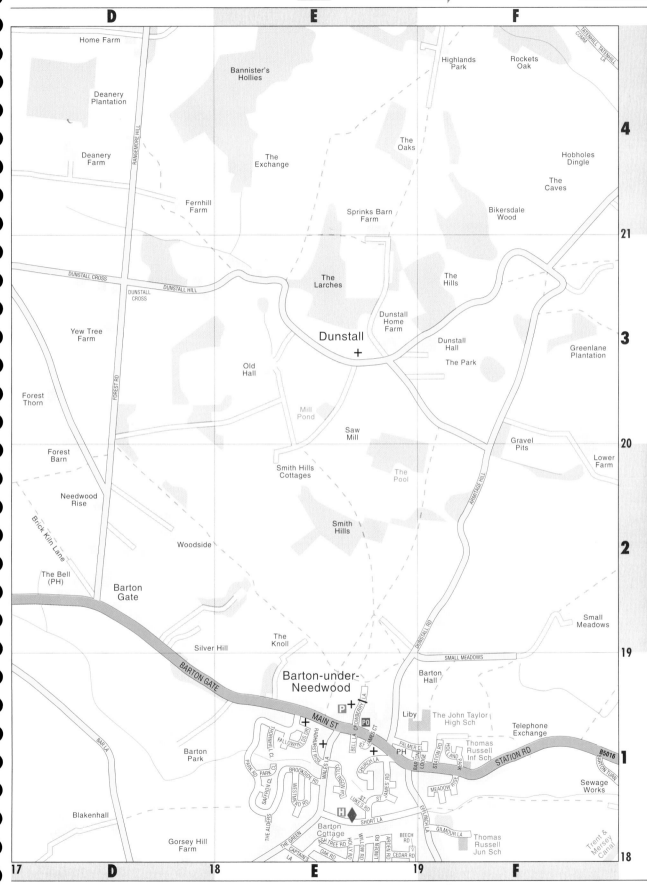

4

Home Farm

Bannister's
Hollies

Highlands
Park

Rockets
Oak

TATENHILL TATENHILL
COMM

Deanery
Plantation

The Exchange

The
Oaks

Hobholes
Dingle

RANGEMORE HILL

Deanery
Farm

The
Caves

Fernhill
Farm

Sprinks Barn
Farm

Bikersdale
Wood

21

Dunstall Cross

Dunstall Hill

The
Larches

The
Hills

Yew Tree
Farm

Dunstall
Cross

Dunstall
Home
Farm

FOREST RD

Dunstall

Dunstall
Hall

Greenlane
Plantation

3

Forest
Thorn

Old
Hall

Mill
Pond

The Park

Saw
Mill

Gravel
Pits

Lower
Farm

20

Forest
Barn

Smith Hills
Cottages

The
Pool

Needwood
Rise

ARMITAGE HILL

Brick Kiln Lane

Smith
Hills

Woodside

2

The Bell
(PH)

Barton
Gate

Small
Meadows

BAR LA

DUNSTALL RD

Silver Hill

The
Knoll

SMALL MEADOWS

19

BARTON GATE

Barton-under-
Needwood

Barton
Hall

Barton
Park

P

CROWBERRY LA

BELLA

ST JAMES CT

Liby

The John Taylor
High Sch

Telephone
Exchange

PO

Main St

FALLOWFIELD

RADHURST RISE

WALES LA

ST JAMES RD

CHURCH RD

PALMER CL

BARTON CL
LODGE

STATION RD

HIGH LAND PARK

Thomas
Russell
Inf Sch

STATION RD

B5016

BARTON TURN

1

PARK RD

PARK CL

BROOKSIDE RD

WILLIAMS RD

CALLINGWOOD

ST LUKE'S RD

ST JAMES
ST

PH

MEADOW RISE

Sewage
Works

SANTRO V CL

Blakenhall

The Alders

H

Barton
Cottage

SHORT LA

EFFLINCH LA

GILMOUR LA

Thomas
Russell
Jun Sch

Trent &
Mersey Canal

Gorsey Hill
Farm

The Green

Captain's
La

ASH TREE RD

OAK RD

HOLLY RD

WILLOW RD

LINDEN RD

ARDEN RD

CEDAR RD

BEECH
RD

18

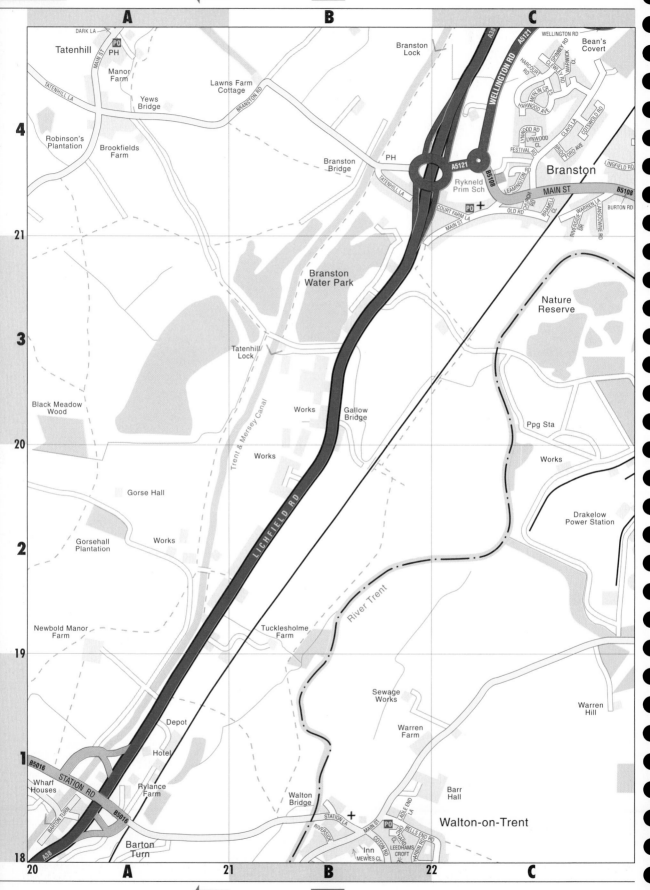

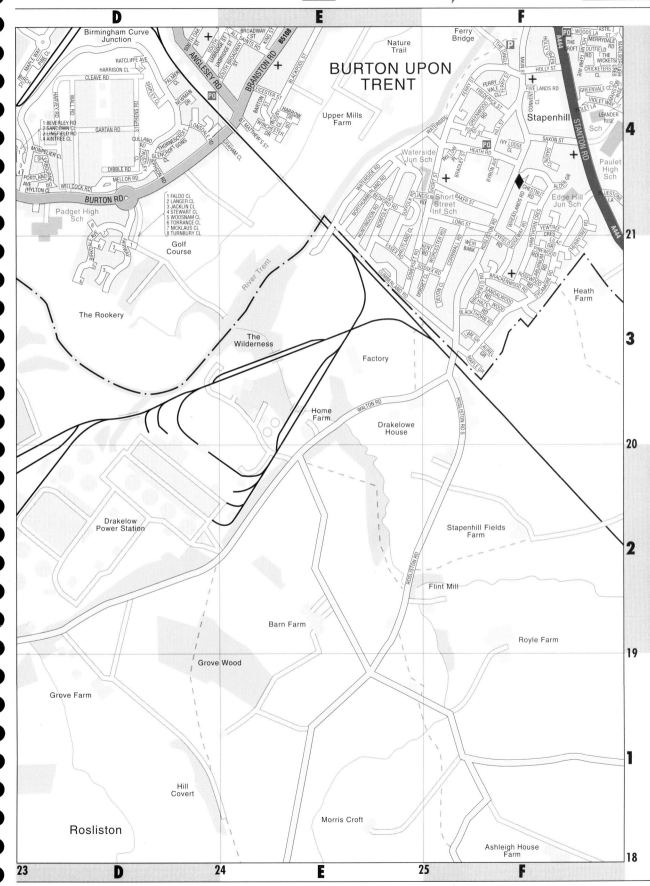

BURTON UPON TRENT

Stapenhill

Roslistown

185
167

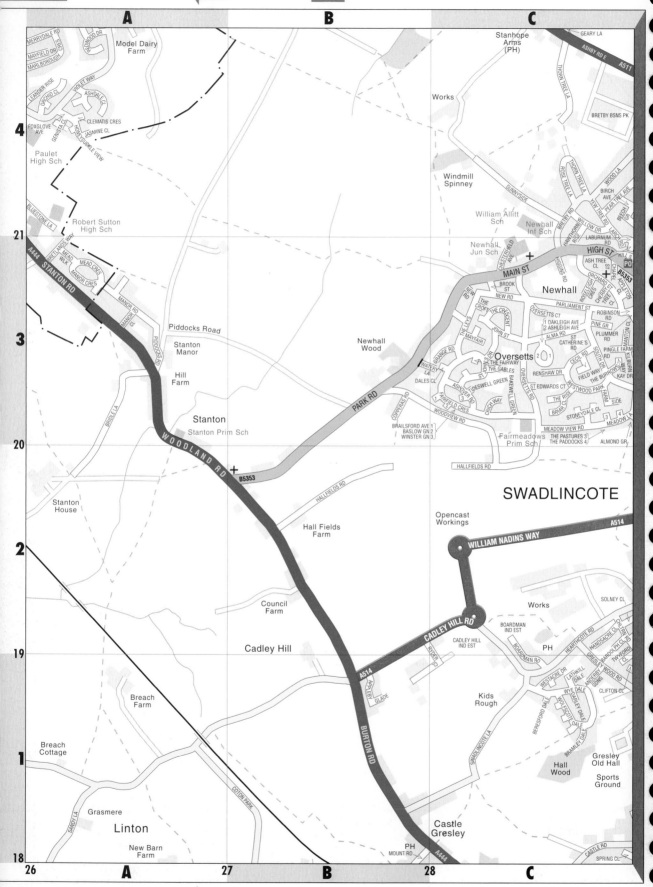

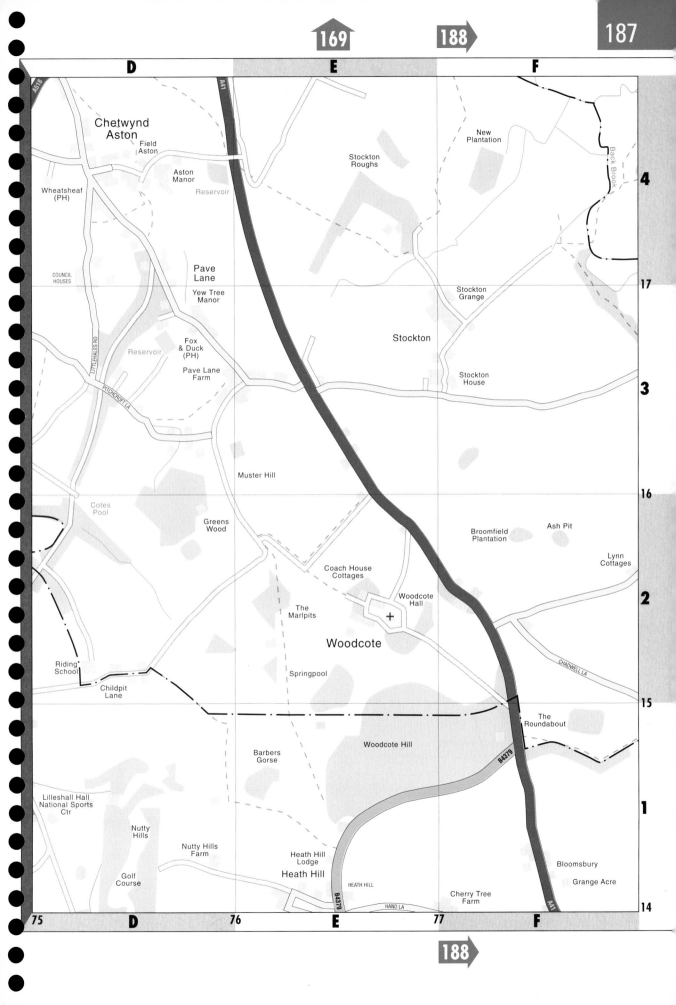

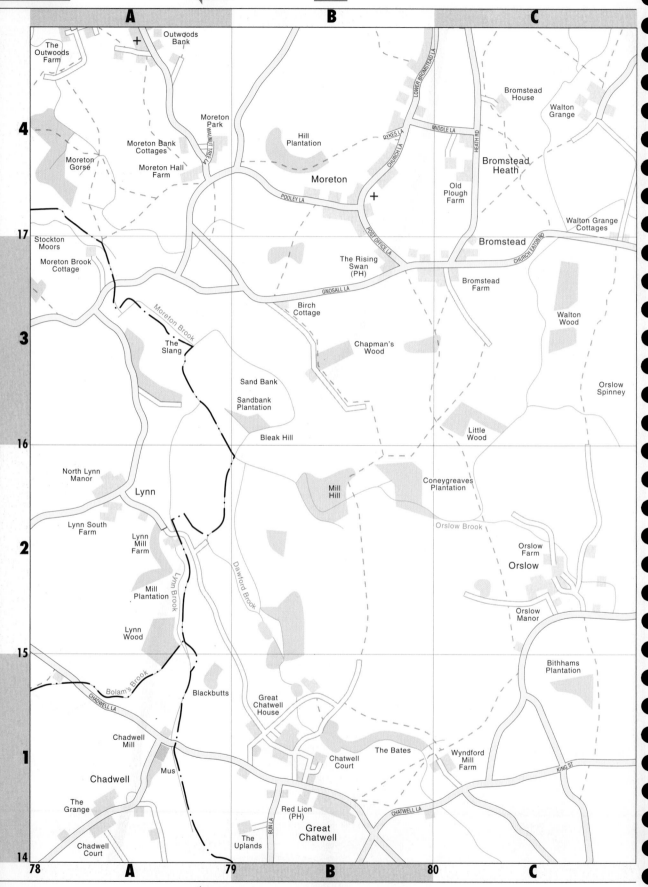

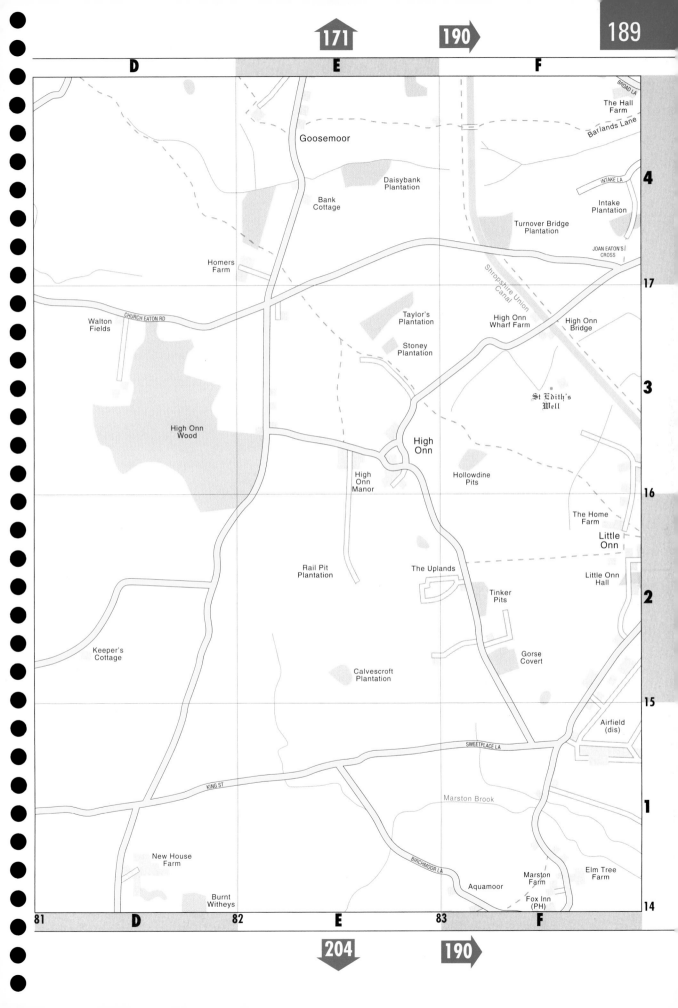

D   E   F

BROAD LA

The Hall
Farm

Barlands Lane

Goosemoor

INTAKE LA

4

Daisybank
Plantation

Intake
Plantation

Bank
Cottage

Turnover Bridge
Plantation

JOAN EATON'S
CROSS

Homers
Farm

Shropshire Union Canal

17

Walton
Fields

CHURCH EATON RD

Taylor's
Plantation

High Onn
Wharf Farm

High Onn
Bridge

Stoney
Plantation

St Edith's
Well

3

High Onn
Wood

High
Onn

High
Onn
Manor

Hollowdine
Pits

16

The Home
Farm

Little
Onn

Rail Pit
Plantation

The Uplands

Little Onn
Hall

2

Tinker
Pits

Keeper's
Cottage

Calvescroft
Plantation

Gorse
Covert

15

Airfield
(dis)

SWEETPLACE LA

Marston Brook

1

KING ST

New House
Farm

BIRCHMOOR LA

Elm Tree
Farm

Aquamoor

Marston
Farm

Burnt
Witheys

Fox Inn
(PH)

14

81   D   82   E   83   F

A   **B**   **C**

ALSTONE LA

Brookhouse
Farm

Wood
Eaton

BROAD LA

Barlands
Lane

INTAKE LA

**Church
Eaton**

Church Eaton
Prim Sch

Barton
Covert

Greenfields
Farm

Middle
Covert

4

ALLEY'S LA

ASHLEY
ST

PO

WOOD EATON RD

HIGH ST

PH

THE OAKLANDS

MALTHOUSE LA

LITTLE ONN RD

PARKERS CL

Church Eaton
Common

Church Eaton
Green

17

Green
Farm

Shredicote
Wood

Park Hall
Farm

Church Eaton Brook

3

Stafford Lane

Woollaston
Farm

Red House
Farm

Wollaston
Cottages

16

Rusty
Pits

**Little
Onn**

Woollaston

2

Upper
Woollaston
Covert

Bagnallditch

Shropshire Union Canal

Airfield
(disused)

15

SLAB LA

Ryehill
Bridge

Little
Onn
Gorse

Longnor Gorse
Farm

Mitton Lodge
Farm

Gorse Lane

Port
Coppice

1

The
Rookery

Barn
Cottage

Shushions
Manor

Wheaton Aston Brook

Longnor
Hall

Stonyford
Bridge

Longnor Brook

Longnor

14

84   **A**   85   **B**   86   **C**

D E F

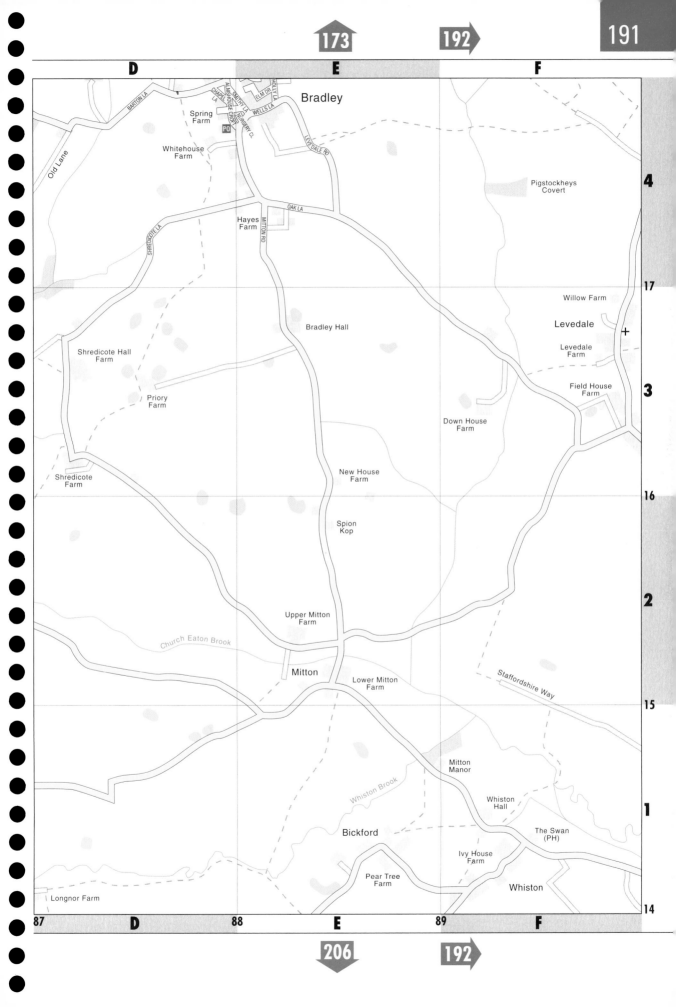

Bradley

Old Lane

BARTON LA

Spring Farm

Whitehouse Farm

ALMSHOUSE CROFT
CHAPEL LA
PO
NURSERY CL
SMITH LA
ELM DR
HOLLY LA
WELLS LA

LEVEDALE RD

OAK LA

Hayes Farm

MITTON RD

SHREDICOTE LA

Pigstockheys Covert

4

17

Willow Farm

Levedale

Bradley Hall

Shredicote Hall Farm

Priory Farm

Levedale Farm

Field House Farm

3

Down House Farm

New House Farm

Shredicote Farm

16

Spion Kop

2

Upper Mitton Farm

Church Eaton Brook

Staffordshire Way

Mitton

Lower Mitton Farm

15

Mitton Manor

Whiston Hall

1

The Swan (PH)

Bickford

Whiston Brook

Ivy House Farm

Whiston

Longnor Farm

Pear Tree Farm

14

A **B** **C**

4

Little
Heath

Yew Tree
Cottage

New Buildings
Farm

Dunston Heath
Farm

Dunston Heath

Stanley
Cottages

Dunston

Dunston House

Dunston
Hall

17

Hay House

Home Farm

SWAN LA

3

Hope Farm

Drayton
Manor

16

Whittemore
Farm

The Whittamoors

Honey
Pots

Lower Drayton
Farm

Longridge

2

Longridge
House

Grassmere
Farm

Chase
View

15

Flax
Ovens

River Penk

Preston Vale

Staffordshire Way

Riverside
Farm

The
Roller Mill

1

Preston
Hill

GOODS STATION LA

STATION RD

NURSERY CL

COOKE CL

GROZOTT CL

THE FLAX OVENS

UPLANDS RD

LEVEDALE RD

STONE CROSS

Penkridge

Marshbrook
Fst Sch

PO

MILL ST

TEDDESLEY RD

FREDERICK RD

HATHERTON
RD

KEMPSON
RD

ROLSTON CL

LITTLE ST

CRES

FREDERICK RD

ORCHARD
CL

GROSVENOR
CL

MARSH LA

ORCHARD

Market
Place

CROWN
BRIDGE

CHURCH RD

STANFORD CL

Sch

BELL BROOK

MARKET ST

HALING RD

SAPLINGS

CHERRY

THE SAPLINGS

MAUDE GR

LITTLE

BERRY CL

DEAN DR

BRIAR CL

Liby

CANNOCK RD

Whiston
Mill

PRESTON VALE LA

Whiston Brook

Monkton
Recn Ctr

PINFOLD LA

St
Michael's
Sq

ST
MICHAEL'S
RD

STATION RD

CLAY ST
A449

NEW RD

14

90 **A** 91 **B** 92 **C**

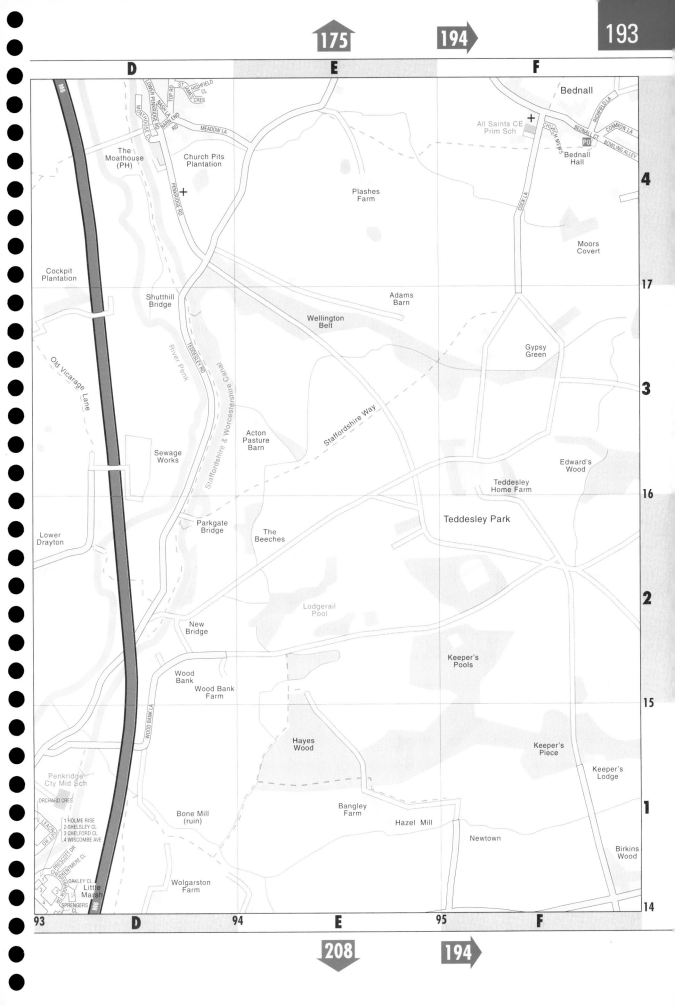

A **B** **C**

Staffordshire Way

Richfield Lane

Staffordshire Way

JOYCE'S LA

Bednall Head

Womere

CHASE RD

Brocton Field

BOWLING ALLEY

COMMON LA

P

Heart of England Way

4

Bednall Head Farm

Bednall Belt Plantation

P

Ansons Bank

Bog Moor

P

Picnic Area

17

Springslade Pool

Bogmoor Farm

Spring Slade

Cannock Chase Country Park

Grenvilles's Wood

Five Oak Hill Plantation

CAMP RD

Heart of England Way

P Meml

3

Dark Slade

Springslade Lodge

Mast

Vivian's Wood

Dark Slade Wood

Edward's Wood

16

Warren Plantation

Warren Hill

P

Cemy

Teddesley Park

P

2

Coppice Farm

Deer Slade

Badger Slade Wood

Cemy

PENKRIDGE BANK

Benty Hill Plantation

P

Badger Slade

Broadhurst Green

15

Bright's Plantation

Pottal Slade

BROADHURST GREEN RD

BROADHURST GREEN

Pottal Valley

Sand and Gravel Pit

Radio Twr

Badger's Hills

PLANTATION RD

BRINDLEY RD

1

Pottal Covert

Great Horsenal Slade

TOWER RD

Yew Tree Farm

Pottal Pool

STAFFORD

Masts

SPRUCE RD

PYE GREEN RD

BROADHURST CL

FISHER ST

Pye Green

Golf Course

A34

14

96   **A**   97   **B**   98   **C**

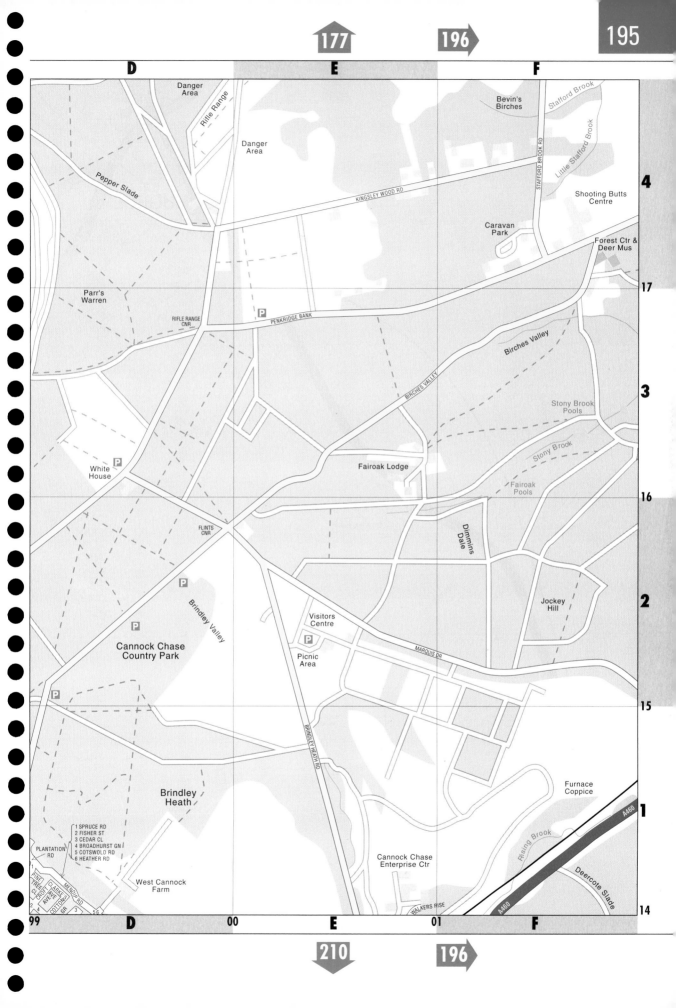

195
178

A   **B**   **C**

4

17

3

16

2

15

1

14

Shooting Butts Farm
STONEHOUSE RD
SHOOTING BUTTS RD
The Stone House
Hagley Farm
PENKRIDGE BANK
QUARRY CL
ST JOHNS CL
FIELD PL
POST OFFICE LA
CHURCH CL
JONES LA
Slitting Mill
SLITTING MILL RD
Lady Hill
Lady Hill Coppice
THE PINGLE
PH
LADY HILL TERR
Fairoak High Sch
CHASE SIDE RD
CHURCH MEADOW
DELL CT
Hagley Park
Hagley Park Cty High Sch
Burnt Hill
Lower Birches Farm
Upper Birches Farm

WESTERN SPRINGS RD
BREWERY
B5013
Mkt Hall
P
P
P
BROOK SQ 1
UPPER BROOK ST 2
ELMORE RD 3
LOWER BROOK ST 4
ALBION ST 5
FORGE RD 6
POWER STATION RD 7
SANDY LA
A460
SARAH CHALONER CT
Sch
BURNTHILL LA
CROSS RD
UPPER CROSS RD
Rugeley Town Sta
P
A513
QUEEN
LOVE LA
HERON
ANTHONYS CL
RICHFIELD RD
KEYSTONE RD
ARCH ST
TALBOT
ST PAULS
WELLINGTON DR
HORSE FAIR
Mossley
Trent & Mersey Canal
ARMITAGE RD
A513
BRERETON RD
A513
Main Road Brereton
Sch
SAXLEY CRES
CARZON PL
Sch
NEWMAN DR
ATTLEE CRES
GEORGE
BREARLEY ST
HADEN AVE
ASHLEIGH
RAVENHILL
SPRINGHILL
McKEE WAY
HEATH RD
WAY

RUGELEY

HIGH FALLS
HADLEY
GREENACRES
HEDNESFORD RD
CANDELAND CT
ST EDWARDS GREEN
PO
MINOR CRES
HILLSIDE
SHAFTESBURY RD
Sch
Stony Brook
Rising Brook
Smart's Buildings
Sheepwash Farm
Flaxley Green
RUTLAND AVE
SOMERSET AVE
SURREY CL
DEVONSHIRE DR
CORNWALL CT
ESSEX DR
DURHAM DR
REDFORD WAY
ST AUGUSTINE'S GREEN
UPLANDS
HILLARY CREST
Flaxley Cty Prim Sch
Ravenhill
ST MICHAEL'S RD 1
ARTHUR EVANS CL 2
Works
Coppice Lane
KIMBERLEY WAY
Chetwynd's Coppice
OAKHURST PARK
THE LEVELS
Cemy
Stilecop Field
Picnic Area
P
Works
India Hills
Mitlins Valley
STILE COP RD
The Glen
Moor's Gorse
Lower Cliff
Regent's Wood
Stile Cop
Picnic Area
P
The Slade
LC
A460
MARQUIS'S DR
Parson's Slade
Heart of England Way
Wandon
Startley Hill
Brereton Hayes Wood
STARTLEY LA
Rainbow Hill
Cannock Chase Forest
Wandon Spur's Plantation
RUGELEY RD
Upper Cliff
Sweakham Covert
Rainbow Valley

02   **A**   03   **B**   04   **C**

195
211

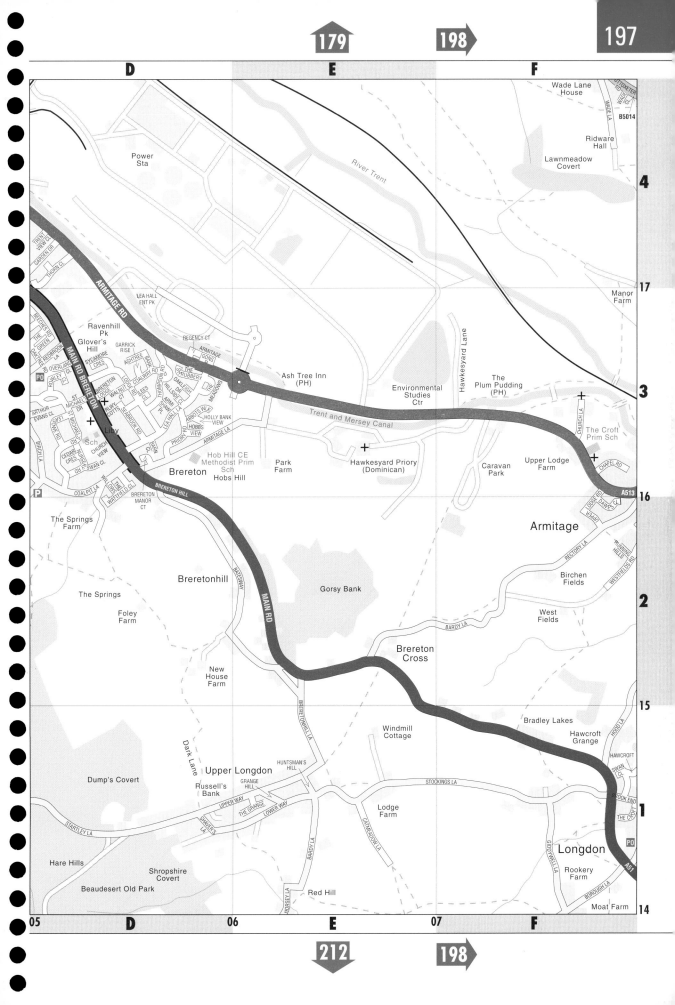

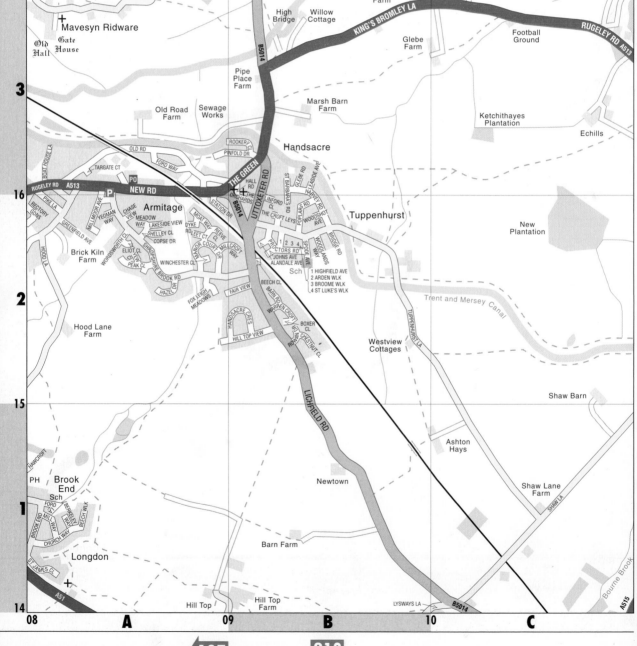

1 HIGHFIELD AVE
2 ARDEN WLK
3 BROOME WLK
4 ST LUKE'S WLK

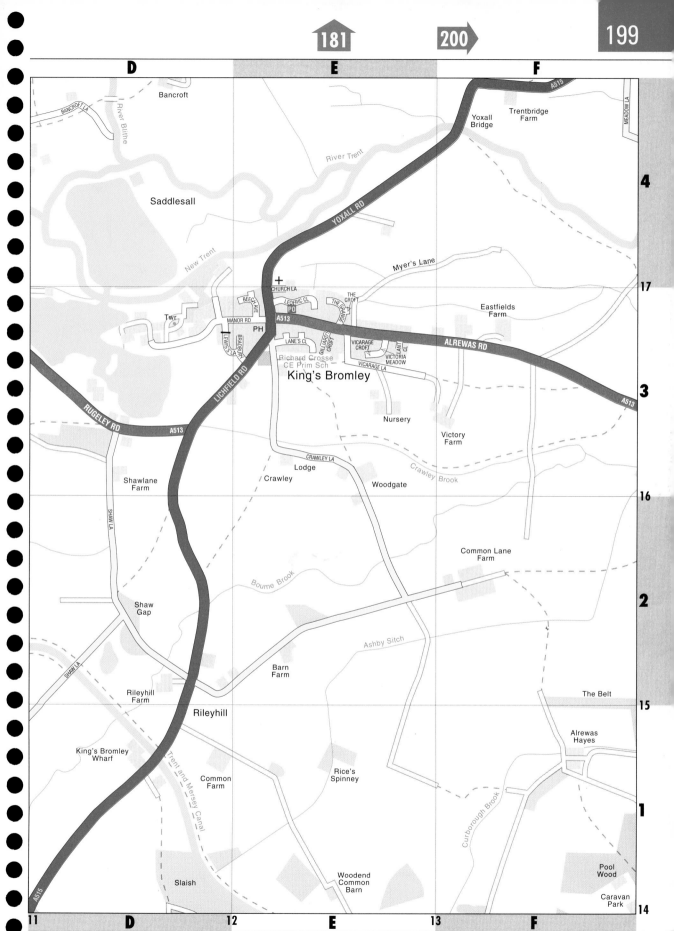

D E F

Bancroft

BANCROFT LA

River Blithe

River Trent

Saddlesall

New Trent

4

YOXALL RD

Yoxall Bridge

Trentbridge Farm

A515

MEADOW LA

Myer's Lane

17

CHURCH LA

BEECA AVE

LEOFRIC CL

THE CROFT

THE GRANGE

Eastfields Farm

Twr

MANOR RD

A513

LEWIS'S LA

BRADBURY

PH

LANE'S CL

GILLIARD'S CROFT

VICARAGE CROFT

LANT CL

Victoria Meadow

ALREWAS RD

Richard Crosse CE Prim Sch

VICARAGE LA

King's Bromley

A513

3

RUGELEY RD

LICHFIELD RD

A513

Nursery

Victory Farm

Crawley Brook

Shawlane Farm

CRAWLEY LA

Lodge

Crawley

Woodgate

16

Common Lane Farm

SHAW LA

Bourne Brook

2

Shaw Gap

Ashby Sitch

SHAW LA

The Belt

Rileyhill Farm

Barn Farm

15

Rileyhill

Alrewas Hayes

King's Bromley Wharf

Trent and Mersey Canal

Common Farm

Rice's Spinney

Curborough Brook

1

Slaish

Woodend Common Barn

Pool Wood

Caravan Park

14

11 D 12 E 13 F

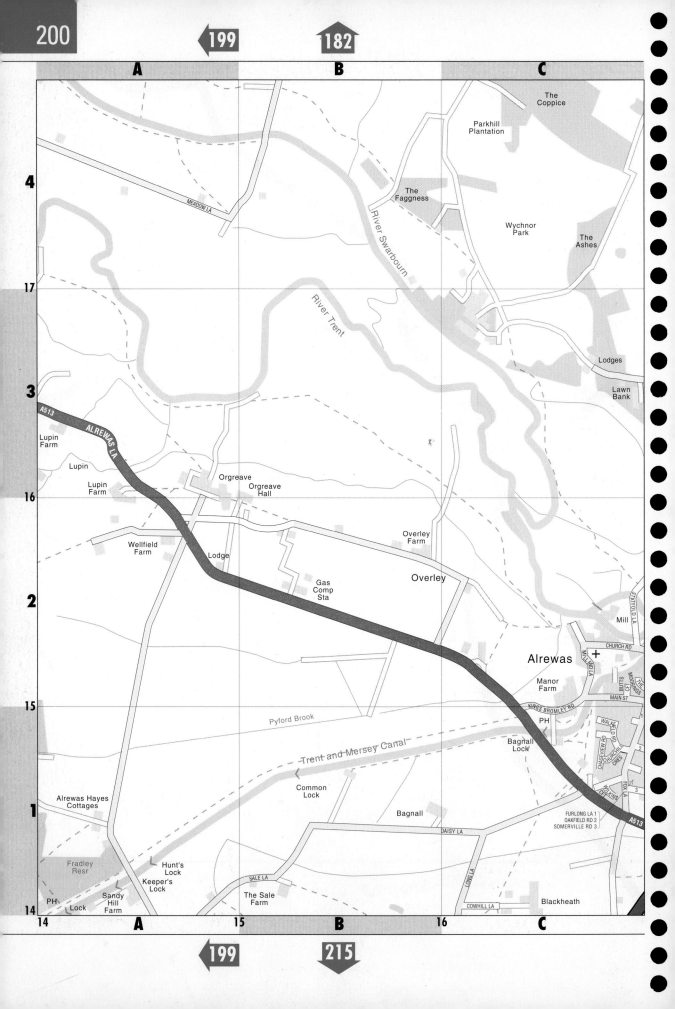

A   B   C

The Coppice

Parkhill Plantation

4

The Faggness

Wychnor Park

The Ashes

River Swarbourn

17

River Trent

Lodges

Lawn Bank

3

A513

ALREWAS LA

Lupin Farm

Lupin

Lupin Farm

Orgreave

Orgreave Hall

16

Overley Farm

Wellfield Farm

Lodge

Gas Comp Sta

Overley

Mill

2

STATFOLD LA

Alrewas

CHURCH RD

Manor Farm

MILL RD LA

THE MOORINGS

BUTTS CFT

MAIN ST

15

Pyford Brook

KINGS BROMLEY RD

PH

WALKE

Bagnall Lock

CHASEVIEW RD

CHURCHILL

Trent and Mersey Canal

Common Lock

Bagnall

WATKINS CFT

FOX LA

Alrewas Hayes Cottages

FURLONG LA 1
OAKFIELD RD 2
SOMERVILLE RD 3

A513

1

DAISY LA

Fradley Resr

Hunt's Lock

Keeper's Lock

LONG LA

Blackheath

PH

Lock

Sandy Hill Farm

SALE LA

The Sale Farm

COWHILL LA

14

14   A   15   B   16   C

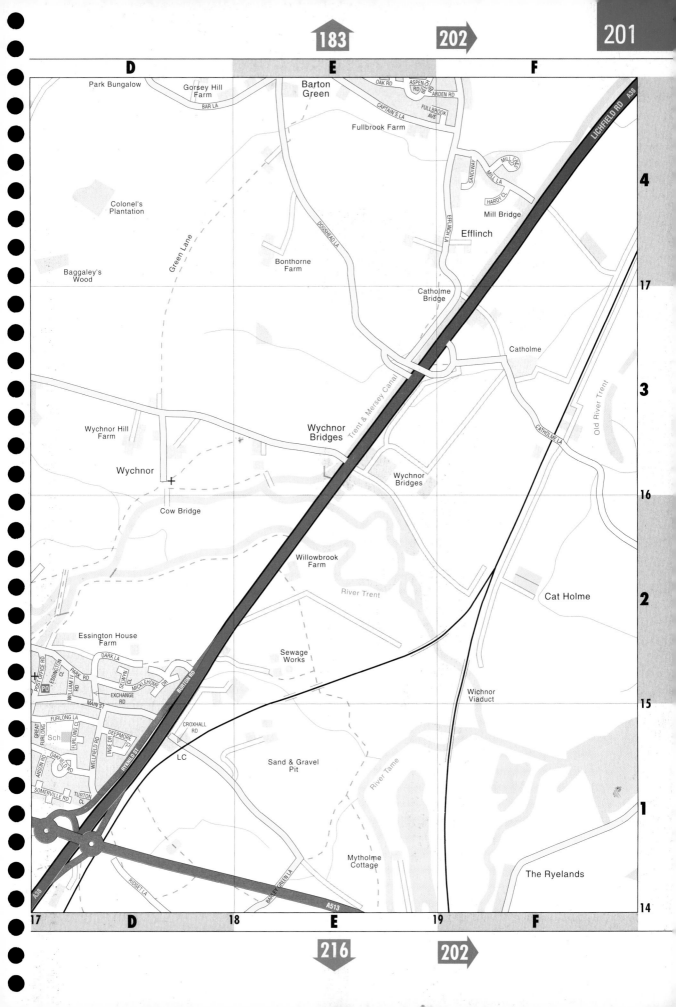

D E F

Park Bungalow
Gorsey Hill Farm
Barton Green
BAR LA
OAK RD
ASPEN
RD
BEECH
ARDEN RD
FULLBROOK AVE
CAPTAIN'S LA
LICHFIELD RD
A38

Fullbrook Farm

MILL C65
SANDIWAY
MILL LA
HARDY CL

Colonel's Plantation

4

Mill Bridge

EFFLINCH LA

Efflinch

Green Lane

Baggaley's Wood

DOGSHEAD LA

Bonthorne Farm

Catholme Bridge

17

Catholme

3

Trent & Mersey Canal

CATHOLME LA

Old River Trent

Wychnor Hill Farm

Wychnor Bridges

Wychnor
+

Wychnor Bridges

16

Cow Bridge

Willowbrook Farm

Cat Holme

2

River Trent

Essington House Farm
DARK LA
PARK RD
WILLIAM IV RD
SELWYN
MICKLEHOME DR
BURTON RD

Sewage Works

Wichnor Viaduct

POST OFFICE RD
PO
+
EXCHANGE RD
MAIN ST

15

GREAT FURLONG
FURLONG LA
DEEPMORE
INGE DR
WELLFIELD RD
Sch
ARSON RD
OAKFIELD RD
SOMERVILLE RD
TURTON CL

CROXHALL RD

LC

Sand & Gravel Pit

River Tame

RYKNILD ST

1

Mytholme Cottage

The Ryelands

A38
RIDGET LA
BAILEY GREEN LA
A513

14

D 18 E 19 F

201
184

A38
LICHFIELD RD

A

B

C

LEEDHAMS CROFT

BELLS END RD

Fairfield

Walton Hall

Walton-on-Trent
CE Prim Sch

STANDING
BUTTS CL

Old Hall

ROSLISTON RD

Fatholme
Farm

The Dumps

Marlpit
Spinney

Old Barn
Farm

4

Walton Hill
Farm

Borough
Hill

Coppershill
Spinney

17

Ryelands
Lodge

Walton
Wood

River Trent

Sand and
Gravel Pit

COTON RD

Oaklands
Farm

Borough Holme

3

Borough Fields
Farm

Old River Trent

Ryelands
Plantation

16

CATHOLME LA

Donkhill
Cottages

Catton Farm
Cottages

The Rough

2

Cat
Holme

Cherry
Holme

Catton
Hall

Summerfields

King's
Covert

Donkhill
Plantation

Donkhill
Farm

15

Mansditch
Farm

Catton
Park

Catton
Wood

1

Croxall
Wood

Pessall Lane

Pessall Brook

Homestall
Wood

14

20

A

21

B

22

C

201
217

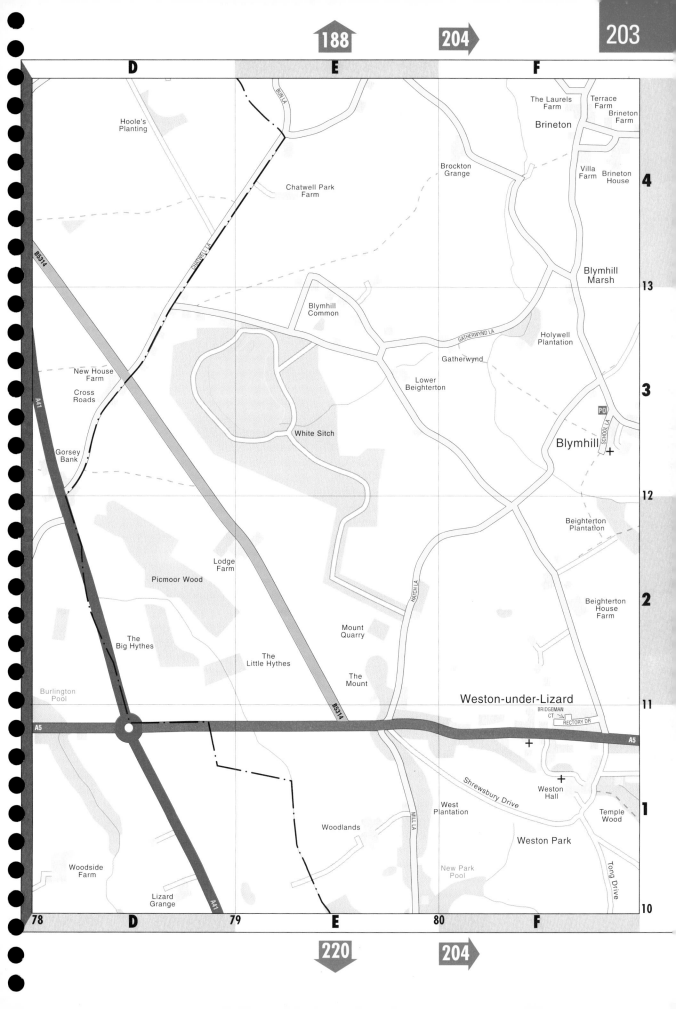

203
189

A   **B**   **C**

Marston

BIRCHMOOR LA

Manor Farm

GAY LA

4

Wet Croft Plantation

Wrestlers Farm

Wrestlers Wood

Mottymeadows Brook

Ryefield Lane

Motty Meadows

13

Broadholes Lane

BROADHOLES LA

Beaudesert Plantation

3

Lower Brockhurst

Lucknow Farm

Hartley's Gorse

Brick Kiln Lane

Blymhill

Grove Farm

Brockhurst Coppice

Lincoln Brook

Blymhill Grange

12

High Hall

Brockhurst

2

Blymhill Lawn

New Buildings Farm

Hurst Plantation

Hurst Farm

IVETSEY RD

Blymhill Lawn Farm

Lawn House

The Hurst

Brickyard Plantation

11

Ivetsey Bank

Wheaton Aston New Hall

A5

Bradford Arms Hotel

Wall Plantations

A5

Wheaton Aston Old Hall

1

Temple Pool

Cottage Wood

Lichfield Drive

East Park

Dogkennel Wood

Ivetsey Bank Farm

Weston Park

Weston Park Farm

10

81   **A**   82   **B**   83   **C**

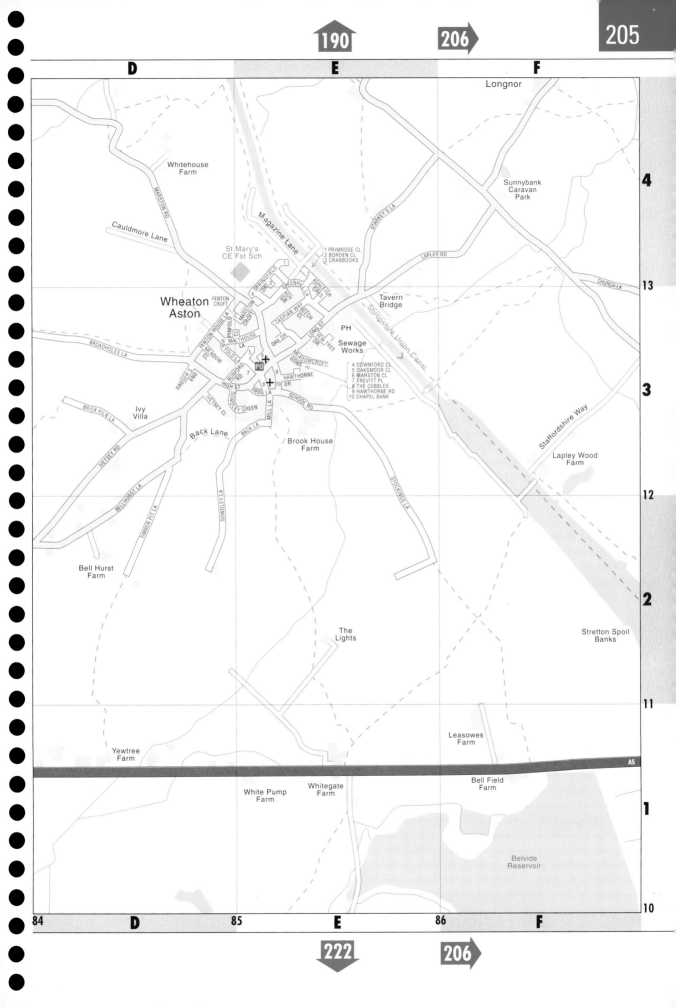

D E F

Longnor

Whitehouse Farm

MARSTON RD

Cauldmore Lane

Magazine Lane

St Mary's CE Fst Sch

STARKEY'S LA

Sunnybank Caravan Park

LAPLEY RD

4

CHURCH LA

13

1 PRIMROSE CL
2 BORDEN CL
3 CRANBOOKS

Wheaton Aston

FENTON CROFT

SPRINGFIELD
DR

MARSTON CROFT

GREENHILL
ASH
DR

ASHLEIGH
CRES

Tavern Bridge

BROADHOLES LA

FENTON HOUSE LA

PINFOLD

PINFOLD LA

MALTHOUSE LA

MARSTON
CL

CASPIAN WAY

BEECH
CL

OAK DR

LONG VIEW
TREE

MEADOWCROFT

GONS

Shropshire Union Canal

PH

Sewage Works

4 DOWNFORD CL
5 OAKSMOOR CL
6 MARSTON CL
7 TREVITT PL
8 THE COBBLES
9 HAWTHORNE RD
10 CHAPEL BANK

BADGER'S END

MEADOW
CL

BURFORD
RD

PO

HAWTHORNE
DR

3

BRICK KILN LA

Ivy Villa

IVETSEY RD

HIGH ST

IVETSEY CL

SOWDLEY GREEN

BACK LA

MILL LA

FROG LA

SCHOOL RD

Staffordshire Way

Lapley Wood Farm

Back Lane

Brook House Farm

STOCKINGS LA

12

BELHURST LA

TIMBER PIT LA

SOWDLEY LA

Bell Hurst Farm

2

The Lights

Stretton Spoil Banks

11

Yewtree Farm

Leasowes Farm

A5

White Pump Farm

Whitegate Farm

Bell Field Farm

1

Belvide Reservoir

10

A · B · C

4

Pool Plantation

Staffordshire Way

Bickford Grange Farm

Bickford Grange

Beacon Hill

MERCIAN WAY

QUEENS COTTAGES

BICKFORD RD

13

CHURCH LA

Lapley

BICKFORD CL

PARK LA

STRETTON RD

Lapley Hall

Lapley Gorse

Stretton Wood

3

Keeper's Cottage

Rabbit Slack

12

The Wilderness

Home Farm

ROWLEYHILL DR

Twenty Acre Pit

LAPLEY LA

WOOD LA

Wood Farm

Stretton Hall

Stretton Park

Rowleyhill Plantation

The Stubblers

SLING LA

GARDEN LA

STONEY LA

The Pool

2

Stretton

Upper Pool

Stretton Spoil Banks

Vernon Lodge Prep Sch

SCHOOL LA

School Farm

Lodge Plantation

11

THE AVENUE

Stretton Mill

Aquaduct House

Stretton Wharf

Road Farm

Crown Farm

The Ivy House

A5

A5

The Bell Inn (PH)

River Penk

1

Shropshire Union Canal Main Line

Horsebrook

Horsebrook Hall

Bell View Farm

Horse Brook

IVY HOUSE LA

Bungalow Farm

Broom Hall Farm

HORSEBROOK LA

Horsebrook Farm

Engleton Hall

10

87 · A · 88 · B · 89 · C

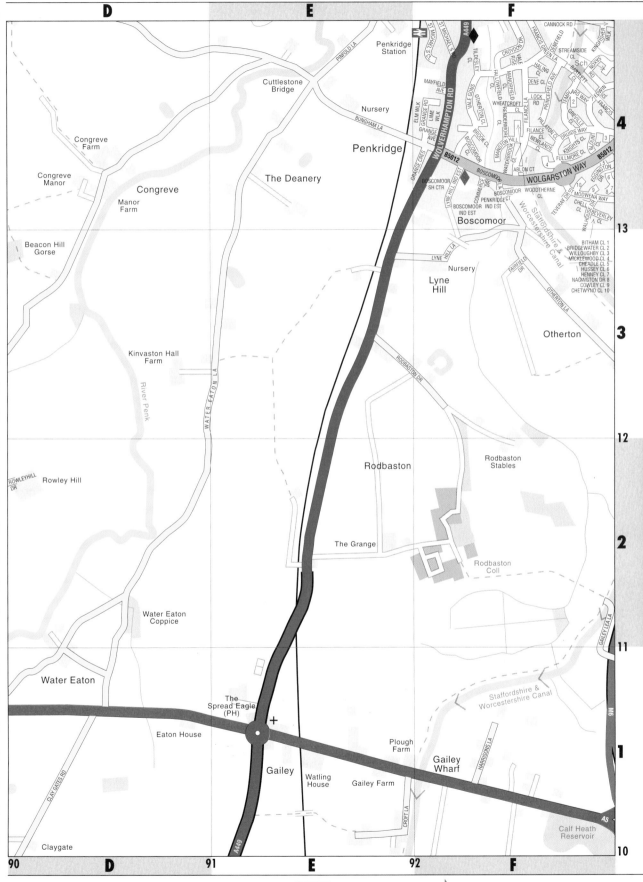

207
193

A **B** **C**

B5012
CANNOCK RD

GREENWAYS
ATHELSTAN CL
Penkridge L Ctr

Quarry Heath

Wolgarston High Sch

KENILWORTH CL

Newlands Wood

FRANCIS CL

4

DRUIDS WAY

Pillaton Farm

WOLGARSTON WAY

M6

MOOR HALL LA

Pillaton Hall Farm

Moor Hall Cottages

Pillaton

SVERDON CL
PAGET CL
MIDWEY WA
ASTON CL
BOYDEN CL
BEDINGTON
THE BRINDLEY
NAGINGTON DR

13

+

Pillaton Old Hall

Mansty Farm

Marina

3

OTHERTON LA

Mansty Wood

Staffordshire & Worcestershire Canal

12

Horsemoor Wood

B5012

MICKLEWOOD LA

Micklewood

2

Fullmoor Wood

Hatherton Wood

Fullmoor Lodge

11

Gailey Lea Farm

GAILEY LEA LA

Hatherton Hall Farm

1

Hatherton

Gailey Upper Reservoir

Gailey Lower Reservoir

Church Farm

A5
12 M6
A5
A5

10

93 **A** 94 **B** 95 **C**

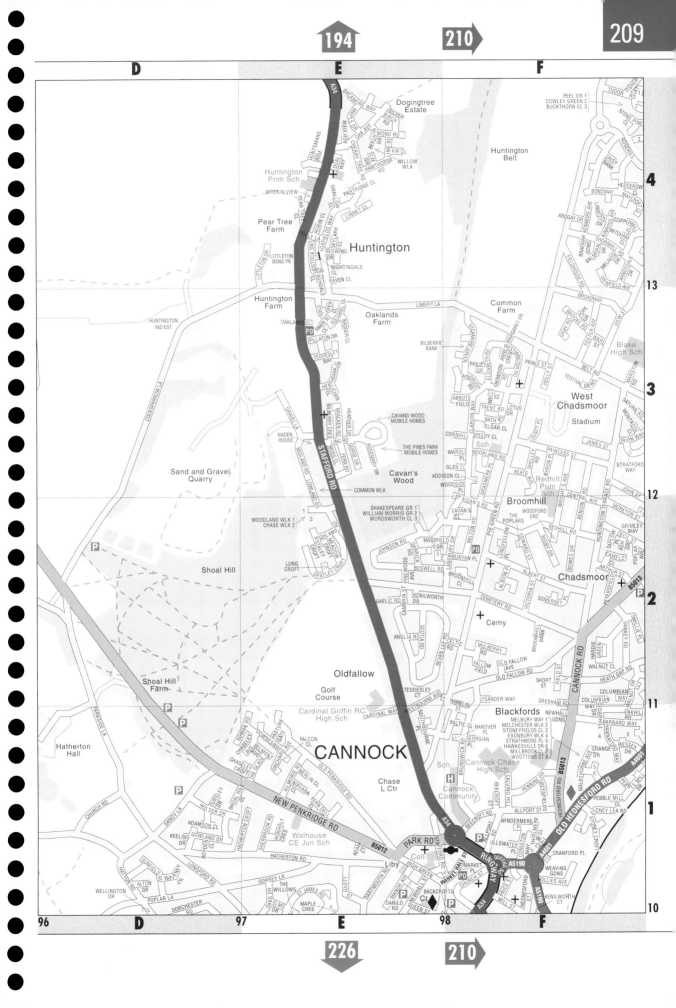

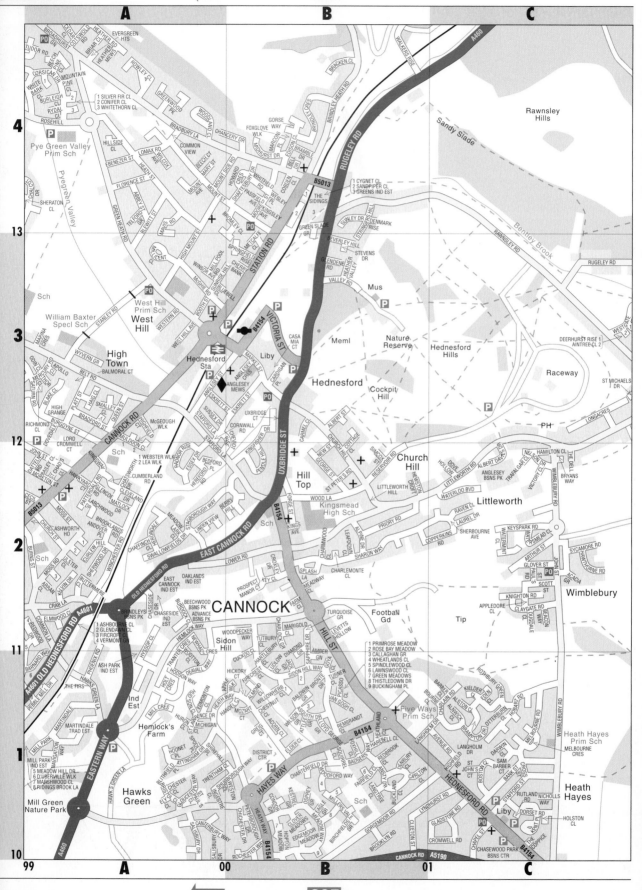

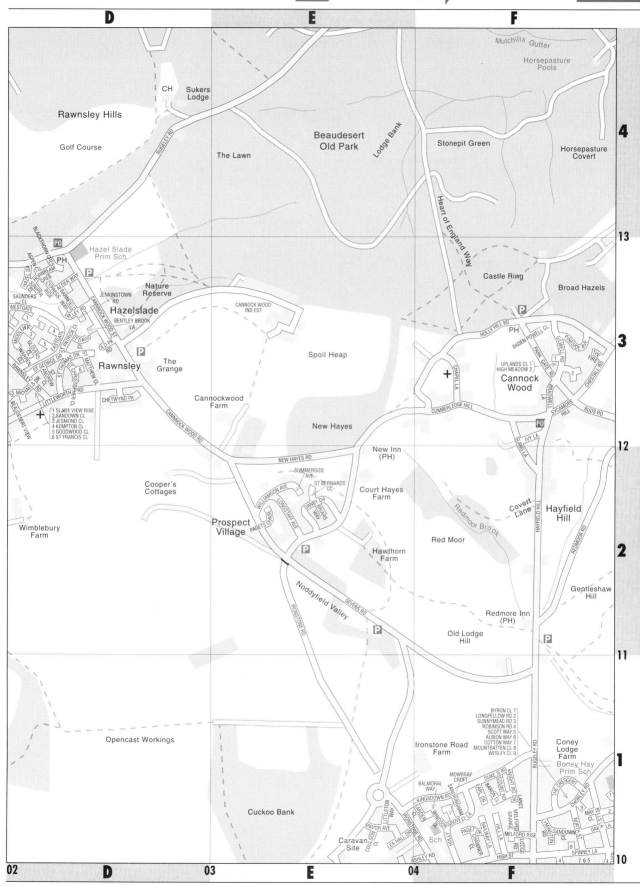

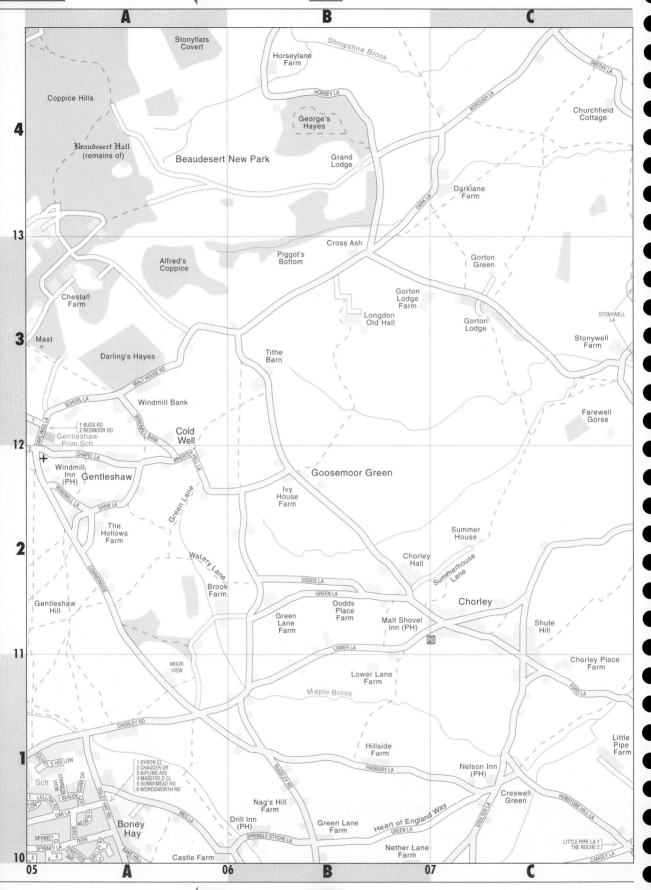

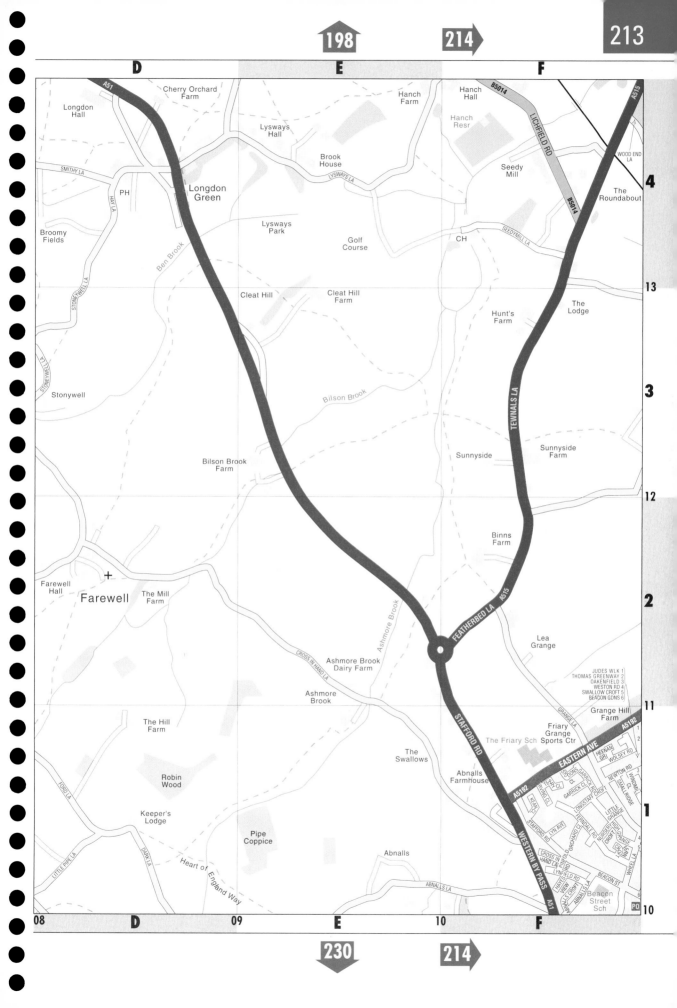

213
199

A · B · C

4

Vicar's Coppice

Black Slough

Cranberry

Shade House Lock

Middle Lock

Ravenshaw Wood

Woodend Lock

Woods Farm

Black Slough Farm

WOOD END LA

Trent and Mersey Canal

Fradley Wood

Tomhay Wood

Wood End Farm

13

New Farm

Full Brook

Big Lyntus

GORSE LA

Fullbrook Farm

Sewage Works

Sprint Course

Little Lyntus

3

Elmhurst Hall Farm

Curborough Brook

NASH LA

FOX LA

Corporation Farm

Curborough

Curborough Farm

Curborough Hall Farm

12

Elmhurst

Apsley House

Curborough House

2

WATERY LA

Brownfield Cottage

1 AUGUSTINES WLK
2 PAULS WLK
3 CHRISTOPHER WLK
4 MATTHEWS WLK
5 STEPHENS WLK
6 MARKS WLK
7 PETERS WLK
8 THOMAS GREENWAY
9 JAMES GREENWAY
10 LUKES WLK

GLOUCESTER CL
SOUTHWARK
WORCESTER CL

RINGWAY IND EST

SALISBURY CL
WINCHESTER CL

Nether Stowe

Brownsfields Farm

11

A5192

ST MARY'S RD
ST HELENS RD
ST CATHERINES RD
ST JAMES RD

GILES RD

TRURO
MEADOWBROOK RD
BARN CL
NORWICH CL
FALLOW FIELD
PUDSEY
MEADOWBROOK RD
JACKSON
PLOUGH
YORK CL
CANTERBURY
CHESTER

York CL

CHADWELL CL

LICHFIELD

FRANCIS RD
SHEFFIELD RD
NEEDWOOD HILL
GARRICK GDNS
HAWKINS
REYNOLDS CL
WILLOW
ANGLESEY
SIMPSON RD
HARWOOD RD

DAVID WILLOWS
Charnwood Prim Sch

Charnwood Prim Sch

THE MILL POND

SPRING RD
AUTUMN RD

NETHERSTOWE LA

OAKENFIELD
COLLINS HILL
BOOTH CL
PIPERS CROFT
GREENCROFT
HEWITT CL
DIMBLE LA

CURBOROUGH RD
ELGAR
OAKLEY CL
STYCHBROOK GDNS
PONESGREEN

PONESFIELD RD

PURCELL AVE

HANDEL WLK

SULLIVAN WLK
VERDI
SAMUEL CL

BOWYER CL
SUMMER GR

Lichfield Bsns Ctr

HERMES RD

WINDMILL LA
WESTON RD
THE GARTH

LEY FIELDS

WALKERS CROFT

STONECROFT

NETHERSTOWE

FECKNAM WAY

HAYWORTH RD

BROWNSFIELD RD
BOYER CL

WINTER CL

FURAVALL CRES

VULCAN

1

MARTIN CROFT
BEACON GDNS
LANGTON CT
FORGE LA
SAINT
Chadsmead Prim Sch

CRANE FIELD

Sch

Wood Ridings

DIMBLES HILL

Netherstowe High Sch

Netherstowe High Sch

AUCHINLECK DR

JOHNSON CL

BENSON CL

STOWE FIELD GDNS

SCOTCH ORCH

WISSAGE RD

PENNY CROFT

Scotch Orchard Prim Sch

Streethay Lodge

BURTON RD

A5127

HILL CREST DR
THISTLEY NOOK
THE FEASOWE
NETHER BEACON
WOODS CROFT
GREENCROFT
THE CHASE
ST CHADS CT

Chadsmead Prim Sch

THE GARTH

GAIALANDS CRES
GAIA STOWE
BULLACE
ST CHADS RD
CHARNWOOD CL

MANLEY RD

HOBS HOLE

TRENT VALLEY RD

A5127

BEXMORE DR

BURTON OLD RD

SWALLOW CROFT
BEACON ST
LITTLE BARROW WLK
LANSTON CROFT
ANSON AVE
LOMAX CL
WINDSOR
GAIA LA
THE ARCHERS
STOWE RD
ST MICHAEL RD
COVEY CL
BROCKLANDS CRES
WISSAGE LA
ORSWORTH VIEW

Stowe

Stowe Pool

BEACON ST
SWAN RD
DARWIN CL
GAIA AVE
VALE CL
GLOVERS CROFT

WISSAGE RD

MALLICOT CL

TRENT VALLEY COTTS

10

11 · A · 12 · B · 13 · C

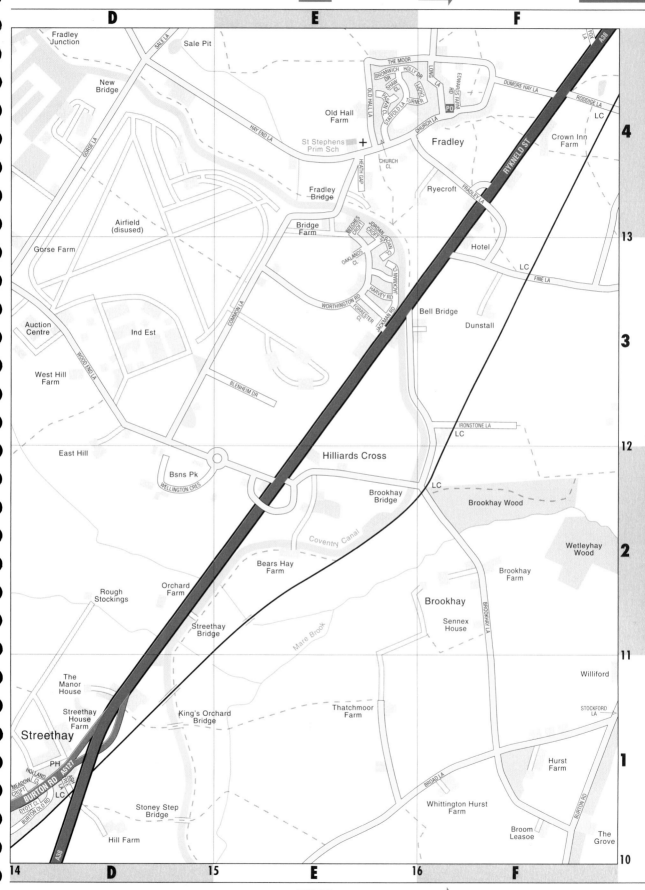

215
201

A   **B**   **C**

RIDGET LA

BARLEY GREEN LA

A513

Chetwynd or
Salter's Bridge

Croxall

CROXALL RD

Dovecote

The
Hall

Roddige

Whitemoor
Haye

Brown's
Island

RODDIGE LA

Broadfields

Oakley
Farm

River Mease

4

13

Croxall
Mill

A513

River Tame

Sittles

Lady
Walk

Elford
Park

New Buildings
Farm

3

12

Park
Farm

The
Bungalow

Sand & Gravel
Pit

STOCKFORD LA

Bisphill
Plantation

2

11

Home
Farm

Greendales
Farm

A513

Elford

BRICKHOUSE LA

The Howard
Prim Sch

P.H.

Old Hall Dr

The Gardens

CHURCH RD

The Square

CROFT CL

The Beck

PO

EDDIES LA

Raddle
Farm

1

Old
Orangery

The
Hill

THE SHRUBBERY

BURTON RD

A513

10

17   **A**   18   **B**   19   **C**

215
233

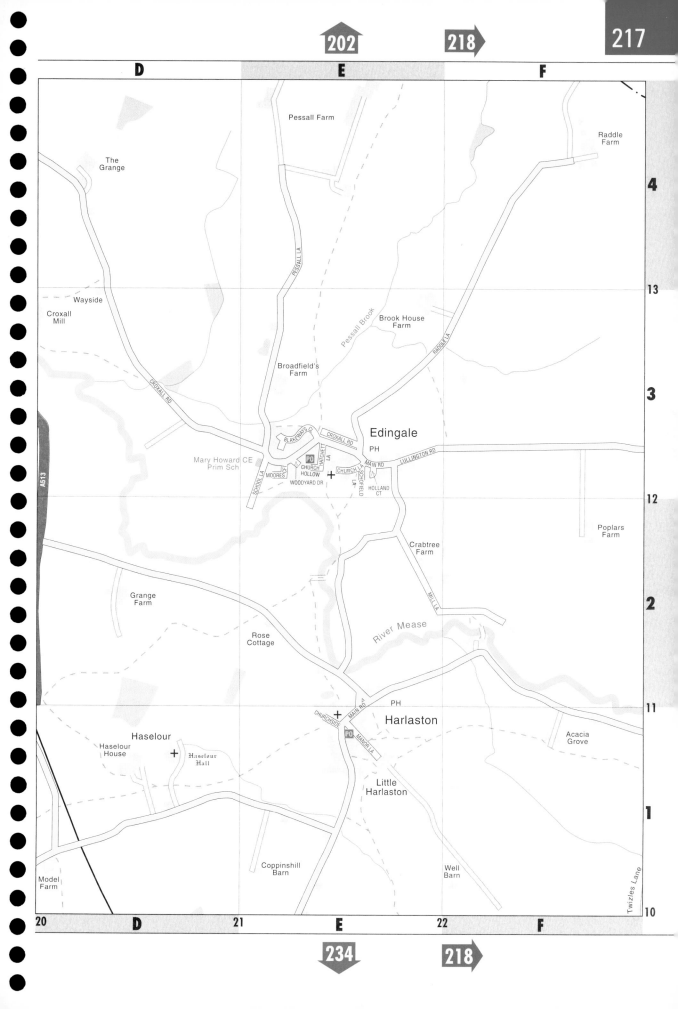

202
218 ▶

D   E   F

Pessall Farm

Raddle Farm

The Grange

PESSALL LA

4

Wayside

Croxall Mill

Pessall Brook

Brook House Farm

RADDLE LA

13

CROXALL RD

Broadfield's Farm

Edingale

3

PH

CROXALL RD

BLAKEWAYS CL

HATCHETT LA

Mary Howard CE Prim Sch

PO

CHURCH HOLLOW

CFT

MOORES

SCHOOL LA

MAIN RD

LULLINGTON RD

CHURCH LA

SCHOFIELD LA

WOODYARD DR

HOLLAND CT

12

Poplars Farm

Crabtree Farm

Grange Farm

MILL LA

2

Rose Cottage

River Mease

PH

11

CHURCHSIDE

MAIN RD

Harlaston

Acacia Grove

Haselour

PO

MANOR LA

Haselour House

Haselour Hall

Little Harlaston

1

Model Farm

Coppinshill Barn

Well Barn

Twizles Lane

20   D   21   E   22   F   10

A513

234
218 ▶

217

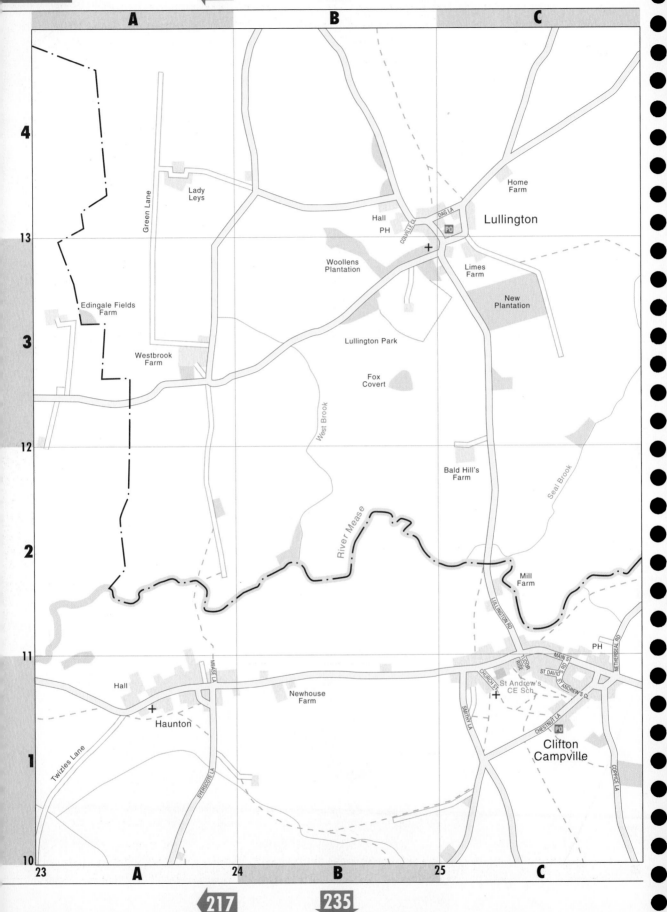

217

235

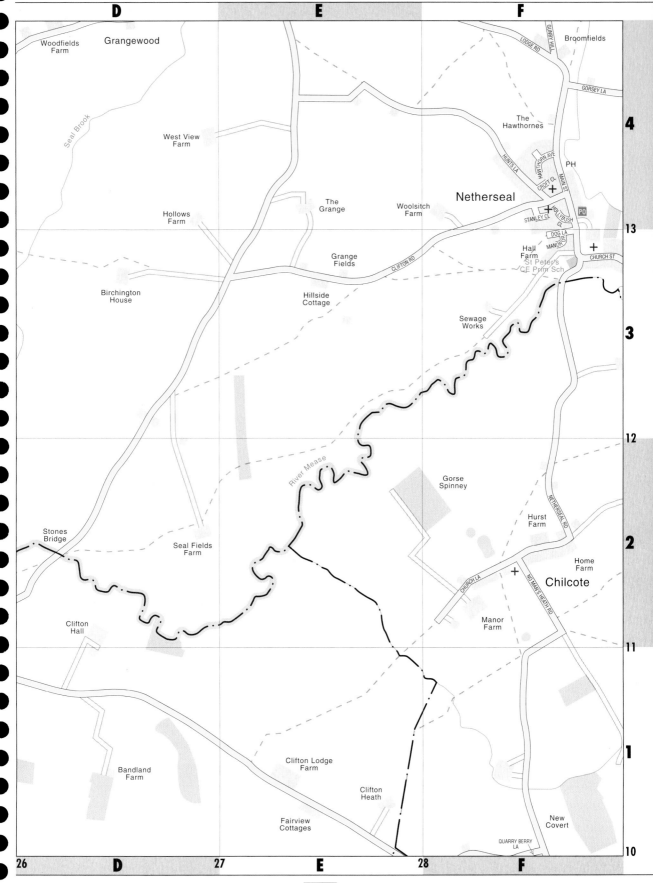

Woodfields Farm

Grangewood

Seal Brook

West View Farm

Hollows Farm

The Grange

Woolsitch Farm

Netherseal

Birchington House

Grange Fields

Hillside Cottage

Clifton Rd

Hall Farm

St Peter's CE Prim Sch

Sewage Works

Stones Bridge

Seal Fields Farm

River Mease

Gorse Spinney

Hurst Farm

Home Farm

Chilcote

Clifton Hall

Church La

Manor Farm

Bandland Farm

Clifton Lodge Farm

Clifton Heath

New Covert

Fairview Cottages

QUARRY BERRY LA

LODGE RD

GUNBY HILL

Broomfields

GORSEY LA

The Hawthornes

HUNTS LA

HAWTHORN AVE

CROFT CL

MAIN ST

PH

STANLEY CL

HOLLYBUSH CL

PO

DOG LA

MANOR

CHURCH ST

NETHERSEAL RD

NO MAN'S HEATH RD

4

13

3

12

2

11

1

10

203

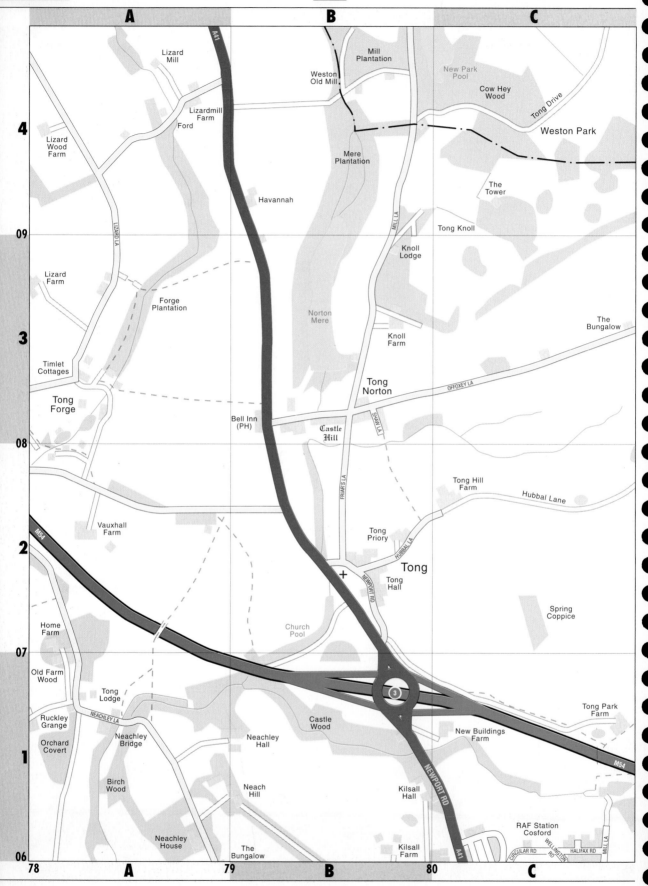

Lizard Mill
Lizardmill Farm
Ford
Lizard Wood Farm
Havannah
Lizard Farm
Forge Plantation
Timlet Cottages
Tong Forge
Bell Inn (PH)
Vauxhall Farm
Home Farm
Old Farm Wood
Tong Lodge
Ruckley Grange
Orchard Covert
Neachley Bridge
Birch Wood
Neachley House
The Bungalow

Mill Plantation
Weston Old Mill
Mere Plantation
Norton Mere
Tong Norton
Castle Hill
Friars La
Tong Priory
Tong Hall
Church Pool
Neachley Hall
Castle Wood
Neach Hill
Kilsall Hall
Kilsall Farm

New Park Pool
Cow Hey Wood
Tong Drive
Weston Park
The Tower
Tong Knoll
Knoll Lodge
The Bungalow
Knoll Farm
Offoxey La
Tong Hill Farm
Hubbal Lane
Tong
Spring Coppice
Tong Park Farm
New Buildings Farm
RAF Station Cosford
Circular Rd
Wellington Rd
Halifax Rd
Mill La

A1
Mill La
Shaw La
Hubbal La
Newport Rd
Neachley La
M54
Lizard La

09
4
3
08
2
07
1
06

78   A   79   B   80   C

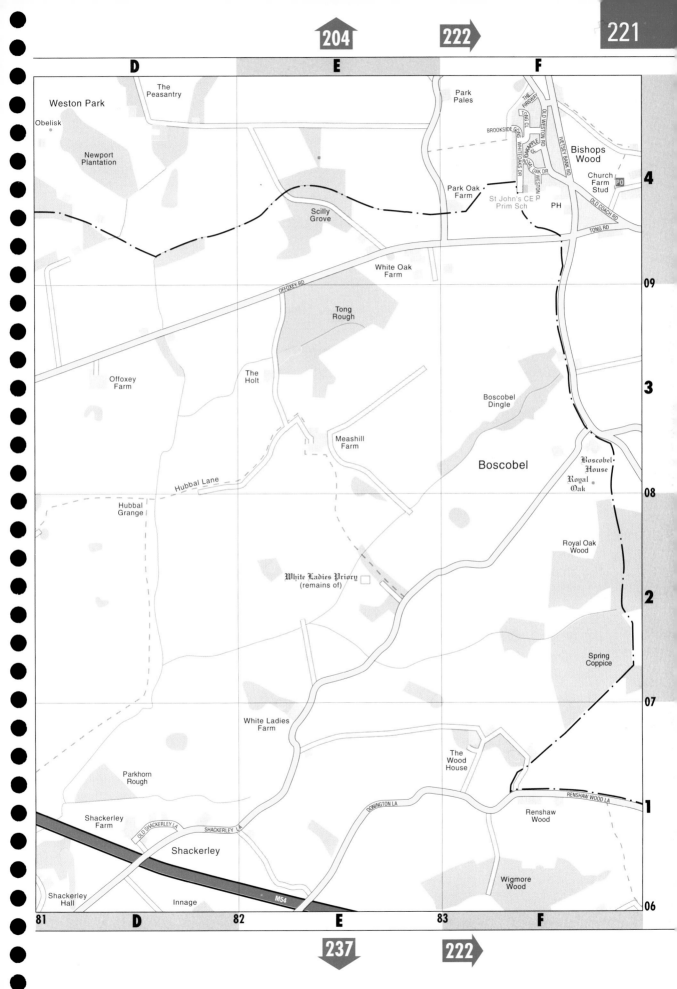

D   E   F

Weston Park

The Peasantry

Obelisk

Newport Plantation

Park Pales

THE FIRSWAY

ING CL

BROOKSIDE GDNS

OLD WESTON RD

WHITOAKS DR

CRABAPPLE CL

OAK DR

OLD WESTON CL

WELSEY BANK RD

Bishops Wood

Church Farm Stud

PO

4

Scilly Grove

Park Oak Farm

St John's CE Prim Sch

PH

OLD COACH RD

TONG RD

White Oak Farm

OFFOXEY RD

09

Tong Rough

Offoxey Farm

The Holt

Boscobel Dingle

3

Meashill Farm

Boscobel

Boscobel House

Royal Oak

Hubbal Lane

08

Hubbal Grange

Royal Oak Wood

White Ladies Priory
(remains of)

2

Spring Coppice

07

White Ladies Farm

The Wood House

RENSHAW WOOD LA

Parkhorn Rough

DONINGTON LA

Renshaw Wood

1

Shackerley Farm

OLD SHACKERLEY LA

SHACKERLEY LA

Shackerley

Wigmore Wood

Shackerley Hall

Innage

M54

06

81   D   82   E   83   F

221
205

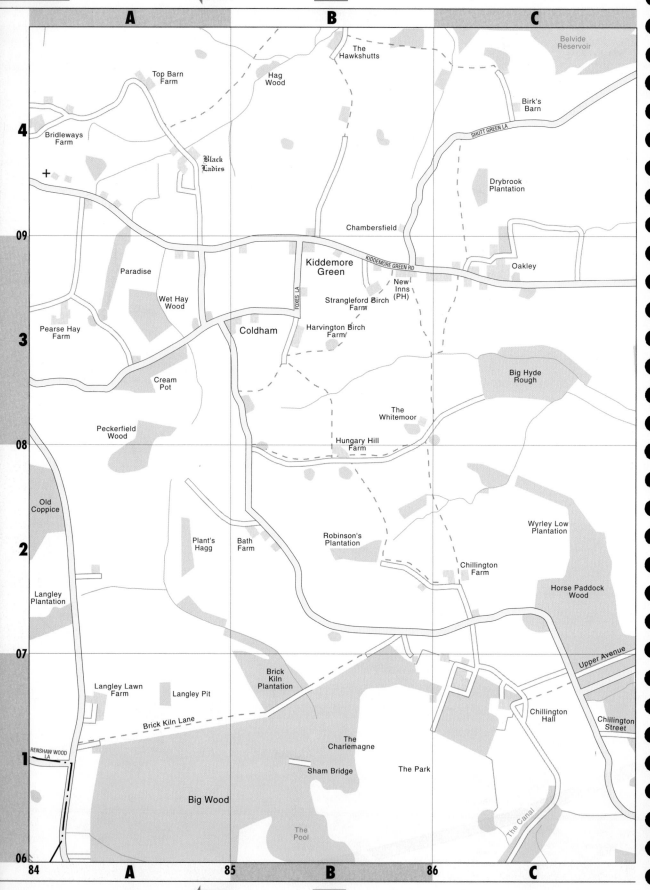

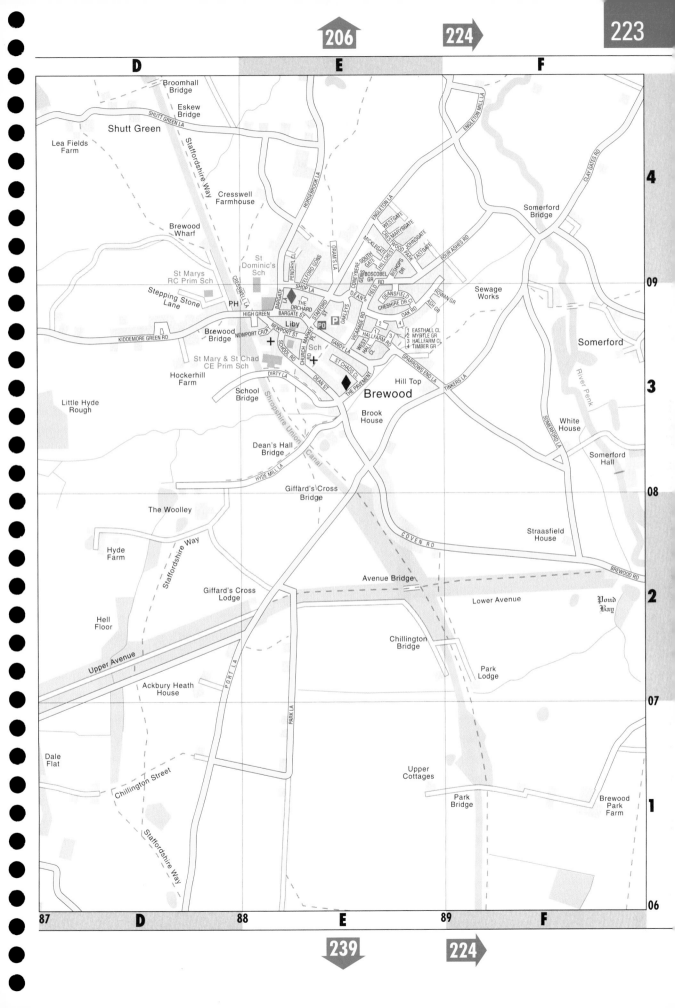

206
224

D

E

F

4

Broomhall
Bridge

Eskew
Bridge

SHUTT GREEN LA

Shutt Green

Lea Fields
Farm

Staffordshire Way

Cresswell
Farmhouse

HORSEBROOK LA

ENGLETON MILL LA

Somerford
Bridge

CLAY GATES RD

09

Brewood
Wharf

St
Dominic's
Sch

St Marys
RC Prim Sch

CRESSWELL LA

PENDRYL CL

STELFORD GDNS

SHOP LA

GRAM'S LA

ENGLETON LA

WESTGATE

MICKLEGATE

CREST-WOOD PARK

JOHNSGATE

CRES'T

ST MARYSGATE

EASTGATE

BISHOP'S
DR

FOUR ASHES RD

ROWAN GR

Sewage
Works

Somerford

Stepping
Stone
Lane

PH

HIGH GREEN

BARGATE LA

THE
ORCHARD

BARGATE ST

STAFFORD ST

Liby

CONEYBERE SOUTH

SGATE

HILL CRES

BOSCOBEL
GR

DEAN'S
FIELD

CRANSFIELD
RD

CHESHIRE DR

OAK RD

EST GR

Brewood
Bridge

NEWPORT CROFT

NEWPORT ST

CHURCH MARKET PL

P0

P

OAKLEYS

VICARAGE RD

DEAN'S

HALLFARM RD

1
2
3

1 EASTHALL CL
2 MYRTLE GR
3 HALLFARM CL
4 TIMBER GR

KIDDEMORE GREEN RD

Sch

SANDY LA

SCHOOL RD

WEST
HALL
CL

SPARROWS END LA

TINKERS LA

River Penk

Somerford

St Mary & St Chad
CE Prim Sch

Hockerhill
Farm

DIRTY LA

DEAN ST

ST CHADS CL

THE PAVEMENT

Hill Top

Brewood

3

Little Hyde
Rough

School
Bridge

Shropshire Union Canal

Brook
House

White
House

SOMERFORD LA

Somerford
Hall

Dean's Hall
Bridge

HYDE MILL LA

Giffard's Cross
Bridge

08

The Woolley

Staffordshire Way

Hyde
Farm

COVEN RD

Straasfield
House

BREWOOD RD

Giffard's Cross
Lodge

Avenue Bridge

Lower Avenue

Pond
Bay

2

Hell
Floor

Chillington
Bridge

Park
Lodge

Upper Avenue

PORT LA

Ackbury Heath
House

PARK LA

07

Dale
Flat

Upper
Cottages

Chillington Street

Park
Bridge

Brewood
Park
Farm

1

Staffordshire Way

06

87

D

88

E

89

F

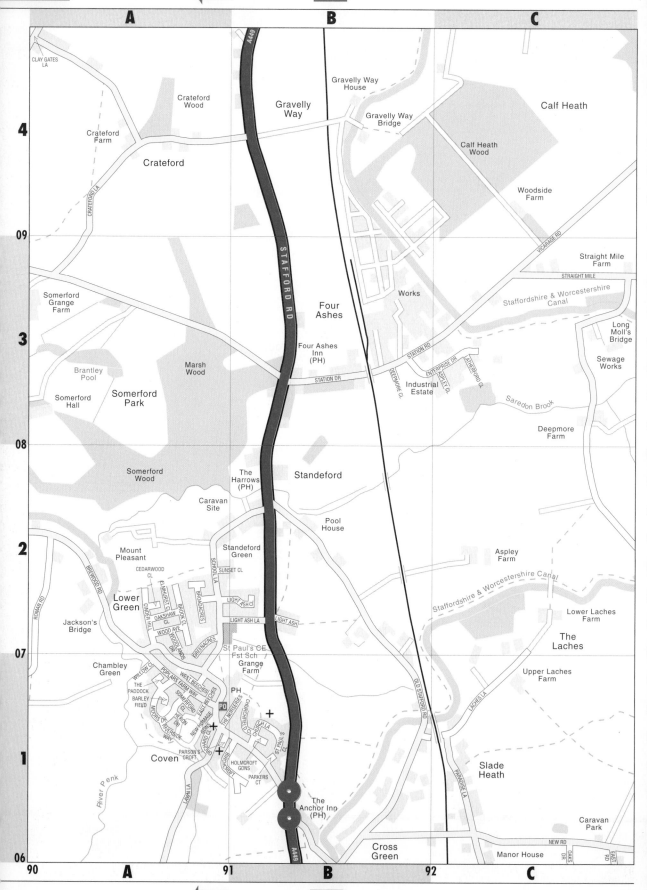

CLAY GATES LA

Crateford Wood

Gravelly Way House

Gravelly Way

Calf Heath

4

Crateford Farm

Gravelly Way Bridge

Calf Heath Wood

CRATEFORD LA

Crateford

Woodside Farm

VICARAGE RD

09

Straight Mile Farm

Somerford Grange Farm

STRAIGHT MILE

Staffordshire & Worcestershire Canal

Works

Four Ashes

Long Moll's Bridge

3

STAFFORD RD

Brantley Pool

Marsh Wood

Four Ashes Inn (PH)

STATION RD

Sewage Works

Somerford Hall

Somerford Park

STATION DR

DEEMORE CL

ENTERPRISE DR

ASHEY CL

LATHERFORD RD

Saredon Brook

Industrial Estate

08

Somerford Wood

The Harrows (PH)

Standeford

Deepmore Farm

ROMAN RD

OLD GROSVENOR LA

Caravan Site

Pool House

Aspley Farm

Staffordshire & Worcestershire Canal

2

Mount Pleasant

Standeford Green

CEDARWOOD CL

SUNSET CL

SCHOOL LA

Lower Laches Farm

Lower Green

ELMHURST CL

BROOK CL

BROADACRES

LIGHT ASH CL

The Laches

Jackson's Bridge

CINDER HILL

OAKSHAW CL

WOOD AVE

WOODLANDS DR

GREENACRES

LIGHT ASH LA

Light Ash

OLD STAFFORD RD

LACHES LA

07

Chambley Green

St Paul's CE Fst Sch

Grange Farm

Upper Laches Farm

WILLOW CL

POPLARS FARM WAY

WEST BEECHES

EAST BEECHES

PH

THE PADDOCK

SOMERFORD CL

MIXONS DR

HERON DR

NEW HIMMAE

THE NURSERIES

CHURCHFIELD CL

ASH LA

ST PAUL'S RD

BARLEY FIELD

PO

+

Slade Heath

RIVERSIDE WAY

PARSON'S CROFT

BIRCH CROFT

HOLMCROFT GDNS

PARADISE LA

Caravan Park

1

Coven

River Penk

LAWN LA

PARKERS CT

Cross Green

NEW RD

OAKS

EAST RD

The Anchor Inn (PH)

Manor House

06

90   A   91   B   92   C

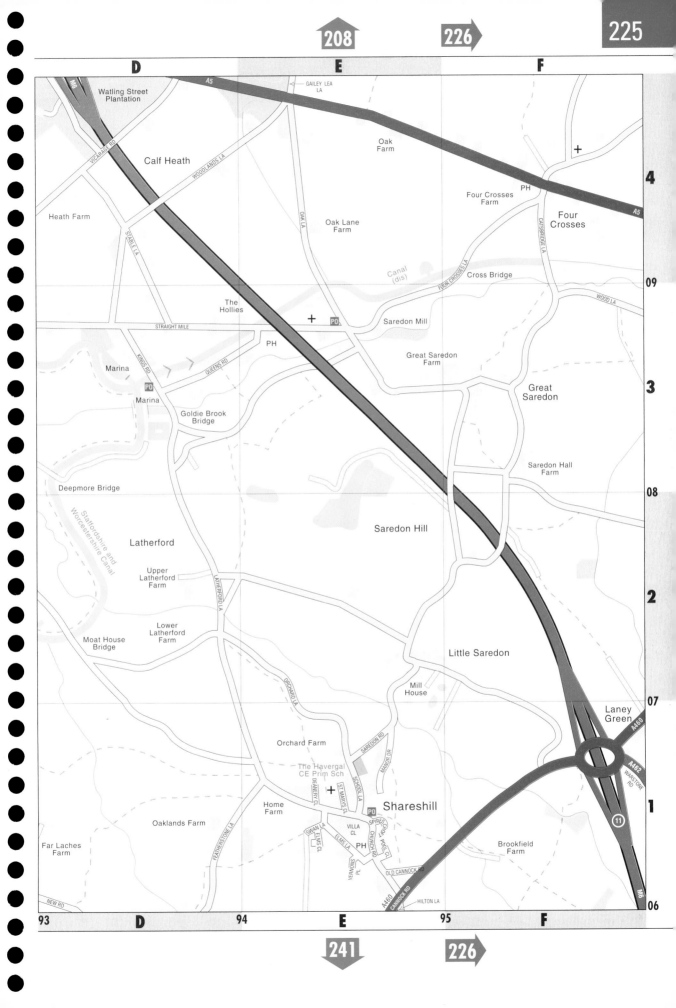

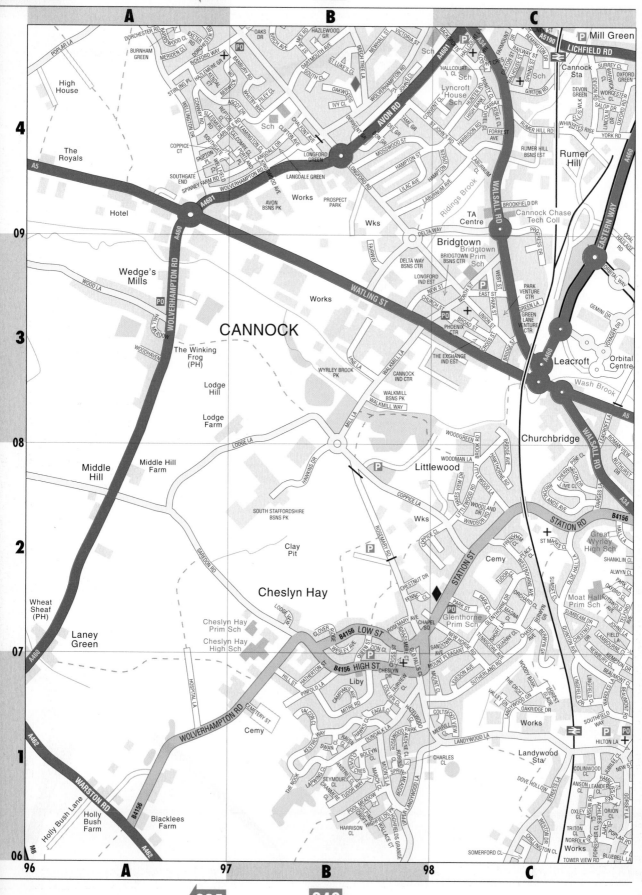

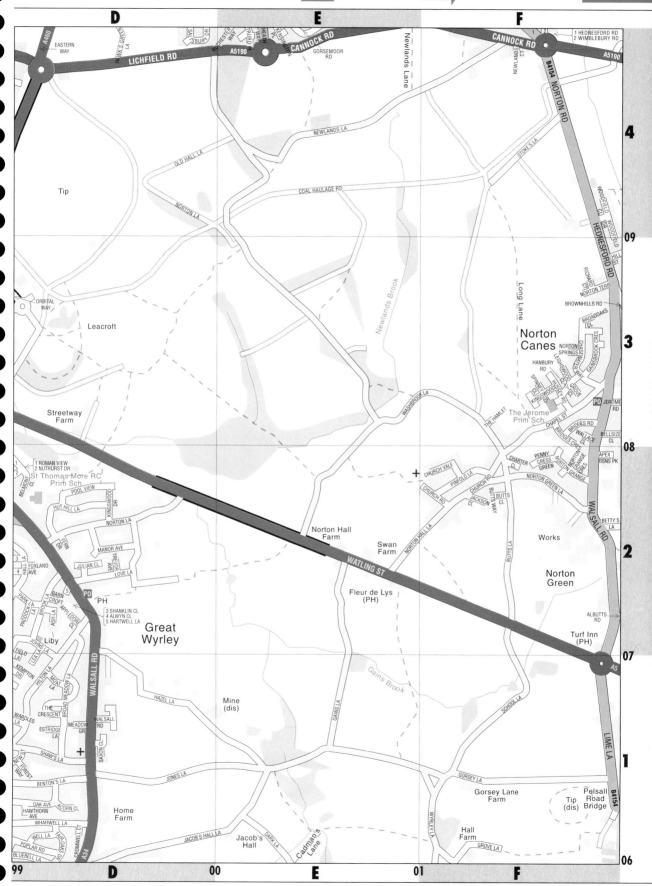

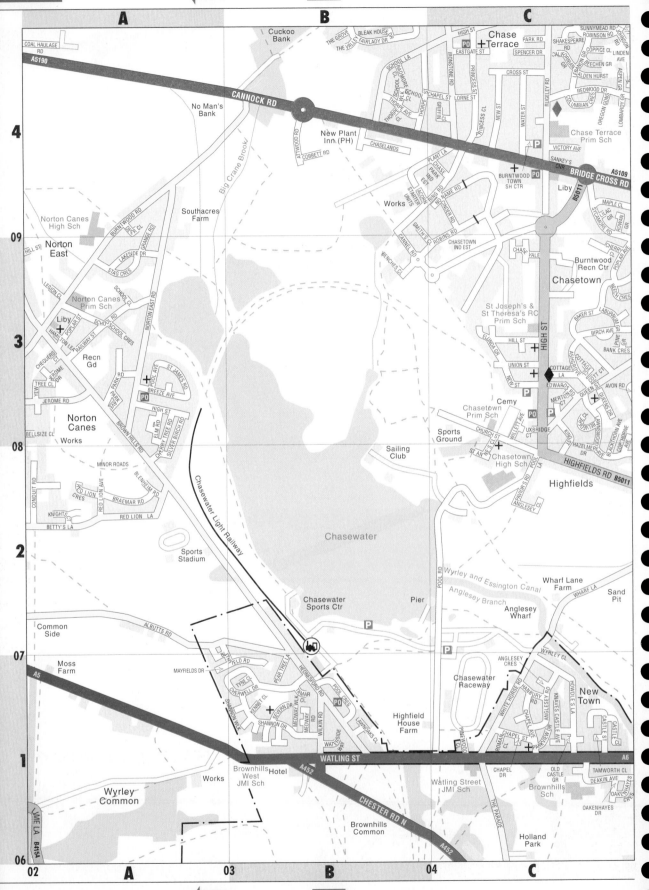

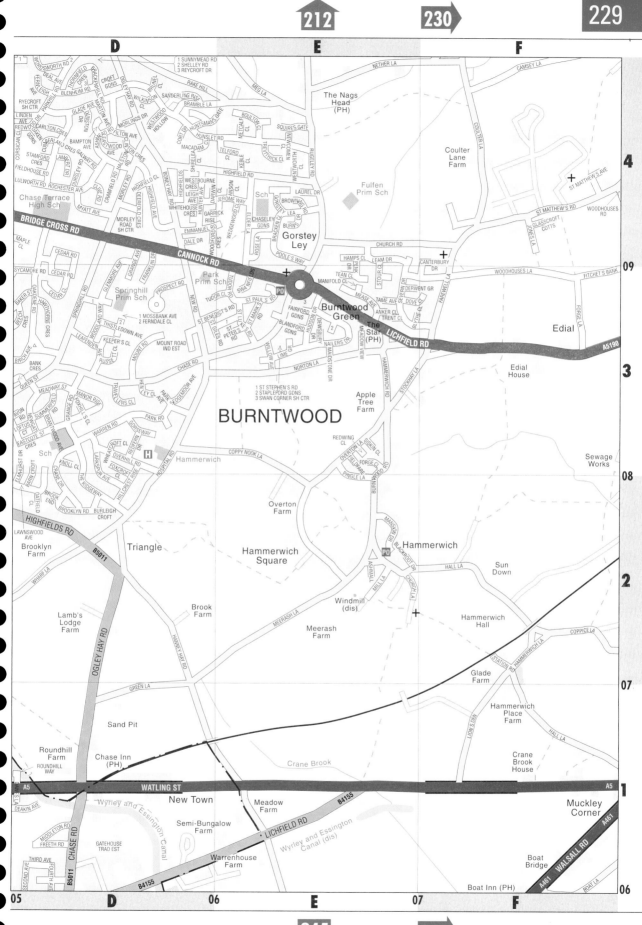

229
213

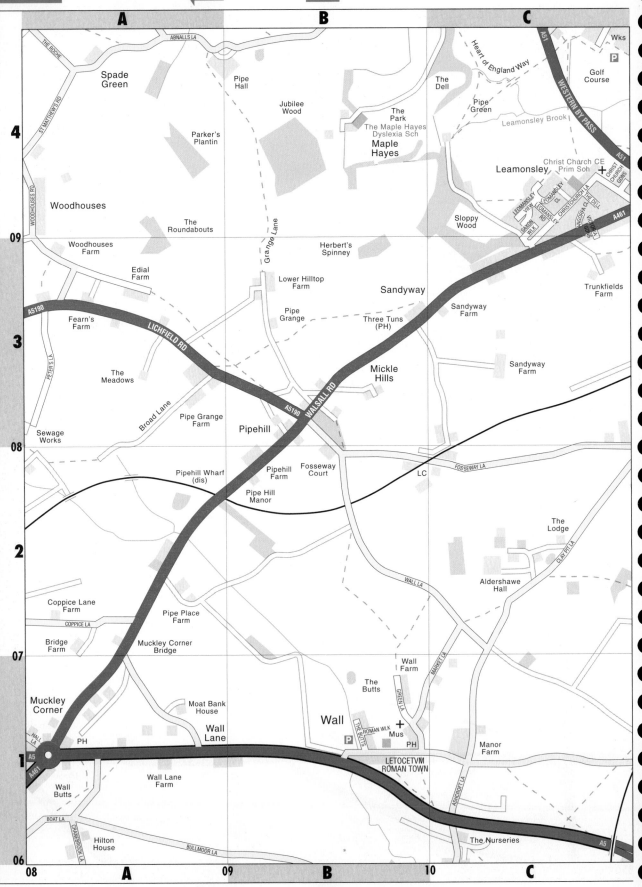

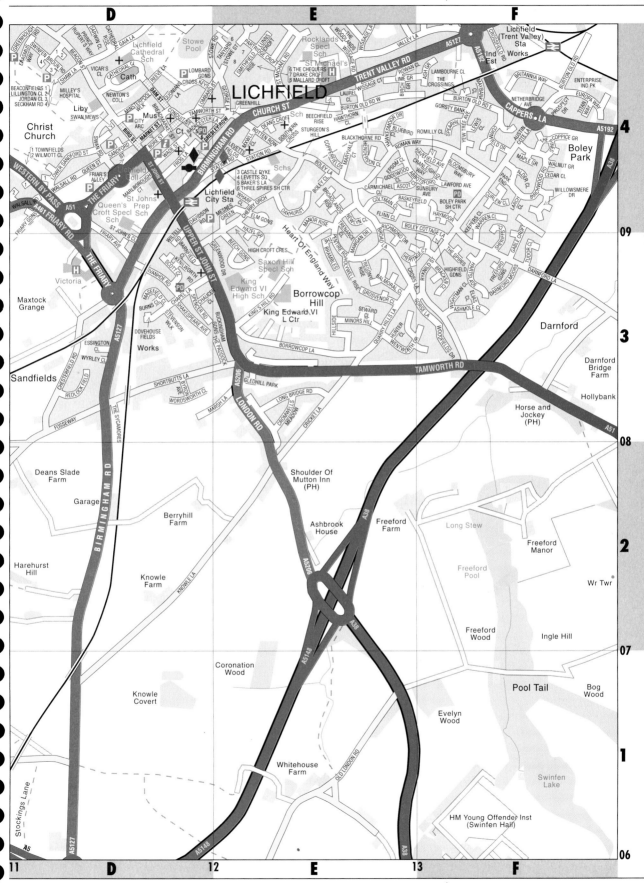

A   B   C

4

3

2

1

09

08

07

06

A38
A5192
A38

Fulfen Wood
Plough Inn (PH)
Huddlesford
PARK LA
Holly Cottage
BROAD LA

Huddlesford Bridge
Huddlesford Grange
Fisherwick Dairy Farm
BURTON RD

Potter's Thatch
Bowman's Bridge
Coventry Canal
Bridge Farm
Fisherwick Brook

Watery Lane Bridge
CAPPER'S LA
HUDDLESFORD LA

Fulfen Farm
Mill Farm
Notington La

SWAN COTTAGES

Marsh Farm
SWAN RD
NODDINGTON LA
NODDINGTON AVE
NEAL CROFT
DARBY AVE
MIDDLETON RD
SPRING LA
FISHERWICK

DARNFORD LA
PASS AVE
ROCK FARM RD
BAILEY CL

Hill Farm
BACK LA
BLACKSMITH
LANGTON CRES
THE GREEN

Ellfield House
MARSH LA
BRAMLEY WAY
CHAPEL LA
MAIN ST
PO
KESTREL CL
MERLIN WAY
FALCON CL
Whittington Bridge

Church Farm
CHURCH ST
Whittington
PH
BABBINGTON CL
CLOISTER WALK
FISHERWICK RD

Ellfield Lodge
BEECHWOOD
WINDMILL HILL LA
Vicarage Lane
Peel Farm

WHITTINGTON COMMON RD
Whittington Prim Sch
Coton House

Bailey's Beating
A51
SANDY LA
Windmill Hill

Brewery Farm
COMMON LA

Golf Course
Whittington Heath
Rifle Range
DANGER AREA

HEATH AVE
Rifle Ranges
Hopwas Hays Lane

Lochranza
TAMWORTH RD
WORCESTER RD
STAFFORD CRES
STAFFORD CRES
DERBY RD
DANGER AREA

CH
PO
CHESTER RD
NOTTINGHAM RD

Freeford Home Farm
Mus
Whittington Barracks
Hopwas Hays Lane

Ingleyhill Farm
Heart of England Way
Packington Hall Farm
Ice House Covert

Horsley Brook Farm
The Bungalow
Botany Bay
LEVETT RD
Packington Hall Works

JERRY'S LA
A51

14   A   15   B   16   C

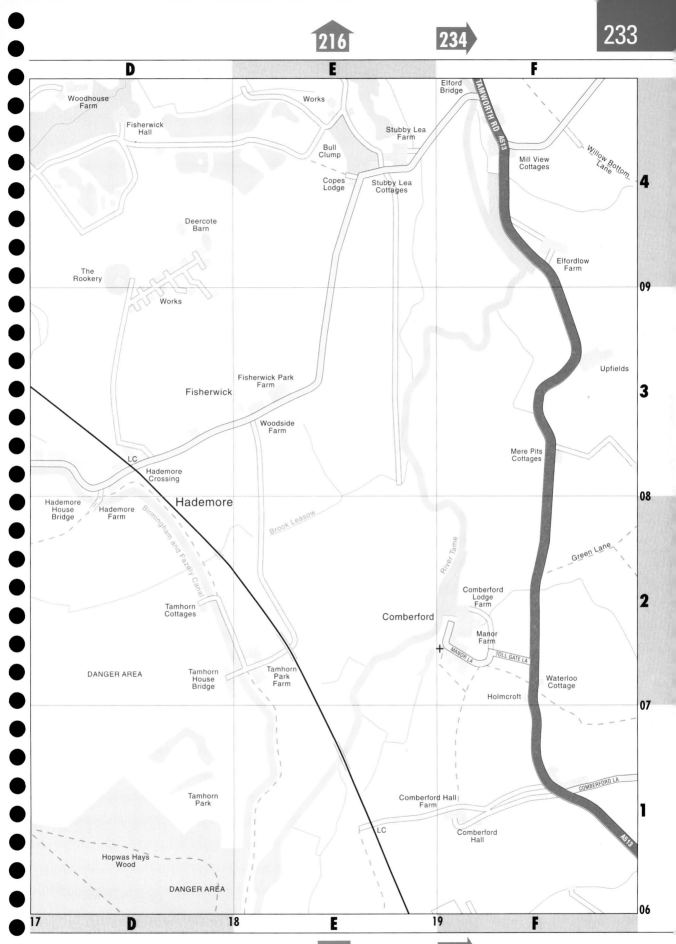

233
217

A
B
C

Twizles Lane

Fishpits Barn

PORTWAY LA

Dunimere Farm

Willow Bottom Lane

Portway

Hogs Hill

09

Winterdyne Farm

3

Birdsley Farm

Green Lane

Mere Pits

08

Wiggington Fields Farm

Cherryfield Cottages

Hanging Hill

Syerscote Manor

2

Watergate Cottage

07

Wigginton Manor

Syerscote Barn

SYERSCOTE LA

+

COMBERFORD LA

PH

World's End Cottages

1

Wigginton

St Leonard's CE Prim Sch

MAIN RD

Bridge Cottages

Arkall Farm

WALRAND CL

A513

SILL GREEN

Rawlett Sports Ctr

Rawlett High Sch

Amington Hall Cottages

ASHBY RD

B5493

06

20
A
21
B
22
C

233
250

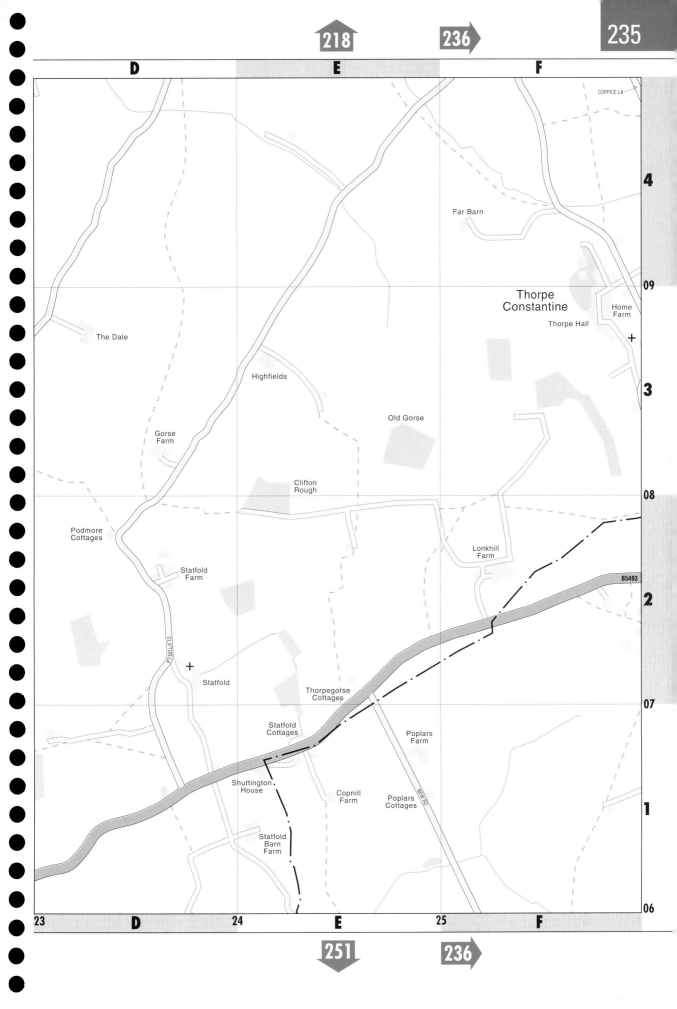

D E F

COPPICE LA

4

Far Barn

09

Thorpe
Constantine

Home
Farm

Thorpe Hall

+

The Dale

Highfields

3

Old Gorse

Gorse
Farm

Clifton
Rough

08

Podmore
Cottages

Lonkhill
Farm

Statfold
Farm

B5493

2

CLIFTON LA

+

Statfold

Thorpegorse
Cottages

07

Statfold
Cottages

Poplars
Farm

Shuttington
House

Copnill
Farm

Poplars
Cottages

NEW RD

1

Statfold
Barn
Farm

06

235
219

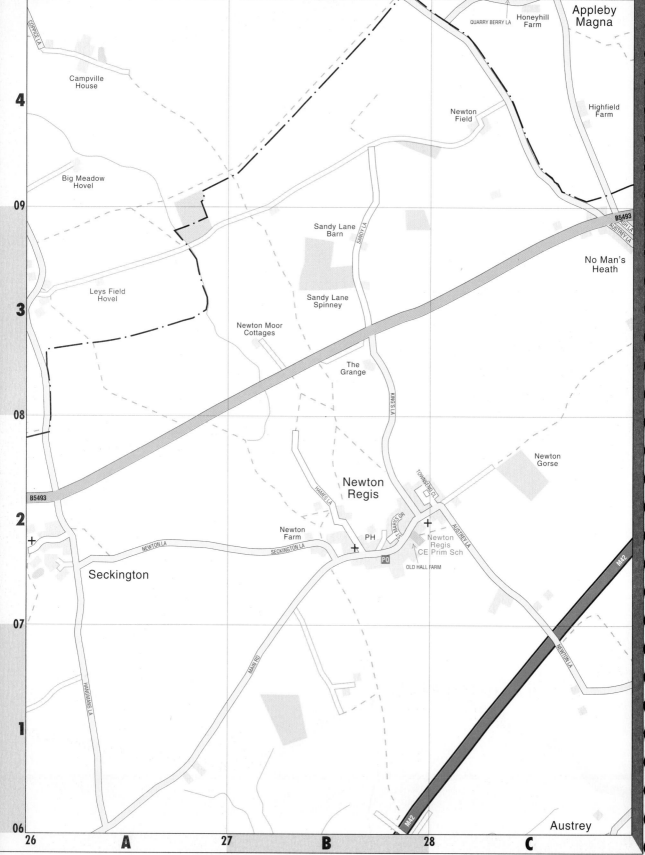

A B C

4

COPPICE LA

Campville
House

Big Meadow
Hovel

09

B5493
AUSTREY LA

Sandy Lane
Barn

SANDY LA

No Man's
Heath

Leys Field
Hovel

3

Sandy Lane
Spinney

Newton Moor
Cottages

The
Grange

KING'S LA

08

Newton
Gorse

TOWNSEND CL.

HAMES LA

Newton
Regis

2

B5493

Newton
Farm

Newton
Regis
CE Prim Sch

AUSTREY LA

KING'S GR

M42

+

Seckington

NEWTON LA

SECKINGTON LA

PH

PO

OLD HALL FARM

+

07

MAIN RD

HANGMANS LA

M42

NEWTON LA

1

06

Austrey

Appleby
Magna

QUARRY BERRY LA

Honeyhill
Farm

Newton
Field

Highfield
Farm

26 A 27 B 28 C

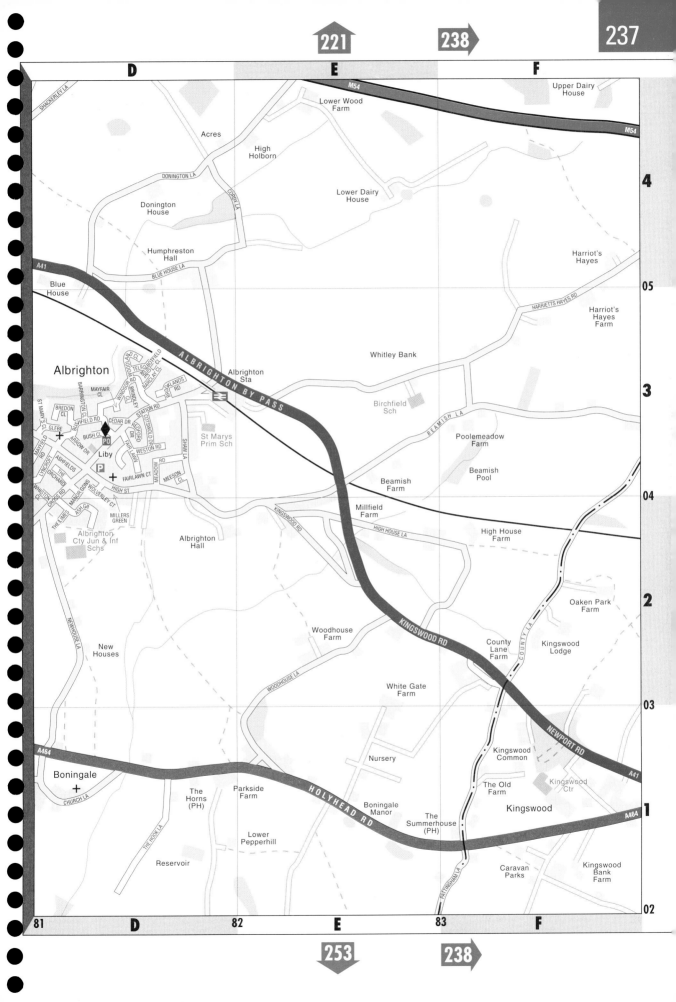

D · E · F

M54

Upper Dairy House

Lower Wood Farm

Acres

High Holborn

DONINGTON LA

Lower Dairy House

Donington House

4

CORDY LA

Harriot's Hayes

Humphreston Hall

BLUE HOUSE LA

A41

Blue House

05

HARRIETTS HAYES RD

Harriot's Hayes Farm

Whitley Bank

Albrighton

ST MARYS CL
BREDON CL
GLEBE
MAYFIELD RD
ASHFIELD RD
LYNCROFT
ASHFIELDS
THE ORCHARD
WINSTON CROSS RD
MANOR GDNS
ASH GA
THE LIMES
MILLERS GREEN
BARRINGTON CL
WINDSOR RD
BRINDLEY CL
CL
TELFORD
AREA
BUSH CL
ARROW DR
WOLVERLEY CT
CEDAR DR
FAIRLAWN CT
BARCLAY CL
FIELD
BROOKLANDS RD
STATION RD
COTSWOLD DR
RETFORD
SHAW LA
MEADOW RD
MEESON CL
HIGH ST
FAIRLAWN
DR

PO
Liby
P

St Marys Prim Sch

Albrighton Sta

Albrighton
BY PASS

Birchfield Sch

3

BEAMISH LA

Poolemeadow Farm

Beamish Pool

Beamish Farm

04

St Marys Prim Sch

Albrighton Hall

Albrighton Cty Jun & Inf Schs

KINGSWOOD RD

Millfield Farm

HIGH HOUSE LA

High House Farm

New Houses

NEWHOUSE LA

Woodhouse Farm

WOODHOUSE LA

KINGSWOOD RD

Oaken Park Farm

2

COUNTY LA

County Lane Farm

Kingswood Lodge

03

A464

White Gate Farm

NEWPORT RD

A41

Boningale

CHURCH LA

THE HOOK LA

The Horns (PH)

Parkside Farm

Nursery

HOLYHEAD RD

Kingswood Common

The Old Farm

Kingswood Ctr

Kingswood

Lower Pepperhill

Boningale Manor

The Summerhouse (PH)

PATTINGHAM LA

Caravan Parks

Kingswood Bank Farm

A464

1

Reservoir

02

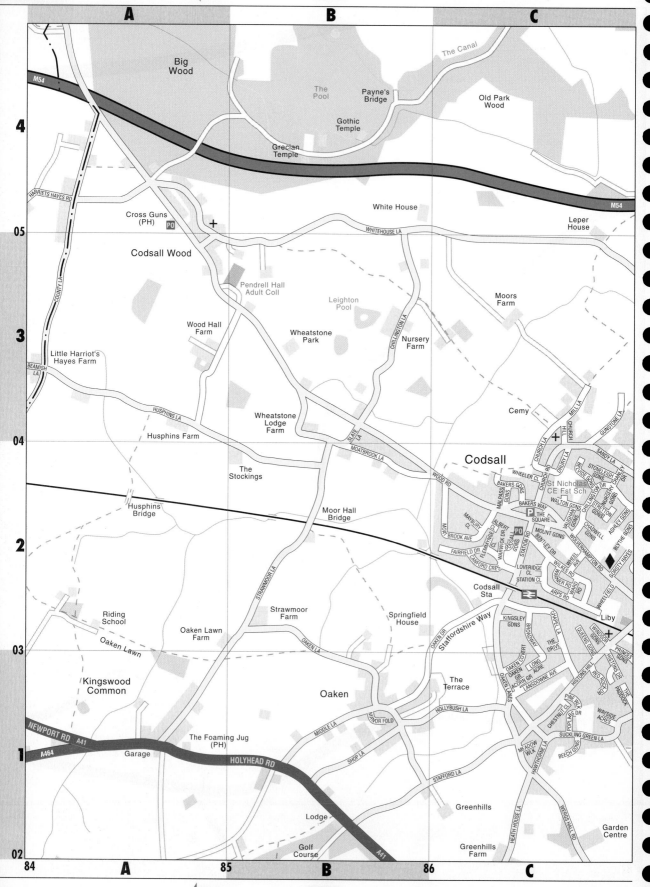

A   B   C

M54

Big Wood

The Canal

Old Park Wood

The Pool

Payne's Bridge

Gothic Temple

Grecian Temple

White House

M54

Leper House

Cross Guns (PH)

PO

WHITEHOUSE LA

Codsall Wood

Pendrell Hall Adult Coll

Leighton Pool

Moors Farm

HARRIETS HAYES RD

COUNTY LA

Wood Hall Farm

Wheatstone Park

CHILLINGTON LA

Nursery Farm

Cemy

MILL LA

GUNSTONE LA

CHURCH HILL

Little Harriot's Hayes Farm

BEAMISH LA

HUSPHINS LA

Husphins Farm

Wheatstone Lodge Farm

SLATE LA

MOATBROOK LA

Codsall

SANDY LA

STONELEIGH GDNS

ASHLEY GDNS

The Stockings

Husphins Bridge

Moor Hall Bridge

WOOD RD

St Nicholas CE Fst Sch

WHEELER CL

BAKERS GDNS

MALPASS

BAKERS WAY

CHURCH RD

CHURCH LA

WALTON GDNS

VAUGHAN

CHADWELL GDNS

BLYTHE GDNS

P

THE SQUARE

MAYBURY CL

ALBERT

MOUNT GDNS

WOLVERHAMPTON RD

PO

Riding School

STRAWMOOR LA

MOOR BROOK AVE

WARWICK DR

FLEMMING

CROFT

STATION RD

BENTLEY LA

WILKES RD

WHEEL

GORSTY HAYES

Oaken Lawn

OAKEN LA

FAIRFIELD DR

CAPFORD CRES

LOVERIDGE CL

STATION CL

WARNER RD

WARD RD

WHEEL FIELD

ARPS RD

Strawmoor Farm

Springfield House

Codsall Sta

Liby

Oaken Lawn Farm

Staffordshire Way

KINGSLEY GDNS

WINDSOR GDNS

PRINCES DR

HISTONS DR

RED ROCK

Kingswood Common

Oaken

OAKEN LA

The Terrace

OAKEN COVERT

OAKEN GR

ACORN GR

LONG ACRE

LANSDOWNE AVE

QUEENS GDNS

THE DRIVE

CHAPEL LA

BROADWAY

HISTONS HILL

THE PADDOCK

NEWPORT RD

A41

A464

Garage

The Foaming Jug (PH)

MIDDLE LA

MANOR FOLD

SHOP LA

HOLLYBUSH LA

CHESTNUT CL

POPLARS DR

PINE WLK

WAYSIDE ACRES

SUCKLING GREEN LA

A464

HOLYHEAD RD

STAFFORD LA

MEADOW WLK

HAWTHORNE LA

BEECH GDNS

Lodge

A41

Greenhills

HEATH HOUSE LA

WERGS HALL RD

Garden Centre

Golf Course

Greenhills Farm

84   A   85   B   86   C

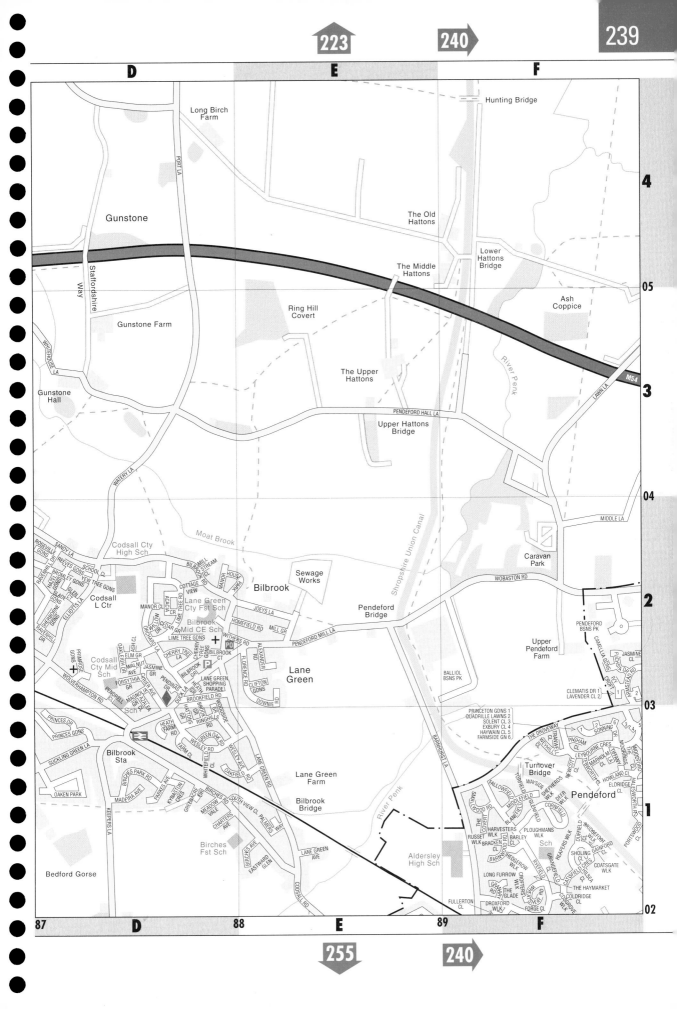

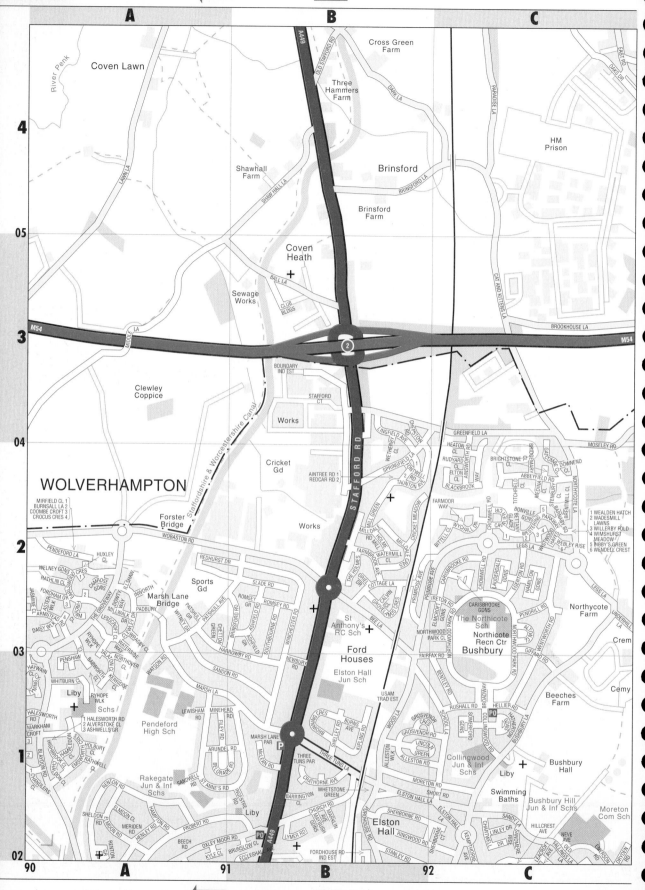

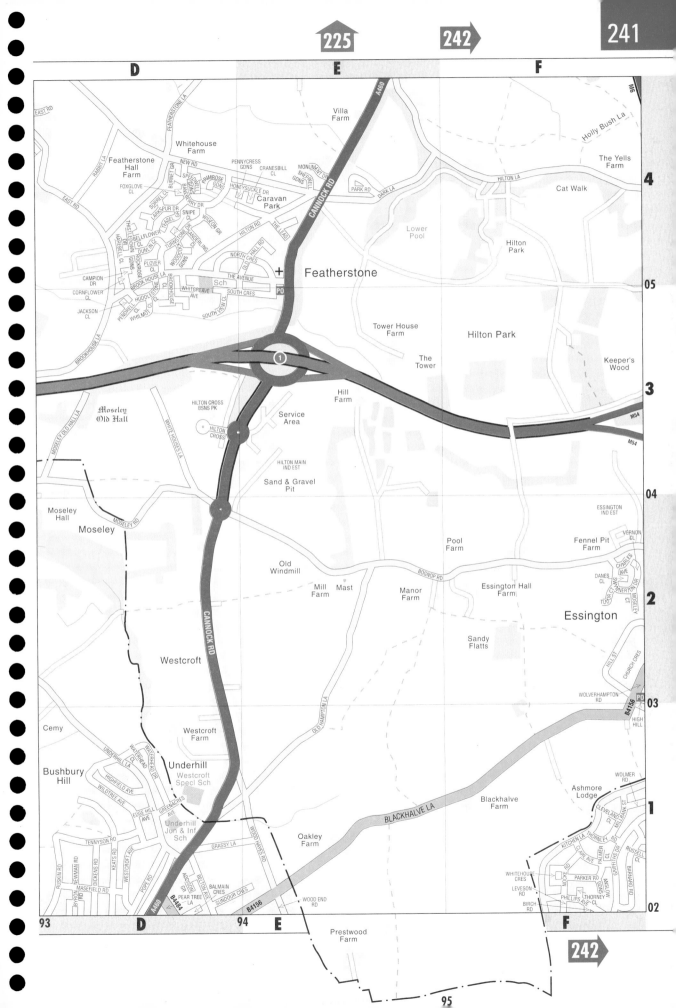

D E F

Villa Farm

Whitehouse Farm

Featherstone Hall Farm

FEATHERSTONE LA

RABBIT LA

EAST RD

EAST RD

FOXGLOVE CL

CAMPION DR

CORNFLOWER CL

JACKSON CL

BROOKHOUSE LA

THISTLEDOWN DR

HAREBELL CL

BELLFLOWER GDNS

PLOVER CL

PENDRIL CL

HUDDLESTONE CL

WHILMOT CL

DUNLIN CL

WOODCOCK GDNS

TURNSTONE DR

TEASEL CL

LARKSPUR DR

SNIPE CL

BANBERRY DR

SORREL CL

SPEEDWELL GDNS

BURNET GR

PRIMROSE GDNS

NEW RD

PENNYCRESS GDNS

CRANESBILL CL

SHEPWELL GDNS

MONUMENT DR

Caravan Park

HONEYSUCKLE DR

SANDERLING CL

WIGEON GR

ROCKROSE CL

BROOK HOUSE LA

WHITGREAVE AVE

BROOKHOUSE CL

HALL RD

HILTON RD

OLD RD

NORTH CRES

THE LEAS

THE AVENUE

SOUTH CRES

SOUTH VW

Sch

PARK RD

DARK LA

PARK RD

CANNOCK RD

A460

M6

Holly Bush La

The Yells Farm

HILTON LA

Cat Walk

Lower Pool

Hilton Park

05

Featherstone

PO

Tower House Farm

Hilton Park

The Tower

Keeper's Wood

3

Moseley Old Hall

HILTON CROSS BSNS PK

HILTON CROSS

WHITE HOUSE LA

MOSELEY OLD HALL LA

Service Area

Hill Farm

Hilton Main Ind Est

Sand & Gravel Pit

1

M54

M54

Moseley Hall

Moseley

MOSELEY RD

Old Windmill

Mill Farm

Mast

Manor Farm

BOGNOP RD

Pool Farm

Essington Hall Farm

ESSINGTON IND EST

Fennel Pit Farm

VERNON CL

CHARLES AVE

DANES CL

SOMERTON RD

MOSELEY CT

TOR CL

Essington

04

2

Westcroft

CANNOCK RD

OLD HAMPTON LA

Sandy Flatts

HILL ST

CHURCH CRES

WOLVERHAMPTON RD

B4156

PO

HIGH HILL

03

Cemy

Bushbury Hill

Westcroft Farm

Underhill

Westcroft Specl Sch

UNDERHILL LA

WATERHEAD DR

WATERHEAD CL

HIGHFIELD AVE

WILDTREE AVE

EDGE HILL AVE

GREENACRES AVE

Ashmore Lodge

WOLMER RD

CLEVELAND CL

MELVERTON AVE

Blackhalve Farm

BLACKHALVE LA

RUSKIN RD

NEWMAN RD

BYRON RD

DICKENS RD

MASEFIELD RD

TENNYSON RD

KEATS RD

WESTCROFT AVE

POPE RD

Underhill Jun & Inf Sch

GRASSY LA

WOOD HAYES RD

BECTON AVE

ADDISON GR

BALMAIN CRES

SUNDOUR CRES

PEAR TREE LA

A460

B4484

Oakley Farm

WOOD END RD

B4156

Whitehouse Cres

LEVESON RD

NOCKE RD

PARKER RD

PHILLIPS AVE

BIRCH RD

KITCHEN LA

CLARE AVE

THORNEY RD

PALMER CL

THORNLEY DR

LEVESON GDNS

ANSLOW GDNS

THORNEY CL

GRIFFITHS DR

RUSSELL CL

BARNARD RD

1

02

93 D 94 E F

Prestwood Farm

242

95

241

226

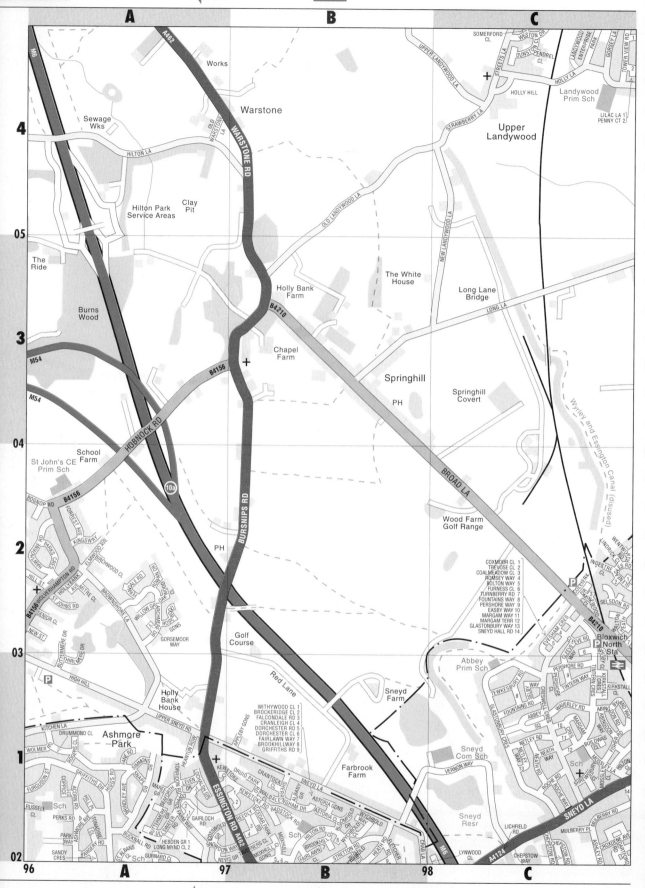

241

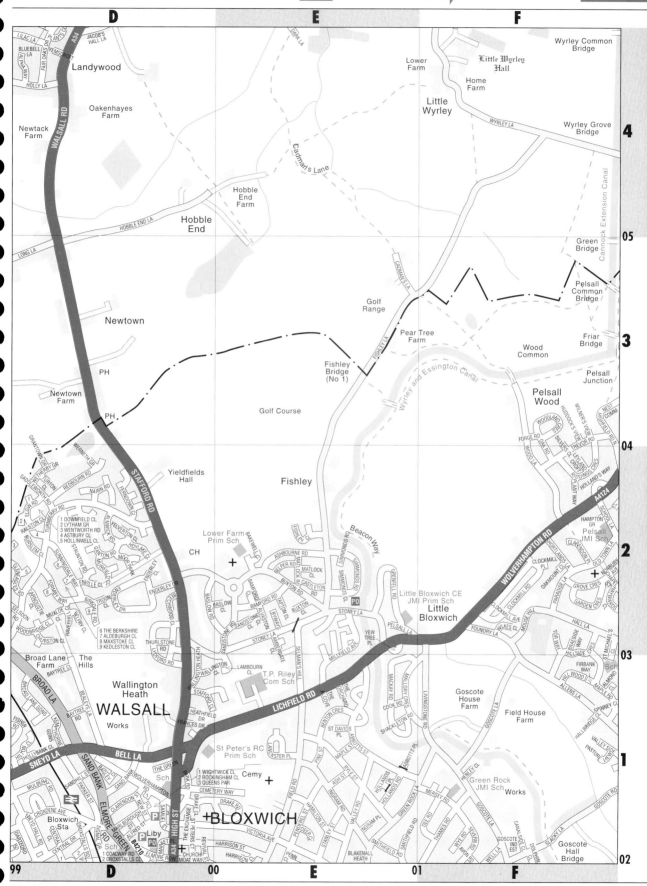

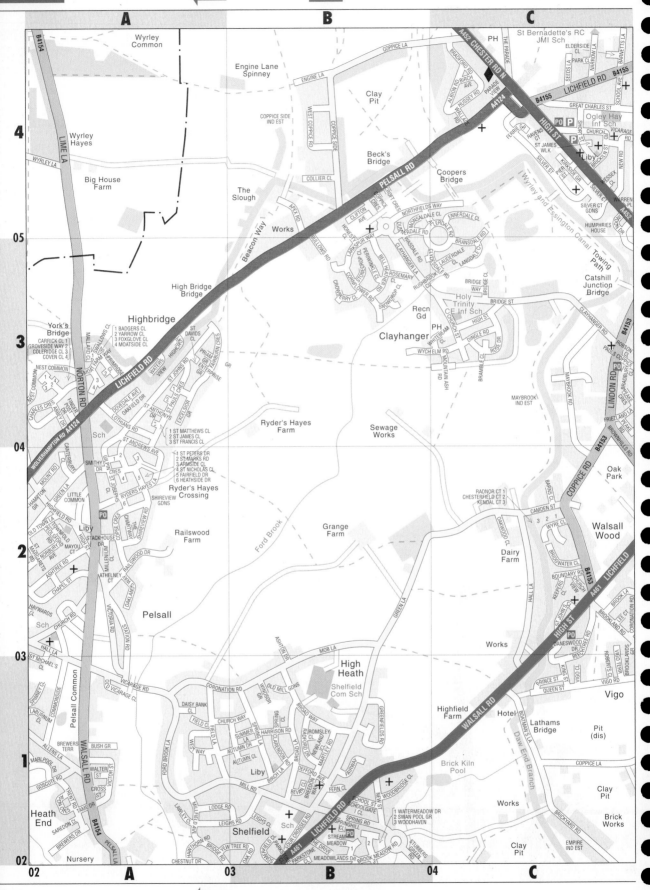

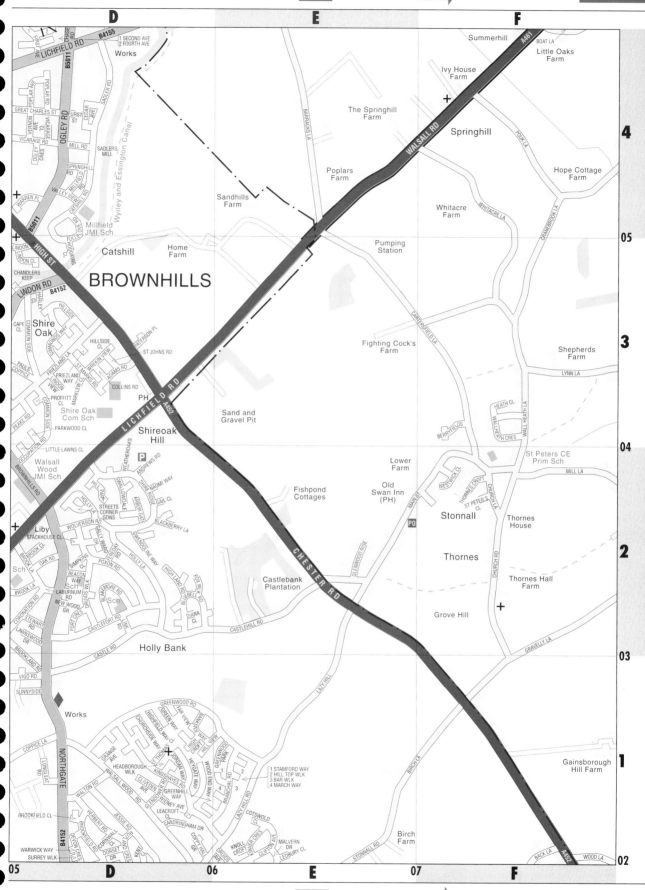

D   E   F

4

05

BROWNHILLS

3

04

2

03

1

02

05   D   06   E   07   F   02

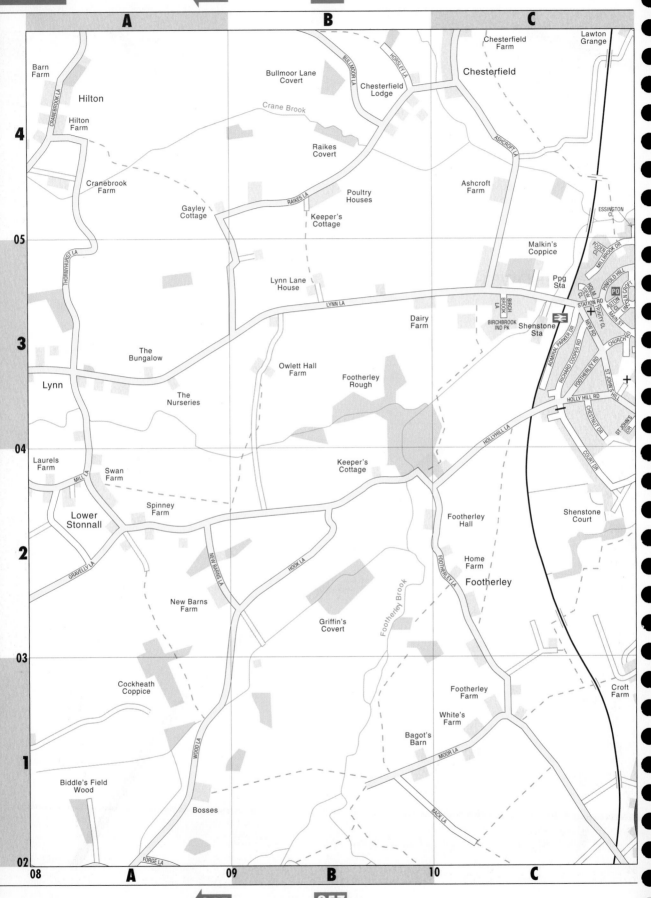

A   B   C

4

05

3

04

2

03

1

02

08   A   09   B   10   C

Barn Farm

Hilton

Hilton Farm

Cranebrook Farm

Gayley Cottage

Lynn

The Bungalow

The Nurseries

Laurels Farm

Swan Farm

Lower Stonnall

Spinney Farm

New Barns Farm

Cockheath Coppice

Biddle's Field Wood

Bosses

Bullmoor Lane Covert

Crane Brook

Raikes Covert

Poultry Houses

Keeper's Cottage

Lynn Lane House

Owlett Hall Farm

Footherley Rough

Keeper's Cottage

Griffin's Covert

Footherley Brook

Chesterfield Lodge

Chesterfield Farm

Chesterfield

Lawton Grange

Ashcroft Farm

Malkin's Coppice

Dairy Farm

Birchbrook Ind Pk

Shenstone Sta

Footherley Hall

Home Farm

Footherley

Footherley Farm

White's Farm

Bagot's Barn

Footherley Farm

Croft Farm

Shenstone Court

Essington Cl

Ppg Sta

Station Rd

Main St

Holly Hill Rd

St John's Dr

THORNYHURST LA

CRANEBROOK LA

BULLMOOR LA

HORSLEY LA

ASHCROFT LA

RAIKES LA

LYNN LA

BIRCH BROOK LA

MILL LA

GRAVELLY LA

NEW BARNS LA

HOOK LA

WOOD LA

HOLLYHILL LA

FOOTHERLEY LA

MOOR LA

BACK LA

FORGE LA

ADMIRAL PARKER DR

RICHARD COOPER RD

FOOTHERLEY RD

NEW RD

CHURCH RD

CHESTNUT DR

COURT DR

ST JOHN'S HILL

FODEN DR

MILLBROOK DR

PINFOLD HILL

ASTON CL

LINCOLN CROFT

HOLM VIEW

TRINITY CL

PO

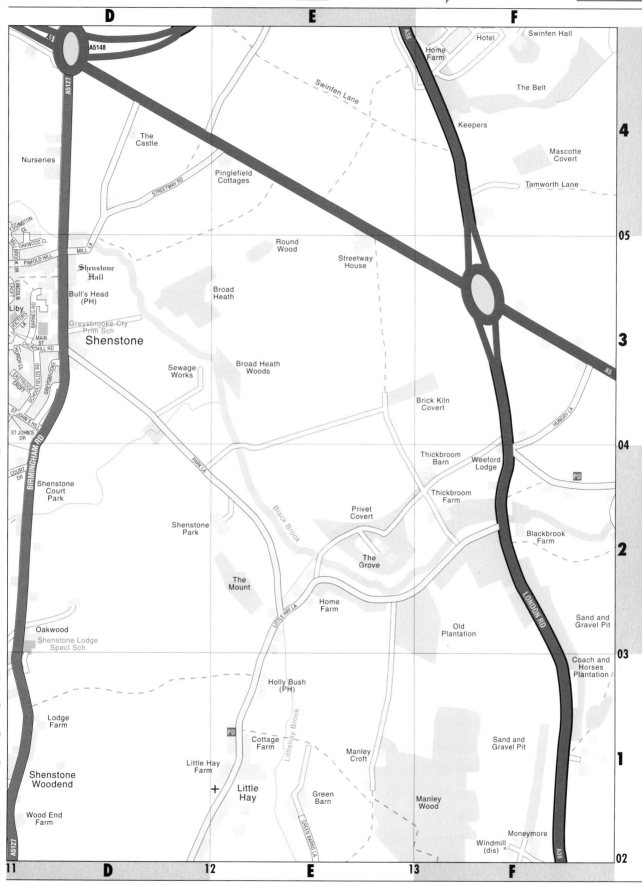

A
B
C

4

05

3

04

2

03

1

02

14
A
15
B
16
C

Broadfields

A51

Packington
Moor

Common
Barn

Moor
Covert

JERRY'S LA

Tamworth Lane

KNOX'S GRAVE LA

Riding
School

A51

HOPWAS HILL

Sand and Gravel
Pit

Packington
Farm

Buck's Head
Cottages

FLATS LA

Hare Park
Wood

Heart of England Way

Mast

Transmitting
Station

PACKINGTON LA

The Devil's
Dressing
Room

Rodbaston
Coll

A5

Buck's Head
Farm

Hanging
Wood

+ Weeford

Church
Wood

Bourne
House

The
Lodge

Long
Island

Sand and Gravel
Pit

Common
Plantation

HINTS LA

Hints Lane
Farm

DOG LA

Black Brook

ROCK HILL

Snake's
Hill

WATLING ST

Hints Hill

A5

Hints

Manor
Farm

Rough
Leasow

Job's
Hill

SCHOOL LA

+

Home
Farm

Bangley
Lodge

ROOKERY LA

Ford

HINTS CT

Botley
House

Gorsey
Hill

Resr

Bourne Brook

Sand and
Gravel Pit

Crow's
Castle

Rookery

New
Plantation

Rookery
Farm

BROCKHURST LA

White Owl
Farm

Roundhill
Wood

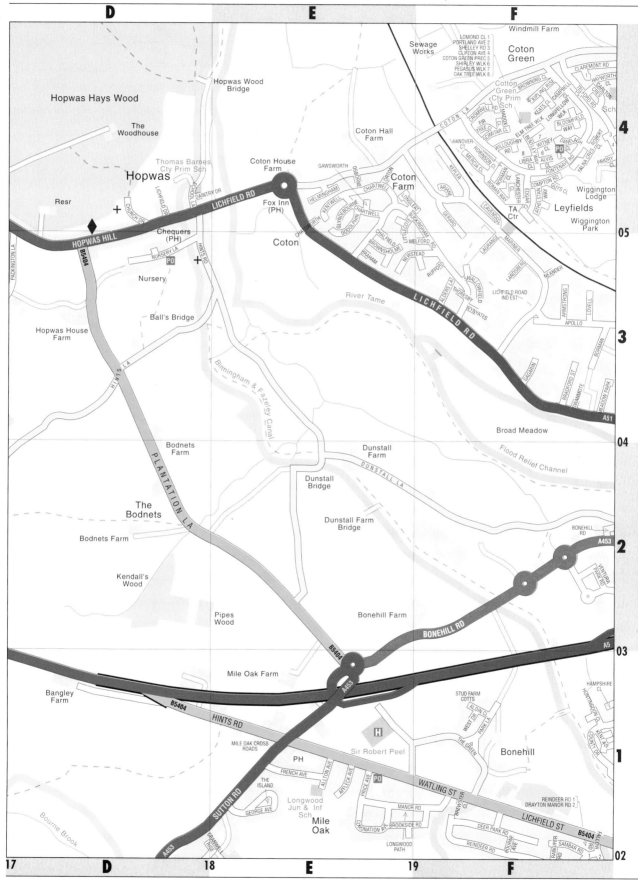

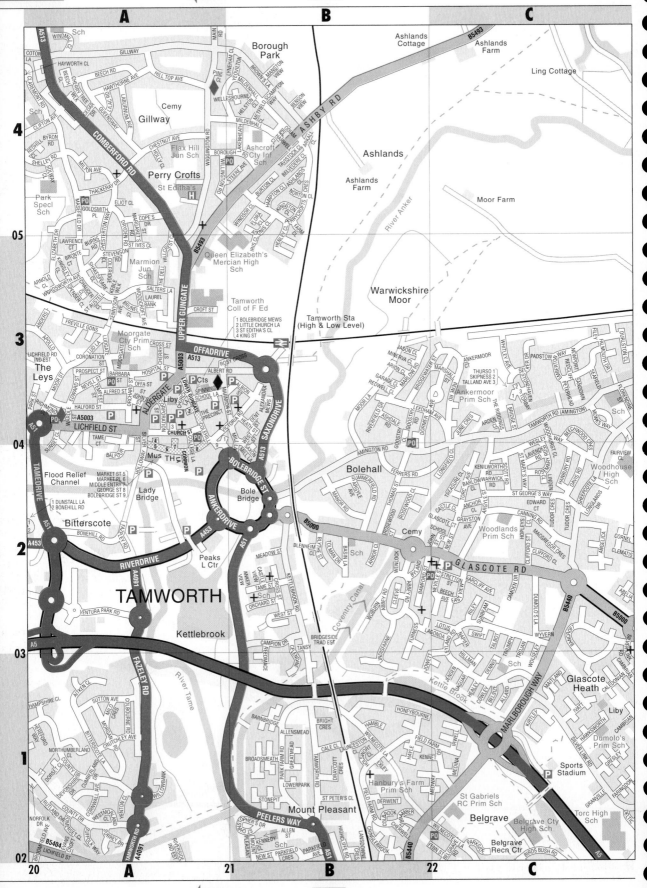

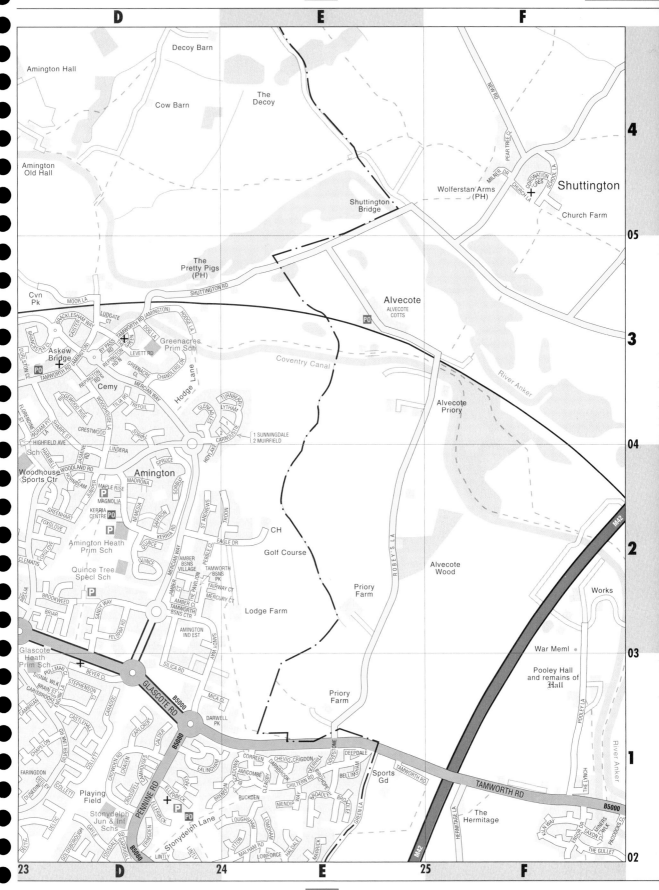

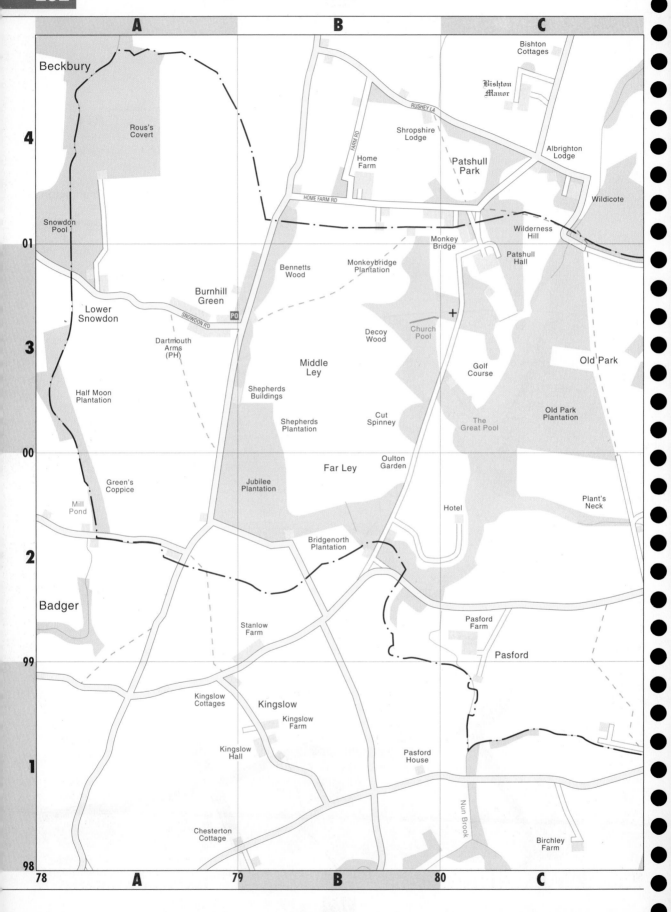

Beckbury

Rous's Covert

4

Snowdon Pool

01

Lower Snowdon

Burnhill Green

PO

SNOWDON RD

Dartmouth Arms (PH)

3

Half Moon Plantation

Shepherds Buildings

Middle Ley

Shepherds Plantation

Cut Spinney

00

Green's Coppice

Mill Pond

Jubilee Plantation

Far Ley

Oulton Garden

2

Badger

Stanlow Farm

Bridgenorth Plantation

99

Kingslow Cottages

Kingslow

Kingslow Farm

Kingslow Hall

Pasford House

1

Chesterton Cottage

Nun Brook

Birchley Farm

98

Bishton Cottages

Bishton Manor

RUSHEY LA

Shropshire Lodge

Patshull Park

Albrighton Lodge

FARM RD

Home Farm

Wildicote

HOME FARM RD

Monkey Bridge

Wilderness Hill

Patshull Hall

Bennetts Wood

Monkeybridge Plantation

Decoy Wood

Church Pool

Old Park

Golf Course

The Great Pool

Old Park Plantation

Hotel

Plant's Neck

Pasford Farm

Pasford

A   B   C

78   79   80

A   B   C

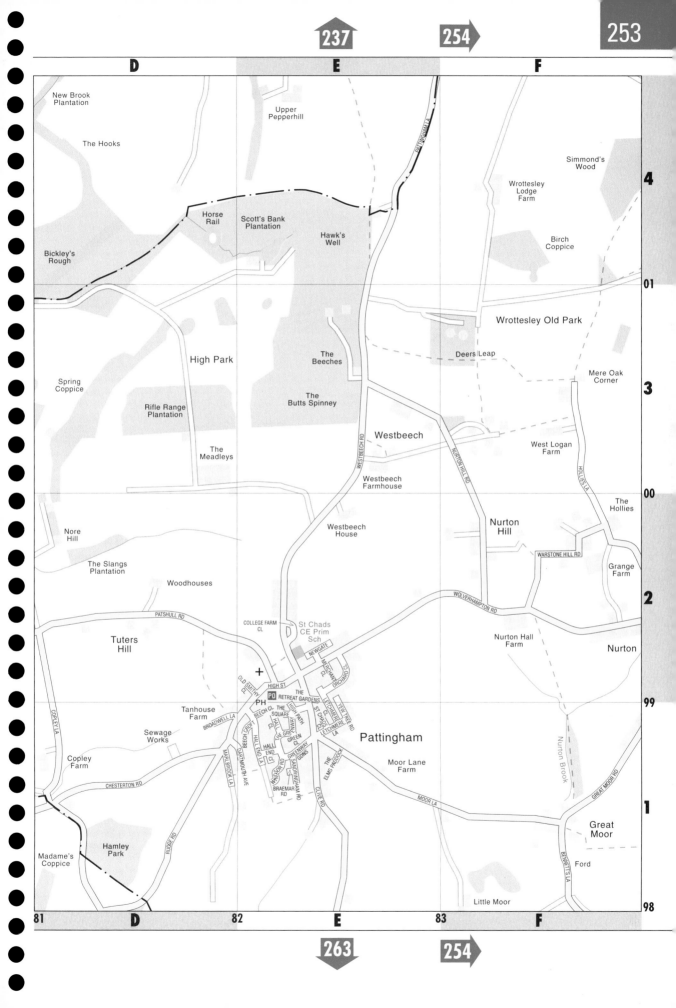

253
238

A   B   C

4

01

3

00

2

99

1

98

84   A   85   B   86   C

Simmond's Wood

Wrottesley Hall

The Bradshaws

Bull Ride

Golf Course

CH

Inland Pool

Heath House Farm

HEATH HOUSE RD

WERGS HALL RD

A41

HOLYHEAD RD

WERGS RD

River Penk

Wergs Hall

Wrottesley Park

The Grange

WESTCROFT RD

YEW TREE LA

A41

Wergs

WROTTESLEY RD W

Salt's Pool

Smith's Rough

SCAMPTON CL 1
HUDSON GR 2
TANGMERE CL 3
LIVINGSTONE DR 4

Dippons Lane

Cranmoor

Cranmoor Lodge

HAWKSTONE CT

TURNBERRY GR

WENTWORTH GR

HEPWORTH CL 1
LOWRY CL 2
MOOR CL 3
THIRLMERE GR 4
WASTWATER CT 5
BUTTERMERE CT 6
CHARTLEY CT 7
KENILWORTH RD 8

SUNNINGDALE AVE

Nurton Brook

Staffordshire Way

Perton

Sch

Sch

Liby

+

PO

THE PADDOCK 1
FALLOWFIELDS 2
THE CARTWAY 3
THE WINDROW 4
THE SADDLESTONES 5
MEADOW CROFT 6
WORCESTER GR 7

HOLLIES LA

NURTON BK

WOLVERHAMPTON RD

Perton Orchard

Golf Course

Boundary Farm

BOUNDARY WAY

THE HIGHFIELDS

GREAT MOOR RD

99

Old Perton

PATTINGHAM RD

Sling Wood

Perton House

Perton Court

PERTON RD

PERTON BROOK VALE

Quail Green

Wightwick Hall Sch

Freehold Wood

Middle Wood

South Perton Farm

JENNY WALKERS LA

Wightwick

Wightwick Manor

Cherringham

BRIDGNORTH RD

A454

Sabrina Rd

CASTLECROFT LA

HEADLAND RD

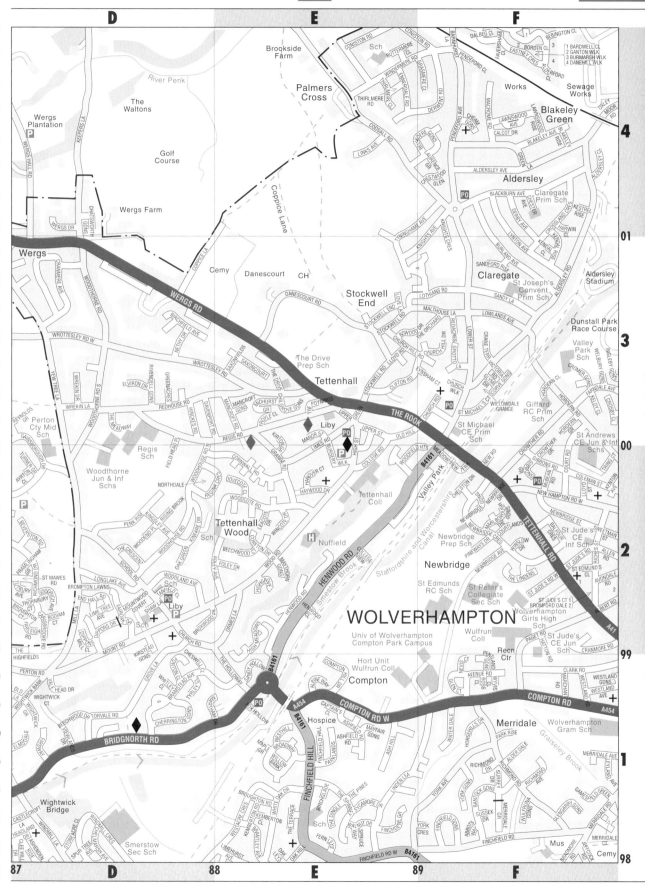

245

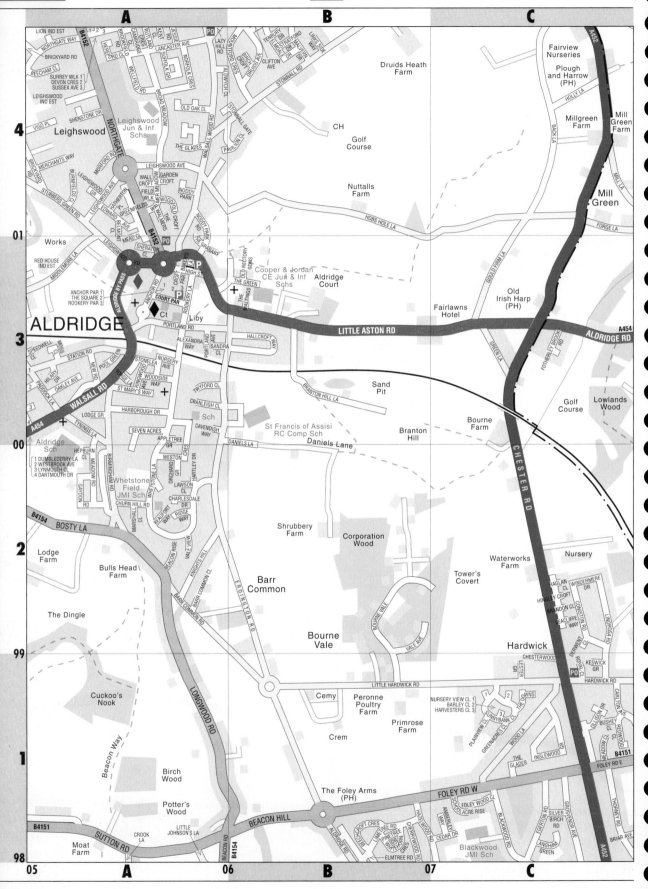

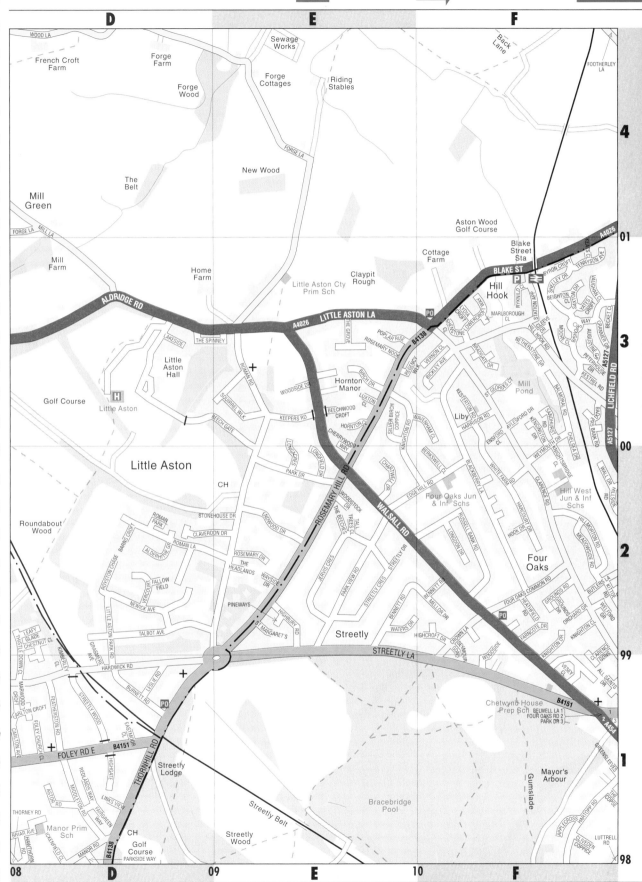

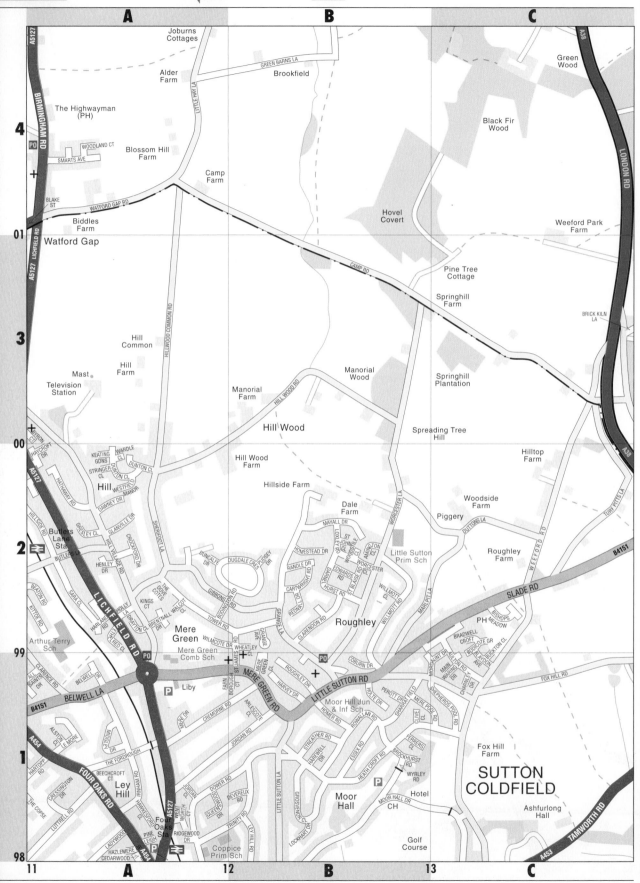

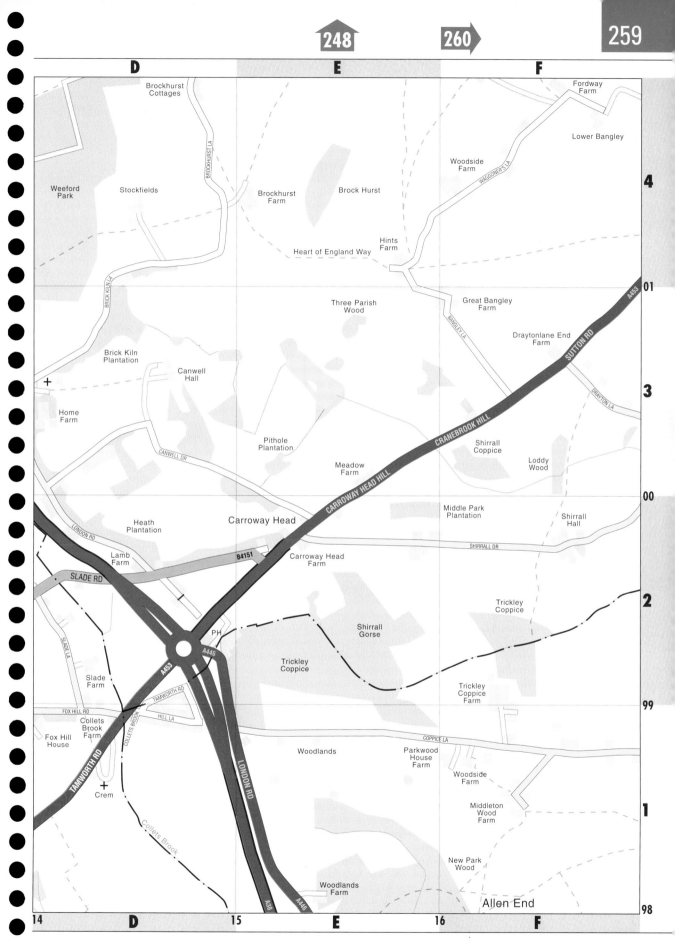

Brockhurst Cottages

Fordway Farm

Lower Bangley

Woodside Farm

WAGGONER'S LA

4

Weeford Park

Stockfields

Brockhurst Farm

Brock Hurst

BROCKHURST LA

Hints Farm

Heart of England Way

01

A453

Three Parish Wood

Great Bangley Farm

BRICK KILN LA

Draytonlane End Farm

SUTTON RD

BANGLEY LA

DRAYTON LA

3

Brick Kiln Plantation

Canwell Hall

+

CRANEBROOK HILL

Shirrall Coppice

Loddy Wood

Home Farm

CANWELL DR

Pithole Plantation

Meadow Farm

CARROWAY HEAD HILL

Middle Park Plantation

Shirrall Hall

00

Heath Plantation

Carroway Head

LONDON RD

SHIRRALL DR

Lamb Farm

B4151

Carroway Head Farm

SLADE RD

Trickley Coppice

2

SLADE LA

PH

A446

Shirrall Gorse

Slade Farm

A453

Trickley Coppice

Trickley Coppice Farm

TAMWORTH RD

HILL LA

99

FOX HILL RD

Collets Brook Farm

COLLETS BROOK

COPPICE LA

Fox Hill House

Woodlands

Parkwood House Farm

LONDON RD

Woodside Farm

TAMWORTH RD

+ Crem

Middleton Wood Farm

1

Collets Brook

New Park Wood

A38

A446

Woodlands Farm

Allen End

98

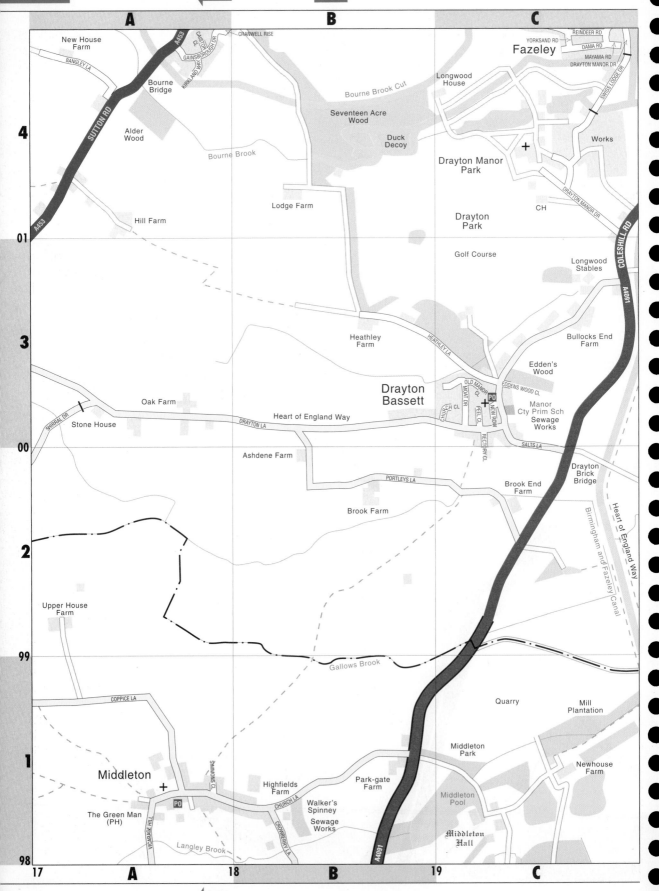

A B C

New House Farm
BANGLEY LA
Bourne Bridge
SUTTON RD
A453
Alder Wood
Bourne Brook
Hill Farm
CASTOR HILL DR
KIRKLAND WAY
GAINSBOROUGH DR
CRANWELL RISE
YORKSAND RD
Fazeley
REINDEER RD
DAMA RD
MAYAMA RD
DRAYTON MANOR DR
SWISS LODGE DR
Longwood House
Bourne Brook Cut
Seventeen Acre Wood
Duck Decoy
Drayton Manor Park
Works
Lodge Farm
Drayton Park
CH
COLESHILL RD
A4091
DRAYTON MANOR DR

4

01

Golf Course
Longwood Stables
Heathley Farm
HEATHLEY LA
Bullocks End Farm
Edden's Wood
EDDENS WOOD CL

3

Oak Farm
SHIRRAL DR
Stone House
DRAYTON LA
Heart of England Way
Drayton Bassett
OLD MANOR CL
MOAT DR
CHURCH CL
PEEL CL
NEW ROW
PO
Manor Cty Prim Sch
Sewage Works

00

Ashdene Farm
RECTORY CT
SALTS LA
Drayton Brick Bridge

PORTLEYS LA
Brook End Farm

Brook Farm

Birmingham and Fazeley Canal
Heart of England Way

2

Upper House Farm

99

Gallows Brook

COPPICE LA
Quarry
Mill Plantation

1

Middleton
SIMMONS CL
VICARAGE HILL
PO
The Green Man (PH)
Highfields Farm
CHURCH LA
Walker's Spinney
CROWBERRY LA
Sewage Works
Park-gate Farm
A4091
Middleton Park
Middleton Pool
Middleton Hall
Newhouse Farm

98

Langley Brook

17 A 18 B 19 C

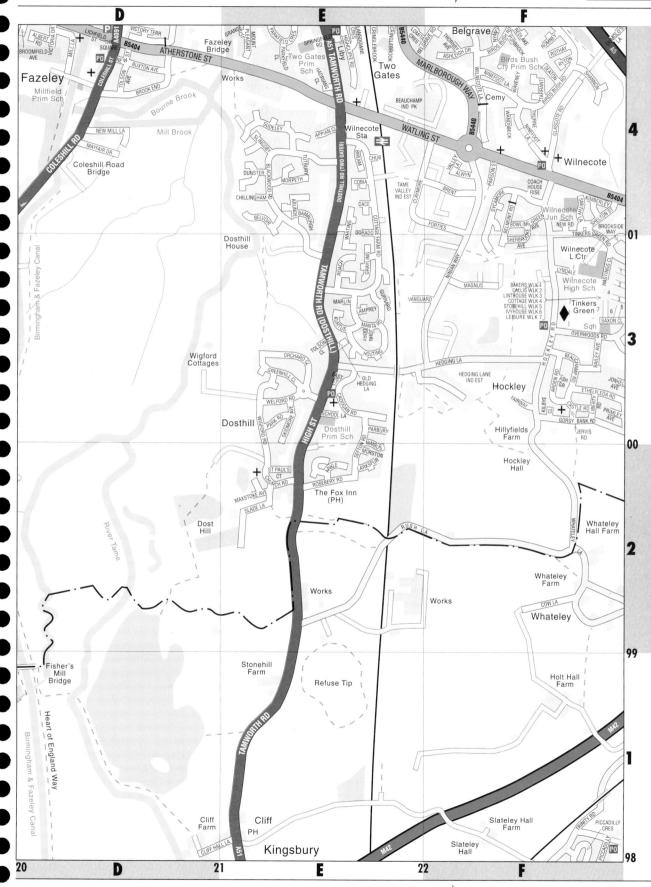

261
251

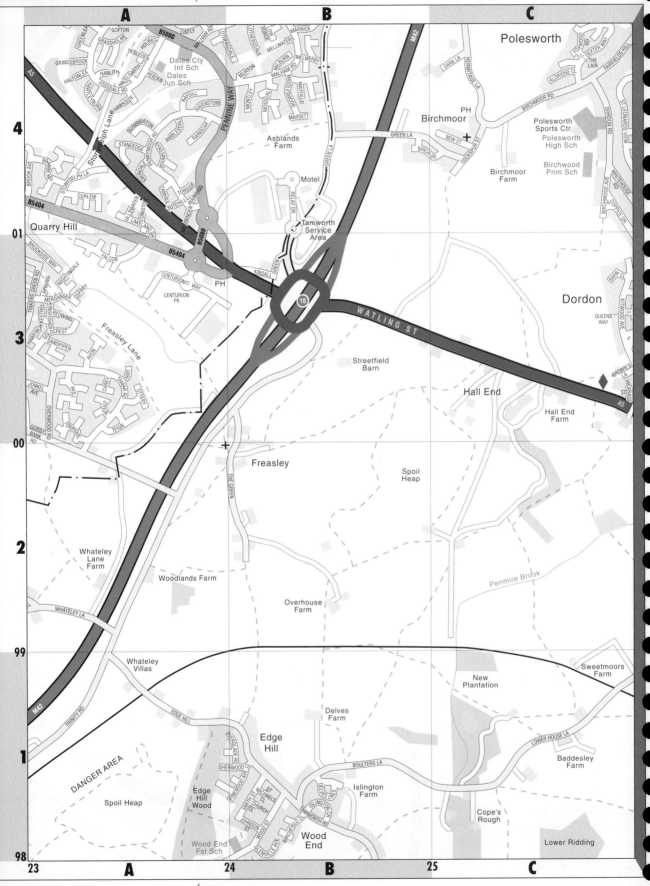

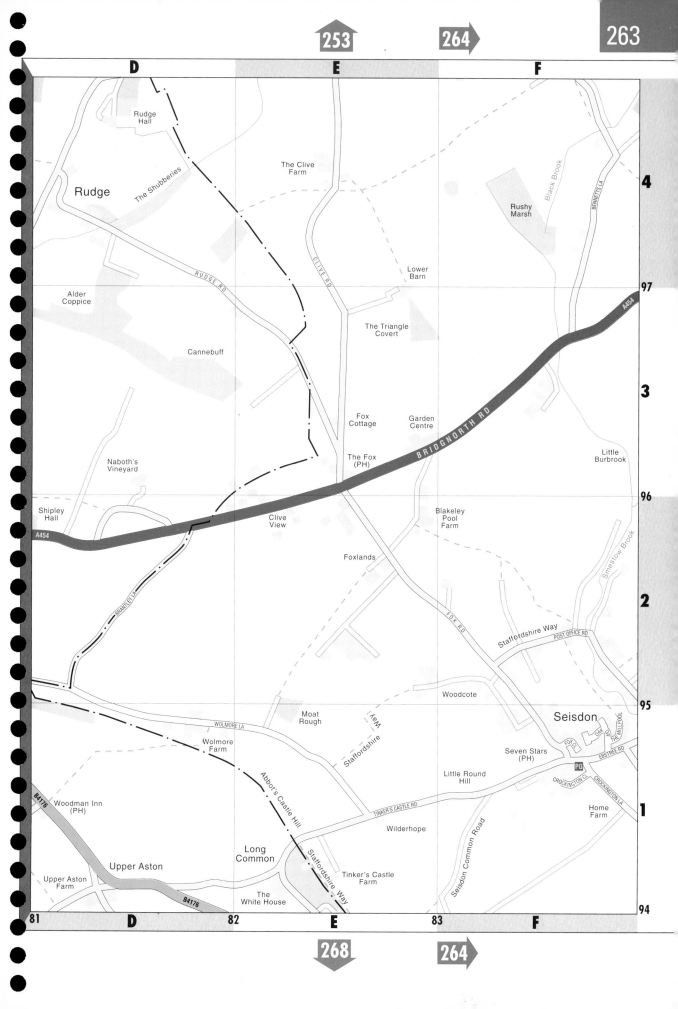

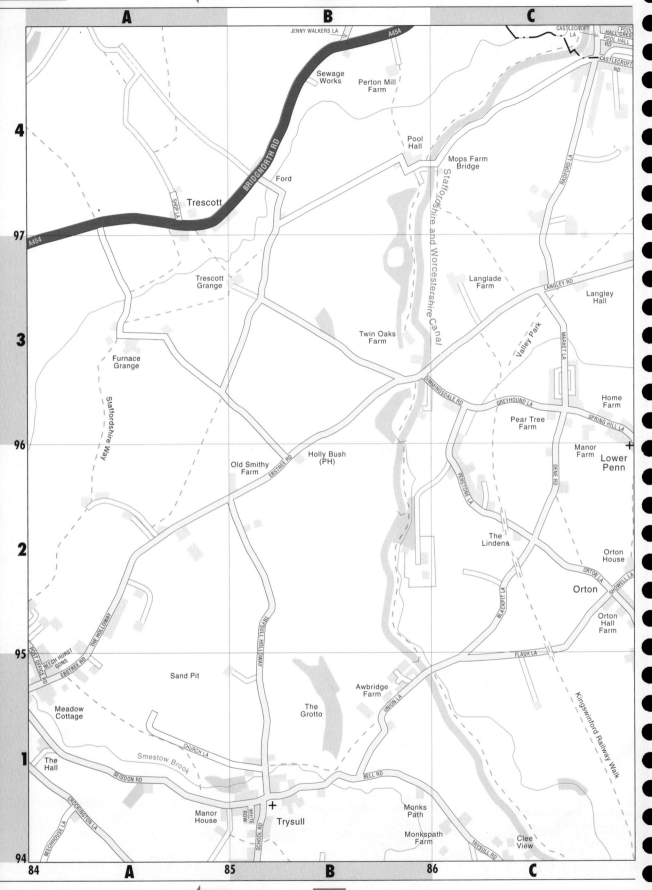

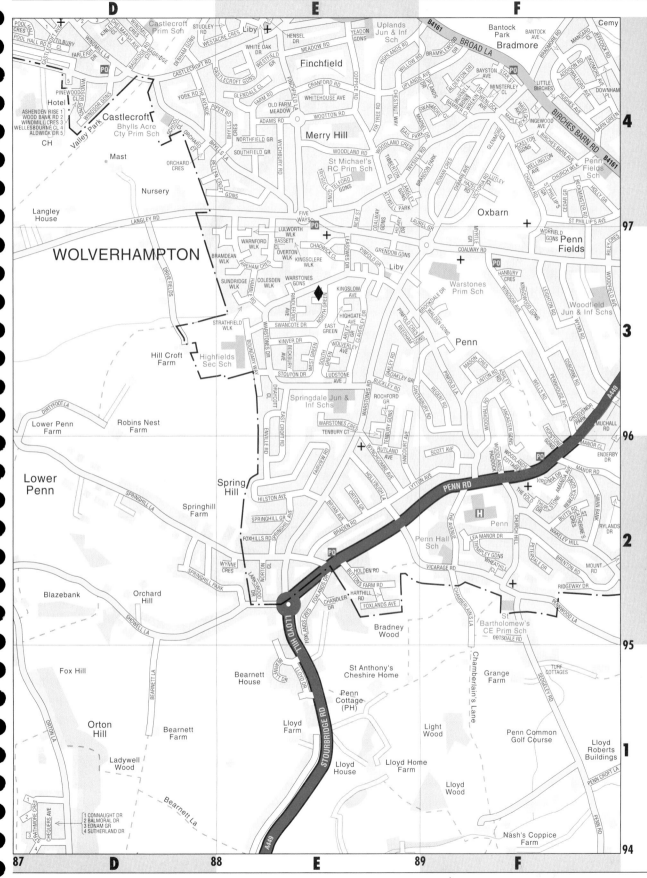

265

B4
1 PAUL ST
2 BLOOMSBURY ST
3 ST JOHNS RET PK
4 GORDON ST
5 GRANVILLE CL
6 LITTLE POUNTNEY ST
7 KING EDWARD'S ROW
8 STEVENS GATE
9 RAINBOW ST

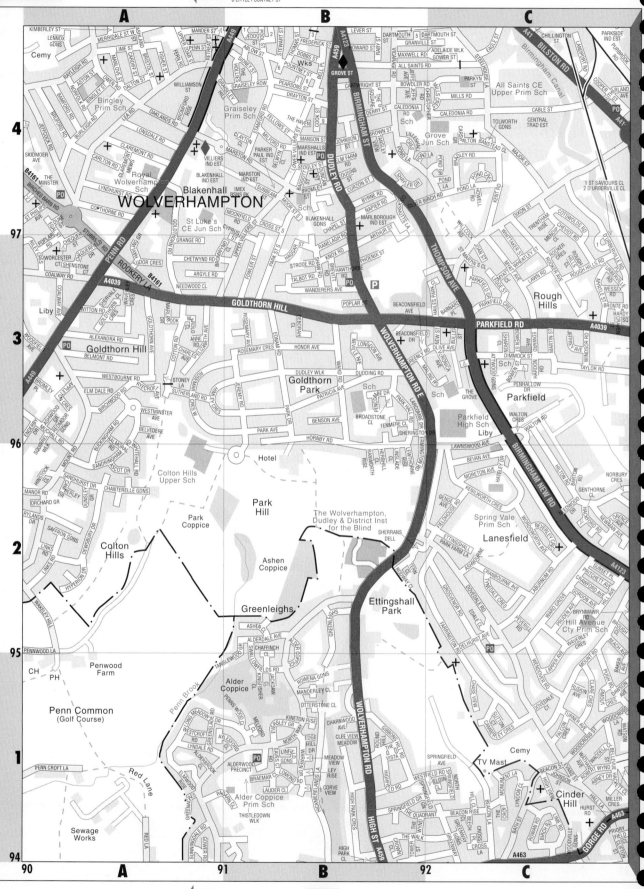

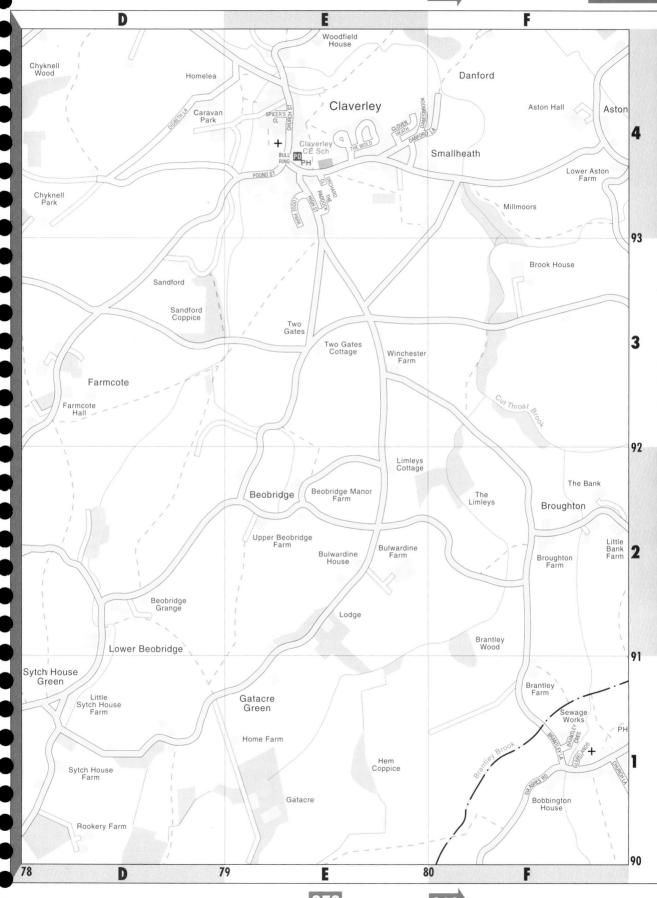

Chyknell Wood

Woodfield House

Danford

Homelea

Aston Hall

Aston

Digbeth La

Caravan Park

Spicer's Cl

Church St

Claverley

Clover Heath

Danessbrook

4

Smallheath

Claverley CE Sch

Danford La

Bull Ring

PO

PH

The Wold

Claverley CE Sch

Lower Aston Farm

Chyknell Park

Pound St

Lodge Park

The Paddock

Orchard

High St

Millmoors

93

Sandford

Brook House

Sandford Coppice

Two Gates

Two Gates Cottage

Winchester Farm

3

Farmcote

Cut Throat Brook

Farmcote Hall

92

Limleys Cottage

Beobridge

Beobridge Manor Farm

The Limleys

The Bank

Broughton

Upper Beobridge Farm

Bulwardine House

Bulwardine Farm

Little Bank Farm

2

Broughton Farm

Beobridge Grange

Lodge

Brantley Wood

Lower Beobridge

91

Sytch House Green

Brantley Farm

Little Sytch House Farm

Gatacre Green

Sewage Works

Brantley La

Brantley Cres

PH

Home Farm

Brantley Brook

Glebelands

1

Sytch House Farm

Hem Coppice

Sxashes Rd

Gatacre

Church La

Rookery Farm

Bobbington House

Church La

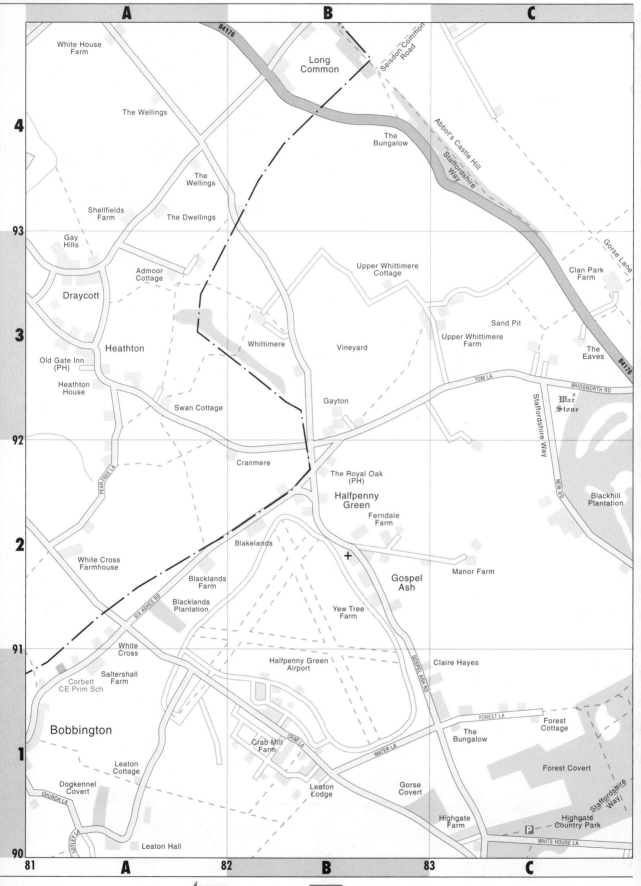

A B C

4

93

3

92

2

91

1

90

81 A 82 B 83 C

White House Farm

The Wellings

The Wellings

Shellfields Farm

The Dwellings

Gay Hills

Draycott

Admoor Cottage

Heathton

Old Gate Inn (PH)

Heathton House

Swan Cottage

Whittimere

Cranmere

PEAR TREE LA

White Cross Farmhouse

Blacklands Farm

Blacklands Plantation

SIX ASHES RD

White Cross

Saltershall Farm

Corbett CE Prim Sch

Bobbington

Leaton Cottage

Dogkennel Covert

CHURCH LA

UTLEY LA

Leaton Hall

B4176

Long Common

The Bungalow

Seisdon Common Road

Abbot's Castle Hill

Staffordshire Way

Upper Whittimere Cottage

Vineyard

Gayton

The Royal Oak (PH)

Halfpenny Green

Ferndale Farm

Blakelands

Yew Tree Farm

Halfpenny Green Airport

Crab Mill Farm

CRAB LA

Leaton Lodge

WATER LA

Gorse Covert

Gorse Lane

Clan Park Farm

Sand Pit

Upper Whittimere Farm

The Eaves

B4176

TOM LA

BRIDGNORTH RD

Staffordshire Way

War Stone

NEW RD

Blackhill Plantation

Gospel Ash

Manor Farm

GOSPEL ASH RD

Claire Hayes

FOREST LA

The Bungalow

Forest Cottage

Forest Covert

Staffordshire Way

Highgate Farm

Highgate Country Park

WHITE HOUSE LA

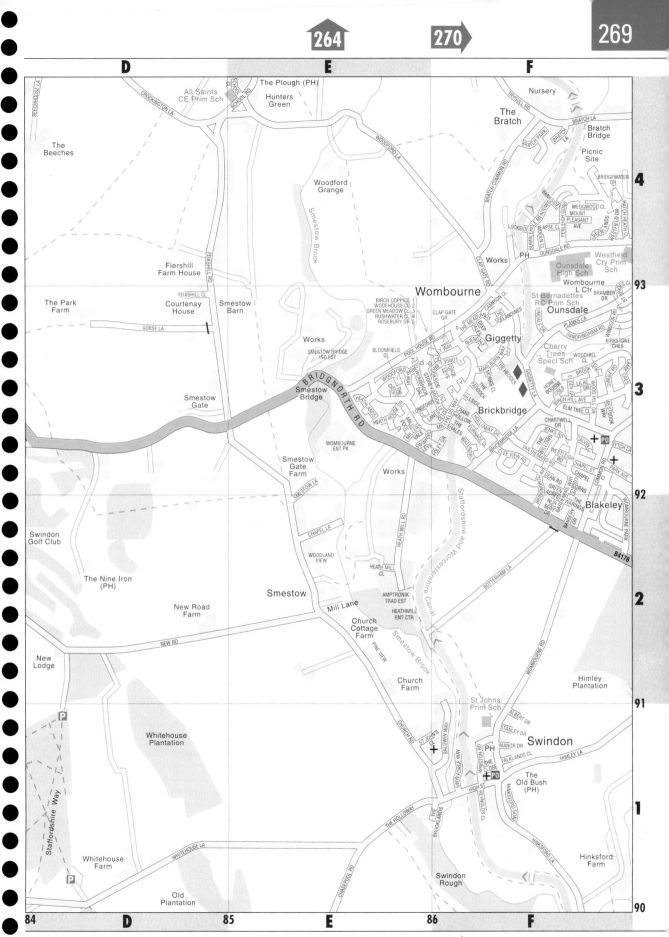

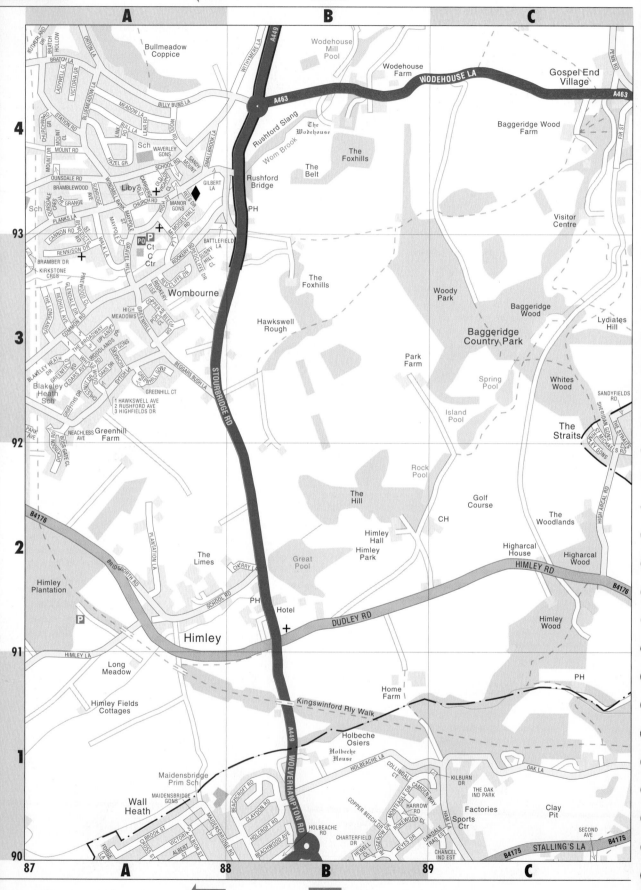

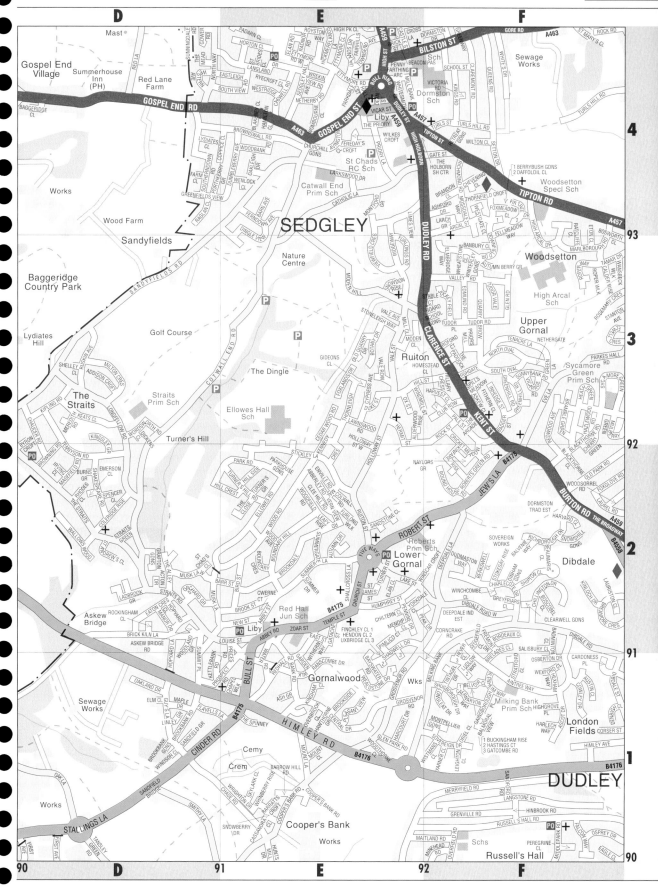

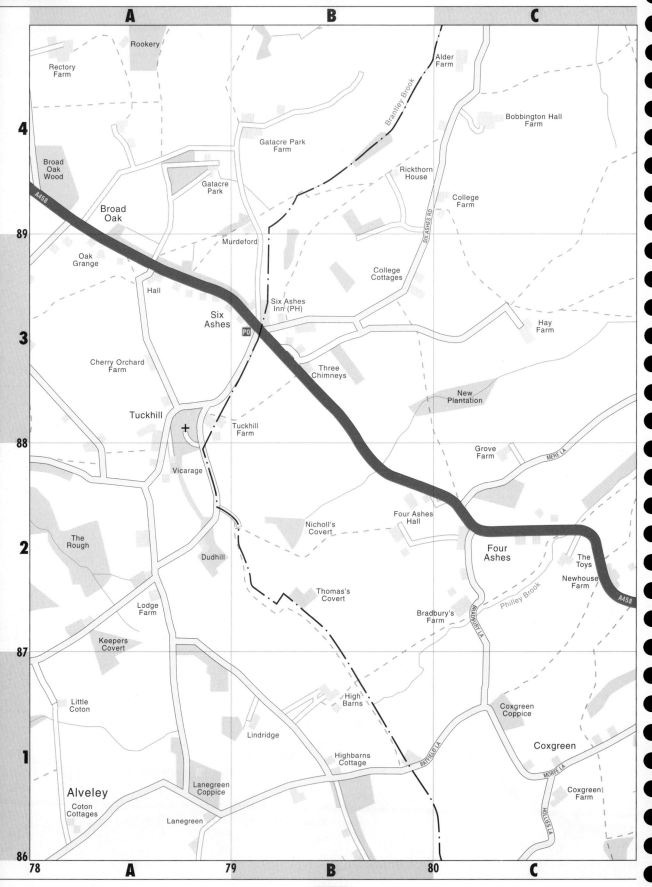

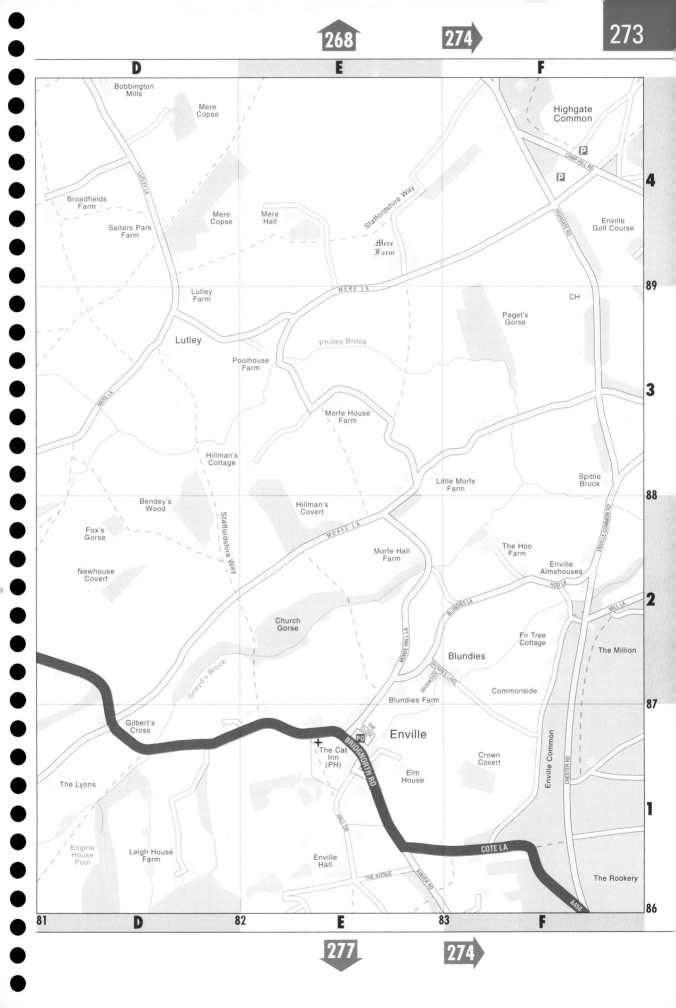

273
269

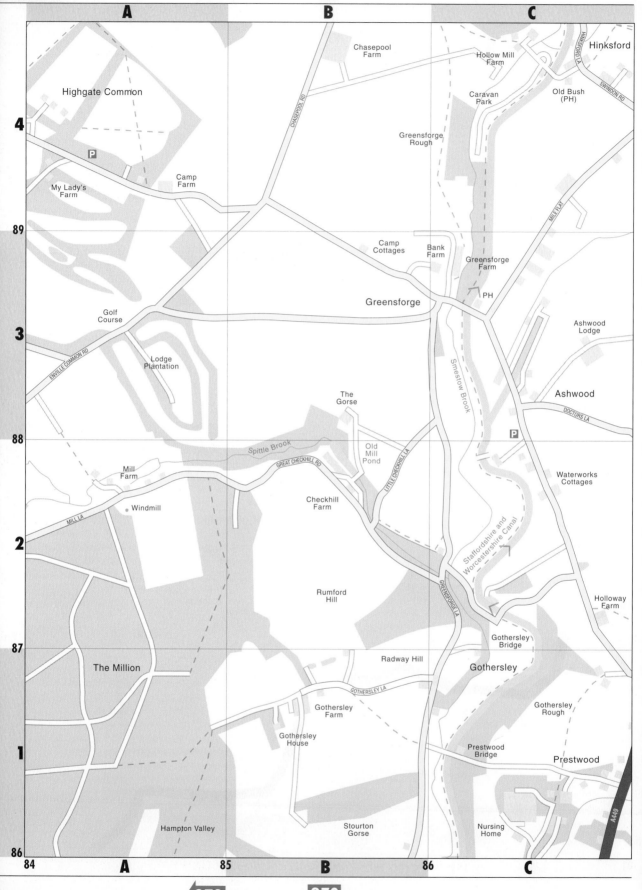

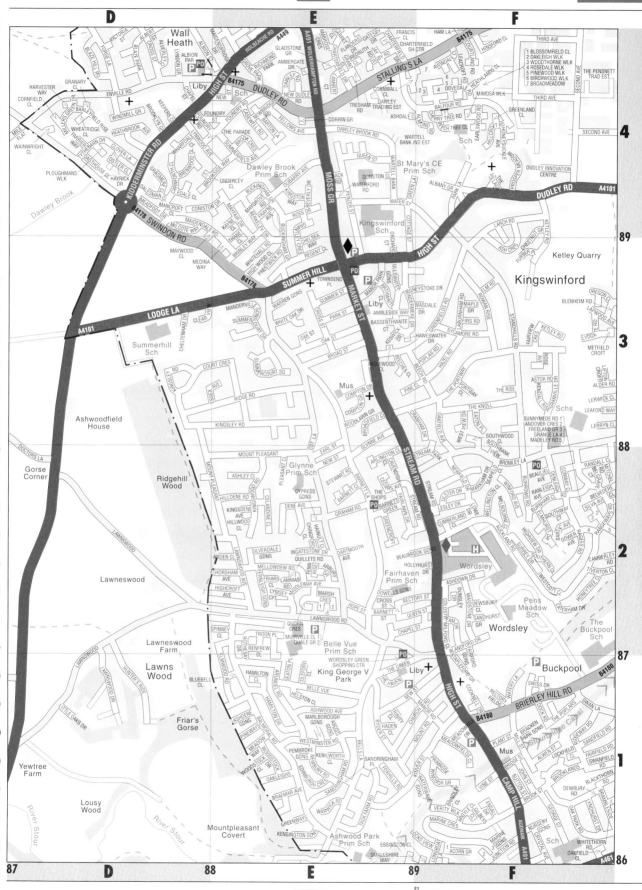

D E F

87 D 88 E 89 F 86

4

89

3

88

2

87

1

F1
1 GREENWAY AVE
2 DIAMOND PARK DR
3 SWEETBRIER DR

272

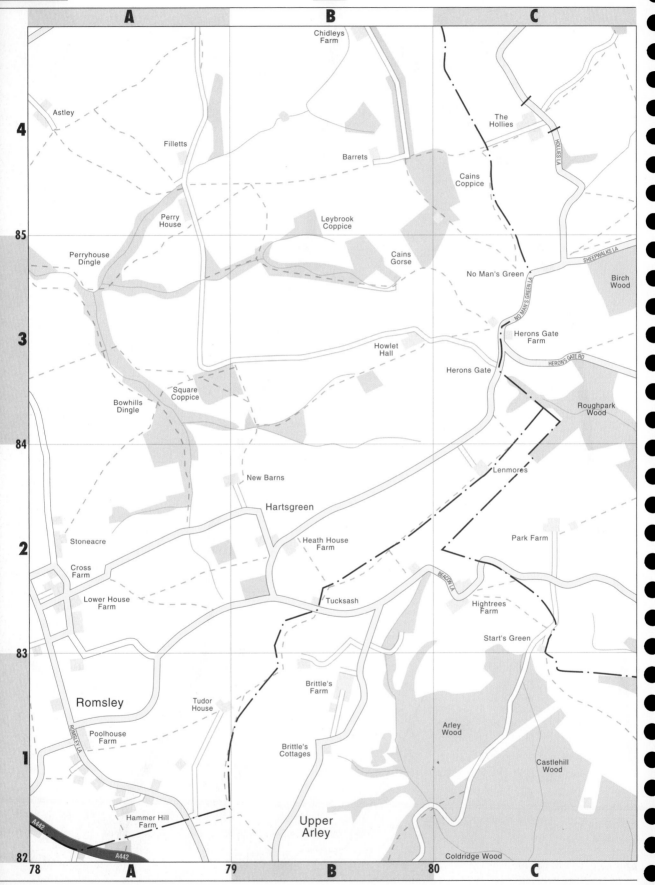

Chidleys Farm

Astley

Filletts

Barrets

The Hollies

HOLLIES LA

Cains Coppice

Perry House

Leybrook Coppice

85

Perryhouse Dingle

Cains Gorse

No Man's Green

SHEEPWALKS LA

Birch Wood

NO MAN'S GREEN LA

Howlet Hall

Herons Gate Farm

3

HERON'S GATE RD

Herons Gate

Square Coppice

Bowhills Dingle

Roughpark Wood

84

Lenmores

New Barns

Hartsgreen

2

Stoneacre

Heath House Farm

Park Farm

Cross Farm

BEACON LA

Lower House Farm

Tucksash

Hightrees Farm

Start's Green

83

Brittle's Farm

Romsley

Tudor House

ROMSLEY LA

Poolhouse Farm

Arley Wood

Brittle's Cottages

Castlehill Wood

1

A442

Hammer Hill Farm

Upper Arley

A442

Coldridge Wood

82

78   A   79   B   80   C

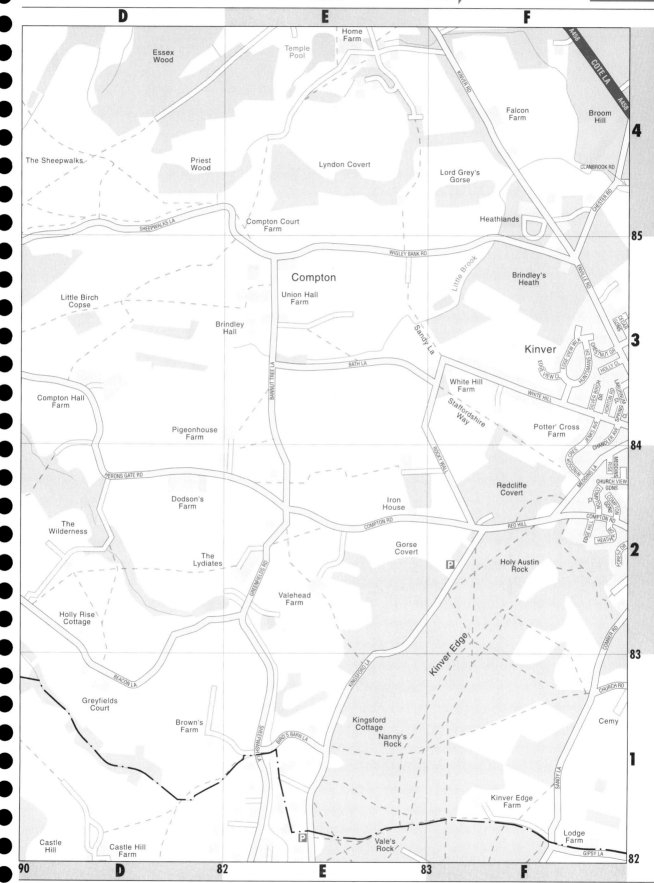

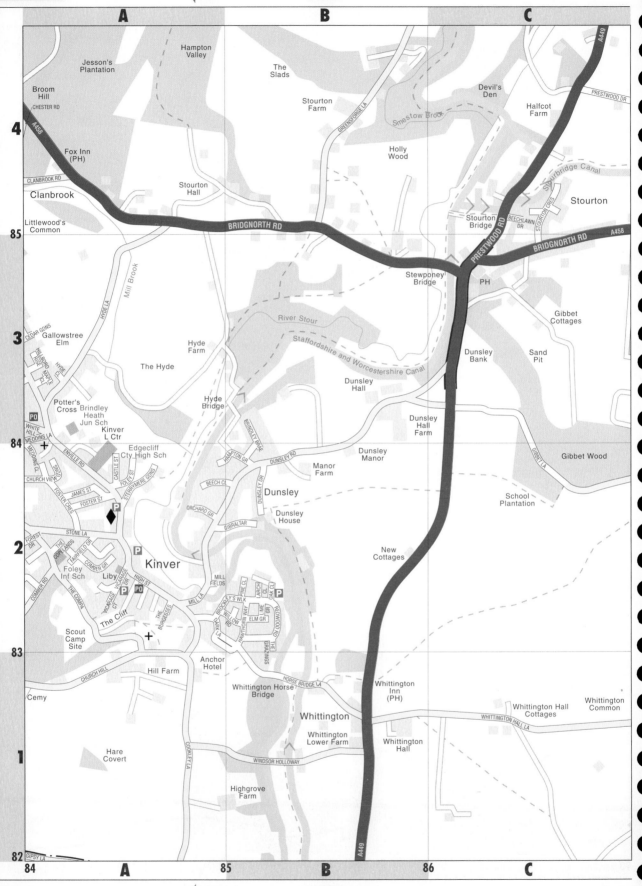

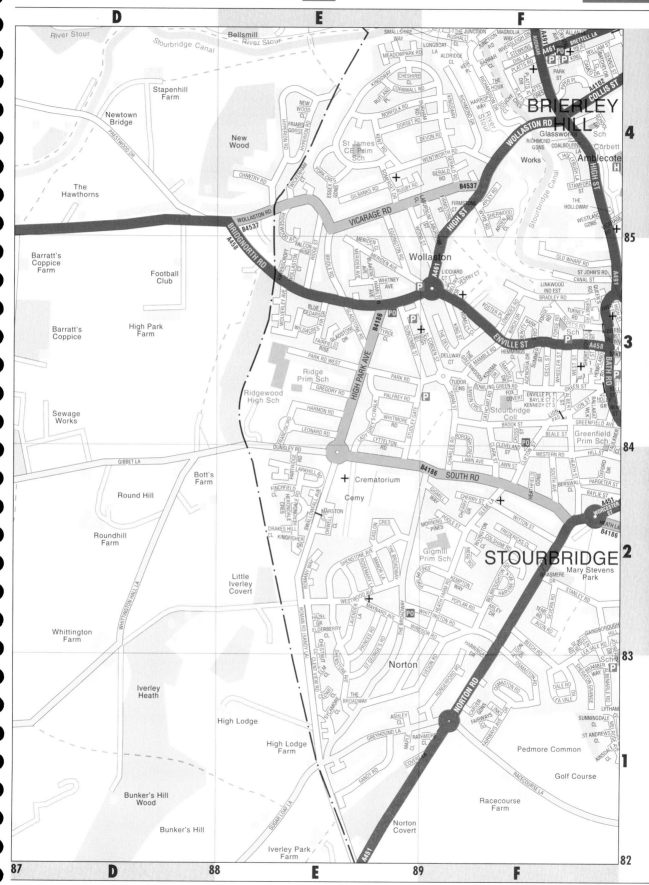

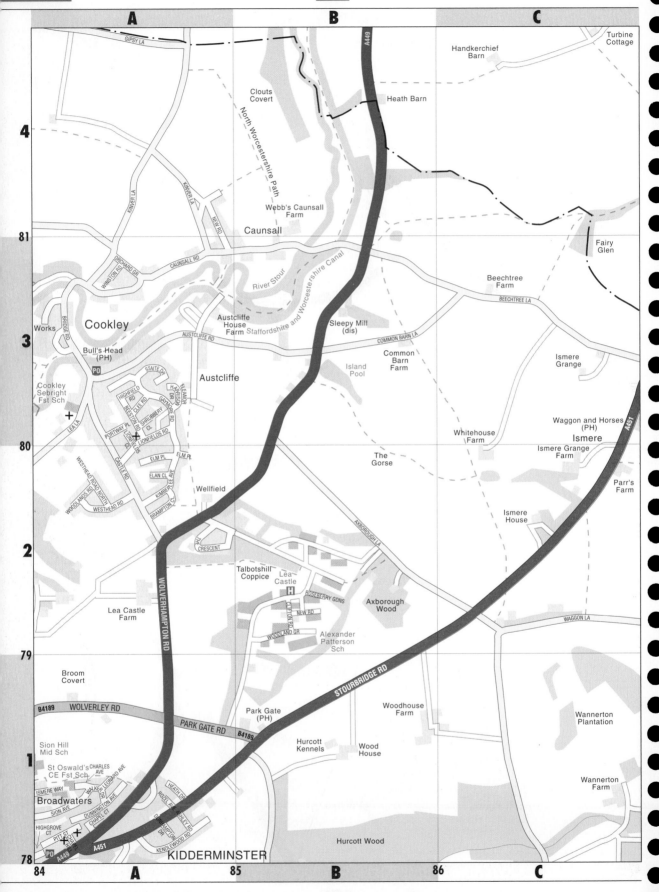

A B C

4

81

Caunsall

GIPSY LA

North Worcestershire Path

Clouts Covert

Heath Barn

Handkerchief Barn

Turbine Cottage

A449

Webb's Caunsall Farm

KINVER LA

KINVER LA

NEW RD

ORCHARD GR

WINSTON RD

CAUNSALL RD

Works

BRIDGE RD

Cookley

River Stour

Staffordshire and Worcestershire Canal

Austcliffe House Farm

AUSTCLIFFE RD

Sleepy Mill (dis)

COMMON BARN LA

Fairy Glen

Beechtree Farm

BEECHTREE LA

A451

3

Bull's Head (PH)

PO

Austcliffe

Common Barn Farm

Island Pool

Ismere Grange

Cookley Sebright Fst Sch

LEA LA

STAITE DR

ELEANOR

HIGHFIELD RD

HARRISON DR

CLEE RD

SHRUBBERY

GAYMORE RD

CL

RD

BELSTONE

PORTWAY PL

LIONFIELDS RD

LIONFIELDS

ELM PL

ELM PL

Whitehouse Farm

Waggon and Horses (PH)

Ismere

Ismere Grange Farm

80

CASTLE RD

KIMBERLEE AVE

ELAN CL LA

The Gorse

Parr's Farm

WESTHEAD ROAD NORTH

WOODLANDS RD

WESTHEAD RD

Wellfield

BRAMPTON

Ismere House

2

THE CRESCENT

Talbotshill Coppice

Lea Castle

H

ROSEBERY GDNS

AXBOROUGH LA

Axborough Wood

WOLVERHAMPTON RD

CLIFTON RD

NEW RD

WOODLAND GR

Alexander Patterson Sch

WAGGON LA

Lea Castle Farm

79

Broom Covert

STOURBRIDGE RD

B4189

WOLVERLEY RD

PARK GATE RD

B4189

Park Gate (PH)

Woodhouse Farm

Wannerton Plantation

Sion Hill Mid Sch

Hurcott Kennels

Wood House

1

St Oswald's CE Fst Sch

CHARLES AVE

WALKER DR

EDWARD AVE

Broadwaters

ISMERE WAY

SION AVE

HIGHGROVE CT

PITT ST

HEATH FM

ROZEL AV

ASHLEY RD

CHAPEL CT

DUNNINGTON AVE

KENDLEWOOD RD

Wannerton Farm

PO

A449

A451

Hurcott Wood

78

KIDDERMINSTER

84 A 85 B 86 C

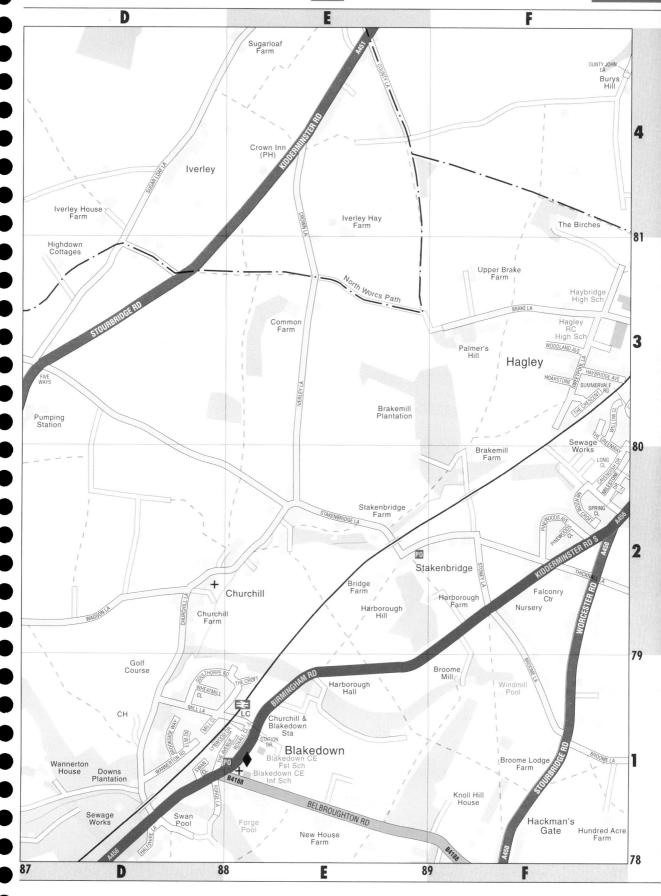

D   E   F

Sugarloaf Farm

A451

COUNTY LA

OUNTY JOHN LA

Burys Hill

4

Crown Inn (PH)

KIDDERMINSTER RD

Iverley

Iverley House Farm

CROWN LA

Iverley Hay Farm

The Birches

81

Highdown Cottages

North Worcs Path

Upper Brake Farm

Haybridge High Sch

STOURBRIDGE RD

BRAKE LA

Hagley RC High Sch

WOODLAND AVE

Common Farm

Palmer's Hill

Hagley

HOARSTONE

SWEETPOOL LA

HAYBRIDGE AVE

SUMMERVALE RD

3

FIVE WAYS

IVERLEY LA

Brakemill Plantation

THE CRESCENT

WILLOW CL

Pumping Station

Brakemill Farm

Sewage Works

THE GREENWAY

LONG CL

80

CAVENDISH DR

MILESTONE

MT PLEASANT

SPRING CL

A456

STAKENBRIDGE LA

Stakenbridge Farm

PINEWOODS AVE

PINEWOODS CL

KIDDERMINSTER RD S

2

PO

Stakenbridge

STONEY LA

Falconry Ctr Nursery

THICKNALL LA

WORCESTER RD

A50

Churchill

Bridge Farm

Harborough Hill

Harborough Farm

WAGGON LA

CHURCHILL LA

Churchill Farm

Golf Course

SOULTHORPE RD

THE CROFT

BIRMINGHAM RD

Broome Mill

BROOME LA

Windmill Pool

79

WHEATMILL CL

Harborough Hall

MILL LA

CH

BROOKSIDE WAY

WANNERTON RD

ELM DR

MILL CL

LYNWOOD DR

THE AVENUE

ROYAL CL

LC

Station DR

Churchill & Blakedown Sta

STATION DR

Blakedown

Broome Lodge Farm

BROOME LA

STOURBRIDGE RD

1

Wannerton House

Downs Plantation

SWAN CL

PO

B4188

Blakedown CE Fst Sch

Blakedown CE Inf Sch

Knoll Hill House

Hackman's Gate

Hundred Acre Farm

Sewage Works

Swan Pool

HALESHIRE LA

FORGE LA

Forge Pool

New House Farm

BELBROUGHTON RD

B4188

A50

A456

78

87   D   88   E   89   F

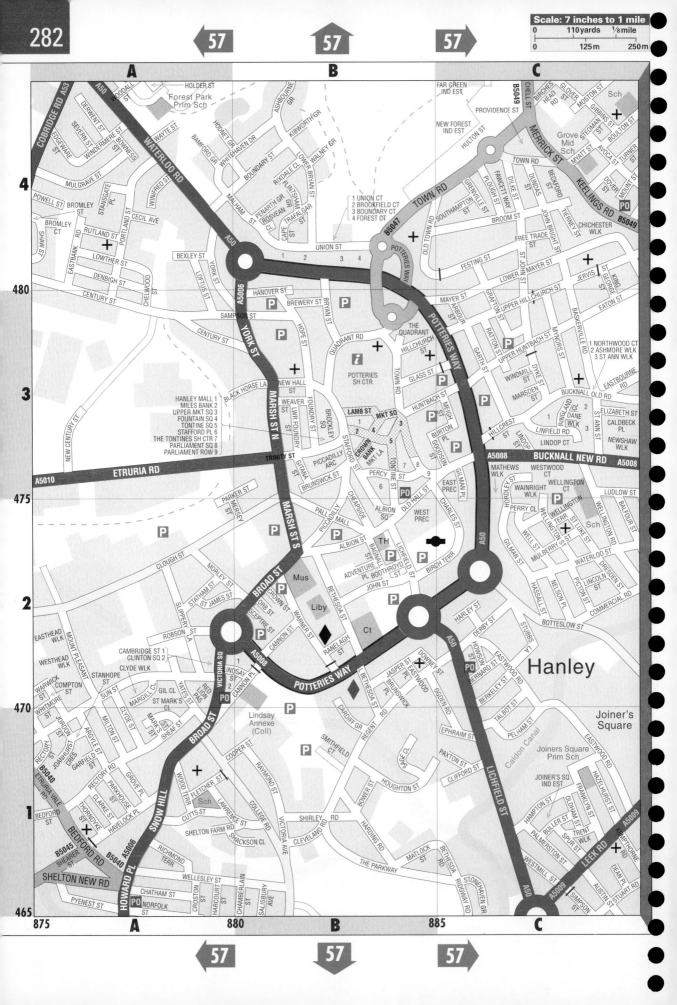

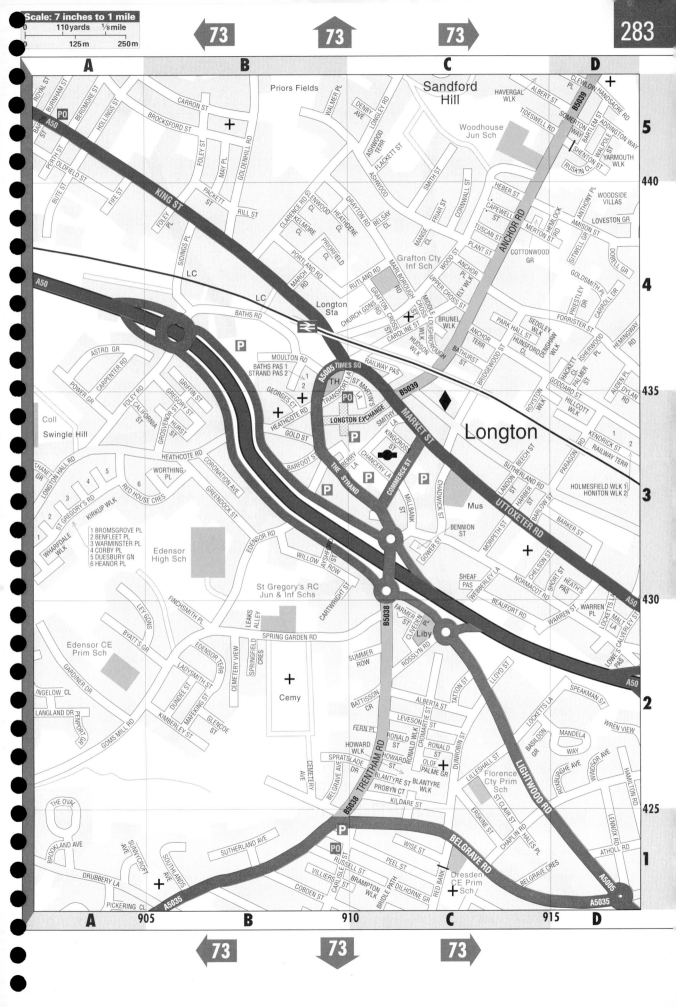

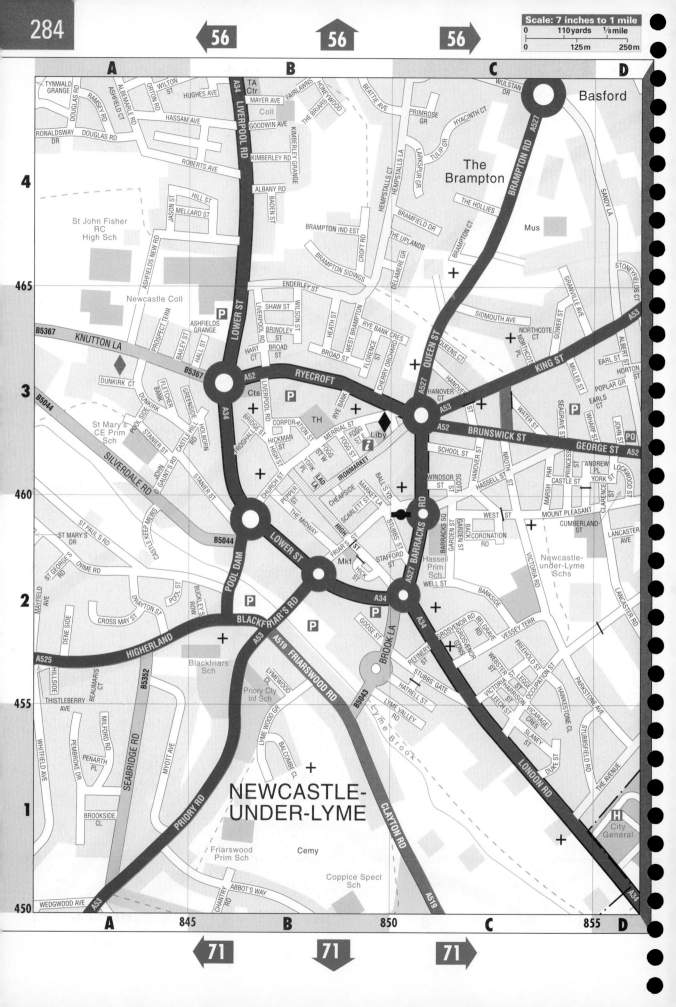

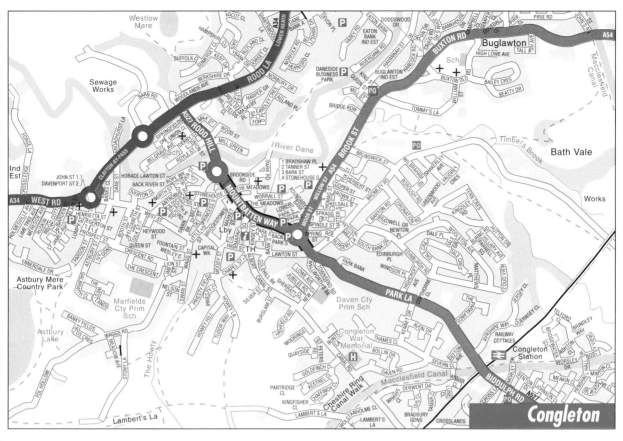

Congleton

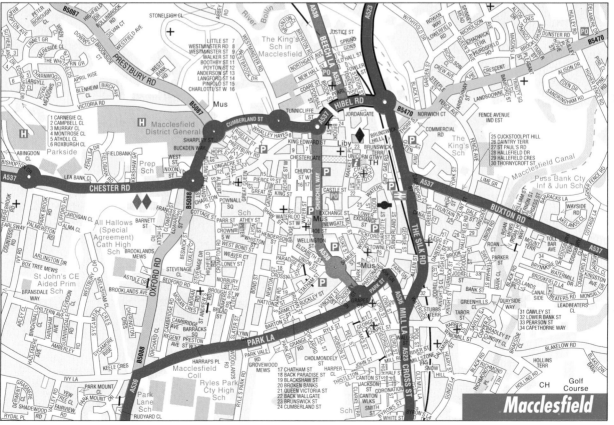

Macclesfield

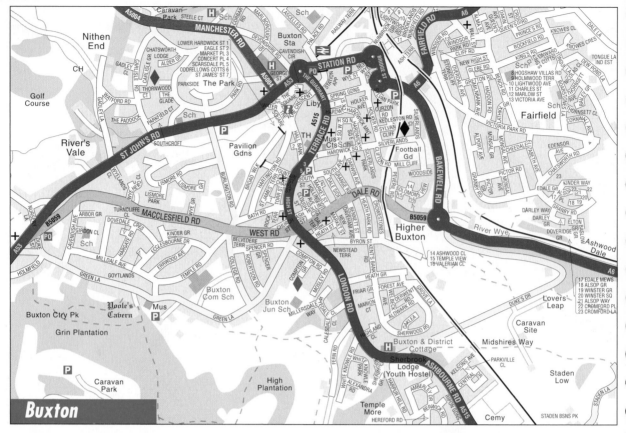

Buxton

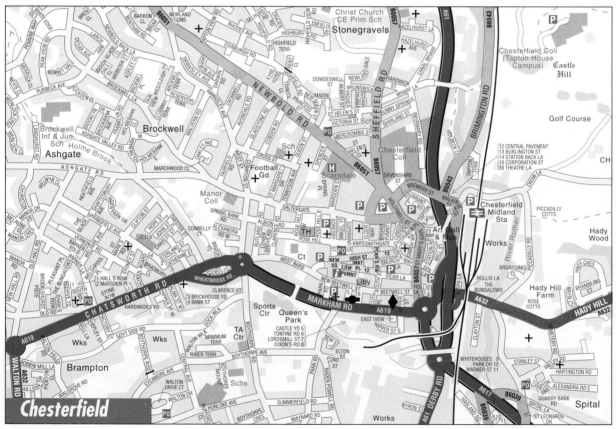

Chesterfield

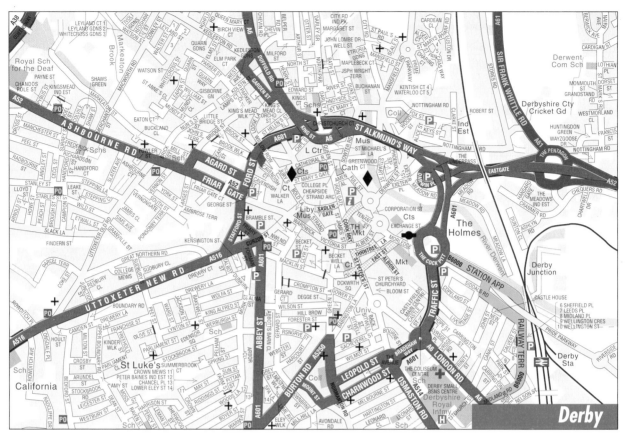

Derby

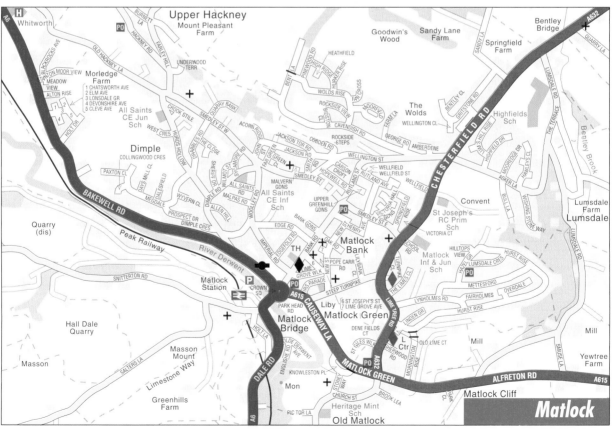

Matlock

Index

Street names are listed alphabetically and show the locality, the Postcode District, the page number and a reference to the square in which the name falls on the map page

Wedgwood St **17** Burslem ST6 .... **56** C4

Full street name
This may have been abbreviated on the map

Location Number
If present, this indicates the street's position on a congested area of the map instead of the name

Town, village or locality in which the street falls.

Postcode District for the street name

Page number of the map on which the street name appears

Grid square in which the centre of the street falls

Schools, hospitals, sports centres, railway stations, shopping centres, industrial estates, public amenities and other places of interest are also listed. These are highlighted in magenta

Abbreviations used in the index

App **Approach**	Comm **Common**	Est **Estate**	N **North**	Sq **Square**
Arc **Arcade**	Cnr **Corner**	Gdns **Gardens**	Orch **Orchard**	Strs **Stairs**
Ave **Avenue**	Cotts **Cottages**	Gn **Green**	Par **Parade**	Stps **Steps**
Bvd **Boulevard**	Ct **Court**	Gr **Grove**	Pk **Park**	St **Street, Saint**
Bldgs **Buildings**	Ctyd **Courtyard**	Hts **Heights**	Pas **Passage**	Terr **Terrace**
Bsns Pk **Business Park**	Cres **Crescent**	Ho **House**	Pl **Place**	Trad Est **Trading Estate**
Bsns Ctr **Business Centre**	Dr **Drive**	Ind Est **Industrial Estate**	Prec **Precinct**	Wlk **Walk**
Bglws **Bungalows**	Dro **Drove**	Intc **Interchange**	Prom **Promenade**	W **West**
Cswy **Causeway**	E **East**	Junc **Junction**	Ret Pk **Retail Park**	Wolv **Wolverhampton**
Ctr **Centre**	Emb **Embankment**	La **Lane**	Rd **Road**	Yd **Yard**
Cir **Circus**	Ent **Enterprise**	Mans **Mansions**	Rdbt **Roundabout**	
Cl **Close**	Espl **Esplanade**	Mdws **Meadows**	S **South**	

Town and village index

Abbots Bromley 161 E3	Cheddleton 45 E2	Fradswell 123 D1	Mappleton 66 C4	Standon 102 B2
Acton Trussell 175 D1	Chell Heath 42 A1	Gayton 138 C3	Marchington 127 F1	Stanton 65 D1
Adbaston 131 E3	Chelmorton 5 D4	Gnosall 171 E4	Market Drayton 97 E1	Stoke-on-Trent 72 A3
Albrighton 237 D3	Cheslyn Hay 226 B1	Great Wyrley 227 D1	Marston 136 C1	Stone 120 A4
Aldridge 256 A3	Cheswardine 130 A4	Grindon 34 A1	Marston Montgomery 96 C1	Stourbridge 279 F3
Allen End 259 D1	Chetwynd 168 C2	Hademore 233 D4	Marston on Dove 147 D4	Stramshall 111 D2
Alrewas 200 C2	Chetwynd Aston 187 D4	Hagley 281 F3	Mayfield 81 E4	Streethay 215 D1
Alsager 39 E4	Chilcote 219 F2	Hamstall Ridware 180 C2	Meir 74 A3	Sudbury 128 A4
Alsop en le Dale 36 C3	Church Broughton 129 F4	Hanbury 145 D1	Middleton 260 B1	Sutton 112 C3
Alstonefield 35 D1	Church Eaton 190 A4	Hanley 57 F4	Millmeece 117 F4	Sutton Coldfield 258 A1
Alton 78 C1	Church Leigh 109 D2	Hanley 282 B3	Milwich 122 B3	Swadlincote 186 C3
Alveley 272 B1	Claverley 267 E4	Harlaston 217 E1	Monyash 14 C4	Swindon 269 F1
Anslow 165 D3	Clifton 81 F3	Hartington 24 B3	Mow Cop 15 F1	Swinscoe 65 E2
Appleby Magna 236 C4	Clifton Campville 218 C1	Hatton 146 B4	Mucklestone 99 D3	Swynnerton 103 E2
Armitage 198 B2	Codsall 238 C1	Haughton 172 C1	Netherseal 219 F3	Tamworth 250 B2
Ashbourne 66 B2	Colton 179 D2	Heathylee 11 A3	Newborough 162 C4	Tatenhill 165 D1
Ashley 100 A3	Colwich 177 E4	Heaton 8 C1	Newcastle-under-Lyme .. 71 D3	The Bank 26 A4
Astbury 15 E4	Congleton 6 C2	Hilderstone 106 B1	Newcastle-under-Lyme .. 284 A1	Thorncliffe 20 C3
Audley 39 F1	Consall 60 A3	Hill Ridware 198 A4	Newport 168 C1	Thorpe 51 E1
Bagnall 43 F2	Cookley 280 B2	Hilton 147 F4	Newton Regis 236 C3	Thorpe Constantine 235 D2
Barlaston 88 C2	Coppenhall 174 B2	Himley 270 C3	Newton Solney 167 F4	Tissington 51 E3
Barthomley 38 C3	Cotton 78 B4	Hints 248 B1	Norbury 151 D3	Tittensor 88 A1
Barton Turn 184 A1	Crewe 37 D4	Hixon 158 B4	Norton Canes 227 F2	Tixall 157 D3
Barton-under-	Croxden 94 D4	Hollinsclough 4 B1	Norton-in-the-Moors 42 C2	Tong 220 B2
Needwood 183 E1	Denstone 95 F3	Hopton 137 E1	Oakamoor 78 C2	Trentham 88 A4
Betley 53 D4	Dilhorne 75 E2	Hopwas 249 D4	Onecote 32 B2	Tunstall 41 E3
Biddulph 27 D4	Dordon 262 C3	Hough Common 37 D1	Pattingham 253 E1	Tutbury 146 B3
Blakedown 281 D1	Doveridge 127 D4	Huntington 209 E4	Penkridge 192 C1	Upper Arley 276 B2
Blakenhall 52 B2	Draycott in the Clay 144 B4	Ilam 50 C1	Perton 254 C2	Upper Tean 92 C2
Blore 99 D2	Draycott in the Moors 91 F3	Ingestre 157 E3	Polesworth 262 C4	Uttoxeter 126 A4
Blymhill 203 F3	Drayton Bassett 260 A4	Ipstones 62 A4	Ranton 153 D2	Wall 230 A1
Blythe Bridge 90 B4	Dudley 271 F2	Keele 69 F4	Repton 148 C1	Walsall 243 E1
Bobbington 268 A1	Dunstall 183 F2	Kidderminster 280 A1	Rocester 96 A2	Walton-on-Trent 184 B1
Boscobel 221 E1	Earl Sterndale 5 D2	Kidsgrove 26 B2	Rolleston 147 D2	Warslow 23 E1
Bosley 7 F3	Eaton 6 A4	King Sterndale 5 C1	Romsley 276 C2	Waterhouses 49 F1
Bradley 191 D4	Eccleshall 133 F3	King's Bromley 199 F3	Roslisten 185 E2	Weeford 248 A2
Bradnop 31 F2	Edgmond 168 A2	Kingsbury 261 D1	Roston 96 C4	Weston 37 D3
Branston 184 C4	Edingale 217 E3	Kingsley 61 E1	Rudge 263 D4	Weston upon Trent 138 C1
Bretby 167 F1	Eggington 148 B3	Kingstone 141 E4	Rudyard 29 D3	Weston-under-Lizard 203 B4
Brewood 223 E3	Elford 216 C1	Kingswinford 275 F4	Rugeley 196 C4	Wetton 34 C1
Bridgemere 67 D2	Ellastone 80 A2	Kinver 278 A3	Rugeley 196 C4	Wheaton Aston 205 E3
Brierley Hill 279 F4	Ellenhall 134 A1	Lawton-gate 25 D3	Salt 137 F1	Whitgreave 135 F4
Brocton 176 B2	Elmhurst 214 A3	Leek 30 B4	Sandon 137 E4	Whitmore 86 A2
Brownhills 245 D3	Endon 43 F3	Lichfield 231 F4	Scholar Green 25 F4	Whittington 232 C3
Bucknall 58 A3	Enville 273 F2	Linton 186 B1	Scropton 129 D3	Wigginton 234 A1
Buerton 82 A4	Essington 241 D1	Little Aston 257 D2	Seckington 236 A1	Wildboarclough 1 C4
Burntwood 229 E3	Etwall 148 B1	Longdon 197 E1	Sedgley 271 F2	Willington 148 C4
Burslem 56 A4	Farewell 213 E2	Longford 168 B1	Seighford 154 C2	Wincle 9 A3
Burton Upon Trent 166 C1	Fawfieldhead 12 C2	Longnor 13 D4	Seisdon 263 D2	Wolverhampton 255 D1
Butterton 33 F3	Fazeley 260 A4	Longsdon 29 F3	Shareshill 225 E1	Wombourne 269 E2
Buxton 4 A4	Featherstone 241 D4	Longton 73 D1	Shavington 37 D3	Woodcote 187 F2
Cannock 209 F3	Fenton 72 C3	Longton 283 B2	Sheen 24 A4	Woodhouse Green 7 E4
Caverswall 74 C1	Flash 3 D2	Lower Penn 265 D3	Shenstone 247 D3	Woodseaves 151 E4
Chapel Chorlton 102 B3	Forsbrook 91 D3	Lullington 218 B4	Shuttington 251 F4	Woore 67 F1
Cheadle 76 C1	Forton 169 F4	Madeley 68 B4	Snelston 81 E2	Wootton 79 F3
Chebsey 134 C3	Foston 129 E4	Maer 85 D2	Stafford 155 F3	Yoxall 182 A1

Aarons Dr ST7 .... 39 F1
Abberley Rd DY3 .... 271 E2
Abbey Arc DE14 .... 166 C1
Abbey Ct ST19 .... 208 A4
Abbey Ct Bucknall ST2 ..... 58 A3
 Newport TF10 .... 168 C1
Abbey Dr Brownhills WS3 .. 244 A3
 Colwich ST18 .... 177 E4
Abbey Green Rd ST13 .... 30 B4
Abbey Hill Specl Sch ST2 .. 58 B3
Abbey Hulton Prim Sch
 ST2 .... 58 A3
Abbey La ST2 .... 58 A3
Abbey Prim Sch WS3 ...... 242 C1
Abbey Rd Bucknall ST2 ..... 58 A3
 Consall ST9 .... 60 A3
 Sedgley DY3 .... 271 E2
 Tamworth B77 .... 250 B2
Abbey Sq WS3 .... 242 C1
Abbey St Bucknall ST2 ...... 58 A3
 Burton u T DE14 .... 166 B1
 Cannock WS12 .... 210 A4
 Newcastle-u-L ST5 .... 55 E1
 Sedgley DY3 .... 271 E2
 Stone ST15 .... 120 A4
Abbey Way TF9 .... 97 E1
Abbeyfield Rd WV10 .... 240 C2
Abbeyfields ST18 .... 158 A1
Abbeyside ST18 .... 153 E3
Abbot Beyne Sch The
 DE15 .... 167 D2
Abbot's Rd ST13 .... 31 D4
Abbot's Way ST5 .... 71 D3
Abbots Field WS11 .... 209 F1
Abbots Pl ST2 .... 58 A3
Abbots Rd ST2 .... 58 A3
Abbots Way WV3 .... 255 F1
Abbots Wlk Rugeley WS15 . 197 D3
 Stafford ST16 .... 155 F3
Abbotsford Rd WS14 .... 231 F4
Abbotsholme Sch ST14 ..... 96 A1
Abbott's Cl CW12 .... 16 A4
Abbotts Ct ST2 .... 58 A4
Abbotts Dr ST1 .... 57 F4
Abbotts Pl WS3 .... 243 E1
Abbotts Rd WS3 .... 243 E1
Abelia B77 .... 250 C2
Aberford Gr ST1 .... 57 F3
Abingdon Rd WS3 .... 242 C1
Abingdon Way
 Trentham ST4 .... 88 A4
 Walsall WS3 .... 242 C1
Ablon Ct ST19 .... 207 F4
Ablow St WV2 .... 266 B4
Abnalls Croft WS13 .... 213 F1
Abnalls La
 Burntwood WS13 .... 213 F1
 Lichfield WS13 .... 213 F1
Abney Dr WV14 .... 266 C1
Acacia Ave ST5 .... 55 F1
Acacia Cres WV8 .... 239 D2
Acacia Gdns ST4 .... 26 B2
Acacia Gr Cannock WS12 .. 210 C2
 Newcastle-u-L ST5 .... 55 F1
Achilles Cl WS6 .... 226 C1
Achilles Way ST7 .... 57 F1
Ackelton Gdns WV3 .... 265 F4
Acorn Cl Ashley TF9 .... 99 E3
 Burntwood WS7 .... 212 A4
 Cannock WS11 .... 210 B1
 Great Wyrley WS6 .... 227 D1
Acorn Gr Brierley Hill DY8 . 275 F1
 Codsall WV8 .... 238 C1
Acorn La CW12 .... 6 C2
Acorn Rd WV11 .... 242 A1
Acorn Rise ST3 .... 89 F4
Acorn Starter Units WS7 .. 228 B4
Acres Nook Rd ST7 .... 41 D3
Acreswood Rd ST6 .... 42 A1
Acton Dr DY3 .... 271 D2
Acton Hill Rd ST17 .... 175 E4
Acton St ST1 .... 57 E3
Adam St WS11 .... 209 E1
Adams Ave ST6 .... 41 E3
Adams Cl TF10 .... 168 C1
Adams Cres TF10 .... 168 C1
Adams Gr ST13 .... 30 B2
Adams Gram Sch TF10 .... 168 C2
Adams Rd Brownhills WS8 . 245 D3
 Wolv WV3 .... 265 F4
Adams St ST5 .... 56 B2
Adamson Cl WS11 .... 209 D1
Adamthwaite Cl ST11 .... 90 B4
Adamthwaite Dr ST11 .... 90 B4
Adbaston Cty Inf Sch ST20 131 E3
Adderley Green
 Cty Inf Sch ST3 .... 73 C1
Adderley Pl ST12 .... 88 C2
Adderley Rd
 Market Drayton TF9 .... 97 D2
 Norton-in-t-M ST8 .... 42 C2
Adderley Road Ind Est
 TF9 .... 97 E1
Addie Rd DE13 .... 166 A3
Addington Way ST3 .... 283 D5
Addison Cl WS11 .... 209 F1
Addison Croft DY3 .... 271 D3
Addison Gr WV11 .... 241 D1
Addison Rd WV3 .... 265 F4
Addison St ST1 .... 57 E3
Adelaide Cres DE15 .... 167 D4
Adelaide St ST6 .... 57 D4
Adelaide Wlk WV2 .... 266 C4
Adkins St ST6 .... 57 E4
Admiral Parker Dr WS14 .. 246 C3
Adonis Cl B79 .... 250 B4
Adrian St ST4 .... 72 C3
Advance Bsns Pk WS11 ... 210 A2

Adventure Pl ST1 .... 282 B2
Adwalton Rd WV6 .... 254 C2
Aegean Cl ST4 .... 88 B4
Aelfgar Sixth Form Ctr
 WS15 .... 178 C1
Affleck Ave B78 .... 249 E1
Agenoria Dr DY8 .... 279 F3
Agger Hill ST5 .... 54 B1
Ainsdale Cl 3 Meir ST3 ...... 73 E1
 Stourbridge DY8 .... 279 F1
Ainsworth Ave ST10 .... 61 E1
Ainsworth Rd WV10 .... 240 C2
Ainsworth St ST4 .... 72 B3
Aintree Cl Branston DE14 . 185 D4
 Cannock WS12 .... 210 C3
 Trentham ST4 .... 88 A4
Aintree Rd Upper Tean ST10 . 92 C2
 Wolv WV10 .... 240 C3
Aintree Way DY1 .... 271 F1
Airdale Gr ST15 .... 105 D1
Airedale Rd ST15 .... 105 D1
Airedale Spinney ST15 .... 105 D1
Aitken Cl B78 .... 250 A1
Aitken St ST6 .... 56 C4
Ajax Cl WS6 .... 226 C1
Ajax Way ST7 .... 57 F1
Akdene Cl Meir ST3 .... 90 B4
Akesmoor La ST8 .... 27 D4
Alan Rd ST2 .... 58 B2
Alanbrooke Gr ST3 .... 89 F4
Alandale Ave WS15 .... 198 B2
Alanley Cl ST6 .... 42 B1
Alastair Rd ST4 .... 71 F2
Albany Dr WS15 .... 178 B2
Albany Gr
 Kingswinford DY6 .... 275 F4
 Stoke-on-T ST4 .... 71 E4
 Walsall WV12 .... 242 B1
Albany Rd
 Newcastle-u-L ST5 .... 284 B4
 Stoke-on-T ST4 .... 71 E4
Albany St ST6 .... 41 E4
Albemarle Rd
 Newcastle-u-L ST5 .... 56 A2
 Stourbridge DY8 .... 279 F1
Albert Ave ST3 .... 73 F2
Albert Cl WV8 .... 238 C2
Albert Davies Dr WS12 ... 210 C2
Albert Dr DY3 .... 269 F1
Albert Pl ST3 .... 73 D1
Albert Rd Fazeley B78 ..... 261 D4
 Tamworth B79 .... 250 A3
 Trentham ST4 .... 88 A3
 Wolv WV6, WV7 .... 255 F2
Albert St Audley ST7 .... 39 F2
 Biddulph ST8 .... 27 E4
 Burton u T DE14 .... 166 B2
 Cannock, Chadsmoor WS11 . 209 F2
 Cannock, Church Hill WS12 . 210 B3
 Kingswinford DY6 .... 275 D4
 Leek ST13 .... 30 C3
 Longton ST3 .... 283 C5
 Newcastle-u-L ST5 .... 284 D3
 Newcastle-u-L, Chesterton
 ST5 .... 55 F4
 Newcastle-u-L, Silverdale ST5 . 55 D1
 Stone ST15 .... 105 D1
 Stourbridge DY8 .... 279 F1
Albert Terr
 Newcastle-u-L ST5 .... 56 B3
 Stafford ST16 .... 155 F3
Alberta St ST3 .... 283 C2
Albion Par WS12 .... 210 C3
Albion Pl WS11 .... 209 D2
Albion Rd WS8 .... 244 C4
Albion Sq ST1 .... 282 B2
Albion St Hanley ST1 .... 282 B2
 Kingswinford DY6 .... 275 D4
 Leek ST13 .... 30 C3
 Rugeley WS15 .... 178 C1
 Tamworth B79 .... 250 B3
Albion Terr DE14 .... 166 C3
Albion Way WS7 .... 211 F1
Albrighton By Pass WV7 .. 237 D2
Albrighton Cty Jun
 & Inf Schs WV7 .... 237 D2
Albrighton Sta WV7 .... 237 D3
Albutts Rd Brownhills WS11 . 228 A2
 Norton Canes WS11 .... 228 A2
Alcester Cl ST6 .... 42 A3
Alcove The WS3 .... 243 E1
Aldbury Cl ST16 .... 136 B1
Aldbury Pl ST3 .... 72 C1
Aldeburgh Dr ST3 .... 243 D2
Alden Hurst WS7 .... 228 C4
Alder Cl Ashley TF9 .... 99 E3
 Kidsgrove ST7 .... 41 D4
 Lichfield WS14 .... 231 F1
Alder Coppice DY3 .... 266 B1
Alder Coppice Prim Sch
 DY3 .... 266 B1
Alder Dale WV3 .... 255 F1
Alder Gr Burton u T DE15 . 185 D4
 Newcastle-u-L ST5 .... 55 E4
 Stafford ST17 .... 174 A4
Alder Rd Kingswinford DY6 . 275 F3
 Market Drayton TF9 .... 112 A4
Alder Way WS12 .... 211 D3
Alder Wlk ST4 .... 71 C2
Alderbrook Cl
 Rolleston DE13 .... 147 D2
 Sedgley DY3 .... 266 A1
Alderdale Ave DY3 .... 266 B2
Alderflat Dr ST4 .... 88 B3
Alderford Cl WV8 .... 255 F4
Aldergate B79 .... 250 A3
Alderhay La ST7 .... 26 B3

Alderhithe Gr B74 .... 257 D2
Alderney Cl ST5 .... 70 C2
Alderney Cres ST3 .... 72 C2
Alders La B79 .... 249 F3
Alders The DE13 .... 183 E1
Aldersea Cl ST6 .... 41 F1
Aldershaw Cl ST16 .... 136 B1
Aldersleigh Dr ST17 .... 175 E3
Aldersley Ave WV6 .... 255 F4
Aldersley Cl WV6 .... 255 D3
Aldersley High Sch WV8 .. 239 E1
Aldersley Rd WV6 .... 255 F3
Aldersley Stadium WV6 ... 255 F3
Alderton Dr WV3 .... 265 F4
Alderton Gr ST3 .... 90 A3
Alderwood Prec DY3 .... 266 B1
Alderwood Rise DY3 .... 271 E3
Aldin Cl B78 .... 249 F1
Aldridge By Pass WS9 ..... 256 A3
Aldridge Cl
 Brierley Hill DY8 .... 279 F4
 Polesworth B78 .... 262 C4
Aldridge Rd Aldridge B74 . 256 B1
 Little Aston B74, WS9 .... 257 D3
Aldridge Sch WS9 .... 256 A2
Aldrin Cl Meir ST3 .... 90 B4
 Stafford ST16 .... 156 A3
Aldwich Cl WV3 .... 265 D4
Aldwych Ave WS6 .... 256 A4
Alexander Patterson Sch
 DY10 .... 280 B2
Alexander Rd WV8 .... 239 D1
Alexandra Cres ST14 .... 126 A4
Alexandra Ct DE15 .... 167 D2
Alexandra Cty Inf Sch ST3 . 73 F1
Alexandra Jun Sch ST3 ..... 73 F1
Alexandra Mews B79 ...... 250 B3
Alexandra Rd
 Burton u T DE15 .... 167 D2
 Longton ST3 .... 73 F1
 Market Drayton TF9 .... 97 D1
 Newcastle-u-L ST5 .... 56 B2
 Stafford ST17 .... 155 F1
 Wolv WV4 .... 266 A3
Alexandra St ST15 .... 104 C1
Alexandra Way WS9 .... 256 A3
Alford Dr ST9 .... 59 D2
Alfred Lyons Cl WS15 ...... 160 C3
Alfred St Burton u T DE14 . 166 B1
 Fenton ST4 .... 72 C4
 Tamworth B79 .... 250 A3
 Walsall WS3 .... 243 D1
Alfreton Rd ST4 .... 73 D3
Algar Pl ST4 .... 71 F3
Alison Dr DY8 .... 279 F2
All Saints CE Fst Sch
 Church Leigh ST10 .... 109 D2
 Denstone ST14 .... 95 F3
 Leek ST13 .... 30 C3
All Saints CE Inf Sch ST18 . 153 E3
All Saints CE Prim Sch
 Acton Trussell ST17 .... 193 D2
 Alrewas DE13 .... 201 D1
 Seisdon WV5 .... 269 D4
 Tatenhill DE13 .... 164 B1
All Saints CE Upper
 Prim Sch WV2 .... 266 C4
All Saints Dr B74 .... 258 A1
All Saints Fst Sch ST21 ... 102 B2
All Saints Rd
 Burton u T DE14 .... 185 E4
 Stoke-on-T ST4 .... 72 A3
 Wolv WV2 .... 266 B4
All Ways ST18 .... 122 B3
Allan Cl DY3 .... 279 F4
Allard B77 .... 250 C1
Allen Birt Wlk WS15 .... 178 B2
Allen Gdns TF9 .... 112 A4
Allen Rd WV6 .... 255 F2
Allen St Cheadle ST10 .... 76 C1
 Stoke-on-T ST4 .... 71 F4
 Tamworth B77 .... 250 B1
Allen's La ST14 .... 127 F1
Allenby Cl ST5 .... 70 C2
Allenby Sq ST4 .... 71 F2
Allendale ST16 .... 155 D4
Allendale Wlk ST3 .... 72 C1
Allens Croft ST14 .... 127 F1
Allens La WS3 .... 243 F1
Allens Rough Jun Mix Sch
 WV12 .... 242 B1
Allensmead B77 .... 250 B1
Allensmore Ave ST4 .... 73 D3
Allensway ST5 .... 70 C2
Allerdale Rd WS8 .... 244 C3
Allerton Rd ST4 .... 87 F4
Alleston Wlk WV10 .... 240 B1
Alley The DY3 .... 271 D2
Alley's La ST20 .... 190 A4
Alleyne Pl ST14 .... 110 C1
Alleynes High Sch ST15 .. 105 D1
Alleynes Sports Ctr ST15 . 105 D2
Alliance St ST4 .... 155 E3
Alliance Works Ind Est
 ST15 .... 120 A4
Alliss Cl ST16 .... 156 B2
Allport Rd WS11 .... 209 F1
Allport St WS11 .... 209 F1
Allsop Cres ST17 .... 175 D1
Allton Ave WS8 .... 249 E1
Allways ST18 .... 122 B3
Allways The ST18 .... 122 B3
Alma Cl ST7 .... 25 D4
Alma Rd DE11 .... 186 C3
Alma St Burton u T DE14 . 166 B1
 Fenton ST4 .... 72 B1
 Leek ST13 .... 30 B3
 Stone ST15 .... 104 C1

Almar Pl ST6 .... 42 A3
Almond Cl Brownhills WS3 . 243 F1
 Cannock WS11 .... 210 B1
Almond Ct DE13 .... 147 F1
Almond Gr Fenton ST3 ...... 72 C2
 Swadlincote DE11 .... 186 C3
Almond Pl ST5 .... 40 C1
Almond Rd
 Huntington WS12 .... 209 E4
 Kingswinford DY6 .... 275 F4
Almshouse Croft ST18 .... 191 D4
Alnwick Cl WS3 .... 210 C1
Alnwick Rd WS3 .... 243 D2
Alpha Way WS6 .... 243 D4
Alpine Dr WS12 .... 210 B2
Alpine Way WV6 .... 255 E1
Alrewas Rd DE13 .... 199 F3
Alsager Rd ST7 .... 39 C3
Alsop St ST3 .... 30 C3
Alston Cl Cannock WS12 .. 210 C1
 Sutton Coldfield B74 ...... 258 A1
Alstone Cl ST16 .... 155 D4
Alstone La Bradley ST18 .. 172 C1
 Haughton ST18 .... 172 C1
Alstonfield Ave ST2 .... 58 B3
Althorp Way DE13 .... 166 B4
Alton Cl Newcastle-u-L ST5 . 55 D1
 Wolv WV10 .... 240 C2
Alton Gr Bucknall ST2 .... 73 E4
 Cannock WS11 .... 209 D1
 Newport TF10 .... 168 C1
Alton Towers Theme Pk
 ST10 .... 78 C2
Altona Cl ST15 .... 120 A4
Alvaston Cl WS3 .... 243 E2
Alvecote Cotts B79 .... 251 E3
Alverley Cl DY6 .... 275 D4
Alverstoke Cl WV9 .... 240 A1
Alvis Cl B79 .... 249 F4
Alwen St DY8 .... 275 F1
Alwyn B77 .... 261 E4
Alwyn Cl WS6 .... 227 D2
Alwyn Cres ST6 .... 57 E4
Alwyn Rd DE13 .... 182 A1
Amanda Ave ST4 .... 265 F2
Amber Bsns Village B77 .. 251 D2
Amber Cl DY3 .... 251 D2
Amber Ct Endon ST9 .... 43 F3
 Tamworth B77 .... 251 D2
Amber Gn WS11 .... 210 B1
Amberfield Cl ST3 .... 73 F2
Ambergate Cl WS3 .... 243 E2
Ambergate Dr DY6 .... 275 E4
Amberley Way B74 .... 256 C1
Amblecote Dr ST3 .... 73 F2
Amblecote Prim Sch DY8 . 279 F4
Amblefield Way ST16 ...... 136 B1
Ambleside Cl ST15 .... 120 B4
Ambleside Pl ST6 .... 42 A2
Ambleside Way DY6 .... 275 D4
Ambrose Cres DY6 .... 275 E4
Ambrose Pl ST7 .... 41 F4
America St ST6 .... 41 E2
Amerton La
 Weston-u-T, Amerton ST18 . 139 D2
 Weston-u-T, Shirleywich
 ST18 .... 138 C1
Amicable St ST6 .... 56 C4
Amicombe B77 .... 251 E1
Amington Cl ST5 .... 258 B2
Amington Heath Prim Sch
 B77 .... 251 D2
Amington Ind Est B77 ..... 251 D2
Amington Rd B77 .... 250 B2
Amison St ST3 .... 73 E2
Ampleforth Dr ST17 .... 156 A1
Ampthill Pl ST4 .... 71 F1
Amptronik Trad Est DY3 .. 269 C2
Ancaster St ST6 .... 41 E4
Anchor Cl B77 .... 250 C2
Anchor Par WS9 .... 256 A3
Anchor Pl ST3 .... 283 C4
Anchor Rd Aldridge WS9 . 256 A3
 Longton ST3 .... 283 C4
Anchor Terr ST3 .... 283 C4
Anchor Way ST20 .... 171 E4
Anderby Gdns DE11 .... 186 C1
Anders B79 .... 250 A3
Anders Sq WV6 .... 254 C2
Anderson St ST6 .... 42 C2
Anderstaff Ind Pk DE14 .. 166 C3
Andover St ST4 .... 73 E2
Andover Cres DY6 .... 275 F2
Andover Pl WS11 .... 210 A2
Andrew Pl ST5 .... 284 D3
Andrew St ST6 .... 41 E4
Andrews Rd WS9 .... 245 D2
Aneurin Bevan Pl WS15 .. 178 B1
Angelica B77 .... 250 C2
Angle St 3 ST13 .... 30 B3
Anglesea Dr ST3 .... 73 D2
Anglesey Bsns Pk WS12 . 210 C2
Anglesey Cl WS7 .... 228 C2
Anglesey Cres
 Brownhills WS8 .... 228 C1
 Cannock WS12 .... 210 B3
Anglesey Ct DE14 .... 166 A1
Anglesey Mews DE14 ..... 210 B3
Anglesey Prim Sch DE14 . 166 B1
Anglesey Rd
 Brownhills WS8 .... 228 C1
 Burton u T DE14 .... 166 A1
 Lichfield WS13 .... 214 A1
Anglesey St
 Burton u T DE13 .... 165 F2
 Cannock WS12 .... 210 A3
Anglia Rd WS11 .... 209 E2
Angorfa Cl WS13 .... 230 C4

Angus Cl ST2 .... 58 B2
Anker Cl WS7 .... 229 E3
Anker View B77 .... 250 B2
Ankerdrive B77 .... 250 A2
Ankermoor Ct B77 .... 250 C3
Ankermoor Prim Sch B77 . 250 C3
Anna Wlk ST6 .... 56 C4
Annan Rd CW12 .... 6 A1
Anne Cres ST11 .... 209 F3
Anne Ct ST7 .... 40 B3
Anne Rd WV4 .... 266 A3
Anne St ST6 .... 41 E4
Annefield Cl TF9 .... 97 E1
Annette Rd ST4 .... 73 D3
Anslow Gdns WV11 .... 241 E1
Anslow La DE13 .... 147 D1
Anslow Rd DE13 .... 145 D1
Ansmead Gr ST3 .... 72 C1
Anson Ave ST13 .... 214 A1
Anson CE Prim Sch ST18 . 158 A1
Anson Cl Burntwood WS7 . 229 E4
 Great Wyrley WS6 .... 226 C1
 Perton WV6 .... 254 C3
Anson Ct DE14 .... 166 C2
Anson Dr ST17 .... 175 F3
Anson Mews WS15 .... 178 C1
Anson Rd Alrewas DE13 .. 201 D1
 Great Wyrley WS6 .... 226 C1
 Meir ST3 .... 90 A4
Anson St ST15 .... 178 C1
Anson's Row ST18 .... 177 E4
Anstree Cl WS6 .... 226 B1
Ansty Dr WS12 .... 210 B1
Anthony Gr ST3 .... 89 F2
Anthony Pl ST3 .... 283 C4
Antler Dr ST15 .... 178 A1
Apedale Bsns Pk ST5 ...... 55 E4
Apedale Rd
 Audley, Chesterton ST5 ... 55 E3
 Audley, Wood Lane ST7 ... 55 E3
 Newcastle-u-L ST5 .... 55 E3
Apex Bsns Pk WS11 .... 227 F2
Apex Rd WS8 .... 244 B4
Apley Pl ST4 .... 87 F4
Apley Rd DY8 .... 279 F4
Apollo B79 .... 249 F3
Apollo Cl WS11 .... 210 A3
Apollo Wlk ST6 .... 42 B1
Appian Cl B77 .... 261 E4
Apple Wlk WS11 .... 210 B1
Appleby Gdns WV11 ...... 242 B1
Appleby Glade DE11 ...... 186 B1
Applecroft Madeley CW3 .. 68 B4
 Newcastle-u-L ST5 .... 40 C4
Applecross B74 .... 257 F1
Appledore Cl
 Cannock WS12 .... 210 C2
 Great Wyrley WS6 .... 227 D2
 Stafford ST17 .... 175 F4
Appledore Gr ST7 .... 41 F4
Appleford Pl ST3 .... 72 C1
Applegarth Cl ST4 .... 73 D3
Appleton Cl Biddulph ST8 . 27 F3
 Congleton CW12 .... 15 F4
 Swadlincote DE11 .... 186 C3
Appleton Cres WV4 .... 266 A3
Appleton Dr ST5 .... 85 E3
Appletree Gr WS9 .... 256 A3
Applewood Cl ST14 .... 111 D1
Applewood Cres ST3 .... 90 B4
Appleyard Ct 12 ST16 ..... 155 F2
Apse Cl WV5 .... 269 F4
Apsley Gr ST12 .... 88 A1
Aqualate Cl TF10 .... 169 D2
Aqualate Ho ST17 .... 174 C1
Aquinas St ST4 .... 72 A4
Arbor Cl B77 .... 250 B2
Arbor Gate WS9 .... 245 D2
Arborfield Rd WS14 .... 143 F4
Arbour Cl CW3 .... 68 C2
Arbour St Hanley ST1 ..... 282 C3
 Kidsgrove ST7 .... 40 B3
Arbourfield Dr ST2 .... 58 A1
Arbury Dr DY8 .... 275 E2
Arcade The DY3 .... 271 D3
Arcal St DY3 .... 271 F4
Arch St WS15 .... 196 C4
Arclid Way ST2 .... 58 A1
Arctic Pl ST4 .... 88 A4
Arden Cl DY8 .... 275 E2
Arden Cl ST13 .... 31 D3
Arden Cl Rugeley WS15 .. 178 B1
 Stourbridge DY8 .... 279 F4
 Tamworth B77 .... 250 C3
Arden Ct CW12 .... 16 A4
Arden Rd DE13 .... 201 D4
Arden Wlk WS15 .... 198 B2
Ardgay Dr WS12 .... 209 F4
Ardingley Ave ST17 .... 156 A1
Argosy Cl ST3 .... 90 A4
Argyle Ave B77 .... 250 B2
Argyle Cl DY8 .... 275 F1
Argyle Rd WV2 .... 266 A3
Argyle St Hanley ST1 ...... 282 C4
 Tamworth B77 .... 250 C2
Argyles Rd ST13 .... 31 D4
Argyll Cl ST11 .... 90 C3
Argyll Rd ST1 .... 73 E1
Ariane B77 .... 249 F4
Aries Cl ST6 .... 41 F1
Arion Cl ST7 .... 250 B3
Arkall Cl B79 .... 250 B4
Arkle B77 .... 261 E2
Arkwright Cl ST2 .... 57 F4
Arlescote Cl B75 .... 258 B1

Arley Dr DY8 279 F2
Arley Gr WV4 265 E3
Arlington Cl DY6 275 E2
Armishaw Pl WS15 197 D3
Armitage Gdns WS15 197 D3
Armitage Hill DE13 183 F2
Armitage La
Armitage WS15 197 D3
Rugeley WS15 197 D3
Armitage Rd WS15 197 D3
Armshead Rd ST9 59 D2
Armside Cl WS3 244 A2
Armstead Rd WV9 240 A2
Armstrong B79 249 F3
Armstrong Ave ST16 156 A2
Armstrong Gn ST6 57 E4
Arnold Cl B79 250 A3
Arnold Gr ST5 56 A4
Arnotdale Dr WS12 209 F4
Arps Rd WV8 238 C2
Arran Cl WS11 210 A2
Arran Dr ST7 41 F4
Arrow Dr WV7 237 D3
Arthur Evans Cl WS15 197 D3
Arthur St Burton u T DE14 166 B3
Cannock, Chadsmoor WS11 209 F2
Cannock, Wimblebury WS12 210 C2
Newcastle-u-L ST5 55 F1
Stone ST15 105 D1
Tunstall ST6 41 F2
Wolv WV2 266 B4
Arthur Terry Sch B74 258 A2
Arthur Wood Pl WS15 178 B1
Arthurs Ct DE13 147 F1
Arundel B77 261 E4
Arundel Gr WV6 254 C2
Arundel Rd
Kingswinford DY8 275 E1
Wolv WV10 240 A1
Arundel Way ST3 73 E3
Ascot Cl Burton u T DE15 167 D2
Lichfield WS14 231 E4
Ascot Dr Cannock WS11 226 A4
Sedgley DY1 271 F1
Wolv WV4 266 A2
Ascot Gdns DY8 275 E1
Ascot Rd ST17 156 B1
Ash Bank Rd ST9 59 D2
Ash Cl Cheadle ST10 76 C1
Codsall WV8 239 D2
Uttoxeter ST14 126 A4
Ash Cres DY6 275 F3
Ash Dr ST18 172 C3
Ash Gr Albrighton WV7 237 D2
Barlaston ST12 88 B1
Blythe Bridge ST11 90 B4
Brewood ST19 223 E3
Cannock WS11 209 F2
Caverswall ST2 58 C2
Fenton ST3 72 C1
Lichfield WS14 231 F4
Newcastle-u-L ST5 55 D1
Sedgley DY3 271 E1
Tamworth B77 261 F3
Wheaton Aston ST19 205 E3
Ash Green Cl ST4 88 A4
Ash Green Cty Prim Sch
ST4 88 A4
Ash Grove La DE65 148 B3
Ash Hill WV3 255 E1
Ash La Great Wyrley WS6 227 D2
Newton Regis B79 236 C3
Swynnerton ST15 118 C3
Ash Park Ind Est WS11 210 A1
Ash Rd ST15 120 A4
Ash Rise ST17 174 C2
Ash St Burton u T DE14 166 A1
Walsall WS3 243 E1
Ash Tree Cl DE11 186 C3
Ash Tree Hill ST10 76 B1
Ash Tree La WS13 215 D1
Ash Tree Rd DE13 183 E1
Ash View WS12 209 E4
Ash Way ST2 58 C2
Ashbourne Cl WS11 210 A2
Ashbourne Dr
Market Drayton TF9 97 E1
Newcastle-u-L ST5 55 D1
Ashbourne Gr ST1 282 B4
Ashbourne La DE6 35 D1
Ashbourne Rd
Alstonefield DE6 35 D2
Cheadle ST10 76 C2
Leek ST13 31 D2
Mayfield DE6 81 E4
Rocester ST14 95 F2
Uttoxeter ST14 111 D1
Walsall WS3 243 E2
Wolv WV4 266 C2
Ashbrook DE15 167 D1
Ashbrook Cl Gnosall ST20 171 E4
Uttoxeter ST14 126 B3
Ashbrook La WS15 161 E3
Ashburton St ST6 57 D4
Ashby Cres ST3 72 C1
Ashby Rd Burton u T DE15 167 D1
Tamworth B79 250 B4
Wigginton B79 250 B4
Ashby Rd E DE15 167 F1
Ashcombe Gr ST3 72 C1
Ashcombe Rd ST13 45 E2
Ashcombe Way ST13 30 C2
Ashcott Wlk ST2 58 B1
Ashcroft Ave ST4 71 F1
Ashcroft Cl ST5 56 A3
Ashcroft Cty Inf Sch B79 250 B4
Ashcroft Gr ST5 56 A3
Ashcroft La
Shenstone WS14 246 C4
Wall WS14 246 C4
Ashcroft Oval ST5 56 A3
Ashcroft Pl ST5 56 A3
Ashcroft Rd ST5 56 A3
Ashdale Cl Burton u T DE15 186 A4
Kingswinford DY6 275 E4
Stone ST15 120 A4
Ashdale Dr ST16 155 E4
Ashdale Pk ST15 118 C3
Ashdale Rd Fenton ST4 72 B3
Leek ST13 31 D3
Tamworth B77 250 B3
Ashdale Rise ST5 71 D2
Ashdene Gdns DY8 275 E1
Ashdene Gr ST4 71 F1
Ashdown Dr DY8 275 F2
Ashe's La DE6 144 B4
Ashen Cl DY3 266 B2
Ashenden Rise WV3 265 D4
Ashendene Gr ST4 87 F4
Ashenhurst Way ST13 30 C2
Ashenough Rd ST7 40 B3
Ashfield Ct ST5 284 A4
Ashfield Gr WV10 240 B2
Ashfield Rd
Wolv, Compton WV3 255 E1
Wolv Ford Houses WV10 240 B2
Ashfield Sq ST2 58 A1
Ashfields WV7 237 D3
Ashfields Grange ST5 284 B3
Ashfields New Rd ST5 284 A4
Ashflats Rd Bradnop ST18 174 C2
Stafford ST17 174 C2
Ashford Dr DY3 271 F4
Ashford Gr ST15 120 B4
Ashford Rd DE13 166 A3
Ashford St ST4 72 B4
Ashgrove WS7 228 C3
Ashland St WV3 266 A4
Ashlands ST18 139 E1
Ashlands Ave ST4 71 F4
Ashlands Cl B79 250 B4
Ashlands Cres ST4 71 F4
Ashlands Gr ST5 71 E4
Ashlands Rd ST4 71 F4
Ashlar Cl ST6 42 A4
Ashlea Dr DE6 81 E4
Ashleigh Ave DE11 186 C3
Ashleigh Cres ST19 205 E4
Ashleigh Dr Tamworth B77 261 F4
Uttoxeter ST14 110 C1
Ashleigh Rd Rugeley WS15 196 C4
Upper Tean ST10 92 C2
Ashley Cl Kingswinford DY6 275 E2
Stafford ST16 155 D2
Stourbridge DY8 279 E1
Ashley Croft ST20 190 A4
Ashley Ct DE15 167 D2
Ashley Gdns WV8 238 C2
Ashley Gr ST5 56 B2
Ashley Rd
Burntwood WS7 211 F1
Kidderminster DY10 280 A1
Walsall WS3 242 C1
Wolv WV4 265 F3
Ashley View TF9 97 E1
Ashmall WS7 229 E2
Ashman St ST6 42 B1
Ashmead Rd WS7 229 D4
Ashmole Cl WS14 231 F3
Ashmore Ave WV11 242 A1
Ashmore Dr ST20 171 E4
Ashmore Wlk ST1 282 C3
Ashoale Cl WS12 209 E4
Ashover Gr ST7 41 F4
Ashover Rd DE11 186 C3
Ashridge Ave ST5 71 D1
Ashridge Gr ST3 73 E3
Ashridge Wlk ST16 136 B1
Ashton Cl CW12 6 A1
Ashton Ct Caverswall ST9 59 D2
Newcastle-u-L ST5 71 E1
Ashton Dr WS4 244 B2
Ashtree Bank WS15 197 D3
Ashtree Cl ST18 177 E4
Ashtree Rd WS3 244 A2
Ashurst Gr ST3 90 A4
Ashwell Rd ST4 71 E4
Ashwells Gr WV9 240 A1
Ashwood ST3, ST4 283 C4
Ashwood Ave DY8 275 E1
Ashwood Cl TF9 97 D1
Ashwood Gr Forsbrook ST11 91 D3
Wolv WV4 266 A3
Ashwood Park Prim Sch
DY8 275 E1
Ashwood Terr ST3 283 C5
Ashworth Ave DE15 167 E1
Ashworth Ho WS11 210 A2
Ashworth St ST4 72 B3
Ashworth Way TF10 168 C1
Askerbank La SK11 8 A1
Askern Cl ST3 73 F1
Askew Bridge Rd DY3 271 D2
Askew Cl DY3 271 F3
Aspen Cft ST17 174 A4
Aspen Cl ST7 26 C2
Aspen Ct WS12 211 D3
Aspen Gr WS7 228 C4
Aspen Rd DE13 201 E4
Aspen Way TF10 168 C1
Aspley Cl WV10 224 C3
Asquith Cl ST8 27 F4
Asquith Dr WS11 210 B1
Astbury CE Aided
Prim Sch CW12 15 E4
Astbury Cl Kidsgrove ST7 26 B2
Walsall WS3 243 D2
Astbury Lane Ends CW12 15 F4
Aster Cl ST3 74 A3
Aster Wlk WV9 240 A2
Astil St DE15 166 C1
Aston Bk Seighford ST18 154 C2
Stafford ST16 154 C2
Aston Chase ST15 120 B4
Aston Cl Colwich ST18 177 E4
Penkridge ST19 208 A4
Shenstone WS14 246 C3
Aston Dr TF10 168 C1
Aston Hill ST18 154 C2
Aston La Maer TF9 83 F4
Stone ST15 120 B2
Sudbury DE6 129 D3
Woore CW3 67 F1
Aston Lodge Parkway
ST15 120 B3
Aston Rd ST5 40 B1
Aston St WV3 266 A4
Aston Terr ST16 155 F3
Astonfields Ind Est ST16 155 F3
Astonfields Rd ST16 155 F3
Astonfields Road Bsns Pk
ST16 155 F3
Astor Rd Aldridge B74 257 D1
Kingswinford DY6 275 F3
Astoria Cl WV12 242 B1
Astoria Dr ST17 174 C3
Astoria Gdns WV12 242 B1
Astro Gr ST3 283 A4
Athelney Ct WS3 244 A2
Athelstan Cl ST19 208 A4
Athelstan Gr WV6 254 C3
Athelstan St ST6 41 E2
Athelstan Way B79 249 F4
Athena Rd ST1 57 F3
Atherstone Rd ST4 88 A4
Atherstone St B78 261 D4
Athlestan Way DE13 147 E1
Athlone St ST6 42 B1
Atholl Rd ST3 283 D1
Atkins Way ST14 95 F2
Atlam Cl ST2 58 A2
Atlantic Gr ST4 88 A4
Atlas St ST4 72 C3
Attingham Dr WS11 210 A1
Attlee Cres Rugeley WS15 196 C4
Stafford ST17 174 B4
Attlee Gr WS11 210 B1
Attlee Rd ST10 76 B1
Attwell Pk WV3 265 E4
Attwood Gdns WV4 266 C3
Attwood Rd WS7 228 B4
Attwood St ST7 26 A1
Aubrey St ST6 41 D4
Auchinleck Dr WS13 214 B1
Auckland Rd DY6 275 F2
Auden Ct WV6 254 C2
Auden Pl ST3 283 D4
Auden Way ST17 174 B4
Audlem Rd CW3 67 D1
Audley Ave TF10 169 D1
Audley Ave Bsns Pk TF10 169 D1
Audley Ho TF10 169 D1
Audley House Mews TF10 169 D1
Audley Pl ST5 71 D3
Audley Rd Alsager ST7 39 E4
Audley ST7 40 A1
Barthomley CW2 38 C3
Kidsgrove ST7 40 A3
Newcastle-u-L ST7 40 A1
Newport TF10 168 C2
Audley St Newcastle-u-L ST5 55 F2
Tunstall ST6 41 E2
Audmore Rd ST20 171 E4
Audnam DY8 275 F1
Augustine Cl ST15 120 B4
Augustine Gr B74 257 F3
Augustines Wlk WS13 214 A2
Aukland St ST6 57 D4
Aulton Rd B75 258 C1
Austcliffe Rd DY10 280 A3
Austin Cl Sedgley DY1 271 F1
Stone ST15 120 A4
Austin Cote La WS14 231 F4
Austin Friars ST17 155 F1
Austin St ST1 282 C1
Austrey La
Newton Regis B79 236 C2
Newton Regis,
No Man's Heath B79 236 C3
Austwick Gr ST4 71 F3
Autumn Berry Gr DY3 271 F3
Autumn Cl WS4 244 B1
Autumn Dr Brownhills WS4 244 B1
Lichfield WS13 214 B1
Sedgley DY3 271 E2
Avarne Pl 14 ST16 155 F2
Aveling Gn ST2 57 F4
Aveling Rd ST2 57 F4
Avenue Rd Cannock WS12 210 C1
Newport TF10 168 C1
Stoke-on-T ST4 57 E1
Wolv WV3 255 F1
Avenue Rd S TF10 168 C1
Avenue The Bagnall ST9 43 F2
Blakedown DY10 281 D1
Cheadle ST10 76 B1
Cheddleton ST13 45 E2
Endon ST9 43 F4
Enville DY7 273 E1
Featherstone WV10 241 D4
Forsbrook ST11 91 D4
Avenue The continued
Kidsgrove ST7 25 F1
Newcastle-u-L, Basford ST5 56 B1
Newcastle-u-L,
City General Hospl ST5 71 E4
Stone ST15 105 D1
Wheaton Aston ST19 206 B2
Wolv, Finchfield WV3 265 D4
Wolv, Penn WV4 265 F2
Wootton DE6 79 F3
Averill Dr WS15 178 B1
Averill Rd ST17 174 B4
Aviation La DE13 165 E2
Avill B77 262 A3
Avington Cl DY3 271 E4
Avion Cl ST3 90 B4
Avoca St ST1 282 C4
Avocet Cl ST14 126 B3
Avon B77 262 A3
Avon Ave ST6 41 F2
Avon Bsns Pk WS11 226 B4
Avon Cl Kidsgrove ST7 26 A1
Newcastle-u-L ST5 71 D2
Perton WV6 254 C2
Stafford ST16 156 A2
Avon Cres WS3 244 A1
Avon Dale TF10 168 C2
Avon Gr Ashley TF9 99 E3
Cheadle ST10 76 C1
Stone ST15 120 A3
Avon Hill ST16 156 B2
Avon Rd Burntwood WS7 228 C3
Cannock WS11 226 B4
Stourbridge DY8 279 F2
Walsall WS3 243 F1
Avon Rise ST16 156 A2
Avon Way DE15 167 D1
Avondale Cl DY6 275 F4
Avondale Rd WV6 255 F2
Avondale St ST6 56 B4
Avonlea Gdns WS15 178 B1
Avonwick Gr ST1 58 A3
Axborough La DY10 280 B2
Axbridge Wlk ST6 42 B1
Axon Cres ST3 74 A2
Aylesbury Rd ST2 58 B1
Aylesford Cl DY3 266 B1
Aylesford Dr B74 257 F3
Aynsley Ave ST5 71 D2
Aynsley Cl ST10 76 B1
Aynsley Rd ST4 57 D1
Aynsley Specl Sch ST11 90 C4
Aynsley's Dr ST11 90 C4
Ayr Rd ST10 76 C3
Ayrshire Way CW12 6 A1
Ayrton Cl WV6 255 D2
Ayshford St ST3 283 B3
Azalea Cl WV8 239 D2

Babbacombe Ave ST17 175 F4
Babbington Cl
Tutbury DE13 146 B3
Whittington WS14 232 C3
Babworth Cl WV9 240 A1
Back Browning St ST16 155 E2
Back Bunt's La ST9 43 E2
Back Cross La CW12 16 A4
Back Ford Green Rd ST6 42 B1
Back Garden St ST5 284 C2
Back Heathcote St ST7 26 A1
Back La
Aldridge WS9 256 C4
Alstonefield DE6 35 F2
Alton ST10 78 C1
Ashley TF9 100 A3
Betley CW3 53 D4
Colwich ST18 177 E4
Ellastone DE6 80 A2
Endon, Brown Edge ST6 43 D4
Endon, Hodgefield ST6 28 A1
Gnosall ST20 171 E3
Haughton ST18 173 D3
Hixon ST18 139 E1
Leek ST13 30 B3
Millmeece ST21 102 B3
Ranton ST18 153 E2
Shenstone WS14 246 C1
Uttoxeter ST14 126 B4
Waterhouses ST10 49 F1
Wheaton Aston ST19 205 E3
Whittington WS14 232 C3
Woodseaves ST20 151 E4
Wootton DE6 79 F4
Back Radfords ST15 105 D1
Back Rd DY6 275 E4
Back Westlands Rd ST14 126 A3
Backcester La WS13 231 D4
Backcrofts WS11 209 E1
Baddeley Green La ST2 43 D1
Baddeley Hall Rd ST2 43 E2
Baddeley Rd ST2 43 D1
Baddeley S
Burslem ST6 41 F1
Cheadle ST10 76 C1
Baddely's Ct TF10 168 C1
Baden Powell Cl WS15 211 F3
Baden Rd ST6 42 B1
Baden St ST5 284 B4
Bader Rd WV6 254 C2
Badger Brow Rd TF9 99 E3
Badger Cl WS12 209 E3
Badger Gr ST3 90 B4
Badger La TF9 84 B2
Badger St DY3 271 F3
Badger's End ST19 205 D3
Badgers Bank Rd B74 257 F3
Badgers Brow ST1 57 F2
Badgers Cl WS3 244 A3
Badgers Croft
Eccleshall ST21 133 F3
Stafford ST17 175 E3
Badgers Hollow SE10 93 D1
Badgers Way WS12 210 B1
Badgery Cl ST14 111 D1
Badminton Cl DY1 271 F2
Badnall Cl ST13 30 B3
Badnall St ST13 30 B3
Bag La Admaston WS15 159 E4
Marchington ST14 127 F1
Roston DE6 96 C4
Baggeridge Cl DY3 271 D4
Baggeridge Ctry Pk DY3 270 C3
Baggott Pl ST5 70 C4
Baggott St WV2 266 B4
Bagnall Hospl ST9 43 F1
Bagnall Rd Bagnall ST2 43 E1
Norton-in-t-M ST2 43 E1
Bagnall St ST1 282 B2
Bagot Gr ST1 57 F4
Bagot St WS15 160 C3
Bagots Oak ST17 174 B4
Bagots View
Abbots Bromley WS15 161 D3
Church Leigh ST10 109 D2
Bagridge Cl WV3 265 D4
Bagridge Rd WV3 265 D4
Bailey Ave B77 261 F3
Bailey Cl WS11 210 A2
Bailey Cres CW12 6 A2
Bailey Rd ST3 72 C2
Bailey St Burton u T DE14 166 B1
Newcastle-u-L ST5 284 A3
Stafford ST17 155 F1
Stoke-on-T ST4 56 C1
Bailey's Bank ST6 16 B2
Bailye Cl WS13 214 C1
Bain Ho ST17 174 C3
Bainbridge Rd ST4 88 A4
Bains Gr ST5 55 F4
Baker Ave WV14 266 C1
Baker Cres ST2 43 E2
Baker Cres N ST2 43 E2
Baker Cres S ST2 43 D2
Baker St Burntwood WS7 228 C3
Burton u T DE15 185 F4
Fenton ST4 72 C3
Baker's La Aldridge WS9 256 A3
Lichfield WS13 231 D4
Norbury TF10 150 B2
Bakers Gdns WV8 238 C2
Bakers Way WV8 238 C2
Bakers Wlk B77 261 F3
Bakewell Cl
Newcastle-u-L ST5 55 D1
Walsall WS3 243 E2
Bakewell Dr ST15 120 B3
Bakewell Gn DE11 186 C3
Bakewell St ST4 71 F3
Bala Gr ST10 76 C2
Balaam's La ST15 106 B3
Balance Hill ST14 126 B4
Balance St ST14 126 B4
Balcombe Cl ST5 284 B1
Baldwin Gr WS11 210 B1
Baldwin Way DY3 269 F1
Baldwin's Gate
CE Prim Sch ST5 85 E3
Balfour B79 250 A2
Balfour Cres WV6 255 F2
Balfour Gr ST8 27 F4
Balfour Rd DY6 275 F4
Balfour St Burton u T DE13 166 B3
Hanley ST1 282 C2
Balk Pas ST16 155 E2
Ball Green Prim Sch ST6 42 B3
Ball Haye Gn ST13 31 D4
Ball Haye Rd ST13 30 C3
Ball Haye St ST13 30 C3
Ball Haye Terr ST13 30 C3
Ball Hayes Rd ST6 42 B3
Ball La
Brewood WV9, WV10 240 B3
Endon ST6 43 D3
Leek ST13 30 C3
Norton-in-t-M ST6 43 D3
Ball's Yd ST5 284 B3
Ballarat Wlk DY8 279 F3
Ballington Gdns ST13 30 C3
Ballington View ST13 30 C2
Ballinson Rd ST3 72 C1
Balliol Bsns Pk WV9 239 F2
Balloon St ST4 56 B1
Balmain Cres WV11 241 D1
Balmoral Cl Lichfield WS14 231 E3
Stone ST15 120 A3
Trentham ST4 72 A1
Balmoral Ct WS11 210 A3
Balmoral Dr Cannock WS12 209 F4
Market Drayton TF9 97 F1
Wombourne WV5 265 D1
Balmoral Rd
Burton u T DE15 167 D2
Kingswinford DY8 275 E1
Stafford ST17 156 B1
Sutton Coldfield B74 257 F3
Wolv WV4 266 A3
Balmoral View DY1 271 F1
Balmoral Way WS7 211 F1
Baltic Cl Cannock WS11 209 F1
Trentham ST4 88 A4
Balvenie Way DY1 271 F2
Bamber Cl WV3 265 F4
Bamber Pl ST5 55 F3
Bamber St ST4 72 A4
Bamborough Cl DE13 166 B4
Bamburgh B77 261 E4

Bambury St Fenton ST3, ST4 . 73 E3
 Longton ST3, ST4 .... 73 E3
Bamford Cl WS3 .... 243 E2
Bamford Gr ST1 .... 282 A4
Bamford Rd Walsall WS3 .... 243 E2
 Wolv WV3 .... 266 A4
Bamford St B77 .... 250 B2
Bampton Ave WS7 .... 229 D4
Bampton Cl ST9 .... 43 F4
Banbery Dr WV5 .... 269 F2
Banbury Dr DY3 .... 271 F3
Banbury Gr ST8 .... 27 E4
Banbury Rd WS11 .... 226 B4
Banbury St ST7 .... 25 E1
Bancroft B77 .... 250 C2
Bancroft La
 Forsbrook ST11 .... 90 C3
 Hamstall Ridware WS15 .. 199 D4
Bandridge La SK11 .... 18 A4
Baneberry Dr WV10 .... 241 D4
Bangley La
 Drayton Bassett B78 ..... 260 A4
 Hints B78 .... 259 F3
Bank Cl ST14 .... 126 B4
Bank Cres WS7 .... 228 C3
Bank End ST6 .... 43 D4
Bank Hall Rd ST6 .... 42 A1
Bank House Dr ST5 .... 56 C1
Bank Pas 9 ST16 .... 155 F2
Bank Rd DY3 .... 271 E4
Bank Side Hartington SK17 .. 24 B3
 Stone ST15 .... 119 F3
Bank St Cannock WS12 .... 210 C1
 Cheadle ST10 .... 76 B2
 Kidsgrove ST7 .... 26 B2
 Tunstall ST6 .... 41 E2
Bank The Gnosall ST20 ..... 171 E3
 The Bank ST7 .... 26 A4
Bank Top WS15 .... 178 B1
Bank Top Ave ST6 .... 42 A2
Bank Wlk DE13 .... 166 A4
Bankerwall La DE6 .... 80 B4
Bankfield Gr ST5 .... 54 C2
Bankfield Rd ST3 .... 89 F4
Bankhouse Dr CW12 .... 6 A3
Bankhouse Rd
 Forsbrook ST11 .... 91 D4
 Trentham ST4 .... 87 F4
Banks La ST10 .... 61 F2
Bankside
 Newcastle-u-L ST5 .... 284 C2
 Stone ST15 .... 104 B2
 Wombourne WV5 .... 269 F4
Bankside Way WS9 .... 245 D1
Banktop Rd DE6 .... 144 A3
Banky Brook Cl ST6 .... 42 B2
Bannut Tree La DY7 .... 277 E3
Banstead Cl WV2 .... 266 C4
Bantock Ave WV3 .... 265 F4
Bantock Gdns WV3 .... 255 F1
Baptist St 9 ST6 .... 57 D4
Bar Hill CW3 .... 68 B2
Bar La DE13 .... 183 D1
Bar Wlk WS9 .... 245 E1
Barbara St B79 .... 250 A3
Barber Cl WS12 .... 210 C1
Barber Dr ST7 .... 25 F4
Barber Pl ST6 .... 41 F3
Barber Rd ST6 .... 41 F3
Barber St ST6 .... 41 F1
Barber's Sq ST5 .... 56 B2
Barbridge Rd ST5 .... 40 B1
Barbrook Ave ST3 .... 73 F2
Barclay Cl WV7 .... 237 D3
Barclay St ST3 .... 73 E3
Barcliff Ave B77 .... 250 C2
Barden Village ST10 .... 92 B2
Bardolph Cl DE11 .... 186 C2
Bardsey Wlk 1 ST3 .... 73 D2
Bardwell Cl WV8 .... 255 F4
Bardy La Armitage WS15 .. 197 F2
 Longdon WS15 .... 197 E1
Barfoot St ST3 .... 283 B3
Barford Rd ST5 .... 70 C2
Bargate La ST13 .... 223 E3
Bargery Rd WV11 .... 242 A1
Bargrave St ST2 .... 58 B1
Barker Cl ST16 .... 155 E2
Barker St Longton ST3 .... 283 D3
 Newcastle-u-L ST5 .... 55 F3
Barks Dr ST6 .... 42 B2
Barlaston CE Fst Sch ST12 . 88 C1
Barlaston Old Rd ST4 ...... 88 A3
Barlaston Rd Barlaston ST3 .. 89 D3
 Longton ST3 .... 88 C2
Barlaston Sta ST12 .... 88 B1
Barley Cl Aldridge B74 .... 256 C1
 Burton u T DE14 .... 166 C3
 Wolv WV8 .... 239 F1
Barley Croft Perton WV6 .. 254 B2
 Whittington WS14 .... 232 C3
Barley Ct ST16 .... 155 D3
Barley Field WV9 .... 224 A1
Barley Green La DE13 ..... 201 E1
Barley Orch ST20 .... 171 F3
Barley Rd ST10 .... 62 A4
Barleycorn Cl DE15 .... 167 D1
Barleycroft ST10 .... 76 C1
Barleycroft Terr ST7 ...... 25 F4
Barleyfield Rise DY6 ...... 275 D4
Barleyfields Audley ST7 .. 39 E1
 Chell Heath ST6 .... 42 B2
Barleyford Dr ST3 .... 73 E3
Barlow Cl DY7 .... 250 C2
Barlow St ST3 .... 283 C3
Barlstone Ave ST11 .... 90 C3
Barmouth Gr ST8 .... 27 D1

Barn Ave DY3 .... 271 E4
Barn Bank La
 Bradnop ST18 .... 174 B3
 Stafford ST17 .... 174 C2
Barn Cl Dordon B78 .... 262 C3
 Lichfield WS14 .... 214 A2
 Rugeley WS15 .... 197 D3
 Stafford ST17 .... 174 C2
Barn Croft Burntwood WS7 . 229 D2
 Great Wyrley WS6 .... 227 D2
Barn Ct ST5 .... 71 E2
Barn End Rd ST17 .... 193 D4
Barn Gn WV3 .... 265 F4
Barn Rd WS15 .... 198 B3
Barnaby Sq WV10 .... 240 C2
Barnard Pl WV2 .... 266 C3
Barnard Rd WV11 .... 241 F1
Barnard Way WS11 .... 209 F4
Barnbridge B77 .... 250 B1
Barnbridge Cl ST7 .... 25 F4
Barncroft Rd ST6 .... 42 B3
Barnes Croft ST15 .... 106 B1
Barnes Rd
 Shenstone WS14 .... 247 D3
 Stafford ST17 .... 174 B4
Barnes Way ST3 .... 73 E1
Barnett Cl DY6 .... 275 E2
Barnett Gn DY6 .... 275 E2
Barnett Gr ST6 .... 41 F3
Barnett La DY6, DY8 ...... 275 E2
Barnett St DY8 .... 275 E2
Barnetts La WS8 .... 244 C4
Barnfield ST4 .... 71 F3
Barnfield Cl Lichfield WS14 . 231 D3
 Stone ST15 .... 119 F4
Barnfield Pl ST13 .... 30 C2
Barnfield Rd Burslem ST6 .. 57 D4
 Leek ST13 .... 30 B2
 Upper Tean ST10 .... 92 C2
Barnfield Way
 Cannock WS12 .... 211 D3
 Stafford ST17 .... 175 E3
Barnfields Cl ST13 .... 30 B2
Barnfields Ind Est ST13 .. 30 B2
Barnfields La ST10 .... 61 E1
Barnfields Prim Sch ST17 . 175 E3
Barngate St ST13 .... 30 B3
Barnhurst La WV8 .... 239 F1
Barnlea Gr ST3 .... 90 A3
Barnmeadow Cl TF10 .... 169 D2
Barnmeadow Rd TF10 ... 169 D1
Barns Cl WS9 .... 244 C2
Barns Croft B74 .... 257 D2
Barnsdale Cl ST4 .... 88 B3
Barnswood Cl WS11 ..... 226 A4
Barnwell Cl ST14 .... 111 D3
Barnwell Gr ST4 .... 72 A1
Barnwood Rd WV8 .... 239 F1
Baron Cl WS7 .... 211 F1
Baron St ST4 .... 283 A5
Baron's Way ST18 .... 158 B4
Barr Common Cl WV3 .... 256 A2
Barr Common Rd WV9 ... 256 A2
Barr St DY3 .... 271 E2
Barracks La WS14 .... 245 E4
Barracks Rd ST5 .... 284 C2
Barracks Sq ST5 .... 284 C2
Barrage Rd ST8 .... 28 A4
Barrar Cl DY8 .... 279 F4
Barratt Gdns ST2 .... 58 A4
Barratts Croft DY5 .... 271 E1
Barrett Cres ST6 .... 57 D3
Barrett Dr ST6 .... 57 D3
Barrie Gdns ST7 .... 40 B4
Barrington Cl
 Albrighton WV7 .... 237 D2
 Burton u T DE13 .... 147 E1
 Wolv WV10 .... 240 B1
Barrington Ct ST5 .... 56 C2
Barrow Hill Rd DY5 ...... 271 E1
Barry Ave ST3 .... 58 A2
Bartholomew Rd ST3 .... 73 F1
Barthomley Rd Audley ST7 . 39 D1
 Barthomley CW2 .... 38 A4
 Betley ST7 .... 38 C2
 Hanley ST1 .... 57 E3
Bartic Ave DY6 .... 275 F2
Bartlem St ST3 .... 283 D5
Bartlett Cl ST19 .... 207 F4
Barton Cottage Hospl
 DE13 .... 183 E1
Barton Cres ST6 .... 41 F1
Barton Gate DE13 .... 183 D1
Barton La Bradley ST18 .. 191 D4
 Kingswinford DY6 ...... 275 D4
Barton Lodge DE13 ...... 183 E1
Barton Rd WV4 .... 266 C2
Barton St DE14 .... 185 E4
Barton Turn DE13 .... 184 A1
Barton's La TF9 .... 112 A4
Barton's Rd TF9 .... 112 A4
Barwood Ave ST7 .... 25 D3
Basford La ST13 .... 45 F4
Basford Lane Ind Est ST13 . 45 F4
Basford Park Rd ST5 ..... 56 B2
Basfordbridge La ST13 .. 45 F3
Basfordbridge Terr ST13 . 45 F3
Basil Cl ST17 .... 174 C3
Basildon Gr ST3 .... 283 C2
Basin La B77 .... 250 B2
Baskerville Rd ST1 ...... 282 C3
Baskeyfield Cl WS14 .... 231 E4
Baskeyfield Pl ST6 ...... 42 A3
Baslow Cl WS3 .... 243 E2
Baslow Gn DE11 .... 186 C3
Baslow Rd WS3 .... 243 D2
Basnett's Wood Rd ST9 . 43 F3
Bass's Bldgs DE14 ...... 166 A2

Bassenthwaite Ct DY6 .... 275 E3
Bassett Cl Cheadle ST10 .. 76 B2
 Wolv WV4 .... 265 E3
Bassilow Rd ST4 .... 72 C4
Baswich Crest ST17 ...... 156 B1
Baswich House Dr ST17 .. 175 E4
Baswich House Way ST17 . 175 D4
Baswich La ST17 .... 175 E4
Batch La DE6 .... 127 D4
Batchelor Cl DY8 .... 279 F4
Bateman Ave ST3 .... 27 D3
Batemans Way ST14 .... 126 B4
Batesway ST12 .... 197 E2
Batfield La Alveley DY7 .. 272 B1
 Enville B77 .... 272 B1
Bath La DY7 .... 277 E4
Bath Rd Cannock WS11 .. 209 F3
 Newcastle-u-L ST5 ..... 54 C1
 Stourbridge DY8 .... 279 F3
Bath St Leek ST13 ...... 30 C3
 Meir ST3 .... 74 A3
 Sedgley DY3 .... 266 C1
 Stoke-on-T ST4 .... 72 A4
Bath Terr ST4 .... 72 A4
Baths La ST18 .... 158 B4
Baths Rd ST3 .... 283 B4
Baths Rd ST3 .... 283 B4
Bathurst St ST3 .... 283 C4
Batten Cl ST3 .... 90 B4
Batten Wlk ST15 ...... 118 C3
Battison Cres ST3 .... 283 C2
Battle Ridge ST16 .... 156 B4
Battlefield La WV5 ... 270 A3
Battlesteads ST10 ... 78 B1
Baulk La ST11 .... 106 C4
Baxter Gn ST16 ...... 155 D2
Bayham Wlk ST2 ..... 58 A4
Bayley Hills TF10 .... 168 A2
Baylie Ct DY8 .... 279 F3
Baylie St DY8 .... 279 F2
Bayston Ave WV3 ... 265 F4
Bayswater Rd
 Rugeley WS15 ...... 178 B1
 Sedgley DY3 .... 271 D1
Baytree Cl Hanley ST1 . 57 F3
Baytree Rd WS3 ..... 243 E1
Baywood Cl ST3 ..... 156 B1
Beach Ave WV14 ... 266 C2
Beachcroft Rd DY6 .. 270 B1
Beachwood Ave DY6 . 270 B1
Beacon Dr DE13 ..... 147 D2
Beacon Gdns WS13 . 214 A1
Beacon Hill B74 ..... 256 B1
Beacon La Kinver DY7 . 277 D1
 Romsley DY7 .... 276 C2
 Sedgley DY3 .... 266 C1
 Upper Arley DY12 .. 276 B2
Beacon Pas ST3 ..... 271 E4
Beacon Rd Aldridge WS9 . 256 A1
 Rolleston DE13 .... 147 D2
 Stone ST15 .... 120 A3
Beacon Rise Aldridge WS9 . 256 A2
 Sedgley DY3 .... 266 C1
 Stone ST15 .... 120 A3
Beacon St Lichfield WS13 . 213 F1
 Wolv DY3 .... 266 C1
Beacon Street Sch WS13 . 213 F1
Beacon Way
 Brownhills WS9 .... 245 D1
 Cannock WS12 ..... 210 C2
Beaconfields WS13 . 231 D4
Beaconsfield ST5 ... 56 B4
Beaconsfield Ave WV4 . 266 B3
Beaconsfield Dr WV4 . 266 B3
Beaconsfield Rd DE13 . 166 A4
Beaconside ST16 ... 156 A3
Beaconside Cl ST16 . 156 A3
Beaconside Sports Ctr
 ST18 .... 156 B2
Beadnell Gr ST3 .... 73 E1
Beale St DY8 .... 279 F3
Bealeys La WS3 ..... 243 D1
Beam Cl DE13 ...... 166 A4
Beamhill Rd DE13 .. 165 F4
Beamish La WV7 ... 237 D3
Beard Gr ST2 .... 58 A4
Bearnett Dr WV4 ... 265 E1
Bearnett La WV4 ... 265 D1
Bearstone Rd
 Mucklestone TF9 .. 83 E2
 Norton in H TF9 .. 82 C2
 Woore TF9 .... 82 C2
Bearwood Hill Rd DE15 . 167 D2
Beasley Ave ST5 ... 55 F4
Beasley Pl ST5 ..... 55 F4
Beat La SK11 .... 17 F4
Beaton Rd B74 ..... 258 A2
Beatrice Wlk ST8 .. 27 D1
Beattie Ave ST5 ... 284 B4
Beatty Dr CW12 ... 6 A2
Beatty Rd ST13 .... 31 D3
Beau Ct WS11 ...... 209 F1
Beaubrook Gdns DY6 . 275 F2
Beauchamp Ind Pk B77 . 261 E4
Beauchamp Rd B77 . 261 F3
Beaudesert WS7 ... 212 A1
Beaudesert View WS12 . 211 D3
Beaufort Ave ST9 .. 59 D2
Beaufort Rd
 Burton u T DE15 .. 167 D1
 Longton ST3 .... 73 E1
Beaufort Way WS9 . 256 A2
Beaulieu Ave DY6 .. 275 F2
Beaulieu Cl ST9 .... 59 D2
Beaumaris Cl
 Sedgley DY1 ...... 271 F2
 Stoke-on-T ST5 .. 71 E4

Beaumaris Ct ST4 ...... 284 A2
Beaumaris Rd TF10 .... 168 C2
Beaumont Cl Biddulph ST6 . 16 B2
 Great Wyrley WS6 .... 226 C1
Beaumont Gdns ST17 .. 174 A4
Beaumont Rd
 Great Wyrley WS6 .... 226 C1
 Tunstall ST6 .... 41 F2
Beauty Bank Cres DY8 . 279 F3
Beauty Bank Prim Sch
 DY8 .... 279 F3
Beaver Dr ST10 .... 76 A2
Bebington Cl WV8 .... 255 F4
Beck Rd CW3 .... 68 C4
Beck The B79 .... 216 C1
Beck's La DE13 .... 162 C1
Beckbury Ave WV4 ... 265 E3
Beckdale St ST4 ..... 126 A4
Beckenham Cl ST3 .. 90 B4
Becket Cl Burton u T DE13 . 166 A3
 Sutton Coldfield B74 . 257 F3
Beckett Ave ST3 ..... 74 A1
Beckfields Cl ST8 ... 17 D1
Beckford St ST1 ..... 282 C4
Beckminster Rd WV3 . 265 F4
Beckton Ave ST6 .... 41 F2
Bedale Pl ST3 .... 72 C1
Bedcroft ST12 ...... 88 C1
Bedford Ave WS14 .. 156 A2
Bedford Cres ST5 ... 71 E2
Bedford Pl WS12 ... 210 A2
Bedford Rd
 Burton u T DE15 ... 185 E4
 Hanley ST1 .... 282 A1
 Kidsgrove ST7 .... 26 A2
Bedford St ST1 ..... 57 D1
Bedford Way WS15 . 196 B3
Bedingstone Dr ST19 . 208 A4
Bednall Ct ST17 .... 193 F4
Bednall Rd ST17 ... 175 E1
Bee La WV10 .... 240 D2
Beech Ave Burton u T DE13 . 166 C4
 Cheddleton ST13 .. 45 E2
 King's Bromley DE13 . 199 E3
 Tamworth B77 .... 250 C2
Beech Cl Armitage WS15 . 198 B2
 Biddulph ST8 ..... 17 D1
 Cheadle ST10 .... 76 C1
 Haughton ST18 .. 172 C3
 Kinver DY7 .... 278 A2
 Leek ST13 .... 30 B1
 Newport TF10 .... 168 C1
 Pattingham WV6 . 253 E1
 Sedgley DY3 ..... 266 C1
 Tamworth B77 ... 250 A4
 Uttoxeter ST14 .. 126 A4
 Wheaton Aston ST19 . 205 E3
Beech Cres WS7 .. 228 C3
Beech Croft Madeley CW3 . 68 C4
 Pattingham WV6 . 253 E1
Beech Ct Cannock WS12 . 210 A4
 Stone ST15 .... 120 A3
Beech Dale Rd
 Swynnerton ST4 .. 87 E1
 Tittenser ST12 .... 103 F4
Beech Dr Burton u T DE13 . 166 C4
 Kidsgrove ST7 .... 40 C4
Beech Gate B74 .. 257 E3
Beech Gdns Codsall WV8 . 238 C1
 Lichfield WS14 ... 231 D3
Beech Gr Ashley TF9 .. 99 E3
 Fenton ST4 .... 72 B2
 Huntington WS12 . 209 E4
 Leek ST13 .... 30 B3
 Newcastle-u-L ST5 . 56 B2
 Swadlincote DE11 . 186 C4
Beech Hurst Gdns WS5 . 264 A1
Beech La Burton u T DE13 . 166 C3
 Coppenhall ST18 .. 174 B2
Beech Pine Ct WS12 . 210 A4
Beech Rd Barton-u-N DE13 . 183 E1
 Eccleshall ST21 ... 133 F3
 Kingswinford DY6 . 275 F3
 Longton ST3 ...... 72 C1
 Stourbridge DY8 . 279 F2
 Tamworth B79 .... 250 A4
 Wolv WV10 .... 240 A1
Beech St Burton u T DE14 . 166 A1
 Longton ST3 ...... 283 C3
Beech Tree Cl DY6 . 275 F4
Beech Tree La WS11 . 226 B4
Beech Wlk WS15 .. 198 A1
Beecham Cl WS9 .. 256 A4
Beechcliff La ST4, ST12 . 87 F1
Beechcroft ST12 .. 88 C1
Beechcroft Ave ST17 . 155 E1
Beechcroft Cres B74 . 256 B1
Beechcroft Ct B74 . 258 A1
Beechen Gr WS7 .. 228 C4
Beeches Croft WS13 . 215 E4
Beeches Cl DY6 ... 275 E3
Beeches, Forsbrook
 Jun Sch The ST11 . 91 D4
Beeches Rd WS15 . 197 D3
Beeches The
 Newcastle-u-L ST5 . 56 B4
 Rugeley WS15 .... 178 B2
 Sutton Coldfield B74 . 257 E2
Beechfield Dr ST17 . 175 F3
Beechfield Rd ST4 . 88 A3
Beechfield Rise WS14 . 231 E4
Beechfields ST12 .. 88 C1
Beechfields Way TF10 . 168 C2
Beechhouse La WV5 . 264 A1
Beechlawn Dr DY7 . 278 C4
Beechmere Rise WS15 . 178 A1
Beechmont Gr ST1 . 57 F3
Beechmount Rise ST17 . 175 E4

Beechtree La
 Blakedown DY10 .... 280 C3
 Cookley DY10 ...... 280 C3
Beechtree Rd WS9 .. 244 C2
Beechway ST16 ..... 155 E3
Beechwood WS14 .. 232 C3
Beechwood Bsns Pk
 WS11 .... 210 A2
Beechwood Cl
 Forsbrook ST11 ... 91 D3
 Newcastle-u-l ST5 . 71 E1
 Walsall WS3 ...... 243 D2
Beechwood Cres B77 . 250 C2
Beechwood Croft B74 . 257 E3
Beechwood Dr WV6 . 255 E2
Beechwood Dr Stone ST15 . 120 A3
 Wolv WV6 .... 255 D1
Beecroft Ave WS13 . 214 A1
Beecroft Ct WS11 .. 209 F1
Beecroft Hill Specl Sch
 WS11 .... 209 F1
Beecroft Rd WS11 . 209 F1
Beelow La ST10 ... 78 B3
Bees La WS15 ..... 178 C1
Beeston Rd DY10 . 280 A3
Beeston Ridge ST17 . 174 A4
Beeston St ST3 ... 73 E3
Beeston View ST7 . 41 D4
Beffcote La ST20 . 171 D2
Beggars Bush La WV5 . 270 A3
Beggars La ST13 .. 30 B3
Beighton Cl B74 .. 257 F3
Belbroughton Rd
 Blakedown DY10 .. 281 E1
 Stourbridge DY8 .. 279 F2
Belfast Cl ST16 ... 42 A1
Belfield Ave ST5 .. 56 B2
Belford Pl ST4 .... 56 C1
Belfry Cl WS3 .... 243 D2
Belfry Dr DY8 .... 279 F3
Belfry The Burton u T DE13 . 147 E1
 Perton WV6 ...... 254 B2
Belgrade Rd WV10 . 240 A1
Belgrave Ave ST3 . 283 B2
Belgrave Cres ST3 . 283 C1
Belgrave Ct DY6 .. 275 F2
Belgrave Cty High Sch
 B77 .... 250 C1
Belgrave Rd Longton ST3 . 283 C1
 Newcastle-u-L ST5 . 284 C2
 Tamworth B77 ... 261 F4
Belgrave Recn Ctr B77 . 250 C1
Bell Ave ST3 ..... 73 E1
Bell Cl ST16 ..... 155 F3
Bell Dr WS12 .... 210 B4
Bell Heather Rd WS8 . 244 B3
Bell La Barlaston B12 . 88 C2
 Barton-u-N DE13 . 183 E1
 Doveridge DE6 .. 127 E4
 Walsall WS3 ..... 243 D1
Bell Orch TF9 .... 100 B3
Bell Pl WV2 ..... 266 B4
Bell Rd WV5 .... 264 B1
Bell St DY8 ..... 279 F2
Bellamour La Colton WS15 . 178 B3
 Colwich WS15 .. 178 B3
Bellamour Way WS15 . 178 C3
Bellaport Rd TF9 . 82 A2
Bellasis St ST5 .. 155 F3
Bellbrook ST19 .. 192 C1
Belle Vue ST5 .. 275 E1
Belle Vue Prim Sch DY8 . 275 E2
Bellefield View ST5 . 56 B2
Bellen Croft Gdns WV3 . 265 E4
Bellerton La ST6 . 42 C1
Bellevue ST4 ... 266 C1
Bellflower Cl WV10 . 241 D4
Bellhouse La DE13 . 164 C3
Bellhurst La ST19 . 205 D3
Bellingham B77 .. 251 E1
Bellringer Cl ST8 . 27 E4
Bells End Rd DE12 . 184 B1
Bells La Burntwood WS7 . 211 B1
 Kingswinford DY8 . 275 E1
Bellsize St WS11 . 227 F3
Bellwood Cl ST3 . 90 A3
Belmont Ave WS11 . 209 E1
Belmont Cl Aldridge WS9 . 256 A4
 Great Wyrley WS11 . 227 D2
Belmont Inf Sch ST5 . 57 D2
Belmont Rd Hanley ST1 . 57 D2
 Ipstones ST10 .. 61 E4
 Tamworth B77 .. 261 F4
 Wolv WV4 ...... 266 A3
Belmot Rd Anslow DE13 . 164 C4
 Tutbury DE13 ... 145 F1
Belper Rd WS3 .. 243 E2
Belsay Cl ST3 ... 283 C4
Belsize B77 ..... 250 C1
Belt Rd WS11 ... 210 A3
Belton Ave WV11 . 241 D1
Belvedere Ave WV4 . 266 A3
Belvedere Cl
 Burntwood WS7 . 228 C3
 Kingswinford DY6 . 275 F2
 Stafford ST17 .. 175 E4
 Tamworth B79 .. 250 B4
Belvedere Cty Jun Sch
 DE14 .... 166 A3
Belvedere Gdns WV6 . 255 F3
Belvedere Rd
 Burton u T DE13 . 166 A3
 Trentham ST4 .. 72 A1

Belvide Gdns WV8 .... 238 C2
Belvoir B77 .... 261 E4
Belvoir Ave ST4 .... 88 B3
Belvoir Cl Burton u T DE13 .. 166 A3
  Sedgley DY1 .... 271 F1
Belvoir Rd DE13 .... 166 A3
Belwell Dr B74 .... 258 A1
Belwell La B74 .... 258 A1
Bemersley Rd
  Chell Heath ST8 .... 27 E1
  Norton-in-t-M ST6 .... 42 C3
Benches Cl WS7 .... 228 B3
Bend Oak Dr DE15 .... 167 E2
Bend Oak Jun Sch DE15 .. 167 E2
Benedict Pl ST2 .... 58 A3
Benenden Cl ST17 .... 156 A1
Benfleet Pl ST3 .... 283 A3
Bengal Gr ST4 .... 88 B4
Bengry Rd ST3 .... 73 F1
Benion Rd WS11 .... 209 F3
Benjamins Way ST7 .... 39 F1
Bennett Pl ST5 .... 56 A4
Bennett Rd B74 .... 257 E2
Bennett St ST6 .... 56 C4
Bennetts La Bosley SK11 .... 7 F4
  Perton WV6 .... 263 F4
  Uttoxeter ST14 .... 125 E3
Bennion St ST3 .... 283 C3
Benson Ave WV4 .... 266 B3
Benson Cl Lichfield WS13 .. 214 B1
  Perton WV6 .... 254 C3
Benson St ST6 .... 41 F3
Benson View B79 .... 250 B4
Bent La Astbury CW12 .... 15 D4
  Whitmore ST5 .... 86 A2
Bentilee Cty Prim Sch ST2 .. 73 E4
Bentley Ave ST5 .... 56 A2
Bentley Brook La WS12 .. 211 D3
Bentley Dr WV8 .... 238 C2
Bentley Rd Chell Heath ST6 .. 42 B3
  Uttoxeter ST14 .... 110 C1
  Wolv WV10 .... 240 C1
Bentley Way B79 .... 249 F4
Bentleys Rd TF9 .... 112 A4
Benton Cres WS3 .... 243 E1
Benton's La WS6 .... 227 D1
Bents La ST10 .... 109 D2
Bentygrange La ST13 .... 48 B2
Beowulf Covert DE13 .... 147 D1
Berdmore St ST4 .... 283 A5
Beresford Cres ST5 .... 71 D3
Beresford Dale DE11 .... 186 C1
Beresford Dell CW3 .... 68 B3
Beresford La SK17 .... 24 B1
Beresford Meml CE
  Fst Sch ST13 .... 31 D4
Beresford St ST1 .... 57 D1
Bergamot Dr ST3 .... 90 A3
Berkeley Cl WV6 .... 254 C2
Berkeley Dr DY6 .... 275 E4
Berkeley St Hanley ST1 .... 282 C2
  Stone ST15 .... 104 C1
Berkeley Way WS15 .... 198 A1
Berkley Cl ST20 .... 171 F4
Berkshire Gr ST5 .... 71 E3
Berkshire The WS3 .... 243 D2
Berkswell Cl Sedgley DY1 .. 271 F1
  Sutton Coldfield B74 .... 257 F2
Berkswich CE Prim Sch
  ST17 .... 175 F3
Bernard Cheadle La ST15 .. 103 E2
Bernard Gr ST3 .... 89 F2
Bernard St ST1 .... 282 C2
Berne Ave ST5 .... 70 C3
Bernwall Cl DY8 .... 279 F2
Berrisford Cl TF9 .... 97 F1
Berrisford Rd TF9 .... 97 F1
Berry Gdns DE15 .... 167 E2
Berry Hedge La DE15 .... 167 E2
Berry Hill WS12 .... 210 B2
Berry Hill High Sch ST2 .. 58 A1
Berry Hill Rd ST4 .... 57 F1
Berry La ST3 .... 283 B3
Berry Rd ST16 .... 155 D4
Berry St ST4 .... 72 A4
Berrybush Gdns DY3 .... 271 F4
Berryfield Gr ST3 .... 73 F2
Berryfields WS9 .... 245 F3
Bert Smith Way TF9 .... 97 E1
Bertlein Rd ST16 .... 155 F4
Berwick Dr WS11 .... 226 A4
Berwick Wlks ST5 .... 70 C4
Berwyn Gr WS6 .... 226 C2
Best Ave DE15 .... 167 D1
Best St ST4 .... 72 C3
Beswick Cl ST10 .... 76 B1
Beswick Rd ST6 .... 41 F3
Beswicks La TF9 .... 82 B1
Bethell Rd ST6 .... 57 E4
Bethesda Rd ST1 .... 282 C1
Bethesda St ST1 .... 282 B2
Betjeman Wlk ST17 .... 174 B4
Betley CE Prim Sch CW3 .. 53 D3
Betley Hall Gdns CW3 .... 53 D3
Betley Pl ST5 .... 71 E3
Betlingspring La DE6 .... 81 E2
Beton Way ST16 .... 155 E4
Bettany Glade WV10 .... 240 C2
Bettany Rd ST6 .... 57 D4
Betton Rd TF9 .... 97 F1
Betty Hatch La ST16 .... 155 E3
Betty's La WS11 .... 228 A2
Bevan Ave Kidsgrove ST7 .. 40 C3
  Wolv WV4 .... 266 C2
Bevan Cl WS4 .... 244 B1

Bevan Lee Rd WS11 .... 209 E2
Bevan Pl CW3 .... 68 C4
Bevandean Cl ST4 .... 88 B3
Beveridge Cl ST3 .... 74 A1
Beverley Cl ST19 .... 207 F4
Beverley Cres
  Forsbrook ST11 .... 91 D4
  Wolv WV4 .... 266 C2
Beverley Dr Bucknall ST2 .. 58 B1
  Stafford ST16 .... 155 E4
Beverley Hill WS12 .... 210 B3
Beverley Rd DE14 .... 185 D4
Beverly Dr DY6 .... 275 E4
Beverston Rd WV6 .... 255 D2
Beville St ST4 .... 72 C3
Bevin La ST2 .... 58 A2
Bew St ST6 .... 42 C3
Bewcastle Gr ST3 .... 90 A4
Bexhill Gr ST1 .... 57 F3
Bexley St ST1 .... 282 A4
Bexmore Dr WS13 .... 214 C1
Beyer Cl B77 .... 251 D1
Bhylls Acre Cty Prim Sch
  WV3 .... 265 D4
Bhylls Cres WV3 .... 265 E4
Bhylls La WV3 .... 265 E4
Bibby's Gn WV10 .... 240 C2
Bickford Cl ST19 .... 206 A3
Bickford Rd ST19 .... 206 A4
Bickley Ave B74 .... 257 F3
Bida La CW12 .... 16 A4
Biddulph Common Rd ST8 .. 17 D3
Biddulph Grange Ctry Pk
  ST8 .... 16 C2
Biddulph Grange Hospl
  ST8 .... 16 C2
Biddulph High Sch ST8 .... 27 E3
Biddulph Park Rd ST8 .... 17 D3
Biddulph Rd Biddulph ST7 .. 26 B3
  Chell Heath ST6 .... 42 A4
  Congleton CW12 .... 16 A4
  Kidsgrove CW7 .... 26 B3
Biddulph St CW12 .... 16 B4
Bideford Ave ST1 .... 175 E4
Bideford Way WS11 .... 226 A4
Biggin Cl WV6 .... 254 C3
Bignall End Rd ST7 .... 40 A2
Bigsbury Wlk ST6 .... 56 C4
Bigwood La Bradley ST18 .. 173 F2
  Coppenhall ST18 .... 173 F2
Bilberry Bank WS11 .... 209 F3
Bilberry Gr WS15 .... 178 B1
Bilberry Cres WS12 .... 209 E3
Bilbrook Ct WV8 .... 239 D2
Bilbrook Gr WV8 .... 239 D2
Bilbrook Mid CE Sch WV8 .. 239 D2
Bilbrook Rd WV8 .... 239 D2
Bilbrook Sta WV8 .... 239 D1
Billinge St ST6 .... 56 C4
Billington Ave ST18 .... 158 B1
Billington Bank ST18 .... 173 E2
Billington La ST18 .... 154 B1
Billy Buns La WV5 .... 270 A4
Bilston Rd WV1, WV2 .... 266 C4
Bilston St DY3 .... 271 F4
Bilton St ST4 .... 72 A4
Bingley Prim Sch WV3 .... 266 A4
Bingley St WV3 .... 266 A4
Birch Ave Biddulph ST8 .... 27 D3
  Brownhills WS8 .... 244 C4
  Burntwood WS7 .... 228 C3
  Cannock WS11 .... 226 B4
Birch Brook La WS14 .... 246 C3
Birch Cl Branston DE14 .. 185 D4
  Colwich ST18 .... 158 B1
  Denstone ST14 .... 95 E3
  Stafford ST17 .... 175 F3
Birch Coppice WV5 .... 269 F3
Birch Croft WS9 .... 256 B4
Birch Dale CW3 .... 68 C3
Birch Dr Little Aston B74 .. 257 E3
  Stourbridge DY8 .... 279 F3
Birch Gr Blythe Bridge ST3 .. 90 A2
  Forsbrook ST11 .... 91 D4
  Lichfield WS14 .... 231 E4
  Polesworth B78 .... 262 B4
Birch Green Gr ST1 .... 57 F4
Birch Hill Ave WV5 .... 269 F3
Birch House La ST21 .... 117 F4
Birch House Rd ST5 .... 55 E4
Birch La Aldridge WS9 .... 245 E1
  Brownhills WS4 .... 244 B1
  Rugeley WS15 .... 197 D3
Birch Mews CW3 .... 68 C3
Birch Rd Audley ST7 .... 39 F1
  Essington WV11 .... 241 F1
  Sedgley DY3 .... 266 C1
  Stone ST15 .... 120 A4
Birch Rise TF9 .... 99 F2
Birch St ST1 .... 57 F3
Birch Terr Burntwood WS7 .. 212 A1
  Hanley ST1 .... 282 B2
Birch Tree La The Bank ST7 .. 26 A4
  Whitmore ST5 .... 85 E4
Birch Wlk ST3 .... 73 D1
Birchall Ave ST6 .... 41 E3
Birchall Cl ST13 .... 30 C1
Birchall La ST13 .... 30 C1
Birchall Park Ave ST13 .... 30 C2
Bircham Wlk ST5 .... 71 D1
Birchbrook Ind Pk WS14 .. 246 C3
Birchcroft WV9 .... 224 B1
Birchdown Ave ST6 .... 42 A2
Birchendale Cl ST10 .... 92 C1
Birchenfields La ST10 .... 75 F3
Birchenwood Rd ST7 .... 41 F1
Birches Ave WV8 .... 239 D1
Birches Barn Ave WV3 .... 265 F4

Birches Barn Rd WV3 .... 265 F4
Birches Cl DE13 .... 166 B4
Birches Fst Sch WV8 .... 239 D1
Birches Head High Sch
  ST1 .... 57 F4
Birches Head Rd
  Bucknall ST1 .... 57 F3
  Hanley ST1 .... 57 F3
Birches Park Rd WV8 .... 239 D1
Birches Rd WV8 .... 239 D1
Birches The ST10 .... 76 B1
Birches Valley WS15 .... 195 E3
Birches Way ST7 .... 26 A1
Birchfield Ave WV6 .... 255 D3
Birchfield Cl CV9 .... 262 B1
Birchfield Rd Bucknall ST2 .. 58 B3
  Burton u T DE15 .... 185 F3
Birchfield Sch WV7 .... 237 E3
Birchfields Cl ST15 .... 119 F3
Birchfields Dr WS12 .... 210 B1
Birchgate ST2 .... 58 B2
Birchgate Gr ST2 .... 58 B2
Birchglade WV3 .... 255 E1
Birchlands Rd ST1 .... 57 F3
Birchmoor La
  Blymhill ST19 .... 189 E1
  Church Eaton ST20 .... 189 E1
Birchmoor Rd B78 .... 262 C4
Birchover Way ST6 .... 42 A4
Birchtree La WS15 .... 196 C3
Birchwood Ave B78 .... 262 C4
Birchwood Cl WV11 .... 242 A2
Birchwood Prim Sch B78 .. 262 C4
Birchwood Rd
  Lichfield WS14 .... 231 F4
  Wolv WV4 .... 266 A3
Birchwood Rise WS15 .... 161 D3
Birchwood Wlk DY6 .... 275 F4
Bird Rd ST3 .... 74 A1
Bird St Lichfield WS13 .... 231 D1
  Sedgley DY3 .... 271 E2
Bird's Barn La DY7 .... 277 E1
Birdhope B77 .... 251 E1
Birds Bush Cty Prim Sch
  B77 .... 261 F4
Birds Bush Rd B77 .... 261 F4
Birdsgrove La Mayfield DE6 .. 66 B2
  Swinscoe DE6 .... 66 B2
Birkdale Dr Kidsgrove ST7 .. 26 B2
  Stafford ST16 .... 156 B2
Birkdale Rd WS3 .... 243 D2
Birkholme Dr ST3 .... 90 A3
Birks St TF9 .... 99 E3
Birks St ST4 .... 72 A4
Birmingham New Rd WV4 .. 266 C2
Birmingham Rd
  Aldridge WS9 .... 256 A2
  Blakedown DY10 .... 281 E1
  Lichfield WS14 .... 231 D2
  Shenstone WS14 .... 247 D2
Birmingham St WV2 .... 266 B4
Birrell St ST2 .... 72 C3
Biscay Gr ST4 .... 88 B4
Bishop Rawle CE Prim Sch
  ST10 .... 76 B2
Bishop Rd ST6 .... 42 A3
Bishop St ST4 .... 73 D3
Bishop's Cl ST7 .... 40 B4
Bishops Ct ST21 .... 133 F4
Bishops Dr ST19 .... 223 E4
Bishops Grange WS15 .. 178 C1
Bishops La TF9 .... 97 D1
Bishops Meadow B75 .... 258 C2
Bishops Way B74 .... 257 F3
Bishton La WS15 .... 178 A3
Bitham Cl ST19 .... 207 F4
Bitham Ct DE13 .... 147 E1
Bitham La DE13 .... 147 E1
Bitham Sch DE13 .... 147 E1
Bittell Cl WV10 .... 240 C2
Bittern La ST10 .... 76 C2
Bitterne Pl ST2 .... 73 E4
Bitterscote La ST19 .... 250 A1
Black Bank Rd ST13 .... 44 B3
Black Dr ST18 .... 157 E3
Black Horse La ST1 .... 282 B3
Black La Forton TF10 .... 150 C1
  Kingsley WS10 .... 62 B2
Blackbank Rd ST5 .... 55 E2
Blackberry La
  Brownhills WS9 .... 245 D2
  Stafford ST16 .... 155 E2
  Sutton Coldfield B74 .... 257 F2
Blackbird Cl ST14 .... 126 B3
Blackbird Way ST8 .... 27 E4
Blackbrook Way WV10 .... 240 C2
Blackbrook World of Birds
  ST13 .... 48 A2
Blackburn Ave WV6 .... 255 F4
Blackdown B77 .... 251 E1
Blackfriar's Rd ST5 .... 284 B2
Blackfriars F Ed Unit ST2 .. 58 A3
Blackfriars St ST5 .... 284 B2
Blackhalve La WV11 .... 241 E1
Blackheath Cl ST4 .... 73 E2
Blackheath La ST18 .... 156 C2
Blackhole La ST18 .... 154 B1
Blackies La ST15 .... 120 C4
Blacklake Dr ST3 .... 90 A2
Blackmere Cl TF10 .... 168 B1
Blackpit La Doveridge DE6 .. 127 D4
  Wombourne WV5 .... 264 C2
Blackpool St DE14 .... 185 E4
Blackroot Dr WS7 .... 229 E2
Blackshaw Cl CW12 .... 6 A1
Blackshaw Moor CE Cty
  Prim Sch ST13 .... 20 C2
Blacksmith La WS14 .... 232 C3

Blacksmith's La
  Eggington DE65 .... 148 A3
  Newton Solney DE15 .... 167 F4
Blackthorn Ave WS7 .... 228 C2
Blackthorn Cres WS12 .... 211 D3
Blackthorn Pl ST5 .... 55 F4
Blackthorn Rd
  Brierley Hill DY8 .... 275 F1
  Burton u T DE15 .... 185 F3
Blackthorne Cl DY1 .... 271 F2
Blackthorne Rd Dudley DY1 .. 271 F3
  Lichfield WS14 .... 231 E4
Blackwell's Row ST5 .... 57 D3
Blackwood Jun Mix
  Inf Sch B74 .... 256 C1
Blackwood Pl ST3 .... 73 F2
Blackwood Rd Aldridge B74 .. 256 C1
  Tamworth B77 .... 261 E4
Bladon Ave ST5 .... 71 D2
Bladon Cl ST6 .... 42 A4
Bladon House Sch DE15 .. 167 D3
Bladon St DE15 .... 167 E2
Bladon View DE13 .... 148 A1
Blaizefield Cl CW3 .... 67 E1
Blake Cl WS13 .... 210 A3
Blake High Sch WS12 .... 209 F3
Blake St Burslem ST6 .... 56 C4
  Shenstone B74 .... 257 F3
  Sutton Coldfield B74 .... 257 F3
Blake Street Sta B74 .... 257 F3
Blakedown CE Fst Sch
  DY10 .... 281 E1
Blakedown CE Inf Sch
  DY10 .... 281 E1
Blakeley Ave WV6 .... 255 F4
Blakeley Heath Cty
  Prim Sch WV5 .... 270 A2
Blakeley Heath Dr WV5 .. 270 A3
Blakeley La Kingsley ST10 .. 63 D1
  Oakamoor ST10 .... 63 D1
Blakeley Rise WV6 .... 255 F4
Blakelow La DE6 .... 65 D1
Blakelow Rd ST2 .... 58 A3
Blakemore Rd WS9 .... 245 D2
Blakenall Heath WS3 .... 243 E1
Blakenhall Gdns WV2 .... 266 B4
Blakenhall Ind Est WV2 .. 266 A4
Blakeways Cl B79 .... 217 E3
Blakiston St ST16 .... 155 F2
Blanchard Cl ST3 .... 90 B4
Blandford Dr ST3 .... 90 B4
Blandford Gdns WS7 .... 229 E3
Blanefield WV8 .... 239 F1
Blanford Mere Prim Sch
  DY6 .... 275 F4
Blantyre Cl ST3 .... 283 C2
Blantyre Wlk ST3 .... 283 C2
Blatchford Cl ST3 .... 74 A1
Blaydon Ave B75 .... 258 C1
Blaydon Rd WV9 .... 240 A1
Blaze Hill Rd DY6 .... 275 D4
Blaze Pk DY6 .... 275 D4
Bleak House Dr WS7 .... 228 B4
Bleak Pl ST6 .... 57 D4
Bleak St ST5 .... 56 B2
Bleakridge Ave ST5 .... 56 A4
Bleeding Wolf La ST7 .... 25 F3
Blencarn Gr ST9 .... 43 E2
Blenheim Cl
  Burton u T DE15 .... 167 E2
  Tamworth B77 .... 250 B2
Blenheim Dr WS13 .... 215 E3
Blenheim Rd
  Burntwood WS7 .... 229 D4
  Kingswinford DY6 .... 275 F4
  Norton Canes WS11 .... 228 A2
Blenheim St ST4 .... 72 B3
Blenheim Way DY1 .... 271 F1
Bleriot Cl ST3 .... 90 B4
Blessed William Howard
  RC High Sch ST17 .... 155 E1
Blewitt St WS12 .... 210 A4
Blithbury Rd Colton WS15 .. 179 D2
  Hamstall Ridware WS15 .. 180 C2
  Hill Ridware WS15 .... 179 E3
Blithfield Cl ST19 .... 59 D1
Blithfield Ho ST17 .... 174 C3
Blithfield Pl WS11 .... 210 A1
Blithfield Rd WS8 .... 228 A1
Bloomfield Cl WV5 .... 269 E3
Bloomfield Cres WS13 .. 214 A1
Bloomfield Dr WV12 .... 242 B1
Bloomfield Way B79 .... 249 F4
Bloomsbury St 2 WV2 .. 266 B4
Bloomsbury Way WS14 .. 231 F4
Blore Rd TF9 .... 98 C1
Blossomfield Cl DY6 .... 275 F4
Blount Cl ST19 .... 207 F4
Blounts Dr ST14 .... 126 A3
Bloxwich CE Prim Sch
  WS3 .... 243 D1
Bloxwich North Sta WS3 .. 242 C1
Bloxwich Sta WS3 .... 243 D1
Blue Cedars DY8 .... 279 E4
Blue House Barns TF10 .. 168 C2
Blue House La WV7 .... 237 D4
Bluebell Cl Biddulph ST8 .. 27 F4
  Cannock WS12 .... 210 A3
  Kingswinford DY6 .... 275 E1
Bluebell La WS6 .... 227 D1
Bluebell Rd WS9 .... 245 D2
Bluebird Cl WS14 .... 231 E4
Bluemeadow La WV5 .... 270 A4
Bluestone Ave ST6 .... 42 A1

Bluestone La DE15 .... 186 A4
Blundies La DY7 .... 273 F2
Blunt St ST5 .... 56 B2
Blunt's Hollow WS15, DE13 162 A2
Blurton High Sch ST3 .... 88 C4
Blurton Prim Sch ST3 .... 72 C1
Blurton Rd Barlaston ST12 .. 89 D2
  Fenton ST3 .... 72 C2
  Longton ST3 .... 72 C2
Blythe Ave ST3 .... 90 A3
Blythe Bridge High Sch
  ST11 .... 90 C4
Blythe Bridge Rd ST11 .... 74 C1
Blythe Bridge Sta ST11 .. 90 C4
Blythe Cl Blythe Bridge ST11 .. 90 B4
  Burntwood WS7 .... 229 E3
Blythe Gdns WV8 .... 238 C2
Blythe Mount Pk ST11 .... 91 D4
Blythe Rd Forsbrook ST11 .. 91 D4
  Stafford ST17 .... 174 C3
Blythe St B77 .... 250 B2
Blythe View
  Blythe Bridge ST11 .... 91 D1
  Forsbrook ST11 .... 90 C3
  Hamstall Ridware WS15 .. 180 C1
Blythebridge Bank ST14 .. 140 C3
Blythfield DE14 .... 166 C2
Board School Gdns DY3 .. 271 F4
Boardman Cres ST16 .... 155 E2
Boardman Ind Est DE11 .. 186 C1
Boardman Rd DE11 .... 186 C1
Boardmans Bank ST6 .... 28 A1
Boat House La WS15 .... 198 A3
Boat La Wall WS14 .... 229 F1
  Weston-u-T ST18 .... 138 B2
Boathorse Rd
  Kidsgrove ST7 .... 41 D4
  Tunstall ST6 .... 41 D3
Boatman's La WS9 .... 244 C1
Bodiam Ct WV6 .... 255 D2
Bodicote Gr ST5 .... 258 C1
Bodington Rd B75 .... 258 B2
Bodmin Ave ST17 .... 175 E4
Bodmin Wlk ST6 .... 42 B1
Bognop Rd WV11 .... 241 E2
Bogs La ST11 .... 90 C3
Bolberry Gr ST3 .... 73 F1
Bold St ST5 .... 57 F3
Bolebridge Mews B79 .... 250 B4
Bolebridge St B79 .... 250 B2
Boley Cl WS14 .... 231 E4
Boley Cottage La WS14 .. 231 F4
Boley La WS14 .... 231 E4
Boley Park Sh Ctr WS14 .. 231 F4
Boleyn Cl WS6 .... 226 B1
Bolina Gr ST4 .... 73 D3
Bollin Gr ST6 .... 16 C1
Bolney Gr ST1 .... 57 F3
Bolsover Cl ST6 .... 42 A4
Bolton Pl ST3 .... 89 F4
Bolton Way WS3 .... 242 C2
Boma Rd ST4 .... 87 F4
Bond End DE13 .... 182 A1
Bond St Burton u T DE14 .. 166 B1
  Tunstall ST6 .... 41 E2
Bondfield La DE13 .... 181 F1
Bondfield Way ST3 .... 74 A1
Bondway WS12 .... 209 F4
Bonehill Rd Fazeley B78 .. 249 F2
  Tamworth B78 .... 249 F2
Boney Hay Prim Sch
  WS7 .... 211 F1
Boney Hay Rd WS7 .... 229 D4
Boningdale Way ST17 .. 174 A4
Bonnard Cl ST3 .... 90 B3
Bonnington Cres ST16 .. 155 E1
Bonville Gdns WV10 .... 240 C2
Boon Ave ST4 .... 72 A4
Boon Gr ST17 .... 174 C3
Boon Hill Rd ST7 .... 39 F1
Boons Ind Est ST18 .... 154 C1
Booth Cl WS13 .... 214 A1
Booth La Admaston ST18 .. 140 C2
  Kingstone ST18 .... 140 C2
Booth St Audley ST7 .... 39 E1
  Cannock WS11 .... 210 A3
  Newcastle-u-L ST5 .... 55 F3
  Stoke-on-T ST4 .... 72 A3
Boothen CE Prim Sch ST4 .. 72 A3
Boothen Gn ST4 .... 72 A3
Boothen Old Rd ST4 .... 72 A3
Boothen Rd ST4 .... 72 A3
Boothenwood Terr ST4 .... 72 A3
Boothroyd St ST1 .... 282 B2
Bordeaux Cl DY1 .... 271 F2
Bordeaux Rd ST3 .... 90 A4
Borden Cl
  Wheaton Aston ST19 .. 205 E4
  Wolv WV8 .... 255 F4
Border Way ST17 .... 174 C3
Bore St WS13 .... 231 D1
Borman B79 .... 249 F3
Borough Cres DY8 .... 279 F3
Borough La WS15 .... 212 C4
Borough Rd
  Burton u T DE14 .... 166 B2
  Tamworth B79 .... 250 B4
Borrowcop La WS14 .... 231 E3
Borrowdale Rd ST6 .... 42 C2
Boscobel Cl DY1 .... 271 F2
Boscobel Gr ST19 .... 223 E4
Boscombe Gr ST4 .... 88 B3
Boscomoor Cl ST19 .... 207 F4
Boscomoor Ind Est ST19 .. 207 F4
Boscomoor La ST19 .... 207 F4
Boscomoor Sh Ctr ST19 .. 207 F4
Bosinney Cl ST4 .... 73 D3

Bosley Gr ST6 .... 41 E3
Bosley View CW12 .... 6 A1
Boss Gate Cl WV5 .... 270 A3
Bostock Cl ST15 .... 120 B3
Boston Cl WS12 .... 210 C1
Bosty La WS9 .... 256 A2
Boswell Rd WS11 .... 209 E3
Boswell St ST4 .... 56 C1
Bosworth Cl DY3 .... 271 E4
Bosworth Dr DE13 .... 166 A4
Botany Bay Rd ST1 .... 57 F3
Botany Dr DY3 .... 271 E4
Botfield Cl WV7 .... 237 D3
Botham Dr ST13 .... 45 E3
Botterham La DY3 .... 269 F2
Botteslow St ST1 .... 282 C2
Bottom La Ipstones ST10 .... 47 E3
  Swynnerton ST15 .... 103 D4
Boucher Rd ST13 .... 45 E2
Boughey Rd Audley ST7 .... 39 F1
  Newport TF10 .... 168 C1
  Stoke-on-T ST4 .... 72 B4
Boughey St ST4 .... 72 A3
Boulevard The ST6 .... 41 F2
Boulters La CV9 .... 262 B1
Boulton Cl WS7 .... 229 E4
Boulton St Hanley ST1 .... 57 E3
  Newcastle-u-L ST5 .... 56 B3
Boundary Cl Leek ST13 .... 30 C2
  Stone ST15 .... 119 F3
Boundary Cres DY3 .... 271 E2
Boundary Ct ST1 .... 282 B4
Boundary Hill DY3 .... 271 E2
Boundary Ind Est WV10 .... 240 B3
Boundary La CW12 .... 16 A4
Boundary Rd
  Brownhills WS9 .... 244 C3
  Etwall DE65 .... 148 B4
Boundary St Hanley ST1 .... 282 B4
  Newcastle-u-L ST5 .... 56 B1
Boundary View ST10 .... 76 A1
Boundary Way
  Wolv, Springhill WV4 .... 265 E3
  Wolv, Wightwick WV6 .... 254 C1
Bourne Ave Fazeley B78 .... 249 F1
  Ranton ST18 .... 153 E3
Bourne Cl WS12 .... 210 C1
Bourne Pl ST13 .... 30 B3
Bourne Rd ST7 .... 25 F1
Bourne St Fenton ST4 .... 72 C2
  Mow Cop ST7 .... 26 B4
Bourne Vale WS9 .... 256 B2
Bournes Bank ST6 .... 56 C4
Bournes Bank S ST6 .... 57 D4
Bournes Bk 10 ST6 .... 57 D4
Bouverie Par ST1 .... 57 F4
Bow St WS15 .... 178 C1
Bowden St ST6 .... 42 A1
Bowdler Rd WV2 .... 266 B4
Bowen St WV4 .... 266 C4
Bowen-cooke Ave WV6 .... 254 C3
Bower Cl WS15 .... 214 B1
Bower End La CW3 .... 68 B3
Bower La WS15 .... 178 B2
Bower Norris RC Prim Sch
  ST17 .... 174 B4
Bowers Ct ST15 .... 120 B3
Bowers La ST15 .... 120 B2
Bowes Dr WS11 .... 209 E3
Bowfell Gr ST4 .... 73 D3
Bowhill La CW3 .... 53 D3
Bowland Ave ST15 .... 55 F1
Bowling Alley ST17 .... 193 F4
Bowling Green Ave B77 .... 261 F4
Bowling Green Rd DY8 .... 279 F3
Bowman Gr ST6 .... 42 A4
Bowmead Cl ST4 .... 88 B3
Bowmere Cl ST6 .... 16 B1
Bowness St ST1 .... 282 A4
Bowood Dr WV6 .... 255 E3
Bowsey Wood Rd CW3 .... 68 C4
Bowstead St ST4 .... 72 A4
Bowyer Ave ST6 .... 42 C3
Box La ST3 .... 73 F1
Boxer Cl WS15 .... 198 B2
Boxwood Pl ST5 .... 55 E4
Boxwood Rd ST10 .... 92 C2
Boyden Cl
  Cannock WS11 .... 209 D1
  Penkridge ST19 .... 208 A4
Boyles Hall Rd ST7 .... 39 F1
Brabazon Cl ST3 .... 90 B4
Bracken Ave TF9 .... 99 E3
Bracken Cl
  Blythe Bridge ST3 .... 89 F3
  Burntwood WS7 .... 229 E4
  Cannock WS12 .... 210 A4
  Lichfield WS14 .... 231 F3
  Stafford ST16 .... 155 D4
  Tittensor ST12 .... 88 A1
  Wolv WV8 .... 239 F1
Bracken Dale ST13 .... 30 A3
Bracken Park Gdns DY8 .... 275 F1
Bracken Rd WS12 .... 209 E3
Bracken St ST4 .... 72 C2
Bracken View ST17 .... 176 B2
Bracken Way
  Newport TF10 .... 168 C2
  Rugeley WS15 .... 178 B1
Brackenberry ST5 .... 56 A2
Brackenfield Ave ST2 .... 58 B1
Brackenfield Rd WS16 .... 155 E4
Brackenhill Rd WS7 .... 229 D4
Brackens The ST5 .... 71 E1
Brackenwood Rd DE15 .... 185 F3
Bracklesham Way B77 .... 251 D4
Brackley Ave ST6 .... 42 A1

Bradbury Cl
  Brownhills WS8 .... 244 C3
  Norton-in-t-M ST6 .... 42 C2
Bradbury La Cannock WS12 .. 210 A4
  Enville DY7 .... 272 C2
  King's Bromley DE13 .... 199 E3
Braden Rd WV4 .... 265 E2
Bradford Rd WS8 .... 244 C4
Bradford St
  Cannock WS11 .... 210 A3
  Tamworth B79 .... 249 F3
Bradford Terr ST1 .... 57 F3
Bradgate Dr B74 .... 257 F3
Bradley Dr ST21 .... 117 F2
Bradley La Bradley ST18 ...... 173 D2
  Bradnop ST18 .... 174 B3
  Haughton ST18 .... 173 D2
Bradley Rd
  Stourbridge DY8 .... 279 F3
  Wolv WV2 .... 266 C4
Bradley St Burton u T DE15 .. 185 F4
  Uttoxeter ST14 .... 126 B4
Bradmore Rd
  Burton u T DE13 .... 166 A3
  Wolv WV3 .... 265 F4
Bradshaw Way ST16 .... 155 E4
Bradwell Croft B75 .... 258 C2
Bradwell Grange ST5 .... 56 A4
Bradwell Hospl ST5 .... 56 A4
Bradwell La
  Cannock WS15 .... 211 F3
  Newcastle-u-L ST5 .... 56 A4
Bradwell Prim Sch ST5 .... 56 B4
Bradwell St ST6 .... 56 B4
Braemar Ave DY8 .... 275 E1
Braemar Cl Bucknall ST2 .... 58 B2
  Sedgley DY3 .... 266 B1
Braemar Gdns WS12 .... 209 E4
Braemar Rd
  Norton Canes WS11 .... 228 A2
  Pattingham WV6 .... 253 E1
Braemore Rd ST2 .... 58 A3
Braeside Way WS3 .... 243 F2
Braham B79 .... 249 E3
Brailsford Ave DE11 .... 186 C3
Brain St B77 .... 251 D1
Braithwaite Cl DY6 .... 275 E3
Brake La DY8 .... 281 F3
Brake Level ST7 .... 26 A4
Brake The ST7 .... 26 A4
Brake Village ST7 .... 26 A4
Brakespeare St ST6 .... 41 E4
Bramber B77 .... 250 B1
Bramber Way DY8 .... 279 F1
Bramble Cl WS8 .... 244 C3
Bramble Dr WS12 .... 210 B4
Bramble Gn DY1 .... 271 F3
Bramble La WS7 .... 229 D4
Bramble Lea CW3 .... 68 C3
Bramble Way WS15 .... 178 B1
Bramble Ct ST8 .... 27 C4
Brambles The
  Lichfield WS15 .... 231 E3
  Newcastle-u-L ST5 .... 71 E1
Brambleside
  Brierley Hill DY8 .... 275 F1
  Stafford ST17 .... 175 E4
Bramblewood WV5 .... 270 A4
Bramblewood Dr WV3 .... 265 F4
Brambling Cl ST14 .... 126 B3
Bramblings The ST7 .... 175 E3
Bramdean Wlk WV4 .... 265 E3
Bramell Cl DE14 .... 184 C4
Bramfield Dr ST5 .... 284 C4
Bramhall Cl ST18 .... 154 A4
Bramhall La ST16 .... 155 E3
Bramley Cl ST10 .... 76 C1
Bramley Dale DE11 .... 186 C1
Bramley Pl ST4 .... 71 F1
Bramley Way ST14 .... 232 B3
Brammall Dr ST11 .... 90 C4
Brammer St ST6 .... 42 B2
Brampton Cl DY10 .... 280 A2
Brampton Ct ST5 .... 284 C4
Brampton Ct WS12 .... 210 C1
Brampton Gdns ST5 .... 56 B2
Brampton Ind Est ST5 .... 284 B4
Brampton Rd ST5 .... 284 C4
Brampton Sidings ST5 .... 284 B4
Brampton Wlk ST3 .... 283 C1
Bramshall Rd ST14 .... 125 F4
Bramshaws The ST10 .... 76 C1
Bramstead Ave WV6 .... 255 D1
Brancaster Cl B77 .... 251 D4
Brandon Aldridge B74 .... 256 C2
  Sedgley DY3 .... 271 F4
Brandon Gr ST4 .... 87 F4
Brandon Pk WV3 .... 265 F4
Brandons The ST7 .... 174 C3
Bransdale Rd WS8 .... 244 C3
Branson Ave ST3 .... 73 F2
Branston Cl Branston DE13 .. 184 B4
  Burton u T DE14 .... 185 D3
Branston Water Pk DE14 .... 184 B3
Bransty Gr ST4 .... 88 B3
Brant Ave ST5 .... 56 A2
Brantley Ave WV3 .... 255 E1
Brantley Cres DY7 .... 267 F1
Brantley La Bobbington DY7 .. 263 D2
  Seisdon WV5 .... 263 D2
Branton Hill La WS9 .... 256 B3
Brantwood Ave WS7 .... 229 D3
Brassington St CW3 .... 53 D3
Brassington Way ST8 .... 58 A3
Bratch Common Rd WV5 .... 269 F4
Bratch Hollow WV5 .... 270 A4

Bratch La WV5 .... 269 F4
Bratch Pk WV5 .... 269 F4
Brattswood Dr ST7 .... 25 D3
Braunton Ave ST17 .... 175 F4
Brawdean Dr ST19 .... 192 C1
Braystones Cl ST7 .... 41 F4
Brazenhill La ST18 .... 172 C4
Breach La Cheadle ST10 ...... 92 B3
  Draycott in t M ST10 .... 92 B3
Breach Rd ST6 .... 43 E4
Breadmarket St WS13 .... 231 D4
Bream ST6 .... 261 E4
Bream Way ST6 .... 42 A2
Bredon Cl WV7 .... 237 D3
Breech Cl ST10 .... 48 C1
Breedon Ct ST5 .... 55 F2
Breedon Way WS4 .... 244 B1
Breeze Ave
  Norton Canes WS11 .... 228 A3
  Tunstall ST6 .... 41 F3
Brelades Cl DY1 .... 271 F1
Brempton Croft ST15 .... 106 B1
Brendale Cl ST4 .... 72 A1
Brendon B77 .... 251 D1
Brendon Cl ST17 .... 175 E4
Brent B77 .... 261 F4
Brentmill Cl WV10 .... 240 C2
Brentnall Dr B75 .... 258 A2
Brentnor Cl ST3 .... 73 F2
Brenton Rd WV4 .... 265 F2
Brentwood Dr ST9 .... 59 D2
Brentwood Gr ST9 .... 43 E2
Brenwood Cl DY6 .... 275 D4
Brereton Hill WS15 .... 197 D3
Brereton Lodge WS15 .... 197 D3
Brereton Manor Ct WS15 ... 197 D3
Brereton Pl ST6 .... 41 F1
Brereton Rd WS15 .... 196 C3
Breretonhill La WS15 .... 197 E1
Bretby Bsns Pk DE15 .... 186 C4
Bretby La DE15 .... 167 F2
Bretby Rd DE11 .... 186 C4
Bretherton Pl ST6 .... 42 A3
Bretlands Way DE15 .... 186 A3
Brettell La DY8 .... 279 F4
Brevitt Rd WV2 .... 266 B3
Brewers Dr WS3 .... 244 A1
Brewers Terr WS3 .... 244 A1
Brewery La ST18 .... 158 A1
Brewery St Hanley ST1 ...... 282 B4
  Rugeley WS15 .... 196 C4
Brewester Rd ST2 .... 57 F2
Brewood CE Mid Sch
  ST19 .... 223 E3
Brewood Rd WV9 .... 224 A2
Brewster Cl B78 .... 249 F1
Brianson Ave ST6 .... 57 E4
Briar B77 .... 251 D2
Briar Ave B74 .... 257 D1
Briar Cl Cannock WS12 ...... 210 A4
  Rugeley WS15 .... 178 B1
  Stafford ST17 .... 175 F3
  Swadlincote DE11 .... 186 C3
Briar Gr ST12 .... 118 C3
Briar Way ST21 .... 102 C1
Briarbank Cl ST4 .... 71 F1
Briars The ST5 .... 284 B4
Briars Way WS12 .... 211 D3
Briarsleigh ST17 .... 175 E4
Briarswood ST7 .... 26 A1
Briarwood Pl ST3 .... 74 A1
Brick House St 9 ST6 .... 56 C4
Brick Kiln La
  Brocton ST17 .... 175 F2
  Hints B75 .... 259 D3
  Rolleston DE13 .... 147 D2
  Salt ST18 .... 137 F1
  Sedgley DY3 .... 271 D2
  Stoke-on-T ST4 .... 56 C1
  Wheaton Aston ST19 ...... 205 D3
Brick Kiln Way WS15 .... 196 C3
Brick St ST3 .... 271 E4
Brick-kiln La ST5 .... 55 F4
Brickbridge La WV5 .... 269 F3
Brickfield Cl ST18 .... 139 E1
Brickfield Pl ST3 .... 73 E3
Brickhill La DE13 .... 163 D3
Brickhouse La B79 .... 216 B1
Brickiln St WS8 .... 244 C4
Brickyard Rd WS9 .... 256 A4
Bridal Path ST9 .... 59 D2
Bridestone Cl ST3 .... 90 A4
Bridge Ave WS11 .... 226 C2
Bridge Cl Audley ST7 .... 39 F1
  Brownhills WS8 .... 244 C3
  Weston-u-T ST18 .... 138 B2
Bridge Cres ST15 .... 120 A4
Bridge Croft ST6 .... 42 A3
Bridge Cross Rd WS7 .... 229 D4
Bridge Farm DE13 .... 147 F1
Bridge La ST18 .... 139 D2
Bridge Rd
  Armitage WS15 .... 198 B2
  Brownhills WS4 .... 244 A1
  Cookley DY10 .... 280 A3
  Stoke-on-T ST4 .... 71 F2
  Uttoxeter ST14 .... 126 B4
Bridge St
  Brierley Hill DY8 .... 275 F1
  Brownhills WS8 .... 244 C3
  Burton u T, Stretton DE13 . 147 F1
  Burton u T, Winshill DE14 . 166 C2
  Cannock WS11 .... 226 C3
  Chell Heath ST8 .... 27 D1

Bridge St continued
  Newcastle-u-L ST5 .... 284 C3
  Newcastle-u-L, Silverdale ST5 . 55 E1
  Stafford ST16 .... 155 F1
  Tamworth B77 .... 250 C3
  Tutbury DE13 .... 146 B4
  Uttoxeter ST14 .... 126 B4
Bridge Street Ind Units
  ST14 .... 126 B4
Bridge Terr ST13 .... 20 C3
Bridge Way WS8 .... 244 C3
Bridgefoot Wlk WV8 .... 239 F1
Bridgeman St ST1 .... 203 F1
Bridgemary Cl WV10 .... 240 C2
Bridgemere Garden World
  CW5 .... 67 D2
Bridges Cres WS11 .... 227 F3
Bridges Rd WS11 .... 227 F3
Bridgeside DE13 .... 147 F1
Bridgeside Trad Est B77 .... 250 B1
Bridgett Cl ST4 .... 71 F3
Bridgewater Cl
  Congleton CW12 .... 6 A1
  Penkridge ST19 .... 207 F4
Bridgewater Dr WV5 .... 269 F4
Bridgewater St Burslem ST6 . 56 B4
  Tamworth B77 .... 250 B3
Bridgewood St ST3 .... 283 C4
Bridgford Ave DE14 .... 184 C4
Bridgnorth Ave WV5 .... 269 F4
Bridgnorth Gr ST5 .... 40 C1
Bridgnorth Rd Enville DY7 .. 273 E1
  Himley DY3 .... 270 C4
  Kinver DY7 .... 278 B4
  Perton WV6 .... 264 B4
  Seisdon WV5 .... 263 F3
  Stourbridge DY8 .... 279 E3
  Wolv WV3, WV6 .... 255 D1
  Wombourne WV5 .... 269 E3
Bridgwater Cl WS9 .... 244 C2
Bridgwood Rd ST11 .... 91 D4
Bridle La Ellenhall ST20 .... 153 E4
  Swadlincote DE15 .... 186 A3
Bridle Path ST3 .... 283 C1
Bridle Path The
  Madeley CW3 .... 68 B3
  Newcastle-u-L ST5 .... 70 C2
Bridle Rd Stafford ST17 ..... 175 E3
  Stourbridge DY8 .... 279 E3
Bridle Wlk WS15 .... 178 A1
Bridleway The TF9 .... 97 D1
Brierley Hill Rd DY8 .... 275 F1
Brierley Rd CW12 .... 6 A1
Brierley St ST6 .... 42 B1
Brierlow Bar SK17 .... 5 D4
Brierley Hill La WS15 .... 212 A2
Brieryhurst ST12 .... 58 B3
Brieryhurst Rd ST7 .... 26 A2
Brindewell Gr ST4 .... 88 B3
Brindley Ave WV11 .... 242 A1
Brindley Bank Rd WS15 .... 178 C2
Brindley Brae DY7 .... 278 B3
Brindley Cl Albrighton WV7 . 237 D3
  Brierley Hill DY8 .... 275 F1
  Kidsgrove ST7 .... 25 F1
  Penkridge ST19 .... 208 A4
  Stafford ST16 .... 155 F4
  Wombourne WV5 .... 269 E3
Brindley Cres
  Cannock WS12 .... 210 B4
  Cheddleton ST13 .... 45 E2
Brindley Heath Jun Sch
  DY7 .... 278 A3
Brindley Heath Rd
  Cannock WS12 .... 210 B4
  Rugeley WS12 .... 195 E1
Brindley La ST9 .... 43 E2
Brindley Pl ST6 .... 42 B3
Brindley Rd Cannock WS12 . 194 C1
  Rugeley WS12 .... 194 C1
Brindley St ST5 .... 284 B3
Brindley Way CW12 .... 6 A1
Brindleys Bsns Pk WS11 ... 210 A2
Brindleys Way ST7 .... 39 F1
Brindleys Way ST7 .... 39 F1
Brindon Cl ST3 .... 74 A2
Brinkburn Cl WS15 .... 178 A1
Brinley Way DY6 .... 275 D3
Brinscall Gn ST6 .... 42 A4
Brinsford La WV10 .... 240 B2
Brinsford Rd WV10 .... 240 B2
Brinsley Ave ST4 .... 88 A3
Brisbane Rd ST16 .... 155 D4
Brisley Hill ST4 .... 71 F3
Bristol Cl WS11 .... 210 A1
Bristol St Newcastle-u-L ST5 . 56 B3
  Wolv WV3 .... 266 A4
Britannia Park Ind Est ST6 . 257 D1
Britannia Way WS13 .... 231 F4
Brittain Ave ST5 .... 55 F1
Brittain Rd ST13 .... 45 E3
Brittania Dr ST16 .... 166 B4
Brittania Stadium
  (Stoke City FC) ST4 .... 72 B2
Brittle Pl ST10 .... 48 B2
Britten St ST4 .... 56 C1
Brixham Cl ST2 .... 57 F1

Brizlincote La DE15 .... 167 E1
Brizlincote St DE15 .... 166 C1
Broad La ST5 .... 71 F4
Broad La Brownhills WS4 .... 244 B1
  Church Eaton ST20 .... 171 F1
  Endon ST6 .... 43 E4
  Great Wyrley WS3 .... 242 C2
  Lichfield WS14 .... 231 E3
  Walsall WS3 .... 243 D1
  Whittington WS13 .... 215 F1
  Wolv WV3 .... 265 F4
Broad Lane Gdns WS3 ...... 243 D1
Broad Meadow WS9 .... 256 A4
Broad Meadow Ct ST16 .... 155 D2
Broad Meadow La WS6 .... 227 D1
Broad Oaks ST17 .... 174 C3
Broad St Cannock WS11 .... 226 C3
  Hanley ST1 .... 282 B2
  Kingswinford DY6 .... 275 E3
  Leek ST13 .... 30 C3
  Newcastle-u-L ST5 .... 284 B3
  Stafford ST16 .... 155 E2
Broad Way WS4 .... 244 B1
Broadacres DY6 .... 275 E3
Broadfield Rd ST5 .... 41 E4
Broadholes La ST19 .... 205 D3
Broadhurst Cl WS12 .... 194 C1
Broadhurst Gn WS12 .... 194 C1
Broadhurst Green Rd
  WS12 .... 194 B1
Broadhurst St ST6 .... 42 A1
Broadlands DE13 .... 166 B4
Broadlands Rise WS14 ...... 231 E4
Broadlee B77 .... 251 E1
Broadmeadow DY6 .... 275 F4
Broadmine St ST4 .... 72 C3
Broadoak Way ST3 .... 72 C1
Broadoaks Cl WS11 .... 227 F3
Broadsmeath B77 .... 250 B1
Broadstone Cl WV4 .... 266 B3
Broadway Cannock WS12 .. 209 F3
  Codsall WV8 .... 238 C2
  Meir ST3 .... 73 F1
  Newport TF10 .... 169 D2
  Wolv, Bushbury WV10 .... 240 C1
  Wolv, Compton WV3 ..... 255 E1
Broadway Ct
  4 Longton ST3 .... 73 F1
  Meir ST3 .... 73 F1
Broadway La ST10 .... 49 D2
Broadway Pl 1 ST3 .... 73 F1
Broadway St DE14 .... 166 B1
Broadway The Dudley DY1 . 271 F2
  Stourbridge DY8 .... 279 E2
  Wombourne WV5 .... 270 A3
Broadwell La WV6 .... 253 D1
Broc Cl ST19 .... 208 A4
Brockbank Pl ST6 .... 42 A3
Brockeridge Cl WV12 ...... 242 B1
Brockhill TF9 .... 99 E3
Brockhurst La B75 .... 259 D4
Brockhurst Rd B75 .... 258 E1
Brocklehurst Way ST1 .... 57 F4
Brockley Sq ST1 .... 282 B3
Brocksford St ST4 .... 283 B5
Brockton La ST21 .... 117 F2
Brockton Cres ST17 .... 175 F3
Brocton Hts ST17 .... 176 B2
Brocton La ST17 .... 175 F3
Brocton Rd ST17 .... 176 B3
Brogan St ST4 .... 72 C3
Bromford Dale WV2 .... 255 F2
Bromford Rise WV3 .... 266 A4
Bromley Cl WS12 .... 210 B4
Bromley Ct ST1 .... 282 A4
Bromley Gdns WV8 .... 239 D2
Bromley Hills Prim Sch
  DY6 .... 275 F3
Bromley Hough ST4 .... 71 F3
Bromley La DY6 .... 275 F3
Bromley Pl WV4 .... 266 A3
Bromley St Hanley ST1 ..... 282 A4
  Wolv WV2 .... 266 B4
Bromleyhedge La ST13 ...... 48 B2
Brompton Dr ST2 .... 43 D2
Brompton Lawns WV6 ..... 255 D2
Bromsberrow Way ST3 .... 283 A3
Bromsgrove Pl ST3 .... 283 A3
Bromwich Dr WS15 .... 215 E4
Bromwynd Cl WV2 .... 266 A3
Bronant Wlk 13 ST6 .... 57 D4
Bronte Cl DE14 .... 166 B4
Bronte Ct ST9 .... 250 A3
Bronte Dr WS11 .... 210 B1
Bronte Gr ST2 .... 43 D1
Bronte Rd WV2 .... 266 C3
Brook Ave B77 .... 262 A4
Brook Cl Brewood WV9 .... 224 A2
  Brownhills WS9 .... 245 D2
  Doveridge DE6 .... 127 E4
  Endon ST9 .... 44 A4
  Forsbrook ST11 .... 91 D4
  Lichfield WS13 .... 214 A1
  Penkridge ST19 .... 207 D3
Brook Cres DY8 .... 275 E4
Brook End Burntwood WS7 . 229 D2
  Fazeley B78 .... 261 D4
  Haughton ST18 .... 172 C3
  Longdon WS15 .... 197 F1
Brook Gdns ST6 .... 16 B1
Brook Glen Rd ST17 .... 174 C4
Brook Gr WV8 .... 239 D1

Brook Ho TF10 168 C2
Brook House La WV10 241 D4
Brook La Brocton ST17 176 B2
Brownhills WS9 244 C2
Church Leigh ST10 108 C3
Endon ST9 43 F4
Great Wyrley WS6 227 D2
Newcastle-u-L ST5 284 B2
Ranton ST18 153 E2
Brook Meadow Rd WS4 244 B1
Brook Pl Newcastle-u-L ST5 71 E3
Stoke-on-T ST4 56 C1
Brook Prim Sch The DY8 275 F1
Brook Rd
Cheslyn Hay WS11 226 C2
Trentham ST4 88 A4
Wombourne WV5 269 F3
Brook Sq WS15 196 C4
Brook St Brierley Hill DY8 275 F1
Burton u T DE14 166 B2
Kidsgrove ST8 27 D3
Kingswinford DY6 270 A1
Leek ST13 30 C3
Newcastle-u-L ST5 55 E1
Sedgley DY3 271 E2
Stoke-on-T ST4 72 A4
Stourbridge DY8 279 F3
Swadlincote DE11 186 C3
Brookbank Gdns DY5 271 D1
Brookbank Rd DY5 271 D1
Brookdale DY3 271 E2
Brookdale Dr WV4 265 F3
Brooke Rd WS12 209 F3
Brookers Ct ST4 72 C3
Brookfield TF9 99 E3
Brookfield Ave ST9 43 F4
Brookfield Cl ST10 62 B2
Brookfield Ct Hanley ST1 282 B4
Stone ST15 120 B3
Brookfield Dr WS11 226 C4
Brookfield Rd
Aldridge WS9 245 D1
Codsall WV8 239 D2
Norton-in-t-M ST2 43 E2
Stoke-on-T ST4 71 F3
Brookfields Rd ST10 62 A4
Brookgate ST11 91 D4
Brookhay La
Alrewas WS13 215 F2
Whittington WS13 215 F2
Brookhill Cl WV12 242 B1
Brookhill Way WV12 242 B1
Brookhouse Cl WV10 241 D3
Brookhouse Dr ST12 88 B1
Brookhouse Green
Prim Sch ST2 58 B1
Brookhouse La Bucknall ST2 58 C2
Caverswall ST2 58 C2
Cheddleton ST13 45 D2
Congleton CW12 6 B1
Featherstone WV10 241 D3
Brookhouse Rd
Cheadle ST10 76 A2
Gnosall ST20 171 E4
Meir ST3 74 A1
Newcastle-u-L ST5 55 F4
Brookhouse Way
Cheadle ST10 76 A1
Gnosall ST20 171 E3
Brookhouses Ind Est ST10 76 A1
Brookland Ave ST3 283 A1
Brookland Rd
Brownhills WS9 244 C2
Chell Heath ST6 41 F3
Brooklands DY8 275 F1
Brooklands Ave WS11 226 C2
Brooklands Cl ST14 126 A3
Brooklands Gr WS9 244 C2
Brooklands Rd
Albrighton WV7 237 D3
Cannock WS11 210 A2
Brooklands Sch ST16 155 E3
Brooklands The DY3 269 F1
Brooklands Way ST13 45 F4
Brooklyn Gr DY6 275 D4
Brooklyn Rd
Burntwood WS7 229 D2
Cannock WS12 210 B1
Brookmead Gr ST4 73 D3
Brookmead Ind Est ST16 155 F4
Brookside Burslem ST6 56 B4
Burton u T DE15 167 D3
Enville DY7 273 E2
Kingsley ST10 62 A2
Ranton ST18 153 E3
Rolleston DE13 147 D2
Sedgley DY3 271 E1
Brookside Ave TF10 168 C1
Brookside Bsns Pk ST14 126 B4
Brookside Cl
Newcastle-u-L ST5 284 A1
Wombourne WV5 269 F3
Brookside Dr Endon ST9 44 A4
Fenton ST3 72 C1
Brookside Gdns ST19 221 F4
Brookside La ST15 119 F4
Brookside Rd
Barton-u-N DE13 183 E1
Fazeley B78 249 E1
Uttoxeter ST14 126 B4
Brookside Way
Blakedown DY10 281 D1
Kingswinford DY6 275 E4
Tamworth B77 262 A3
Brookview Dr ST3 73 F2
Brookweed B77 251 D2
Brookwillows ST17 175 E4
Brookwood Cl ST5 71 D2
Brookwood Dr ST3 74 A1
Broom Lea TF9 99 E2
Broom St ST1 282 C4
Broom's La DE6 129 D1
Broome Hill ST5 71 E1
Broome La Blakedown DY9 281 F1
Hagley DY9 281 F1
Broome Wlk WS15 198 B2
Broomfield Ave B78 261 D4
Broomfield Cl
Newport TF10 168 B2
Stone ST15 120 A3
Broomfield Ct ST15 105 D1
Broomfield La DE6 79 F1
Broomfield Pl TF10 168 B2
Broomfield Pl N ST1 57 D2
Broomfield Pl S ST1 57 D2
Broomfield Rd
Newport TF10 168 B2
Norton-in-t-M ST6 42 B3
Broomfields ST8 17 D1
Broomhill Bank WS11 209 F2
Broomhill Cl WS11 209 F2
Broomhill St ST6 41 E2
Brooms Rd ST15 120 A3
Broomstead Cres ST16 155 D3
Broomyclose La ST14 111 D2
Brough Cl WV14 266 C2
Brough La ST4 88 A4
Brough Park L C tr ST13 30 C4
Brough Rd DE15 167 E2
Broughton Cl ST16 155 E4
Broughton Cres ST12 88 C1
Broughton Ct WV6 255 D2
Broughton Rd Bucknall ST2 57 F2
Newcastle-u-L ST5 56 B1
Wolv WV3 255 E1
Brow Hill ST13 30 C3
Brown Ave ST7 25 D3
Brown Lees Ind Est ST8 27 D2
Brown Lees Rd
Biddulph ST8 27 D2
Kidsgrove ST8 27 D3
Brown St Burslem ST6 57 D4
Wolv WV2 266 B4
Brown's La Tamworth B79 250 B4
Yoxall DE13 182 A1
Brown's Lake DY7 273 E2
Brownfield Rd ST3 74 A1
Brownhill Rd ST6 43 D4
Brownhills High Sch ST6 41 F1
Brownhills Rd
Brownhills WS9 245 D2
Norton Canes WS11 228 A2
Tunstall ST6 41 E1
Brownhills Sch WS8 228 C1
Brownhills West Jun Mix
Inf Sch WS8 228 B1
Browning Cl Cheadle ST10 76 B1
Tamworth B79 249 F4
Browning Cres WV10 240 B1
Browning Gr Kidsgrove ST7 40 B4
Perton WV6 254 C2
Browning Rd
Burntwood WS7 229 E4
Longton ST3 72 C1
Sedgley DY3 271 D2
Browning St ST16 155 E2
Brownley Rd ST6 42 B1
Browns Wlk WS15 178 B1
Brownsea Pl ST3 72 C2
Brownsfield Rd WS13 214 B1
Brownsholme B79 249 E3
Brownshore La WV11 242 A2
Brownswall Rd DY3 271 E4
Broxwood Pk WV6 255 E2
Bruford Rd WV3 266 A4
Brund La ST13 45 D2
Brundall Oval ST2 58 B1
Brundle Ave ST16 155 D2
Brunel Cl Burntwood WS7 229 D4
Stafford ST16 155 F4
Tamworth B79 250 A3
Brunel Gr WV6 254 C3
Brunel Wlk ST3 283 C4
Brunslow Cl WV10 240 B1
Brunswick Pl ST1 282 B2
Brunswick Rd WS11 209 F1
Brunswick St Hanley ST1 282 B3
11 Leek ST13 30 C3
Newcastle-u-L ST5 284 C3
Brunswick Terr ST17 155 E1
Brunt St ST6 56 B4
Brutus Rd ST5 55 E3
Bryan Ave WV4 265 E2
Bryan St ST1 282 B3
Bryans La WS15 178 C1
Bryans Way WS12 210 C2
Bryant Rd ST2 58 A3
Brymbo Rd ST5 55 F3
Brynmawr Rd WV14 266 C2
Buccleuch Rd ST3 73 E1
Buckden B77 251 E1
Buckingham Cl
Burton u T DE13 166 B4
Stafford ST17 156 B1
Buckingham Cres ST4 72 A1
Buckingham Ct DE15 167 E2
Buckingham Gdns WS14 231 D3
Buckingham Gr DY6 275 E4
Buckingham Pl WS11 210 B1
Buckingham Rd
Tamworth B79 249 F4
Wolv WV4 266 A3
Buckingham Rise DY1 271 F1
Buckland Cl WS12 210 B1
Buckland Gr ST4 88 B3
Buckland Rd ST16 136 B1
Buckley Cl ST14 125 E4
Buckley Rd
Chell Heath ST6 42 B3
Wolv WV4 265 E3
Buckley's Row ST5 284 B2
Buckmaster Ave ST5 71 E3
Bucknall Hospl ST2 58 A2
Bucknall New Rd ST1 282 C3
Bucknall Old Rd ST1 282 C3
Bucknall Rd Bucknall ST1 57 F2
Hanley ST1 57 F2
Wolv WV11 242 A1
Buckpool Sch The DY8 275 F2
Buckthorn Cl WS12 209 F4
Buckton Cl B75 258 C1
Buds Rd WS15 211 F3
Buglawton Cty Prim Sch
CW12 6 A2
Buglawton Hall Sch
CW12 6 B3
Buildwas Cl WS3 242 C1
Bull Hill ST16 155 F2
Bull La Chell Heath ST8 27 D1
Wombourne WV5 270 A4
Bull Ring Claverley WV5 267 E4
Sedgley DY3 271 E4
Bull Ring The ST18 138 B1
Bull St DY3 271 E1
Bulldog La WS13 214 A1
Buller St Hanley ST1 282 C1
Wolv WV4 266 C3
Bullgap La Stanton DE6 65 E2
Swinscoe DE6 65 E2
Bullmoor La WS14 230 A1
Bullocks House Rd ST7 26 C2
Bullows Rd WS8 244 B3
Bulstrode St 24 ST6 56 C4
Bumblehole Mdws WV5 269 F4
Bun La Blymhill TF10 188 B1
Sheriffhales TF10 203 E4
Bungalows The ST20 131 E2
Bungham La ST19 207 E4
Bunny Hill ST5 71 E3
Bunt's La ST9 43 E2
Bunting Cl ST14 126 A3
Bunting The
Cheddleton ST9 60 A4
Kingsley ST10 61 E2
Buntingdale Rd TF9 112 A4
Bunyan Pl WS11 209 F2
Burcham Cl ST16 155 D4
Burdock Cl WS11 210 A2
Burford Rd Stafford ST17 156 B1
Wheaton Aston ST19 205 D3
Burford Way ST2 58 A1
Burgage Cl TF9 97 E1
Burgage Ct TF10 168 C1
Burgage The
Eccleshall ST21 133 F4
Market Drayton TF9 97 E1
Burgess St ST6 56 C4
Burgesses The DY7 278 A2
Burgis Cl ST13 45 E2
Burgoyne St WS11 210 A3
Burgundy Gr ST3 90 A4
Burland Ave WV6 255 F3
Burland Rd ST5 40 B1
Burleigh Cl WS12 210 A4
Burleigh Croft WS7 229 D2
Burleigh Gr ST5 56 B2
Burleigh Rd WV3 266 A4
Burlidge Rd ST6 42 A3
Burlington Ave ST5 56 B2
Burlington Dr ST17 174 A4
Burmarsh Wlk
16 Burslem ST6 56 C4
Wolv WV8 255 F4
Burnaby Rd ST6 41 E3
Burnell Gdns WV3 265 F4
Burnet Gr WV10 241 D4
Burnett Ct ST16 155 D3
Burnett Pl ST6 42 B2
Burnett Rd B74 257 D1
Burnfield Dr WS15 178 B1
Burnfields Cl WS9 256 A4
Burnham Ave ST17 175 E3
Burnham Cl DY6 275 F2
Burnham Gn WS11 226 A4
Burnham St ST4 283 A5
Burnhays Rd ST6 41 F1
Burnley St ST1 57 E3
Burns Ave Stafford ST17 174 A4
Wolv WV10 240 B1
Burns Cl Kidsgrove ST7 41 D4
Lichfield WS14 231 D3
Burns Dr WS7 229 E4
Burns Gr DY3 271 D2
Burns Rd
Congleton CW12 6 A1
Tamworth B79 250 A3
Burns Row ST3 74 A1
Burns St WS11 210 A2
Burnsall Cl WV9 240 A2
Burnside DE13 147 D2
Burnside Cl ST3 90 A4
Burnthill La WS15 196 C4
Burntwood Rd
Burntwood WS7 229 E3
Norton Canes WS11 228 A4
Burntwood Recn Ctr
WS7 228 C3
Burntwood Town Sh Ctr
WS7 228 C4
Burnwood Ct ST6 42 B1
Burnwood Pl ST6 42 A3
Burnwood Prim Sch ST6 42 A3
Burrington Dr ST4 88 B3
Burrows Rd DY6 275 F2
Burrows The DE11 186 C3
Burslem Cl WS3 243 D2
Burslem Ent Ctr ST6 57 D4
Bursley Cl ST17 174 B3
Bursley Prim Sch ST5 56 A4
Bursley Rd ST6 57 D4
Bursley Way ST5 56 A4
Bursnips Rd
Essington WV11 242 B2
Great Wyrley WV11 242 B2
Burt St ST3 74 A2
Burton Bank La
Bradnop ST18 174 B3
Stafford ST17 174 C3
Burton Borough Sch The
TF10 169 D1
Burton Cl B79 250 B4
Burton Cres Hanley ST1 57 F4
Kingsley ST10 76 C4
Burton Ct ST17 174 C4
Burton District Hospl Ctr
DE13 166 A3
Burton District Hospl Ctr
Outwoods Branch DE13 166 A3
Burton Ent Pk DE14 166 C3
Burton Manor Cty
Prim Sch ST17 174 B3
Burton Manor Rd
Bradnop ST17 174 B3
Stafford ST17, ST18 174 B3
Burton Old Rd
Lichfield WS14 231 F4
Streethay WS13 214 C1
Burton Old Rd E WS14 231 F4
Burton Old Rd W WS14 231 E4
Burton Pl ST1 282 C3
Burton Rd Alrewas DE13 201 D2
Branston DE14 185 D4
Dudley DY1 271 F2
Elford B79 216 C1
Linton DE11 186 B1
Repton NG17 148 C1
Streethay WS13 214 C1
Tutbury DE13 146 B2
Whittington WS13 232 C4
Willington DE65 148 C4
Burton Sq ST17 174 C4
Burton St Leek ST13 30 B3
Tutbury DE13 146 B3
Burton Tech Coll
(Annexe) DE13 147 E2
Burton upon Trent Sta
DE14 166 B2
Burton upon Trent
Tech Coll DE14 166 C1
Bury Ring ST18 173 E3
Bush Cl WV7 237 D3
Bush Dr WS15 178 C1
Bush Gr WS3 244 A1
Bushberry Cl ST15 119 F3
Bushbury Hill Jun
& Inf Schs WV10 240 C1
Bushbury La WV10 240 C1
Bushey Cl B74 256 C1
Bushfield Rd WV7 237 D3
Bushton La DE13 146 A1
Business Pk DE14 166 C3
Bustomley La ST10 108 A2
Bute St ST4 283 A4
Butler Ct DE14 166 A2
Butler St ST4 72 A3
Butlers La B74 258 A2
Butlers Lane Sta B74 258 A2
Butt La ST18 153 E1
Butter Bk ST18 154 A2
Butterbank La ST18 154 A1
Butterfield Cl WV6 254 B2
Butterfield Pl ST6 41 F2
Butterhill Bank ST18 121 D1
Butterhill La ST15 121 F3
Buttermere Cl
Burslem ST6 56 C4
Cannock WS11 210 A2
Wolv WV6 255 E4
Buttermere Ct WV6 254 C2
Buttermere Dr WV11 242 A2
Buttermere Gr WV11 242 A1
Butthouse La ST5 102 B3
Buttons Farm Rd WV4 265 E2
Butts Cl WS11 227 F2
Butts Croft DE13 200 C2
Butts Gn ST2 58 B3
Butts La
Norton Canes WS11 227 F2
Warslow SK17 23 E1
Butts Rd
Market Drayton TF9 97 D1
Wolv WV4 265 F2
Butts The Betley CW3 53 D3
Wall WS14 230 B1
Butts Way WS11 227 F2
Butts's La ST13 63 F4
Buxton Ave
Fazeley B78 261 D4
Newcastle-u-L ST5 55 D1
Buxton Cl WS3 243 E2
Buxton Old Rd CW12 6 A2
Buxton Rd
Alstonefield DE6 35 D3
Congleton CW12 6 B3
Leek ST13 31 D4
Longnor SK17 13 D4
Walsall WS3 243 E2
Buxton St ST1 57 E4
By Pass Rd B77 251 D3
Byatt's Gr ST3 283 A2
Bycars La Burslem ST6 42 A1
Chell Heath ST6 42 A1
Bycars Rd ST6 41 F1
Byland B77 250 B2
Byland Pl ST5 71 D3
Byland Way WS3 242 C1
Byrd's Cl ST14 125 F4
Byrd's La ST14 125 F4
Byrkley Park Ctr DE13 164 A2
Byrkley St DE14 166 B2
Byrne Rd WV2 266 B4
Byron Ave
Burton u T DE15 185 F4
Lichfield WS14 231 D3
Byron Cl Burntwood WS7 211 F1
Cheadle ST10 76 A1
Market Drayton TF9 112 A4
Stafford ST16 156 A3
Byron Croft Sedgley DY3 271 D3
Sutton Coldfield B74 257 F3
Byron Ct Kidsgrove ST7 41 D4
Sutton Coldfield B74 258 A3
Byron Pl Cannock WS11 209 F3
Rugeley WS15 178 B1
Byron Rd Essington WV10 241 D1
Tamworth B79 250 A4
Byron St Leek ST13 30 B3
Stoke-on-T ST4 56 B1
Bywater Gr 3 ST3 73 E3
Byways WS3 243 E2

Cable St WV2 266 C4
Cacklehill La DE6 81 E1
Cadeby Gr ST2 43 D1
Cadley Hill Ind Est DE11 186 C2
Cadley Hill Rd DE11 186 C2
Cadman Cres ST6 42 C2
Cadman's La WS3 243 E3
Cadogan Rd B77 261 E3
Caernarvon Cl
Burton u T DE13 166 B4
Market Drayton TF9 97 F1
Stone ST15 120 B3
Caernarvon Way DY1 271 F1
Cairn Cl ST2 58 B2
Cairns Cl DE15 167 E2
Cairns Dr ST16 156 A3
Caister B77 251 D4
Caistor Cl Fazeley B78 260 A4
Norton-in-t-M ST2 43 D1
Calais Rd DE13 166 A3
Calcot Dr WV6 255 F4
Caldbeck Pl ST1 282 C3
Calder B77 251 D1
Calder Rise DY3 271 F3
Caldercrofts TF10 168 C2
Caldervale Dr ST17 175 E3
Caldew Gr ST4 88 B3
Cale Cl B77 250 B1
Caledonia Rd Hanley ST1 57 D1
Wolv WV2 266 B4
Wolv WV2 266 C4
Caledonian B77 250 C1
Calgary Cres DE15 167 E2
California St ST3 283 A3
Californian Gr WS7 228 C4
Callaghan Gr WS11 210 B1
Callender Pl ST6 57 D4
Callingwood La DE13 164 C2
Callis Wlk B77 261 F3
Callow Hill La ST10 75 E2
Calrofold Dr ST5 40 B1
Calvary Cres ST2 73 E4
Calveley Cl ST15 118 C3
Calver St ST6 41 E2
Calverley St ST3 283 D2
Calvert Gr ST5 56 A4
Calvin Cl Wolv WV10 240 B2
Wombourne WV5 269 F3
Calving Hill WS11 209 F1
Camberley Cres DY3 266 C1
Camberley Dr WV4 266 A2
Camberley Rd DY6 275 F2
Camberwell Gr ST4 88 B3
Camborne Cl ST17 175 F4
Camborne Cres ST5 71 D3
Cambourne Cl CW12 15 F4
Cambria St WS11 209 E2
Cambrian B77 251 D1
Cambrian La WS15 178 B2
Cambridge Cl
Aldridge WS9 256 A4
Biddulph ST6 16 B1
Cambridge Ct ST5 71 E2
Cambridge Dr ST5 71 E2
Cambridge St
Burton u T DE14 166 A1
Hanley ST1 282 A2
Stafford ST16 156 A2
Camden Dr B77 250 C2
Camden St
Brownhills WS9 244 C2
Fenton ST4 72 C2
Camden Way DY6 270 B1
Camelford Cl ST17 175 F4
Camellia Gdns WV9 239 F2
Camelot Cl
Burton u T DE13 147 F1
Cannock WS11 209 F2
Trentham ST4 88 B2
Cameo Dr DY8 279 F4
Cameo Way ST16 155 D4
Cameron Cl DE15 167 D1
Camhouses B77 251 D1
Camillus Rd ST5 55 F1
Camoys Ct 15 ST6 57 D4
Camoys Rd ST6 57 D4

Camp Hill
Brierley Hill DY8 .... 275 F1
Maer ST5 .... 84 C3
Camp Hill Rd DY7 .... 273 F4
Camp Rd Brocton WS12 .. 194 B3
Chell Heath ST6 .... 42 B1
Shenstone B75 .... 258 B3
Weeford B75 .... 258 B3
Campbell Ave ST13 .... 30 B2
Campbell Cl
Congleton CW12 .... 6 A1
Rugeley WS15 .... 178 B1
Tamworth B79 .... 249 F4
Campbell Pl ST4 .... 72 A4
Campbell Rd
Market Drayton TF9 ...... 97 E1
Stoke-on-T ST4 .... 72 A3
Campbell Terr ST1 ...... 57 F3
Campian's Ave WS6 .... 226 B1
Campion Ave ST5 .... 56 B2
Campion Cl
Eccleshall ST21 .... 133 E1
Wombourne WV5 .... 269 F3
Campion Dr
Featherstone WV10 ...... 241 D4
Tamworth B77 .... 250 B2
Camrose Gdns WV9 .... 240 A4
Camsey La WS7 .... 229 F4
Canal Cl ST12 .... 88 B1
Canal La ST6 .... 41 E1
Canal Mews The ST4 .. 88 B3
Canal Rd Congleton CW12 .. 15 F4
Stone ST15 .... 104 C1
Canal St Brierley Hill DY8 .. 279 F3
Burslem ST6 .... 56 B4
Burton u T DE14 .... 166 B1
Canalside Cl WS3 .... 243 F1
Canaway Wlk WS15 .... 178 B1
Canberra Cres ST3 .... 90 B4
Canberra Dr ST16 ...... 156 A2
Candle La CW3 .... 67 D1
Canford Cres WV8 ...... 238 C2
Cannel Rd WS7 .... 228 B3
Canning Rd B77 .... 250 C2
Canning St ST4 .... 72 C3
Cannnock Wood Rd WS12 .. 211 D3
Cannnock Wood St ST17 .. 211 D3
Cannock Chase Ctry Pk
Brocton ST17, WS15 ...... 176 C2
Rugeley WS12 .... 195 D2
Cannock Chase Ent Ctr
WS12 .... 195 E1
Cannock Chase High Sch
WS11 .... 209 F1
Cannock Chase Tech Coll
Cannock WS11 .... 209 E1
Cannock, Bridgtown WS11 .. 226 C4
Cannock Com Hospl
WS11 .... 209 F1
Cannock Ind Ctr WS11 .. 226 B3
Cannock Rd Brocton ST17 .. 176 A2
Burntwood, Chase Terrace
WS7 .... 228 B4
Burntwood, Gorstey Ley
WS7 .... 229 D4
Cannock,
Heath Hayes WS11 ...... 227 E4
Cannock, High Town WS11 .. 210 A3
Featherstone WV10 ...... 241 D4
Huntington ST19 .... 208 A4
Penkridge ST19 .... 192 C1
Stafford ST17 .... 175 E3
Wolv WV10, WV11 ...... 241 D2
Cannock Sta WS11 ...... 226 C4
Cannock Wood Ind Est
WS12 .... 211 E3
Cannock Wood Rd WS12 .. 211 D3
Cannock Wood St WS12 .. 211 D3
Cannon Pl ST1 .... 282 B2
Cannon Rd WV5 .... 270 A4
Cannon St ST1 .... 282 B2
Canons ST15 .... 120 A3
Canterbury Cl
Brownhills WS3 .... 244 A2
Lichfield WS13 .... 214 B2
Canterbury Dr
Burntwood WS7 .... 229 F4
Chell Heath ST6 .... 42 A2
Perton WV6 .... 254 C2
Canterbury Rd
Burton u T DE15 .... 167 E2
Wolv WV4 .... 265 F3
Canterbury Way WS12 .. 210 A1
Canvey Gr ST3 .... 90 A4
Canwell Dr B75 .... 259 D3
Cape Ave ST17 .... 174 A4
Cape Cl WS8 .... 245 D3
Cape St ST1 .... 282 B4
Capesthorne Cl ST9 .... 59 D2
Capewell St ST3 .... 283 C4
Capper Cl ST7 .... 26 A1
Capper St ST6 .... 41 F2
Capper's La WS14 ...... 232 A4
Cappers La WS13, WS14 .. 231 F4
Capricorn Way ST6 ...... 41 F3
Captain's Cl WV3 .... 255 E1
Captain's La DE13 ...... 201 E4
Caradoc B77 .... 251 D1
Caraway Pl ST3 .... 90 A3
Carberry Way ST3 ...... 74 A2
Card St ST6 .... 57 D4
Carder Ave ST15 ...... 155 D4
Carder Gn SK17 .... 13 D3
Cardiff Gr ST1 .... 282 B1
Cardiff St WV3 .... 266 A4
Cardigan Ave WS15 .... 196 B3
Cardigan Gr ST4 .... 88 B3
Cardigan Pl WS12 ...... 210 B3

Cardinal Griffin RC
High Sch WS11 .... 209 E1
Cardinal Way WS11 .... 209 E1
Cardington Cl ST5 ...... 71 D2
Cardoness Pl DY1 ...... 271 F1
Cardway ST5 .... 56 A4
Cardwell St ST1 .... 57 F3
Carey B77 .... 262 A3
Carfax WS11 .... 226 C4
Carier Ave WV8 .... 239 D2
Carina Gdns ST6 .... 42 B1
Carisbrooke B77 .... 251 D1
Carisbrooke Dr
Burton u T DE13 .... 147 F1
Stafford ST17 .... 174 A4
Carisbrooke Gdns WV10 .. 240 C2
Carisbrooke Rd
Perton WV6 .... 255 D2
Wolv WV10 .... 240 C2
Carisbrooke Way ST4 .. 88 B3
Carlcroft B77 .... 251 D1
Carling Cl ST16 .... 155 D1
Carling Gr ST4 .... 73 D3
Carlisle Rd WS11 ...... 226 B4
Carlisle St ST3 .... 283 B1
Carlos Cl ST10 .... 76 B2
Carlos Pl ST5 .... 41 D1
Carlton Ave Aldridge B74 .. 257 D1
Chell Heath ST6 .... 42 A2
Endon ST6 .... 43 D3
Newcastle-u-L ST5 ...... 71 D2
Carlton Cft B74 .... 257 D1
Carlton Cl Cannock WS12 .. 210 B1
Cheadle ST10 .... 76 B1
Endon ST6 .... 43 D3
Carlton Cres
Burntwood WS7 .... 229 D4
Tamworth B79 .... 249 F4
Carlton Ct DE14 .... 166 A2
Carlton Rd Stoke-on-T ST4 .. 72 B4
Wolv WV3 .... 266 A4
Carlton Sq ST17 .... 174 A4
Carlton St DE13 .... 166 A3
Carlton Terr ST13 ...... 31 D3
Carlyon Pl ST1 .... 57 E4
Carmel Cl WS12 .... 210 B3
Carmichael St WS14 .. 231 E4
Carmount Rd ST2 ...... 58 A4
Carmountside Prim Sch
ST2 .... 58 A4
Carnation Cl ST3 .... 74 A3
Carnforth Cl DY6 ...... 275 D4
Carnforth Gr ST4 ...... 41 F4
Carnoustie B77 .... 251 E3
Carnoustie Cl WS3 .... 243 D2
Caroline Cl ST9 .... 59 D2
Caroline Cres ST6 ...... 43 D3
Caroline St ST3 .... 283 C4
Caroline Terr DE14 .... 166 B1
Carpenter Cl DE15 .... 167 E1
Carpenter Rd ST3 ...... 283 A4
Carr Bank ST10 .... 78 A4
Carr La Audley ST7 ...... 39 D1
Wetton DE6 .... 34 C1
Carr St ST7 .... 26 C1
Carriage Dr ST6 .... 16 C1
Carrick Cl WS3 .... 244 A3
Carrick Pl ST4 .... 72 A1
Carriers Fold WV5 ...... 270 A4
Carriers Rd DE65 ...... 148 B3
Carroll Dr ST3 .... 283 D4
Carron St ST4 .... 283 B5
Carroway Head Hill B78 .. 259 E3
Carryer Pl ST5 .... 70 C4
Carshalton Gr WV2 .... 266 C4
Carson Rd ST6 .... 41 F2
Carson Way ST16 ...... 155 C2
Carter St ST14 .... 126 B4
Carters Croft ST7 ...... 92 C2
Cartersfield La WS14 .. 245 E3
Cartlich St ST6 .... 41 E3
Cartledge St ST4 ...... 56 B1
Cartmel Pl ST6 .... 42 A2
Cartway The WV6 ...... 254 B2
Cartwright Dr ST20 .... 171 E4
Cartwright Rd B75 .... 258 B2
Cartwright St Longton ST3 .. 283 B1
Wolv WV2 .... 266 B4
Carver Gdns DY8 ...... 279 F1
Carver Rd
Burton u T DE13 .... 166 B3
Stafford ST16 .... 155 F1
Casa Mia Ct WS12 .... 210 B3
Casewell Rd Hanley ST6 .. 57 F4
Kingswinford DY6 .... 275 E4
Casey La Burton u T DE14 .. 166 A2
Shavington CW2 .... 37 D3
Casey The ST13 .... 48 A1
Cash La ST21 .... 132 C2
Caslon Cres DY8 .... 279 E2
Caspian Gr ST4 .... 88 A4
Caspian Way ST19 .... 205 E3
Cassandra Cl DY5 ...... 271 E1
Castel Cl ST5 .... 70 C2
Castle Acre ST17 ...... 174 A4
Castle Bank ST17 ...... 174 A4
Castle Cl Brownhills WS8 .. 228 C1
Tamworth B77 .... 250 C2
Castle Ct DE13 .... 146 B4
Castle Dyke WS13 ...... 231 D4
Castle Gr ST17 .... 58 A3
Castle Hayes La DE13 .. 146 B4
Castle Hill Rd Alton ST10 .. 78 C1
Newcastle-u-L ST5 ...... 56 B2
Castle House Sch TF10 .. 168 C2
Castle Inn Rd CW12 .... 16 B4
Castle Keep Mews ST5 .. 284 C3
Castle La CW3 .... 68 C3

Castle Park Inf Sch DE13 .. 166 A4
Castle Park Rd DE13 .. 166 A4
Castle Prim Sch ST7 .... 26 B3
Castle Rd Brownhills WS9 .. 245 D1
Cookley DY10 .... 280 A2
Kidsgrove ST7 .... 26 B4
Swadlincote DE11 .... 186 C1
Tamworth B77 .... 261 F3
Castle Ridge ST5 .... 70 C4
Castle St Brownhills WS8 .. 228 C1
Eccleshall ST21 .... 133 C4
Kinver DY7 .... 278 A2
Newcastle-u-L ST5 ...... 284 C3
Newcastle-u-L, Chesterton
ST5 .... 55 F4
Sedgley DY3 .... 271 E4
Stafford ST16 .... 155 E2
Tutbury DE13 .... 146 B3
Castle View Biddulph ST8 .. 27 E3
Seighford ST18 .... 154 C1
Stafford ST16 .... 155 E2
Tamworth B77 .... 250 B2
Castle View Est ST18 .. 154 C1
Castle Way ST16 .... 155 E1
Castle Way The DE65 .. 148 C3
Castlechurch Cty
Prim Sch ST17 .... 174 A4
Castlecroft Ave WV3 .. 265 D4
Castlecroft Gdns WV3 .. 265 D4
Castlecroft La WV3 .... 254 C1
Castlecroft Prim Sch
WV3 .... 265 D4
Castlecroft Rd WV3 .... 265 D4
Castledene Dr ST16 .... 155 E1
Castledine Gr ST3 ...... 73 F2
Castlefield St ST1 ...... 57 F1
Castlefields ST16 ...... 155 E1
Castlefort Jun Mix
Inf Sch WS3 .... 245 D2
Castlefort Rd WS9 ...... 245 D2
Castlehall B77 .... 251 D1
Castlehill Rd WS9 ...... 245 E2
Castleton Rd Meir ST3 .. 89 F4
Walsall WS3 .... 243 E2
Castleview DE65 .... 146 B4
Castleview Gr ST7 ...... 41 F4
Castleview Rd ST7 ...... 26 A2
Caswell Rd DY3 .... 271 E4
Cat And Kittens La WV10 .. 240 C3
Catalina Pl ST3 .... 90 B3
Caterham Dr DY6 ...... 275 F2
Caterham Pl ST3 .... 90 A3
Catesby Dr DY6 .... 275 E4
Catharine Rd ST6 ...... 42 B3
Cathcart Rd DY8 .... 279 F3
Cathedral Cl WS13 .... 231 D4
Cathedral Rise WS13 .. 231 D4
Catherine St ST5 ...... 56 B2
Catholic La DY3 .... 271 E4
Catholme La
Barton Turn DE13 .... 202 A2
Barton-u-N DE13 .... 201 F3
Catisfield Cres WV8 .... 239 F1
Catkin Wlk WS15 ...... 178 A1
Catmeadow La WS15 .. 197 E1
Caton Cres ST6 .... 42 C1
Catsbridge La WS11 .... 225 F4
Catshill Rd WS8 .... 245 D4
Catwall End Prim Sch
DY3 .... 271 E4
Cauldon Ave
Cheddleton ST13 .... 45 E3
Newcastle-u-L ST5 ...... 56 A4
Cauldon Cl ST13 .... 30 C2
Cauldon Pl ST1 .... 57 D1
Cauldon Prim Sch ST4 .. 57 E1
Cauldon Rd ST4 .... 57 E1
Caulton St ST6 .... 41 F1
Caunsall Rd DY11 ...... 280 A3
Causeley Gdns ST2 .... 58 A2
Causeley Rd ST2 .... 58 A2
Causeway Pl ST13 ...... 33 F3
Cavalier Cir WV10 ...... 240 C2
Cavan's Cl WS11 .... 209 F2
Cavans Wood
Mobile Homes WS12 .. 209 E3
Cavendish B79 .... 249 E3
Cavendish Cl DY6 ...... 275 E2
Cavendish Dr DY9 ...... 281 F2
Cavendish Gr ST5 ...... 71 D2
Cavendish St ST1 ...... 57 D2
Cavendish Way WS9 .. 256 A3
Caverswall La ST3 ...... 90 B4
Caverswall Old Rd ST11 .. 90 C4
Caverswall Rd
Dilhorne ST10 .... 75 D2
Forsbrook ST11 .... 90 C4
Meir ST3 .... 74 A2
Cavour St ST1 .... 56 C2
Caxton St WS11 .... 226 C4
Cayley Pl ST3 .... 90 B3
Cecil Ave ST1 .... 282 A4
Cecil Payton Cl WS15 .. 160 C3
Cecil Rd DE11 .... 186 C1
Cecil St Cannock WS11 .. 209 F2
Stourbridge DY8 .... 279 F3
Cecilly St ST10 .... 76 C2
Cecilly Terr ST10 ...... 76 C2
Cedar Ave Brownhills WS8 .. 245 D4
Forsbrook ST11 .... 91 D3
Kidsgrove ST7 .... 25 E1
Cedar Cl Burntwood WS7 .. 229 D3
Cannock WS11 .... 195 D1
Cheadle ST10 .... 76 C1
Lichfield WS14 .... 231 F4
Market Drayton TF9 ...... 97 D1
Stourbridge DY8 .... 279 E1
Uttoxeter ST14 .... 110 C1

Cedar Cres Audley ST7 .. 39 F1
Endon ST9 .... 43 D3
Rugeley WS15 .... 197 D3
Cedar Ct CW12 .... 15 F4
Cedar Dr Albrighton WV7 .. 237 D3
Aldridge B74 .... 256 C1
Tamworth B79 .... 250 A4
Cedar Gdns DY7 .... 277 F3
Cedar Gr Biddulph ST8 .. 17 D1
Codsall WV8 .... 239 D2
Fenton ST3 .... 72 C2
Wolv WV3 .... 265 F4
Cedar Park Rd ST15 .... 120 A4
Cedar Pk ST15 .... 120 A4
Cedar Rd Barton-u-N DE13 .. 183 E1
Burntwood WS7 .... 229 D4
Newcastle-u-L ST5 ...... 40 B1
Cedar Wood Rd DY3 .... 271 E3
Cedarhill ST10 .... 78 B1
Cedarhill Dr WS11 ...... 209 F2
Cedars Ave
Kingswinford DY6 .... 275 E2
Wombourne WV5 .... 270 A3
Cedars Gr ST15 .... 120 A3
Cedarwood B74 .... 258 A1
Cedarwood Cl WV9 .... 224 A2
Celandine Cl
Kingswinford DY6 .... 275 E2
Norton-in-t-M ST2 ...... 43 D1
Celandines The WV5 .. 269 F3
Celendine DE13 .... 250 B2
Cellarhead Rd
Cheddleton, Cellarhead ST9 .. 59 F2
Cheddleton,
Wetley Rocks ST9 ...... 60 A4
Celtic Ave ST7 .... 41 F4
Celtic Rd WS11 .... 209 F2
Cemetery Ave ST3 ...... 283 B2
Cemetery Rd
Cannock WS11 .... 209 F2
Hanley ST1 .... 57 D1
Market Drayton TF9 ...... 97 D1
Newcastle-u-L, Knutton ST5 .. 55 E1
Newcastle-u-L, Silverdale ST5 .. 55 E1
Weston ST20 .... 37 D3
Cemetery St WS6 ...... 226 B1
Cemetery View
Longton ST3 .... 283 B2
Newcastle-u-L ST5 ...... 55 F2
Cemetery Way WS3 .... 243 D1
Cemlyn Ave ST3 .... 72 C2
Central Ave Bucknall ST2 .. 58 A2
Cannock WS11 .... 209 F3
Central Cl WS3 .... 243 D1
Central Dr Fenton ST3 .. 72 C2
Sedgley DY3 .... 271 E1
Walsall WS3 .... 243 D1
Central St ST7 .... 26 A3
Central Trad Est WV2 .. 266 C4
Central Way DE13 ...... 166 A4
Centre Rd ST15 .... 104 C1
Centurion Pk B77 ...... 262 A3
Centurion Way B77 .... 262 A3
Century St ST1 .... 282 B3
Chadsfield Rd WS15 .. 178 C1
Chadsmead Prim Sch
WS13 .... 214 A1
Chadsmoor CE Jun Sch
WS11 .... 210 A2
Chadsmoor Inf Sch
WS11 .... 210 A2
Chadswell Hts WS13 .. 214 A1
Chadwell Gdns WV8 .. 238 C2
Chadwell La Gnosall TF10 .. 188 A1
Woodcote TF10 .... 187 F2
Chadwell Way ST2 .... 58 B1
Chadwick Cl
Hill Ridware WS15 ...... 198 A4
Wolv WV4 .... 265 E4
Chadwick St WS15 .... 196 C4
Chadwick St ST3 .... 283 C1
Chadwyn Dr ST2 .... 43 D1
Chaff La DE6 .... 65 E1
Chaffinch Cl
Cannock WS12 .... 210 A2
Sedgley DY3 .... 266 B1
Chaffinch Dr Biddulph ST8 .. 27 E4
Uttoxeter ST14 .... 126 B3
Chain La ST17 .... 174 C2
Chain St ST6 .... 42 B1
Chalcot Dr WS12 ...... 210 A4
Chaldon Cl WV9 .... 240 A1
Chalfield B79 .... 249 E3
Chalfont Ave WS11 .... 226 B4
Chalfont Gn ST2 .... 58 B1
Challinor Ave ST4 ...... 72 A3
Challinor St ST6 .... 41 F2
Chamberlain Ave ST4 .. 72 A3
Chamberlain St ST1 .... 282 B1
Chamberlain Way ST8 .. 27 F4
Chamberlain's La
Wolv WV4 .... 265 F2
Wombourne WV5 .... 265 F2
Chance Hall La ST7 .... 25 D4
Chancel Cty Inf Sch
WS15 .... 178 C1
Chancel Ind Est DY6 .. 270 C1
Chancery Dr WS12 ...... 210 B4
Chancery La ST3 .... 283 C3
Chandler Dr DY7 .... 277 F3
Chandler Dr WV4 ...... 265 E2
Chandlers Cl WV9 ...... 240 A1
Chandlers Dr B77 ...... 251 D3
Chandlers Keep WS8 .. 245 D3
Chanterelle Gdns WV4 .. 266 A2
Chantry Rd Kinver DY7 .. 279 E4
Newcastle-u-L ST5 ...... 284 B1
Chapel Ave WS8 .... 228 C1

Chapel Bank Kidsgrove ST7 .. 26 B3
Wheaton Aston ST19 .... 205 E3
Chapel Cl
Mount Pleasant ST7 ...... 26 A3
Wombourne WV5 .... 269 F3
Chapel Ct Gnosall ST20 .. 171 E3
Kidderminster DY10 ...... 280 A1
Newcastle-u-L ST5 ...... 55 E1
Chapel Dr WS8 .... 228 C1
Chapel Gn DE6 .... 127 E4
Chapel Hill DY10 ...... 280 A1
Chapel La Anslow DE13 .. 165 D3
Ashley, Ashley TF9 ...... 100 A3
Ashley, Hookgate ST7 .. 99 F2
Audley ST7 .... 39 E1
Biddulph ST8 .... 17 D1
Bradley ST18 .... 191 D4
Burslem ST6 .... 57 D4
Cannock WS15 .... 211 F3
Codsall WV8 .... 238 C2
Endon ST6 .... 28 A1
Hanbury DE13 .... 144 C1
Kidsgrove ST7 .... 26 C2
Kingsley ST10 .... 62 A1
Lichfield WS14 .... 231 D3
Longdon WS15 .... 212 A2
Mucklestone TF9 .... 83 E3
Newborough DE13 ...... 162 C4
Norton in H TF9 .... 82 B1
Rolleston DE13 .... 147 D2
Rudyard ST9 .... 29 D3
Tatenhill DE13 .... 164 B2
Whittington WS14 ...... 232 C3
Chapel Rd WS15 .... 197 F3
Chapel Sq WS6 .... 226 B2
Chapel St Audley ST7 .. 39 F2
Brownhills, New Town WS8 .. 228 C1
Brownhills, Pelsall WS3 .. 244 A4
Bucknall ST2 .... 58 A2
Burntwood WS7 .... 228 C4
Cannock WS12 .... 210 C1
Cheadle ST10 .... 76 B2
Forsbrook ST11 .... 91 D4
Kidsgrove ST7 .... 25 E1
Kingsley ST10 .... 61 E2
Kingswinford, Wall Heath
DY6 .... 275 D4
Kingswinford, Wordsley DY8 .. 275 E2
Longnor SK17 .... 13 D3
Mount Pleasant ST7 ...... 26 A3
Newcastle-u-L, Knutton ST5 .. 55 E1
Newcastle-u-L,
May Bank ST5 ...... 56 B2
Newcastle-u-L,
Silverdale ST5 ...... 55 E1
Norton Canes WS11 .... 227 F3
Stafford ST16 .... 155 F1
Swadlincote DE12 ...... 186 C3
Wolv WV2 .... 266 B4
Wombourne WV5 .... 269 F3
Chapel Terr ST16 ...... 155 F2
Chapel Wlk DY5 .... 271 E1
Chapelon B77 .... 251 D1
Chapelside WS15 ...... 178 B1
Chaplain Rd WS12 .... 210 C1
Chaplin Rd ST3 .... 283 C1
Chapter Wlk ST2 ...... 58 A3
Charlecote Dr DY1 .... 271 F2
Charlemonte Cl WS12 .. 210 B2
Charles Ave
Essington WV11 .... 241 F2
Kidderminster DY10 ...... 280 A1
Wolv WV4 .... 266 A3
Charles Cl WS6 .... 226 B1
Charles Cotton Dr CW3 .. 68 B3
Charles Cotton St ST16 .. 155 E3
Charles Cres ST3 ...... 244 A3
Charles Rd DY8 .... 279 F2
Charles St Biddulph ST8 .. 27 E4
Cheadle ST10 .... 76 B2
Hanley ST1 .... 282 C2
Newcastle-u-L ST5 ...... 56 B2
Charlesdale Dr WS9 .. 256 A2
Charlesway TF9 .... 112 A4
Charlock Gr WS11 ...... 210 B2
Charlotte Cl ST18 ...... 177 E4
Charlotte St ST6 .... 41 E4
Charlton St ST4 .... 72 A4
Charminster Rd ST3 .. 90 A4
Charmouth Cl ST1 ...... 58 A3
Charnwood Cl WS12 .. 210 B2
Charnes Rd TF9 .... 100 B3
Charnley Dr B75 .... 258 C1
Charnley Rd ST16 ...... 155 F3
Charnock Pl ST5 .... 42 A4
Charnsford La TF9 .... 100 A2
Charnwood ST7 .... 26 A1
Charnwood Ave DY3 .. 266 B1
Charnwood Cl Leek ST13 .. 30 B2
Lichfield WS13 .... 214 B1
Rugeley WS15 .... 178 B1
Charnwood Prim Sch
WS13 .... 214 A1
Charnwood Rd
Burton u T DE13 .... 166 A4
Meir ST3 .... 73 F1
Charsley Pl ST3 .... 72 C1
Charter Cl WS11 .... 227 F2
Charter Ct TF9 .... 97 E1
Charter Rd ST6 .... 56 A2
Charterfield Dr
Cannock WS11 .... 210 B1
Kingswinford DY6 .... 275 E4
Charterfield Sh Ctr DY6 .. 275 E4
Charterhouse Dr ST17 .. 156 A1

Charters Ave WV8 ... 239 D1
Charters The WS13 ... 214 A1
Chartley Cl
  Blythe Bridge ST11 ... 90 C3
  Perton WV6 ... 254 C2
  Stafford ST16 ... 155 E4
Chartley Hall Cotts ST18 ... 139 E3
Chartway The WS3 ... 244 A2
Chartwell B79 ... 249 E4
Chartwell Cl ST9 ... 59 D2
Chartwell Dr
  Sutton Coldfield B74 ... 257 E2
  Wolv WV10 ... 240 C1
  Wombourne WV5 ... 269 F3
Chartwell Rd ST17 ... 175 E4
Chartwood TF9 ... 99 E3
Chase Ave WS6 ... 226 C2
Chase Cres ST17 ... 176 A2
Chase L Ctr WS11 ... 209 E1
Chase La ST15 ... 103 F3
Chase Park Ind Est WS7 ... 228 C4
Chase Rd
  Brocton ST17, WS15 ... 176 B1
  Brownhills WS8 ... 229 D1
  Burntwood WS7 ... 229 D3
  Sedgley DY5 ... 271 E1
Chase Side Rd WS15 ... 196 B4
Chase Terrace High Sch
  WS7 ... 229 D4
Chase Terrace Prim Sch
  WS7 ... 228 C4
Chase Vale WS7 ... 228 C3
Chase View Armitage WS15 ... 198 A2
  Wolv DY3 ... 266 C1
Chase View La ST18 ... 174 B2
Chase Wlk WS12 ... 209 E2
Chaselands WS7 ... 228 B4
Chaseley Ave WS11 ... 209 E1
Chaseley Cl WS15 ... 178 A1
Chaseley Croft WS11 ... 209 E1
Chaseley Gdns WS11 ... 229 E4
Chaseley Rd WS11 ... 178 A1
Chasepool Rd DY3 ... 274 B4
Chaseside Dr WS11 ... 210 A2
Chaseside Ind Est WS11 ... 210 A2
Chasetown High Sch WS7 228 C2
Chasetown Ind Est WS7 228 C3
Chasetown Prim Sch WS7 228 C3
Chaseview Rd DE13 ... 200 C1
Chasewater WS7 ... 228 B2
Chasewater Dr ST10 ... 76 C2
Chasewater Light Rly
  WS11 ... 228 A2
Chasewater Sports Ctr
  WS8 ... 228 B2
Chasewater Way WS11 ... 227 F3
Chasewood Park
  Bsns Ctr WS12 ... 210 C1
Chatfield Cl DE15 ... 167 E1
Chatfield Pl ST3 ... 73 E1
Chatham St ST1 ... 282 A1
Chatsworth B79 ... 249 E4
Chatsworth Dr
  Cannock WS11 ... 210 A2
  Caverswall ST9 ... 59 D2
  Norton-in-t-M ST6 ... 42 C3
  Tutbury DE13 ... 146 B3
Chatsworth Gdns WV6 ... 255 D4
Chatsworth Pl Meir ST3 ... 73 F1
  Newcastle-u-L ST5 ... 55 F4
Chatteris Cl ST3 ... 90 A3
Chatterley Cl ST5 ... 56 A4
Chatterley Dr ST7 ... 41 D4
Chatterley Rd ST6 ... 41 E2
Chatterley St ST6 ... 41 F1
Chatterton Pl ST3 ... 73 E2
Chatwell La Blymhill TF10 ... 188 B1
  Sheriffhales TF10, TF11 ... 203 D4
Chaucer Cl
  Burton u T DE14 ... 166 B3
  Lichfield WS14 ... 231 D3
  Tamworth B79 ... 250 A3
Chaucer Dr WS7 ... 212 A1
Chaucer Rd Sedgley DY3 ... 271 D3
  Stafford ST17 ... 174 B4
Chaulden Rd ST16 ... 136 B1
Chawner Cl WS7 ... 211 F1
Cheadle Cl ST19 ... 207 F4
Cheadle High Sch ST10 ... 76 B1
Cheadle Hospl ST10 ... 76 B2
Cheadle Prim Sch ST10 ... 76 B1
Cheadle Rd Alton ST10 ... 78 C1
  Cheddleton ST13 ... 45 E2
  Draycott in t M ST11 ... 91 F3
  Forsbrook ST11 ... 91 D4
  Leek ST13 ... 45 F4
  Upper Tean ST10 ... 92 B3
  Uttoxeter ST14 ... 111 D1
Cheam Gdns WV6 ... 255 D1
Cheapside Hanley ST1 ... 282 B2
  Newcastle-u-L ST5 ... 284 B3
Chebsey Dr ST16 ... 155 D3
Checkley Dr ST6 ... 16 B1
Checkley Gr [6] ST3 ... 73 E3
Checkley La CW3 ... 52 C1
Checkley Rd ST5 ... 40 B1
Chedale Rd ST10 ... 61 E1
Cheddar Dr ST5 ... 54 C1
Cheddleton Flint Mill Mus
  ST13 ... 45 E3
Cheddleton Heath Rd ST13 45 F4
Cheddleton Park Ave ST13 ... 45 E4
Cheddleton Rd ST13 ... 30 C2
Cheedale Cl DE15 ... 167 D3
Chelford Cl ST19 ... 193 D1

Chell Cl ST19 ... 207 F4
Chell Gr ST5 ... 56 A4
Chell Green Ave ST6 ... 42 A3
Chell Heath Rd ST6 ... 42 B2
Chell Rd ST16 ... 155 E2
Chell St ST1 ... 57 E3
Chelmarsh Ave WV3 ... 265 D4
Chelmorton Dr ST3 ... 73 F1
Chelmsford Dr ST2 ... 58 B1
Chelmsford Rd ST5 ... 56 B3
Chelsea Cl ST6 ... 16 B1
Chelsea Dr B74 ... 257 F2
Chelsea Way
  Kingswinford DY6 ... 275 E3
  Stafford ST16 ... 155 E1
Chelson St ST3 ... 283 C3
Chelston Dr WV6 ... 255 F2
Cheltenham Ave ST10 ... 76 C3
Cheltenham Dr
  Kingswinford DY6 ... 275 D3
  Stafford ST17 ... 175 E4
Cheltenham Gr Hanley ST1 ... 57 F3
  Newcastle-u-L ST5 ... 54 C1
Chelwood St ST1 ... 282 A4
Chemical La ST6 ... 41 E1
Chepstow Cl Biddulph ST6 ... 16 B1
  Perton WV6 ... 254 C2
Chepstow Dr ST17 ... 175 E4
Chepstow Rd Walsall WS3 ... 242 C1
  Wolv WV10 ... 240 B3
Chepstow Way WS3 ... 242 C1
Chequer St WV3 ... 266 A3
Chequerfield Dr WV4 ... 266 A3
Chequers Ave WS5 ... 265 D1
Chequers Ct WS11 ... 228 A3
Chequers The WS13 ... 231 E4
Cheriton Gn ST2 ... 58 B1
Cheriton Gr WV6 ... 254 C2
Cherrington Dr WS11 ... 226 C2
Cherrington Gdns WV6 ... 255 D1
Cherry Bank WS12 ... 210 B3
Cherry Cl Blythe Bridge ST11 106 C4
  Burntwood WS7 ... 228 C3
  Newcastle-u-L ST5 ... 40 B1
Cherry Gn DY1 ... 271 F2
Cherry Gr Fenton ST3 ... 72 C2
  Stourbridge DY8 ... 279 F2
Cherry Hill CW3 ... 68 C3
Cherry Hill Ave ST3 ... 74 A1
Cherry Hill Jun Sch ST5 ... 55 F1
Cherry Hill La ST5 ... 55 F1
Cherry La Cheadle ST10 ... 77 D3
  Congleton CW12 ... 16 C4
  Gayton ST18 ... 138 C3
  Himley DY3 ... 270 B2
  Seighford ST18 ... 135 E2
Cherry Leys DE15 ... 167 E2
Cherry Orch Lichfield WS14 . 231 E4
  Newcastle-u-L ST5 ... 284 B3
  Stone ST15 ... 120 B4
Cherry St Stourbridge DY8 ... 279 F2
  Tamworth B79 ... 250 A3
Cherry Tree Ave ST7 ... 25 D3
Cherry Tree Cl
  Eccleshall ST21 ... 133 F4
  Stone ST15 ... 119 F3
  Swadlincote DE11 ... 186 C3
  Trentham ST4 ... 88 A3
Cherry Tree Gdns WV8 ... 239 D2
Cherry Tree La
  Biddulph ST8 ... 17 D1
  Codsall WV8 ... 239 D2
  Woore CW3 ... 67 E1
Cherry Tree Rd Audley ST7 .. 39 F1
  Huntington WS12 ... 209 E4
  Kingswinford DY6 ... 275 F4
  Newcastle-u-L ST5 ... 40 C1
  Norton Canes WS11 ... 228 A3
  Rugeley WS15 ... 196 C3
Cherry Tree Wlk B79 ... 250 A4
Cherry Trees Specl Sch
  WV5 ... 269 F3
Cherry Way TF9 ... 97 E1
Cherrybrook Dr ST19 ... 193 D1
Cherrytree Cres ST18 ... 135 D1
Cherrytree Rd DE15 ... 185 F4
Cherrywood Cl ST17 ... 175 E3
Cherrywood Gr ST3 ... 89 F3
Cherrywood Rd B74 ... 256 B1
Cherrywood Way B74 ... 257 E2
Chertsey Pl ST1 ... 57 E4
Chervil Cl ST3 ... 90 A3
Cherwell B77 ... 250 B1
Cherwell Dr WS8 ... 228 B1
Chesham Gr ST3 ... 90 A3
Chesham Rd ST16 ... 155 F3
Cheshire Cl DY8 ... 279 E4
Cheshire Dr ST19 ... 223 E3
Cheshire Gdns TF9 ... 97 E1
Cheshire Gr WV6 ... 254 C2
Cheshire St TF9 ... 97 E1
Chesley Dr WS6 ... 226 B1
Cheslyn Hay High Sch
  WS6 ... 226 B2
Cheslyn Hay Prim Sch
  WS6 ... 226 B2
Chessington Cres ST4 ... 88 B4
Chestall Rd WS15 ... 211 F3
Chester Ave WV6 ... 255 F4
Chester Cl Cannock WS11 ... 210 A4
  Kidsgrove ST7 ... 40 C4
  Lichfield WS13 ... 214 B2
Chester Cres ST5 ... 71 D3
Chester Rd Aldridge WS9 ... 256 C2
  Audley ST7 ... 39 E1
  Brownhills WS9 ... 245 E4
  Chetwynd TF10 ... 168 B4
  Enville DY7 ... 273 F1

Chester Rd continued
  Kidsgrove ST7 ... 40 B4
  Kinver DY7 ... 277 F4
  Whittington WS14 ... 232 B2
Chester Rd N WS8 ... 228 B1
Chesterfield Ave DE11 ... 186 C3
Chesterfield Ct WS9 ... 244 C2
Chesterfield Rd WS14 ... 231 D3
Chesterton High Sch ST5 ... 55 F4
Chesterton Prim Sch
  Newcastle-u-L, Beasley ST5 ... 55 F4
  Newcastle-u-L,
    Broad Meadow ST5 ... 55 F3
Chesterton Rd
  Burton u T DE14 ... 166 B3
  Pattingham WV6 ... 253 D1
Chesterton Stadium ST5 ... 55 F3
Chesterton Way B79 ... 250 A4
Chesterwood B74 ... 256 C1
Chesterwood Rd ST6 ... 42 A2
Chestnut Ave B79 ... 250 A4
Chestnut Cl Aldridge B74 .... 257 D2
  Armitage WS15 ... 198 B2
  Cannock WS11 ... 210 B1
  Gnosall ST20 ... 171 E4
  Seighford ST18 ... 154 C1
  Stourbridge DY8 ... 279 E1
  Upper Tean ST10 ... 92 C2
Chestnut Cres ST11 ... 91 D3
Chestnut Ct ST21 ... 102 B2
Chestnut Dr
  Brownhills WS4 ... 244 A1
  Cheslyn Hay WS6 ... 226 B2
  Great Wyrley WS6 ... 226 C2
  Shenstone WS14 ... 246 A3
  Wombourne WV5 ... 270 A3
Chestnut Gr
  Kingswinford DY6 ... 275 F3
  Kinver DY7 ... 277 F3
  Newcastle-u-L ST5 ... 40 C1
Chestnut La B79 ... 218 C1
Chestnut Rd Ashley TF9 ... 99 E3
  Burton u T DE15 ... 185 F4
  Endon ST6 ... 43 E4
  Market Drayton TF9 ... 112 A4
Chestnut Way WV3 ... 265 D4
Chestow Pl ST3 ... 73 E3
Cheswardine City
  Prim Sch TF9 ... 130 A4
Cheswardine Rd ST5 ... 56 A4
Cheswell Cl WV6 ... 255 D1
Chetton Gn WV10 ... 240 A2
Chetwode Cl TF9 ... 83 E3
Chetwynd Ave
  Caverswall ST9 ... 59 D2
  Norton-in-t-M ST6 ... 42 C3
Chetwynd Cl
  Penkridge ST19 ... 207 F4
  Rugeley WS15 ... 196 C3
Chetwynd End TF10 ... 168 C2
Chetwynd Gr TF10 ... 168 C2
Chetwynd House
  Prep Sch B74 ... 257 F1
Chetwynd Pk
  Cannock WS12 ... 211 D3
  Chetwynd TF10 ... 168 B4
Chetwynd Rd
  Chetwynd TF10 ... 168 B3
  Edgmond TF10 ... 168 B3
  Newcastle-u-L ST5 ... 56 A3
  Newport TF10 ... 168 C2
  Wolv WV2 ... 266 A3
Chetwynd St
  Chell Heath ST6 ... 42 B1
  Newcastle-u-L ST5 ... 56 B3
Chevening Cl DY3 ... 271 F4
Chevin The DE13 ... 147 E1
Cheviot ST7 ... 251 E1
Cheviot Cl ST5 ... 55 F2
Cheviot Dr
  Chell Heath ST6 ... 42 B2
  Rugeley WS15 ... 178 B2
Cheviot Rd WV2 ... 266 C4
Cheviot Rise WS12 ... 210 B3
Chichester Dr WS12 ... 210 B1
Chichester Wlk ST1 ... 282 C4
Chieveley Cl WS15 ... 178 B1
Childerplay Rd ST8 ... 27 E4
Chilgrove Cl ST1 ... 57 F3
Chilgrove Gdns WV6 ... 255 E3
Chillingham B77 ... 261 E4
Chillington Cl WS6 ... 226 C1
Chillington Dr
  Codsall WV8 ... 238 C2
  Sedgley DY1 ... 271 F2
Chillington La WV8 ... 238 B3
Chillington St WV1 ... 266 C4
Chiltern Cl DY3 ... 271 E2
Chiltern La ST21 ... 133 F3
Chiltern Pl ST5 ... 55 F2
Chiltern Rd
  Swadlincote DE11 ... 186 C2
  Tamworth B77 ... 251 E1
Chilton St ST3 ... 72 C2
Chilwell Ave ST18 ... 177 F4
Chilworth Gr ST3 ... 72 C1
China St ST4 ... 72 C2
Chingford Cl DY8 ... 275 E2
Chivelstone Cl ST4 ... 88 B3
Cholerton Cl ST4 ... 72 C3
Chorley Ave ST6 ... 42 A3
Chorley Rd WS7 ... 212 A1
Chorley St ST13 ... 30 C3
Chorlton La CW2 ... 37 D3
Chorlton Rd ST1 ... 57 E3
Chorlton Terr ST14 ... 111 E1
Christ Church CE Fst Sch
  ST15 ... 105 D1

Christ Church CE Inf Sch
  WV6 ... 255 D2
Christ Church CE Jun Sch
  WV6 ... 255 D3
Christ Church CE Mid Sch
  ST15 ... 105 D1
Christ Church CE Prim Sch
  WS13 ... 230 C4
Christ Church Gdns WS13 . 230 C4
Christ Church La TF9 ... 112 A4
Christchurch CE Mid Sch
  ST4 ... 72 C3
Christchurch Inf Sch
  DE14 ... 166 B1
Christchurch La WS13 ... 230 C4
Christchurch St ST4 ... 72 C3
Christchurch Way WS15 ... 105 D1
Christie Ave ST16 ... 155 E2
Christie Pl ST3 ... 73 F3
Christine St ST2 ... 58 A2
Christopher Rd WV2 ... 266 C4
Christopher Sq ST4 ... 72 C3
Christopher Terr ST17 ... 156 A1
Christopher Wlk WS13 ... 214 A2
Chub B77 ... 261 E4
Chubb Way ST4 ... 71 F2
Chumleigh Gr ST6 ... 42 A1
Church Ave Grindon ST13 ... 34 A1
  Hatton DE65 ... 146 B4
  Norton-in-t-M ST2 ... 43 D1
Church Bank Audley ST7 ... 39 E1
  Keele ST5 ... 69 F4
  Oakamoor ST10 ... 78 A3
  Waterhouses ST13 ... 63 F4
Church Cl Alrewas WS13 ... 215 E4
  Biddulph ST8 ... 27 E3
  Blythe Bridge ST3 ... 89 F3
  Burton u T DE15 ... 167 D2
  Coppenhall ST18 ... 192 C4
  Drayton Bassett B78 ... 260 C3
  Gnosall ST20 ... 171 F3
  Haughton ST18 ... 172 C3
  Kingsbury CV9 ... 262 B1
  Kingstone ST14 ... 141 E4
  Marchington ST14 ... 127 F1
  Ranton ST18 ... 153 E3
  Rugeley WS15 ... 196 A4
  Shenstone WS14 ... 247 D3
  Stafford ST17 ... 174 C3
  Stone ST15 ... 120 A4
Church Cres WV11 ... 241 F2
Church Croft ST14 ... 125 E4
Church Dr B78 ... 249 D4
Church Eaton Prim Sch
  ST20 ... 190 A4
Church Eaton Rd
  Church Eaton TF10 ... 189 D3
  Gnosall TF10 ... 188 D3
Church Farm TF9 ... 100 B3
Church Fields Keele ST5 ... 69 F4
  Norton in H TF9 ... 82 B1
Church Gdns ST3 ... 283 C4
Church Gr ST21 ... 133 E4
Church Hill
  Cannock WS12 ... 210 B3
  Codsall WV8 ... 238 C3
  Kinver DY7 ... 278 A1
  Wolv WV4 ... 265 F2
Church Hill Dr WV6 ... 255 F3
Church Hill Rd WV6 ... 255 F3
Church Hill St DE15 ... 167 D2
Church Hollow B79 ... 217 E3
Church La
  Albrighton WV7 ... 237 D1
  Alrewas WS13 ... 215 E4
  Armitage WS15 ... 197 F3
  Barton-u-N DE13 ... 183 E1
  Betley CW3 ... 53 E3
  Biddulph ST8 ... 17 D1
  Bobbington DY7 ... 268 A1
  Bradley ST18 ... 173 E1
  Brewood WV9 ... 224 A1
  Burntwood WS7 ... 229 E2
  Cheddleton ST10 ... 46 C1
  Chilcote DE12 ... 219 F2
  Codsall WV8 ... 238 C2
  Draycott in t M ST11 ... 91 F3
  Eccleshall ST21 ... 116 A3
  Edingale DE6 ... 217 E3
  Ellastone DE6 ... 80 A2
  Endon ST9 ... 43 F4
  Gayton ST18 ... 138 B3
  Gnosall TF10 ... 188 B4
  Hanbury DE13 ... 145 D2
  Hill Ridware WS15 ... 198 A4
  Hixon ST18 ... 158 B4
  Ipstones ST10 ... 46 C1
  Kidsgrove ST7 ... 26 C1
  King's Bromley DE13 ... 199 E3
  Kingstone ST14 ... 141 E4
  Leek ST13 ... 30 C3
  Marchington ST14 ... 127 F1
  Mayfield DE6 ... 81 E3
  Middleton B78 ... 260 B1
  Newcastle-u-L, Knutton ST5 .... 55 F1
  Newcastle-u-L, Wolstanton
    ST5 ... 56 B3
  Newton Solney DE15 ... 167 E4
  Rocester ST14 ... 96 A3
  Roston DE6 ... 96 B4
  Rugeley WS15 ... 178 B1
  Scholar Green ST7 ... 25 D3
  Seighford ST18 ... 154 C1
  Seisdon WV5 ... 264 A1
  Shenstone WS9 ... 245 F2
  Shuttington B79 ... 251 E4
  Stafford ST16 ... 155 F2
  Standon ST21 ... 102 A2

Church La continued
  Stone ST15 ... 105 E2
  Tamworth B79 ... 250 A3
  Thorpe DE6 ... 51 F1
  Trentham ST4 ... 71 F1
  Upper Tean ST10 ... 109 D4
  Uttoxeter ST14 ... 125 E4
  Waterhouses ST13 ... 63 F4
  Wheaton Aston ST19 ... 206 A3
Church Lawton Gate
  Cty Prim Sch ST7 ... 25 D3
Church Meadow
  Ipstones ST10 ... 46 C1
  Norton in H TF9 ... 82 B1
Church Mews
  Acton Trussell ST17 ... 193 F4
  Tutbury DE13 ... 146 B4
Church Moat Way WS3 ... 243 D1
Church of the Ascension
  Prim Sch ST5 ... 275 D4
Church Plantation ST5 ... 70 A4
Church Rd Alrewas DE13 ... 200 C2
  Ashley TF9 ... 100 B3
  Biddulph ST8 ... 27 E4
  Branston DE14 ... 184 C4
  Brewood ST19 ... 223 E3
  Brownhills, Catshill WS8 ... 244 C4
  Brownhills, Pelsall WS3 ... 244 A2
  Burntwood WS7 ... 229 E4
  Burton u T DE13 ... 147 F1
  Codsall WV8 ... 238 C2
  Eggington DE65 ... 148 A2
  Elford B79 ... 216 B1
  Endon ST6 ... 43 D4
  Hixon ST18 ... 139 E4
  Huntington WS11 ... 209 D1
  Kingswinford DY8 ... 275 F1
  Longton ST3 ... 88 C4
  Norton Canes WS11 ... 227 F2
  Penkridge ST19 ... 192 C1
  Rolleston DE13 ... 147 D2
  Shareshill WV10 ... 225 D1
  Shenstone WS14 ... 246 C3
  Shenstone, Thornes WS9 ... 245 F2
  Snelston DE6 ... 81 E2
  Swindon DY3 ... 269 E1
  Tamworth B77 ... 261 E2
  Wolv, Elston Hall WV10 ... 240 B1
  Wolv, Penn Fields WV3 ... 265 F4
  Wolv, Stockwell End WV6 ... 255 F3
  Wolv, Tettenhall Wood WV6 255 D2
  Wombourne WV5 ... 270 A4
Church Sq ST6 ... 56 C4
Church St
  Abbots Bromley WS15 ... 160 C3
  Alstonefield DE6 ... 35 F2
  Audley ST7 ... 40 A1
  Brownhills WS8 ... 244 C3
  Burntwood WS7 ... 228 C3
  Cannock WS11 ... 209 F1
  Cannock, Bridgmoor WS11 ... 226 B3
  Cannock, Chadsmoor WS11 . 210 A2
  Cheadle ST10 ... 76 B2
  Claverley WV5 ... 267 E4
  Clifton Campville B79 ... 218 C1
  Eccleshall ST21 ... 133 E4
  Hartington SK17 ... 24 B3
  Kidsgrove, Butt Lane ST7 ... 25 E1
  Kidsgrove, The Rookery ST7 ... 26 A2
  Kingsley ST10 ... 61 F1
  Leek ST13 ... 30 C3
  Lichfield WS13, WS14 ... 231 E4
  Longnor SK17 ... 13 D3
  Market Drayton TF9 ... 97 E1
  Mount Pleasant ST7 ... 26 B3
  Netherseal DE12 ... 219 F3
  Newcastle-u-L, ST5 ... 284 B3
  Newcastle-u-L, Chesterton
    ST5 ... 55 F4
  Newcastle-u-L, Silverdale ST5 55 D1
  Rugeley WS15 ... 178 C1
  Sedgley DY3 ... 271 E2
  Stoke-on-T ST4 ... 72 A4
  Stone ST15 ... 120 A4
  Tamworth B79 ... 250 A3
  Tutbury DE13 ... 146 B4
  Uttoxeter ST14 ... 126 B4
  Whittington WS14 ... 232 B3
Church Terr Burslem ST6 ... 57 D3
  Caverswall ST11 ... 74 C1
  Warslow SK17 ... 23 D1
Church Vale WS11 ... 227 F2
Church View Gdns DY7 ... 278 A2
Church Way
  Brownhills WS4 ... 244 A1
  Longdon WS15 ... 198 A1
Church Wlk
  Newcastle-u-L ST5 ... 55 F4
  Wolv, Penn Fields WV3 ... 265 F4
  Wolv, Stockwell End WV6 ... 255 F3
Churchcroft Gdns WS15 ... 178 C1
Churchfield Ave ST3 ... 73 E1
Churchfield Cl
  Brewood WV9 ... 224 B1
  Stafford ST17 ... 156 B1
Churchfield Ct ST10 ... 46 C1
Churchfield Rd ST21 ... 133 E3
Churchfields DE13 ... 182 A1
Churchfields CE Jun Sch
  WS15 ... 196 C4

Churchill Ave
Cheddleton ST13 ..... 45 E3
Trentham ST4 ..... 87 F4
Churchill & Blakedown Sta DY10 ..... 281 E1
Churchill Cl ST11 ..... 90 C3
Churchill Cres DE13 ..... 200 C1
Churchill Gdns DY3 ..... 271 E4
Churchill La DY10 ..... 281 D2
Churchill Rd Cheadle ST10 ..... 76 C2
Shenstone WS14 ..... 247 D1
Stone ST15 ..... 119 F4
Churchill Way
Stafford ST17 ..... 174 C3
Trentham ST4 ..... 87 F4
Churchside B79 ..... 217 E1
Churchside Way WS3 ..... 245 D1
Churchward Gr WV5 ..... 270 A4
Churn Hill Rd WS9 ..... 256 A2
Churnet Cl ST13 ..... 45 D2
Churnet Ct DE14 ..... 166 C2
Churnet Gr WV6 ..... 254 C2
Churnet Rd Cheadle ST10 ..... 76 C1
Forsbrook ST11 ..... 91 D4
Churnet Valley Rd ST10 ..... 62 A1
Churnet Valley Rly Ctr ST13 ..... 45 F3
Churnet View ST13 ..... 31 D4
Churnet View Mid Sch ST13 ..... 31 D4
Churnet View Rd ST10 ..... 78 A4
Churnetside Bsns Pk ST13 ..... 45 E3
Churston Cl
Newcastle-u-L ST5 ..... 71 D1
Walsall WS3 ..... 243 D2
Churston Pl ST1 ..... 57 E4
Cinder Hill WV9 ..... 224 A2
Cinder Hill La ST7 ..... 25 F4
Cinder Rd Burntwood WS7 ..... 228 C4
Sedgley DY5 ..... 271 D1
Cinderhill Ind Est ST3 ..... 73 F2
Cinderhill La ST3 ..... 73 E2
Circular Rd WV7 ..... 220 C1
City Arc WS13 ..... 231 D4
City Bank ST6 ..... 16 B1
City General Hospl ST4 ..... 71 E4
City La ST9 ..... 30 A2
City Rd Fenton ST4 ..... 72 B3
Stoke-on-T ST4 ..... 72 B3
Clamgoose La ST10 ..... 76 B4
Clanbrook Rd DY7 ..... 278 A4
Clandon Ave ST6 ..... 41 F2
Clanford Cl ST17 ..... 174 C3
Clanford La ST18 ..... 154 A3
Clanford Rd ST18 ..... 154 A3
Clanway St ST6 ..... 41 F3
Clap Gate Gr WV5 ..... 269 F3
Clap Gate Rd WV5 ..... 269 F4
Clare Ave Essington WV11 ..... 241 F1
Newcastle-u-L ST5 ..... 56 A3
Clare Cres WV14 ..... 266 C1
Clare Rd ST16 ..... 155 F4
Clare St Kidsgrove ST7 ..... 26 C2
Mount Pleasant ST7 ..... 26 B3
Stoke-on-T ST4 ..... 56 B1
Claregate Prim Sch WV6 ..... 255 F4
Claremont Cl
Newcastle-u-L ST5 ..... 56 B4
Stone ST15 ..... 120 A4
Claremont Gr ST17 ..... 174 A4
Claremont Mews WV3 ..... 266 A4
Claremont Rd
Eccleshall ST21 ..... 133 F3
Sedgley DY3 ..... 271 E4
Tamworth B79 ..... 250 A4
Wolv WV3 ..... 266 A4
Clarence Gdns B74 ..... 257 F1
Clarence Rd
Longton ST3, ST4 ..... 283 B4
Sutton Coldfield B74 ..... 257 F2
Clarence St
Burton u T DE14 ..... 166 B1
Fenton ST4 ..... 72 C3
Newcastle-u-L ST5 ..... 284 D3
Newcastle-u-L, Porthill ST5 ..... 56 A3
Clarendon Dr ST17 ..... 174 A4
Clarendon Pl WS3 ..... 243 F2
Clarendon Rd
Brownhills WS8 ..... 244 B1
Sutton Coldfield B75 ..... 258 B2
Clarendon St Fenton ST4 ..... 72 B3
Walsall WS3 ..... 243 D1
Claridge Rd ST4 ..... 56 C1
Clarion Way WS11 ..... 209 F3
Clark Rd WV3 ..... 255 F1
Clark St Stafford ST16 ..... 155 F2
Stourbridge DY8 ..... 279 F2
Clark's Cres WS15 ..... 161 D3
Clarke Ind Est DE14 ..... 166 C2
Clarke St ST1 ..... 282 A1
Clarke's Ave WS12 ..... 195 D1
Clarke's Cl ST14 ..... 111 D1
Claud St ST4 ..... 72 B2
Claverdon Dr B74 ..... 257 F2
Claverhouse Rd DE15 ..... 167 D1
Claverley CE Sch WV5 ..... 267 E4
Claverley Dr WV4 ..... 265 E3
Clay Gates Rd ST19 ..... 207 D1
Clay Hills ST6 ..... 41 E2
Clay La ST9 ..... 43 F4
Clay Pit La Lichfield WS14 ..... 230 C1
Wall WS14 ..... 230 C1
Clay St Burton u T DE15 ..... 166 C1
Penkridge ST19 ..... 192 C1
Clay St E DE15 ..... 167 D1
Clayalders Bank ST21 ..... 101 F3
Claydon Cres ST5 ..... 71 D1
Claydon Rd DY6 ..... 270 B1

Clayfield Gr ST3 ..... 73 E3
Clayfield Gr W ST3, ST4 ..... 73 E3
Claygate Rd WS12 ..... 210 C2
Clayhanger Cl ST5 ..... 56 A4
Clayhanger La WS8 ..... 244 B3
Clayhanger Rd WS8 ..... 244 C3
Clayhanger St ST6 ..... 56 C4
Claymills Rd DE13 ..... 148 A1
Claymore B77 ..... 261 E4
Clays La DE14 ..... 184 C4
Clayton Av CW12 ..... 6 A3
Clayton Cl WV2 ..... 266 B4
Clayton High Sch ST5 ..... 71 E2
Clayton La
Newcastle-u-L ST5 ..... 71 E2
Stoke-on-T ST5 ..... 71 E2
Clayton Rd ST5 ..... 71 E2
Claytonwood Rd ST4 ..... 71 F2
Cleadon Pl ST2 ..... 58 A3
Clear View DY6 ..... 275 D4
Clearwell Gdns DY1 ..... 271 F2
Cleasby B77 ..... 251 E1
Cleave Rd DE14 ..... 185 D4
Clee Hill Dr WV3 ..... 255 D1
Clee Hill Rd DY3 ..... 271 E2
Clee View Rd WV5 ..... 269 F3
Cleeton St WS12 ..... 210 B1
Cleeve B77 ..... 250 B2
Cleeve Dr B74 ..... 257 F3
Cleeve Rd WS3 ..... 242 C2
Cleeve Way WS3 ..... 242 C2
Clematis B77 ..... 250 C2
Clematis Ave ST11 ..... 90 C3
Clematis Cl ST18 ..... 135 D1
Clematis Cres DE15 ..... 186 A4
Clematis Dr WV9 ..... 239 F2
Clement Cl ST16 ..... 155 F3
Clement Pl ST6 ..... 42 C3
Clement St ST6 ..... 42 A3
Clent View Rd DY8 ..... 279 E1
Clerk Bank ST13 ..... 30 C3
Clermont Ave ST4 ..... 72 A1
Clevedon Ave ST17 ..... 175 E4
Cleveland Cl WV11 ..... 241 F1
Cleveland Dr WV11 ..... 210 A2
Cleveland Rd Hanley ST1 ..... 282 B1
Newcastle-u-L ST5 ..... 55 F2
Cleveland St 11
Burslem ST6 ..... 56 C4
Stourbridge DY8 ..... 279 F2
Cleveland Wlk ST17 ..... 174 A4
Cleves Cres WS6 ..... 226 B1
Clewley Dr WV9 ..... 240 A2
Clewley Rd DE14 ..... 184 C4
Clewlow Pl ST3 ..... 283 D5
Clewlows Bank ST9 ..... 43 F2
Clews St ST6 ..... 56 C4
Clews Wlk ST5 ..... 56 B3
Cley Gr ST5 ..... 71 D1
Cliff Hall La B78 ..... 261 D1
Cliff Rd ST18 ..... 158 B1
Cliff St ST6 ..... 42 B1
Cliff Vale Rd ST4 ..... 56 C1
Cliffe Pl ST6 ..... 42 C1
Clifford Cl ST6 ..... 250 C2
Clifford Rd TF9 ..... 112 A4
Clifford St Hanley ST1 ..... 282 C1
Tamworth B77 ..... 250 C2
Cliffs La TF10 ..... 150 C1
Clifton Ave Aldridge WS9 ..... 245 E1
Brownhills WS8 ..... 244 B4
Cannock WS11 ..... 226 B4
Tamworth B79 ..... 250 A4
Clifton CE Prim Sch DE6 ..... 81 F3
Clifton Cl Fenton ST4 ..... 72 C3
Stafford ST16 ..... 156 A2
Swadlincote DE11 ..... 186 C1
Clifton Dr ST16 ..... 156 A2
Clifton Gdns WV8 ..... 239 E2
Clifton La B79 ..... 235 D2
Clifton Rd Clifton DE6 ..... 81 F4
Cookley DY10 ..... 280 B2
Netherseal DE12 ..... 219 E3
Wolv WV6 ..... 255 E4
Clifton St Fenton ST4 ..... 72 C3
Newcastle-u-L ST5 ..... 56 B2
Sedgley DY3, WV14 ..... 266 C1
Stourbridge DY8 ..... 279 F2
Clinton Cres WS7 ..... 229 D4
Clinton Gdns ST15 ..... 120 A4
Clinton Sq ST1 ..... 282 A2
Clive Ave ST2 ..... 43 D2
Clive Cl B75 ..... 258 B1
Clive Rd Burntwood WS7 ..... 229 D4
Market Drayton TF9 ..... 97 E1
Newcastle-u-L ST5 ..... 56 B3
Pattingham WV6 ..... 263 E4
Clive St ST6 ..... 41 F2
Cliveden Ave WS9 ..... 245 D1
Cliveden Coppice B74 ..... 257 F1
Cliveden Pl ST3 ..... 283 C2
Clockmill Ave WS3 ..... 243 F2
Clockmill Pl WS3 ..... 243 F2
Clockmill Rd WS3 ..... 243 F2
Cloister Wlk Bucknall ST2 ..... 58 A3
Whittington WS14 ..... 232 C4
Cloisters The
Burton u T DE15 ..... 166 C1
Gnosall ST20 ..... 171 F3
Close Bank DE13 ..... 146 B3
Close Jun Sch ST4 ..... 71 F4
Close The Enville DY7 ..... 273 C4
Madeley CW3 ..... 69 D3
Meir ST3 ..... 74 A3
Sedgley DY3 ..... 271 E2
Stafford, Moss Pit ST17 ..... 174 C3

Close The continued
Stafford, Rowley Park ST16 ..... 155 E1
Swindon DY3 ..... 269 F1
Tutbury DE13 ..... 146 A3
Cloud The CW12 ..... 7 D2
Cloud View CW12 ..... 6 A1
Clough Hall Dr ST7 ..... 40 C3
Clough Hall Rd ST7 ..... 40 C4
Clough Hall Sch The ST7 ..... 25 F1
Clough La ST9 ..... 59 D1
Clough St ST1 ..... 282 A2
Clovelly Wlk 2 ST6 ..... 56 C4
Clover Heath WV5 ..... 267 E4
Clover La DY6 ..... 275 D4
Clover Mdws WS12 ..... 210 B1
Clover Rd ST5 ..... 56 B3
Clover Ridge WS6 ..... 226 B2
Cloverdale Perton WV6 ..... 254 B2
Stafford ST17 ..... 175 E4
Cloverdale Pl ST7 ..... 73 F2
Cloverdale Rd ST5 ..... 56 A2
Clowes St ST4 ..... 58 A2
Clowes Way ST4 ..... 71 F4
Club Bldgs WV10 ..... 240 B3
Club Row DY3 ..... 271 F3
Club St ST4 ..... 72 A3
Clumber Ave ST5 ..... 71 E3
Clumber Gr ST5 ..... 71 E3
Cluny Pl ST2 ..... 58 A3
Clyde Ave ST6 ..... 16 C1
Clyde Pl ST5 ..... 71 D2
Clyde Rd ST6 ..... 57 D4
Clyde St ST1 ..... 282 A1
Clyde Wlk ST1 ..... 282 A2
Clydesdale Rd WS8 ..... 244 C3
Clynes Way ST3 ..... 74 A2
Co-operative St ST16 ..... 155 E3
Coach House La WS15 ..... 178 C1
Coach House Rise ST7 ..... 261 F4
Coal Haulage Rd WS11 ..... 227 E4
Coal Way Rd WV4 ..... 265 F3
Coalbourne La DY8 ..... 279 F4
Coalmeadow Cl WS3 ..... 242 C2
Coalpit Hill ST7 ..... 40 B4
Coalpit La WS15 ..... 197 D3
Coalpitford La ST13 ..... 44 C2
Coalport Cl ST10 ..... 76 B1
Coalville Rd ST3 ..... 74 A3
Coalway Ave WV3, WV4 ..... 266 A3
Coalway Gdns WV3 ..... 265 E4
Coalway Rd Rugeley WS15 ..... 197 D3
Walsall WS3 ..... 243 D1
Coates Pl ST6 ..... 42 A4
Coatsgate Wlk WV8 ..... 239 F1
Cob Moor Rd
Kidsgrove ST7 ..... 26 A2
Lawton-gate ST7 ..... 26 A2
Cobbett Rd WS7 ..... 228 B4
Cobbles The ST19 ..... 205 E4
Cobden Cl WS12 ..... 210 B4
Cobden St Longton ST3 ..... 283 B1
Newcastle-u-L ST5 ..... 56 B3
Stourbridge DY8 ..... 279 F3
Cobham Cl ST15 ..... 118 C3
Cobham Pl ST3 ..... 90 A4
Cobia B77 ..... 261 E4
Cobridge Rd ST1 ..... 57 D3
Coburn Dr B75 ..... 258 B3
Cock La ST4 ..... 193 F4
Cocketts Nook WS15 ..... 178 B2
Cocknage Rd Longton ST3 ..... 73 D1
Meir ST3 ..... 89 E3
Cocks La ST9 ..... 43 E2
Cockshutts La WV2 ..... 266 B4
Cocksparrow La SW12 ..... 209 D3
Cockspur St B78 ..... 262 C4
Cockster Brook La ST3 ..... 72 C2
Cockster Rd ST3 ..... 72 C2
Cockstubbles ST14 ..... 126 A4
Cocton Cl WV6 ..... 254 C3
Codsall Cty High Sch WV8 ..... 239 D2
Codsall Cty Mid Sch WV8 ..... 239 D2
Codsall L Ctr WV8 ..... 239 D2
Codsall Rd Codsall WV8 ..... 239 E1
Wolv WV6 ..... 255 D1
Codsall Sta WV8 ..... 238 C2
Coghlan Rd ST17 ..... 174 B4
Colbourne Rd B78 ..... 250 A1
Colbrook B77 ..... 250 B1
Colclough Ave ST5 ..... 56 A4
Colclough La ST6 ..... 41 E4
Colclough Rd ST3 ..... 74 A1
Coldridge Cl WV8 ..... 239 F1
Coldstream Dr DY8 ..... 275 F2
Cole Dr ST5 ..... 155 E1
Cole St ST8 ..... 27 E4
Coleford Cl DY8 ..... 275 E1
Colehill B79 ..... 250 A3
Coleman St WV6 ..... 255 F3
Colenso Way ST5 ..... 56 A4
Coleridge Cl
Brownhills WS3 ..... 244 A3
Tamworth B79 ..... 250 A3
Coleridge Ct DE14 ..... 166 B3
Coleridge Dr Cheadle ST10 ..... 76 B1
Perton WV6 ..... 254 C2
Stafford ST17 ..... 174 B4
Coleridge Rd ST3 ..... 73 D1
Coleridge Rise DY3 ..... 271 D2
Colesden Wlk WV4 ..... 265 D1
Coleshill Rd B78 ..... 261 D4
Coleshill St B78 ..... 261 D4
Coley Gr ST18 ..... 177 E4
Coley La ST18 ..... 158 B1
Colin Cres ST3 ..... 74 A2
Colindene Gr ST4 ..... 72 A3
Colinwood Cl WS6 ..... 226 C1

Collard Ave ST5 ..... 56 A2
College Cl CW3 ..... 68 C2
College Farm Cl WV6 ..... 253 E2
College Fields ST15 ..... 118 C3
College La B79 ..... 250 A3
College Rd Denstone ST14 ..... 95 E3
Hanley ST1 ..... 57 E1
Stoke-on-T ST1 ..... 282 B1
Wolv WV6 ..... 255 E2
College View WV6 ..... 255 E2
Collet Rd WV6 ..... 254 C3
Collets Brook B75 ..... 259 D1
Collett B77 ..... 251 D1
Colley Rd ST6 ..... 41 F3
Collier Cl Brownhills WS8 ..... 244 B4
Cheslyn Hay WS6 ..... 226 B1
Colliery Dr WS3 ..... 242 C2
Colliery Rd WS15 ..... 196 C2
Collin Rd ST4 ..... 71 F3
Collin St ST4 ..... 126 A4
Collindale Ct DY6 ..... 270 B1
Collingwood Gr ST4 ..... 71 F4
Collingwood Jun & Inf Schs WV10 ..... 240 C1
Collingwood Rd WV10 ..... 240 C1
Collins Hill WS13 ..... 214 A1
Collins Rd WS8 ..... 245 D3
Collinson Rd
Barton-u-N DE13 ..... 183 E1
Tunstall ST6 ..... 41 E4
Collis Ave ST5 ..... 56 B1
Collis St DY8 ..... 279 F4
Colne Mount ST14 ..... 126 A4
Colonnade The 13 ST16 ..... 155 F2
Colshaw Rd DY8 ..... 279 F2
Coltman Cl ST14 ..... 231 E4
Colton Hills Upper Sch WV4 ..... 266 A2
Colton Rd WS15 ..... 178 C2
Coltsfoot Way WS7 ..... 228 C4
Columbian Cres WS7 ..... 228 C4
Columbian Way WS11 ..... 209 F4
Colville Cl DE12 ..... 218 B4
Colville St ST4 ..... 72 C3
Colwall Rd DY3 ..... 271 E2
Colwich Cres ST16 ..... 156 B2
Colwich Prim Sch ST17 ..... 177 E4
Colwyn Dr ST8 ..... 27 E3
Combe Dr ST3 ..... 90 A3
Comber Gr DY7 ..... 278 A2
Comber Pl DY7 ..... 277 F2
Comberford La B79 ..... 234 A1
Comberford Rd B79 ..... 250 A4
Combermere TF9 ..... 97 E1
Comfrey Cl ST3 ..... 90 A3
Commerce Dr ST19 ..... 207 F4
Commerce St ST3 ..... 283 C3
Commercial Rd ST1 ..... 282 C2
Commercial St ST4 ..... 57 D4
Common Barn La DY10 ..... 280 B3
Common La
Acton Trussell ST17 ..... 194 A4
Alrewas WS13 ..... 215 E3
Betley CW3 ..... 52 B3
Cannock WS11 ..... 210 A2
Kingstone ST14 ..... 124 B1
Meir ST3 ..... 89 F2
Stone ST15 ..... 119 F3
Tamworth B79 ..... 250 A2
Waterhouses ST10 ..... 64 C4
Whitmore ST5 ..... 85 E3
Whittington WS14 ..... 232 B2
Common Rd Stafford ST16 ..... 155 F4
Wombourne WV5 ..... 270 A3
Common Road Ind Est ST16 ..... 155 F4
Common Side WS8 ..... 245 D3
Common The ST10 ..... 75 C2
Common View
Burntwood WS7 ..... 212 A1
Cannock WS12 ..... 210 A1
Common Wlk WS12 ..... 209 E3
Commonside
Brownhills WS3 ..... 244 A1
Longdon WS7, WS15 ..... 212 A2
Community Dr ST6 ..... 42 B1
Como St ST5 ..... 70 C3
Compton ST3 ..... 30 C3
Compton Cl DY7 ..... 277 F2
Compton Dr DY6 ..... 275 E3
Compton Gdns DY7 ..... 277 F2
Compton Gr DY6 ..... 275 E3
Compton Hill Dr WV3 ..... 255 E1
Compton Park Recn Ctr WV6 ..... 255 F2
Compton Rd Kinver DY7 ..... 277 E2
Stafford ST17 ..... 156 B1
Tamworth B79 ..... 249 F4
Wolv WV3 ..... 255 F1
Compton Rd W WV3 ..... 255 E1
Compton St ST1 ..... 282 A1
Comptons The TF9 ..... 130 A4
Condlyffe Rd ST13 ..... 30 C2
Condor Gr WS12 ..... 210 B1
Conduit Rd WS11 ..... 228 A2
Conduit St WS13 ..... 231 D4
Conewood Pl ST3 ..... 72 C1
Coney Gr ST3 ..... 74 A2
Coneybere Gdns ST19 ..... 223 E4
Coneygreave Cl ST10 ..... 76 B1
Coneygreave La ST5 ..... 85 E3
Conford St ST7 ..... 57 F1
Congleton Edge Rd CW12 ..... 16 A3
Congleton Rd
Biddulph ST6 ..... 16 B2
Kidsgrove ST7 ..... 25 E1
Mow Cop CW12 ..... 15 F1

Congleton Rd N
Lawton-gate ST7 ..... 25 F3
Scholar Green ST7 ..... 25 F3
Congleton Rd S ST7 ..... 25 E2
Congleton Sta CW12 ..... 6 A1
Congreve Cl ST17 ..... 175 F4
Congreve Rd ST3 ..... 72 C1
Conifer Cl WS12 ..... 210 A4
Conifer Gr Longton ST3 ..... 72 C1
Stafford ST17 ..... 174 A4
Coniston B77 ..... 262 A4
Coniston Cl ST15 ..... 120 B4
Coniston Dr Cheadle ST10 ..... 76 C2
Kingswinford DY6 ..... 275 D4
Coniston Gr ST5 ..... 71 D2
Coniston Pl ST4 ..... 87 F4
Coniston Rd Aldridge B74 ..... 256 C2
Wolv WV6 ..... 255 E4
Coniston Way WS11 ..... 209 F1
Connaught Dr WV5 ..... 265 D1
Connaught St ST6 ..... 41 E1
Conners La TF10 ..... 168 A2
Conrad Cl ST3 ..... 73 E2
Consall Gr ST4 ..... 88 B3
Consall La ST9 ..... 60 B3
Consett Rd ST3 ..... 88 C4
Consort St ST4 ..... 72 A4
Constable Ave ST5 ..... 55 F3
Constable Cl ST4 ..... 90 A4
Constance Ave ST4 ..... 88 A4
Convent Cl
Burton u T DE15 ..... 185 F4
Cannock WS11 ..... 226 B4
Colwich ST18 ..... 177 E4
Stoke-on-T ST4 ..... 72 A4
Convent St ST4 ..... 72 A4
Convent La WS15 ..... 105 D2
Conway Cl Burton u T DE13 ..... 166 B4
Kingswinford DY6 ..... 275 F2
Conway Gr ST10 ..... 76 C1
Conway Rd Biddulph ST8 ..... 27 E3
Cannock WS11 ..... 226 A4
Perton WV6 ..... 254 C2
Stafford ST16 ..... 155 D2
Conway St ST4 ..... 72 B4
Conygree La DE6 ..... 81 E4
Cook Cl WV6 ..... 254 C2
Cook's Bank ST17 ..... 175 D1
Cook's Hollow ST13 ..... 47 D4
Cook's La ST13 ..... 32 A1
Cooke Cl ST19 ..... 192 C1
Cookley La DY7 ..... 278 A1
Cookley Sebright Fst Sch DY10 ..... 280 A3
Cooknell Dr DY8 ..... 275 F1
Cookson Ave ST3 ..... 73 E1
Coombe Croft WV9 ..... 240 A2
Coombe Park Rd ST15 ..... 119 F3
Coombesdale ST5 ..... 85 F1
Cooper Ave ST5 ..... 56 C1
Cooper Cl ST15 ..... 120 B4
Cooper & Jordan CE Inf Sch WS9 ..... 256 B3
Cooper & Jordan CE Jun Sch WS9 ..... 256 B3
Cooper St Hanley ST1 ..... 282 A1
Newcastle-u-L ST5 ..... 55 F3
Wolv WV1 ..... 266 C4
Cooper's Bank Rd DY5 ..... 271 E1
Cooper's Sq DE14 ..... 166 B1
Coopers Cl ST13 ..... 30 B3
Coopers Way ST8 ..... 27 D4
Cope St
Norton-in-t-M ST2 ..... 43 D1
Stafford ST16 ..... 155 F2
Cope's Dr B79 ..... 250 A4
Copeland Ave
Newcastle-u-L ST5 ..... 71 D2
Tittensor ST12 ..... 88 A4
Copeland Cl ST10 ..... 76 B1
Copeland Dr WS15 ..... 120 B3
Copeland St ST4 ..... 72 A4
Copelands The DY7 ..... 278 A2
Copes Ave ST6 ..... 41 F2
Copes Way ST14 ..... 111 D1
Copley La WS14 ..... 253 D1
Coplow Ave ST10 ..... 92 B2
Coplow La DE6 ..... 129 E3
Copp La ST6 ..... 41 E1
Copper Beech Dr
Kingswinford DY6 ..... 270 B1
Wombourne WV5 ..... 270 A3
Copper Glade ST16 ..... 156 A2
Copperas Rd DE11 ..... 186 B3
Copperfields WS14 ..... 231 E4
Copperhill Rd CW12 ..... 16 A4
Copperkins Rd WS12 ..... 210 C2
Coppermill Cl WS12 ..... 209 F4
Coppice Ave ST5 ..... 55 C1
Coppice Brook ST17 ..... 176 B2
Coppice Cl Biddulph ST8 ..... 27 E4
Burntwood WS7 ..... 228 C4
Cheslyn Hay WS11 ..... 226 C2
Sedgley DY3 ..... 271 E4
Stone ST15 ..... 105 D1
Coppice Cres WS8 ..... 244 B4
Coppice Ct WS11 ..... 226 A4
Coppice Dr TF10 ..... 168 C3
Coppice Farm Way WV11 ..... 242 A1
Coppice Gdns WS15 ..... 105 D1
Coppice Gr
Lichfield WS14 ..... 231 F4
Meir ST3 ..... 73 F2

Coppice La Aldridge WS9 .... 244 C1
Allen End B75, B78 .... 259 E1
Brownhills WS8 .... 244 B4
Burntwood WS7 .... 230 A2
Cheslyn Hay WS11 .... 226 B2
Clifton Campville B79 .... 218 C1
Middleton B78 .... 260 A1
Wolv WV6 .... 255 D3
Coppice Prim Sch B75 ... 258 A1
Coppice Rd
Brownhills WS9 .... 244 C2
Kidsgrove ST7 .... 40 B4
Rugeley WS15 .... 196 C3
Stone ST15 .... 105 D1
Wolv WV3 .... 265 E4
Coppice Side WS8 .... 244 B4
Coppice Side Ind Est
WS8 .... 244 B4
Coppice Specl Sch ST5 ... 284 B1
Coppice The
Cannock WS12 .... 210 C1
Hanley ST6 .... 57 E4
Market Drayton TF9 .... 97 D1
Coppice View ST5 .... 56 A2
Coppins The Leek ST13 ..... 30 B3
Stafford ST17 .... 175 E4
Copplestone Gr ST3 .... 73 F2
Coppull Pl ST6 .... 42 A4
Coppy Hall Gr WS9 .... 245 D1
Coppy Nook La WS7 .... 229 E3
Copse Cres WS3 .... 244 A2
Copse Dr WS15 .... 198 A2
Copse The B74 .... 257 F1
Copthorne Ave WS7 .... 228 C2
Copthorne Rd WV3 .... 266 A4
Coral Gr ST4 .... 88 A4
Corbet Ct TF9 .... 97 E1
Corbett CE Prim Sch DY7 .. 268 A1
Corbett Hospl DY8 .... 279 F4
Corby Pl ST3 .... 283 A3
Corden Ave DE13 .... 166 C4
Cordy La WV7 .... 237 D4
Corfe Cl WV6 .... 254 C2
Corfe Gn ST3 .... 73 E3
Corfield Pl ST3 .... 42 B3
Corfton Dr WV6 .... 255 E2
Corina Ct ST3 .... 73 E2
Corina Way ST3 .... 73 E2
Cormie Cl ST6 .... 42 A3
Corncrake Rd DY1 .... 271 F1
Cornel B77 .... 250 C2
Cornelious St ST3 .... 74 A1
Cornes St ST1 .... 57 F1
Corneville Rd ST2 .... 58 B2
Cornfield WV8 .... 239 F1
Cornfield Cl DY6 .... 275 D4
Cornfield Dr WS14 .... 231 F4
Cornfield Rd ST8 .... 27 F4
Cornflower Cl WV10 .... 241 D4
Cornflower Rd WS8 .... 244 B3
Cornhill WS11 .... 209 F3
Cornhill Cl ST5 .... 40 B1
Cornhill Gdns ST13 .... 30 C2
Cornhill Rd ST6 .... 42 B3
Cornhill St 🖲 ST13 .... 30 C3
Cornmell Lea TF10 .... 168 C2
Cornmill Gr WV6 .... 254 B2
Cornmill La DE13 .... 146 C3
Cornovian Cl WV6 .... 254 C3
Corns Gr WV5 .... 269 F3
Cornwall Ave
Newcastle-u-L ST5 .... 71 E2
Tamworth B78 .... 250 A1
Cornwall Cl Aldridge WS9 ... 245 D1
Congleton CW12 .... 6 A1
Kingswinford DY6 .... 275 D4
Cornwall Ct WS15 .... 196 B3
Cornwall Rd
Burton u T DE15 .... 185 F3
Cannock WS12 .... 210 A3
Stourbridge DY8 .... 279 E4
Wolv WV6 .... 255 E2
Cornwall St ST3 .... 283 C4
Cornwallis St ST4 .... 72 A3
Cornwood Gr ST3 .... 89 F4
Coronation Ave
Biddulph ST8 .... 27 D3
Fazeley B78 .... 249 E1
Longton ST3 .... 283 B3
Coronation Cres
Kidsgrove ST7 .... 25 F1
Rocester ST14 .... 96 A2
Shuttington B79 .... 251 E4
Coronation Rd
Brownhills WS9 .... 245 D2
Newcastle-u-L ST5 .... 284 C2
Stafford ST16 .... 156 A3
Stoke-on-T, Hartshill ST4 ... 71 F4
Coronation St
Cheadle ST10 .... 76 B2
Tamworth B79 .... 250 A3
Tunstall ST6 .... 41 F2
Corporation St
Newcastle-u-L ST5 .... 284 B3
Stafford ST16 .... 155 F2
Stoke-on-T ST4 .... 72 A3
Tamworth B79 .... 250 A3
Corran Rd ST17 .... 174 B3
Correen B77 .... 251 E1
Corrin Gr DY6 .... 275 E4
Corser St DY1 .... 271 F1
Corsham Pl ST14 .... 143 F4
Corsican Cl WS7 .... 229 D4
Corsican Dr WS12 .... 210 A4
Corsty La ST18 .... 154 A2

Cort Dr WS7 .... 229 D4
Corve Gdns WV6 .... 255 F3
Corve View DY3 .... 266 B1
Coseley St ST6 .... 42 B1
Cosford Ct WV6 .... 254 C3
Cosgrove Wlk WV8 .... 239 F1
Cot La DY6, DY8 .... 275 E3
Cote La DY7 .... 273 F1
Cotehill Rd ST9 .... 59 D2
Cotesheath St ST4 .... 57 E1
Coton Ave ST16 .... 156 A2
Coton Green Cty Prim Sch
B79 .... 249 F4
Coton Green Prec B79 ..... 249 F4
Coton La Ranton ST18 ..... 153 F2
Seighford ST18 .... 154 A2
Tamworth B79 .... 249 F4
Coton Pk DE11 .... 186 B1
Coton Rd DE12 .... 202 C3
Coton Rise ST12 .... 88 C1
Cotsdale Rd WV4 .... 265 F2
Cotswold Ave
Great Wyrley WS6 .... 226 C2
Newcastle-u-L ST5 .... 55 F2
Cotswold Cl WS9 .... 245 E1
Cotswold Cres ST2 .... 43 D1
Cotswold Dr WV7 .... 237 D3
Cotswold Gr WV12 .... 242 A1
Cotswold Rd
Branston DE14 .... 184 C4
Cannock WS12 .... 210 A4
Meir ST3 .... 73 F1
Cotswolds Rd WV2 .... 266 C4
Cottage Cl Burntwood WS7 . 228 C3
Cannock WS12 .... 210 B3
Meir ST3 .... 73 F1
Cottage Ct WS7 .... 228 C3
Cottage Farm Rd B77 ...... 261 E4
Cottage La Biddulph ST8 .... 28 A4
Burntwood WS7 .... 228 C3
Wolv WV10 .... 240 B2
Cottage St DY6 .... 275 E4
Cottage View WV8 .... 239 D2
Cottage Wlk B77 .... 261 F3
Cotterill Dr ST5 .... 56 A4
Cotterill Gr ST6 .... 56 C4
Cotters Hill Cl ST18 .... 177 E4
Cottesmore Rd DE15 .... 167 D1
Cotton Gr WS12 .... 195 D1
Cotton La ST10 .... 63 D1
Cotton Rd Tunstall ST6 ..... 41 E3
Wolv WV4 .... 266 A3
Cotton Way WS7 .... 211 F1
Cottonwood Dr ST7 .... 26 C2
Cottonwood Gr ST3 .... 283 C4
Cotwall End Rd DY3 .... 271 D3
Coulson Cl WS7 .... 211 E1
Coulter Gr WV6 .... 254 B2
Coulter La WS7 .... 229 F4
Coulthwaite Way WS15 ..... 196 C3
Council Hos
Chetwynd Aston TF10 ...... 187 D4
Kingstone ST14 .... 140 C3
County Dr B78 .... 250 A1
County La Codsall WV7 ..... 237 F2
Stourbridge DY7 .... 281 E4
County Rd ST16 .... 155 F2
Coupe Dr ST3 .... 74 A3
Court Cres DY6 .... 275 E3
Court Dr WS14 .... 246 C2
Court Farm La DE14 .... 184 C4
Court La ST5 .... 56 A2
Court No 1 ST3 .... 73 F1
Court Par WS9 .... 256 A3
Court Rd WV6 .... 255 F2
Court Wlk WS3 .... 53 D3
Courtland Rd DY6 .... 275 E4
Courtlands The WV6 .... 255 F2
Courtney Pl ST3 .... 89 F4
Courtway Dr ST1 .... 57 E4
Cousins St WV2 .... 266 B4
Coven Cl WS3 .... 244 A3
Coven Rd WV9 .... 223 E2
Coventry Ct ST16 .... 155 D2
Coverdale Cl ST3 .... 90 A4
Coverley Pl ST4 .... 71 F3
Covert Cl ST18 .... 158 A1
Covert Gdns ST7 .... 40 B4
Covert La DY8 .... 279 E1
Covert The Keele ST5 .... 70 A4
Newcastle-u-L ST5 .... 71 E1
Wolv WV8 .... 239 F1
Covey Cl WS13 .... 214 B1
Cow La ST13 .... 63 F4
Cowallmoor La ST9 .... 28 B3
Cowan Dr ST16 .... 156 A2
Cowen St ST6 .... 42 C3
Cowhill La DE13 .... 200 C1
Cowhouse La ST10 .... 109 D2
Cowley B77 .... 250 C1
Cowley Cl Penkridge ST19 ... 207 F4
Stafford ST17 .... 174 B4
Cowley Dr DY1 .... 271 F1
Cowley Gn WS12 .... 209 F4
Cowley La ST20 .... 171 E3
Cowley Way ST2 .... 73 F4
Cowlishaw Cl ST8 .... 27 D3
Cowlishaw Rd ST6 .... 42 A3
Cowlishaw Way WS15 ...... 196 C3
Cowlow La SK17 .... 23 E2
Cowper St ST4 .... 72 C3
Coxmoor Cl WS3 .... 242 C1
Crab La Bobbington DY7 .... 268 B1
Cannock WS11 .... 210 A2
Enville DY7 .... 268 B1
Stafford ST18 .... 155 D4
Walsall WV12 .... 242 B1
Crabbery St ST16 .... 155 F2
Crabtree Ave ST8 .... 27 E4

Crabtree Cl ST4 .... 72 C4
Crabtree Way WS15 .... 178 B1
Crackley Bank Prim Sch
ST5 .... 55 F4
Crackley La ST5 .... 54 C2
Cracow Moss CW3 .... 53 D2
Craddock Rd ST16 .... 155 E4
Craftdown Cl ST17 .... 174 C2
Craigside ST8 .... 27 E4
Cramer St ST1 .... 155 F1
Cranberry Ave SE10 .... 93 D1
Cranberry Cl ST16 .... 155 D3
Cranberry Dr ST5 .... 40 B1
Cranbourne Ave
Norton-in-t-M ST2 .... 43 D1
Wolv WV4 .... 266 C2
Cranbrook Cl ST4 .... 88 A4
Cranbrook Gr WV6 .... 254 C2
Cranbrook Wlk ST17 ...... 174 A4
Cranbrooks ST19 .... 205 E4
Crane Dr WS7 .... 229 D2
Crane Field WS13 .... 214 A1
Crane Hollow WV5 .... 269 F3
Crane St ST1 .... 57 D3
Crane Terr WV6 .... 255 E3
Cranebrook Hill B78 .... 259 F3
Cranebrook La
Shenstone WS14 .... 245 F4
Wall WS14 .... 246 A4
Cranesbill WV10 .... 241 E4
Cranfield Cl ST4 .... 58 A1
Cranfield Rd WS7 .... 229 D4
Cranford Pl WS11 .... 209 F1
Cranford Rd WV3 .... 265 E4
Cranford Way ST2 .... 58 B2
Cranham Dr DY6 .... 275 F3
Cranleigh Ave ST1 .... 57 E4
Cranleigh Cl
Aldridge WS9 .... 256 A3
Walsall WV12 .... 242 B1
Cranleigh Way WS14 .... 231 F4
Cranley Dr WV8 .... 238 C2
Cranmer Gr B74 .... 257 F3
Cranmer St ST4 .... 72 A4
Cranmere Ave WV6 .... 255 D3
Cranmere Gr WS6 .... 226 B1
Cranmore Cl ST15 .... 120 B4
Cranmore Rd WV3 .... 255 F2
Cranswick Gr ST2 .... 58 B1
Crantock Cl WV12 .... 242 B1
Cranwell Pl ST3 .... 89 F4
Cranwell Rise B78 .... 249 E1
Cranwood Rd ST12 .... 88 A1
Cranworth Gr ST3 .... 89 F4
Crateford La ST19 .... 224 A4
Crathorne Ave WV10 .... 240 B1
Crauford Rd CW12 .... 6 A4
Craven B77 .... 251 D1
Craven Cl ST4 .... 42 B1
Craven St Burton u T DE13 .. 166 B3
Wolv WV2 .... 266 C3
Crawford Ave WV4 .... 266 C2
Crawford St ST4 .... 72 B3
Crawley La DE13 .... 199 E3
Crayford Ave CW12 .... 6 A3
Craythorne Rd
Burton u T DE13 .... 147 E2
Rolleston DE13 .... 147 E2
Crediton Cl ST6 .... 42 B2
Creighton La ST14 .... 111 D3
Cremorne Dr ST17 .... 175 E4
Cremorne Rd B75 .... 258 A1
Crescent Gr ST4 .... 56 C1
Crescent Rd ST17 .... 155 E1
Crescent The Ashley TF9 ... 100 B3
Burntwood WS7 .... 211 F1
Cookley DY10 .... 280 A2
Eccleshall ST21 .... 133 E3
Great Wyrley WS6 .... 227 D1
Hagley DY8 .... 281 F3
Leek ST13 .... 31 D4
Mayfield DE6 .... 81 E4
Newcastle-u-L, Silverdale ST5 55 D1
Newcastle-u-L, Westlands
ST5 .... 71 D3
Rudyard ST9 .... 18 B1
Stafford ST17 .... 175 F4
Stoke-on-T ST4 .... 71 F2
Stone ST15 .... 105 D1
Swadlincote DE11 .... 186 C3
Wolv WV6 .... 255 D2
Cressington St B74 .... 258 A1
Cresswell Ave ST5 .... 40 B1
Cresswell La
Brewood ST19 .... 223 E3
Draycott in t M ST11 .... 91 F2
Cresswell Old La ST11 ...... 91 F2
Cresswell Rd Hanley ST1 .... 57 F2
Hilderstone ST15 .... 106 C2
Crest Cl DE13 .... 147 F1
Crestbrook Rd ST2 .... 58 B3
Crestfield Rd ST3 .... 89 F4
Crestway Rd ST2 .... 43 E2
Crestwood B77 .... 251 D3
Crestwood Cl DE13 .... 166 B4
Crestwood Dr ST15 .... 119 F3
Crestwood Glen WV6 .... 255 F4
Crestwood Pk ST19 .... 223 E4
Crestwood Rise WS15 ...... 178 B1
Crestwood Sch The DY6 .... 275 E4
Creswell Cres WS3 .... 242 C1
Creswell Dr ST18 .... 154 C4
Creswell Farm Dr ST16 .... 155 D4
Creswell Gr ST18 .... 154 C4
Crich Way DE11 .... 186 C3
Crichton Ave DE13 .... 166 B4
Crick Rd ST1 .... 57 F1
Cricket Cl DE15 .... 167 F4

Cricket La WS14 .... 231 E3
Cricket Meadow
Sedgley DY3 .... 271 F2
Wolv WV10 .... 240 B2
Cricketers Cl DE15 .... 185 F4
Crigdon B77 .... 251 E1
Crinan Gr ST17 .... 174 B3
Cringlebrook B77 .... 250 B1
Crispin Cl ST16 .... 155 E4
Critchlow Gr ST3 .... 73 D1
Crockford Dr B75 .... 258 A2
Crockington Cl WV5 .... 263 F1
Crockington La WV5 .... 264 A1
Crocus Cres WV9 .... 240 A2
Croft Ave Cannock WS12 ... 195 D1
Newcastle-u-L ST5 .... 56 A3
Croft Cl Elford B79 .... 216 C1
Netherseal DE12 .... 219 F4
Rolleston DE13 .... 147 D2
Croft Cres Brownhills WS8 .. 244 B4
Stoke-on-T ST4 .... 72 A3
Croft Ct ST6 .... 42 B1
Croft Gdns WS7 .... 229 D4
Croft Gr ST14 .... 111 E1
Croft La ST19 .... 207 E1
Croft Leys The WS15 ...... 198 B2
Croft Par WS7 .... 256 A3
Croft Prim Sch The
WS15 .... 197 F3
Croft Rd Cheadle ST10 ..... 76 B2
Newcastle-u-L ST5 .... 284 B4
Stone ST15 .... 119 F3
Croft St Burslem ST6 .... 56 C4
Tamworth B79 .... 250 A3
Croft The Blakedown DY10 .. 281 E1
Burton u T DE15 .... 166 C1
Cheadle ST10 .... 76 B2
Cheddleton ST13 .... 45 E2
Cheslyn Hay WS6 .... 226 C1
Colwich ST18 .... 158 B1
Hixon ST18 .... 158 B4
King's Bromley DE13 ...... 199 E3
Longdon WS15 .... 197 F1
Maer TF9 .... 84 B1
Sedgley DY3 .... 266 C1
Stoke-on-T ST4 .... 71 F3
Swadlincote DE11 .... 186 A4
Wombourne WV5 .... 269 E3
Croft Way TF9 .... 97 D1
Crofter Cl ST8 .... 27 D4
Crofters Wlk WV8 .... 239 F1
Croftfield St ST2 .... 73 E4
Croftstead Ave ST14 .... 95 C3
Cromartie St ST3 .... 283 C4
Cromer Cres ST1 .... 57 F2
Cromer Gdns WV6 .... 255 F3
Cromer Rd ST1 .... 57 F2
Cromer St ST5 .... 56 B2
Crompton Cl ST15 .... 177 F4
Crompton Gr ST4 .... 88 B3
Crompton Rd ST15 .... 120 A4
Cromwell Cl Hopton ST18 ... 137 E1
Tutbury DE13 .... 146 B3
Cromwell Ct WS6 .... 227 D1
Cromwell Rd
Cannock WS12 .... 210 C1
Tamworth B79 .... 249 F4
Wolv WV10 .... 240 C1
Cromwell St Biddulph ST8 ... 27 E4
Hanley ST1 .... 57 E3
Cromwell Terr 🖲 ST13 ..... 30 C3
Cromwells Meadow
WS14 .... 231 E3
Crony Cl ST13 .... 45 E2
Crook La WS9 .... 256 A1
Crooked Bridge Rd ST16 ... 155 F2
Crosby Cl WV6 .... 255 F3
Crosby Rd ST4 .... 71 F2
Cross Butts ST21 .... 133 E3
Cross Edge ST6 .... 43 D4
Cross Hill ST6 .... 56 C4
Cross In Hand La
Farewell WS13 .... 213 E2
Lichfield WS13 .... 213 F1
Cross Keys ST3 .... 231 D4
Cross La Audley ST7 .... 39 F3
Congleton CW12 .... 6 A1
Lichfield WS13 .... 231 E3
Rolleston DE13 .... 147 D1
Sedgley DY3 .... 266 B1
Stone ST15 .... 105 D1
Waterhouses ST13 .... 48 C2
Cross May St ST5 .... 284 A2
Cross of the Hand WS15 .... 161 D1
Cross Pl DY3 .... 266 C1
Cross Rd Albrighton WV7 ... 237 D2
Rugeley WS15 .... 196 C4
Uttoxeter ST14 .... 111 D1
Cross Side DE6 .... 81 F4
Cross St Biddulph ST8 ...... 27 E4
Brownhills WS3 .... 244 A1
Burntwood WS7 .... 228 C4
Burton u T DE14 .... 166 B2
Cannock, Bridgtown WS11 .. 226 C3
Cannock, Hayes Heath
WS12 .... 210 C1
Cheadle ST10 .... 76 B2
Cheslyn Hay WS6 .... 226 B2
Gnosall ST20 .... 171 E3
Kingsley ST10 .... 61 E2
Kingswinford DY6 .... 275 E3
Kingswinford, Wall Heath
DY6 .... 275 D4
Kingswinford,
Wordsley DY6 .... 275 E2
Leek ST13 .... 30 C3
Longton ST3 .... 283 C4
Market Drayton TF9 .... 97 E1

Cross St continued
Meir ST3 .... 74 A3
Newcastle-u-L ST5 .... 55 F4
Stafford ST16 .... 155 E4
Stourbridge DY8 .... 279 F3
Tamworth, Kettlebrook B77 . 250 B2
Tamworth, The Leys B79 .... 250 A3
Tunstall ST6 .... 56 B4
Cross St S WV2 .... 266 B4
Crossdale Ave ST2 .... 43 D1
Crossfell B77 .... 251 D1
Crossfield Ave Biddulph ST8 . 27 E3
Forsbrook ST11 .... 90 C3
Crossfield Rd WS13 .... 231 F4
Crosshill Bank ST16 .... 122 C3
Crossing La ST18 .... 154 B4
Crossings The WS14 .... 231 F4
Crossland Cres WV6 .... 255 D3
Crossland Pl E ST3 .... 90 A4
Crossland Pl W ST3 .... 74 A1
Crosslands CW3 .... 6 A1
Crossley Rd ST6 .... 42 A2
Crossley Stone WS15 ...... 178 C2
Crosslow La DE6 .... 36 C3
Crossman St DE14 .... 166 A2
Crossmead Gr ST1 .... 57 F3
Crossway ST16 .... 156 A2
Crossway Rd ST6 .... 57 E4
Crossway The ST5 .... 56 B2
Crossways ST6 .... 16 C1
Crossways Rd ST7 .... 25 D2
Croston ST1 .... 282 A1
Crotia Ave CW2 .... 37 D3
Crouch Ave ST6 .... 42 A2
Crouch La CW12 .... 6 B2
Crowberry Cl WS8 .... 244 B3
Crowberry La
Barton-u-N DE13 .... 183 E1
Middleton B78 .... 260 B1
Crowborough Rd ST8 ...... 28 A3
Crowcrofts Rd ST3 .... 88 C4
Crowden Rd B77 .... 251 D1
Crowfoot La DE65 .... 129 F4
Crowland Ave WV6 .... 254 C2
Crown Bank ST1 .... 282 B3
Crown Bank Cres ST7 ...... 40 B3
Crown Bridge ST19 .... 192 C1
Crown Cl DY3 .... 266 B1
Crown Ind Est DE14 ...... 166 A1
Crown La Kinver DY10 ..... 281 E3
Stourbridge DY8 .... 279 F3
Sutton Coldfield B74 ...... 257 F2
Crown Specl Sch The
DE13 .... 147 E1
Crown St Hanley ST1 ...... 282 B2
Newcastle-u-L ST5 .... 55 F4
Stone ST15 .... 120 A4
Crowndale Pl ST7 .... 41 F4
Crowther Gr WV6 .... 255 F2
Crowther Rd WV6 .... 255 F3
Crowther St ST4 .... 72 B4
Crowtrees Farm Ind Est
ST10 .... 48 C1
Croxall B B79, WS13 ...... 217 D3
Croxden Rd ST2 .... 58 A3
Croxdene Ave WS3 .... 243 D1
Croxhall Rd DE13 .... 201 D1
Croxley Dr WS12 .... 210 B2
Croxstalls Cl WS3 .... 243 D1
Croxstalls Rd WS3 .... 243 D1
Croyde Pl ST3 .... 90 A3
Croydon Dr ST19 .... 207 F4
Cruso St ST13 .... 30 C3
Crutchley Ave B78 .... 250 A1
Crystal Ave DY8 .... 275 F1
Crystal St ST6 .... 57 D3
Cubley La DE6 .... 96 C1
Cuckoo Cage La DE13 ..... 164 C1
Cuckoo Cl WS11 .... 210 B1
Cull Ave ST16 .... 156 A2
Cullamore La ST14 .... 126 A2
Culland Rd DE14 .... 185 D4
Cumberland Cl
Kidsgrove ST7 .... 40 C4
Kingswinford DY6 .... 275 F2
Cumberland Cres WS7 ..... 229 D4
Cumberland Dr B78 .... 250 A1
Cumberland Rd
Burton u T DE15 .... 185 E3
Cannock WS11 .... 210 A2
Cumberland St
Fenton ST4 .... 72 C3
Newcastle-u-L ST5 .... 284 D3
Cumberledge Hill WS15 .... 211 F3
Cumberpatch Ave ST6 ..... 42 A4
Cumbers The ST18 .... 154 A3
Cumming St ST4 .... 71 F4
Cunningham Rd WV6 ..... 254 C2
Curborough Rd WS13 ..... 214 A1
Curland Pl ST3 .... 73 F1
Curlew B77 .... 250 C1
Curlew Cl Lichfield WS14 ... 231 E4
Uttoxeter ST14 .... 126 B3
Curlew Hill WS11 .... 210 A2
Curtis Way DE14 .... 166 A2
Curtiss St ST3 .... 90 B3
Curzon Pl WS15 .... 196 C4
Curzon Rise ST13 .... 30 A3
Curzon St Burton u T DE14 .. 166 B2
Newcastle-u-L ST5 .... 56 B1
Wolv WV2 .... 266 B4
Curzon St W DE14 .... 166 A2
Cutts St ST1 .... 282 A1
Cwerne Ct DY3 .... 271 E2
Cygnet Cl Cannock WS12 ... 210 B4
Keele CW3 .... 69 D4
Cynthia Gr ST6 .... 42 A1

Cypress Ave DY3 ... 271 E3
Cypress Cl TF9 ... 97 D1
Cypress Gdns DY6 ... 275 E2
Cypress Gr
Forsbrook ST11 ... 91 D3
Newcastle-u-L ST5 ... 55 E4
Cypress Rise WS12 ... 211 D3
Cyprus St WV2 ... 266 B3

D'Urberville Cl WV2 ... 266 C3
D'Urberville Rd WV2 ... 266 C3
D'Urberville Wlk WS11 ... 210 A1
Dace B77 ... 261 E4
Dace Gr ST6 ... 42 A2
Daffodil Cl DY3 ... 271 F4
Daffodil Wlk WS15 ... 178 B1
Dag La DE12 ... 218 C4
Dahlia Cl ST3 ... 74 A3
Dain Pl ST5 ... 56 A3
Dain St ST6 ... 56 C4
Daintry Cl ST13 ... 30 C3
Daintry Dr B78 ... 249 D4
Daintry St Leek ST13 ... 30 C3
Stoke-on-T ST4 ... 71 F2
Dairyfields Way ST1 ... 57 E4
Dairyhouse La
Cheadle ST10 ... 60 C1
Dilhorne ST10 ... 60 A1
Daist Bank ST13 ... 30 C3
Daisy Ave ST10 ... 62 A4
Daisy Bank WS12 ... 209 F4
Daisy Bank Cl WS4 ... 244 A1
Daisy La DE13 ... 200 B1
Daisy Pl ST4 ... 72 C2
Daisy Wlk WV9 ... 240 A2
Dalbeg Cl WV8 ... 255 F4
Dale Ave ST6 ... 42 C3
Dale Cl Cheadle ST10 ... 76 C1
Whitmore ST5 ... 85 E3
Dale Cres CW12 ... 6 A1
Dale Dr WS7 ... 229 D4
Dale Gr CW12 ... 6 A1
Dale La Haughton ST18 ... 173 D4
Seighford ST18 ... 154 A1
Stanton ST10 ... 64 C2
Dale Rd DY8 ... 279 F1
Dale St Burslem ST6 ... 56 C4
Burton u T DE14 ... 166 B1
Dale The Ashley TF9 ... 100 A3
Blythe Bridge ST11 ... 90 C1
Warslow SK17 ... 23 E1
Dale View
Earl Sterndale SK17 ... 5 D2
Meir ST3 ... 74 A2
Dale View Ct ST11 ... 90 C1
Dale View Dr ST5 ... 55 E1
Dalebrook Rd DE15 ... 167 D3
Dalecot Gn ST2 ... 73 E4
Dalegarth Gr ST3 ... 89 F4
Dalehall Gdns 23 ST6 ... 56 C4
Dalehead Ct ST3 ... 89 F4
Dalehouse Rd ST13 ... 45 E2
Dalelands Est TF9 ... 112 A4
Dalelands W TF9 ... 112 A4
Dales Cl Biddulph ST8 ... 28 A4
Swadlincote DE11 ... 186 C3
Dales Cty Inf Sch B77 ... 262 A4
Dales Green Rd ST7 ... 26 B3
Dales Jun Sch B77 ... 262 A4
Daleside DE15 ... 167 D1
Dalesman Cl DY6 ... 275 D4
Dallow Cl DE14 ... 166 B3
Dallow Cres DE14 ... 166 B3
Dallow St DE14 ... 166 B3
Dalton Ave DE15 ... 167 D1
Dalton Gr ST2 ... 58 B1
Dalton St WV3 ... 266 A4
Daltry Way CW3 ... 68 C4
Daly Cres ST5 ... 55 D1
Dam La Alsop en le D DE6 ... 36 C2
Biddulph ST8 ... 17 D1
Dam St WS13 ... 231 D4
Dama Rd B78 ... 260 C4
Dampier St ST13 ... 30 C3
Dams The ST11 ... 74 B1
Danby Crest ST17 ... 174 A4
Danby Dr WS12 ... 211 E2
Dandillion Ave ST10 ... 92 B4
Dane Dr ST6 ... 16 C1
Dane Gdns ST7 ... 26 B1
Dane Gr ST10 ... 76 C1
Dane Wlk ST1 ... 282 C3
Danebower Rd ST4 ... 88 A3
Danebridge Gr ST1 ... 57 F3
Danehill Gr ST4 ... 71 F1
Danehill Hollow WV8 ... 255 F4
Danelagh Cl B79 ... 249 F4
Danemead Cl ST3 ... 90 A4
Danes Cl WV11 ... 241 F2
Danes Croft ST4 ... 88 A4
Danesbrook WV5 ... 267 E4
Danescourt Rd WV6 ... 255 E3
Danesgate 10 ST13 ... 30 C3
Danesmore Park
Prim Sch WV11 ... 242 A1
Daneswood Dr WS9 ... 244 C2
Danford La WV5 ... 267 E4
Daniels Cross TF10 ... 169 D2
Daniels La WS9 ... 256 B3
Danilo Rd WS11 ... 209 E1
Danta Way ST17 ... 156 B1
Darby Ave WS14 ... 232 C3
Darges La WS11 ... 226 C2
Darius Cl ST5 ... 56 A4
Dark La Alrewas DE13 ... 201 D2
Farewell WS13 ... 213 D1
Featherstone, Brinsford
WV10 ... 240 B4
Dark La continued
Featherstone, Hilton Park
WV10, WV11 ... 241 E4
Great Wyrley WS6 ... 227 E1
Kinver DY7 ... 278 A2
Longdon WS15 ... 212 B4
Newborough DE13 ... 162 B4
Newport TF10 ... 168 C1
Polesworth B78 ... 262 C4
Darley Dale DE11 ... 186 C1
Darley Gr ST10 ... 76 C1
Darlings La WS15 ... 212 A3
Darnbrook B77 ... 251 E1
Darnel Hurst Rd B75 ... 258 B2
Darnford Cl ST16 ... 155 E4
Darnford La
Lichfield WS14 ... 231 F3
Whittington WS14 ... 232 A3
Darnford Moors WS14 ... 231 F3
Darnford View WS13 ... 214 C1
Darnley St ST4 ... 72 B4
Darrall Gdns ST4 ... 71 F2
Darsham Gdns ST5 ... 71 E1
Dart B77 ... 262 A3
Dart Ave ST6 ... 42 A2
Dart Cl ST6 ... 16 B1
Dart Gr ST10 ... 76 C1
Dart Pl ST5 ... 71 D2
Dartford Pl ST6 ... 42 B2
Dartford Rd WS3 ... 242 C1
Dartmouth Ave
Cannock WS11 ... 226 B4
Kingswinford DY8 ... 275 E2
Newcastle-u-L ST5 ... 71 D3
Pattingham WV6 ... 253 E1
Dartmouth Dr WS9 ... 256 A3
Dartmouth Pl ST3 ... 89 F4
Dartmouth Rd WS11 ... 209 E1
Dartmouth St
Chell Heath ST6 ... 42 A1
Stafford ST16 ... 156 A2
Wolv WV2 ... 266 B4
Darwell Pk B77 ... 251 D1
Darwin Cl Burntwood WS7 ... 229 D4
Burton u T DE15 ... 167 E1
Cannock WS12 ... 210 C1
Lichfield WS13 ... 231 D4
Stafford ST16 ... 156 B2
Darwin Ct WV6 ... 254 C2
Dash Gr ST6 ... 42 B1
Datteln Rd WS11 ... 210 A2
Davenport Cl ST13 ... 30 A2
Davenport Rd WV6 ... 255 D3
Davenport St Burslem ST6 ... 56 B4
Tunstall ST6 ... 41 F1
Daventry Cl ST2 ... 57 F1
David Garrick Gdns
WS13 ... 214 A1
David Rd ST3 ... 73 F1
Davidson Ave CW12 ... 6 A3
Davidson Rd WS14 ... 231 D4
Davies Dr ST14 ... 110 C1
Davis Cl ST16 ... 156 A2
Davis Rd B77 ... 250 C2
Davis St ST1 ... 57 D1
Davison St ST6 ... 57 D4
Davy Cl ST2 ... 58 A2
Davy Pl WS15 ... 196 B3
Dawes Cl WS15 ... 197 F2
Dawes La WS8 ... 229 D1
Dawley Brook Prim Sch
DY6 ... 275 E4
Dawley Brook Rd DY6 ... 275 E4
Dawley Rd DY6 ... 275 E4
Dawley Trad Est DY6 ... 275 E4
Dawlish Ave ST17 ... 175 E4
Dawlish Dr ST2 ... 58 B1
Dawn Ave ST6 ... 42 A2
Dawn View ST3 ... 74 A2
Dawney Dr B75 ... 258 A2
Dawson Ave WV14 ... 266 C1
Dayson Pl ST5 ... 56 A4
Dayton Dr WS15 ... 178 B1
Daywell Rise WS15 ... 178 B2
De Ferrers Croft DE13 ... 166 B4
De Ferrers High Sch
DE13 ... 166 B4
De Havilland Dr ST15 ... 118 C3
De-Wint Rd ST15 ... 120 A4
Deacon Way WS15 ... 178 C1
Deakin Ave WS8 ... 228 C1
Deakin Gr ST5 ... 71 E3
Deakin Rd ST6 ... 42 A3
Deal Ave WS7 ... 229 D4
Dean Ct WV6 ... 254 C3
Dean Hollow ST7 ... 39 E1
Dean Pl ST1 ... 282 C1
Dean Rd WV5 ... 269 F3
Dean St Brewood ST19 ... 223 E3
Bucknall ST2 ... 58 B2
Sedgley DY3 ... 271 E4
Dean's La ST5 ... 40 B1
Deanery Cl
Rugeley WS15 ... 178 C1
Shareshill WV10 ... 225 E1
Deans Croft WS14 ... 231 E4
Deans La CW2 ... 38 B2
Deansberry Cl ST4 ... 88 A4
Deanscroft Way ST3 ... 73 F2
Deansfield Cl ST19 ... 223 E3
Deansfield Rd ST19 ... 223 E3
Deanshill Cl ST16 ... 155 E1
Deansway ST4 ... 88 A3
Dearnsdale Cl ST16 ... 155 D4
Deavall Way WS11 ... 210 A1
Deaville Rd ST2 ... 58 B2
Debenham Cres ST2 ... 58 A1
Deborah Cl WV4 ... 266 B3
Dee Cl Biddulph ST6 ... 16 C1
Kidsgrove ST7 ... 40 C4
Dee Gr WS11 ... 226 B4
Dee La ST5 ... 71 D2
Dee Rd WS3 ... 243 F1
Deebank Ave ST13 ... 31 D3
Deeley B77 ... 251 D1
Deep Cut Rd DE6 ... 144 A4
Deepdale B77 ... 251 E1
Deepdale Cl
Burton u T DE15 ... 167 D3
Norton-in-t-M ST6 ... 42 C1
Deepdale Ind Est DY1 ... 271 F2
Deepdale La Sedgley DY1 ... 271 F2
Snelston DE6 ... 81 D1
Deepdales Stafford ST17 ... 175 E3
Wombourne WV5 ... 269 F3
Deepmore Cl
Alrewas DE13 ... 201 D1
Featherstone WV10 ... 224 B3
Deer Cl Huntington WS12 ... 209 E3
Norton Canes WS11 ... 228 A4
Walsall WS3 ... 243 E1
Deer Hill ST17 ... 176 B2
Deer Park Dr TF10 ... 168 C3
Deer Park Rd B78 ... 249 F1
Deer Pk ST20 ... 171 F4
Deer Wlk WV8 ... 239 F1
Deerfold Cres WS7 ... 229 D4
Deerhill B77 ... 251 E1
Deerhurst Rise WS12 ... 210 C3
Deerleap Way WS15 ... 178 B1
Defford Ave WS4 ... 244 B1
Defoe Dr ST3 ... 73 F2
Delafield Way WS15 ... 178 B1
Delamere Gr
Newcastle-u-L ST5 ... 284 C4
Trentham ST4 ... 88 A4
Delamere La ST17 ... 174 A4
Delaney Dr ST3 ... 73 F2
Delhi Cl DE15 ... 167 E2
Delhurst Ave DY3 ... 266 C2
Delius Gr ST1 ... 57 F3
Dell Cl ST16 ... 155 D4
Dell The Cannock WS12 ... 210 C2
Lichfield WS13 ... 230 C4
Newcastle-u-L ST5 ... 55 E1
Stourbridge DY8 ... 279 F3
Tamworth B79 ... 250 A3
Dellway Ct DY8 ... 279 F3
Dellwood Gr 2 ST3 ... 73 E3
Delph Wlk ST4 ... 72 C3
Delphouse Rd
Cheadle ST10 ... 76 A1
Forsbrook ST10 ... 75 F1
Delphside ST7 ... 39 F1
Delta Way WS11 ... 226 C4
Delta Way Bsns Ctr
WS11 ... 226 B3
Deltic B77 ... 251 D1
Delves Cres CV9 ... 262 B1
Delves Pl ST5 ... 71 D3
Den La CW3 ... 52 B2
Denbigh Cl Biddulph ST8 ... 27 E3
Burton u T DE13 ... 166 B4
Dudley DY1 ... 271 F1
Newcastle-u-L ST5 ... 71 E2
Denbigh St ST1 ... 282 A4
Denbury Cl WS12 ... 210 B1
Denby Ave ST3 ... 283 C5
Dency Gr ST6 ... 42 A2
Dene Ave DY6 ... 275 E2
Dene Cl ST19 ... 207 F4
Dene Rd Lower Penn WV4 ... 264 C2
Stourbridge DY8 ... 279 F2
Dene Side ST5 ... 284 A2
Denefield ST19 ... 207 F4
Denehurst Cl ST3 ... 74 A1
Denewood Pl ST3 ... 74 A1
Denford Rd ST9 ... 44 C4
Denham Gdns WV3 ... 265 D4
Denham Sq ST3 ... 72 C1
Denleigh Rd DY6 ... 275 F2
Denmark Rise WS12 ... 210 B4
Dennington Cres ST3 ... 72 C1
Dennis B77 ... 250 C1
Dennis St Brierley Hill DY8 ... 279 F4
Fenton ST4 ... 72 C3
Denry Cres ST5 ... 56 A4
Denshaw Wlk ST3 ... 283 C4
Denstone Ave ST17 ... 156 A1
Denstone Coll ST14 ... 95 D3
Denstone Cres ST3 ... 72 C1
Denstone La ST14 ... 95 E4
Dent St B79 ... 250 B3
Dentdale Cl ST3 ... 90 A4
Denton Cl ST5 ... 71 E2
Denton Gr ST3 ... 73 F2
Denton Rd DE13 ... 166 A3
Denton Rise DE13 ... 166 A4
Denver Fold ST17 ... 174 A4
Denzil Gn ST17 ... 174 A4
Derby Ave WV6 ... 255 F4
Derby Pl ST5 ... 71 E2
Derby Rd Burton u T DE13 ... 166 C4
Doveridge DE6 ... 127 E4
Eggington DE65 ... 148 B2
Kidsgrove ST7 ... 40 B4
Uttoxeter ST14 ... 111 E1
Whittington WS14 ... 232 B2
Derby St Burton u T DE14 ... 166 B2
Hanley ST1 ... 282 C2
Leek ST13 ... 30 C3
Stafford ST16 ... 155 E2
Derby St E DE14 ... 166 B2
Derby Turn DE14 ... 166 B3
Dereham Way ST2 ... 58 B1
Derek Dr ST1 ... 57 F3
Derrington La
Bradley ST18 ... 173 F4
Seighford ST18 ... 154 C1
Derry St Fenton ST4 ... 72 C2
Wolv WV2 ... 266 B4
Derwent B77 ... 250 B1
Derwent Ave ST15 ... 120 B4
Derwent Cl Aldridge B74 ... 256 C2
Burton u T DE14 ... 166 C2
Derwent Cres ST7 ... 26 B1
Derwent Dr Ashley TF9 ... 99 E3
Biddulph ST6 ... 16 C1
Cheadle ST10 ... 76 C1
Derwent Gr
Burntwood WS7 ... 229 E3
Cannock WS11 ... 226 B4
Derwent Ho ST17 ... 174 C4
Derwent Pk DE14 ... 166 C3
Derwent Pl ST5 ... 56 A2
Derwent Rd
Burton u T DE15 ... 167 D1
Wolv WV6 ... 255 F4
Derwent St ST1 ... 282 A4
Devall Cl WS15 ... 196 C4
Devana Wlk ST3 ... 74 B1
Devereux Rd B75 ... 258 B1
Deveron Cl DE13 ... 147 E1
Devil's La ST9 ... 29 F3
Devon Cl Burton u T DE15 ... 185 F3
Newcastle-u-L ST5 ... 71 E2
Devon Cres WS9 ... 245 D1
Devon Gn WS11 ... 226 C4
Devon Gr ST6 ... 16 B1
Devon Rd Cannock WS11 ... 226 C4
Stourbridge DY8 ... 279 F4
Devon Way ST17 ... 174 B3
Devonshire Dr
Rugeley WS15 ... 196 B3
Tamworth B78 ... 250 A1
Devonshire Sq ST2 ... 58 B1
Dewbury Rd DY8 ... 275 F1
Dewsbury Cl DY8 ... 275 F2
Dewsbury Dr
Burntwood WS7 ... 229 E3
Wolv WV4 ... 266 A2
Dewsbury Rd ST4 ... 72 C4
Dexter Way B78 ... 262 C4
Dexton Rise ST17 ... 174 A4
Dial La Biddulph CW12 ... 7 D1
Brierley Hill DY8 ... 279 F4
Diamond Cl
Barlaston ST12 ... 104 B4
Biddulph ST8 ... 27 E4
Blythe Bridge ST3 ... 90 A2
Diamond Gr WS11 ... 210 B1
Diamond Jubilee Cotts
DE6 ... 81 F4
Diamond Park Dr 2 DY8 ... 275 F1
Diamond Ridge ST12 ... 104 B4
Diamond Way ST15 ... 120 A3
Diana Cl WS9 ... 245 D2
Diana Rd ST1 ... 57 F3
Diarmid Rd ST4 ... 71 F1
Dibble Rd DE14 ... 185 D4
Dibdale Rd DY1 ... 271 F2
Dibdale Rd W DY1 ... 271 F2
Dibdale St DY1 ... 271 F1
Dickens Cl
Burton u T DE14 ... 166 B3
Sedgley DY3 ... 271 D3
Dickens Rd WV10 ... 241 D1
Dickens St ST2 ... 58 B2
Dickenson Rd E ST6 ... 57 E4
Dickenson Rd W ST6 ... 57 E4
Dickinson Rd WV5 ... 270 A3
Dickson Rd ST16 ... 156 A3
Dicky's La ST20 ... 151 F4
Didcot Dr ST14 ... 143 F4
Dig St SK17 ... 24 B3
Digbeth La WV5 ... 267 D4
Digby Rd DY6 ... 275 E4
Diglake St ST7 ... 39 F2
Digmire La DE6 ... 51 E1
Dilhorne Endowed
Prim Sch ST10 ... 75 E3
Dilhorne Gr ST3 ... 283 C1
Dilhorne La
Caverswall ST11 ... 74 C2
Dilhorne ST11 ... 75 D1
Dilhorne Rd Cheadle ST10 ... 76 A2
Dilhorne ST11 ... 75 D1
Forsbrook ST11 ... 75 D1
Dilke St ST1 ... 282 C4
Dill Gr ST3 ... 90 A3
Dimble La ST10 ... 94 C4
Dimbles Hill WS13 ... 214 A1
Dimbles La WS13 ... 214 A1
Dimensions L Ctr ST6 ... 41 F1
Dimmelow St ST3 ... 74 A3
Dimmingsdale Rd WV4 ... 264 C3
Dimmock St WV4 ... 266 C3
Dimsdale Par E ST5 ... 56 B3
Dimsdale Par W ST5 ... 56 A3
Dimsdale St ST6 ... 56 C4
Dimsdale View ST5 ... 55 F3
Dimsdale View E ST5 ... 56 A3
Dimsdale View W ST5 ... 56 A3
Dingle La SK11 ... 17 F4
Dingle Rd Brownhills WS8 ... 244 C3
Wombourne WV5 ... 269 F3
Dingle The
Burton u T DE15 ... 185 F4
Endon ST6 ... 43 D4
Wolv WV3 ... 255 E1
Dingle View DY3 ... 271 E3
Dippons Dr WV6 ... 255 D2
Dippons Mill Cl WV6 ... 255 D2
Dirty La ST19 ... 223 E3
Dirtyfoot La WV4 ... 265 D3
District Ctr WS11 ... 210 B1
Ditch The SK17 ... 5 F4
Dividy Rd ST2 ... 58 A1
Dixon Rd CW12 ... 6 A3
Dixon St WV2 ... 266 C4
Dixon's Row ST5 ... 55 E4
Dobbinhorse La DE6 ... 81 F3
Dobbs St WV2 ... 266 B4
Dobell Gr ST3 ... 283 D4
Dobree Cl ST17 ... 177 F4
Dobson St ST6 ... 57 E4
Dock Rd DY8 ... 275 F1
Doctor's Bank TF9 ... 100 B3
Doctors Cl ST8 ... 27 E4
Doctors La Kinver DY6 ... 274 C3
Shenstone WS14 ... 247 D3
Doddington Pl ST5 ... 71 D3
Dodds La Astbury CW12 ... 15 E3
Farewell WS13 ... 212 B2
Dodslow Ave DE13 ... 147 D2
Dog Kennel La TF9 ... 112 B4
Dog La Butterton ST13 ... 33 F4
Leek ST13 ... 30 C3
Netherseal DE12 ... 219 F3
Ranton ST18 ... 153 E2
Swynnerton ST5 ... 86 B2
Tamworth B77 ... 251 D3
Waterhouses ST10 ... 50 A1
Weeford WS14 ... 248 A2
Dogcroft Rd ST6 ... 42 B3
Doglands Rd ST18 ... 123 D1
Dogmoor La ST10 ... 64 C4
Dogshead La DE13 ... 201 E4
Dolefoot La DE13 ... 163 D2
Dolespring Cl ST11 ... 91 D4
Doley Cl ST20 ... 171 E3
Dolphin Cl Stafford ST17 ... 156 B1
Walsall WS3 ... 243 F1
Dominic St Stoke-on-T ST4 ... 72 A4
Stone ST15 ... 104 C1
Don Gr WS11 ... 226 B4
Donald Rd ST1 ... 57 F3
Doncaster La ST4 ... 71 F4
Donington La
Albrighton WV7 ... 237 D4
Boscobel WV8 ... 221 E1
Donithorne Cl DE13 ... 166 B4
Donkey La ST10 ... 76 C3
Dorado B77 ... 261 E3
Dorcas Dr ST3 ... 72 C2
Dorchester Cl WV12 ... 242 B1
Dorchester Rd
Cannock WS11 ... 209 D1
Walsall WV12 ... 242 B1
Dorchester Wlk ST2 ... 58 B1
Dordon Rd B78 ... 262 C4
Doreen Ave CW12 ... 16 A4
Dorian Way ST9 ... 43 F4
Dorking Cl ST2 ... 57 F1
Dorlan Cl ST9 ... 43 E2
Dormer Ave B77 ... 250 B3
Dormston Dr DY3 ... 271 F4
Dormston Sch DY3 ... 271 F4
Dormston Trad Est DY1 ... 271 F2
Dorridge Gr ST5 ... 56 C2
Dorrington Cl ST2 ... 43 D1
Dorrington Dr ST16 ... 155 F3
Dorrington Gr ST5 ... 56 B3
Dorrington Ind Pk ST16 ... 155 F3
Dorset Cl Bucknall ST2 ... 58 B2
Burton u T DE15 ... 185 F3
Tamworth B78 ... 250 A1
Dorset Dr Aldridge WS9 ... 245 D1
Biddulph ST8 ... 27 D4
Dorset Pl Kidsgrove ST7 ... 26 A1
Newcastle-u-L ST5 ... 71 E2
Dorset Rd Cannock WS12 ... 210 C1
Stourbridge DY8 ... 279 E4
Dosthill Prim Sch B77 ... 261 E3
Dosthill Rd (Two Gates)
B77 ... 261 E4
Douglas Ave Biddulph ST8 ... 27 E4
Stoke-on-T ST4 ... 71 F3
Douglas Pl ST1 ... 57 F1
Douglas Rd
Newcastle-u-L ST5 ... 56 A2
Stafford ST16 ... 156 A3
Douglas Rd W ST16 ... 156 A3
Douglas St ST1 ... 57 D3
Doulton Cl ST10 ... 76 B1
Doulton Dr ST5 ... 56 A4
Doulton Rd ST18 ... 156 A4
Doulton St 4 ST6 ... 57 D4
Douse La Bradnop ST13 ... 32 B2
Onecote ST13 ... 32 B2
Dove Bank ST14 ... 126 B4
Dove Bank Prim Sch ST7 ... 26 A1
Dove Cl Burntwood WS7 ... 229 E3
Stafford ST17 ... 174 C3
Dove Fields ST14 ... 126 B4
Dove Fst Sch ST14 ... 96 A2
Dove Gr Biddulph ST6 ... 16 B1
Eggington DE65 ... 148 A3
Dove Hollow
Cannock WS12 ... 210 C2
Great Wyrley WS6 ... 226 C1
Dove La ST14 ... 96 A2
Dove Lea DE13 ... 147 D2
Dove Pl ST5 ... 71 D2
Dove Rd ST11 ... 91 D4
Dove Ridge SK17 ... 13 E3
Dove Side DE65 ... 146 B4
Dove St DE6 ... 80 A1
Dove View DE13 ... 146 B3

Dove Wlk ST14 .... **126** B4
Dovebank Gr ST3 .... **90** A3
Dovecliff Cres DE13 .... **147** F1
Dovecliff Rd
  Burton u T DE13 .... **147** F2
  Rolleston DE13 .... **147** F2
Dovecote ST14 .... **255** E2
Dovecote Pl ST3 .... **89** F4
Dovecotes Jun Sch WV8 .. **239** F1
Dovecotes The B75 .... **258** A2
Dovedale ST11 .... **210** A3
Dovedale Ave WS3 .... **244** A3
Dovedale Cl
  Burton u T DE15 .... **167** D3
  Cheadle ST10 .... **76** C3
  Congleton CW12 .... **6** A2
  Tunstall ST6 .... **41** D4
Dovedale Ct WV4 .... **266** C3
Dovedale Pl ST5 .... **55** D1
Dovedale Rd Kingsley ST10 .. **61** F3
  Kingswinford DY6 .... **275** F4
  Wolv DY3, WV4 .... **266** C2
Dovefields ST14 .... **95** F2
Dovehouse Fields WS14 .. **231** D3
Dover Ct DE13 .... **166** B4
Dover Rd DE13 .... **166** A4
Dover St ST1 .... **282** C4
Doveridge ST6 .... **167** D1
Doveridge Prim Sch DE6 .. **127** E4
Doveside DE6 .... **81** E4
Dovestone B77 .... **251** E1
Dowells Gdns DY8 .... **275** E2
Dower Rd B75 .... **258** A1
Downderry Cl ST17 .... **174** A4
Downend Cl WV10 .... **240** C2
Downesway WS11 .... **209** E1
Downey St ST1 .... **282** B2
Downfield Cl WS3 .... **243** D2
Downfield Dr DY3 .... **271** F3
Downfield Gr ST16 .... **155** E4
Downfield Pl ST2 .... **42** C1
Downford ST19 .... **205** E3
Downham Pl WV3 .... **265** F4
Downham Rd ST5 .... **55** F1
Downie Rd WV8 .... **239** E2
Downing Ave ST5 .... **56** C2
Downing Gdns ST15 .... **120** A4
Downs The Aldridge B74 .. **256** C1
  Stafford ST17 .... **175** E4
Downsview Gr ST3 .... **72** C2
Dowty Way WV9 .... **240** A2
Doxey Cres ST16 .... **155** D2
Doxey Cty Prim Sch
  ST16 .... **155** D2
Doxey Fields ST16 .... **154** C2
Doxey Rd ST16 .... **155** D2
Dragon Sq ST5 .... **55** F4
Drake Cl Bucknall ST2 .... **57** F1
  Walsall WS3 .... **243** D1
Drake Croft WS13 .... **231** E4
Drake Rd WS3 .... **243** D1
Drakeford Gr ST6 .... **42** C2
Drakes Hill Cl DY8 .... **279** E2
Draw-well La
  Caverswall ST9 .... **59** D2
  Caverswall ST9 .... **59** E2
Draycott Cl WV4 .... **265** E3
Draycott Cliff DE6 .... **144** B3
Draycott Cres B77 .... **250** B1
Draycott Cross Rd
  Cheadle ST10 .... **76** A1
  Draycott in t M ST11 .... **91** E4
Draycott Dr Cheadle ST10 .. **76** B1
  Newcastle-u-L ST5 .... **40** B1
Draycott Manor Prim Sch
  ST11 .... **91** E3
Draycott Old Rd
  Draycott in t M ST11 .... **91** E4
  Forsbrook ST11 .... **91** E4
Draycott Rd ST10 .... **92** B2
Drayton Gn ST2 .... **58** A1
Drayton Gr TF9 .... **97** E1
Drayton La
  Drayton Bassett B78 .... **260** B3
  Hints B78 .... **259** F3
Drayton Manor Dr
  Drayton Bassett B78 .... **260** C4
  Fazeley B78 .... **260** C4
Drayton Manor Pk B78 .. **260** C4
Drayton Rd
  Longton ST3 .... **283** C4
  Swynnerton ST4 .... **87** D3
Drayton St
  Newcastle-u-L ST5 .... **284** A2
  Wolv WV2 .... **266** B4
Dreieich Cl ST16 .... **155** F3
Drenfell Rd ST7 .... **25** F4
Dresden CE Prim Sch
  ST3 .... **283** C1
Dresden St ST1 .... **282** C2
Dreys The ST4 .... **88** A4
Driffield Cl ST2 .... **58** C1
Drive Fields WV4 .... **265** D3
Drive Prep Sch The WV6 .. **255** E4
Drive The Burntwood WS7 .. **54** C3
  Brownhills WS4 .... **244** B4
  Codsall WV8 .... **238** C2
  Stafford ST16 .... **155** D2
  Wolv WV6 .... **255** E3
Drointon La ST18 .... **139** E2
Droitwich Cl ST5 .... **54** C1
Droveway The WV9 .... **239** F2
Droxford Wlk WV8 .... **239** F1
Drubbery La ST3 .... **283** A1
Druid Park Rd WV12 .... **242** B1

Druids Ave WS9 .... **256** B4
Druids Way ST19 .... **207** F4
Druids Wlk WS9 .... **245** D2
Drumber La ST7 .... **26** A4
Drumburn Cl ST7 .... **41** F4
Drummond Cl WV11 .... **242** A1
Drummond Rd ST16 .... **155** F3
Drummond St ST6 .... **41** E4
Drury La WV8 .... **238** C2
Dryberg Wlk ST2 .... **58** A2
Dryburgh Cl ST17 .... **174** A4
Dryden Cres ST17 .... **155** E1
Dryden Rd Burslem ST6 .... **57** D3
  Tamworth B79 .... **250** A3
  Wolv WV10 .... **240** C1
Dryden Way ST10 .... **76** B1
Dual Way WS12 .... **209** E4
Dubarry Ave DY6 .... **275** E4
Duchy Cl DE13 .... **166** C4
Duchy Rd CW1 .... **37** D4
Duck La WV8 .... **239** D2
Duck St DE65 .... **148** A3
Duddell Rd ST6 .... **42** B1
Dudding Rd WV4 .... **266** B3
Dudley Innovation Ctr
  DY6 .... **275** F4
Dudley Pl ST3 .... **90** A4
Dudley Rd Himley DY3 .... **270** B2
  Kingswinford, Ketley Quarry
  DY6 .... **275** F4
  Kingswinford, Wall Heath
  DY6 .... **275** E4
  Sedgley DY3 .... **271** E3
  Wolv WV2 .... **266** B4
Dudley St DY3 .... **271** E4
Dudley Wlk WV4 .... **266** B3
Dudmaston Way DY1 .... **271** F2
Duesbury Gn ST3 .... **283** A3
Duffield Cl WV8 .... **239** F1
Dugdale Cl WS12 .... **210** C2
Dugdale Cres B75 .... **258** B2
Duke Bank Terr ST6 .... **42** C2
Duke Cl ST5 .... **55** E1
Duke Rd WS7 .... **211** F1
Duke St Biddulph ST8 .... **27** E4
  Burton u T DE14 .... **166** B1
  Fenton ST4 .... **72** C3
  Leek ST13 .... **30** C3
  Newcastle-u-L ST5 .... **284** C1
  Sedgley DY3 .... **271** E3
  Wolv WV3 .... **266** A4
Dukes La ST13 .... **63** E4
Dulverton Ave ST5 .... **71** D3
Dumbleberry Ave DY3 .. **271** E4
Dumbledery La WS9 .... **256** A3
Dumolo's La ST5 .... **250** C2
Dumolo's Prim Sch B77 .. **250** C1
Dumore Hay La WS13 .. **215** F4
Duncalf Gr ST5 .... **56** A4
Duncalf St ST6 .... **56** C4
Duncalfe Dr B75 .... **258** A2
Duncan St Fenton ST4 .... **72** C3
  Wolv WV2 .... **266** B4
Duncombe St DY8 .... **279** E3
Dundalk La WS6 .... **226** B1
Dundas St ST1 .... **282** C4
Dundee Rd ST1 .... **57** D2
Dundee St ST3 .... **283** B2
Dunedin B77 .... **251** D1
Dunedin Cres DE15 .... **167** E1
Dungarven Dr TF10 .... **168** B1
Dunhampton Dr DY10 .. **280** A1
Dunkirk ST5 .... **284** A3
Dunkirk Cl ST5 .... **284** A3
Dunlin Cl WV10 .... **241** D4
Dunnerdale Rd WS8 .... **244** B3
Dunning St ST6 .... **41** E2
Dunnington Ave WV10 .. **280** A1
Dunnock Way ST8 .... **27** F4
Dunrobin St ST3 .... **283** C2
Dunsany Gr ST1 .... **57** F3
Dunsford Ave ST2 .... **43** D1
Dunsley Dr
  Kingswinford DY8 .... **275** F2
  Kinver DY7 .... **278** B2
Dunsley Gr WV4 .... **266** A2
Dunsley Rd Kinver DY7 .. **278** B2
  Stourbridge DY8 .... **279** E2
Dunstall Brook DE15 .... **167** D1
Dunstall Cross DE13 .... **183** D3
Dunstall Hill DE13 .... **183** D3
Dunstall La Hopwas B78 .. **249** F2
  Tamworth B78 .... **249** E2
Dunstall Park
  Race Course WV6 .... **255** F3
Dunstall Rd DE13 .... **183** F2
Dunster B77 .... **261** E4
Dunster Cl ST17 .... **174** A4
Dunster Gr WV6 .... **254** C2
Dunster Rd ST3 .... **73** E3
Dunston Cl
  Great Wyrley WS6 .... **242** C4
  Kingswinford DY6 .... **275** E4
Dunston Dr WS7 .... **229** D4
Dunton Cl B75 .... **258** A2
Dunwood Dr ST6 .... **42** A2
Dunwood La Longsdon ST9 .. **29** E3
  Rudyard ST9 .... **29** E3
Durban Rd DE15 .... **167** E2
Durber Cl Audley ST7 .... **39** E1
  Stoke-on-T ST4 .... **71** F2
Durfield La DE13 .... **163** D4
Durham Dr WS15 .... **196** B3
Durham Gr ST5 .... **71** D3
Durham Rd DY8 .... **279** E4
Durlston Cl B77 .... **250** C3
Dursley Dr WS11 .... **209** D1
Dursley Rd WS7 .... **229** D4

Durston Pl ST3 .... **73** F2
Dutton Way ST15 .... **119** F3
Duttons La B75 .... **258** C2
Dyke Rd WS15 .... **198** A2
Dyke St ST1 .... **282** C3
Dykes La TF10 .... **188** B4
Dylan Rd ST3 .... **73** E2
Dyott Ave WS14 .... **232** C3
Dyott Cl WS13 .... **215** D1

Eagle Cl Cheslyn Hay WS6 .. **226** B1
  Dudley DY1 .... **271** F1
  Uttoxeter ST14 .... **126** A3
Eagle Cres ST21 .... **133** E3
Eagle Dr B77 .... **251** E2
Eagle Gr WS12 .... **210** B1
Eagle Hts ST6 .... **167** E2
Eagle St Hanley ST1 .... **57** F2
  Wolv WV2 .... **266** C4
Ealingham B77 .... **251** D1
Eamont Ave ST6 .... **42** A2
Eardleyend Rd ST7 .... **39** F4
Earl Dr WS7 .... **211** F1
Earl St Kingswinford DY6 .. **275** E2
  Leek ST13 .... **30** C3
  Newcastle-u-L ST5 .... **284** D3
  Newcastle-u-L,
  Silverdale ST5 .... **55** E1
  Stafford ST16 .... **155** F2
Earl Sterndale CE
  Prim Sch SK17 .... **5** E2
Earl's Dr ST5 .... **71** D3
Earls Ct Burton u T DE13 .. **166** B4
  Newcastle-u-L ST5 .... **284** D3
Earls Rd ST4 .... **88** A4
Earls Way ST18 .... **158** B1
Earlsbrook Dr ST4 .... **88** B4
Earlsway ST10 .... **64** A4
Earlswood Cres WV9 .... **240** A2
Earlswood Dr ST1 .... **58** A3
Earlswood Rd DY6 .... **275** F4
Early La ST15 .... **103** E2
Easby Cl ST17 .... **174** A4
Easby Way WS3 .... **242** C1
Easdale Pl ST5 .... **71** D3
Easedale Cl ST2 .... **43** D1
Easing La ST13 .... **31** F4
East Ave CW2 .... **37** E3
East Bank Ride ST11 .... **91** D4
East Beeches WV6 .... **224** A1
East Butts Rd WS15 .... **178** A1
East Cannock Ind Est
  WS12 .... **210** A2
East Cannock Rd WS12 .. **210** A2
East Cl ST15 .... **119** F4
East Cres Hanley ST1 .... **57** F4
  Newcastle-u-L ST5 .... **56** B2
East Croft Rd WV4 .... **265** E3
East Dr Biddulph ST8 .... **27** E4
  Cheddleton ST13 .... **45** E4
East Gn WV4 .... **265** E3
East Gr ST3 .... **74** A1
East Prec ST1 .... **282** C3
East Rd WV10 .... **241** D4
East St Burton u T DE15 .. **167** E2
  Cannock WS11 .... **226** C3
  Leek ST13 .... **31** D3
  Meir ST3 .... **74** A3
  Sedgley DY3 .... **271** E3
  Tamworth B77 .... **261** E3
East Terr ST6 .... **42** A3
East View Burslem ST6 .. **56** C4
  Tamworth B77 .... **250** C2
Eastbank Rd ST1 .... **282** A4
Eastbourne Cl ST13 .... **30** B3
Eastbourne Rd ST1 .... **57** F2
Eastbridge Ave ST1 .... **57** E4
Eastcote Cres WS7 .... **229** D3
Eastdean Ave ST2 .... **58** A1
Eastern Ave WS13 .... **214** B1
Eastern Way WS11 .... **210** A1
Easters Gr ST3 .... **43** D1
Eastfield Cl ST3 .... **88** C4
Eastfields Rd ST14 .... **126** B4
Eastgate Brewood ST19 .. **223** E4
  Cannock WS12 .... **211** D3
Eastgate St
  Burntwood WS7 .... **228** C4
  Stafford ST16 .... **155** F2
Easthall Cl ST19 .... **223** E3
Easthead Wlk ST1 .... **282** A2
Eastholme ST15 .... **106** B1
Eastlands ST17 .... **174** C4
Eastlands Cl ST17 .... **174** C4
Eastlands Gr ST17 .... **174** C4
Eastleigh DY3 .... **271** E4
Eastmoor Cl B74 .... **257** D1
Eastney Cres WV8 .... **255** F4
Eastridge Croft WS14 .. **247** D3
Eastward Glen WV8 .... **239** E1
Eastwick Cres ST4 .... **88** A4
Eastwood Ave
  Burntwood WS7 .... **229** D4
  Chell Heath ST6 .... **42** A4
Eastwood Pl ST1 .... **282** B2
Eastwood Rd ST1 .... **282** C1
Eastwood Rise ST5 .... **85** D4
Easy Lawns CW3 .... **53** D3
Eaton Cres DY3 .... **271** D2
Eaton Park Prim Sch ST2 .. **58** A1
Eaton Pl DY6 .... **275** F3
Eaton Rd ST14 .... **95** F2
Eaton St ST1 .... **282** C3
Eaves Ct Rd DY3 .... **266** C3
Eaves La Bucknall ST2 .... **58** B3
  Cheadle ST10 .... **76** C3
  Oakamoor ST10 .... **78** A4
Eaveswood Rd ST2 .... **58** B3

Ebenezer St WS12 .... **210** A4
Ebstree Rd WV5 .... **264** A2
Ebury Gr ST3 .... **73** F1
Eccleshall Ave WV10 .. **240** B1
Eccleshall Rd Ashley TF9 .. **99** F2
  Mucklestone ST9 .... **99** D3
  Seighford ST18 .... **135** E1
  Stafford ST16 .... **155** E3
  Stone ST15 .... **119** F3
Eccleston Pl ST6 .... **42** A3
Ecdale B77 .... **251** D1
Edale Cl Kingswinford DY6 .. **275** D4
  Newcastle-u-L ST5 .... **55** F4
  Tunstall ST6 .... **41** D4
  Wolv DY3 .... **266** C2
Eddens Wood Cl B78 .. **260** C3
Eddies La B79 .... **216** C1
Eddisbury Dr ST5 .... **40** B1
Eden Cl Biddulph ST6 .... **16** C1
  Cannock WS12 .... **210** C1
  Kidsgrove ST7 .... **26** A1
Eden Gr Ashley TF9 .... **99** E3
  Cheadle ST10 .... **76** C1
  Meir ST3 .... **73** F1
Edenhurst Ave ST3 .... **74** B1
Edensor CE Prim Sch
  ST3 .... **283** A2
Edensor Ct ST5 .... **55** F4
Edensor High Sch ST3 .. **283** B3
Edensor Rd ST3 .... **283** B3
Edensor St ST5 .... **55** F4
Edensor Terr ST3 .... **283** B3
Edes Farm Dr ST14 .... **95** F2
Edgar Cl B79 .... **249** F4
Edgar Pl ST3 .... **73** E3
Edge Ave ST6 .... **42** A3
Edge Hill Kingsbury B78 .. **262** A1
  Kinver DY7 .... **277** F2
Edge Hill Ave WV10 .... **241** D1
Edge Hill Dr Perton WV6 .. **254** C2
  Sedgley DY3 .... **266** B3
Edge Hill Jun Sch DE15 .. **185** A4
Edge La ST9 .... **43** E4
Edge St ST6 .... **41** F1
Edge View Cl Kinver DY7 .. **277** F3
  Norton-in-t-M ST7 .... **43** E1
Edge View Ct ST8 .... **27** E4
Edge View Rd ST2 .... **43** E1
Edge View Wlk DY7 .... **277** F3
Edgecliff Cty High Sch
  DY7 .... **278** A2
Edgefield La ST9 .... **43** E3
Edgefield Rd ST3 .... **73** E3
Edgeley Rd ST8 .... **27** E4
Edgemoor Meadow WS12 . **210** B1
Edgeview Rd CW12 .... **16** A4
Edgeware St ST1 .... **282** A4
Edghill Rd ST13 .... **30** B3
Edgmond Hall Sch TF10 .. **168** A2
Edgmond Rd TF10 .... **168** C2
Edinburgh Cres DY8 .... **275** E1
Edinburgh Rd CW12 .... **6** A1
Edinburgh Way DE13 .. **166** B4
Edision St ST4 .... **72** B3
Edison Cl WS12 .... **210** B4
Edison Rd ST16 .... **155** F3
Edmonton Cl WS13 .... **210** A1
Edmonton Gr ST2 .... **42** C1
Edmonton Pl DE15 .... **167** E1
Edmund Ave ST17 .... **174** A4
Edmund Rd DY3 .... **271** E4
Ednam Gr WV5 .... **265** D1
Ednam Pl ST3 .... **74** A1
Ednam Rd WV4 .... **266** B3
Edwal Rd ST3 .... **74** A2
Edward Ave Aldridge WS9 .. **256** A4
  Newcastle-u-L ST5 .... **71** D3
  Trentham ST4 .... **88** A4
  Wolv WV4 .... **266** C3
Edward Ct B77 .... **250** C2
Edward Davies Rd ST6 .. **42** B1
Edward Rd WV6 .... **254** C3
Edward St Audley ST7 .... **39** F2
  Burton u T DE14 .... **166** B2
  Cannock WS11 .... **209** F2
  Fenton ST4 .... **72** C4
  Newcastle-u-L ST5 .... **56** B2
  Stone ST15 .... **105** D1
  Tamworth B79 .... **250** A3
Edwards Dr ST16 .... **155** E2
Edwards Farm Rd WS13 .. **215** F4
Edwards Rd
  Burntwood WS7 .... **228** C3
  Sutton Coldfield B75 .... **258** B2
Edwin Cl Penkridge ST19 .. **207** F4
  Stafford ST17 .... **155** D1
Efflinch La DE13 .... **201** F4
Egal St WV3 .... **266** A4
Egelwin Cl WV6 .... **254** C3
Egerton Rd Aldridge B74 .. **256** C1
  Stoke-on-T ST4 .... **71** F4
  Wolv WV10 .... **240** C2
Egerton St ST4 .... **57** E1
Egg La ST18 .... **158** C4
Eggington Prim Sch
  DE65 .... **148** A3
Eggington Rd DY8 .... **279** D3
Egginton Dr ST19 .... **207** F4
Egginton Rd
  Eggington DE65 .... **148** A4
  Hilton DE55 .... **147** F4
Elan Cl Cookley DY10 .... **280** A2
  Sedgley DY3 .... **271** D2
Elan Rd DY3 .... **271** D2
Elburton Rd ST4 .... **73** D3
Elder Cl WS11 .... **210** B1
Elder Gr WV5 .... **269** F3

Elder La WS7 .... **229** E4
Elder Pl ST6 .... **57** D3
Elder Rd ST6 .... **57** D3
Elderberry Cl DY8 .... **279** E2
Elderside Cl WS8 .... **244** C4
Eldertree La Ashley TF9 .. **100** A4
  Ashley TF9 .... **100** B3
Eldon St Burton u T DE15 .. **167** D2
  Hanley ST1 .... **57** E3
Eldridge Cl WV9 .... **239** F1
Eleanor Cres ST5 .... **71** D3
Eleanor Harrison Dr
  DY10 .... **280** A3
Eleanor Pl ST5 .... **71** D3
Eleanor View ST5 .... **71** D3
Electric Ind Est DE14 .. **166** C3
Electric St DE14 .... **166** C3
Elenora St ST4 .... **72** A4
Elford Cl ST16 .... **155** E4
Elgar Cl Cannock WS11 .. **209** F3
  Lichfield WS13 .... **214** A1
Elgar Cres ST1 .... **58** A3
Elgin Cl DY3 .... **266** C1
Elgin Ct WV6 .... **254** C2
Elgin Rd WS3 .... **243** D2
Elgin St ST4 .... **57** D1
Elgood La ST6 .... **41** E4
Elias Cl WS14 .... **231** F3
Eliases La ST8 .... **17** D1
Eliot Cl Armitage WS15 .. **198** A4
  Tamworth B79 .... **250** A4
Eliot Way ST17 .... **155** E1
Elizabeth Ave
  Rolleston DE15 .... **147** D3
  Wolv WV4 .... **266** A3
Elizabeth Cl Kidsgrove ST7 .. **40** B3
  Market Drayton TF9 .... **112** B4
Elizabeth Dr
  Newcastle-u-L ST5 .... **55** F4
  Tamworth B79 .... **250** A3
Elizabeth Rd WS11 .... **209** F3
Elizabeth St ST1 .... **282** C3
Elkington Cl TF10 .... **168** C1
Elkington Rise CW3 .... **68** C4
Elkstone Cl ST6 .... **41** F2
Ellam's Pl ST5 .... **55** F1
Ellastone Gr ST4 .... **71** F3
Ellastone Rd ST13 .... **63** E3
Elldawn Ave ST6 .... **42** C1
Ellerbeck B77 .... **251** D1
Ellerby Rd ST3 .... **88** C4
Ellers Gr ST6 .... **56** C4
Ellesmere Ct TF10 .... **168** C1
Ellesmere Gr TF9 .... **112** A4
Ellesmere Rd WS11 .... **226** A4
Ellgreave St ST6 .... **56** C4
Ellington Ave ST16 .... **156** A3
Ellington Cl ST2 .... **58** A1
Elliot Cl WS3 .... **42** A3
Elliot Dr ST9 .... **59** D2
Elliot Rd ST4 .... **72** C3
Elliott St ST5 .... **56** B1
Elliotts La WV8 .... **239** D2
Ellis St ST6 .... **57** E4
Ellison Prim Sch ST5 .. **56** B3
Ellison St ST5 .... **56** B3
Ellowes Hall Sch DY3 .. **271** E3
Ellowes Rd DY3 .... **271** E2
Elm Ave ST17 .... **175** F3
Elm Cl Colwich ST18 .... **158** A1
  Doveridge DE6 .... **127** E4
  Kidsgrove ST7 .... **41** D4
  Leek ST13 .... **30** B3
  Newport TF10 .... **168** C1
  Sedgley DY3 .... **271** D1
  Stourbridge DY8 .... **279** E1
Elm Cres ST18 .... **158** B4
Elm Ct ST18 .... **174** B3
Elm Dr Blakedown DY10 .. **281** D1
  Bradley ST4 .... **191** E4
  Cheadle ST10 .... **76** C1
  Market Drayton TF9 .... **112** A4
Elm Farm Rd WV2 .... **266** B4
Elm Gdns ST4 .... **231** E4
Elm Gr Codsall WV8 .... **239** D2
  Huntington WS12 .... **209** E4
  Kinver DY7 .... **278** A2
Elm Pl Cookley DY10 .... **280** A2
  Longton ST3 .... **72** C1
Elm Rd Kingswinford DY6 .. **275** F3
  Norton Canes WS11 .... **228** A3
  Stone ST15 .... **120** A4
Elm St Burslem ST6 .... **57** D4
  Newcastle-u-L ST5 .... **56** B2
Elm Tree Cl WV5 .... **269** F3
Elm Tree Dr ST7 .... **39** F1
Elm Tree Wlk B79 .... **249** F4
Elm View ST14 .... **95** F3
Elm Wlk ST19 .... **207** F4
Elmbridge Way DY3 .... **271** F3
Elmbrook Cl ST3 .... **89** F4
Elmcroft Gdns WV10 .. **240** C2
Elmcroft Rd ST2 .... **58** A3
Elmdale Dr WS9 .... **256** B4
Elmdon Cl
  Penkridge ST19 .... **208** A4
  Wolv WV10 .... **240** A1
Elmdon Pl ST3 .... **90** A4
Elmdon Rd WV10 .... **240** A1
Elmhurst DE65 .... **148** A3
Elmhurst Cl
  Brewood WV9 .... **224** C1
  Bucknall ST2 .... **57** F1
  Stafford ST16 .... **155** E4
Elmhurst Dr
  Burntwood WS7 .... **229** D2
  Kingswinford DY6 .... **275** F2

Elmley Gr WV6 .... 254 C2
Elmore Green Jun Sch WS3 .... 243 D1
Elmore Green Rd WS3 .... 243 D1
Elmore Ho WS3 .... 178 C1
Elmore La WS15 .... 178 C1
Elmore Row WS3 .... 243 D1
Elms CI WV10 .... 225 E1
Elms Dr WS11 .... 209 E1
Elms La WV10 .... 225 E1
Elms Paddock The WV6 .... 253 E1
Elms Rd DE15 .... 166 C1
Elms The ST5 .... 56 B4
Elms Way ST3 .... 74 A1
Elmsdale WV6 .... 255 D1
Elmsmere Rd ST2 .... 58 A3
Elmstead CI ST4 .... 71 F1
Elmstone CI ST17 .... 175 E4
Elmtree Rd B74 .... 256 B1
Elmwood Ave WV11 .... 242 A2
Elmwood CI
  Cannock WS11 .... 210 A2
  Forsbrook ST11 .... 91 D3
  Gnosall ST20 .... 171 E4
  Lawton-gate ST7 .... 25 C2
Elmwood Dr ST11 .... 91 D3
Elmwood Gr ST14 .... 110 C1
Elmwood Rd DY8 .... 275 E1
Elmwood Rise DY3 .... 266 A1
Elphinstone Rd ST4 .... 71 F2
Elsby PI ST6 .... 42 A3
Elsdon Rd ST17 .... 174 B3
Elsing St ST4 .... 72 B3
Elsmere Ave ST3 .... 73 C1
Elston Hall Jun Sch WV10 .... 240 B1
Elston Hall La WV10 .... 240 B1
Elstree CI ST3 .... 73 F1
Elstree Gr ST1 .... 58 A3
Elswick Rd ST4 .... 72 C4
Eltham Gdns ST5 .... 56 B2
Elton CI Newborough DE13 .... 162 C4
  Wolv WV10 .... 240 C2
Elton La DE13 .... 162 C4
Elton Terr ST6 .... 41 E4
Elton Way ST20 .... 171 C4
Elunda Gr WS7 .... 228 C3
Elviron Dr WV6 .... 255 D3
Elwell Cres DY3 .... 271 F3
Elworthy CI ST16 .... 156 A3
Elwyn CI DE13 .... 147 E1
Ely CI WS11 .... 210 A1
Ely Wlk ST3 .... 283 C1
Embers Way ST9 .... 44 A4
Emberton St
  Newcastle-u-L, Chesterton ST5 .... 55 F3
  Newcastle-u-L, Wolstanton ST5 .... 56 B3
Emberton Way B77 .... 250 C3
Embleton Wlk 1 ST6 .... 56 C4
Embry Ave ST16 .... 156 A3
Emerald Way ST15 .... 120 A2
Emerson CI DY3 .... 271 D2
Emerson Rd Burslem ST6 .... 57 D3
  Wolv WV10 .... 240 C1
Emery Ave Hanley ST1 .... 57 F4
  Newcastle-u-L ST5 .... 71 D4
Emery St ST6 .... 57 D3
Emmanuel Rd WS7 .... 229 D4
Empire Ind Est WS9 .... 244 C1
Empire Pas ST4 .... 72 A3
Empire Rd DE15 .... 167 E2
Empire St ST4 .... 72 A3
Emstone CI ST3 .... 88 C4
Emsworth Cres WV9 .... 240 A1
Emsworth Rd ST3 .... 88 C4
Encounter PI ST1 .... 57 F3
End Hall Rd WV6 .... 255 D2
End The ST6 .... 167 F4
Enderby Dr WV4 .... 266 A4
Enderby Rise DE13 .... 166 A4
Enderley CI WS3 .... 243 D2
Enderley Dr WS3 .... 243 D2
Enderley St ST5 .... 284 B4
Endon Dr ST8 .... 27 D3
Endon Hall Prim Sch ST9 .... 43 F4
Endon High Sch ST9 .... 43 F4
Endon Rd
  Norton-in-t-M, Duke Bank ST6 .... 42 C2
  Norton-in-t-M, Norton Green ST6 .... 42 C3
Endwood Dr B74 .... 257 E2
Engelsea Brook La CW2 .... 38 A3
Engine La Brownhills WS8 .... 244 B4
  Tamworth B77 .... 251 D1
Englesea Ave ST3 .... 74 A3
Engleton La ST19 .... 223 F4
Engleton Mill La ST19 .... 223 F4
English Martyrs RC Prim Sch ST8 .... 27 D1
Ennerdale CI
  Brownhills WS8 .... 244 C3
  26 Burslem ST6 .... 56 C4
Ennerdale Dr WV6 .... 254 C2
Ennerdale Rd WV6 .... 255 E4
Enoch St ST6 .... 56 C4
Ensall Dr DY8 .... 275 F1
Ensford B74 .... 257 F3
Enson La Marston ST18 .... 137 D3
  Salt ST18 .... 137 D4
  Stone ST18 .... 120 D1
Ensor Dr B78 .... 251 F1
Enstone Ct ST5 .... 71 D2
Enterprise Dr WV10 .... 224 B3
Enterprise Sq ST4 .... 244 A3
Enterprise Ind Pk WS13 .... 231 F4

Enville CI WS3 .... 243 D2
Enville Common Rd DY7 .... 273 F2
Enville PI DY8 .... 279 F3
Enville Rd
  Kingswinford DY6 .... 275 D4
  Kinver DY7 .... 278 A3
  Sedgley DY3 .... 271 E2
  Wolv WV4 .... 265 E2
Enville St DY8 .... 279 F3
Ephraim St ST1 .... 282 C1
Epping Rd ST4 .... 71 F2
Epsley's Yd ST16 .... 155 F1
Epsom CI Kingsley ST10 .... 76 C3
  Lichfield WS14 .... 231 E4
  Wolv WV6 .... 254 C2
Epsom Dr ST17 .... 175 E4
Epworth St ST4 .... 72 A4
Erasmus Way WS13 .... 231 D4
Erdington Rd WS9 .... 256 B2
Eringden B77 .... 251 D1
Ermington Rd WV4 .... 266 B2
Erneley Gdns ST15 .... 120 A4
Eros Cres ST1 .... 57 F3
Errill Ct ST4 .... 72 B3
Erskine St ST3 .... 283 C1
Eskdale PI
  Newcastle-u-L ST5 .... 71 D3
  Trentham ST4 .... 88 A4
Eskrett St WS12 .... 210 B3
Esperanto Way ST6 .... 57 E4
Esselie Ave TF9 .... 100 B3
Essex Ave DY6 .... 275 D3
Essex Dr Biddulph ST6 .... 16 B1
  Cannock WS12 .... 210 A2
  Colwich ST18 .... 158 B1
  Kidsgrove ST7 .... 25 F1
  Rugeley WS15 .... 196 B3
  Stone ST15 .... 119 F3
Essex Gdns DY8 .... 279 E4
Essex PI ST5 .... 71 D3
Essex Rd Burton u T DE15 .... 185 E3
  Sutton Coldfield B75 .... 258 B1
Essington CI
  Alrewas DE13 .... 201 D2
  Brierley Hill DY8 .... 275 F1
  Lichfield WS14 .... 231 D3
  Shenstone WS14 .... 247 D3
Essington Ind Est WV11 .... 241 F2
Essington Rd WV12 .... 242 A1
Estridge La WS6 .... 227 D1
Etching Hill CE Prim Sch WS15 .... 178 B1
Etching Hill Rd WS15 .... 178 A1
Ethelfleda Rd B77 .... 261 F3
Ethelred CI B74 .... 258 A2
Eton Ave ST5 .... 70 C2
Eton CI Burton u T DE14 .... 166 B4
  Sedgley DY3 .... 271 F3
  Stafford ST17 .... 156 A1
Eton Park Jun Sch DE14 .... 166 B4
Eton Pk DE14 .... 166 B4
Eton Rd DE14 .... 166 B3
Etruria Old Rd ST1 .... 56 C2
Etruria Rd Hanley ST1 .... 282 A3
  Newcastle-u-L ST5 .... 56 C2
Etruria Sta ST4 .... 56 C1
Etruria Vale Rd ST1 .... 57 D2
Etruria Way ST5 .... 56 C1
Etruscan St ST1 .... 56 C1
Etruscan Wlk ST12 .... 88 C2
Ettingshall Park Farm La WV4 .... 266 C2
Ettymore CI DY3 .... 271 E4
Ettymore Rd DY3 .... 271 E4
Ettymore Rd W DY3 .... 271 E4
Etwall Rd DE65 .... 148 A4
Europa Way WS13 .... 231 F4
Eva Gr ST5 .... 87 E4
Evans Croft B78 .... 250 A1
Evans St Burslem ST6 .... 41 F1
  Wolv DY3, WV14 .... 266 C1
Eve La DY3 .... 271 E4
Evelyn St ST4 .... 72 B3
Everest Rd ST7 .... 26 B2
Everglade Rd CV9 .... 262 B1
Evergreen Hts WS12 .... 210 A4
Eversley Ave WS13 .... 30 C3
Eversley Gr DY3 .... 266 B1
Eversley Rd ST5 .... 73 F1
Evesham Cres WS3 .... 242 C2
Evesham Way ST3 .... 73 F2
Eveson Rd DY8 .... 279 F1
Ewe Dale La DE6 .... 35 D2
Exbury CI WV9 .... 239 F1
Excelsior Gr WS3 .... 244 A3
Exchange Ind Est The WS11 .... 226 C3
Exchange Rd DE13 .... 201 D2
Exchange The WS3 .... 243 D1
Exeter Gn ST2 .... 58 B1
Exeter Rd WS11 .... 226 A4
Exeter St ST17 .... 174 C4
Exley B77 .... 250 B1
Exmouth Gr ST6 .... 57 D4
Exonbury Wlk WS11 .... 209 F1
Eynsham Ct WV6 .... 255 F3
Eyre St ST6 .... 56 C4
Eyrie The DE15 .... 167 E2

Faber RC Prim Sch The ST10 .... 78 B4
Faceby Gr ST3 .... 90 B4
Fair Lady Dr WS7 .... 211 E1
Fair Lawn WV7 .... 237 D3
Fair Oak TF10 .... 168 C2
Fair Oak Rd ST5 .... 40 B1
Fair Oaks Dr WS6 .... 243 D4

Fair View Armitage WS15 .... 198 B2
  Mayfield DE6 .... 81 E4
Fair View Rd ST13 .... 31 D2
Fairbank Ave ST4 .... 72 A3
Fairbanks Wlk ST15 .... 103 D2
Fairburn Cres WS3 .... 244 A3
Fairclough PI ST6 .... 42 A2
Fairfax W WV10 .... 240 C2
Fairfax St ST1 .... 57 E3
Fairfield Ave Endon ST6 .... 43 D4
  Longton ST3 .... 89 E4
  Newcastle-u-L ST5 .... 56 B2
  Rolleston DE13 .... 147 E2
Fairfield CI WS12 .... 210 B1
Fairfield Cres DE11 .... 186 C3
Fairfield Ct ST16 .... 155 F3
Fairfield Dr
  Brownhills WS3 .... 244 A2
  Codsall WV8 .... 238 C2
  Kinver DY7 .... 278 A2
  Penkridge ST19 .... 207 F3
Fairfield Rd
  Brierley Hill DY8 .... 275 F1
  Uttoxeter ST14 .... 126 A4
Fairfield Rise DY8 .... 279 E3
Fairfields ST7 .... 39 F1
Fairfields Hill B78 .... 262 C4
Fairfields Rd Biddulph ST8 .... 17 D1
  Market Drayton TF9 .... 97 E1
Fairford Gdns
  Burntwood WS7 .... 229 E3
  Kingswinford DY8 .... 275 F2
Fairgreen Way B74 .... 257 D1
Fairham Rd DE13 .... 147 F1
Fairhaven Gr ST1 .... 57 F3
Fairhaven Prim Sch DY8 .... 275 E2
Fairhills DY3 .... 271 E4
Fairlady Dr WS7 .... 228 B4
Fairlawn CI Meir ST3 .... 89 F4
  Walsall WV12 .... 242 B1
Fairlawn Ct WV7 .... 237 D3
Fairlawn Dr DY6 .... 275 E2
Fairlawn Way WV12 .... 242 B1
Fairlawns ST5 .... 284 B4
Fairlight Gr ST3 .... 90 A4
Fairmead CI ST17 .... 175 E3
Fairmeadows Prim Sch DE11 .... 186 C3
Fairmount Way WS15 .... 178 B1
Fairoak Ave ST4 .... 155 E4
Fairoak Dr WV6 .... 255 D2
Fairoak High Sch WS15 .... 196 B4
Fairview Ave CW2 .... 37 D3
Fairview CI
  Cheslyn Hay WS6 .... 226 B1
  Tamworth B77 .... 250 C3
Fairview Cres DY6 .... 275 D3
Fairview Rd WV4 .... 265 E2
Fairview Way ST17 .... 156 B1
Fairway Branston DE14 .... 185 D4
  Brownhills WS4 .... 244 B1
  Cannock WS11 .... 226 B3
  Stafford ST16, ST17 .... 156 A1
  Tamworth B77 .... 261 F3
  Trentham ST4 .... 87 F4
Fairway Gr B77 .... 251 D2
Fairway Rd ST6 .... 42 A2
Fairway The Clifton DE6 .... 81 F3
  Swadlincote DE11 .... 186 C3
Fairways Ave DY8 .... 279 F1
Fairways CI DY8 .... 279 F1
Falcon B77 .... 262 A3
Falcon CI Burton u T DE14 .... 166 B4
  Cannock WS11 .... 209 E1
  Cheslyn Hay WS6 .... 226 B1
Falcon Cres WV14 .... 266 C1
Falcon Dr WS14 .... 232 C3
Falcon Rd ST3 .... 90 A3
Falcon Rise DY8 .... 279 E3
Falcon Way DY1 .... 271 F1
Falcondale Rd WV12 .... 242 B1
Faldo Ct DE14 .... 185 D3
Falkirk Grange ST5 .... 70 C4
Falklands CI DY3 .... 269 F1
Fallow Deer Lawn TF10 .... 168 C3
Fallow Field
  Cannock WS11 .... 209 F2
  Lichfield WS13 .... 214 A4
  Little Aston B74 .... 257 D2
Fallow Rd B78 .... 249 F1
Fallowfield Longton ST3 .... 88 C4
  Perton WV6 .... 254 B3
  Stafford ST17 .... 175 E3
  Wolv WV6 .... 239 F1
Fallowfield CI ST19 .... 207 F4
Fallowfields Dr DE13 .... 183 E1
Falmouth Ave ST17 .... 175 F4
Falmouth CI ST17 .... 175 F4
Falmouth Ct ST5 .... 71 E3
Falmouth Dr B77 .... 250 C3
Falmouth Rd CW12 .... 15 F4
Falna Cres B79 .... 249 F4
Fancourt Ave WV4 .... 265 E2
Fancy Wlk ST16 .... 155 F3
Fane Rd WV11 .... 242 A1
Fanlizard La ST20 .... 171 E2
Faraday PI ST4 .... 71 F4
Faraday Rd ST16 .... 155 F1
Farcroft Ave ST3 .... 55 F3
Farcroft Dr TF9 .... 97 D1
Fareham Cres WV4 .... 265 E2
Fareham Gr ST3 .... 89 F4
Farewell La WS7 .... 229 E3
Faringdon B77 .... 250 C1
Farington PI ST6 .... 42 A2

Farland Gr ST6 .... 42 A4
Farleigh Dr WV3 .... 265 D2
Farleigh Rd WV2 .... 58 B1
Farleigh Rd WV6 .... 255 D2
Farley La ST10 .... 78 B2
Farley Rd ST10 .... 78 A3
Farm CI Burton u T DE13 .... 166 A4
  Cannock WS12 .... 210 B2
  Codsall WV8 .... 239 D1
  Market Drayton TF9 .... 97 E1
  Rugeley WS15 .... 178 B1
  Sedgley DY3 .... 271 D4
  Tamworth B79 .... 250 B4
Farm Gr TF10 .... 168 B2
Farm La DE15 .... 167 F4
Farm Lea ST15 .... 106 B1
Farm Rd Albrighton WV6 .... 252 B4
  Burton u T DE13 .... 166 B4
  Wolv WV3 .... 265 D2
Farm Side DE11 .... 186 C3
Farm View ST15 .... 106 B1
Farmadine ST4 .... 88 A4
Farman CI ST3 .... 90 B4
Farmbrook Ave WV10 .... 240 B2
Farmdown Rd ST17 .... 156 B1
Farmer St ST3 .... 283 C2
Farmers Bank ST5 .... 55 E1
Farmfields Rise CW3 .... 67 E1
Farmoor Way WV10 .... 240 C2
Farmount Dr WS11 .... 226 C4
Farmside Gn WV9 .... 239 F1
Farmside La ST3 .... 17 D1
Farmwood CI ST3 .... 74 A1
Farnborough Ct B75 .... 258 B1
Farnborough Dr ST3 .... 90 B4
Farncote B74 .... 257 F2
Farndale Ave WV6 .... 255 F3
Farne Gr ST3 .... 73 D2
Farnham Dr ST8 .... 27 D3
Farnworth CI ST3 .... 27 D3
Farnworth Rd ST3 .... 73 F2
Farrier CI ST15 .... 120 B4
Farrier Way DY6 .... 275 D4
Farrington CI ST6 .... 42 C2
Farrington Rd DY3 .... 266 C2
Farwall La ST10 .... 49 F1
Fauld Ind Pk DE13 .... 145 F3
Fauld La Hanbury DE13 .... 145 E4
  Tutbury, Fauld DE13 .... 145 E4
  Tutbury, Owen's Bank DE13 .... 146 A3
Faulkner CI DY8 .... 279 F2
Faulkner PI ST3 .... 73 F2
Faversham CI WV8 .... 239 D2
Faversham Rd DE13 .... 166 A4
Fawcett Way ST1 .... 282 C4
Fawfield Dr ST6 .... 41 E3
Fawn CI Huntington WS12 .... 209 E3
  Meir ST3 .... 90 A4
Fazeley Rd B78 .... 250 A1
Fearns Ave ST5 .... 41 D1
Fearon Gn ST6 .... 42 C2
Featherbed La
  Elmhurst WS13 .... 213 F2
  Hixon ST18 .... 158 B4
Featherston Rd DE13 .... 166 A4
Featherstone Gr ST4 .... 72 A4
Featherstone La
  Featherstone WV10 .... 241 D4
  Shareshill WV10 .... 225 D1
Fecknam Way WS13 .... 214 B1
Federation Rd ST6 .... 41 F1
Fegg Hayes Rd ST6 .... 42 A4
Feiashill CI WV5 .... 269 D3
Feiashill Rd WV5 .... 269 D4
Felcourt Gdns ST1 .... 57 F3
Felden CI ST16 .... 136 B1
Fell St ST6 .... 42 B1
Fellbrook Ct ST2 .... 58 A2
Fellbrook La ST2 .... 58 A2
Fellfield Way ST16 .... 155 E4
Fellmeadow Way DY3 .... 271 F4
Fellows Ave DY6 .... 275 E4
Fellows St WV2 .... 266 B4
Felspar Rd B77 .... 251 D2
Felsted St ST2 .... 43 D2
Felthouse La ST13 .... 45 D1
Fence La CW12 .... 15 E2
Fenlow Ave ST3 .... 57 F1
Fenmere CI WV4 .... 266 B3
Fenn Rise ST8 .... 275 E2
Fenn St B77 .... 250 C1
Fennel CI
  Cheslyn Hay WS6 .... 226 B2
  Uttoxeter ST14 .... 126 A3
Fennel Dr ST17 .... 174 C3
Fennel Gr ST3 .... 90 A3
Fennel Wlk DE14 .... 166 B1
Fenpark Ind Est ST4 .... 73 D3
Fenpark Rd ST4 .... 73 D3
Fenton CI CW12 .... 6 A1
Fenton Croft ST19 .... 205 E3
Fenton House La ST19 .... 205 D3
Fenton Ind Es
  Bucknall ST4 .... 57 F1
  Stoke-on-T ST4 .... 72 C4
Fenton Pk ST4 .... 73 D3
Fenton Rd ST4 .... 57 F1
Fereday Rd WS9 .... 245 D2
Fereday's Croft DY3 .... 271 E4
Fermain CI ST5 .... 70 C2
Fern CI WS4 .... 244 B1
Fern Cres CW12 .... 6 A2
Fern Croft WS13 .... 213 F1
Fern Dell CI WS11 .... 209 E1
Fern Dene CW3 .... 68 B4
Fern Dr WS6 .... 227 D2
Fern Leys WV3 .... 255 E1

Fern PI ST3 .... 283 C2
Fern Rd Huntington WS12 .... 209 E3
  Wolv WV3 .... 266 A4
Ferncombe Dr WS15 .... 178 B1
Ferncroft CI ST4 .... 88 A4
Ferndale CI
  Burntwood WS7 .... 229 D3
  Caverswall ST9 .... 59 D2
  Forsbrook ST11 .... 90 C3
  Weston CW2 .... 37 D3
Ferndale Rd
  Essington WV11 .... 242 A2
  Lichfield WS13 .... 213 F1
Ferndown Ave DY3 .... 271 E4
Ferndown CI Meir ST3 .... 73 E1
  Walsall WS3 .... 243 D2
Ferndown Dr S ST5 .... 71 E1
Ferney PI ST6 .... 41 E3
Fernhurst CI ST15 .... 120 B4
Fernhurst Gr ST3 .... 89 F4
Fernie CI ST15 .... 120 B3
Fernlea Cres ST9 .... 43 F4
Fernlea Gr
  Blythe Bridge ST3 .... 90 A2
  Meir ST3 .... 74 A3
Fernleigh Ave WS7 .... 229 D4
Fernleigh Gdns
  Kingswinford DY8 .... 275 E2
  Stafford ST16 .... 155 D3
Fernwood ST16 .... 155 E4
Fernwood Croft ST13 .... 30 B2
Fernwood Dr Leek ST13 .... 30 B2
  Newcastle-u-L ST5 .... 71 E1
  Rugeley WS15 .... 178 B1
Fernwood Gn ST4 .... 88 B4
Ferrand CI ST4 .... 72 A4
Ferrers Ave DE13 .... 146 A3
Ferrers CI B75 .... 258 B1
Ferrers Rd Tamworth B77 .... 250 B2
  Weston-u-T ST18 .... 138 B1
  Yoxall DE13 .... 182 A1
Ferrie Gr WS8 .... 244 C4
Ferry St DE15 .... 185 F4
Ferry Vale CI DE15 .... 185 F4
Festing St ST1 .... 282 C4
Festival Mews WS11 .... 209 E4
Festival Rd DE14 .... 184 C4
Festival Way ST6 .... 56 C3
Fiddler's La DE13 .... 146 C2
Fiddlers Bank ST6 .... 43 D4
Field Ave DE65 .... 166 B4
Field CI Blythe Bridge ST11 .... 90 C3
  Brownhills WS4 .... 244 A1
  Burton u T DE13 .... 166 A4
  Whitmore ST5 .... 85 E3
Field Ct ST18 .... 154 B1
Field Dr DE13 .... 147 D2
Field End ST4 .... 88 A4
Field Farm Rd B77 .... 250 B1
Field Head PI WV6 .... 255 D2
Field House CI ST15 .... 104 C1
Field La Brownhills WS4 .... 244 A1
  Burton u T DE13 .... 165 F4
  Church Leigh ST10 .... 109 D1
  Great Wyrley WS6 .... 226 C2
  Stanton DE6 .... 80 B4
Field PI Longton ST3 .... 73 E3
  Rugeley WS15 .... 196 A4
  Stafford ST16 .... 155 F3
Field Rd Lichfield WS13 .... 214 A2
  Walsall WS3 .... 243 E1
Field Rise ST3 .... 166 A4
Field St Cannock WS11 .... 209 F2
  Leek ST13 .... 30 C3
Field Terr ST15 .... 105 D1
Field View Biddulph ST6 .... 16 B1
  Meir ST3 .... 74 A2
Field Way DE11 .... 186 C3
Field Wlk WS9 .... 256 A4
Fielden CI ST16 .... 42 C1
Fieldfare WS7 .... 229 E3
Fieldhouse Rd
  Burntwood WS7 .... 229 D4
  Cannock WS12 .... 209 F4
  Wolv WV4 .... 266 C2
Fielding St ST4 .... 72 A3
Fields Rd CW12 .... 15 F4
Fieldside Stafford ST17 .... 175 E3
  Swynnerton ST18 .... 118 C3
Fieldsway ST15 .... 119 F4
Fieldway
  Blythe Bridge ST11 .... 90 B4
  Caverswall ST2 .... 58 C2
  Fenton ST3 .... 72 C2
  Trentham ST4 .... 87 F4
Fife St ST4 .... 283 A4
Fifth Ave ST7 .... 25 F1
Filance CI ST19 .... 207 F4
Filance La ST19 .... 207 F4
Filey B77 .... 250 C3
Filey CI Bucknall ST2 .... 58 B1
  Cannock WS11 .... 226 B4
Filey Rd WV10 .... 240 A1
Fillybrooks CI ST15 .... 119 F4
Fillybrooks The ST15 .... 119 F4
Filton Ave WS7 .... 229 D4
Finch PI ST8 .... 27 D1
Finch St ST8 .... 27 D1
Fincham CI WV9 .... 240 A2
Finchdean CI ST3 .... 90 A4
Finchdene Gr WV3 .... 255 D3
Finches Hill ST15 .... 178 B1
Finchfield CI DY8 .... 279 E2
Finchfield Gdns WV3 .... 255 F1
Finchfield Hill WV3 .... 255 E1

Finchfield La WV3 .... 265 E4
Finchfield Rd WV3 .... 255 F1
Finchfield Rd W WV3 .... 255 F1
Finchley Cl DY3 .... 271 E1
Finchsmith Pl ST3 .... 283 B2
Fine La WS13 .... 215 F3
Finger Post Dr WS3 .... 244 A3
Finney Gr ST2 .... 58 A2
Finstock Ave ST3 .... 88 C4
Fir Cl WS12 .... 209 E4
Fir Gr DY8 .... 279 E3
Fir St DY3 .... 270 C4
Fir Tree Cl B79 .... 249 F4
Fir Tree Dr DY3 .... 271 F4
Fir Tree Pl ST5 .... 55 F4
Fir Tree Rd Meir ST3 .... 89 F4
  Wolv WV3 .... 265 E4
Firbank Pl ST3 .... 73 F2
Firbank Way WS3 .... 243 F1
Firbeck Gdns ST17 .... 175 E4
Firbob La ST10 .... 94 A2
Fircroft Cl WS11 .... 210 A2
Firecrest Cl WS11 .... 210 B1
Firmstone Ct DY8 .... 279 F4
Firmstone St DY8 .... 279 F4
Firs Cl The ST17 .... 175 E4
Firs Rd DY6 .... 275 F3
Firs The
  Cannock, Cannock Wood
  WS15 .... 211 F3
  Cannock, Hawks Green
  WS11 .... 210 A1
First Ave Brownhills WS8 .... 245 D4
  Bucknall ST2 .... 58 B2
  Kidsgrove ST7 .... 25 F1
  Newcastle-u-L ST5 .... 56 B4
  Sedgley DY6 .... 271 D1
  Stafford ST16 .... 155 E4
Firsway WV6 .... 255 D1
Firsway The ST19 .... 221 F4
Firtree Cl ST18 .... 174 B2
Firwood Rd WS6 .... 16 C1
Fisher Rd WS3 .... 242 C1
Fisher St Cannock WS12 .... 194 C1
  Chell Heath ST8 .... 27 D1
  Wolv WV3 .... 266 A4
Fishers Lock TF10 .... 168 C2
Fisherwick Cl WS14 .... 232 C3
Fisherwick Rd WS14 .... 232 C3
Fishley Cl WS3 .... 243 E2
Fishley La
  Great Wyrley WS3 .... 243 E3
  Norton Canes WS3 ...... 243 E3
  Walsall WS3 .... 243 E3
Fishpond La DE65 .... 148 A3
Fishpond Way ST2 .... 58 A4
Fistral Cl ST3 .... 73 E2
Fitchet's Bank WS7 .... 229 F3
Fithern Cl DY3 .... 271 F3
Fitzgerald Cl ST3 .... 74 A2
Fitzherbert Cl ST3 .... 103 D2
Fitzherbert Rd ST1 .... 57 F4
Five Lands Rd DE15 .... 185 F4
Five Lanes End ST20 .... 153 E4
Five Oaks Cl ST5 .... 70 C2
Five Ways
  Blakedown DY10 .... 281 D3
  Sedgley DY6 .... 271 E2
  Wolv WV3 .... 265 E4
Five Ways Prim Sch
  WS12 .... 210 B1
Flackets La
  Doveridge DE6 .... 128 A4
  Sudbury DE6 .... 128 A4
Flackett St ST3 .... 283 C5
Flamborough Gr ST6 .... 56 C4
Flanders Dr DY6 .... 275 E4
Flash CE Prim Sch SK17 .... 3 D2
Flash La Blore TF9 .... 98 C1
  Norton-in-t-M ST2 ...... 43 E1
  Stoke-on-T ST4 .... 71 F2
  Wombourne WV4 .... 264 C1
Flashes The ST20 .... 171 F4
Flather La DE6 .... 65 E1
Flats La WS14 .... 248 A3
Flatts Cl DE13 .... 166 A3
Flatts Rd ST6 .... 42 C3
Flavells La DY5 .... 271 D1
Flax Croft WS15 .... 120 A4
Flax Hill Jun Sch B79 ...... 250 A4
Flax Ovens The ST19 .... 192 C1
Flax St ST4 .... 72 A3
Flaxley Cty Prim Sch
  WS15 .... 196 C3
Flaxley Rd WS15 .... 196 B3
Flaxman Cl ST12 .... 88 C2
Fleckney Ave ST3 .... 73 F2
Fleet St DE14 .... 166 B1
Fleets La ST13 .... 49 D4
Fleming Rd ST4 .... 72 A4
Flemmynge Cl WV8 .... 238 C2
Fletcher Bank ST5 .... 284 A3
Fletcher Cres ST2 .... 43 D1
Fletcher Rd
  Stoke-on-T ST4 .... 72 A3
  Walsall WV12 .... 242 B1
Fletcher St ST1 .... 282 A1
Fletches The DE13 .... 147 D1
Fleur Dr ST4 .... 73 D3
Flinn Cl WS14 .... 231 E4
Flint St ST4 .... 74 A3
Flints Cnr WV12 .... 195 D2
Flintsham Gr ST1 .... 282 B4
Flora Cl B79 .... 250 B4
Florence Ave WV4 .... 266 C2

Florence Cty Prim Sch
  ST3 .... 283 C2
Florence Dr DE6 .... 127 E4
Florence Rd Codsall WV8 .. 239 C2
  Trentham ST4 .... 71 F1
Florence St
  Cannock WS12 .... 210 A4
  Newcastle-u-L ST5 ..... 284 B3
Florendine Cty Prim Sch
  B77 .... 250 C3
Florendine St B77 .... 250 C3
Florida Cl ST6 .... 57 D4
Floyd St ST4 .... 72 A4
Flynn Row ST4 .... 72 C4
Foden Ave ST7 .... 25 D2
Foden Cl WS14 .... 246 C3
Foden St ST4 .... 72 A3
Fogg St ST5 .... 284 B3
Fogg St E ST5 .... 284 B3
Fogg St W ST5 .... 284 B3
Fold La ST6 .... 16 C2
Fold Terr ST11 .... 45 E3
Fold The Stone ST15 .... 105 E3
  Wolv WV4 .... 265 F2
Foley Ave WV6 .... 255 E2
Foley Church Cl B74 .... 257 D1
Foley Dr WV6 .... 255 E2
Foley Gr WV5 .... 269 F3
Foley Inf Sch DY7 ...... 278 A2
Foley Pl ST4 .... 283 B4
Foley Rd ST3 .... 283 A3
Foley Rd E B74 .... 257 D1
Foley Rd W B74 .... 256 C1
Foley St Kinver DY7 .... 278 A2
  Longton ST4 .... 283 B5
Foley Wood Cl B74 ..... 256 C1
Folly Fields ST13 ...... 45 D1
Folly La Cheddleton ST9 .. 60 B4
  Consall ST9 .... 60 B4
Fontaine Pl ST14 ...... 72 A3
Fontenaye Rd B79 ..... 249 F4
Fonthill Rd ST16 ...... 155 F3
Fonthill Wlk ST2 ...... 58 A2
Fontwell Rd WV10 .... 240 B2
Footherley La WS14 ... 246 C2
Footherley Rd WS14 .. 246 C3
Forber Rd ST4 .... 71 F2
Forbisher Cl WS6 ..... 226 C1
Ford Ave ST6 .... 42 A3
Ford Brook La WS4 ... 244 A1
Ford Cl ST15 .... 120 A4
Ford St ST15 .... 118 C3
Ford Green Rd
  Chell Heath ST6 ..... 42 B1
  Norton-in-t-M ST6 ... 42 B1
Ford Hayes La Bucknall ST2 .. 58 C1
  Caverswall ST3 ...... 58 C1
Ford La Farewell WS13 .. 212 C1
  Longdon WS15 .... 198 A1
Ford Rd TF10 .... 168 C1
Ford St Burton u T DE15 .. 185 F4
  Leek ST13 .... 30 C3
  Newcastle-u-L ST5 ... 55 D1
  Stoke-on-T ST4 ...... 56 C1
Ford Way WS15 .... 198 A3
Fordham Gr WV9 ..... 240 A2
Fordhouse Rd WV10 .. 240 B1
Fordhouse Road Ind Est
  WV10 .... 240 B1
Fordrough The B74 ... 258 A1
Fords La ST7 .... 26 B3
Foregate Ct ST16 ..... 155 F2
Foregate St ST16 ..... 155 E2
Forest Cl Colwich ST18 .. 177 E4
  Newcastle-u-L ST5 ... 70 C2
Forest Ct ST1 .... 282 B4
Forest Ctr & Deer Mus
  WS15 .... 195 F4
Forest Dr DY7 .... 277 F2
Forest Glade WS6 .... 226 C1
Forest La DY7 .... 268 C1
Forest Park Prim Sch
  ST1 .... 282 A4
Forest Rd Burton u T DE13 .. 165 F2
  Draycott in t C DE13 .. 144 A2
  Dunstall DE13 .... 183 D3
  Market Drayton TF9 .. 112 A4
  Meir ST3 .... 89 F4
Forest Way WS6 ...... 227 D1
Foresters Bk ST4 .... 43 E2
Forestside Gr ST4 ... 72 A1
Forge Cl Burntwood WS7 .. 229 E3
  Wolv WV8 .... 239 F1
Forge La Aldridge, WS9 .. 256 C4
  Aldridge, Mill Green WS9 .. 256 C4
  Blakedown DY10 .... 281 D1
  Burntwood WS7 ..... 229 F3
  Burslem ST1 .... 56 C2
  Burton u T DE13 .... 148 A1
  Kingswinford DY6 ... 275 D4
  Lichfield WS13 ...... 214 A1
  Little Aston WS14 ... 257 E4
  Norton in H TF9 .... 82 B1
  Shenstone WS14 .... 257 E4
Forge Leys WV5 ..... 269 F3
Forge Mews WS15 ... 178 C1
Forge Rd Brownhills WS3 .. 243 F3
  Rugeley WS15 ...... 178 C1
  Stourbridge DY8 .... 279 F3
Forge Side ST9 ...... 44 A4
Forge St WS12 .... 210 B2
Forge Valley Way WV5 .. 269 F3
Forge Way ST4 ...... 72 D2
Formby Ave WV6 .... 254 B2
Formosa Way WS3 .. 243 D2
Forrest Ave
  Cannock WS11 ...... 226 C4
  Essington WV11 .... 242 A2

Forrester Cl
  Alrewas WS13 .... 215 E3
  Biddulph ST8 .... 27 E4
Forrester Rd ST15 ... 120 A4
Forrister St ST3 ..... 73 E2
Forsbrook CE Inf Sch
  ST11 .... 91 D4
Forster St ST6 ...... 41 E2
Forsyte Rd ST3, ST4 .. 73 E3
Forsythia Gr WV8 .... 239 D2
Fort Cres WS9 .... 245 D2
Fortescue La WS15 .. 178 C1
Forties B77 .... 261 F4
Forton Cl WV6 ...... 255 D1
Forton Rd TF10 ..... 168 C3
Forty Acre Cl TF9 ... 99 E3
Forum Rd ST5 ...... 55 E3
Fosbrooke Pl ST4 ... 71 E4
Fossdale Rd B77 .... 262 A4
Fosseway WS14 ..... 231 D3
Fosseway La WS14 .. 230 C2
Foster Ave WS12 ... 209 F3
Foster Cres DY7 .... 278 A2
Foster Ct ST3 ...... 72 C2
Foster Gr WV6 ..... 254 C2
Foster Pl DY8 ...... 279 F3
Foster St DY7 ...... 278 A2
Fosters Rd CW12 ... 6 A3
Foston Ave DE13 ... 166 A3
Foston Cl DE65 ..... 146 B4
Fotherley Brook Rd WS9 .. 256 C3
Foundry La
  Brownhills WS3 ..... 243 F2
  Bucknall ST2 .... 58 A1
  Scholar Green ST7 .. 25 F4
Foundry Rd DY6 .... 275 E4
Foundry Sq ST6 .... 43 D3
Foundry St Hanley ST1 .. 282 B3
  Kingswinford DY6 .. 275 E4
Fountain Ct ST6 .... 16 B1
Fountain Fold ST20 .. 171 E3
Fountain Rd DE6 .... 144 B3
Fountain Sq ST1 .... 282 B3
Fountain St Fenton ST4 .. 72 C3
  Leek ST13 .... 30 C3
Fountains Ave ST5 .. 71 D3
Fountains Rd WS3 .. 242 C1
Fountains Way WS3 .. 242 C1
Four Ashes Rd ST19 .. 223 F4
Four Crosses La WS3 .. 225 F4
Four Crosses Rd WS4 .. 244 B1
Four Lane Ends
  Eccleshall ST21 .... 134 A3
  Milwich ST18 ...... 122 A4
Four Lanes End
  Betley CW2 .... 37 F1
  Haughton ST18 .... 173 D3
  Seighford ST18 .... 153 F4
  Uttoxeter ST14 .... 126 B2
Four Oaks Common Rd
  B74 .... 257 F2
Four Oaks Inf Sch B74 .. 257 F2
Four Oaks Jun Sch B74 .. 257 F2
Four Oaks Rd B74 ... 258 A1
Four Oaks Sta B74 .. 258 A1
Fourlane Ends ST21 .. 131 F4
Fourth Ave
  Brownhills WS8 .... 229 D1
  Bucknall ST2 .... 58 C2
  Kidsgrove ST7 ..... 25 F1
Fowlchurch Rd ST13 .. 30 C4
Fowler Cl WV6 ..... 254 C3
Fowler St WV2 ..... 266 B3
Fowler's La ST3 ... 43 E1
Fox Cl WV5 .... 263 F1
Fox Covert DY8 .... 279 F3
Fox Gdns ST7 ..... 40 B4
Fox Gr ST5 .... 71 E1
Fox Hill Rd B75 ... 258 C1
Fox Hollow Ashley TF9 .. 99 E3
  Eccleshall ST21 .... 133 F3
  Wolv WV3 .... 255 E1
Fox La Alrewas DE13 .. 200 C1
  Elmhurst WS13 .... 214 A3
Fox Leigh Mdws WS15 .. 198 A2
Fox Rd WV5 .... 263 F2
Fox Wlk WS9 ...... 245 D2
Foxcote ST17 ..... 175 F3
Foxcroft Cl WS7 ... 229 D3
Foxes La ST19 .... 222 B3
Foxfield Cl ST10 .. 76 C3
Foxfield Way ST3 .. 88 C4
Foxfields Way WS12 .. 209 E4
Foxglove B77 ..... 251 D2
Foxglove Ave
  Burton u T DE15 ... 186 A4
  Uttoxeter ST14 .... 126 A3
Foxglove Cl
  Brownhills WS3 .... 244 A3
  Featherstone WV10 .. 241 D4
  Meir ST3 .... 74 A3
  Rugeley WS15 ..... 178 B1
Foxglove La ST5 ... 71 E1
Foxglove Rd DY1 .. 271 F2
Foxglove Wlk WS12 .. 210 B4
Foxhill Cl WS12 ... 210 B1
Foxhills Cl WS7 ... 229 D3
Foxhills Rd
  Kingswinford DY8 .. 275 D4
  Wolv WV4 .... 265 E2
Foxland Ave WS6 .. 227 D2
Foxlands Ave WV4 .. 265 E2
Foxlands Cl ST2 ... 58 B2
Foxlands Cres WV4 .. 265 E2
Foxlands Dr Sedgley DY3 .. 271 E3
  Wombourne WV4 .. 265 E2
Foxley La ST2 ..... 43 D1
Foxmeadow Cl DY3 .. 271 F4

Foxwood Cl ST15 ... 119 F3
Foxwood Rd B78 ... 262 C4
Fradley La WS13 ... 215 F4
Fradswell Cl ST18 .. 123 D1
Framlingham Gr WV6 .. 255 D2
Frampton Gr ST6 ... 41 F3
Frances Dr WS3 .... 243 D1
Francis Cl
  Kingswinford DY6 .. 275 E4
  Penkridge ST19 .... 208 A4
Francis Green La ST19 .. 207 F4
Francis Rd
  Lichfield WS13 ..... 214 A1
  Stourbridge DY8 ... 279 E3
Francis St ST6 .... 41 F3
Frank Gee Cl WS15 .. 178 B1
Frank Rogers Wlk WS15 .. 178 B1
Frank St ST4 ...... 72 A3
Franklin Cl
  Burton u T DE15 ... 167 D1
  Perton WV6 .... 254 C3
Franklin Dr WS7 ... 229 D4
Franklin Rd ST4 ... 71 F4
Franklyn St ST1 ... 282 C1
Fraser Cl ST15 .... 119 F3
Fraser St ST6 ..... 57 D4
Frayne Ave DY6 ... 275 E4
Freckleton Pl ST3 .. 90 B4
Frederick Ave ST4 .. 72 A4
Frederick Rd ST19 .. 192 C1
Frederick St
  Burton u T DE15 ... 185 F4
  Fenton ST4 .... 72 C3
  Wolv WV2 .... 266 B4
Fredericks Cl DY8 .. 279 F2
Free Trade St ST1 .. 282 C4
Freebridge Cl ST3 .. 73 F2
Freeford Gdns WS14 .. 231 F3
Freehold St ST5 .. 284 C2
Freeland Gr DY6 ... 275 F2
Freemen St ST16 .. 155 F3
Freeth Rd WS8 .... 229 D1
Fremantle Rd ST4 .. 71 F2
Fremont Dr DY1 ... 271 F2
French Ave B78 ... 249 E1
Frenchmore Gr ST3 .. 73 F1
Frensham WS6 .... 226 C2
Freshwater Gr ST2 .. 57 F2
Freville Gdns B79 .. 250 A3
Frew Cl ST4 ...... 156 A2
Friar St Longton ST3 .. 283 C4
  Stafford ST16 ...... 155 E3
Friar's Alley WS13 .. 231 D4
Friar's La TF11 .... 220 B2
Friar's St ST5 ..... 284 B2
Friars Ave ST15 ... 120 A4
Friars Cl Cheadle ST10 .. 76 B2
  Kingswinford DY8 .. 275 E2
Friars Gorse DY7 .. 279 E4
Friars Pl ST2 ..... 58 A4
Friars Rd ST2 ..... 58 A4
Friars' Rd ST17 ... 155 F1
Friars' Terr ST17 .. 155 F1
Friars' Wlk
  Newcastle-u-L ST5 .. 71 D3
  Stafford ST17 ...... 155 F1
Friarswood Prim Sch
  ST5 .... 284 B1
Friarswood Rd ST5 .. 284 B2
Friary Ave
  Abbots Bromley WS15 .. 160 C3
  Lichfield WS13 ..... 231 D4
Friary Gdns WS13 .. 231 D4
Friary Grange Sports Ctr
  WS13 .... 213 F1
Friary Rd WS13 ... 231 D4
Friary Sch The WS13 .. 213 F1
Friary St WS13 .... 231 D4
Friday Acre WS13 .. 214 A1
Friendly Ave ST5 .. 56 A4
Friesian Gdns ST5 .. 40 B1
Friezland La WS8 .. 245 D3
Friezland Way WS8 .. 245 D3
Frinton Cl ST16 ... 155 F3
Frith St ST13 ..... 30 B3
Frobisher Dr ST15 .. 103 E2
Frobisher St ST6 .. 43 D3
Frodingham Rd ST2 .. 58 B1
Frog La Lichfield WS13 .. 231 D4
  Market Drayton TF9 .. 97 E1
  Wheaton Aston ST19 .. 205 E3
Froghall ST5 ...... 284 B3
Froghall Rd Cheadle ST10 .. 76 C3
  Ipstones ST10 ..... 62 A3
  Kingsley ST10 ..... 76 C3
Froghall Wharf ST10 .. 62 A2
Frogmore Rd TF9 .. 97 E1
Frome Wlk ST6 ... 42 A2
Froyle Cl WV6 .... 255 E3
Fuchsia Dr WV9 .. 239 F2
Fulfen Prim Sch WS7 .. 229 E4
Fulford Cty Prim Sch
  ST11 .... 106 C4
Fulford Rd ST11 ... 106 C4
Fullbrook Ave DE13 .. 201 F4
Fullelove Rd WS8 .. 245 D4
Fuller St ST6 ..... 41 F2
Fullerton Cl WV8 .. 239 F1
Fullmore Cl ST19 .. 207 F4
Fullwood Wlk ST2 .. 58 B1
Fulmer Pl ST3 .... 90 A4
Furber Pl DY6 .... 275 F3
Furguson St ST1 .. 282 A1
Furlong Ave ST10 .. 92 C2
Furlong Cl Alrewas DE13 .. 201 D1
  Upper Tean ST10 .. 92 C2
  Weston-u-T ST18 .. 138 B1
Furlong Dr ST10 .. 92 C2

Furlong La
  Alrewas DE13 ...... 201 D1
  Alstonefield DE6 ... 35 E2
  Bradley ST18 ...... 173 E1
  Burslem ST6 .... 56 C4
Furlong Par **5** ST6 ... 56 C4
Furlong Pas **6** ST6 .. 56 C4
Furlong Rd ST6 ... 41 F2
Furlong The ST15 .. 118 C3
Furlong Wlk DY3 .. 271 E2
Furlongs Rd DY3 .. 271 E3
Furmston Pl TF13 .. 31 D4
Furnace Cl WV5 .. 269 F3
Furnace La CW3 .. 68 C4
Furnace Rd ST3 .. 73 E1
Furness B77 ...... 250 B2
Furness Cl WS3 .. 242 C2
Furness Gr ST17 .. 174 A4
Furnival St ST6 .. 57 D3
Furnivall Cres WS13 .. 214 B1
Furst St WS8 ..... 245 D4
Fyfield Rd ST6 ... 185 F3
Fynney Fields ST13 .. 45 F4
Fynney St ST13 ... 30 C3
Gable Croft WS14 .. 231 F3
Gable St ST4 ..... 72 A3
Gables The DE11 .. 186 C3
Gaelic Rd WS11 .. 209 E2
Gag La DE6 ...... 51 E3
Gagarin B79 ..... 249 F3
Gaia La WS13 .... 231 D4
Gaia Stowe WS13 .. 214 A1
Gaiafields Rd WS13 .. 214 A1
Gaialands Cres WS13 .. 214 A1
Gail Cl WS9 ..... 245 D2
Gail Pk WV3 ..... 265 E4
Gailey Lea La
  Huntington ST19 .. 208 A1
  Penkridge ST19 ... 207 F2
Gainford Cl WV8 .. 239 F1
Gains La WS3 .... 227 E2
Gainsborough Dr
  Fazeley B78 .... 260 A4
  Perton WV6 .... 255 D2
Gainsborough Hill DY8 .. 279 E4
Gainsborough Pl DY1 .. 271 F1
Gainsborough Rd
  Longton ST3 ...... 88 C4
  Newcastle-u-L ST5 .. 55 F1
Gainsborough Way DE15 .. 167 D2
Gainsbrook Cres WS11 .. 227 F3
Gairloch Rd WV11 .. 242 A1
Galahad Dr DE13 .. 147 F1
Galleys Bank ST7 .. 26 A2
Gallimore Cl ST6 .. 41 F1
Galloway Rd ST2 .. 73 F4
Gallowstree La
  Mayfield DE6 ...... 81 E4
  Newcastle-u-L ST5 .. 70 C4
Galsworthy Rd ST4 .. 73 D3
Galway Rd WS7 ... 229 D4
Gamesfield Gn WV3 .. 255 F1
Ganton Rd WS3 ... 243 D2
Ganton Wlk WV8 .. 255 F4
Gaol Butts ST21 .. 133 E3
Gaol Rd ST16 .... 155 F2
Gaol Sq ST16 .... 155 F2
Gaolgate St **5** ST16 .. 155 F2
Garage Cl B77 ... 250 B3
Garbett St ST6 ... 41 E4
Garden Cotts ST20 .. 171 E3
Garden Cres WS3 .. 243 F2
Garden Croft WS9 .. 256 A4
Garden Dr WS15 .. 197 D4
Garden La ST19 .. 206 B2
Garden Pl Stafford ST17 .. 155 F1
  Stoke-on-T ST4 ... 71 F4
Garden St Leek ST13 .. 30 B3
  Newcastle-u-L ST5 .. 284 C2
  Stafford ST17 ..... 155 F1
  Stoke-on-T ST4 ... 71 F3
Garden View WS15 .. 178 B1
Garden Wlk DY3 .. 271 E1
Gardeners Cl ST8 .. 27 D3
Gardeners Way WV5 .. 269 F3
Gardenholm Cl ST3 .. 89 F4
Gardens The B79 .. 216 B1
Gardiner Dr ST3 .. 283 A2
Gardner Pl ST14 .. 111 D1
Garfield Ave ST4 .. 71 F1
Garfield Cres ST4 .. 71 F1
Garfield Rd ST1 .. 282 A1
Garibaldi St ST1 .. 56 C2
Garlick St ST6 ... 42 A1
Garner St Burslem ST5 .. 56 C2
  Stoke-on-T ST4 ... 56 C1
Garners Way CW3 .. 68 C4
Garnet St ST1 .... 57 D2
Garnett Rd E ST5 .. 56 A3
Garnett Rd W ST5 .. 56 A3
Garret Cl DY6 .... 275 E4
Garrick Cl WS13 .. 213 F1
Garrick Rd Cannock WS11 .. 209 E2
  Lichfield WS13 .... 213 F1
Garrick Rise
  Burntwood WS7 ... 229 D4
  Rugeley WS15 .... 197 D3
Garrigill B77 ..... 251 D1
Garrod Sq ST16 .. 156 A3
Garsdale Cres ST3 .. 88 C4
Gartan Rd DE14 .. 185 D4
Garth Cl ST17 ... 174 C3
Garth Rd ST17 ... 174 C3
Garth St ST1 ..... 282 C3
Garth The WS13 .. 214 A1
Gas St ST14 ..... 111 E1
Gaskell Rd ST2 .. 58 B2

Gatacre St DY3 271 E2
Gatcombe Cl
Burton u T DE13 147 F1
Wolv WV10 240 C2
Gatcombe Rd DY1 271 F1
Gate St Meir ST3 74 A3
Sedgley DY3 271 F4
Gatehouse Trad Est WS8 229 D1
Gateway Ave ST5 85 E3
Gatherwynd La TF11 203 F3
Gatley Gr ST3 90 A3
Gauledge La SK17 13 D3
Gaunt St 2 ST13 30 B3
Gawain Gr DE13 147 F1
Gawsworth B79 249 E4
Gawsworth Cl ST3 73 E3
Gay La ST20 204 C4
Gaydon Rd WS9 256 A2
Gayle B77 251 D1
Gaymore Rd DY10 280 A3
Gayton Ave ST2 43 D1
Geary La DE15 167 F1
Gedney Gr ST5 71 D1
Geen St ST4 72 A4
Gemini Dr WS11 226 C3
Gemini Gr ST6 41 F3
Geneshall Cl ST20 171 E4
Geneva Dr Hanley ST1 57 F3
Newcastle-u-L ST5 70 C3
Genge Ave WV4 266 C2
Genista Cl DE15 186 A4
Genthorne Cl WV4 266 C2
Gentleshaw Prim Sch WS15 212 A3
Geoffrey Ave ST13 30 B3
Geoffrey Gr ST3 74 A2
George Ave Fazeley B78 249 E1
Meir ST3 74 A1
George Baily Ct ST17 155 F1
George Brealey Cl WS15 196 C4
George Elliott Cl ST14 126 B3
George La Lichfield WS13 231 E4
Stone ST15 120 B4
George St Audley ST7 39 E1
Brierley Hill DY8 275 F1
Burton u T DE14 166 B2
Cannock WS12 210 B2
Fenton ST4 72 C4
Newcastle-u-L ST5 284 D3
Newcastle-u-L, Chesterton ST5 55 F4
Newcastle-u-L, Porthill ST5 56 B3
Newcastle-u-L, Silverdale ST5 55 D1
Stafford ST16 155 E3
Tamworth B79 250 A2
George Walker Ct DE14 166 B2
Georges Ct ST3 283 B3
Georges Way ST7 39 F1
Georgian Pl WS11 209 F1
Gerald Rd DY8 279 F4
Gerard B79 249 F4
Gerards Way TF9 100 B3
Gerrard St ST4 72 A4
Gibb La DE6 128 C3
Gibbet La DY7 279 D2
Gibbins St ST1 282 C4
Gibbons Gr WV6 255 F2
Gibbons Hill Rd DY3 266 B1
Gibbons Rd
Sutton Coldfield B75 258 A2
Wolv WV6 255 F2
Gibraltar DY7 278 B2
Gibson Gr ST5 55 E4
Gibson Pl ST3 74 A1
Gibson Rd WV6 254 C2
Gibson St ST6 41 F1
Giddywell La WS15 197 F1
Gideons Cl DY3 271 E3
Giffard RC Prim Sch WV6 255 F3
Giffard Rd WV10 240 C1
Gifford Pl ST4 71 F3
Giffords Croft WS13 214 A1
Giggetty La WV5 269 F3
Gigmill Prim Sch DY8 279 F2
Gigmill Way DY8 279 F2
Gil Cl ST1 282 A2
Gilbanks Rd DY8 279 E4
Gilbern Dr ST8 27 D3
Gilbert Cl Kidsgrove ST7 26 A1
Newport TF10 168 B1
Gilbert La WV5 270 A4
Gilbert Rd WS13 214 B1
Gilbert St ST6 41 E4
Gilbert Wlk WS13 214 B1
Gilbeys Cl DY8 275 F1
Gilchrist Pl 17 ST6 57 D4
Giles Cl ST10 76 B2
Giles Rd WS13 214 A2
Giles Wlk ST1 57 F3
Gill Bank Rd Kidsgrove ST6 41 D4
Tunstall ST6 41 D4
Gill Wlk ST1 57 D2
Gilliard's Croft DE13 199 E3
Gilliat Wlk ST2 58 B1
Gillingham Cres ST16 155 D1
Gillway B79 250 A4
Gilman Ave ST2 43 D1
Gilman Pl ST1 282 C3
Gilman St ST1 282 C2
Gilmour La DE13 183 F1
Gilpin Cres WS3 244 A2
Gilpins Croft WS6 226 B1
Gilwell Rd WS15 211 F3
Gimson St ST4 72 C3
Ginger Hill ST20 171 E3
Ginger La ST21 116 A2
Gipsy La Alstonefield DE6 35 F2
Cookley DY11 280 A4
Girsby Cl ST4 88 B3
Girton Rd WS11 226 C4
Gisbourne Cl DE13 182 A2
Gitana St ST1 282 B3
Glade The Cannock WS11 209 E1
Newcastle-u-L ST5 71 D1
Stafford ST17 175 D4
Wolv WV8 239 F1
Glades The
Aldridge, Hardwick B74 256 C1
Aldridge, Leighswood WS9 256 A4
Gladstone Dr DY8 279 E3
Gladstone Gr Biddulph ST8 27 E4
Kingswinford DY6 275 E4
Gladstone Pl ST4 71 F3
Gladstone Rd
Cannock WS12 210 C1
Stourbridge DY8 279 E3
Gladstone St Leek ST13 30 C3
Stoke-on-T ST4 56 C1
Gladstone Way ST16 156 A3
Gladwyn St ST2 58 B2
Glaisher Dr ST3 90 B4
Glamis Cl DE13 166 B4
Glamis Dr ST15 120 B3
Glandore Rd ST3 73 F2
Glanville Dr B75 258 A2
Glascote Ct B77 250 C2
Glascote Heath Prim Sch B77 251 D1
Glascote Rd
Tamworth, Glascote Heath B77 250 C2
Tamworth, Wilnecote B77 261 F4
Glass La WS15 161 F1
Glass St ST1 282 B3
Glasscroft Cotts WS7 229 F4
Glastonbury Cl
Norton-in-t-M ST9 43 E2
Stafford ST17 175 E3
Glastonbury Cres WS3 242 C1
Glastonbury Way WS3 242 C1
Glebe WV7 237 D3
Glebe Ave ST16 155 E3
Glebe Cl Cheswardine TF9 130 A4
Doveridge DE6 127 D4
Forsbrook ST11 91 D3
Rolleston DE13 147 D2
Glebe Ct ST4 72 B4
Glebe La Gnosall ST20 171 F4
Stourbridge DY8 279 F2
Glebe Prim Sch ST4 72 C3
Glebe Rd Armitage WS15 198 B3
Cheadle ST10 76 B2
Glebe St Kidsgrove ST7 25 E1
Stoke-on-T ST4 72 A4
Glebe The ST15 135 D4
Glebedale Rd ST4 72 C3
Glebefields ST20 151 E4
Glebelands
Bobbington DY7 267 F1
Stafford ST17 174 C3
Glebeville ST13 30 C2
Gledhill Pk WS14 231 E3
Glen Cl WS11 209 F3
Glen Ct Codsall WV8 239 D2
Wolv WV6 255 F1
Glen Dr ST10 94 C4
Glen Park Rd DY1 271 E1
Glen Rd Sedgley DY3 271 F3
Stourbridge DY8 279 F2
Glen Rise DE13 166 A4
Glen The ST15 120 A4
Glencastle Way ST4 88 B3
Glencoe Rd WS11 210 A2
Glencoe St ST3 283 B2
Glencroft Cl DE14 185 D4
Glendale Cl WV3 265 E4
Glendale Ct ST5 71 E1
Glendale Dr WV5 270 A3
Glendale St ST6 57 D4
Glendawn Cl WS11 210 A2
Glendene Rd WS12 210 B3
Glendon Cl TF9 112 A4
Glendower Cl ST20 171 E3
Glendower Rd WS9 245 D1
Glendue Gr ST4 88 B3
Gleneagles B77 251 D3
Gleneagles Cres ST1 57 F3
Gleneagles Dr
Burton u T DE13 147 E1
Stafford ST16 156 B2
Gleneagles Rd
Perton WV6 254 B3
Walsall WS3 242 C2
Glenfield WV8 239 F1
Glenfield Rise DE13 166 A4
Glenfield Way ST2 73 F4
Glengarry Gdns WV3 255 F1
Glenhaven WS15 178 B1
Glenmore Ave WS7 229 D3
Glenmore Cl WV3 265 F4
Glenroyd Ave ST2 58 A1
Glenroyd Wlk ST2 58 B1
Glenthorne Cl ST17 175 E3
Glenthorne Dr WS6 226 C2
Glenthorne Prim Sch WS6 226 C2
Glenville Ave CV9 262 B1
Glenwood Cl Longton ST3 283 B4
Newcastle-u-L ST5 55 E1
Glenwood Rise WS9 245 E2
Globe Ave ST17 174 C3
Globe St ST6 56 C4
Gloucester Cl WS13 214 A2
Gloucester Grange ST5 71 E3
Gloucester Rd ST7 25 F1
Gloucester Way
Burton u T DE15 167 D1
Cannock WS11 210 A1
Glover St Cannock WS12 210 C2
Hanley ST1 282 C4
Stafford ST16 155 E2
Glovers Cl WS12 211 D3
Glyme Dr WV6 255 F3
Glyn Pl ST6 41 F2
Glyndebourne B79 249 E4
Glynne Ave DY6 275 E3
Glynne Prim Sch DY6 275 E2
Gnosall La TF10 188 B3
Gnosall Rd
Gnosall, Beffcote TF10 170 B1
Gnosall, Knightley Dale ST20 152 A2
Goddard St ST3 283 D4
Godfrey Rd ST2 58 A2
Godley La ST10 75 E3
Godleybarn La ST10 75 F3
Godolphin B79 249 E4
Godsall Gdns WV8 238 C2
Gofton B77 262 A4
Golborn Ave ST3 90 A2
Golborn Cl ST3 90 A2
Gold St ST3 283 B3
Goldcrest B77 262 A3
Goldcrest Way ST8 27 F4
Goldenhill Prim Sch ST6 41 E4
Goldenhill Rd ST4 283 B5
Goldenhill St Joseph's RC Prim Sch ST6 41 E4
Goldfinch View TF9 99 E2
Goldhurst Dr ST10 92 C1
Goldsborough B77 251 D1
Goldsmith Pl Longton ST3 283 D4
Tamworth B79 250 A4
Goldthorn Ave WV4 266 A3
Goldthorn Cres WV4 266 A3
Goldthorn Hill WV2, WV4 266 B3
Goldthorn Park Prim Sch WV4 266 B3
Goldthorn Rd WV2 266 A4
Goldthorne Ave WS11 209 F1
Golf Links Cl ST6 41 E4
Goms Mill Rd ST3 283 A2
Goodfellow St ST6 41 E2
Goodill Cl ST15 119 F3
Goodman St DE14 166 B3
Goodrich Ave WV6 255 D2
Goods Station La ST19 192 C1
Goodson St ST1 282 C3
Goodwick Cl ST4 88 B3
Goodwin Ave ST5 284 B4
Goodwin Rd ST3 74 A1
Goodwood Ave ST10 76 C2
Goodwood Cl
Burton u T DE13 147 E1
Cannock WS12 211 D3
Lichfield WS14 231 E4
Goodwood Pl ST4 88 A4
Goose La WS15 160 C3
Goose St ST5 284 B2
Goosefield Cl TF9 97 D1
Goosemoor Gr ST3 90 A4
Goostry Cl B77 250 B3
Goostry Rd B77 250 B3
Gordale Cl CW12 6 A3
Gordon Ave Cheadle ST10 76 A2
Hanley ST6 57 E4
Stafford ST16 155 E4
Wolv WV4 266 C2
Gordon Cl ST13 30 B2
Gordon Cres ST1 57 E4
Gordon Rd ST6 41 E3
Gordon St Burton u T DE14 166 B2
Chell Heath ST6 42 A1
Newcastle-u-L ST5 55 F2
4 Wolv WV2 266 B4
Gore Rd DY3 271 F4
Gorse Cres TF9 99 E3
Gorse Dr WS12 209 E3
Gorse La Alrewas WS13 215 D4
Astbury CW12 15 E3
Gnosall ST20 152 A4
Lichfield WS14 231 F3
Rugeley WS15 196 C3
Seisdon WV5 269 D3
Gorse Rd WS15 196 C3
Gorse St ST4 72 C2
Gorse Way WS12 210 B4
Gorsebrook Leys ST16 155 D3
Gorseburn Way WS15 178 B1
Gorsemoor Prim Sch WS12 210 B1
Gorsemoor Rd WS12 210 B1
Gorsemoor Way WV11 242 A2
Gorseway WS7 229 D3
Gorsey Bank ST6 42 C3
Gorsey La Cannock WS11 209 E1
Great Wyrley WS6 226 C1
Millmeece ST21 102 C3
Netherseal DE12 219 F4
Norton Canes WS3 227 F1
Gorsley Dale ST17 175 E3
Gorstey Lea WS7 229 E4
Gorsty Bank WS14 231 F4
Gorsty Hayes WV8 238 C2
Gorsty Hill Rd ST10 92 C3
Gorsy Bank Rd B77 261 F3
Gorsy La TF10 150 A2
Gort Rd ST5 55 F2
Gosberryhole La CW12 7 D1
Goscote Ind Est WS3 243 F1
Goscote La WS3 243 F1
Goscote Rd WS3 244 A1
Gosforth Gr ST3 90 B4
Gospel Ash Rd
Bobbington DY7 268 B1
Enville DY7 268 B1
Gospel End Rd
Himley DY3 271 D4
Sedgley DY3 271 D4
Gospel End St DY3 271 E4
Gothersley La DY7 274 B1
Gough Cl ST16 155 E4
Gough Side DE14 166 B1
Gould Firm La WS9 256 C3
Govan Rd ST4 72 C4
Gowan Ave ST6 42 A2
Gower Ave DY6 275 F2
Gower Rd Sedgley DY3 266 A1
Stone ST15 120 A4
Gower St Longton ST3 283 C3
Newcastle-u-L ST5 284 C3
Wolv WV2 266 C4
Gowland Dr WS11 209 D1
Goya Cl WS11 210 B1
Grace St ST13 30 B3
Graffam Gr ST10 76 C2
Grafton Ave ST6 42 A1
Grafton Cty Inf Sch ST3 283 C4
Grafton Gdns DY3 271 D2
Grafton Rd Burton u T DE15 167 D1
Longton ST3 283 C4
Grafton St ST1 282 C3
Graham Cl DE14 185 E4
Graham Rd DY6 275 E2
Graham St ST2 58 A2
Graiseley Hill WV2 266 B4
Graiseley Prim Sch WV2 266 B4
Graiseley Row WV2 266 B4
Granary Cl DY6 275 D4
Granary Rd WV8 239 F1
Granary The WS9 256 A3
Granby Wlk ST4 71 F3
Granchester Cl ST3 90 A3
Grange Ave Aldridge WS9 245 D1
Burntwood WS7 229 D4
Penkridge ST19 207 F4
Sutton Coldfield B75 258 B2
Grange Cl Burton u T DE14 166 A2
Ellenhall ST21 134 A1
Tamworth B77 261 E4
Grange Cres ST19 207 F4
Grange Ct Biddulph ST6 16 B1
Eggington DE65 148 A3
Grange Cty Inf Sch DE14 166 A2
Grange Cty Prim Sch ST3 90 A4
Grange Dr WS11 209 F1
Grange Gdns ST13 30 B2
Grange Hill WS15 197 E1
Grange La
Kingswinford DY6 275 F2
Lichfield WS13 213 F1
Newcastle-u-L ST5 56 B3
Sutton Coldfield B75 258 B2
Grange Rd Biddulph ST6 16 C2
Burntwood WS7 229 D3
Cheddleton ST13 45 E2
Gnosall ST20 151 F3
Meir ST3 90 A3
Norton Canes WS11 228 A3
Penkridge ST19 207 F4
Stone ST15 120 B4
Swadlincote DE11 186 C3
Uttoxeter ST14 111 D1
Wolv, Blakenhall WV2 266 A3
Wolv, Tettenhall WV6 255 E2
Grange St Burslem ST6 57 D3
Burton u T DE14 166 A2
Grange The
Burton u T DE14 166 A2
King's Bromley DE13 199 E3
Longdon WS15 197 E1
Meir ST3 74 A1
Stafford ST18 174 B3
Wombourne WV5 270 A4
Grangefield Cl
Cheddleton ST13 45 E2
Wolv WV8 239 F1
Grangefields ST6 16 C2
Grangewood Ave ST3 89 E3
Grangewood Rd ST3 74 A1
Granstone Cl ST6 42 A4
Grant Cl DY6 275 E4
Grant St ST4 72 B4
Grantham Pl ST2 58 A3
Grantley Cl ST3 73 D1
Grantley Cres DY6 275 E4
Grantown Gr WS3 243 D2
Granville B77 250 C1
Granville Ave Hanley ST1 57 E4
Newcastle-u-L ST5 284 C3
Newport TF10 168 C1
Granville Cl Newport TF10 168 C1
Wolv WV2 266 B4
Granville Dr DY6 275 F3
Granville Rd Bucknall ST2 58 A3
Newport TF10 168 C1
Granville Sq ST15 105 D1
Granville St 5 WV2 266 B4
Granville Terr ST15 105 D1
Granville Vilas TF10 168 C1
Grasmere Ave
Little Aston B74 257 D1
Newcastle-u-L ST5 71 D2
Perton WV6 254 C2
Grasmere Cl
Burton u T DE15 167 D1
Kingswinford DY6 275 D4
Wolv WV6 255 F4
Grasmere Dr DY8 279 F2
Grasmere Pl WS11 209 F3
Grasmere Terr ST6 42 A2
Grassholme B77 262 A4
Grassmere Ct WS6 226 B2
Grassmere Hollow ST16 154 C3
Grassy La WV11 241 D1
Grassygreen La ST7 39 F1
Gratley Croft WS12 209 E2
Gratton La Endon ST9 29 D2
Rudyard ST9 29 D2
Gratton Rd ST2 58 B2
Gravel Hill WV5 270 A3
Gravel La
Huntington WS12 209 E3
Stafford ST17 174 C3
Gravelly Bank ST3 89 F4
Gravelly Dr TF10 168 C1
Gravelly Hill TF9 100 A3
Gravelly La WS9 245 F2
Gray Rd WS12 209 F3
Gray Wlk ST17 174 B4
Gray's Cl ST7 26 A4
Grayling B77 261 E3
Grayling Gr ST6 42 A2
Grayling Willows CW3 68 C3
Grayshott Rd ST6 41 F3
Grayston Ave B77 250 C2
Grazings The DY7 278 B2
Greasley Rd ST2 58 A3
Great Charles St WS8 244 C4
Great Checkhill Rd DY7 274 B2
Great Furlong DE13 201 D1
Great Hales St TF9 97 E1
Great Moor Rd WV6 253 F1
Great Wood Prim Sch ST10 92 C2
Great Wood Rd ST10 92 C2
Great Wyrley High Sch WS6 226 C2
Greatbatch Ave ST4 71 F4
Greatmead B77 250 B1
Greatoak Rd ST7 39 F2
Greaves La DE13 144 C2
Green Acres WV5 269 F3
Green Barns La
Shenstone WS14 258 B4
Weeford WS14 258 B4
Green Brook Ct ST5 56 A2
Green Cl Barlaston ST12 88 B1
Blythe Bridge ST11 90 B4
Pattingham WV6 253 E1
Stone ST15 119 F4
Green Gore La ST17 175 F4
Green Heath Rd WS12 210 A4
Green La Aldridge WS9 256 C3
Ashley TF9 100 B3
Brownhills, High Heath WS9 244 B2
Brownhills, Pelsall WS3 244 A2
Burntwood, Creswell Green WS7 212 B1
Burntwood, Triangle WS7 229 D1
Cannock WS11 226 C3
Clifton DE6 81 F4
Dordon B77, B78 262 B4
Eccleshall ST21 133 F3
Farewell WS13 212 B2
Forsbrook ST11 91 D3
Forton TF10 150 C1
Hamstall Ridware WS15 181 D2
Heaton ST13 18 C1
Kingswinford DY6 275 E4
Marchington ST14 128 A1
Newport TF10 168 C2
Polesworth B77, B78 262 B4
Roston DE6 96 C4
Rugeley WS15 178 B1
Sedgley DY3 271 F3
Stafford ST18 174 B2
Tissington DE6 36 B1
Tutbury DE13 146 B3
Wall WS14 230 B1
Waterhouses DE6 65 D4
Whitgreave ST18 135 F4
Wolv WV6 255 F4
Green Lane Venture Ctr WS11 226 C3
Green Lea Fst Sch ST18 122 B2
Green Mdws WS11 210 B1
Green Meadow Cl WV5 269 F3
Green Oak Rd WV8 239 D1
Green Pk Blythe Bridge ST11 90 C1
Eccleshall ST21 133 F3
Green Rd Stoke-on-T ST4 71 F2
Weston-u-T ST18 138 B1
Green Rock Jun Mix Inf Sch WS3 243 F1
Green Rock La WS3 243 E1
Green Slade Gr WS12 210 B4
Green St Burton u T DE14 166 B1
Stourbridge DY8 279 F3
Green The Aldridge WS9 256 B3
Armitage WS15 198 B3
Barton-u-N DE13 183 E1
Brocton, Milford Common ST17 176 B4
Brocton, Old Acre ST17 176 A2
Burton u T DE13 147 F1
Caverswall ST11 74 B2
Cheadle ST10 76 A1
Chebsey ST21 134 C3
Dordon B78 262 B2
Endon ST6 43 D4
Fazeley B78 249 F1
Kingsley ST10 61 E1

Green The continued
Kingswinford DY8 .... 275 E1
Lawton-gate ST7 .... 25 D2
Newcastle-u-L, Clayton ST5 .... 71 E2
Rugeley WS15 .... 197 D3
Stoke-on-T ST4 .... 71 F4
Tamworth B77 .... 251 D3
Walsall WS3 .... 243 D1
Weston-u-T ST18 .... 138 B1
Whittington WS14 .... 232 C3
Green Way Aldridge WS9 ..... 245 D1
Burton u T DE13 .... 166 A4
Uttoxeter ST14 .... 126 A4
Green's La ST2 .... 58 C2
Greenacre Cl B77 .... 251 D3
Greenacre Dr WV8 .... 239 D1
Greenacre The DE6 .... 81 F4
Greenacres Brewood WV9 ..... 224 A2
Rugeley WS15 .... 196 C4
Sedgley DY3 .... 266 A1
Wolv WV6 .... 255 D3
Greenacres Ave
Blythe Bridge ST11 .... 90 B4
Essington WV10 .... 241 D1
Greenacres Cl B74 .... 256 C1
Greenacres Dr ST14 .... 111 D1
Greenacres Prim Sch
B77 .... 251 D3
Greenacres Way TF10 .... 168 B2
Greenbank Rd
Chell Heath ST6 .... 42 A2
Newcastle-u-L ST5 .... 56 B2
Greencroft
Kingswinford DY6 .... 275 D3
Lichfield WS13 .... 214 A1
Greendale Dr ST5 .... 40 B1
Greendale La ST10 .... 77 E2
Greendock St ST3 .... 283 B3
Greenfield ST8 .... 27 E3
Greenfield Ave
Armitage WS15 .... 198 A2
Endon ST6 .... 43 E4
Stourbridge DY8 .... 279 F3
Greenfield Cl ST6 .... 43 E4
Greenfield Cres ST10 .... 76 C2
Greenfield Dr ST14 .... 126 A4
Greenfield La WV10 .... 240 C3
Greenfield Pl ST6 .... 43 E4
Greenfield Prim Sch DY8 .. 279 F3
Greenfield Rd
Stafford ST17 .... 175 E3
Tunstall ST6 .... 41 F3
Greenfields
Aldridge WS9 .... 256 A4
Cannock WS11 .... 209 F1
Denstone ST14 .... 95 E3
Gnosall ST20 .... 171 F4
Greenfields Dr WS15 .... 178 B1
Greenfields La TF9 .... 97 D1
Greenfields Rd
Brownhills WS4 .... 244 B1
Endon ST9 .... 43 F4
Hixon ST18 .... 139 E1
Kingswinford DY6 .... 275 F3
Kinver DY7 .... 277 E2
Wombourne WV5 .... 270 A3
Greenfields View DY3 .... 271 D4
Greenfinch Cl ST14 .... 126 B3
Greengate St ST16 .... 155 F2
Greengates St ST6 .... 41 F2
Greenhart B77 .... 251 D2
Greenhead St ST6 .... 56 C4
Greenhill Lichfield WS13 .... 231 E4
Wombourne WV5 .... 270 A3
Greenhill Cl B77 .... 261 E3
Greenhill Ct WV5 .... 270 A3
Greenhill Gdns WV5 .... 270 A3
Greenhill La ST19 .... 205 E4
Greenhill Rd
Norton-in-the-M ST6 .... 42 C3
Sedgley DY3 .... 271 F3
Greenhill Way WS9 .... 245 D1
Greenhough Rd WS13 .... 231 D4
Greenland Cl DY6 .... 275 F4
Greenlands WV5 .... 269 F4
Greenlea B77 .... 262 A4
Greenlea Cl ST4 .... 88 B3
Greenleighs DY3 .... 266 B2
Greenly Rd WV4 .... 266 B3
Greenmeadow Gr ST9 .... 43 F3
Greenmeadows Rd CW3 ..... 68 C4
Greenmoor Ave ST5 .... 42 A4
Greenock St ST5 .... 70 C4
Greens Ind Est WS12 .... 210 B4
Greensforge La DY6, DY7 .. 274 C2
Greenside
Newcastle-u-L ST5 .... 284 A3
Swynnerton ST15 .... 118 C3
Greenside Ave ST9 .... 43 E2
Greenside Cl ST7 .... 41 D4
Greenslade Rd DY3 .... 266 A1
Greensome Cl ST16 .... 155 D2
Greensome Cres ST16 .... 155 D3
Greensome Ct ST16 .... 155 D2
Greensome La ST16 .... 155 D3
Greenvale Cl DE15 .... 185 F4
Greenway Burton u T DE15 .. 167 D2
Eccleshall ST21 .... 133 F3
Fenton ST3 .... 72 C2
Sedgley DY3 .... 266 C1
Stafford ST16 .... 156 A2
Greenway Ave ⬜1
Brierley Hill DY8 .... 275 F4
Chell Heath ST6 .... 42 A1
Stone ST15 .... 120 A3

Greenway Bank
Biddulph ST8 .... 27 E2
Norton-in-the-M ST2 .... 43 E1
Greenway Gdns
Pattingham WV6 .... 253 E1
Sedgley DY3 .... 266 C1
Greenway Hall Rd ST9 .... 43 E2
Greenway Pl ST2 .... 58 A4
Greenway Rd ST6 .... 16 C1
Greenway The
Hagley DY9 .... 281 F3
Newcastle-u-L ST5 .... 56 B2
Pattingham WV6 .... 253 E1
Trentham ST4 .... 87 F4
Greenways Audley ST7 .... 39 F1
Bradnop ST13 .... 184 B3
Kingswinford DY8 .... 275 E1
Penkridge ST19 .... 208 A4
Greenways Dr ST10 .... 76 B2
Greenways Prim Sch ST9 ... 43 E2
Greenwood Ave ST4 .... 71 F1
Greenwood Dr WS14 .... 231 E3
Greenwood Gr ST17 .... 174 B4
Greenwood Pk
Aldridge WS9 .... 245 E1
Cannock WS12 .... 210 A4
Greenwood Rd
Aldridge WS9 .... 245 D1
Burton u T DE15 .... 185 F4
Forsbrook ST11 .... 91 D4
Greenwoods The DY8 .... 279 F3
Gregory La
Norbury ST20 .... 150 B3
Woodseaves ST20 .... 150 B3
Gregory Rd DY8 .... 279 E3
Gregory St ST3 .... 283 B3
Greig Ct WS11 .... 210 B1
Grenadier Cl ST4 .... 88 B2
Grendon Gdns WV4 .... 265 E3
Grendon Gn ST2 .... 58 B1
Grenfell Rd WS3 .... 243 E2
Grenville Cl ST14 .... 110 C1
Grenville Rd DY1 .... 271 F1
Grenville St ST1 .... 282 C4
Gresham Rd WS11 .... 209 F2
Gresley B77 .... 250 C1
Gresley Cl B74 .... 258 A2
Gresley Row WS13 .... 231 E4
Gresley Way ST7 .... 39 F1
Gresley Wood Rd DE11 ... 186 C1
Gresty St ST4 .... 72 A4
Gretton Ave DE13 .... 147 F1
Greville Cl ST19 .... 207 F4
Grey Friars ST16 .... 155 E1
Grey Friars' Pl ST16 .... 155 E2
Grey Friars Way ST16 ...... 155 E3
Greyfriars Cl DY1 .... 271 F2
Greyfriars Rd ST2 🡖 58 A3
Greyhound La
Lower Penn WV4 .... 264 C3
Stourbridge DY8 .... 279 E1
Greyhound Way ST1 .... 57 D3
Greylarch La ST17 .... 175 E4
Greysan Ave ST7 .... 41 F4
Greysbrooke WS14 .... 247 D3
Greysbrooke Cty Prim Sch
WS14 .... 247 D3
Greystoke Dr DY6 .... 275 E3
Greyswood Rd ST4 .... 71 F2
Grice Rd ST4 .... 71 F4
Griffin Cl
Burntwood WS7 .... 228 C4
Norton in H TF9 .... 82 B1
Griffin St ST3 .... 283 B3
Griffiths Dr Wolv WV11 ... 242 A1
Wombourne WV5 .... 270 A3
Griffiths Rd WV12 .... 242 B1
Griffiths Way ST15 .... 120 B3
Grimley Way WS11 .... 209 F2
Grindcobbe Gr WS15 ...... 178 B2
Grindley Bank ST18 .... 140 C3
Grindley La ST3 .... 90 A3
Grindley Pl ST4 .... 71 F3
Grindsbrook B77 .... 262 A4
Grisedale Cl ST3 .... 90 A4
Grissom Cl ST3 .... 156 A3
Gristhorpe Way ST2 .... 58 B1
Gritton St ST9 .... 41 E1
Grocott Cl ST19 .... 192 C1
Grosvenor Ave
Aldridge B74 .... 256 C1
Stoke-on-T ST4 .... 71 F2
Grosvenor Cl Endon ST9 .... 43 F4
Lichfield WS14 .... 231 E3
Penkridge ST19 .... 192 C1
Sutton Coldfield B75 .... 258 B1
Grosvenor Cres WV10 ...... 240 B1
Grosvenor Gdns ST5 .... 284 C2
Grosvenor Pk WV4 .... 265 F3
Grosvenor Pl
Newcastle-u-L ST5 .... 56 B3
Tunstall ST6 .... 41 E2
Grosvenor Rd
Market Drayton TF9 .... 97 E1
Meir ST3 .... 73 F1
Newcastle-u-L ST5 .... 284 C2
Sedgley DY1 .... 271 E1
Wolv, Bushbury WV10 .... 240 B1
Wolv, Ettingshall Park DY3 .. 266 C2
Grosvenor St Leek ST13 ...... 30 C3
Longton ST3 .... 283 B3
Grosvenor Way ST17 .... 175 F3
Grotto La WV6 .... 255 F3
Grotto Rd TF9 .... 112 A4
Grounds Dr B74 .... 257 F2
Grounds Rd B74 .... 257 F2
Groundslow Hospl ST12 .. 103 F4

Grove Ave Fenton ST4 .... 72 C2
Kidsgrove ST7 .... 25 F1
Lawton-gate ST7 .... 25 D2
Grove Cl WS11 .... 227 F3
Grove Comp Sch TF9 .... 97 E1
Grove Cres
Brownhills WS3 .... 243 A3
Woore CW3 .... 83 E4
Grove Cty Prim Sch The
ST17 .... 174 B4
Grove Gdns TF9 .... 97 E1
Grove Jun Sch WV2 .... 266 C4
Grove La Doveridge DE6 ..... 127 F4
Norton Canes WS3 .... 227 F1
Wolv WV6 .... 255 D1
Grove Mid Sch ST1 .... 57 E3
Grove Park Ave ST7 .... 25 D2
Grove Pk DY6 .... 275 E4
Grove Pl ST1 .... 282 A1
Grove Rd Fenton ST4 .... 72 B2
Stone ST15 .... 119 F4
Grove St Burslem ST6 .... 57 D3
Leek ST13 .... 30 B3
Newcastle-u-L ST5 .... 55 F2
Wolv WV2 .... 266 B4
Grove The
Blythe Bridge ST11 .... 90 C3
Burntwood WS7 .... 228 B4
Chell Heath WS7 .... 42 A1
Lawton-gate ST7 .... 25 D2
Little Aston B74 .... 257 E3
Newcastle-u-L ST5 .... 71 D3
Stone ST15 .... 120 B2
Wolv WV4 .... 266 C3
Grovebank Rd ST4 .... 71 F2
Grovelands Cres WV10 ..... 240 B2
Groveside Way WS3 .... 244 A3
Grub St Norbury ST20 .... 151 D3
Woodseaves ST20 .... 151 D3
Grunmore Dr DE13 .... 147 F1
Guernsey Cl CW12 .... 6 A1
Guernsey Dr ST5 .... 70 C2
Guernsey Wlk 🔲2 ST3 ...... 73 D2
Guild La TF10 .... 169 F4
Guild St DE14 .... 166 B2
Guildford St ST4 .... 72 B4
Guinevere Ave DE13 .... 147 F1
Gullet The B78 .... 251 F1
Gun Battery La ST8 .... 28 A4
Gunby Hill DE12 .... 219 F4
Gungate B79 .... 250 A3
Gunn St ST8 .... 27 E4
Gunnel Cl ST16 .... 155 E1
Gunstone La WV8 .... 238 C3
Gurnard B77 .... 261 E3
Gurnard Cl WV11 .... 242 A1
Guthrum Cl WV6 .... 254 C1
Guy St ST2 .... 58 A2
Guy's La DY5 .... 271 D1
Guys Cl B79 .... 249 F4
Gwendoline Way WS9 ..... 245 D2
Gwenys Cres ST3 .... 72 C2
Gwyn Ave ST8 .... 27 E3
Gypsum Way DE6 .... 144 B3

Hackett Cl Longton ST3 .... 283 D4
Wolv WV14 .... 266 C1
Hackford Rd WV4 .... 266 C2
Hackwood Cl WS12 .... 88 C2
Hadden Cl ST9 .... 59 D1
Haddon Gr ST5 .... 55 F3
Haddon La ST5 .... 85 F1
Haddon Pl Bucknall ST2 ..... 58 B3
Stone ST15 .... 120 B4
Haden Cl DY8 .... 275 E1
Hadfield Gn ST6 .... 42 B1
Hadleigh Cl ST5 .... 71 D1
Hadleigh Rd ST2 .... 58 A3
Hadley Park Gdns WS15 .. 196 B4
Hadley St DE13 .... 181 F2
Hadrian Way ST5 .... 55 E3
Hadrians Cl B77 .... 261 E4
Haggar St WV2 .... 266 B3
Hagley Dr WS15 .... 178 B1
Hagley Park Cty High Sch
WS15 .... 196 B4
Hagley RC High Sch DY8 .. 281 F3
Hagley Rd WS15 .... 178 B1
Haig Cl WS11 .... 210 A3
Haig Rd ST13 .... 31 D4
Haig St ST3 .... 73 E1
Haigh Cl ST13 .... 45 E3
Hailes Park Cl WV2 .... 266 C3
Hailsham Cl ST6 .... 41 F3
Hainult Cl DY8 .... 275 E2
Halcyon Cl DE14 .... 166 A2
Halcyon Way DE14 .... 166 A2
Haldale B77 .... 251 E1
Hales Hall Rd ST10 .... 76 C2
Hales Pl ST3 .... 283 C1
Halesworth Cres ST5 .... 71 D1
Halesworth Rd WV9 .... 239 F1
Halford Ave ST1 .... 57 E4
Halford St B79 .... 250 A3
Halfpenny Green Airport
DY7 .... 268 B1
Halfshire La DY10 .... 281 D1
Halfway Pl ST5 .... 55 F1
Halifax Cl ST3 .... 90 B4
Halifax Rd WV7 .... 220 C1
Haling Cl ST19 .... 207 F4
Haling Rd ST19 .... 192 C1
Hall Ave ST13 .... 31 D4
Hall Bank SK17 .... 24 C3
Hall Cl Pattingham WV6 .... 253 E1
Stafford ST17 .... 175 D4
Hall Dr Enville DY7 .... 273 E1
Meir ST3 .... 74 A2

Hall End Cl WV6 .... 253 E1
Hall End La WV6 .... 253 E1
Hall Farm Cres ST18 .... 137 F2
Hall Gdns ST14 .... 127 F1
Hall Green Ave DE13 .... 147 F1
Hall Hill Dr ST2 .... 73 D4
Hall La
Brownhills WS3 .... 243 F2
Burntwood WS7 .... 229 F2
Doveridge DE6 .... 127 D4
Great Wyrley WS6 .... 227 D2
Hilderstone ST15 .... 106 C2
Swynnerton ST15 .... 103 E2
Wolv DY3, WV14 .... 266 C1
Hall Meadow WS11 .... 226 A3
Hall Orch Cheadle ST10 ..... 76 B2
Uttoxeter ST14 .... 125 D4
Hall Pl ST5 .... 56 B3
Hall Rd Armitage WS15 ... 198 B3
Marchington ST14 .... 127 F1
Rolleston DE13 .... 146 C2
Uttoxeter ST14 .... 126 A4
Hall St Audley ST7 .... 39 E1
Burslem ST6 .... 56 C4
Newcastle-u-L ST5 .... 284 B3
Sedgley DY3 .... 271 E4
Hall Yd ST10 .... 92 C2
Hallahan Cl ST15 .... 120 B3
Hallahan Gr ST4 .... 72 A4
Hallam Rd ST14 .... 110 C1
Hallam St ST4 .... 72 B3
Hallams Row DE14 .... 166 B2
Hallbridge Cl WS3 .... 243 F1
Hallcourt Cl WS11 .... 226 C4
Hallcourt Cres WS11 ...... 226 C4
Hallcourt La WS11 .... 226 C4
Hallcroft Cl TF10 .... 168 C2
Hallcroft Gdns TF10 .... 168 C2
Hallcroft Way WS9 .... 256 B3
Halldearn Ave ST11 .... 74 B2
Hallfarm Cl ST19 .... 223 E3
Hallfarm Rd ST19 .... 223 E3
Hallfield Gr ST6 .... 41 F3
Hallfields Rd
Swadlincote, Newhall DE11 . 186 C2
Swadlincote, Stanton DE11 . 186 B2
Hallhill La WS15 .... 161 D3
Halls Rd Biddulph ST6 .... 16 B1
Mow Cop ST7 .... 26 B4
Halston Rd WS7 .... 229 D4
Halton Gn ST3 .... 88 C4
Haltonlea B77 .... 262 A4
Ham La DY6 .... 270 C1
Hamble B77 .... 250 B1
Hamble Gr WV6 .... 254 C2
Hamble Rd WV4 .... 265 E3
Hamble Way ST2 .... 58 B1
Hambledon Cl WV9 .... 240 A1
Hambleton Pl ST8 .... 27 D3
Hambridge Cl ST17 .... 174 B4
Hambro Pl ST6 .... 42 A4
Hamelin St WS11 .... 209 F2
Hames La B79 .... 236 B2
Hamil Dr ST13 .... 30 B3
Hamil Rd Burslem ST6 .... 42 A1
Chell Heath ST6 .... 42 A1
Hamilton Ave DY8 .... 279 E3
Hamilton Cl
Cannock WS12 .... 210 C2
Kingswinford DY8 .... 275 E1
Sedgley DY3 .... 271 E4
Hamilton Ct ST5 .... 71 E1
Hamilton Dr ST8 .... 275 E1
Hamilton Fields DE15 ..... 167 D1
Hamilton Gdns WV10 ..... 240 C2
Hamilton Inf Sch ST1 .... 57 E3
Hamilton Lea WS11 .... 228 A3
Hamilton Rd
Burton u T DE15 .... 167 D1
Longton ST3 .... 283 D2
Hamilton Rise ST2 .... 43 D1
Hamilton St Fenton ST4 ...... 72 B3
Walsall WS3 .... 243 E1
Hamlet The WS11 .... 227 F3
Hamlett Pl ST6 .... 42 C2
Hammerley Hayes Rd
ST10 .... 76 C3
Hammersley St ST1 .... 57 F3
Hammerton Ave ST2 .... 57 F1
Hammerwich La WS7 ...... 229 F2
Hammerwich Rd WS7 ...... 229 E3
Hammond Ave ST6 .... 43 D4
Hammond Rd ST5 .... 55 F4
Hammonds St ST18 .... 158 B4
Hammoon Gr ST2 .... 58 A1
Hamner Gr ST2 .... 73 E4
Hamps Cl WS7 .... 229 E4
Hamps Valley Rd ST10 .... 48 C1
Hampshire Cl
Endon ST9 .... 43 F4
Tamworth B78 .... 250 A1
Hampstead Gr ST4 .... 88 B4
Hampton Cl
Newport TF10 .... 169 D2
Tamworth B79 .... 250 B4
Hampton Dr TF10 .... 169 D2
Hampton Gn WS11 .... 226 C4
Hampton Gr
Brownhills WS3 .... 244 A2
Kinver DY7 .... 278 B2
Hampton Rd WV10 .... 240 A1
Hampton St
Cannock WS11 .... 282 C1
Hanley ST1 .... 282 C1
Hams Cl ST9 .... 27 E4
Hanbridge Ave ST5 .... 56 A4
Hanbury Cres WV4 .... 265 F3
Hanbury Hill DE13 .... 145 D3

Hanbury Rd
Brownhills WS8 .... 228 C1
Norton Canes WS11 .... 227 F3
Tamworth B77 .... 250 C2
Hanbury's Farm Prim Sch
B77 .... 250 B1
Hanch Hall WS15 .... 213 A1
Hanchurch La ST4 .... 87 D4
Hancock St ST4 .... 72 B4
Hand La TF11 .... 187 E1
Hand St ST6 .... 41 F1
Handel Ct WS11 .... 210 B1
Handel Gr ST1 .... 58 A3
Handel Wlk WS13 .... 214 B1
Handley Banks ST11 .... 74 C2
Handley Dr ST8 .... 27 D1
Handley St DE11 .... 27 D1
Handsacre Cl DE11 .... 186 C2
Handsacre Cres WS15 ..... 198 B2
Handsacre Rd ST3 .... 283 D5
Hangmans La B79 .... 236 A1
Hankin Heys La TF9 .... 82 A4
Hanley Mall ST1 .... 282 B3
Hanley Rd
Chell Heath ST6, ST1 .... 57 E4
Hanley ST6, ST1 .... 57 E4
Hanlith B77 .... 262 A4
Hannaford Way WS11 ...... 209 F1
Hanney Hay Rd WS7 .... 229 D2
Hanover Ct
Newcastle-u-L ST5 .... 284 C3
Tamworth B79 .... 249 F4
Wolv WV6 .... 255 E2
Hanover Pl WS11 .... 209 F1
Hanover St Hanley ST1 ...... 282 B3
Newcastle-u-L ST5 .... 284 C3
Hanyards La ST18 .... 157 D3
Harald Cl WV6 .... 254 C3
Harber St ST3 .... 283 C3
Harbin Rd DE12 .... 184 B1
Harborough Dr WS9 .... 256 A3
Harbourne Cres ST10 .... 76 C2
Harbourne Rd ST10 .... 76 C2
Harbury St DE13 .... 166 A3
Harcourt Ave ST3 .... 73 F1
Harcourt Dr
Newport TF10 .... 169 D2
Sedgley DY1 .... 271 E1
Sutton Coldfield B74 .... 257 F2
Harcourt Rd DE14 .... 184 C4
Harcourt St ST1 .... 282 A1
Harcourt Way ST16 .... 155 D4
Hardewick Cl ST9 .... 59 D2
Hardie Ave WS15 .... 196 C4
Hardie Gn WS11 .... 209 F2
Hardince St ST4 .... 72 B3
Harding Rd ST1 .... 282 B1
Hardingswood Rd ST7 .... 25 F1
Hardington Cl ST13 .... 30 C2
Hardnam St ST2 .... 43 D1
Hardon Rd WV4 .... 266 C3
Hardwick Rd B74 .... 257 D1
Hardy Cl Barton-u-N DE13 . 201 F4
Cheadle ST10 .... 76 B1
Hardy Rd ST17 .... 174 A4
Hardy Sq WV2 .... 266 C3
Hardy St ST6 .... 41 E2
Harebell B77 .... 251 D2
Harebell Cl Cannock WS12 . 210 B1
Featherstone WV10 .... 241 D4
Harebell Gr ST7 .... 26 C1
Harecastle Ave ST7 .... 25 F1
Haregate Rd ST13 .... 31 D4
Haregate Terr ST13 .... 31 D4
Harehedge La DE13 .... 166 A4
Hareshaw Gr ST6 .... 42 A4
Harewell Dr B75 .... 258 B1
Harewood Cl ST10 .... 76 B2
Harewood Est ST10 .... 76 B3
Harewood Rd ST6 .... 41 E1
Hargreave Cl ST3 .... 90 B4
Hargreaves La ST17 .... 155 E1
Harington Dr ST3 .... 73 F3
Harland Cl ST18 .... 177 E4
Harland Rd B74 .... 258 A2
Harlaxton St DE13 .... 166 A3
Harlech Ave ST3 .... 73 F1
Harlech Dr ST8 .... 27 E3
Harlech Way
Burton u T DE13 .... 166 B4
Sedgley DY1 .... 271 F1
Harlequin Dr ST6 .... 42 B1
Harley Cl Brownhills WS8 .. 245 D3
Rugeley WS15 .... 196 C3
Harley La
Abbots Bromley WS15 .... 160 C4
Swynnerton ST4 .... 87 E1
Harley St ST3 .... 282 C2
Harley Thorn La ST4 .... 87 D2
Harmon Rd DY8 .... 279 E3
Harmony Gn ST4 .... 174 A4
Harney Ct WS15 .... 178 B2
Harold St ST8 .... 42 B1
Harper Ave
Burton u T DE13 .... 166 B4
Newcastle-u-L ST5 .... 56 A2
Harper Ct DE13 .... 166 B4
Harper St ST6 .... 56 C4
Harpfield Rd ST4 .... 71 F3
Harplow La ST10 .... 76 A1
Harptree Wlk ST4 .... 71 F1
Harrier Cl ST3 .... 90 A3
Harrietts Hayes Rd WV8 ... 237 F3
Harringay Dr DY8 .... 279 F2
Harris Rd ST16 .... 156 A2
Harris St ST4 .... 72 A4
Harriseahead La ST7 .... 26 B2

Harrison Cl Audley ST7 .... 54 B4
  Branston DE14 .... 185 D4
  Great Wyrley WS6 .... 226 B1
  Walsall WS3 .... 243 E1
Harrison Rd
  Brownhills WS4 .... 244 B1
  Cannock WS11 .... 226 C4
  Norton-in-t-M ST6 .... 42 C2
  Sutton Coldfield B74 .... 257 F3
Harrison St
  Newcastle-u-L ST5 .... 284 C2
  Walsall WS3 .... 243 E1
Harrison Way ST13 .... 45 E3
Harrisons La ST19 .... 207 F1
Harrogate Gr ST5 .... 54 C1
Harrop St ST1 .... 57 E3
Harrop Way DY8 .... 279 F4
Harrots La SK17 .... 24 B3
Harrow Dr DE14 .... 185 E4
Harrow Pl ST15 .... 120 B4
Harrow Rd DY6 .... 270 C2
Harrowby Dr ST5 .... 70 C2
Harrowby Rd Meir ST3 .... 90 A4
  Wolv WV10 .... 240 B1
Harrowby St ST16 .... 156 A2
Hart Ct ST5 .... 284 B3
Harthill Rd WV4 .... 265 E2
Hartill St ST4 .... 72 B4
Hartington CE Prim Sch
  SK17 .... 24 B3
Hartington St Leek ST13 .... 30 C3
  Newcastle-u-L ST5 .... 56 A3
Hartland Ave
  Chell Heath ST6 .... 42 B2
  Stafford ST17 .... 175 F4
Hartlands Rd ST3 .... 133 F4
Hartlebury Cl WS11 .... 210 B1
Hartley Dr WS9 .... 256 A2
Hartleyburn B77 .... 262 A4
Hartopp Rd B74 .... 257 F1
Hartsbourne Way ST17 .... 175 E4
Hartshill Rd ST4 .... 71 F4
Hartslade WS14 .... 231 F3
Hartwell Gr ST16 .... 155 D3
Hartwell La Barlaston ST12 ...... 89 E1
  Great Wyrley WS6 .... 227 D2
Hartwell Rd ST3 .... 90 A4
Harvard Cl DY1 .... 271 F2
Harvest Cl DY3 .... 271 F4
Harvester Way DY6 .... 275 D4
Harvesters Cl B74 .... 256 C1
Harvesters Wlk WV8 .... 239 F1
Harvey Dr B75 .... 258 B1
Harvey Pl ST14 .... 111 D1
Harvey Rd Alrewas WS13 .... 215 E3
  Armitage WS15 .... 198 B2
  Branston DE14 .... 185 D4
  Congleton CW12 .... 6 A3
  Meir ST3 .... 74 A1
Harvine Wlk DY8 .... 279 F2
Harwell Cl B79 .... 250 B4
Harwin Cl WV6 .... 255 F4
Harwood Ave DE14 .... 184 C4
Harwood Rd WS14 .... 214 A2
Haslemere Ave ST2 .... 43 D1
Hassall St ST1 .... 282 C2
Hassam Ave ST5 .... 284 A4
Hassam Par ST5 .... 56 A3
Hassell Prim Sch ST5 .... 284 C2
Hassell St ST5 .... 284 C3
Haste Hill La ST10 .... 61 F1
Hastings Cl B77 .... 261 F3
Hastings Ct DY1 .... 271 F1
Hatch Heath Cl WV5 .... 269 F4
Hatch La TF11 .... 203 E2
Hatchett La B79 .... 217 E3
Hateley Dr WV4 .... 266 C2
Hatfield Cres ST3 .... 88 C4
Hathaway Rd B74 .... 258 A2
Hathersage Cl ST3 .... 73 E3
Hatherton Cl ST5 .... 40 B1
Hatherton Croft WS11 .... 209 E1
Hatherton Gdns WV10 .... 240 C1
Hatherton Pl WS9 .... 256 A4
Hatherton Rd
  Cannock WS11 .... 209 E1
  Penkridge ST19 .... 192 C1
Hatherton St
  Cheslyn Hay WS6 .... 226 B1
  Stafford ST16 .... 156 A2
Hatrell St ST5 .... 284 C2
Hatton Rd Cannock WS11 .... 209 D1
  Wolv WV3 .... 255 F2
Hatton Waterworks Cotts
  ST21 .... 102 B4
Hattons Gr WV8 .... 239 D1
Haughton CE Prim Sch
  ST18 .... 172 C3
Havana La CW12 .... 6 A3
Havannah Cty Prim Sch
  CW12 .... 6 A3
Havefield Ave WS14 .... 231 F4
Havelet Dr ST5 .... 70 C2
Havelock Ave WV3 .... 265 F4
Havelock Gr ST8 .... 27 E4
Havelock Pl ST1 .... 282 A1
Haven Ave ST5 .... 57 E4
Haven Cres ST9 .... 59 D2
Haven Gr ST5 .... 56 B4
Haven The
  Kingswinford DY8 .... 275 D1
  Wolv WV2 .... 266 B4
Havergal CE Prim Sch The
  WV10 .... 225 E1
Havergal Wlk ST3 .... 283 C5
Haverhill Cl WS3 .... 243 D2
Havisham Ct TF10 .... 168 C2
Hawcroft WS15 .... 197 F1

Hawes St ST6 .... 41 E2
Haweswater Dr DY6 .... 275 E3
Hawfield La
  Burton u T DE15 .... 167 E2
  Newton Solney DE15 .... 167 F2
Hawfinch B77 .... 262 A3
Hawfinch Rd ST10 .... 76 C2
Hawke Rd ST16 .... 155 E4
Hawke's Dr DE15 .... 167 E2
Hawkesford Cl B74 .... 258 A1
Hawkesmoor Dr
  Lichfield WS14 .... 231 E4
  Perton WV6 .... 254 B2
Hawkesmore Dr ST18 .... 177 E4
Hawkestone Cl ST5 .... 284 C1
Hawkesville Dr WS11 .... 209 F1
Hawkins Cl WS13 .... 214 A1
Hawkins Dr WS11 .... 226 B2
Hawkins La
  Burton u T DE14 .... 166 C3
  Fradswell ST18 .... 122 C1
2 Meir ST3 .... 73 F1
Hawkins St ST4 .... 72 B3
Hawks Cl WS6 .... 226 B1
Hawks Green La WS11 .... 210 A1
Hawksdale Cl ST3 .... 90 A4
Hawkside B77 .... 262 A4
Hawksley Dr DE13 .... 147 D2
Hawksmoor Rd ST17 .... 174 C4
Hawkstone Ave TF10 .... 168 C1
Hawkstone Ct WV6 .... 254 B3
Hawkswell Ave WV5 .... 270 A3
Hawksworth B77 .... 250 C1
Hawksworth Ave ST13 .... 30 B2
Hawksworth Cl ST13 .... 30 B2
Hawkyard Ct WS11 .... 210 A2
Hawley Cl ST15 .... 120 B3
Haworth Ave CW12 .... 6 A3
Hawthorn Ave
  Great Wyrley WS6 .... 227 D1
  Netherseal DE12 .... 219 F4
  Stone ST15 .... 119 F4
Hawthorn Cl
  Denstone ST14 .... 95 F3
  Gnosall ST20 .... 171 F4
  Lichfield WS14 .... 231 E4
  Seighford ST18 .... 135 D1
Hawthorn Cres DE15 .... 185 F4
Hawthorn Gdns ST7 .... 40 B4
Hawthorn Pl ST3 .... 89 F4
Hawthorn Rd
  Aldridge B74 .... 257 D1
  Brownhills WS4 .... 244 A1
  Newcastle-u-L ST5 .... 40 C1
Hawthorn Rise DE11 .... 186 C4
Hawthorn St ST6 .... 57 D3
Hawthorn Way
  Kinver DY7 .... 278 A2
  Market Drayton TF9 .... 97 E1
  Rugeley WS15 .... 178 B1
  Stafford ST17 .... 156 A1
Hawthornden Ave ST14 .... 126 A4
Hawthornden Cl ST14 .... 126 A4
Hawthornden Gdns ST14 .... 125 F4
Hawthornden Manor
  Mews ST14 .... 126 A4
Hawthorne Ave Audley ST7 ...... 39 F1
  Stoke-on-T ST4 .... 71 F3
  Tamworth B79 .... 250 A4
Hawthorne Cl
  Haughton ST18 .... 172 C3
  Upper Tean ST10 .... 92 C2
Hawthorne Cres WS7 .... 229 D3
Hawthorne Dr ST19 .... 205 E3
Hawthorne Gr DY3 .... 271 E1
Hawthorne La WV8 .... 238 C1
Hawthorne Rd
  Cannock WS12 .... 210 C2
  Cheslyn Hay WS11 .... 226 C2
  Essington WV11 .... 242 A2
  Huntington WS12 .... 209 E4
  Wheaton Aston ST19 .... 205 E3
  Wolv WV2 .... 266 B3
Hawthorne Terr ST13 .... 30 C3
Hawthorns The ST5 .... 69 F4
Hay Barns The ST15 .... 103 D3
Hay End La WS13 .... 215 E4
Hay La Ellastone DE6 .... 79 F2
  Foston DE65 .... 129 F3
  Longdon WS15 .... 213 D4
Haybarn The ST16 .... 155 F4
Haybridge Ave DY8 .... 281 F3
Haybridge High Sch DY8 .... 281 F3
Haycroft Dr B74 .... 258 A2
Haydock Cl ST10 .... 76 C3
Haydon Ct ST4 .... 56 C1
Haydon St ST4 .... 56 C1
Hayes Cl ST13 .... 30 C3
Hayes Meadow Prim Sch
  WS15 .... 198 B2
Hayes St ST6 .... 42 B1
Hayes View WS13 .... 213 F1
Hayes View Dr WS11 .... 226 C2
Hayes Way ST10 .... 210 B1
Hayeswood La ST7 .... 54 C3
Hayfield Cres ST14 .... 72 C4
Hayfield Hill WS15 .... 211 F2
Hayfield Rd ST5 .... 55 D1
Hayhead Cl ST7 .... 26 A1
Hayle B77 .... 250 B1
Hayling Gr WV2 .... 266 A3
Hayling Pl ST3 .... 72 C2
Haymarket The WV8 .... 239 F1
Haymoor WS14 .... 231 F4
Hayner Gr ST3 .... 74 A2
Hayrick Dr DY6 .... 275 D4
Hays La ST10 .... 48 C2

Haywain Cl WV9 .... 239 F1
Haywards Cl WS3 .... 243 F2
Haywood Dr WV6 .... 255 E2
Haywood Grange ST18 .... 177 E4
Haywood High Sch ST6 .... 42 A1
Haywood Hts ST18 .... 177 E4
Haywood La TF9 .... 113 E1
Haywood Rd ST4 .... 42 A1
Haywood St Leek ST13 .... 30 C3
  Stoke-on-T ST4 .... 57 D1
Hayworth Cl B79 .... 249 E4
Hayworth Rd WS13 .... 214 B4
Hazel Cl Kidsgrove ST7 .... 26 A2
  Stoke-on-T ST4 .... 71 F3
  Uttoxeter ST14 .... 126 A3
Hazel Dr Armitage WS15 .... 198 A2
  Cannock WS12 .... 211 D3
Hazel Gdns WV8 .... 239 D2
Hazel Gr Alsager ST7 .... 25 D2
  Biddulph ST8 .... 17 D1
  Leek ST13 .... 30 B2
  Lichfield WS14 .... 231 E4
2 Meir ST3 .... 73 F1
  Stafford ST16 .... 155 E4
  Stourbridge DY8 .... 279 E2
  Wombourne WV5 .... 270 A4
Hazel La WS6 .... 227 D1
Hazel Rd Kingswinford DY6 ..... 275 F3
  Newcastle-u-L ST5 .... 55 E4
  Wolv WV3 .... 265 F4
Hazel Slade Prim Sch
  WS12 .... 211 D3
Hazeldene ST18 .... 158 B1
Hazeldene Rd ST4 .... 88 B4
Hazelgarth B77 .... 262 A4
Hazelhurst Dr ST13 .... 45 E2
Hazelhurst Rd ST6 .... 41 F3
Hazelhurst St ST1 .... 282 C1
Hazelmere Dr WS7 .... 228 C2
Hazelton Gr ST17 .... 174 B3
Hazelwood Cl
  Cheslyn Hay WS6 .... 226 B1
  Hanley ST6 .... 57 E3
Hazelwood Gr WS11 .... 226 B4
Hazelwood Rd
  Aldridge B74 .... 256 B1
  Burton u T DE15 .... 185 F3
  Endon ST9 .... 43 F3
Hazlemere Dr B74 .... 258 A1
Hazlemere Gr WS11 .... 226 A4
Hazlescross Rd ST10 .... 61 E2
Hazlewood Gr WS11 .... 226 B4
Hazlewood Rd DY1 .... 271 F3
Hazlitt Way ST3 .... 73 F3
Headborough Wlk WS9 .... 245 D1
Headland Dr WV3 .... 255 D1
Headland Way ST10 .... 78 C1
Headlands The B74 .... 257 E2
Heakley Ave ST6 .... 42 C2
Healey B77 .... 250 C1
Healey Ave ST8 .... 27 D3
Heanor Pl ST3 .... 283 A3
Heantun Row WV11 .... 242 A1
Hearn Ct ST17 .... 174 B4
Hearthcote Rd DE11 .... 186 C2
Heath Ave Cheddleton ST9 .... 59 F2
  Newcastle-u-L ST5 .... 56 B2
  Whittington WS14 .... 232 B2
Heath Cl WS14 .... 245 F3
Heath Croft Rd B75 .... 258 B1
Heath Cross ST14 .... 126 A4
Heath Dr
  Kidderminster DY10 .... 280 A1
  Stafford ST16 .... 155 D4
Heath Farm Rd
  Codsall WV8 .... 239 D1
  Stourbridge DY8 .... 279 F2
Heath Gap Rd WS11 .... 215 E4
Heath Gap Rd WS11 .... 209 F2
Heath Gdns ST15 .... 119 F3
Heath Gn DY1 .... 271 F3
Heath Gr Ashley TF9 .... 99 F2
  Blythe Bridge ST3 .... 90 A3
  Codsall WV8 .... 239 D2
Heath Hayes Prim Sch
  WS12 .... 210 C1
Heath Hill TF11 .... 187 E1
Heath Hill Rd WV6 .... 254 C1
Heath House Dr WV5 .... 269 F4
Heath House La
  Bucknall ST2 .... 58 A2
  Codsall WV8 .... 238 C1
  Hanley ST2 .... 58 A2
  Upper Tean SE10 .... 93 D2
Heath La Admaston WS15 .... 140 B1
  Stourbridge DY8 .... 279 F2
Heath Mill Cl WV5 .... 269 E2
Heath Mill Rd WV5 .... 269 E2
Heath Pl ST5 .... 56 B2
Heath Rd Burton u T DE15 ...... 185 F4
  Gnosall ST20 .... 188 C4
  Rugeley WS15 .... 196 C3
  Uttoxeter ST14 .... 111 D1
  Walsall WV12 .... 242 B1
  Whitmore ST5 .... 85 E4
Heath Row CW3 .... 69 D4
Heath St Biddulph ST8 .... 27 E4
  Cannock WS12 .... 210 A4
  Newcastle-u-L ST5 .... 284 B3
  Newcastle-u-L,
   Broad Meadow ST5 .... 55 F3
  Stourbridge DY8 .... 279 F2
  Tamworth B79 .... 250 B3
  Tunstall ST6 .... 41 E4
Heath Top TF9 .... 99 F2
Heath Way Cannock WS11 ...... 210 A1
  Hatton DE65 .... 146 B4
Heath's Pas ST3 .... 283 D3

Heathbank Dr WS12 .... 209 E3
Heathbrook Ave DY6 .... 275 E4
Heathcote Ave TF9 .... 99 F2
Heathcote Cl **10** ST3 .... 73 E4
Heathcote Prim Sch ST7 .... 54 C3
Heathcote Rd Audley ST7 .... 54 C4
  Longton ST3 .... 283 B3
Heathcote Rise ST3 .... 74 A3
Heathcote St
  Fenton ST3, ST4 .... 73 E3
  Kidsgrove ST7 .... 26 A1
  Longton ST3, ST4 .... 73 E3
  Newcastle-u-L ST5 .... 55 F4
Heathdene Cl ST3 .... 283 B4
Heather Cl Brocton ST17 .... 176 B2
  Caverswall ST9 .... 59 D2
  Rugeley WS15 .... 196 C3
  Seighford ST18 .... 135 E1
Heather Cres ST3 .... 90 A2
Heather Dr
  Huntington WS12 .... 209 E3
  Kinver DY7 .... 277 F2
Heather Glade CW3 .... 68 B4
Heather Hill WS12 .... 176 B2
Heather Hills ST9 .... 43 E3
Heather Mews WS12 .... 210 A4
Heather Rd WS12 .... 210 A4
Heather Valley WS12 .... 210 B3
Heatherlands ST13 .... 89 F3
Heatherleigh Gr ST1 .... 57 F3
Heathfield Ave WS15 .... 120 A4
Heathfield Ct ST6 .... 41 E4
Heathfield Dr
  Newcastle-u-L ST5 .... 40 B1
  Walsall WS3 .... 243 D1
Heathfield Gdns DY8 .... 279 F2
Heathfield Gr ST3 .... 89 F3
Heathfield Rd
  Chell Heath ST6 .... 42 B3
  Sutton Coldfield B74 .... 257 F2
  Uttoxeter ST14 .... 126 A4
Heathfield Specl Sch ST6 .... 42 B3
Heathfields Inf Sch B77 .... 261 F3
Heathland Cl WS12 .... 210 B1
Heathlands WV5 .... 269 E3
Heathlands Cl DY6 .... 275 E4
Heathlands Dr ST14 .... 111 D1
Heathley La B78 .... 260 C3
Heathmill Ent Ctr DY3 .... 269 E2
Heathside Dr WS3 .... 244 A2
Heathside La ST6 .... 41 E4
Heathview WS13 .... 45 F4
Heathway Colton WS15 .... 179 D4
  Gnosall ST20 .... 171 E3
Heathwood Rd TF10 .... 168 C1
Heatley Back La WS15 .... 141 E2
Heatley La WS15 .... 141 E1
Heaton Cl WV10 .... 240 C3
Heaton Terr ST5 .... 56 A3
Hebden B77 .... 262 A4
Hebden Gr WV11 .... 242 A1
Heber St ST3 .... 283 C4
Hedgerow Cl WS12 .... 209 F4
Hedgerow Dr DY6 .... 270 B1
Hedgerow Wlk WV8 .... 239 F1
Hedges The WV5 .... 269 F3
Hedging La B77 .... 261 F3
Hedging Lane Ind Est
  B77 .... 261 F3
Hedley Pl ST5 .... 70 C4
Hednesford Rd
  Brownhills WS8 .... 228 B1
  Cannock, Blackfords WS11 ... 209 F1
  Cannock, Little Hayes WS12 ... 210 C1
  Norton Canes WS11 .... 227 F3
  Rugeley WS15 .... 196 B3
Hednesford St WS11 .... 209 F1
Hednesford Sta ST17 .... 210 A3
Heenan Gr Lichfield WS13 ...... 213 F1
  Stafford ST17 .... 174 C3
Heighley Castle Way CW3 .... 68 C4
Heighley La CW3 .... 53 F2
Heights The ST13 .... 30 A1
Helen Sharman Dr ST16 .... 156 A3
Helford Rd DY3 .... 174 A4
Helligan B79 .... 249 E4
Hellier Rd WV10 .... 240 C1
Helmingham B79 .... 249 E4
Helmshaw Gr ST3 .... 73 F2
Helston Ave ST6 .... 56 A3
Helston Cl
  Kingswinford DY8 .... 275 E1
  Tamworth B79 .... 250 B4
Heming Rd ST3 .... 73 E2
Hemingway Rd ST3 .... 73 E2
Hemlock Rd ST3 .... 283 D4
Hemlock Way WS11 .... 210 A2
Hemmings Cl DY8 .... 279 F3
Hempbutts The ST15 .... 120 A4
Hempits Gr ST17 .... 175 D1
Hemplands Rd DY8 .... 279 F2
Hempstalls Ct ST5 .... 284 B4
Hempstalls Gr ST5 .... 56 A2
Hempstalls La ST5 .... 284 C4
Hempstalls Prim Sch ST5 .... 56 A2
Hemsby Way ST5 .... 71 D1
Hen La ST10 .... 108 B3
Hencroft ST3 .... 30 C3
Henderson Cl WS14 .... 231 E4
Henderson Gr ST3 .... 74 A1
Hendon Cl DY3 .... 271 E1
Henhurst Hill DE13 .... 165 E2
Henhurst Ridge DE13 .... 165 E3
Henley Ave ST8 .... 27 D3
Henley Cl Barlaston ST12 .... 88 C2
  Burntwood WS7 .... 229 D3
  Tamworth B79 .... 250 A3
  Walsall WS3 .... 243 F1
Henley Dr Newport TF10 .... 169 D2
  Sutton Coldfield B74 .... 258 A2

Henley Grange WS15 .... 178 A1
Henley Rd WV10 .... 240 A1
Henney Cl ST19 .... 207 F4
Henry Chadwick
  Prim Sch The WS15 .... 198 A4
Henry Prince CE
  Fst Sch The DE6 .... 81 E4
Henry St Stafford ST16 .... 155 F3
  Tunstall ST6 .... 41 E2
Hensel Dr WV3 .... 265 E4
Henshall Hall Dr CW12 .... 6 A1
Henshall Pl ST6 .... 41 E3
Henshall Rd ST5 .... 55 F4
Henshaw Way WS15 .... 119 D3
Henwood Cl WV6 .... 255 E2
Henwood Rd WV6 .... 255 E2
Hepburn Cl WS9 .... 256 A2
Hepworth Cl WV6 .... 254 C2
Herbert Rd Aldridge WS9 .... 245 D1
  Stafford ST17 .... 155 F1
Herbert St
  Burton u T DE15 .... 167 D2
  Fenton ST4 .... 72 B3
Herbhill Cl WV4 .... 266 B2
Herd St ST6 .... 41 F1
Hereford Ave ST5 .... 71 E2
Hereford Cl WS9 .... 256 A4
Hereford Gr ST2 .... 58 B1
Hereford Rd WS12 .... 210 A2
Hereford Way B78 .... 250 A1
Heritage Ct WS14 .... 231 E3
Heritage Way DE15 .... 167 D1
Herm Cl ST5 .... 70 C2
Hermes Cl ST3 .... 90 B4
Hermes Rd WS13 .... 214 B1
Hermit St DY3 .... 271 E3
Hermit Rd CW3 .... 68 C4
Heron Cross Prim Sch
  ST4 .... 72 B2
Heron Dr WV9 .... 224 A1
Heron Pool Dr ST5 .... 85 E2
Heron St Fenton ST4 .... 72 C3
  Rugeley WS15 .... 196 C4
Heron Way TF10 .... 168 C3
Herondale WS12 .... 210 A2
Herondale Rd DY8 .... 279 E2
Heronry The WV6 .... 254 C1
Herons Cl ST17 .... 175 E4
Herons Gate Rd DY7 .... 277 D2
Heronswood ST17 .... 175 E4
Hertford Gr ST5 .... 71 E2
Hertford St ST4 .... 72 C2
Hesketh Ave ST6 .... 42 B3
Hesketh Rd ST17 .... 174 C3
Heskin Way ST6 .... 42 A3
Hesleden B77 .... 262 A4
Hester Cl ST3 .... 73 E3
Hethersett Wlk ST2 .... 58 B1
Hever Cl DY1 .... 271 F2
Hewell Cl DY6 .... 270 B1
Hewitt Cl WS13 .... 214 A1
Hewitt Cres ST9 .... 59 D2
Hewitt St ST6 .... 41 F3
Hewston Croft WS12 .... 210 B2
Hexham Way DY1 .... 271 F1
Hextall La ST18 .... 153 E3
Heybridge Cl ST10 .... 92 C1
Heyburn Cres ST6 .... 56 C4
Heygate Way WS9 .... 245 D1
Heysham Cl ST3 .... 74 A2
Hick St ST5 .... 284 B2
Hickman St ST5 .... 284 B3
Hickmerelands La DY3 .... 266 B1
Hickory Ct WS11 .... 210 B1
Hidden Hills CW3 .... 68 C4
Hide La SK17 .... 24 C4
Hide St ST4 .... 72 A4
Higgins Rd DE11 .... 186 C3
Higgs Rd WV11 .... 242 A1
High Arcal Dr DY3 .... 271 F4
High Arcal Rd DY3 .... 270 C2
High Arcal Sch DY3 .... 271 F3
High Bank WS11 .... 226 C4
High Bank Pl ST6 .... 42 A1
High Bank Rd DE15 .... 167 D2
High Chase Rise ST18 .... 177 E4
High Croft WS9 .... 245 D1
High Croft Cres WS14 .... 231 E4
High Cross SK17 .... 24 C3
High Falls WS15 .... 196 C4
High Gn ST19 .... 223 E3
High Grange
  Cannock WS11 .... 210 A3
  Lichfield WS13 .... 213 F1
High Grn WS11 .... 209 E1
High Hill WV11 .... 242 A1
High Holborn DY3 .... 271 E4
High House La WV7 .... 237 E2
High La Audley ST5 .... 55 D3
  Chell Heath ST6 .... 42 A2
  Endon ST6 .... 43 D3
  Leek ST13 .... 45 F4
  Newcastle-u-L ST5 .... 55 D3
High Land Rd WS9 .... 245 D2
High Lowe Ave CW12 .... 6 A2
High Lows La WS15 .... 118 C3
High Mdws Newport TF10 .... 169 D2
  Wolv WV6 .... 255 E2
  Wombourne WV5 .... 270 A4
High Meadow
  Cannock WS11 .... 211 D3
  Norbury ST20 .... 151 D2
High Mount St WS12 .... 210 A3
High Offley Rd ST20 .... 151 E4

High Park Ave DY8 .... 279 E3
High Park Cl DY3 .... 271 E4
High Park Cres DY3 .... 266 B1
High Path WV6 .... 253 E1
High Pk ST16 .... 155 E1
High St
  Abbots Bromley WS15 .... 161 D3
  Albrighton WV7 .... 237 D3
  Aldridge WS9 .... 256 A3
  Alton ST10 .... 78 C1
  Audley, Alsagers Bank ST7 .... 54 C3
  Audley, Wood Lane ST7 .... 40 A1
  Biddulph ST8 .... 27 E4
  Brierley Hill DY8 .... 279 F4
  Brownhills, Catshill WS8 .... 244 B4
  Brownhills, Clayhanger WS8 244 C3
  Brownhills, Pelsall WS3 .... 244 A2
  Brownhills, Walsall Wood
  WS9 .... 244 C2
  Burntwood, Chase Terrace
  WS7 .... 211 F1
  Burton u T DE14 .... 166 C1
  Caverswall ST11 .... 74 C2
  Cheadle ST10 .... 76 B2
  Cheslyn Hay WS6 .... 226 B1
  Cheswardine TF9 .... 130 A4
  Church Eaton ST20 .... 190 A4
  Claverley WV5 .... 267 E4
  Colton WS15 .... 179 D3
  Dilhorne ST10 .... 75 E2
  Eccleshall ST21 .... 133 F4
  Edgmond TF10 .... 168 A2
  Gnosall ST20 .... 171 E3
  Hixon ST18 .... 158 B4
  Ipstones ST10 .... 47 D1
  Kidsgrove, Harriseahead
  ST7 .... 26 B3
  Kidsgrove, Newchapel ST7 .... 26 C1
  Kidsgrove, Talke ST7 .... 40 B3
  Kidsgrove, The Rookery ST7 ... 26 B2
  Kingsley ST10 .... 61 F1
  Kingswinford DY6 .... 275 F1
  Kingswinford, Wall Heath
  DY6 .... 275 E4
  Kingswinford, Wordsley DY8 275 F1
  Kinver DY7 .... 278 A2
  Leek ST13 .... 30 C3
  Longdon WS15 .... 197 F1
  Longnor SK17 .... 13 E3
  Marchington ST14 .... 127 F1
  Market Drayton TF9 .... 97 E1
  Mow Cop ST7 .... 26 B4
  Newcastle-u-L ST5 .... 284 B2
  Newcastle-u-L, Chesterton
  ST5 .... 55 E4
  Newcastle-u-L, Knutton
  ST5 .... 55 F2
  Newcastle-u-L,Silverdale
  ST5 .... 55 E1
  Newcastle-u-L, Wolstanton
  ST5 .... 56 B3
  Newport TF10 .... 168 C2
  Norton Canes WS11 .... 228 A3
  Pattingham WV6 .... 253 E2
  Rocester ST14 .... 95 F2
  Sedgley DY3 .... 271 E4
  Stone ST15 .... 120 A4
  Stourbridge DY8 .... 279 F4
  Swadlincote DE11 .... 186 C3
  Swindon DY3 .... 269 F1
  Tamworth B79 .... 261 E3
  Tunstall ST6 .... 41 E2
  Tunstall, Goldenhill
  ST6 .... 41 E4
  Tutbury DE13 .... 146 B3
  Upper Tean ST10 .... 92 C2
  Uttoxeter ST14 .... 126 B4
  Walsall WS3 .... 243 D1
  Wheaton Aston ST19 .... 205 D3
  Wolv WV6 .... 255 E1
  Wombourne WV5 .... 270 A4
High St (May Bank) ST5 .. 56 B2
High St (Sandyford) ST6 .... 41 E3
High View
  Blythe Bridge ST3 .... 90 A3
  Mount Pleasant ST7 .... 26 A3
  Wolv DY3 .... 266 C1
High View Rd
  Endon ST9 .... 43 F4
  Leek ST13 .... 31 D3
High Wood Cl DY6 .... 275 E3
Highbrook Cl WV9 .... 240 A1
Highbury Rd
  Caverswall ST9 .... 59 E2
  Sutton Coldfield B74 .... 257 E2
Highcliffe Rd B77 .... 261 E4
Highcroft WS3 .... 244 A3
Highcroft Ave DY8 .... 275 E2
Highcroft Dr
  Burton u T DE13 .... 165 F2
  Sutton Coldfield B74 .... 257 F2
Highcroft Wlk ST6 .... 42 A1
Higher Ash Rd ST7 .... 40 B4
Higher Woodcroft WS13 .. 30 B2
Higherland ST5 .... 284 A2
Highfield TF10 .... 168 A2
Highfield Ave
  Armitage WS15 .... 198 B2
  Burntwood WS7 .... 229 D4
  Cheadle ST10 .... 76 B2
  Essington WV10 .... 241 D1
  Kidsgrove ST7 .... 26 A1
  Meir ST3 .... 73 D1
  Newcastle-u-L ST5 .... 56 B2
  Tamworth B77 .... 251 D3

Highfield Cl
  Acton Trussell ST17 .... 193 D4
  Blythe Bridge ST11 .... 90 B4
  Burntwood WS7 .... 229 D4
  Burton u T DE13 .... 166 A4
Highfield Cres ST10 .... 76 B2
Highfield Ct
  Cannock WS11 .... 210 A3
  Newcastle-u-L ST5 .... 71 E3
Highfield Dr Colwich ST18 .. 177 E4
  Fenton ST3 .... 72 C2
Highfield Gdns WS14 .... 231 F3
Highfield Gr ST7 .... 174 B4
Highfield Grange ST5 .... 56 C2
Highfield La SK17 .... 24 C3
Highfield Rd
  Brownhills WS3 .... 244 A2
  Burntwood WS7 .... 229 E4
  Cannock WS12 .... 210 C1
  Cookley DY10 .... 280 A3
  Hixon ST18 .... 158 B4
  Sedgley DY3 .... 266 B1
Highfield Rd E ST8 .... 27 E4
Highfield Rd N WS3 .... 243 F3
Highfield Rd W ST8 .... 27 E4
Highfield Way WS9 .... 245 D1
Highfields
  Burntwood WS7 .... 229 D4
  Market Drayton TF9 .... 112 A4
Highfields Dr WV5 .... 270 A3
Highfields Grange WS6 .. 226 B1
Highfields Pk WS6 .... 226 B1
Highfields Prim Sch WS7 .. 229 E4
Highfields Rd WS7 .... 228 C2
Highfields Sec Sch WV4 .. 265 E3
Highfields The
  Eccleshall ST21 .... 116 A3
  Wolv WV6 .... 255 D1
Highgate Aldridge B74 .... 257 D1
  Sedgley DY3 .... 271 F3
Highgate Ave WV4 .... 265 E3
Highgate Cl ST6 .... 42 C2
Highgate Rd DY7 .... 273 F4
Highgrove Stone ST15 .... 120 B3
  Wolv WV6 .... 255 E2
Highgrove Cl DE13 .... 147 E1
Highgrove Pl DY1 .... 271 F1
Highland Cl Biddulph ST8 ..... 28 A4
  Blythe Bridge ST11 .... 90 C3
Highland Rd
  Huntington WS12 .... 209 E2
  Newport TF10 .... 168 C1
Highland Way WS15 .... 178 B2
Highlands Stafford ST17 .. 174 B4
  Stone ST15 .... 119 F3
Highlands Dr DE15 .... 167 D2
Highlands Rd WV3 .... 265 E4
Highlanes ST21 .... 116 B3
Highton St ST2 .... 43 E1
Highup Rd ST13 .... 19 E1
Highview Dr DY6 .... 275 F2
Highview Rd ST11 .... 106 C4
Highway La ST5 .... 69 F4
Highwood Rd ST14 .... 126 B3
Higson Ave ST4 .... 72 A4
Hilary Dr Aldridge WS9 ..... 256 A3
  Wolv WV4 .... 265 E3
Hilcote Hollow ST16 .... 155 D3
Hilderstone Rd
  Hilderstone ST15 .... 106 B3
  Stone ST15 .... 106 B3
Hill Ave WV4 .... 266 C2
Hill Avenue Cty Prim Sch
  WV4 .... 266 C2
Hill Cl Sedgley DY3 .... 266 C1
  Uttoxeter ST14 .... 110 C1
Hill Cres Audley ST7 .... 54 C3
  Stone ST15 .... 120 A3
Hill Crest Sedgley DY3 .... 271 E2
  Stafford ST17 .... 174 B4
Hill Crest Dr WS13 .... 214 A1
Hill Croft ST18 .... 158 B4
Hill Dr ST15 .... 120 A3
Hill Hook Rd B74 .... 257 F3
Hill La Allen End B75 .... 259 D1
  Burntwood WS7 .... 211 F1
  Church Leigh ST10 .... 108 B2
Hill Pk WS9 .... 245 D2
Hill Pl WV11 .... 242 A1
Hill Rise ST18 .... 137 F2
Hill Side DY3 .... 271 E2
Hill St Brierley Hill DY8 .... 279 F4
  Burntwood WS7 .... 228 C3
  Burton u T DE15 .... 185 F4
  Cannock WS12 .... 210 B2
  Cheslyn Hay WS6 .... 226 B1
  Essington WV11 .... 241 F2
  Newcastle-u-L ST5 .... 284 B4
  Norton Canes WS11 .... 227 F3
  Rugeley WS15 .... 196 C4
  Sedgley DY3 .... 271 E3
  Stoke-on-T ST4 .... 72 A4
  Stourbridge DY8 .... 279 F2
  Swadlincote DE11 .... 186 C3
Hill Terr ST7 .... 39 E1
Hill Top Ave B79 .... 250 A4
Hill Top Cl ST6 .... 28 A1
Hill Top Cres ST3 .... 90 A3
Hill Top Prim Sch ST6 .... 56 C4
Hill Top Wlk WS9 .... 245 E1
Hill View Aldridge WS9 .. 245 D1
  Norton-in-t-M ST2 .... 43 D1
Hill Village Rd B75 .... 258 A2
Hill West Inf Sch B74 .... 257 F2
Hill West Jun Sch B74 .. 257 F2
Hill Wood WS3 .... 243 F1
Hill Wood Rd B75 .... 258 B3

Hillary Ave CW12 .... 6 A1
Hillary Crest
  Rugeley WS15 .... 196 C3
  Sedgley DY3 .... 271 F3
Hillary Rd ST7 .... 26 A2
Hillary St ST6 .... 57 D3
Hillberry Cl ST2 .... 58 A1
Hillboro Rise DY7 .... 278 A3
Hillchurch St ST1 .... 282 B3
Hillcott Wlk ST3 .... 283 D3
Hillcrest Brewood ST19 .... 223 E4
  Hixon WS15 .... 140 A1
  Leek ST13 .... 30 B3
  Tutbury DE13 .... 146 A3
Hillcrest Ave
  Burton u T DE15 .... 167 D2
  Kingsley WS10 .... 62 A1
Hillcrest Cl Kingsley ST10 .. 62 A1
  Tamworth B79 .... 250 A3
Hillcrest Rise WS7 .... 229 D2
Hillcrest St ST1 .... 282 C3
Hillcroft Ave ST17 .... 175 F4
Hillcroft Rd DY6 .... 275 E4
Hilldene Rd DY6 .... 275 E2
Hillfarm Cl ST17 .... 174 C3
Hillfield Ave ST4 .... 71 F2
Hillfield La DE13 .... 147 F1
Hillgreen Rd ST3 .... 73 E3
Hillman ST2 .... 250 C1
Hillman St ST2 .... 43 D1
Hillmorton Rd B74 .... 257 F2
Hillport Ave ST5 .... 56 A4
Hillrise ST10 .... 94 C4
Hillsdale La ST13 .... 33 F2
Hillsdale Rd DE15 .... 167 D3
Hillside
  Abbots Bromley WS15 .... 161 D3
  Brownhills WS8 .... 245 D3
  Eccleshall ST21 .... 133 F4
  Lichfield WS14 .... 231 E3
  Newcastle-u-L ST5 .... 284 A2
  Tutbury DE13 .... 146 B3
  Wombourne WV5 .... 269 F3
Hillside Ave Endon ST9 .... 43 F4
  Forsbrook ST11 .... 91 D4
  Kidsgrove ST7 .... 41 D4
  Meir ST3 .... 73 F1
Hillside Cl Biddulph ST8 .... 17 D1
  Blythe Bridge ST11 .... 106 C4
  Brownhills WS8 .... 245 D3
  Cannock WS12 .... 210 A4
  Kidsgrove ST7 .... 26 B4
  Norton-in-t-M ST2 .... 43 E2
  Rugeley WS15 .... 197 D3
Hillside Cres WS3 .... 243 F2
Hillside Dr Colwich ST18 .. 177 E4
  Leek ST13 .... 30 B2
Hillside Prim Sch ST2 .... 43 D1
Hillside Rd Caverswall ST9 .. 59 D2
  Cheddleton ST13 .... 45 E3
  Norton-in-t-M ST2 .... 43 E2
  Sutton Coldfield B74 .... 258 A2
Hillside Wlk ST4 .... 71 E4
Hillswood Ave WS13 .... 30 B3
Hillswood Dr ST9 .... 43 F4
Hilltop WS15 .... 196 C4
Hilltop Ave ST5 .... 56 C1
Hilltop Prim Sch ST7 .... 40 B4
Hillview Cres ST5 .... 85 E3
Hillway ST5 .... 178 B1
Hillwood Cl DY6 .... 275 E2
Hillwood Common Rd
  B75 .... 258 A3
Hillwood Rd CW3 .... 69 D4
Hilsea Cl WV8 .... 239 F1
Hilsea Cres ST14 .... 143 F4
Hilston Ave WV4 .... 265 E2
Hilton Cl Stafford ST17 .. 174 C3
  Walsall WS3 .... 243 D1
Hilton Cross WV10 .... 241 D3
Hilton Cross Bsns Pk
  WV10 .... 241 D3
Hilton Dr ST21 .... 117 F2
Hilton La
  Featherstone WV10, WV11 .. 241 F4
  Great Wyrley WS6 .... 227 D1
  Great Wyrley, Warstone
  WV11 .... 242 A4
Hilton Main Ind Est
  WV11 .... 241 E3
Hilton Park Service Area
  WV11 .... 242 A4
Hilton Rd Eggington DE65 .. 148 A4
  Featherstone WV10 .... 241 E4
  Stoke-on-T ST4 .... 71 F4
  Walsall WV12 .... 242 B1
  Wolv WV4 .... 266 C2
Himley Ave ST5 .... 271 F1
Himley Cres WV4 .... 266 A3
Himley Gdns DY3 .... 270 B2
Himley La Himley DY3 .... 270 A2
  Swindon DY3 .... 269 F1
Himley Rd Dudley DY5 .... 271 E1
  Himley DY5 .... 271 E1
  Sedgley DY5 .... 271 E1
Hinbrook Rd DY1 .... 271 F1
Hinchco ST6 .... 42 C2
Hinckes Rd WV6 .... 255 D3
Hinckley Gr ST4 .... 88 A3
Hines St ST4 .... 72 C3
Hingley Croft B74 .... 256 C2
Hinksford Gdns DY3 .... 269 F1
Hinksford La DY6 .... 269 E1
Hinsford Cl DY6 .... 275 F4
Hinsley Mill La TF9 .... 97 F1
Hinstock Cl WV4 .... 266 A2
Hinton Cl ST3 .... 88 C3

Hints Ct B78 .... 248 B1
Hints La Hints B78 .... 248 C2
  Hopwas B78 .... 249 D3
Hints Rd Fazeley B78 .... 249 E1
  Hopwas B78 .... 249 D3
Hislop Rd WS15 .... 196 C4
Histons Dr WV8 .... 238 C1
Histons Hill WV8 .... 238 C1
Hitchman St ST4 .... 72 C3
Hixon Airfield Est ST18 .. 139 D1
Hixon Ind Est ST18 .... 158 A4
HM Young Offender Inst
  (Swinfen Hall) WS14 .... 231 F1
Hoarstone ST18 .... 281 F3
Hob Hill CE Methodist
  Prim Sch 197 D3
Hob's Rd WS13 .... 214 C1
Hobart Cl DE15 .... 167 E1
Hobart Rd WS12 .... 210 C1
Hobart St ST6 .... 57 D4
Hobb La ST14 .... 142 A4
Hobble End La WS6 .... 243 D4
Hobbs View WS15 .... 197 D3
Hobby Cl ST3 .... 90 A4
Hobfield La WS15 .... 161 D4
Hobnock Rd
  Essington WV11 .... 242 A3
  Great Wyrley WV11 .... 242 A3
Hobs Hole La WS9 .... 256 B4
Hobson St ST6 .... 57 D4
Hobstone Hill La
  WS7, WS13 .... 212 C1
Hockley Rd
  Tamworth B77 .... 261 F3
  Uttoxeter ST14 .... 126 A4
Hodge La B77 .... 251 D3
Hodgkins Cl WS8 .... 245 D3
Hodgkinson St ST5 .... 55 F3
Hodnet Gr ST1 .... 282 A4
Hodnet Pl WS11 .... 210 A1
Hodson Way WS11 .... 210 A1
Hogan Way ST16 .... 156 B2
Hogarth Pl ST5 .... 55 F3
Holbeach Ave ST2 .... 58 A1
Holbeache La DY6 .... 270 B1
Holbeache Rd DY6 .... 275 E4
Holborn ST5 .... 284 B3
Holborn Sh Ctr The DY3 .. 271 E4
Holborn The CW3 .... 68 C3
Holbrook Wlk ST2 .... 58 A1
Holbury Cl WV9 .... 240 A1
Holcroft Rd DY6 .... 270 B1
Holdcroft Rd ST2 .... 58 B3
Holden Ave ST5 .... 56 B2
Holden Ave N ST6 .... 57 E4
Holden Ave S ST6 .... 57 E4
Holden Lane High Sch
  ST2 .... 57 F4
Holden Lane Prim Sch
  ST1 .... 57 F4
Holden Rd WV4 .... 265 E2
Holder Dr WS11 .... 209 D1
Holder St ST1 .... 57 D3
Holdiford Rd
  Brocton ST17, ST18 .... 176 B4
  Tixall ST18 .... 157 E1
Holding Cres ST7 .... 54 B4
Holditch Rd ST5 .... 55 F3
Holecroft St ST6 .... 57 D4
Holehouse La Endon ST9 .. 28 B1
  Scholar Green ST7 .... 25 E4
Holehouse Rd ST2 .... 58 A3
Holland Cl WS13 .... 215 D1
Holland Ct B79 .... 217 E3
Holland Pk DE13 .... 183 F1
Holland St ST6 .... 41 E2
Holland's Way WS3 .... 243 F2
Hollands Pl WS3 .... 243 D1
Hollands Rd WS3 .... 243 E1
Hollands The ST8 .... 17 E2
Hollies Ave WS11 .... 209 F1
Hollies Brook Cl ST20 .. 171 E4
Hollies Cl Clifton DE6 .... 81 F3
  Newton Solney DE15 .... 167 F4
Hollies Dr ST3 .... 90 A2
Hollies La Enville DY7 .... 276 C4
  Pattingham WV6 .... 253 F3
Hollies The
  Newcastle-u-L ST5 .... 284 C4
  Wolv WV2 .... 266 B4
Hollings St ST4 .... 283 A5
Hollington Dr ST6 .... 42 A4
Hollington La ST14 .... 110 C3
Hollington Rd SE10 .... 93 D2
Hollins Cres ST7 .... 25 F1
Hollins Grange ST7 .... 40 B4
Hollins La ST10 .... 61 D2
Hollinsclough CE Prim Sch
  SK17 .... 4 B1
Hollinsclough Rake SK17 .. 4 A1
Hollinshead Ave ST5 .... 56 A2
Hollinshead Cl ST7 .... 25 F4
Hollinwell Cl WS3 .... 243 D2
Hollinwood Cl ST7 .... 40 C4
Hollinwood Rd ST7 .... 40 C4
Hollis La ST14 .... 95 D3
Hollow Cres DE15 .... 167 E2
Hollow La Burton u T DE15 .. 167 E2
  Cheddleton ST13 .... 45 E3
  Colton WS15 .... 179 D3
  Draycott in t C DE6 .... 144 B3
  Mayfield DE6 .... 66 B1
Hollow The
  Caverswall ST11 .... 74 C2
  Mount Pleasant ST7 .... 26 A3
  Roston DE6 .... 96 C3
  Uttoxeter ST14 .... 126 B3
Holloway B79 .... 250 A2

Holloway Dr WV5 .... 269 F3
Holloway La ST5 .... 84 B3
Holloway St DY3 .... 271 E2
Holloway St W DY3 .... 271 E2
Holloway The
  Brierley Hill DY8 .... 279 F4
  Seisdon WV5 .... 264 A2
  Swindon DY3 .... 269 E1
  Wolv WV6 .... 255 E1
Hollowood Pl ST6 .... 42 C3
Hollowood Wlk ST6 .... 42 B3
Holly Ave ST13 .... 45 E2
Holly Bank View WS15 .. 197 D3
Holly Bush Cotts ST13 .. 44 C4
Holly Bush La ST5 .... 85 D2
Holly Bush Rd DE13 .... 143 F1
Holly Cl Kinver DY7 .... 277 F3
  Market Drayton TF9 .... 112 A4
  Tamworth B79 .... 250 A4
Holly Dr Alrewas WS13 .. 215 E4
  Caverswall ST9 .... 59 D2
  Stafford ST17 .... 175 F3
Holly Fields ST15 .... 118 C3
Holly Gn DE15 .... 185 F4
Holly Gr Stone ST15 .... 120 A4
  Stourbridge DY8 .... 279 F3
  Wolv WV3 .... 265 F4
Holly Grove La WS7 .... 211 F1
Holly Grove Prim Sch
  WS7 .... 211 F1
Holly Hill WS6 .... 242 C4
Holly Hill Rd
  Cannock WS15 .... 211 F3
  Shenstone WS14 .... 246 C3
Holly La Aldridge WS9 .... 256 C4
  Bradley ST18 .... 173 E1
  Brownhills WS9 .... 245 D2
  Great Wyrley WS6 .... 242 C4
  Huntington WS12 .... 209 E4
  Kidsgrove ST7 .... 26 B3
  Seighford ST18 .... 153 F1
  Sutton Coldfield B74 .... 258 A2
  Uttoxeter ST14 .... 125 E1
Holly Pl ST4 .... 72 C2
Holly Rd Barton-u-N DE13 .. 183 E1
  Newcastle-u-L ST5 .... 40 C1
Holly St Burton u T DE15 .. 185 F4
  Cannock WS11 .... 209 F3
Holly Tree Dr ST6 .... 16 B1
Hollybank Ave WV11 .... 242 A2
Hollybank Cl WS3 .... 243 D1
Hollybank Cres ST4 .... 72 A3
Hollybush Cl DE12 .... 219 F4
Hollybush Cres ST3 .... 72 C2
Hollybush La
  Brierley Hill DY8 .... 279 F4
  Codsall WV8 .... 238 C1
  Wolv WV4 .... 265 E2
Hollybush Rd ST3 .... 72 C2
Hollyhill La WS14 .... 246 C3
Hollyhurst ST17 .... 175 E3
Hollyhurst Dr DY6 .... 275 F2
Hollyhurst La ST18 .... 140 C3
Hollys Rd DE13 .... 182 A1
Hollywall La ST6 .... 41 E3
Hollywall Prim Sch ST6 .... 41 E2
Hollywood La ST5 .... 54 B1
Holm Oak Dr CW3 .... 68 C4
Holm Rd ST10 .... 78 B1
Holm View Cl WS14 .... 246 C3
Holmcroft Gdns WV9 .... 224 B1
Holmcroft Rd ST16 .... 155 E3
Holme Farm Ave DE15 .. 185 F4
Holme Mill WV10 .... 240 B2
Holme Rise ST19 .... 193 D1
Holmes Bank DE6 .... 81 E4
Holmes Cl ST16 .... 155 D1
Holmes The WV10 .... 240 B2
Holmes Way ST6 .... 42 A4
Holmesfield Wlk ST3 .... 283 D3
Holst Dr ST1 .... 58 A3
Holston Cl WS12 .... 210 C1
Holsworth Cl B77 .... 250 B1
Holt Cres WS11 .... 210 A1
Holt La ST10 .... 61 F1
Holt's La DE13 .... 146 A3
Holte Dr B75 .... 258 B1
Holwich B77 .... 262 A4
Holy Austin Rock DY7 .... 277 F2
Holy Rosary RC
  Prim Sch The DE15 .... 167 D2
Holy Trinity CE Inf Sch
  WS8 .... 244 C3
Holy Trinity CE Prim Sch
  DE14 .... 166 C2
Holyhead Cres ST3 .... 74 A2
Holyhead Rd
  Albrighton WV7 .... 237 E1
  Codsall WV8 .... 238 B1
Holyoake Pl WS15 .... 178 B2
Holyrood Cl ST15 .... 120 B3
Holywell Rise WS14 .... 231 E3
Home Farm Rd WV6 .... 252 B4
Homefield Rd WV8 .... 239 E2
Homer Pl ST6 .... 42 A3
Homer Rd B75 .... 258 B1
Homer St ST1 .... 57 F2
Homestead Cl DY3 .... 271 F3
Homestead Ct ST16 .... 155 F4
Homestead Dr B75 .... 258 B2
Homestead Rd ST2 .... 73 E4
Homestead The ST2 .... 43 E2
Honesty Cl WS8 .... 244 B3
Honeybourne B77 .... 250 B1
Honeybourne Cres WV5 .. 269 F3
Honeysuckle Ave
  Forsbrook ST11 .... 90 C3
  Kingswinford DY6 .... 275 F4

Honeysuckle Cl ST10 .... 92 C2
Honeysuckle Dr WV10 .... 241 E4
Honeysuckle La ST9 .... 29 F1
Honeysuckle View DE15 .... 186 A4
Honeywall ST4 .... 72 A4
Honeywall La Keele CW3 .... 69 D4
  Stanton DE6 .... 80 C4
Honeywood ST5 .... 284 B4
Honiton ST17 .... 175 E4
Honiton Wlk ST3 .... 283 D3
Honor Ave WV4 .... 266 B3
Hoo La DY7 .... 273 F2
Hood La Armitage WS15 .... 198 A2
  Longdon WS15 .... 197 F1
Hook Dr B74 .... 257 F2
Hook La Shenstone WS14 .... 246 B2
  Stramshall ST14 .... 111 D3
Hook La The WV7 .... 237 D1
Hoomill La Colwich ST18 .... 158 A3
  Ingestre ST18 .... 158 A3
Hoon Ave ST5 .... 56 A2
Hoon Rd DE65 .... 146 B4
Hoover St ST6 .... 41 E2
Hope La B77 .... 251 D3
Hope St Audley ST7 .... 39 F2
  Hanley ST1 .... 282 B3
  Kingswinford DY8 .... 275 E2
Hopedale Cl Fenton ST4 .... 73 D3
  Newcastle-u-L ST5 .... 71 D2
Hopley Rd Anslow DE13 .... 165 D3
  Branston DE13 .... 165 D1
Hopleys Cl B77 .... 250 C2
Hopstone Gdns WV4 .... 265 F2
Hopton Cl WV6 .... 254 C2
Hopton Ct ST16 .... 155 E3
Hopton La ST18 .... 137 E1
Hopton Meadow WS12 .... 210 B1
Hopton St ST16 .... 155 E3
Hopton Way ST6 .... 42 A4
Hoptonhall La ST18 .... 137 E1
Hopwas Hill B78 .... 249 D3
Hopwood Pl ST2 .... 58 A2
Hopyard Cl DY3 .... 271 D2
Hopyard La DY3 .... 271 D2
Horatius Rd ST5 .... 55 E3
Hordern Cl WV6 .... 255 F3
Hordern Gr WV6 .... 255 F3
Hordern Rd WV6 .... 255 F3
Hordley St ST1 .... 282 C3
Hornbeam B77 .... 251 D2
Hornbeam Cres WS12 .... 211 D3
Hornbeams The ST14 .... 111 D1
Hornbrook Cl DE13 .... 166 A4
Hornbrook Rd DE13 .... 166 A4
Hornby Rd WV4 .... 266 B3
Hornby Row ST4 .... 72 A4
Horninglow Inf Sch
  DE13 .... 166 B3
Horninglow Rd DE14 .... 166 B4
Horninglow Rd N DE13 .... 166 B4
Horninglow St DE14 .... 166 B2
Hornton Cl B74 .... 257 E3
Hornton Rd DE13 .... 166 A4
Horse Bridge La DY7 .... 278 B1
Horse Fair Eccleshall ST21 .... 132 F4
  Rugeley WS15 .... 196 C4
Horse Rd ST10 .... 78 C1
Horsebrook La ST19 .... 223 E4
Horsecroft Cres ST13 .... 31 D4
Horsehills Dr WV3 .... 255 F1
Horseshoe Dr WS15 .... 178 A1
Horsey La WS15 .... 212 B4
Horsham Ave DY8 .... 275 E2
Horsley Gr ST3 .... 88 C4
Horsley La Eccleshall ST21 .... 132 C3
  Wall WS14 .... 246 B4
Hort Unit Wulfrun Coll
  WV6 .... 255 E1
Horton Ave DE13 .... 166 C4
Horton Cl DY3 .... 271 E4
Horton Dr ST4 .... 74 A3
Horton Lodge Sch ST9 .... 18 B1
Horton Rd DY7 .... 277 F3
Horton St Leek ST13 .... 30 C3
  Newcastle-u-L ST5 .... 284 D3
Horwood ST5 .... 70 B3
Horwood Gdns ST6 .... 42 B1
Hose St ST6 .... 41 E2
Hoskins Cl ST15 .... 120 B4
Hoskins Rd ST6 .... 41 F3
Hospital La WS6 .... 226 A1
Hospital Rd WS7 .... 229 D3
Hospital St ST9 .... 250 A3
Hot La Biddulph ST8 .... 17 E1
  Burslem ST6 .... 57 D4
Hot Lane Ind Est ST6 .... 57 D4
Hothill La ST10 .... 109 E1
Hough Hill ST6 .... 43 D4
Hougher Wall Rd ST7 .... 39 E1
Houghton St ST1 .... 282 B1
Houghwood La ST9 .... 43 E2
Houldsworth Dr ST6 .... 42 A4
Housefield Rd ST2 .... 73 E4
Houseman Dr ST3 .... 73 F2
Houting B77 .... 261 E3
Houx The DY8 .... 279 F4
Hoveringham Dr ST2 .... 57 F1
Howard Cl Caverswall ST9 .... 59 D2
  Leek ST13 .... 30 B2
Howard Cres
  Cannock WS12 .... 210 B4
  Hanley ST1 .... 57 F1
Howard Gr ST5 .... 71 D3
Howard Pl Hanley ST1 .... 282 A1
  Newcastle-u-L ST5 .... 71 D3
Howard Prim Sch The
  B79 .... 216 B1

Howard Rd ST17 .... 174 C4
Howard St Longton ST3 .... 283 C2
  Wolv WV2 .... 266 B4
Howard Wlk ST3 .... 283 C2
Howdle's La WS8 .... 228 C1
Howe Gr ST5 .... 55 F1
Howell Rd WV2 .... 266 C4
Howitt Cres ST14 .... 111 D1
Howitt House Sch DE13 .... 144 C2
Howland Cl WV9 .... 239 F1
Howson St ST1 .... 282 C3
Hoylake B77 .... 251 D2
Hoylake Cl WS3 .... 243 D2
Hoylake Rd WV6 .... 254 B3
Hubbal La TF11 .... 220 B2
Huddlesford La WS13 .... 232 B4
Huddlestone Cl WV10 .... 241 D3
Huddock's View WS3 .... 243 F3
Hudson Cl Cannock WS11 .... 210 A1
  Gnosall ST20 .... 171 F4
Hudson Dr WS7 .... 229 D3
Hudson Gr WV6 .... 254 C3
Hudson Wlk ST3 .... 283 C4
Hugh Bourne Pl ST8 .... 27 D1
Hughes Ave
  Newcastle-u-L ST5 .... 284 B4
  Wolv WV3 .... 265 F4
Hughes St ST6 .... 57 D4
Hughson Gr ST6 .... 42 C2
Hugo Meynell CE
  Prim Sch The TF9 .... 99 F2
Hugo St ST13 .... 30 C3
Hulland Cl ST5 .... 55 D1
Hullock's Pool Rd ST7 .... 39 F3
Hulme Cl ST5 .... 55 D1
Hulme La ST9 .... 59 D1
Hulme Rd ST3 .... 73 F3
Hulme St ST4 .... 71 F4
Hulse St ST4 .... 73 D3
Hulton Rd ST2 .... 58 A3
Hulton St ST1 .... 282 C4
Humber Dr ST8 .... 27 F4
Humber Way ST5 .... 71 D2
Humbert St ST1 .... 56 C2
Humphrey St DY3 .... 271 E2
Humphries Ho WS8 .... 244 C4
Hungerford La CW3 .... 69 D3
Hungerford Rd DY8 .... 279 F1
Hungry La WS14 .... 247 F3
Hunsford Cl ST3 .... 283 C4
Hunslet Rd WS7 .... 229 D4
Hunt St ST6 .... 41 F2
Huntbach St ST1 .... 282 C3
Hunter Ave WS7 .... 229 D4
Hunter Cl ST14 .... 231 E3
Hunter Rd WS11 .... 226 C4
Hunter St ST4 .... 166 B3
Hunter's Point TF9 .... 99 E3
Hunter's Ride DY7 .... 275 D1
Hunters Ct ST8 .... 27 E4
Hunters Ct ST18 .... 137 F2
Hunters Dr ST4 .... 71 F3
Hunters Rise ST17 .... 174 C2
Hunters Way ST4 .... 72 A3
Huntilee Rd ST6 .... 41 F2
Huntingdon Cl B78 .... 249 F1
Huntingdon Pl ST1 .... 57 F3
Huntingdon Rd DE15 .... 185 E4
Huntington Ind Est
  SW12 .... 209 D3
Huntington Prim Sch
  WS11 .... 209 E4
Huntington Terrace Rd
  WS11 .... 209 F2
Huntley Ave ST4 .... 72 A3
Huntley Cl ST10 .... 76 B1
Huntley La ST10 .... 92 B4
Huntley Rd ST13 .... 44 C4
Hunts La DE12 .... 219 F4
Hunts Mill Dr DY5 .... 271 E1
Huntsbank Dr ST5 .... 40 B1
Huntsman's Hill WS11 .... 197 E1
Huntsmans Dr DY7 .... 277 F3
Huntsmans Gate WS7 .... 229 D4
Huntsmans Rise WS12 .... 209 E4
Huntsmans Wlk WS15 .... 178 B1
Hurlingham Rd ST16 .... 155 E4
Huron Cl WS11 .... 210 A1
Huron Gr ST4 .... 88 A4
Hurst Cl ST7 .... 40 B3
Hurst Dr DE13 .... 147 F1
Hurst Rd Biddulph ST8 .... 17 D2
  Sedgley WV14 .... 266 C4
Hurst St ST3 .... 283 B3
Hurstbourne Cl WS15 .... 178 A1
Hurstmead Dr ST17 .... 175 E3
Hurstons La ST10 .... 78 C1
Hurstons The ST10 .... 78 C1
Husphins La WV8 .... 238 A3
Hussey Cl ST19 .... 207 F4
Hussey Rd Brownhills WS8 .... 244 C4
  Norton Canes WS11 .... 227 D3
Huston Ave ST9 .... 43 F4
Hut Hill La WS11 .... 227 D2
Hutchinson Cl WS15 .... 178 A1
Hutchinson Meml CE
  Fst Sch ST10 .... 109 D4
Hutchinson Wlk ST3 .... 73 D2
Hutton Cl CW12 .... 6 A1
Hutton Dr WV12 .... 240 A2
Hutton Way ST12 .... 58 B1
Huxley Cl WV9 .... 240 A2
Huxley Pl ST3 .... 73 E2
Hyacinth Ct ST5 .... 284 C4
Hyde Cl DY7 .... 278 A3
Hyde Ct ST17 .... 174 B4
Hyde La DY7 .... 278 A3
Hyde Lea Bank ST18 .... 174 B3

Hyde Mill La ST19 .... 223 E3
Hylton Cl DE14 .... 185 D4
Hyndley Cl ST2 .... 58 A2
Hyperion Rd DY7 .... 279 E4
Hyssop Cl WS11 .... 210 A2

I-Mex Bsns Pk ST4 .... 72 C3
Ian Rd ST7 .... 26 B1
Ibsen Rd ST3 .... 74 A2
Ibstock St DE13 .... 166 A3
Ickenfield Cl B74 .... 257 D1
Idonia Rd WV6 .... 254 C3
Ikins Dr ST7 .... 39 F1
Ilam CE Prim Sch DE6 .... 50 C1
Ilam Cl ST5 .... 55 D1
Ilam Ctry Pk ST10 .... 50 C2
Ilam-moor La DE6 .... 50 C3
Ilford Side ST3 .... 88 C4
Ilkley Pl ST5 .... 54 C1
Illshaw WV9 .... 240 A2
Imandra Cl ST4 .... 88 A4
Imex Bsns Pk
  Burton u T DE14 .... 166 A2
  Wolv WV2 .... 266 B4
Imogen Cl ST3 .... 73 D3
Impstones ST20 .... 171 E3
Ingatestone Dr DY8 .... 275 E2
Inge Dr DE13 .... 201 D1
Ingelow Cl ST3 .... 73 D1
Ingestre Cl
  Cannock WS11 .... 210 A1
  Newport TF10 .... 168 B1
  Walsall WS3 .... 242 C2
Ingestre Rd Stafford ST17 .... 155 F1
  Wolv WV10 .... 240 B1
Ingestre Sq ST3 .... 88 C4
Ingleborough Ave WV3 .... 265 F4
Ingleborough Pl ST2 .... 43 E1
Ingleby Gdns WV6 .... 255 F3
Ingleby Rd ST3 .... 88 C4
Inglefield Ave ST5 .... 42 A1
Ingleside WS15 .... 178 B1
Ingleton Gr ST3 .... 90 A4
Inglewood Cl ST17 .... 155 E1
Inglewood Cl DY6 .... 275 E3
Inglewood Dr ST5 .... 56 B3
Inglewood Gr
  Aldridge B74 .... 256 C1
  Newcastle-u-L ST5 .... 56 B3
Inglis St ST4 .... 72 B4
Ingram Pit La B77 .... 251 D3
Ingram Pl WS3 .... 243 E1
Ingram Rd WS3 .... 243 E1
Inhedge St DY3 .... 271 F3
Intake La ST20 .... 190 A4
Intake Rd ST6 .... 42 B2
Intakes La ST10 .... 108 C2
Inworth WV9 .... 240 A2
Iona Pl ST3 .... 72 C2
Irene Ave Chell Heath ST6 .... 41 F2
  Newcastle-u-L ST5 .... 56 B1
Ireton Rd WV10 .... 240 C2
Iris Cl Meir ST3 .... 74 B3
  Tamworth B79 .... 250 B3
Irnham Rd B74 .... 258 A1
Ironmarket ST5 .... 284 B3
Ironstone La WS13 .... 215 F3
Ironstone Rd WS12 .... 211 E2
Ironwalls La DE13 .... 146 B3
Irvine Rd ST9 .... 59 E2
Irving Cl Lichfield WS13 .... 213 F1
  Sedgley DY3 .... 271 D2
Irwell B77 .... 250 C1
Irwell St ST6 .... 56 C3
Isabel Cl ST17 .... 174 A4
Isherwood Pl ST3 .... 283 D4
Island Cl ST4 .... 175 E3
Island The Fazeley B78 .... 249 E1
  Upper Tean ST10 .... 92 B2
Islay Wlk 3 ST3 .... 73 D2
Islington Cl TF10 .... 168 C2
Islington Cres CV9 .... 262 B1
Ismere Way CV10 .... 280 A1
Itchen Gr WV6 .... 254 C2
Ivanhoe Rd WS14 .... 231 D3
Ivatt B77 .... 250 C1
Iverley La Blakedown DY10 .... 281 E3
  Kinver DY10 .... 281 E3
Ivetsey Bank Rd ST19 .... 221 F4
Ivetsey Cl ST19 .... 205 D3
Ivetsey Rd ST19 .... 204 C2
Ivy Cl Acton Trussell ST17 .... 175 D1
  Cannock WS11 .... 226 B4
  Forsbrook ST11 .... 90 C3
  Uttoxeter ST14 .... 126 A4
Ivy Croft WV9 .... 239 F2
Ivy Ct Acton Trussell ST17 .... 175 D1
  Hixon ST18 .... 158 A4
Ivy Gr ST4 .... 87 F4
Ivy House La ST19 .... 206 C1
Ivy House Rd
  Biddulph ST6 .... 16 B1
  Hanley ST1 .... 57 F2
Ivy La WS15 .... 211 F3
Ivy Lodge Cl DE15 .... 185 F4
Ivyhouse Dr ST12 .... 88 C2
Ivyhouse Wlk B77 .... 261 E3
Izaac Walton Way CW3 .... 68 C3
Izaak Walton Cl ST16 .... 155 E3
Izaak Walton St ST16 .... 155 E3
Izaak Walton's Cottage
  & Mus ST15 .... 135 D4

Jack Haye La ST2 .... 43 E1
Jack Hayes La ST2 .... 58 C4
Jack La CW2 .... 37 E3
Jack's La ST14 .... 127 F1

Jackdaw Cl DY3 .... 266 B1
Jackfield Inf Sch ST6 .... 42 A1
Jackfield St ST6 .... 42 A1
Jacklin Cl DE14 .... 185 D3
Jackman Cl WS13 .... 215 E3
Jackman Rd WS13 .... 215 E3
Jackson Ave DE13 .... 166 C4
Jackson Cl
  Featherstone WV10 .... 241 D3
  Norton Canes WS11 .... 227 F2
Jackson Rd WS13 .... 214 A2
Jackson St 2 ST6 .... 57 D4
Jacob's Hall La WS6 .... 227 D1
Jacobean Ct DE15 .... 167 E2
Jacobs Croft ST5 .... 155 E4
Jacqueline St ST6 .... 41 E2
Jade Cl ST3 .... 73 E2
Jade Gr ST9 .... 210 B1
Jaguar B77 .... 250 C1
Jamage Rd ST7 .... 40 B3
James Brindley Cl ST1 .... 57 D1
James Brindley High Sch
  ST6 .... 41 F3
James Ct DE14 .... 166 B1
James Greenway WS13 .... 214 A1
James St
  Burton u T DE14 .... 166 B1
  Cannock WS11 .... 209 F3
  Kinver DY7 .... 278 A2
  Leek ST13 .... 30 C3
  Newcastle-u-L ST5 .... 56 B3
  Stoke-on-T ST4 .... 72 A3
  Uttoxeter ST14 .... 126 A4
James Warner Cl WS15 .... 178 B1
James Way ST7 .... 27 D3
Janet Pl ST1 .... 57 F2
Janson St ST4 .... 71 F1
Jasmin Way ST7 .... 26 C1
Jasmine Cl
  Burton u T DE15 .... 186 A4
  Wolv WV2 .... 240 A2
Jasmine Ct ST11 .... 90 C3
Jasmine Gr WV8 .... 239 D2
Jasmine Rd
  Seighford ST18 .... 135 E1
  Tamworth B77 .... 251 D2
Jason Cl B77 .... 250 B3
Jason St ST5 .... 56 A4
Jasper Cl Barlaston ST12 .... 88 C2
  Newcastle-u-L ST5 .... 56 A4
Jasper St ST1 .... 282 B2
Java Cres ST4 .... 88 A4
Jay Rd DY6 .... 275 E4
Jaycean Ave ST6 .... 41 F2
Jean Cl ST6 .... 42 A1
Jedburgh Ave WV6 .... 254 C2
Jeddo St WV2 .... 266 B4
Jeffcock Rd WV3 .... 266 A4
Jefferson St ST6 .... 41 E2
Jeffrey Ave WV4 .... 266 C3
Jeffrey Cl WS15 .... 178 B2
Jeffs Ave WV2 .... 266 B4
Jenkins St ST6 .... 56 C4
Jenkinson Ct ST5 .... 70 C4
Jenkinstown Rd WS12 .... 211 D3
Jenks Ave DY7 .... 277 F3
Jenks Rd WV5 .... 269 F3
Jennet's La WS15 .... 179 F1
Jenny Walkers La WV6 .... 254 B1
Jensen Rd DE14 .... 185 D4
Jephson Rd DE14 .... 185 D4
Jerbourg Cl ST5 .... 70 C2
Jeremy Cl ST4 .... 71 F3
Jeremy Rd WV4 .... 266 B3
Jerningham St ST16 .... 155 E2
Jerome Dr WS11 .... 228 A3
Jerome Prim Sch The
  WS11 .... 227 F3
Jerome Rd WS11 .... 228 A3
Jerome Way WS7 .... 229 E4
Jerry's La WS14 .... 248 A4
Jersey Cl Congleton CW12 .... 6 A1
  Newcastle-u-L ST5 .... 70 C2
Jervis Cres B74 .... 257 E2
Jervis La ST15 .... 104 B2
Jervis Rd Stone ST15 .... 120 A4
  Tamworth B77 .... 261 F3
Jervis St ST1 .... 282 C4
Jervison St ST3 .... 73 E3
Jesmond Cl WS12 .... 211 D3
Jesmond Gr ST3 .... 88 C4
Jessie Rd WS9 .... 245 D1
Jew's La DY1 .... 271 F2
Jinny Cl DE65 .... 146 B4
Joan Eaton's Cross ST20 .... 189 F4
Joan St WV2 .... 266 C3
Joanhurst Cres ST1 .... 282 A1
Jockey Field DY3 .... 271 E4
Jodrell View ST7 .... 41 D4
Joeys La WV8 .... 239 E2
John Amery Dr ST17 .... 174 B3
John Ball Ct WS15 .... 178 B2
John Bamford Cty
  Prim Sch ST6 .... 178 B1
John Bright St ST1 .... 282 C4
John Donne St ST5 .... 178 B1
John O' Gaunt's Rd ST5 .... 284 A3
John of Rolleston
  Prim Sch DE13 .... 147 D2
John Offley Rd CW3 .... 68 C3
John St Biddulph ST8 .... 27 E4
  Brierley Hill DY8 .... 275 F1
  Cannock, High Town WS11 .... 210 A2
  Cannock, Wimblebury WS12 .... 210 C2
  Hanley ST1 .... 282 B2
  Leek ST13 .... 30 C3
  Newcastle-u-L ST5 .... 284 D3
  Newcastle-u-L, Knutton ST5 .... 55 F1

John St continued
  Stafford ST16 .... 156 A2
  Swadlincote DE11 .... 186 C3
  Tamworth B77 .... 250 C2
  Uttoxeter ST14 .... 126 A4
John Taylor High Sch The
  DE13 .... 183 F1
John Till St WS11 .... 178 C1
John Wheeldon Cty
  Prim Sch ST16 .... 155 F3
John Wood CE Inf Sch
  WS11 .... 226 C4
Johndory B77 .... 261 E3
Johns Ave WS15 .... 198 B2
Johns La WS6 .... 227 D2
Johnsgate ST19 .... 223 E4
Johnson Ave ST5 .... 56 A2
Johnson Cl
  Congleton CW12 .... 6 A1
  Lichfield WS13 .... 214 B1
  Ranton ST18 .... 153 E3
  Rugeley WS11 .... 178 B1
Johnson Cres ST10 .... 61 E1
Johnson Gr ST15 .... 120 B3
Johnson Rd
  Burntwood WS7 .... 228 C4
  Cannock WS11 .... 209 E2
  Uttoxeter ST14 .... 111 D1
Johnson St
  Kingsbury CV9 .... 262 B1
  Newcastle-u-L ST5 .... 55 E4
  Wolv, Blakenhall WV2 .... 266 B4
  Wolv, Cinder Hill DY3 .... 266 C1
Johnstone Ave ST9 .... 59 E2
Joiner's Square Ind Est
  ST1 .... 282 C1
Joiner's Square Prim Sch
  ST1 .... 282 C1
Jolley St ST6 .... 42 B1
Jolliffe St 7 ST13 .... 30 C3
Jolpool La ST18 .... 121 E2
Jolt La ST18 .... 172 C3
Jolyon St ST4 .... 73 D3
Jonathan Rd ST4 .... 88 B3
Jones Cl ST17 .... 174 B4
Jones La
  Burntwood WS7 .... 229 F4
  Great Wyrley WS6 .... 227 D1
  Rugeley WS15 .... 196 B4
Jones Rd WV12 .... 242 B1
Jonkel Ave B77 .... 262 A3
Jordan Ave DE13 .... 147 F1
Jordan Cl Alrewas WS13 .... 215 E3
  Lichfield WS13 .... 231 D4
  Sutton Coldfield B75 .... 258 A1
Jordan Croft WS13 .... 215 E4
Jordan Rd B75 .... 258 B1
Jordan Way
  Aldridge WS9 .... 245 D1
  Stone ST15 .... 120 A4
Jordon St ST1 .... 282 A1
Joseph Dix Dr WS15 .... 178 B1
Joseph St 22 ST6 .... 56 C4
Josiah Wedgwood St ST1 .... 57 D2
Jowett B77 .... 250 B1
Joyberry Dr DY8 .... 279 F2
Joyce Ave ST6 .... 42 A1
Joyce's La ST17 .... 194 A4
Jubilee Ave ST1 .... 57 D2
Jubilee Cl Biddulph ST8 .... 27 E4
  Great Wyrley WS6 .... 226 C1
Jubilee Ct ST14 .... 126 A4
Jubilee Dr ST10 .... 62 B2
Jubilee Rd
  Newcastle-u-L ST5 .... 56 B2
  Trentham ST4 .... 87 F4
Jubilee Sq DE6 .... 81 E4
Jubilee St WS13 .... 178 B1
Jubilee Terr ST13 .... 30 B3
Judes wlk WS13 .... 213 F1
Judgefield La ST6 .... 28 A1
Judith Gr ST4 .... 72 B3
Jug Bank Ashley TF9 .... 100 A2
  Hanley ST6 .... 57 D3
Julian Cl WS6 .... 227 D2
Junction Rd
  Brierley Hill DY8 .... 275 F1
  Leek ST13 .... 30 C2
Junction The DY8 .... 279 F4
June Cres B77 .... 250 C2
June Rd ST4 .... 73 D3
Juniper B77 .... 251 D2
Juniper Cl Cannock WS12 .... 211 D3
  Meir ST3 .... 90 A3
Juniper Row TF10 .... 168 C1
Jupiter St ST6 .... 42 B1
Justin Cl ST5 .... 56 B3

Kara Pl ST4 .... 88 A4
Kay Dr DE11 .... 186 C3
Kaydor Cl ST9 .... 59 D2
Kayne Cl DY6 .... 275 E4
Kean Cl WS13 .... 213 F1
Kearsley Way ST3 .... 88 C4
Kearyn St ST4 .... 72 A3
Keates St 8 ST6 .... 56 C4
Keating Gdns B75 .... 258 A2
Keats Ave
  Cannock WS11 .... 209 F3
  Stafford ST17 .... 174 B4
Keats Cl Sedgley DY3 .... 271 D3
  Sutton Coldfield B74 .... 257 F3
  Tamworth B79 .... 249 F4
Keats Gdns ST7 .... 41 D4
Keats Rd WV10 .... 241 D1

Keble CI Burntwood WS7 ...... **229** E4
Burton u T DE15 .... **167** E1
Cannock WS11 .... **226** C4
Keble Way ST3 .... **73** D1
Keble Wlk B79 .... **250** A3
Kedleston CI
Burton u T DE13 .... **147** E1
Walsall WS3 .... **243** D2
Kedleston Rd ST6 .... **42** A1
Keele L Ctr ST5 .... **70** A4
Keele Rd Keele ST5 .... **70** B4
Newcastle-u-L ST5 .... **70** B4
Keele Service Area ST5 ..... **69** F2
Keele St ST6 .... **41** E2
Keeling Dr WS11 .... **209** D1
Keeling Rd ST10 .... **76** C2
Keeling St ST5 .... **56** B3
Keelings Dr ST4 .... **71** F2
Keelings Rd ST1 .... **57** F3
Keene CI ST6 .... **42** C2
Keeper's CI WS7 .... **229** D3
Keepers CI
Brownhills WS9 .... **244** C2
Kingswinford DY6 .... **275** D4
Lichfield WS14 .... **231** F4
Keepers La Codsall WV8 .... **239** D1
Wolv WV8 .... **255** D4
Keepers Rd B74 .... **257** E3
Keir PI DY8 .... **279** F4
Keld Ave ST17 .... **174** A4
Keldy CI WV6 .... **255** F3
Kelham Rd ST4 .... **73** D3
Kelly Ave WS15 .... **196** C3
Kelly Gn ST6 .... **42** A3
Kelmore CI ST3 .... **283** B4
Kelsall CI ST3 .... **42** A1
Kelsall Way ST7 .... **39** E1
Kelsow Gdns WV6 .... **254** B2
Kelvedon Way WS15 .... **178** B3
Kelvin Ave ST1 .... **57** E4
Kelvin Dr WS11 .... **210** A2
Kelvin St ST5 .... **56** B2
Kemball Ave ST4 .... **72** B2
Kemball Specl Sch ST4 ..... **72** C3
Kemberton CI WV3 .... **255** E1
Kemberton Rd WV3 .... **255** E1
Kemnay Ave ST4 .... **42** A4
Kempson Rd ST19 .... **192** C1
Kempthorne Ave WV10 .... **240** C1
Kempthorne Gdns WS3 .... **243** D1
Kempthorne Rd ST1 .... **282** C1
Kempton CI WS12 .... **211** D3
Kempton Dr WS6 .... **226** C1
Kempton Gr ST10 .... **76** C3
Kempton Rd DE15 .... **167** D2
Kempton Way DY8 .... **279** F2
Kendal Stafford ST17 .... **174** A4
Wolv WV6 .... **255** F3
Kendal Ct Brownhills WS9 .. **244** C2
Cannock WS11 .... **226** A4
Kendal Gr ST2 .... **58** B1
Kendal PI ST5 .... **71** D3
Kendal Rise WV6 .... **255** F3
Kendall Rise DY6 .... **275** F3
Kendlewood Rd DY10 ...... **280** A1
Kendrick St ST3 .... **283** D3
Kenelyn Cres ST3 .... **72** C2
Kenilworth Ave DE13 ...... **166** B4
Kenilworth CI
Kingswinford DY6 .... **275** E1
Market Drayton TF9 .... **97** F1
Penkridge ST19 .... **208** A4
Kenilworth Cres WS11 ..... **266** C2
Kenilworth Ct WS11 .... **209** E1
Kenilworth Dr WS11 .... **209** E2
Kenilworth Gr 🗉 Meir ST3 .. **73** F1
Newcastle-u-L ST5 .... **56** C2
Kenilworth Rd
Perton WV6 .... **254** C2
Tamworth B77 .... **250** C2
Kenley Ave ST9 .... **43** F4
Kenmore Ave WS12 .... **209** F4
Kennedy CI B77 .... **250** B1
Kennedy Cres DY3 .... **271** E2
Kennedy Ct DY8 .... **279** F3
Kennedy Rd ST4 .... **88** A4
Kennedy Way ST16 .... **155** D4
Kennedy Wlk ST9 .... **59** D2
Kennermont Rd ST2 .... **58** B3
Kennet B77 .... **250** B1
Kennet CI Brownhills WS8 .. **228** B1
Newcastle-u-L ST5 .... **71** D2
Kenrick CI CW3 .... **67** E1
Kensington CI ST15 .... **120** B3
Kensington Ct ST4 .... **71** F2
Kensington Dr B79 .... **257** F3
Kensington Gdns DY8 ...... **275** E1
Kensington PI WS11 .... **227** E4
Kensington Rd
Burton u T DE15 .... **167** D2
Stoke-on-T ST4 .... **72** A2
Kensworth CI ST5 .... **71** D2
Kent Ave B78 .... **249** F1
Kent CI WS9 .... **245** D1
Kent Dr ST9 .... **43** F3
Kent Gr Newcastle-u-L ST5 .. **55** F4
Stone ST15 .... **104** C1
Kent PI Cannock WS12 ...... **210** C1
Fenton ST4 .... **72** C3
Kent Rd Burton u T DE15 .. **185** F3
Stafford ST17 .... **175** D4
Stourbridge DY8 .... **279** E4
Wolv WV2 .... **266** C4
Kent St DY3 .... **271** F3
Kentish CI ST17 .... **174** A4

Kentmere CI Longton ST4 ...... **73** D3
Penkridge ST19 .... **193** D1
Stafford ST17 .... **174** A4
Kentmere PI ST5 .... **71** D3
Kenton Ave WV6 .... **255** F2
Kentwell B79 .... **249** E4
Kenworthy Rd ST16 .... **155** F3
Kenworthy St ST6 .... **41** F2
Kepler B79 .... **249** F4
Kerria Ctr B77 .... **251** D2
Kerria Rd B77 .... **251** D2
Kerridge CI WV9 .... **240** A1
Kerry La ST1 .... **133** E3
Kersbrook CI ST4 .... **88** B3
Kervis Gr ST3 .... **90** A3
Kesterton Rd B74 .... **257** F3
Kesteven Rd ST2 .... **58** A2
Kestrel B77 .... **262** A3
Kestrel Ave ST3 .... **90** B4
Kestrel CI Biddulph ST8 ..... **27** D3
Newport TF10 .... **169** D3
Stafford ST17 .... **156** B1
Uttoxeter ST14 .... **126** A3
Whittington WS14 .... **232** C3
Kestrel Dr TF9 .... **99** E2
Kestrel Gr WS12 .... **210** B1
Kestrel La ST10 .... **76** C2
Kestrel Rd B74 .... **257** F3
Kestrel Rise WV6 .... **255** F4
Kestrel Way
Burton u T DE15 .... **167** E2
Cheslyn Hay WS6 .... **226** B1
Keswick Dr DY6 .... **275** E3
Keswick Gr Aldridge B74 .... **256** C1
Stafford ST17 .... **174** A4
Keswick PI ST5 .... **71** D3
Ketley Rd DY6 .... **275** F4
Kettering Ct ST1 .... **57** F1
Kettlebank Rd DY3 .... **271** D1
Kettlebrook Rd B77 .... **250** B2
Ketton CI ST5 .... **42** A4
Kewstoke CI WV12 .... **242** B1
Kewstoke Rd WV12 .... **242** B1
Key CI WS12 .... **210** B2
Keyes Dr WS12 .... **270** B1
Keynsham Wlk ST6 .... **42** B1
Keyspark Rd WS12 .... **210** C2
Keystone La WS15 .... **196** C4
Keystone Rd WS15 .... **196** C4
Keyworth Wlk ST2 .... **58** A1
Kibblestone Rd ST15 .... **105** E2
Kibworth Gr ST1 .... **282** B4
Kidbrooke PI ST4 .... **88** B4
Kiddemore Green Rd
ST19 .... **222** B3
Kidderminster Rd
Kingswinford DY6 .... **275** D4
Kinver DY7, DY10 .... **281** E2
Kidderminster Rd S DY9 ... **281** F2
Kidsgrove Bank ST7 .... **41** D4
Kidsgrove Rd ST6 .... **41** E4
Kidsgrove Sports Ctr ST7 .. **25** F1
Kidsgrove Sta ST7 .... **25** F1
Kielder CI WS12 .... **210** C1
Kilburn Dr DY6 .... **270** C1
Kilburn PI ST2 .... **57** F1
Kilburn Way DE11 .... **186** C3
Kilbye CI B77 .... **261** F3
Kildare St ST3 .... **283** C2
Kilmorie Rd WS11 .... **209** E1
Kiln La ST13 .... **30** B3
Kiln Way B78 .... **251** F1
Kilnbank Cres TF9 .... **112** B4
Kilnbank Rd TF9 .... **112** B4
Kilndown CI ST1 .... **57** D1
Kilsby Gr ST2 .... **43** D1
Kimberlee Ave DY10 .... **280** A2
Kimberley B77 .... **261** F4
Kimberley CI B74 .... **257** D1
Kimberley Dr
Burton u T DE15 .... **167** D2
Uttoxeter ST14 .... **110** C1
Kimberley Grange ST5 ..... **284** B4
Kimberley Rd Hanley ST1 .. **57** D2
Newcastle-u-L ST5 .... **284** B4
Kimberley St
Longton ST3 .... **283** B2
Wolv WV3 .... **266** A4
Kimberley Way
Rugeley WS15 .... **196** C3
Stafford ST17 .... **174** A4
Kinder CI ST5 .... **55** D1
Kineton Rise DY3 .... **266** B1
Kinfare Dr WV6 .... **255** D2
Kinfare Rise DY3 .... **271** F2
King Edward PI DE14 ...... **166** A2
King Edward St ST10 .... **76** C2
King Edward VI Cty
High Sch ST17 .... **155** E1
King Edward VI High Sch
WS14 .... **231** E3
King Edward VI L Ctr
WS14 .... **231** E3
King Edward's Row
🗉 WV2 .... **266** B4
King George St ST1 .... **282** C4
King St Audley ST7 .... **39** E1
Biddulph ST8 .... **27** E4
Blymhill TF10 .... **189** D1
Brownhills WS9 .... **244** C4
Burntwood WS7 .... **228** C3
Burton u T DE14 .... **166** B1
Fenton ST4 .... **72** C3
Kidsgrove, Dove Bank ST7 .. **26** A1
Kidsgrove, Talke Pits ST7 .. **40** B3
Leek ST13 .... **30** C4
Longton ST3, ST4 .... **283** B4
Newcastle-u-L ST5 .... **284** C3

King St continued
Newcastle-u-L, Chesterton
ST5 .... **55** F4
Newcastle-u-L, Cross Heath
ST5 .... **56** A2
Rugeley WS15 .... **196** C4
Stourbridge DY8 .... **279** F3
Tamworth B79 .... **250** A3
Yoxall DE13 .... **182** A2
King William St
Brierley Hill DY8 .... **279** F4
Tunstall ST6 .... **41** F2
King's Ave
Newcastle-u-L ST5 .... **56** B3
Stone ST15 .... **105** D1
King's Bromley La WS15 .. **198** B3
King's Croft ST4 .... **56** B1
King's Hill Rd WS14 .... **231** E3
King's La B79 .... **236** B3
Kingcross St ST3 .... **283** C3
Kingcup Rd ST17 .... **174** C3
Kingfisher B77 .... **262** A3
Kingfisher CI
Madeley ST3 .... **68** C4
Newport TF10 .... **168** C3
Sedgley DY3 .... **266** B1
Kingfisher Cres
Blythe Bridge ST11 .... **106** C4
Cheadle ST10 .... **76** C2
Kingfisher Dr
Cannock WS12 .... **210** B3
Stourbridge DY8 .... **279** E2
Kingfisher Gr ST6 .... **42** B2
Kingfisher Way ST4 .... **126** A3
Kingfisher Wlk ST19 .... **207** F4
Kingham CI DY3 .... **271** E1
Kings Ave Cannock WS12 .. **210** B3
Market Drayton TF9 .... **112** A4
Kings Bromley Rd DE13 ... **200** C1
Kings Ct B75 .... **258** A2
Kings PI ST4 .... **56** B1
Kings Rd Hopton ST16 ..... **156** B4
Sedgley DY3 .... **271** F4
Shareshill WV10 .... **225** D3
Trentham ST4 .... **72** A1
Kings Terr ST4 .... **56** B1
Kingsbridge Ave ST5 .... **71** D3
Kingsbridge Gr DE15 ...... **167** D2
Kingsbury Gr ST1 .... **57** F3
Kingsclere Gr ST1 .... **57** F4
Kingsclere Wlk WV4 .... **265** E3
Kingsdale CI ST3 .... **90** A4
Kingsdale Croft DE13 ...... **166** B4
Kingsdene Ave DY6 .... **275** E2
Kingsdown Mews ST5 ...... **71** E2
Kingsdown Rd WS7 .... **211** F1
Kingsfield CI ST8 .... **27** E4
Kingsfield Fst Sch ST8 ..... **27** E4
Kingsfield Oval ST4 .... **56** B1
Kingsfield Rd
Biddulph ST8 .... **27** E4
Stoke-on-T ST4 .... **56** B1
Kingsford La
Cookley DY7 .... **277** E1
Kinver DY7 .... **277** E1
Kingsford PI ST4 .... **90** A4
Kingshayes Rd WS9 .... **245** D1
Kingside Gr ST4 .... **88** B3
Kingsland Ave ST4 .... **71** F3
Kingsland CI ST15 .... **120** B4
Kingsland Ct ST15 .... **120** B4
Kingsland Rd ST15 .... **120** B4
Kingsley Ave
Cannock WS12 .... **210** B4
Wolv WV6 .... **255** D2
Kingsley CI Kidsgrove ST7 .. **40** B3
Stafford ST17 .... **174** C4
Tamworth B79 .... **250** A3
Kingsley Gdns WV8 .... **238** C2
Kingsley Gr DY3 .... **271** F2
Kingsley Rd
Burton u T DE14 .... **166** B3
Cheddleton ST13 .... **60** A2
Congleton CW12 .... **6** A2
Consall ST9 .... **60** A2
Kidsgrove ST7 .... **40** B3
Kingswinford DY6 .... **275** D3
Stafford ST17 .... **174** C4
Kingsley St ST3 .... **74** A1
Kingsley View ST15 .... **45** E3
Kingsley Wood Rd WS15 .. **195** E4
Kingslow Ave WV6 .... **265** E3
Kingsmead High Sch
WS12 .... **210** B2
Kingsmead Hospl ST16 .... **155** F2
Kingsmead Rd ST3 .... **89** F4
Kingsnorth PI ST3 .... **90** A3
Kingston Ave Hanley ST1 .. **57** F4
Stafford ST16 .... **156** A2
Kingston CI B79 .... **250** B4
Kingston Dr ST5 .... **120** A3
Kingston Hill Ct ST16 ...... **156** B2
Kingston PI Biddulph ST6 .. **16** C1
Norton-in-t-M ST6 .... **42** C2
Kingston Rd DE15 .... **167** D1
Kingston Way DY6 .... **275** E4
Kingsway Cannock WS11 .. **210** A2
Essington WV11 .... **242** A2
Stafford ST16 .... **155** E1
Stoke-on-T ST4 .... **72** A4
Stourbridge DY8 .... **279** E4
Kingsway E ST5 .... **71** D3
Kingsway W ST5 .... **71** D3
Kingswear Ave WV6 .... **254** C2
Kingswell Rd ST4 .... **56** B1
Kingswinford PI ST1 .... **57** E4
Kingswinford Sch DY6 ..... **275** E4
Kingswood ST7 .... **26** A1

Kingswood Ave WS11 ...... **226** B4
Kingswood Ctr WV7 .... **237** F1
Kingswood Dr
Great Wyrley WS11 .... **227** D2
Norton Canes WS11 .... **227** F3
Kingswood Gdns WV4 ..... **265** F3
Kingswood Rd
Albrighton WV7 .... **237** E2
Kingswinford DY6 .... **275** E2
Kinlet CI WV3 .... **265** D4
Kinloch Dr DY1 .... **271** F2
Kinnersley Ave ST7 .... **40** C4
Kinnersley St ST1 .... **26** A1
Kinross Ave WS12 .... **209** F4
Kinsall Gn B77 .... **262** B3
Kinsey St ST5 .... **55** D1
Kinver Cres WS9 .... **245** E1
Kinver Dr WV4 .... **265** E3
Kinver Edge DY7 .... **277** F2
Kinver L Ctr DY7 .... **278** A3
Kinver La DY11 .... **280** A4
Kinver Rd Enville DY7 ...... **277** F4
Kinver DY7 .... **277** F4
Kinver St
Chell Heath ST6 .... **42** B1
Kingswinford DY8 .... **275** F1
Kiplass La ST18 .... **121** E2
Kipling Ave WS7 .... **212** A1
Kipling Rd Sedgley DY3 .... **271** D3
Wolv WV10 .... **240** B1
Kipling Rise B79 .... **249** F4
Kipling Way ST2 .... **58** B1
Kirby St ST6 .... **57** D3
Kirk St ST6 .... **42** B1
Kirkbride CI ST3 .... **73** E2
Kirkham St ST4 .... **72** A3
Kirkland La ST4 .... **72** A3
Kirkland Way B78 .... **260** A4
Kirkside Gr WS8 .... **244** C4
Kirkstall CI WS3 .... **242** C1
Kirkstall Cres WS3 .... **242** C1
Kirkstall PI ST5 .... **71** D3
Kirkstone Cres WV5 .... **269** F3
Kirkup Wlk ST3 .... **283** A3
Kirkwall Gr ST2 .... **43** D1
Kirstead Gdns WV6 .... **255** D2
Kirtley B77 .... **250** C1
Kirton Gr WV6 .... **255** E2
Kitchen La WV11 .... **241** F1
Kite Gr Kidsgrove ST7 ...... **26** B1
Meir ST3 .... **90** A3
Kitling Greaves La DE13 ... **166** A4
Kitlings La ST17 .... **175** F4
Kittoe Rd B74 .... **258** A2
Kitwood Ave B78 .... **262** C3
Knarsdale CI 🗉 ST3 .... **73** E3
Knaves Castle Ave WS8 .... **228** C1
Knenhall WS15 .... **105** F4
Knenhall La ST15 .... **89** F1
Knight Ave ST16 .... **156** A2
Knight La ST10 .... **78** C1
Knight Rd WS7 .... **211** F1
Knight St ST6 .... **41** E2
Knightley CW3 .... **68** C3
Knightley CI ST20 .... **171** E3
Knightley Rd ST20 .... **171** E4
Knightley Way ST20 .... **171** E4
Knighton CI B74 .... **257** F2
Knighton Dr B74 .... **257** F2
Knighton Rd
Cannock WS12 .... **210** A2
Sutton Coldfield B74 ...... **257** E2
Knights Ave WV6 .... **255** F3
Knights CI ST19 .... **207** F4
Knights Cres WV6 .... **255** F4
Knights Croft ST5 .... **69** F4
Knights Ct
Burton u T DE13 .... **147** F1
Norton Canes WS11 .... **228** A2
Knights Hill WS9 .... **256** A4
Knightsbridge CI B74 ...... **257** F2
Knightsbridge Way DE13 .. **166** B4
Knightsfield Rd DE13 ...... **144** C1
Knivedon La ST13 .... **31** D3
Knoll CI WS7 .... **229** D3
Knoll Croft WS9 .... **245** E1
Knoll The DY6 .... **275** F3
Knotty La CW12, ST8 ...... **17** D4
Knowl St ST4 .... **72** A4
Knowlbank Rd ST7 .... **53** F4
Knowle La WS14 .... **231** D2
Knowle Rd Biddulph ST8 .. **27** E4
Stafford ST17 .... **175** E4
Knowle Wood View ST3 ... **72** C3
Knowles Hill DE13 .... **147** D2
Knowsley La ST7 .... **25** F2
Knowsley Rd ST9 .... **44** B2
Knox Rd WV2 .... **266** B3
Knox's Grave La WS14 ..... **248** B4
Knutsford Rd ST7 .... **25** D3
Knutton CE Jun Sch ST5 .. **55** E1
Knutton Inf Sch ST5 .... **55** F1
Knutton La ST5 .... **55** F1
Knutton Rd ST5 .... **56** B3
Knutton Recn Ctr ST5 ..... **55** F1
Knype CI ST5 .... **56** A4
Knype Way Biddulph ST8 ... **27** D3
Newcastle-u-L ST5 .... **56** A4
Knypersley Fst Sch ST8 .... **27** D3
Kohima Dr DY8 .... **279** F3
Kurtus B77 .... **261** D2
Kyffin Rd ST2 .... **58** A2
Kyle CI WV10 .... **240** A1
Kynaston Cres WV8 .... **239** D1

Laburnam CI ST7 .... **40** C4
Laburnham Rd DY6 .... **275** F1

Laburnum Ave
Cannock WS11 .... **226** C4
Tamworth B79 .... **250** A4
Laburnum CI
Brownhills WS3 .... **244** A1
Cannock WS11 .... **226** C4
Forsbrook ST11 .... **91** D3
Kinver DY7 .... **277** F3
Market Drayton TF9 .... **97** F3
Seighford ST18 .... **135** D1
Stourbridge DY8 .... **279** F4
Laburnum Gr
Burntwood WS7 .... **228** C3
Fenton ST3 .... **72** C2
Laburnum PI Meir ST3 ..... **89** F4
Newcastle-u-L ST5 .... **40** B1
Laburnum Rd
Brownhills WS9 .... **245** D2
Burton u T DE15 .... **185** F3
Swadlincote DE11 .... **186** C3
Wolv WV4 .... **266** C2
Laburnum St DY8 .... **279** F4
Laches La WV10 .... **224** C1
Lad La ST5 .... **284** B3
Ladbrook Gr DY3 .... **271** D2
Ladderedge Leek ST13 ..... **30** B1
Longsdon ST13 .... **30** B1
Ladford Covert Ind Pk
ST18 .... **134** C1
Ladfordfields Ind Est
ST18 .... **134** B1
Ladfordfields Ind Pk
ST18 .... **153** F4
Ladle End La DE12 .... **184** B1
Lady Grey's Wlk DY8 .... **279** E3
Lady Hill Terr WS15 .... **196** A4
Ladybank Gr ST3 .... **88** C4
Ladydale CI ST13 .... **30** C2
Ladygates CW3 .... **53** D3
Ladymoor La ST6 .... **28** A2
Ladysmith Rd ST1 .... **57** D2
Ladysmith St ST3 .... **283** B2
Ladywell CI
Burton u T DE13 .... **147** F1
Wombourne WV5 .... **270** A4
Ladywell Rd ST6 .... **41** E2
Ladywood Rd B74 .... **258** A1
Lagonda B77 .... **250** C2
Lagonda CI ST8 .... **27** D3
Lagrange B79 .... **249** F3
Lair The B78 .... **262** C4
Lakeland Dr B77 .... **262** A4
Lakenheath B79 .... **250** B4
Lakeside Betley CW3 .... **53** D3
Bosley SK11 .... **7** E4
Little Aston B74 .... **257** D3
Lakeside ST5 .... **85** E2
Lakeside Dr WS11 .... **228** A3
Lakeside Prim Sch B77 .... **250** C1
Lakeside View WS15 .... **198** A2
Lakewood Dr ST12 .... **88** C2
Lakewood Gr ST1 .... **57** D2
Lamb Cres WV5 .... **269** F3
Lamb La ST15 .... **119** F4
Lamb St Hanley ST1 .... **282** B3
Kidsgrove ST7 .... **26** A1
Lambert Ct DY6 .... **275** E4
Lambert Dr WS7 .... **229** D4
Lambert Rd ST14 .... **110** C1
Lambert St ST4 .... **41** F2
Lambert's La CW12 .... **15** F4
Lambourn CI WS3 .... **243** E1
Lambourn PI ST3 .... **88** C4
Lambourne CI
Great Wyrley WS6 .... **226** C2
Lichfield WS14 .... **231** F4
Lamborne Dr ST2 .... **43** E1
Lamerton Gr ST3 .... **73** F1
Lammas Rd DY8 .... **275** E2
Lammascote Rd ST16 ...... **155** F2
Lamotte CI ST4 .... **73** D3
Lamprey B77 .... **261** E3
Lanark Wlks ST5 .... **70** C4
Lancaster Ave
Aldridge WS9 .... **256** A4
Blythe Bridge ST11 .... **90** C1
Leek ST13 .... **30** C4
Newcastle-u-L ST5 .... **284** D2
Lancaster Cres ST5 .... **71** E4
Lancaster Dr
Norton-in-t-M ST6 .... **42** C2
Tutbury DY3 .... **146** A3
Lancaster Gdns WV4 ...... **265** F3
Lancaster PI WS3 .... **243** E1
Lancaster Rd
Newcastle-u-L ST5 .... **284** D2
Stafford ST17 .... **175** D4
Lance Dr WV2 .... **211** F1
Lancelot Dr DE13 .... **147** F1
Lanchester CI
Biddulph ST8 .... **27** D3
Tamworth B79 .... **249** F4
Lancia CI ST8 .... **27** D3
Lancing Ave ST17 .... **175** D4
Lander CI ST15 .... **120** B4
Lander PI ST6 .... **42** A3
Landon St ST3 .... **283** C3
Landor Cres WS15 .... **196** C4
Landport Rd WV1 .... **266** C4
Landrake Gr ST6 .... **41** F4
Landsberg B79 .... **249** F3
Landseer PI ST5 .... **55** F3
Landywood Ent Pk WS6 ... **242** C4
Landywood Gn WS6 .... **226** C1
Landywood La WS6 .... **226** C1
Landywood Prim Sch
WS6 .... **242** C4

Landywood Sta WS6 226 C1
Lane Farm Gr ST1 57 F4
Lane Green Ave WV8 239 E1
Lane Green Cty Fst Sch WV8 239 D2
Lane Green Rd WV8 239 E1
Lane Green Sh Par WV8 239 D2
Lane Head SK17 13 D4
Lane The ST18 174 A2
Lane's Cl DE13 199 E3
Lanehead Rd ST1 56 C2
Lanehead Wlk WS15 178 B1
Lanes Cl WV5 269 F3
Langdale Cl WS8 244 C3
Langdale Cres ST1 57 E4
Langdale Dr WS11 226 B4
Langdale Gn WS11 226 B4
Langdale Jun & Inf Schs ST5 71 D3
Langdale Rd ST5 71 D3
Langer Cl DE14 185 D3
Langford Rd Bucknall ST2 58 B2
Newcastle-u-L ST5 71 D2
Langford St ST13 30 B3
Langham Gn B74 256 C1
Langham Rd ST2 43 D1
Langholm Dr WS12 210 C1
Langland Dr Longton ST3 73 D1
Sedgley DY3 271 E4
Langley Cl ST5 40 B1
Langley Gdns WV3 265 E4
Langley Rd
Lower Penn WV3 265 D4
Wolv WV3 265 D4
Langley St ST4 56 B1
Langot La ST21 115 E2
Langstone Rd DY1 271 F1
Langton Cres WS14 232 C3
Langton Ct Caverswall ST9 59 D2
Lichfield WS13 214 A1
Langtree Cl WS12 210 B1
Lanrick Gdns WS15 178 C1
Lansbury Cl ST17 174 C4
Lansbury Dr WS11 209 F2
Lansbury Gr ST3 74 A2
Lansbury Rd WS15 196 C3
Lansdell Ave ST5 56 A3
Lansdown Cl ST15 119 F3
Lansdowne Ave WV8 238 C1
Lansdowne Cl ST13 30 B3
Lansdowne Cres
Caverswall ST9 59 D2
Tamworth B77 261 E4
Lansdowne Cty Inf Sch DE14 166 B3
Lansdowne Rd
Branston DE14 184 C4
Stoke-on-T ST4 56 C1
Lansdowne St ST3 73 D1
Lansdowne Terr DE14 166 B3
Lansdowne Way
Rugeley WS15 178 B1
Stafford ST17 175 E3
Lant Cl DE13 199 E3
Lapley Ave ST16 155 D4
Lapley La ST19 206 B2
Lapley Rd ST19 205 E4
Lapper Ave WV4 266 C1
Lapwing B77 262 A3
Lapwing Cl WS6 226 B1
Lapwing Rd ST7 26 B2
Lapwood Ave DY6 275 F3
Lapworth Way TF10 169 D2
Lara Cl ST16 155 D2
Larch Cl Kidsgrove ST7 41 D4
Kinver DY7 278 B2
Lichfield WS14 231 F4
Larch Gr Fenton ST3 72 C1
Sedgley DY3 271 F4
Larch Pl ST5 55 F4
Larch Rd
Kingswinford DY6 275 F4
Rugeley WS15 196 C3
Swadlincote DE11 186 C3
Larches The TF10 168 C1
Larchfields ST15 120 A3
Larchmere Dr WV11 242 A2
Larchmount Cl ST4 88 A4
Larchwood Keele ST5 70 A3
Stafford ST17 175 E3
Larchwood Dr WS11 210 A2
Larcombe Dr WV4 266 B3
Lark Hall Cty Inf Sch B79 250 A4
Lark Rise ST14 126 A3
Larkfield ST7 26 A1
Larkhill La TF9 100 A2
Larkhill Rd DY8 279 E2
Larkholme Cl WS15 178 A1
Larkin Ave ST3 73 E2
Larkin Cl ST17 174 B4
Larksfield Rd ST6 42 B1
Larksmeadow Vale ST17 175 E3
Larkspur B77 261 E2
Larkspur Ave WS7 229 D2
Larkspur Dr WV10 241 D4
Larkspur Gr ST5 284 C4
Larkspur Way WS8 244 B3
Larkstone La DE6 34 C1
Larkswood Dr
Sedgley DY3 271 E4
Wolv WV4 265 E2
Lascelles St ST6 41 E1
Lask Edge Rd ST9 28 B4
Laski Cres ST3 74 A1
Latebrook Cl ST6 41 E4
Latham Cl DE15 167 E1
Latham Gr ST6 42 A4
Latherford Cl WV10 224 C3
Latherford La WV10 225 D2
Lathkill Dale DE11 186 C1
Latimer Way ST2 58 B1
Lauder Cl DY3 266 B1
Lauder Pl N ST2 73 F4
Lauder Pl S ST2 73 F4
Lauderdale Cl WS8 244 C3
Lauderdale Gdns WV10 240 C2
Launceston Cl B77 250 B1
Laurel Bank B79 250 A3
Laurel Cl WS14 231 E4
Laurel Cres ST9 59 D2
Laurel Dr Burntwood WS7 229 E4
Cannock WS12 210 C2
Kidsgrove ST7 26 C2
Newport TF10 168 C2
Laurel Gr Burton u T DE15 185 F3
Fenton ST3 72 B1
Stafford ST17 174 C4
Wolv WV4 265 F3
Laurel Rd DY1 271 F2
Laurels The WS15 196 C4
Lauren Cl ST4 72 C3
Laurence Gr WV6 255 F4
Lauriston Cl DY1 271 F2
Lavender Ave ST11 90 C3
Lavender Cl Codsall WV9 239 F2
Meir ST3 74 B3
Seighford ST18 135 E1
Lavender La DY8 279 E2
Lavender Lodge ST17 177 F4
Lavender Rd B77 250 C2
Laverock Gr CW3 68 C3
Lawford Ave WS14 231 F4
Lawley Cl WS4 244 A1
Lawley St ST3 73 E2
Lawn Ave DY8 279 F2
Lawn La Brewood WV9 240 A4
Cheswardine TF9 113 F1
Lawn Rd Stafford ST17 155 E1
Wolv WV2 266 C3
Lawn St DY8 279 F2
Lawnoaks Cl WS8 228 B1
Lawns The
Market Drayton TF9 97 E1
Rolleston DE13 147 D2
Uttoxeter ST14 111 D1
Lawnsfield Wlk ST16 136 B1
Lawnswood DY7 275 D2
Lawnswood Ave
Burntwood WS7 228 C3
Kingswinford DY8 275 E2
Wolv, Blakeley Green WV6 255 F4
Wolv, Parkfield WV4 266 C2
Lawnswood Cl WS11 210 B1
Lawnswood Dr
Brownhills WS9 245 D2
Kinver DY7 275 D1
Lawnswood Rd
Kingswinford DY8 275 E2
Sedgley DY3 271 E3
Lawnswood Rise WV6 255 F4
Lawrence Ct B79 250 A3
Lawrence Dr ST15 103 D2
Lawrence St Hanley ST1 282 A1
Stafford ST17 155 F1
Lawson Cl WS9 256 A2
Lawton Ave ST7 25 E2
Lawton Coppice ST7 25 F2
Lawton Cres ST8 27 E4
Lawton St Biddulph ST8 27 E4
Chell Heath ST6 42 A1
Kidsgrove ST7 26 B2
Lawtongate Est ST7 25 D2
Laxey Rd ST5 56 A2
Laxton Gr ST4 88 B2
Lazar La ST17 176 A3
Lazy Hill WS9 245 E1
Le More B74 258 A1
Lea Castle Hospl DY10 280 B2
Lea Cl ST5 85 E3
Lea Cres ST17 174 B4
Lea Gn ST16 155 E4
Lea Hall Dr WS7 211 E1
Lea Hall Ent Pk WS15 197 D3
Lea Hall La WS15 197 D3
Lea La Colton WS15 159 F1
Cookley DY10 280 A3
Great Wyrley WS6 227 D2
Lea Manor Dr WV4 265 F2
Lea Pl ST3 74 A1
Lea Rd Hixon ST18 139 F1
Stone ST15 119 F3
Wolv WV3 266 A4
Lea The ST4 88 A4
Lea Vale Rd DY8 279 E1
Lea Wlk WS11 210 A2
Leacliffe Way B74 256 C2
Leacote Dr WV6 255 E2
Leacroft ST15 120 B4
Leacroft Ave WV10 240 C1
Leacroft Cl WS9 245 D1
Leacroft La WS11 226 C3
Leacroft Rd
Kingswinford DY6 275 F4
Meir ST3 90 A4
Penkridge ST19 193 D1
Leadbeater Ave ST4 71 F3
Leadendale La ST3 89 F2
Leafdown Cl WS12 210 B2
Leafenden Ave WS7 229 D3
Leaford Way DY6 275 F3
Leaford Wlk ST2 57 F1
Leafy Glade B74 257 D2
Leafy Rise DY3 271 E2
Leahurst cl ST17 175 E3
Leaks Alley ST3 283 B2
Leam Dr WS7 229 E4
Leamington Cl WS11 226 B4
Leamington Gdns ST5 56 C2
Leamington Rd DE14 184 C4
Leander Cl
Burntwood WS7 211 F1
Great Wyrley WS6 226 C1
Leander Rise DE15 186 A4
Lear Rd WV5 270 A4
Leas The WV10 241 E4
Leasawe Cl ST18 158 B1
Leaside Ave WS15 198 B3
Leaside Rd ST4 71 F3
Leason Rd ST3 74 A1
Leason St ST4 72 A4
Leasowe Rd WS15 197 D3
Leasowe The WS13 214 A1
Leasowes Cty Jun & Inf Schs ST17 175 E4
Leasowes Dr Perton WV6 254 B2
Wolv WV4 265 E3
Leaswood Cl ST5 71 E1
Leaswood Pl ST5 71 E1
Leathermill La WS15 178 C1
Leathersley La
Scropton DE6 129 E1
Sudbury DE6 129 E1
Leawood Rd ST4 71 F2
Lebanon Gr WS7 228 C4
Ledbury Cl WS9 245 E1
Ledbury Cres ST1 57 F3
Ledstone Way ST3 73 F2
Lee Ct WS9 244 C2
Lee Gr ST5 71 D2
Leech Ave ST5 55 F3
Leech St ST5 284 C1
Leedham Ave B77 250 B3
Leedhams Croft DE12 202 B4
Leeds St ST4 72 C3
Leek Coll of F Ed ST13 30 C3
Leek Fst Sch ST13 31 D3
Leek High Sch ST13 31 D3
Leek La ST8 28 A4
Leek Morlands Hospl ST13 31 D3
Leek New Rd
Chell Heath ST6, ST1 57 E4
Norton-in-t-M ST6 42 C1
Leek Rd Bucknall ST2 58 A3
Caverswall ST9 59 F2
Cheadle ST10 76 B3
Cheddleton, Cellarhead ST9 59 F2
Cheddleton, Cheddleton Heath ST13 45 E4
Congleton CW12 16 A4
Consall ST10 60 B2
Endon ST9 43 F3
Endon, Brown Edge ST9 43 E4
Hanley ST1 57 F1
Kingsley ST10 60 B2
Longnor SK17 13 D3
Norton-in-t-M ST6 42 C2
Stoke-on-T ST4 72 B4
Wetton DE6 34 B2
Leekbrook Ind Est
Cheddleton ST13 45 F4
Leek ST13 30 C1
Leekbrook Way ST13 30 C1
Lees Cl WS15 197 D3
Lees La ST10 108 C1
Leese La
Acton Trussell ST17 175 D1
Stone ST15 105 F3
Leese St ST4 72 A4
Leet Ct WS15 198 A2
Legge La ST18 139 E1
Legge St
Newcastle-u-L ST5 284 C2
Wolv WV2 266 C3
Legion Cl WS11 228 A3
Legs La WV10 240 C2
Leicester Cl ST5 71 E3
Leicester Pl ST2 58 B1
Leicester St DE14 185 E4
Leigh Ave WS7 229 D4
Leigh Bank ST10 108 C4
Leigh Cl ST17 174 C3
Leigh La
Church Leigh ST10 108 B3
Tunstall ST6 41 E1
Upper Tean ST10 92 C1
Uttoxeter ST14 125 D4
Leigh Rd Congleton CW12 6 A3
Newport TF10 168 C1
Leigh St ST6 42 A1
Leighs Cl WS4 244 B1
Leighs Rd WS4 244 A1
Leighswood ST17 175 E4
Leighswood Ave WS9 256 A4
Leighswood Cl WS11 227 F3
Leighswood Gr WS9 256 A4
Leighswood Ind Est WS9 256 A4
Leighswood Inf Sch WS9 256 A4
Leighswood Jun Sch WS9 256 A4
Leighswood Rd WS9 256 A3
Leighton Cl
Norton-in-t-M ST9 43 E2
Sedgley DY1 271 F1
Uttoxeter ST14 126 B3
Leighton Rd
Uttoxeter ST14 126 B3
Wolv WV4 265 F3
Leisure La SK17 24 C3
Leisure Wlk B77 261 F3
Lema Way ST16 156 B2
Lennox Gdns WV3 266 A4
Lennox Rd ST3 283 D1
Lenthall Ave CW12 15 F4
Leofric Cl DE13 199 E3
Leomansley Cl WS13 230 C4
Leomansley Rd WS13 230 C4
Leomansley View WS13 230 C4
Leonard Ave
Kidderminster DY10 280 A1
Norton-in-t-M ST2 43 D2
Leonard Dr ST6 43 D4
Leonard Rd DY8 279 E3
Leonard St Chell Heath ST6 42 A1
Leek ST13 30 C3
Leonora St ST6 56 C4
Leopold St ST4 72 C3
Lerridge La ST20 131 F3
Lerryn Cl DY6 275 F3
Lerwick Cl DY6 275 F3
Lesley Dr DY6 275 F2
Leslie Rd B74 257 D1
Lesscroft Cl WV9 240 A2
Lessways Cl ST5 56 A4
Lessways Wlk 13 ST6 56 C4
Lester Gr B74 256 C1
Letchmere Cl WV6 253 E1
Letchmere La WV6 253 E1
Lethbridge Gdns ST17 174 A4
Levedale Cl ST16 155 D4
Levedale Rd
Bradley ST18 191 E4
Penkridge ST19 192 C1
Levels The WS15 196 C3
Leven Dr WV11 242 A1
Lever St WV2 266 B4
Leveson Ave WS6 226 C1
Leveson Rd
Essington WV11 241 F1
Trentham ST4 71 F1
Levett Rd Hopwas WS14 232 B1
Tamworth B77 251 D3
Levetts Fields WS14 231 E4
Levetts Hollow WS11 210 B2
Levetts Sq WS13 231 D4
Levington Cl WV6 254 C2
Levita Rd ST4 71 F2
Lewis Cl WS14 231 F4
Lewis Dr DE13 166 A4
Lewis St ST4 72 A4
Lewis's La DE13 199 E3
Lewisham Dr ST6 41 E4
Lewisham Rd WV10 240 A1
Lewthorne Rise WV4 266 B2
Lexham Pl ST3 73 F1
Lexington Gn ST17 174 A4
Ley Gdns ST3 283 A2
Ley Hill Rd B75 258 B1
Ley Rise DY3 266 B1
Leybourne Cres WV9 239 F1
Leycett La ST5 54 B1
Leycett Rd ST5 54 C2
Leyfield Rd ST4 88 A3
Leyfields WS13 214 A1
Leyfields Farm Mews DE13 165 E4
Leyland Ave WV3 255 F1
Leyland Croft WS3 243 F2
Leyland Dr WS15 178 C1
Leyland Gn ST6 42 A3
Leyland Rd B77 250 C2
Leys Dr ST5 70 C2
Leys La ST2 43 E2
Leys The DE11 186 C3
Liberty Pk ST17 174 A4
Liberty Rd B77 261 F3
Libra Cl B79 249 F4
Libra Pl ST6 41 F3
Lichen Cl WS12 209 E3
Lichfield Bsns Ctr WS13 214 B1
Lichfield Cathedral Sch WS13 231 D4
Lichfield City Sta WS14 231 D4
Lichfield Cl ST5 55 E1
Lichfield Coll WS13 231 D4
Lichfield Ct ST17 155 F1
Lichfield Dr Colwich ST18 158 A1
Hopwas B78 249 D4
Lichfield Rd
Abbots Bromley WS15 161 D2
Armitage WS15 198 B2
Barton Turn DE14 184 B2
Branston DE14 184 B2
Brownhills, Gatehouse Trad Est WS8 245 D4
Brownhills, Highbridge WS3 244 A3
Brownhills, Shelfield WS4 244 B1
Burntwood, Burntwood Green WS7 229 E3
Burntwood, New Town WS7 229 E1
Cannock WS11 226 C4
Hamstall Ridware WS15 180 C1
Kidsgrove ST7 40 B4
King's Bromley DE13 199 D3
Sandon ST18 137 E4
Stafford ST17 155 F1
Stone ST15 120 A4
Sutton Coldfield B74 258 A2
Tamworth B78, B79 249 F3
Walsall, New Invention WS3, WS4, WS8, WS9 242 C1
Walsall, Wallington Heath WS3 243 E1
Lichfield Road Ind Est B79 249 F3
Lichfield St
Burton u T DE14 166 B1
Fazeley B78 249 F1
Hanley ST1 282 C1
Rugeley WS15 196 C4
Stone ST15 120 A4
Lichfield (Trent Valley) Sta WS13 231 F4
Lid La Cheadle ST10 76 B2
Roston DE6 96 C4
Liddiard Ct DY8 279 F3
Liddle St ST4 72 A3
Lidgate Gr ST3 72 C1
Lidgate Wlk ST5 71 D1
Liffs Rd DE6 36 B4
Lifton Croft DY6 275 F3
Light Ash WV10 224 B2
Light Ash Cl WV9 224 B2
Light Ash La WV9 224 B2
Light Oaks Ave ST2 43 E1
Lightfoot Rd ST14 110 C1
Lightwater Gr ST2 42 C1
Lightwood Rd Longton ST3 283 C2
Meir ST3 89 E3
Newcastle-u-L ST5 40 B1
Yoxall DE13 181 F1
Lilac Ave WS11 226 B4
Lilac Cl Meir ST3 74 B3
Newcastle-u-L ST5 40 B1
Seighford ST18 135 E1
Uttoxeter ST14 126 A3
Lilac Dr WV5 269 F3
Lilac Gr Burntwood WS7 228 C4
Burton u T DE15 185 F3
Fenton ST3 72 C2
Stafford ST17 174 C4
Lilac La WS6 243 D4
Lilac Rd B79 250 A4
Lilleshall Cres WV2 266 B4
Lilleshall Hall National Sports Ctr TF10 187 D1
Lilleshall Rd ST5 71 E3
Lilleshall St ST3 283 C2
Lilleshall Way ST17 174 B4
Lillington Cl WS13 231 D4
Lillydale Rd ST2 58 A2
Lily St ST5 56 B3
Lime Cl Church Leigh ST10 109 D3
Doveridge DE6 127 D4
Great Wyrley WS11 226 C2
Meir ST3 74 B3
Lime Gr Barlaston ST12 88 C2
Burntwood WS7 229 E3
Burton u T DE15 185 F3
Kinver DY7 278 A2
Lichfield WS14 231 E4
Waterhouses ST10 48 C2
Lime Kiln La Alton ST10 78 C1
Kidsgrove ST7 25 F1
Lime La WS3 244 A4
Lime Rd Huntington WS12 209 E4
Sedgley DY3 266 C1
Lime St Stoke-on-T ST4 72 A3
Wolv WV3 266 A4
Lime Tree Ave WV6 255 D2
Lime Tree Gdns WV8 239 D2
Lime Tree Rd WV8 239 D2
Lime Wlk ST19 207 F4
Limeheath Pl ST6 41 F3
Limehurst Ave WV3 255 E1
Limepit La Cannock WS12 209 E3
Huntington WS12 209 E3
Limes Ave ST9 30 A1
Limes Rd WV6 255 E2
Limes The Albrighton WV7 237 D2
Newcastle-u-L ST5 56 B4
Limes View DY3 271 E4
Limetree Ave ST16 155 E3
Limetree Rd B74 256 B1
Limewood Cl ST11 91 D3
Linacre Rd ST21 133 F3
Linacre Way ST3 73 F3
Lincoln Ave ST5 71 E3
Lincoln Cl WS13 214 B2
Lincoln Croft WS14 247 D3
Lincoln Dr WS11 226 C4
Lincoln Gn WV10 240 B1
Lincoln Gr ST5 71 E3
Lincoln Meadow ST17 174 A4
Lincoln Rd Burslem ST6 57 D4
Burton u T DE15 185 E4
Kidsgrove ST7 25 F1
Lincoln St ST1 282 C2
Linda Rd ST6 41 F3
Lindale Cl CW12 6 A3
Lindale Dr WV5 269 F3
Lindale Gr ST3 90 A4
Linden Ave WS7 229 D4
Linden Cl Congleton CW12 16 A4
Newcastle-u-L ST5 56 A2
Stafford ST17 174 A4
Tamworth B77 250 C2
Linden Dr ST6 16 B1
Linden Gr ST5 56 A2
Linden Lea WV3 255 E1
Linden Pl ST3 72 C1
Linden Rd DE13 183 E1
Linden View WS12 210 A2
Linden Way TF9 97 E1
Lindenbrook Vale ST17 175 E4
Lindens The Stone ST15 120 A3
Wolv WV6 255 F2
Lindera B77 251 D2
Lindisfarne B77 250 B2
Lindley Pl ST3 90 A2
Lindley St ST6 57 D4
Lindon Dr WS8 245 D3
Lindon Rd WS8 244 C3
Lindon View WS8 245 D3
Lindop Ct ST1 282 C3
Lindop St ST1 282 C3

Lindops La CW3 .... 68 C4
Lindrick Cl WS3 .... 242 C2
Lindrosa Rd B74 .... 256 C2
Lindsay St ST1 .... 282 A2
Lindum Ave ST4 .... 88 B4
Lineker Cl ST16 .... 155 D2
Linfield Gdns DY3 .... 266 B1
Linfield Rd ST1 .... 282 C3
Linford Cl WS15 .... 198 B2
Ling Rd WS12 .... 209 E3
Lingard St ST6 .... 57 D4
Lingfield Ave Endon ST6 .. 43 D4
   Wolv WV10 .... 240 B3
Lingfield Cl WS6 .... 226 C1
Lingfield Dr WS6 .... 226 C1
Lingfield Gr WV6 .... 254 C2
Lingfield Rd DE14 .... 184 C4
Linhope Gr ST3 .... 90 A4
Link Rd Brownhills WS9 .. 245 D2
   Wombourne WV5 .... 270 A4
Linkend Cl ST1 .... 57 F3
Links Ave
   Newcastle-u-L ST5 .... 56 A2
   Wolv WV5 .... 255 E4
Links Dr DY8 .... 279 F1
Links Rd WV4 .... 266 A2
Links Side Way WS9 ...... 256 B4
Links View B74 .... 257 D1
Linksfield Dr ST16 .... 155 E4
Linksway CW12 .... 15 F4
Linksway Cl CW12 .... 15 F4
Linkwood Ind Est DY8 ... 279 F3
Linley Dr WV10 .... 240 C1
Linley Gr Alsager ST7 .... 25 D2
   Sedgley DY5 .... 271 D1
Linley La ST7 .... 25 D1
Linley Rd Alsager ST7 .... 25 D1
   Kidsgrove ST7 .... 40 B4
   Stoke-on-T ST4 .... 71 F4
Linley Trad Est ST7 ...... 25 E1
Linnburn Rd ST3 .... 73 F2
Linnet Cl SW12 .... 209 E4
Linnet Way ST8 .... 27 F4
Linslade Cl WV4 .... 266 B2
Lintake Dr WS15 .... 160 C3
Linthouse Wlk B77 .... 261 F3
Lintly B77 .... 262 A4
Linton Rd WV4 .... 265 F3
Linwood Dr WS12 .... 209 F4
Linwood Way ST6 .... 41 F3
Lion Gr ST5 .... 55 F4
Lion Ind Est WS9 .... 256 A4
Lion Pas DY8 .... 279 F3
Lion St Rugeley WS15 .... 178 C1
   Stoke-on-T ST4 .... 72 A4
   Stourbridge DY8 .... 279 F3
Lion's Den WS14 .... 229 F1
Lionel Gr ST4 .... 71 F3
Lionfields Cl DY10 .... 280 A3
Lionfields Rd DY10 ...... 280 A3
Lisbon Pl ST5 .... 70 C4
Liskeard Cl ST2 .... 58 A1
Lister Rd ST16 .... 155 F3
Litley Dr ST10 .... 92 B4
Little Aston Cty Prim Sch
   WS14 .... 257 E3
Little Aston Hospl B74 .. 257 D3
Little Aston La B74 ...... 257 E3
Little Aston Park Rd B74 257 D2
Little Aston Rd WS9 ..... 256 B3
Little Barrow Wlk WS13 .. 214 A1
Little Birches WV3 .... 265 F4
Little Bloxwich CE Jun Mix
   Inf & Prim Sch WS3 ... 243 E2
Little Burton E DE14 .... 166 B2
Little Burton W DE14 ... 166 B2
Little Checkhill La DY6 .. 274 B2
Little Chell La
   Chell Heath ST6 .... 41 F3
   Tunstall ST6 .... 41 F3
Little Church Rd B79 .... 250 A3
Little Cliffe Rd ST4 ...... 72 C2
Little Common WS3 ...... 244 A2
Little Eaves La ST2 .... 58 B3
Little Field ST4 .... 71 F2
Little Grange WS13 ...... 213 F1
Little Hardwick Rd
   B74, WS9 .... 256 B1
Little Hay La
   Shenstone WS14 .... 247 E2
   Weeford WS14 .... 247 E2
Little Johnson's La WS9 .. 256 A1
Little La ST3 .... 89 F2
Little Lawns Cl WS9 ..... 245 D2
Little Marsh Gr WS19 ... 192 C1
Little Moss Cl ST5 .... 25 F3
Little Moss La ST7 .... 25 F3
Little Oaks Dr DY7 ...... 275 D1
Little Onn Rd ST20 ...... 190 A4
Little Orch WS15 .... 178 C1
Little Pipe La WS13 ..... 213 D1
Little Pountney St
   ⑥ WV2 .... 266 B4
Little Row ST4 .... 72 C4
Little Sutton La B75 .... 258 B1
Little Sutton Prim Sch
   B75 .... 258 B2
Little Sutton Rd B75 .... 258 B1
Little Tixall La ST18 .... 158 C1
Littlecote B79 .... 249 E4
Littlefield La
   Ellastone DE6 .... 80 A1
   Snelston DE6 .... 81 D3
Littlehales Rd TF10 ...... 187 D3

Littleton Bsns Pk WS12 .. 209 E4
Littleton Cl ST19 .... 156 A2
Littleton Cres ST19 ...... 192 C1
Littleton Dr WS12 .... 209 E4
Littleton Way WS7 .... 211 E1
Littlewood La WS11 ...... 226 C2
Littlewood Rd WS11 ..... 226 C2
Littleworth Hill WS12 .... 210 B2
Littleworth Rd WS12 ..... 210 C2
Litton B77 .... 251 E1
Littondale Cl CW12 ...... 6 A3
Littywood La ST18 .... 173 E1
Liverpool Rd
   Kidsgrove ST7 .... 26 A1
   Newcastle-u-L ST5 ...... 284 B3
   Newcastle-u-L, Cross Heath
   ST5 .... 56 A2
   Newcastle-u-L, Red Street
   ST5 .... 40 B1
   Stoke-on-T ST4 .... 72 A4
Liverpool Rd E
   Kidsgrove ST7 .... 25 F1
   Lawton-gate ST7 .... 25 F1
Liverpool Rd W ST7 ...... 25 D2
Livingstone Dr WV6 ...... 254 C3
Livingstone Rd WS3 ..... 243 F1
Livingstone St
   Chell Heath ST6 .... 42 B1
   Leek ST13 .... 30 C3
Lizard La TF11 .... 220 A3
Llewellyn Roberts Way
   TF9 .... 97 E1
Lloyd Dr WV4 .... 265 E2
Lloyd George Gr WS11 .. 210 B1
Lloyd Hill WV4 .... 265 E2
Lloyd Rd WV6 .... 255 E3
Lloyd St Cannock WS11 .. 209 E1
   Longton ST3 .... 283 C2
   Stafford ST16 .... 155 F2
   Wolv WV6 .... 255 F3
Lochalsh Gr WV11 .... 242 A1
Lock Rd ST19 .... 207 F4
Locke Way ST14 .... 156 A2
Lockerbie Cl ST13 .... 31 D3
Lockett St ST1 .... 57 E3
Locketts La ST3 .... 283 C2
Lockfield Cl DY8 .... 275 F1
Lockington Ave ST2 ...... 58 B1
Lockley St ST1 .... 57 F3
Locks View DY8 .... 275 F1
Lockside WV5 .... 269 E4
Lockwood Cl ST10 .... 62 A1
Lockwood Rd
   Cheadle ST10 .... 77 D3
   Kingsley ST10 .... 77 D3
Lockwood St
   Newcastle-u-L ST5 ...... 284 D3
   Norton-in-t-M ST2 ..... 43 D2
Lode La DE6 .... 35 F2
Lodge Barn Rd ST8 ...... 27 F3
Lodge Gr Aldridge WS9 .. 256 A3
   Newcastle-u-L ST5 ...... 56 B3
Lodge Hill DE13 .... 146 C2
Lodge La
   Alstonefield DE6 .... 35 D3
   Cheslyn Hay WS11 ..... 226 B3
   Eccleshall ST21 .... 115 F3
   Ilam ST14 .... 50 B2
   Kingswinford DY6 ...... 275 D3
   Netherseal DE12 .... 219 F4
   Woodseaves ST20 ...... 151 F3
   Yoxall DE13 .... 182 A4
Lodge Pk WV5 .... 267 E4
Lodge Rd
   Brownhills WS4 .... 244 A1
   Burntwood WS7 .... 211 F1
   Kidsgrove ST7 .... 40 B1
   Rugeley WS15 .... 197 D3
   Stoke-on-T ST4 .... 71 F4
Lodge View WS6 .... 226 B2
Loftus St ST4 .... 72 C4
Loftus St ST1 .... 282 A4
Loganbeck Gr ST3 .... 73 F3
Lohengrin Ct DE13 ...... 147 F1
Lomas St ST1 .... 57 D1
Lomax Cl WS13 .... 214 A1
Lomax Rd WS12 .... 210 A4
Lombard Gdns WS13 .... 231 D4
Lombard St WS13 .... 231 D4
Lombardy Gr
   Burntwood WS7 .... 228 A4
   Meir ST3 .... 74 A1
Lomita Cres B77 .... 261 E4
Lomond Cl WS11 .... 226 C2
Lomond Gr ST10 .... 76 C2
Lomond Rd DY3 .... 266 B1
Lomond Wlk ST3 .... 88 C4
London Rd
   Allen End B75 .... 259 E1
   Bridgemere CW5 .... 67 D3
   Hints B75 .... 259 D2
   Lichfield WS14 .... 231 E3
   Mucklestone CW3 ...... 83 E3
   Newcastle-u-L, Chesterton
   ST5 .... 55 F4
   Newcastle-u-L,
   City General Hospl ST5 .. 284 D1
   Stoke-on-T ST4 .... 72 A3
   Weeford WS14 .... 247 F2
   Weston-u-T ST18 ...... 138 B1
   Woore CW5 .... 67 D3
   Woore, Dorrington CW3 83 E3
London St ST3 .... 30 C3
Long Acre WV8 .... 238 C1
Long Bridge Rd WS14 .. 231 E3
Long Cl DY9 .... 281 F2
Long Croft WS12 .... 209 E2
Long Furrow WV8 .... 239 F1

Long La Alrewas DE13 .. 200 C1
   Alstonefield DE6 .... 35 D3
   Great Wyrley WS6 ..... 242 C3
   Haughton ST18 .... 154 B1
   Kidsgrove ST7 .... 26 C2
   Seighford ST18 .... 154 B1
Long Meadow
   Newcastle-u-L ST5 ..... 71 E2
   Stafford ST17 .... 174 C3
Long Meadow Dr DY3 .. 266 A1
Long Mynd Cl WV11 .... 242 A1
Long Row Caverswall ST11 74 B2
   Kidsgrove ST7 .... 26 A1
Long St Burton u T DE15 185 F4
   Wheaton Aston ST19 .. 205 E3
Long Valley Rd ST6 ..... 16 B1
Longacres Cannock WS12 210 C3
   Little Aston B74 .... 257 E2
Longboat La DY8 .... 275 F1
Longbow Cl DE13 .... 147 E1
Longbow Gr DE13 ...... 147 E1
Longbridge Hayes Rd
   ST5 .... 56 A4
Longbrook Ave ST3 .... 72 C1
Longclough Rd ST5 .... 40 B1
Longcroft La DE13 ..... 182 A2
Longdon Ave WV4 ..... 266 B3
Longdon Dr B74 .... 257 F2
Longfellow Cl DE14 ... 166 B4
Longfellow Pl WS11 ... 209 F2
Longfellow Rd
   Burntwood WS7 ...... 212 A1
   Sedgley DY3 .... 271 D3
Longfellow Wlk B79 ... 249 F4
Longfield Ave WS15 ... 119 F4
Longfield Cl B77 .... 250 C2
Longfield Dr B74 .... 257 E2
Longfield Rd ST4 ...... 71 F4
Longford Cl WV5 ...... 269 E3
Longford Gn WS11 .... 226 B4
Longford Ind Est WS11 .. 226 B3
Longford Prim Sch
   WS11 .... 226 B4
Longford Rd
   Cannock WS11 .... 226 B4
   Longford TF10 .... 168 B1
   Newport TF10 .... 168 B1
Longford Wlk ST2 ..... 58 A1
Longhedge La DE13 ... 146 C1
Longhope Dr ST15 .... 119 F3
Longhurst Dr ST16 .... 156 B2
Longlake Ave WV6 .... 255 D2
Longlands City
   Prim Sch The TF9 ... 97 E1
Longlands Dr B77 ..... 250 C2
Longlands La TF9 ..... 97 E1
Longlands The WV5 .. 270 A3
Longleat Dr DY1 ...... 271 F1
Longleat Rd WS9 ..... 245 D1
Longley Rd ST3 .... 73 E3
Longmead Rd DE13 .. 166 B3
Longnor Pl ST2 .... 58 A1
Longport Rd ST6 ..... 56 B4
Longport Sta ST6 .... 56 B4
Longsdon Cl ST3 .... 40 B1
Longsdon Gr ST3 ... 73 F2
Longshaw Ave WS5 . 56 A4
Longshaw La
   Oakamoor, Farley ST10 .. 78 C3
   Oakamoor, Longshaw ST10 78 C4
   Stockton ST6 .... 56 B4
Longshore Cl ST17 .. 174 B3
Longslow Cl TF9 .... 97 D1
Longslow Rd TF9 ... 97 D1
Longstaff Ave WS12 . 211 E2
Longstaff Croft WS13 213 F1
Longton Exchange ST3 283 C3
Longton Hall Rd ST3 . 72 C1
Longton High Sch ST3 73 F1
Longton Hospl ST3 .. 73 E1
Longton Rd
   Barlaston ST12 .... 88 C1
   Stone ST15 .... 105 E2
   Trentham ST4 .... 88 A3
Longton Sta ST3 ..... 283 B4
Longview ST3 .... 73 E3
Longwood Jun & Inf Sch
   B78 .... 249 E1
Longwood Path B78 . 249 E1
Longwood Rd WV6 .. 256 A1
Lonsdale CE Prim Sch
   ST21 .... 133 E3
Lonsdale Ct TF9 ..... 97 E1
Lonsdale Rd
   Branston DE14 .... 185 D4
   Wolv WV3 .... 266 A4
Lonsdale St ST4 ...... 72 A3
Lootle Rd ST5 .... 55 F3
Loomer Road Ind Est ST5 .. 55 F3
Lord Cromwell Ct WS11 210 A3
Lord St Biddulph ST8 .. 27 E4
   Chell Heath ST6 ...... 42 B1
Lordship La ST7 ...... 72 B4
Lordshire Pl ST7 ..... 26 C1
Lordsley Rd TF9 ...... 100 A4
Lordswell Rd DE13 .. 165 F2
Lorien Cl ST13 .... 30 B2
Loring Rd ST5 .... 56 A3
Loring Terr S ST5 ... 56 B3
Lorne St Burntwood WS7 .. 228 C4
   Chell Heath ST6 ...... 42 A1
Lorraine Cl ST5 ...... 26 C1
Lorton B77 .... 249 E4
Lothersdale B77 ..... 262 B4
Lothians Rd
   Brownhills WS3 ...... 244 A3
   Wolv WV6 .... 255 F3
Lotus B77 .... 250 C2

Lotus Ave ST8 .... 27 D3
Lotus Ct ST15 .... 105 D1
Lotus Dr WS11 .... 209 F3
Loughborough Wlk ST3 283 C4
Loughshaw B77 .... 251 E1
Louise Dr ST3 .... 72 C2
Louise St Chell Heath ST6 .. 42 A1
   Sedgley DY3 .... 271 E2
Lount La DE13 .... 146 C1
Louvain Ave ST1 ...... 57 E4
Lovage Gr ST2 .... 58 A2
Lovatt Ave ST5 .... 56 A2
Lovatt Cl DE13 .... 147 F1
Lovatt Pl WS11 .... 209 F3
Lovatt St Stafford ST16 155 E3
   Stoke-on-T ST4 .... 72 A4
Love La
   Great Wyrley WS6 ..... 227 D2
   Rugeley WS15 .... 178 C1
   Wolv WV6 .... 255 E3
Lovelace Ct ST17 ...... 174 B4
Lovell B77 .... 249 F3
Lovell Rd DE13 .... 182 A1
Loveridge Cl WV8 ..... 238 C2
Loveston Gr ST3 ...... 283 D4
Lovett Ct WS15 .... 178 B1
Low St WS5 .... 226 B2
Lowdham B77 .... 251 E1
Lowe Dr DY6 .... 275 F2
Lowe St ST4 .... 72 A4
Lowe's Pas ST3 .... 283 D2
Lowell Dr ST3 .... 73 F2
Lower Ash Rd ST7 .... 25 F1
Lower Bar TF10 .... 168 C2
Lower Bedford St ST1 .. 57 D1
Lower Bethesda St ST1 282 C2
Lower Bromstead La
   TF10 .... 188 B4
Lower Brook St WS15 178 C1
Lower Bryan St ST1 .. 282 B4
Lower Cres ST4 .... 71 F4
Lower Farm Prim Sch
   WS3 .... 243 E2
Lower Foundry St ST1 282 B3
Lower Hadderidge ❸ ST6 .. 56 C4
Lower High St
   Mow Cop ST7 .... 26 B4
   Stourbridge DY8 ...... 279 F3
   Tutbury DE13 .... 146 B4
Lower La WS13 .... 212 B2
Lower Mayer St ST1 . 282 C4
Lower Milehouse La ST5 .. 55 F2
Lower Outwoods Rd
   DE13 .... 165 F3
Lower Oxford St ST5 . 56 C1
Lower Penkridge Rd ST17 175 E1
Lower Rd Ashley TF9 . 100 A2
   Cannock WS12 .... 210 B2
   Gnosall ST20 .... 152 A3
Lower Sandford St
   WS13 .... 231 D4
Lower Spring Rd ❷ ST3 .. 73 E1
Lower St ❶ Burslem ST6 .. 57 D4
   Doveridge DE6 .... 127 D4
   Newcastle-u-L ST5 ... 284 B3
   Wolv WV6 .... 255 F3
Lower Villiers St WV2 266 B4
Lower Way WS15 ..... 197 E1
Lowercroft Way B74 . 257 F3
Lowerpark B77 .... 250 B1
Lowfield La WS20 ... 171 F3
Lowforce B77 .... 251 E1
Lowhurst Dr ST5 .... 42 A4
Lowland Rd WS12 ... 209 E3
Lowlands Ave WV6 . 255 F3
Lowlands Rd ST6 ... 41 D2
Lowndes Cl ST4 .... 71 F3
Lowndes Rd DY8 ... 279 F3
Lowry Cl WV6 .... 254 C2
Lowther Pl ST13 .... 31 D3
Lowther St ST1 ..... 282 A4
Lowthorpe Way ST2 58 C1
Loxdale Hall Specl Sch
   ST14 .... 125 E3
Loxley La ST14 .... 125 E3
Loxley Pl ST3 ..... 89 F4
Loxley Rd B75 .... 258 B2
Loynton Cl ST16 .. 155 D4
Loynton Sands ST20 .. 151 D2
Lucas St ST6 ..... 56 C4
Lucepool La DE13 . 182 B2
Lucerne Pl ST5 .. 70 C4
Lud La B79 ...... 250 A3
Ludbrook Rd ST4 . 73 D3
Ludford Cl ST5 .. 40 B1
Ludgate B79 .... 250 A4
Ludgate Ct B77 . 251 D3
Ludgate St DE13 146 B3
Ludlow Cl WS11 . 210 B1
Ludlow St ST1 .. 282 C3
Ludlow Way DY1 271 F1
Ludstone Ave WV4 265 E3
Ludwall Rd ST3 . 73 F1
Lugano Cl ST5 .. 70 C3
Luke St ST6 .... 56 C4
Lukes Wlk WS13 214 A1
Lukesland Ave ST4 71 F3
Lullington Rd
   Clifton Campville B79 218 C2
   Edingale B79 .... 217 E3
Lulworth Gr ST3 ... 41 F3
Lulworth Rd WS7 . 229 D4
Lulworth Wlk WV4 265 E3
Lundy Rd ST3 .... 72 C2
Lune Cl CW12 ... 6 A1
Lunns Croft WS13 231 E4
Lutley Cl WV3 ... 265 F4
Lutley La DY7 ... 273 D4

Luttrell Rd B74 .... 258 A1
Luxton Cl B74 .... 257 E3
Lydford Pl ST3 .... 73 F2
Lydford Rd WS3 ...... 243 D2
Lydgate Rd DY6 ...... 275 D4
Lydia Croft B74 ...... 257 F3
Lydia Dr ST1 .... 57 F3
Lydiates Cl DY3 ...... 271 D4
Lyme Brook Pl ST4 .. 71 F2
Lyme Gr ST5 .... 56 B2
Lyme Rd ST5 .... 74 A1
Lyme Valley Rd ST5 . 284 C1
Lyme Wood Gr ST5 . 284 B1
Lymer Rd WV10 ..... 240 B1
Lymer's La ST18 .... 123 D1
Lymes Rd Keele ST5 70 A2
   Whitmore ST5 ...... 70 A2
Lymevale Rd ST4 ... 71 F2
Lymewood Cl ST5 .. 284 B2
Lymington Rd
   Burntwood WS7 ... 211 F1
   Stafford ST16 ..... 156 B2
Lyminster Gr ST2 .. 43 D1
Lymsey Croft DY8 . 275 E2
Lyn Ave WS13 ..... 213 F1
Lynam St ST4 ..... 72 A4
Lynam Way CW3 . 68 C4
Lynch The B78 ... 251 F1
Lyncroft WV7 .... 237 D3
Lyncroft House Sch
   WS11 .... 226 C4
Lyndale B77 ..... 261 F3
Lyndham Ave DE15 166 C1
Lyndhurst Dr
   Biddulph ST8 .... 27 D3
   Brierley Hill DY8 .. 275 F1
Lyndhurst Gr WS15 120 B3
Lyndhurst Rd
   Cannock WS12 ... 210 C1
   Wolv WV3 .... 266 A4
Lyndhurst St ST6 . 56 C4
Lyndon Cl DY3 ... 266 C1
Lyndon Gr DY6 .. 275 D4
Lyne Ct DE14 ... 166 A2
Lyne Hill Ind Est ST19 207 F4
Lyneham Ct ST19 250 B4
Lyneham La ST19 207 F3
Lyneside Rd ST4 . 27 D3
Lynfield Rd WS13 213 F1
Lynmouth Cl
   Aldridge WS9 ... 256 A3
   Biddulph ST8 .... 27 E3
Lynmouth Gr ST6 41 F4
Lynn Ave ST7 ... 40 B4
Lynn La WS14 .. 246 B3
Lynn St ST3 .... 74 A3
Lynsey Cl ST7 .. 54 C4
Lynton Ave Stafford ST17 175 E4
   Wolv WV6 .... 255 F3
Lynton Gr ST3 .. 89 F4
Lynwood Ave DY6 275 D4
Lynwood Cl
   Branston DE14 .. 184 C4
   Walsall WS5 .... 242 C1
Lynwood Dr DY10 281 E4
Lynwood Rd DE14 184 C4
Lyric Cl ST17 .. 174 C3
Lysander Rd ST3 90 A4
Lysander Way WS11 209 F2
Lysways La WS15 213 D4
Lytham B77 .... 251 E3
Lytham Cl DY8 . 279 F1
Lytham Dr ST16 156 B2
Lytham Gr WS3 243 D2
Lytham Rd WV6 254 B2
Lyttelton Rd DY8 279 E3
Lytton Ave WV4 265 F2
Lytton St ST4 .. 72 B4

Macadam Cl WS7 ... 229 D4
Macclesfield Rd
   Eaton CW12 .... 6 A4
   Leek ST13 .... 30 B4
Macclesfield St ST6 42 A1
Macdonald Cres ST3 74 A2
Mace St ST4 .... 71 F2
Macgregor Cres B77 250 C2
Machin Cres ST5 ... 56 A4
Machin St ST6 .... 41 F2
Macintyre St ST6 . 57 D4
Mackay Rd WS3 .. 243 E1
Mackenzie Cres ST10 76 C1
Maclagan St ST4 . 72 A3
Macrome Rd WV6 255 F4
Madden Cl WS15 . 196 C3
Maddock St Audley ST7 39 E1
   Burslem ST6 ..... 56 C4
Madeira Ave WV8 239 D1
Madeira Pl ST5 .. 41 E2
Madeley High Sch CW3 68 C3
Madeley Rd DY6 .. 275 F2
Madeley St
   Newcastle-u-L ST5 55 D1
   Tunstall ST6 ..... 41 E2
Madeley St N ST5 55 D1
Madison St ST6 .. 41 E2
Madox Cl B79 ... 249 F4
Madras Rd DE15 167 E2
Madrona B77 ... 251 D2
Maer La TF9 .... 97 E1
Maerway La ST5 84 B3
Maesfield Cl TF9 112 A4
Maesfield Dr ST17 155 E1
Mafeking St ST6 283 D2
Magdalen ST3 .. 88 C4
Magdalen Wlk ST3 88 C4
Magna Cl WS6 . 226 C2
Magnolia B77 .. 251 D2

Magnolia Cl ST18 .... 135 D1
Magnolia Dr ST6 .... 42 C1
Magnolia Gr WV8 .... 239 D2
Magnolia Way DY8 .... 279 F4
Magnus B77 .... 261 F3
Magnus ST6 .... 56 C4
Magpie Cres ST7 .... 26 A1
Maidendale Rd DY6 .... 275 D4
Maidensbridge Dr DY6 .... 275 E4
Maidensbridge Gdns
  DY6 .... 270 A1
Maidensbridge Prim Sch
  DY6 .... 270 A1
Maidensbridge Rd DY6 .... 270 A1
Maidstone Dr
  Burntwood WS7 .... 229 E3
  Kingswinford DY8 .... 275 F2
Maidstone Gr ST2 .... 58 B1
Main Rd Adbaston ST20 ... 131 E3
  Armitage WS15 .... 197 E2
  Betley CW3 .... 53 D3
  Brocton ST17 .... 176 A4
  Cheddleton ST9 .... 60 A4
  Cotton ST10 .... 63 F2
  Edingale B79 .... 217 E3
  Harlaston B79 .... 217 E1
  Meir ST3 .... 74 B2
  Newton Regis B79 .... 236 B1
  Norton in H TF9 .... 82 B1
  Stafford ST17 .... 176 A4
  Sudbury, Aston DE6 .... 129 D2
  Sudbury, Sudbury DE6 .... 128 C3
  Weston CW2 .... 37 E4
  Wigginton B79 .... 234 A1
Main Rd Brereton WS15 ... 197 D3
Main St Alrewas DE13 ...... 201 D2
  Anslow DE13 .... 165 E4
  Barton-u-N DE13 .... 183 E1
  Branston DE14 .... 184 C4
  Burton u T, Stapenhill DE15 .. 185 F4
  Burton u T, Stretton DE13 .. 147 F1
  Clifton Campville B79 ..... 218 C1
  Eggington DE65 .... 148 A3
  Meir ST3 .... 74 A3
  Netherseal DE12 .... 219 F4
  Newton Solney DE15 .... 167 F4
  Shenstone WS14 .... 246 C3
  Shenstone, Stonnall WS9 .. 245 E2
  Swadlincote DE12 .... 186 C3
  Tatenhill DE13 .... 165 D1
  Walton-on-T DE12 .... 184 B4
  Whittington WS14 .... 232 C3
  Yoxall DE13 .... 182 A1
Mainwaring Dr B75 .... 258 C1
Maitland B77 .... 250 C1
Maitland Rd DY1 .... 271 F1
Major St WV2 .... 266 C4
Majors Barn ST10 .... 76 B1
Maker La DE13 .... 162 B1
Malcolm Cl ST2 .... 43 D1
Malcolm Ct ST2 .... 58 B3
Malcolm Dr ST2 .... 58 B3
Malcolm Rd ST17 .... 174 B3
Malham Rd
  Newcastle-u-L ST5 .... 55 E1
  Tamworth B77 .... 251 E1
Malham St ST1 .... 282 B1
Malhamdale Rd CW12 .... 6 A3
Malins Rd WV4 .... 266 C3
Malkin Way ST6 .... 56 C3
Mallard Ave ST17 .... 175 D4
Mallard Cl
  Brownhills WS3 .... 244 A3
  Uttoxeter ST14 .... 126 A4
Mallard Croft WS13 .... 231 E4
Mallard Way ST6 .... 42 B2
Mallens Croft ST14 .... 125 E4
Mallicot Cl WS13 .... 214 B1
Mallorie Rd ST6 .... 42 B2
Mallory Cl ST15 .... 120 A3
Mallory Cres WS3 .... 243 E1
Mallory Rd WV6 .... 254 C2
Mallory Way ST6 .... 76 C2
Mallow Cl ST21 .... 133 F3
Mallowdale Cl ST4 .... 88 B3
Malpas Gdns WV8 .... 238 C2
Malpass Wlk ST6 .... 41 E4
Malt House Rd WS15 .... 212 B1
Malt La ST3 .... 283 D2
Malt Mill La ST16 .... 155 F2
Malthouse La
  Barlaston ST12 .... 88 C1
  Bradley ST18 .... 173 E1
  Caverswall ST3 .... 74 B4
  Church Eaton ST20 .... 190 A4
  Wheaton Aston ST19 ...... 205 A4
  Wolv WV6 .... 255 F3
Malthouse Rd ST2 .... 58 A2
Maltings Ind Est DE14 ..... 166 C3
Maltings The
  Aldridge WS9 .... 256 B3
  Burton u T DE15 .... 167 D1
  Uttoxeter ST14 .... 126 B4
Malton Gr ST6 .... 41 E3
Malvern Ave
  Burton u T DE15 .... 167 D1
  Newcastle-u-L ST5 .... 54 C1
Malvern Cl Stafford ST17 .. 156 A1
  Trentham ST4 .... 88 A4
Malvern Dr Aldridge WS9 .. 256 B4
  Rugeley WS15 .... 178 B1
Malvern St DE15 .... 166 C1
Malvern View Rd DY3 ...... 271 E2
Mamble Rd DY8 .... 279 F3
Mancroft Rd DY6 .... 275 D4
Mancroft Gdns WV6 .... 255 E3
Mancroft Rd WV6 .... 255 E3
Mandela Way ST3 .... 283 D2

Mander St WV3 .... 266 A4
Manderley CI DY3 .... 266 B1
Manderville Gdns DY6 ..... 275 E3
Mandeville Ct ST6 .... 42 B2
Manifold CE Prim Sch
  SK17 .... 23 D1
Manifold Cl
  Burntwood WS7 .... 229 E3
  Newcastle-u-L ST5 .... 55 D1
Manifold Dr ST10 .... 76 C1
Manifold Rd ST11 .... 90 C4
Manifold Wlk ST2 .... 58 B1
Manley Rd WS13 .... 214 B1
Manlove St WV3 .... 266 A4
Mannin Cl ST3 .... 74 A2
Manor Ave
  Cannock WS11 .... 209 E1
  Great Wyrley WS6 .... 227 D4
Manor Cl Codsall WV8 ...... 239 D2
  Colwich ST18 .... 158 A1
  Congleton CW12 .... 6 A1
  Draycott in t M ST11 .... 91 E3
  Market Drayton TF9 .... 97 E1
  Swadlincote DE15 .... 186 A3
  Uttoxeter ST14 .... 126 A4
  Weston-u-T ST18 .... 138 B1
  Wolv WV4 .... 265 F2
Manor Court Dr WS15 ...... 198 A2
Manor Cres DE15 .... 186 A3
Manor Croft DE14 .... 166 C1
Manor Ct ST4 .... 71 F3
Manor Cty Prim Sch B78 .. 260 C3
Manor Dr Netherseal DE12 .. 219 F3
  Shareshill WV10 .... 225 D2
  Swindon DY3 .... 269 F1
Manor Farm Cres ST17 ..... 174 C3
Manor Farm Rd ST18 .... 177 E4
Manor Fold WV8 .... 238 B1
Manor Gdns
  Albrighton WV7 .... 237 D3
  Market Drayton TF9 .... 97 E1
  Wombourne WV5 .... 270 A4
Manor Glade ST5 .... 85 D4
Manor Gn ST17 .... 174 B4
Manor Hill Fst Sch ST15 .. 119 F4
Manor House Pk WV8 ...... 239 D2
Manor La Harlaston B79 ... 217 E1
  Stourbridge DY8 .... 279 E2
  Wigginton B79 .... 233 F2
Manor Pk DY6 .... 275 E3
Manor Prim Sch B74 .... 257 D1
Manor Rd Aldridge B74 .... 257 D1
  Edgmond TF10 .... 168 A2
  Fazeley B78 .... 249 E1
  Gnosall ST20 .... 171 F4
  King's Bromley DE13 ...... 199 E3
  Kingswinford DY8 .... 275 F1
  Madeley CW3 .... 68 C2
  Mow Cop ST7 .... 26 B4
  Swadlincote DE15 .... 186 A3
  Tamworth B77 .... 250 B2
  Uttoxeter ST14 .... 126 A4
  Walsall WS3 .... 243 D1
  Whitmore ST5 .... 85 D4
  Wolv WV4 .... 265 F2
Manor Rise
  Burntwood WS7 .... 229 D3
  Lichfield WS14 .... 231 E4
  Stone ST15 .... 119 F4
Manor Sq ST17 .... 174 B4
Manor St Fenton ST4 .... 72 C3
  Wolv WV6 .... 255 E3
Manor Way ST5 .... 179 D3
Manorfield Cl ST19 .... 207 F4
Mansard Cl WV3 .... 265 F4
Manse Cl ST3 .... 283 C4
Mansell Ct ST16 .... 155 E1
Mansfield Cl ST1 .... 71 E1
Mansfield Dr ST8 .... 27 D3
Mansion Cl ST10 .... 76 C1
Mansion Dr WS7 .... 229 E2
Manson St WV2 .... 266 B4
Manston Dr WV6 .... 254 C3
Manston Hill ST19 .... 207 F4
Manston View B79 .... 250 B4
Manta Rd B77 .... 261 E3
Manton Cl DE11 .... 186 C3
Maple Ave Kidsgrove ST7 ... 40 B4
  Newcastle-u-L ST5 .... 40 C1
Maple Cl Burntwood WS7 .. 228 C4
  Cheadle ST10 .... 76 B3
  Kinver DY7 .... 278 A3
  Norton-in-t-M ST6 .... 43 D3
  Stourbridge DY8 .... 279 E1
  Swynnerton WS15 .... 118 C3
Maple Cres Cannock WS11 .. 209 E1
  Forsbrook ST11 .... 91 D3
Maple Dr Ashley TF9 .... 99 E3
  Huntington WS12 .... 209 E4
  Sedgley DY5 .... 271 D4
  Seighford ST18 .... 154 C1
Maple Gdns ST15 .... 120 A3
Maple Gr Burton u T DE15 .. 185 F3
  Kingswinford DY6 .... 275 F3
  Lichfield WS14 .... 231 F4
  Stafford ST17 .... 174 C4
  Wolv WV3 .... 255 E1
Maple Hayes
  Dyslexia Sch The WS13 .. 230 B4
Maple Pl ST3 .... 74 A1
Maple Rd Brownhills WS3 .. 243 F1
  Wolv WV3 .... 265 F4
Maple Rise B77 .... 251 D2
Maple St WS3 .... 243 F1
Maple Way ST17 .... 185 D4
Maple Wood ST17 .... 175 E3
Mapledene Cl ST17 .... 175 E3
Maplehurst Cl ST6 .... 57 D4

Marcel Cl ST4 .... 72 A1
March Banks WS15 .... 178 B1
March Cl WS6 .... 226 B1
March La Dilhorne ST9 .... 60 A2
  Whitgreave ST18 .... 135 F3
March Rd ST3 .... 283 B4
March Way WS9 .... 245 C3
Marchant Rd WV4 .... 255 F1
Marchington Ind Est
  ST14 .... 127 F1
Marchwood Ct ST4 .... 71 F3
Marcia Rice Ct WS15 .... 161 D3
Marconi WS12 .... 210 B4
Marcus Ind Est ST1 .... 57 F2
Mardale Cl CW12 .... 6 A3
Maree Gr WV11 .... 242 A1
Margam Cres WS3 .... 242 C1
Margam Way WS3 .... 242 C1
Margaret Ave ST4 .... 87 F4
Margaret Dr ST1 .... 209 F3
Margaret St Hanley ST1 ..... 57 F2
  Stone ST15 .... 104 C1
Margery Ave ST7 .... 25 C4
Margill Cl ST1 .... 282 A2
Marholm Cl WV9 .... 239 F1
Marigold Cl WS11 .... 210 B2
Marina Cres WS3 .... 210 A3
Marina Dr Burslem ST1 ...... 57 D2
  Newcastle-u-L ST1 .... 56 C2
Marina Rd ST4 .... 71 F2
Marine Cres DY8 .... 275 F1
Marine Gdns DY8 .... 275 F1
Mariner B79 .... 249 F3
Market Drayton
  Cottage Hospl TF9 .... 112 B4
Market Drayton Cty
  Inf Sch TF9 .... 97 E1
Market Drayton Cty
  Jun Sch TF9 .... 112 A4
Market Drayton Rd TF9 ..... 99 E2
Market Hall DE14 .... 166 C1
Market Hall St WS11 .... 209 F1
Market La Hanley ST1 ...... 282 B3
  Lower Penn WV4 .... 264 C2
  Newcastle-u-L ST5 .... 284 B3
  Wall WS14 .... 230 C1
Market Mews TF10 .... 168 C2
Market Pl Brewood ST19 .. 223 E3
  Burslem ST6 .... 56 C4
  Burton u T DE14 .... 166 C1
  Cannock WS11 .... 209 E1
  Cheadle ST10 .... 76 B2
  Hartington SK17 .... 24 B3
  5 Leek ST13 .... 30 C3
  Longnor SK17 .... 13 D3
  Tamworth B79 .... 250 A2
  Uttoxeter ST14 .... 126 B4
  Walsall WS3 .... 243 D1
Market Sq Hanley ST1 ..... 282 B3
  Rugeley WS15 .... 178 C1
  10 Stafford ST16 .... 155 F2
Market St Cannock WS12 .. 210 B3
  Kidsgrove ST7 .... 26 A1
  Kingswinford DY6 .... 275 E3
  Leek ST13 .... 30 C3
  Lichfield WS13 .... 231 D4
  Longton ST3 .... 283 C4
  Penkridge ST19 .... 192 C1
  Rugeley WS15 .... 178 C1
  Stafford ST16 .... 155 F2
  Tamworth B79 .... 250 A2
  Uttoxeter ST14 .... 126 B4
Marketfields ST21 .... 133 F4
Markham Croft WV9 .... 240 A1
Markham Dr DY6 .... 275 F2
Marklew Cl WS8 .... 245 D3
Marklin Ave WV10 .... 240 B1
Marks Wlk WS13 .... 214 A1
Marlborough Ave ST16 .... 156 B2
Marlborough Cl
  Colwich ST18 .... 158 B1
  Endon ST9 .... 43 F4
  Sutton Coldfield B74 .... 257 F3
Marlborough Cres DE15 .. 186 A4
Marlborough Ct WS13 ..... 231 D4
Marlborough Gdns
  Kingswinford DY8 .... 275 E1
  Wolv WV6 .... 255 D1
Marlborough Ind Est
  WV2 .... 266 B4
Marlborough Rd
  Longton ST3 .... 283 C4
  Sedgley DY3 .... 271 D2
  Stone ST15 .... 119 F3
Marlborough St
  Fenton ST4 .... 72 B3
  Walsall WS3 .... 243 D1
Marlborough Way
  Tamworth B77 .... 250 C1
  Uttoxeter ST14 .... 110 C2
Marlbrook La WV6 .... 253 D1
Marlbrook Rd WV4 .... 266 A3
Marlburn Way WV5 .... 269 F3
Marldon Pl ST6 .... 41 E3
Marlin B77 .... 261 E3
Marlow Cl ST3 .... 73 E3
Marlow Rd Longton ST3 .... 73 E3
  Tamworth B79 .... 250 B3
Marlowe Rd ST17 .... 174 A4
Marlpit La Denstone ST14 .. 95 E3
  Ellastone DE6 .... 80 A1
  Stone ST15 .... 105 D3
  Sutton Coldfield B75 ...... 258 B2
Marlpool Dr WS3 .... 244 A1
Marmion Jun Sch B79 ..... 250 A3
Marmion St B79 .... 250 A3
Marnel Dr WV3 .... 265 F4
Marney Wlk ST6 .... 42 A1

Marquis Dr WS12 .... 195 E2
Marrick B77 .... 251 E3
Marriott St ST4 .... 73 D1
Mars B77 .... 42 B1
Marsden St ST1 .... 282 C3
Marsett B77 .... 262 B4
Marsh Ave Chell Heath ST6 .. 42 A1
  Kidsgrove ST7 .... 26 C1
  Newcastle-u-L ST5 .... 56 B3
Marsh Cl ST9 .... 59 D2
Marsh Cres DY8 .... 275 E2
Marsh Ct ST16 .... 155 E3
Marsh Gr ST6 .... 16 B2
Marsh Green Cl ST6 .... 16 B1
Marsh Green Rd ST6 .... 16 B1
Marsh La
  Cheswardine TF9 .... 130 A4
  Ellenhall ST21 .... 134 A1
  Lichfield WS14 .... 231 E3
  Penkridge ST19 .... 192 C1
  Stanton DE6 .... 80 B4
  Whittington WS14 .... 232 A3
  Wolv WV10 .... 240 A1
Marsh Lane Par WV10 ..... 240 B1
Marsh Par ST5 .... 284 C3
Marsh Prim Sch The
  ST11 .... 91 D3
Marsh St ST16 .... 155 E3
Marsh St N ST1 .... 282 B3
Marsh St S ST1 .... 282 B3
Marsh View ST3 .... 90 A3
Marsh Way ST5 .... 56 B3
Marshall Ave ST6 .... 43 D4
Marshall Cl WS3 .... 256 A2
Marshall Cl Burslem ST6 ... 41 F1
  Tamworth B77 .... 250 C3
Marshalls Ind Est WV2 .... 266 B4
Marshbrook Fst Sch
  ST19 .... 192 C1
Marshfield La ST6 .... 16 B1
Marshland Gr ST6 .... 42 A4
Marshlands Specl Sch
  ST17 .... 175 E3
Marshwood Cl WS11 .... 210 A1
Marsland Cl ST16 .... 155 D2
Marsland Rd ST16 .... 155 D2
Marston Cl
  Stourbridge DY8 .... 279 E2
  Wheaton Aston ST19 ...... 205 E3
Marston Croft ST19 .... 205 E3
Marston Ct ST16 .... 155 E3
Marston Dr ST16 .... 155 E3
Marston Gr ST1 .... 57 E4
Marston Ind Est WV2 ...... 266 B4
Marston La Hatton DE65 .. 146 B4
  Marston ST18 .... 136 C1
  Rolleston DE13 .... 147 D2
  Stafford ST18 .... 136 C1
Marston Old La DE65 ...... 146 B4
Marston Rise DE15 .... 185 F4
Marsworth Way ST16 ...... 136 B1
Martham Dr WV6 .... 255 D1
Martin Croft WS14 .... 214 A1
Martin Dale TF9 .... 99 E3
Martin Dr ST16 .... 155 E2
Martin St Hanley ST6 .... 57 D4
  Stafford ST16 .... 155 F2
  Wolv WV4 .... 266 C3
Martin's La DE13 .... 145 D2
Martindale
  Cannock WS11 .... 210 A1
  Stafford ST17 .... 175 E3
Martindale Cl ST3 .... 89 F4
Martindale Trad Est
  WS11 .... 210 A1
Martins Way ST18 .... 158 B4
Martinslow La ST13 .... 48 C2
Martley Rd WS4 .... 244 B1
Marton Ave WS7 .... 229 D4
Marwood Cft B74 .... 257 D1
Mary Howard CE Prim Sch
  B79 .... 217 E3
Mary Rand Cl ST17 .... 174 A4
Mary Rose Ct ST2 .... 58 A2
Mary St WS12 .... 210 A4
Marychurch CE Prim Sch
  ST2 .... 58 A2
Marychurch Rd ST2 .... 58 A2
Maryfield Wlk ST4 .... 71 F4
Maryhill Cl ST7 .... 26 A2
Maryhill High & Prim Sch
  ST7 .... 26 A2
Marysgate ST19 .... 223 E4
Maryvale Ct WS14 .... 231 E4
Masefield Cl
  Burntwood WS7 .... 212 A1
  Cheadle ST10 .... 76 B3
  Lichfield WS14 .... 231 D3
Masefield Cres DE14 .... 166 B4
Masefield Dr B79 .... 250 A4
Masefield Gr WS11 .... 209 F2
Masefield Rd
  Essington WV10 .... 241 D1
  Longton ST3 .... 73 D1
  Sedgley DY3 .... 271 D2
Mason Cres WV4 .... 265 F3
Mason Dr ST8 .... 27 D4
Mason St ST4 .... 72 C3
Mason's Pl TF10 .... 168 C3
Masons Lawn ST20 .... 171 E3
Masterson St ST4 .... 72 B3
Mathews Wlk ST1 .... 282 C3

Matlock Cl WS3 .... 243 E2
Matlock Dr WS11 .... 210 A2
Matlock Pl ST5 .... 55 D1
Matlock Rd WS3 .... 243 E2
Matlock St ST1 .... 282 B1
Matthews Pl CW12 .... 6 A1
Matthews Rd ST17 .... 174 B4
Matthews Wlk WS13 .... 214 A1
Maud St ST4 .... 72 C4
Maunders Rd ST2 .... 43 D1
Maureen Ave ST6 .... 41 E3
Maureen Gr ST5 .... 56 B2
Mavesyn Cl WS15 .... 198 A4
Mavis Rd WS12 .... 210 A4
Mavor Ave WS7 .... 211 E1
Mawdesley St ST6 .... 57 D3
Mawgan Dr WS14 .... 231 E3
Mawson Gr ST4 .... 57 E1
Maxstoke Ave B77 .... 261 E2
Maxstoke Cl WS3 .... 243 D2
Maxton Way ST3 .... 74 A1
Maxwell Cl WS14 .... 231 E4
Maxwell Pl ST4 .... 71 F4
Maxwell Rd
  Congleton CW12 .... 16 A4
  Wolv WV2 .... 266 B4
May Ave
  Newcastle-u-L ST5 .... 56 B2
  Tunstall ST6 .... 41 F2
May Bank Inf Sch ST5 .... 56 B2
May Cl WS7 .... 211 F1
May Pl Longton ST4 .... 283 B5
May St Chell Heath ST6 ...... 42 A1
  Newcastle-u-L ST5 .... 55 E1
Mayall Dr B75 .... 258 B2
Mayama Rd B78 .... 260 C4
Maybank WS14 .... 231 F4
Maybrook Ind Est WS8 .... 244 C3
Maybrook Rd WS8 .... 244 C3
Maybury Cl WV8 .... 238 C2
Maybury Way ST2 .... 43 D1
Maybush Gdns WV10 ...... 240 B1
Maycroft Cl ST17 .... 209 F4
Mayer Ave ST5 .... 284 B4
Mayer Bank 6 ST6 .... 57 D4
Mayer St ST1 .... 282 C3
Mayfair DE11 .... 186 C3
Mayfair Ave ST10 .... 62 A4
Mayfair Cl WV7 .... 237 D3
Mayfair Dr
  Drayton Bassett B77 .... 261 D4
  Kingswinford DY6 .... 275 E4
Mayfair Gdns WV3 .... 255 E1
Mayfair Gr ST9 .... 43 F4
Mayfield B77 .... 262 B4
Mayfield Ave
  Hanley ST1 .... 57 F3
  Mayfield DE6 .... 81 E4
  Newcastle-u-L ST5 .... 284 A2
  Penkridge ST19 .... 207 F4
Mayfield Cl ST13 .... 30 A3
Mayfield Cres ST1 .... 57 F2
Mayfield Dr
  Blythe Bridge ST11 .... 90 B4
  Burton u T DE15 .... 186 A4
Mayfield Pl E ST4 .... 71 F3
Mayfield Pl W ST4 .... 71 F3
Mayfield Rd
  Albrighton WV7 .... 237 D3
  Biddulph ST8 .... 27 E3
  Burton u T DE15 .... 167 D2
  Stafford ST17 .... 156 B1
Mayfield Terr DE6 .... 81 E3
Mayfields Dr WS8 .... 228 A1
Mayflower Dr WS15 .... 178 B1
Maygrove Rd DY6 .... 275 F4
Maylea Cres ST6 .... 57 E4
Maynard Ave DY8 .... 279 E2
Maynards Croft TF10 .... 169 D2
Mayne St ST4 .... 71 F1
Mayneford Pl ST4 .... 71 F1
Mayock Cres ST16 .... 155 D2
Mayou Ct WS3 .... 244 A2
Maypole Ct WV5 .... 270 A3
Maypole Dr DY8 .... 279 F3
Maypole St WV5 .... 270 A4
Mayswood Dr WV6 .... 254 C1
Maythorn Gdns WV6 .... 255 D1
Maythorne Rd ST3 .... 73 D1
Maywood Cl DY6 .... 275 D3
McAdam Cl DE15 .... 167 D1
McBean Rd WV6 .... 255 F2
McGeough Wlk WS11 ...... 210 A3
Mcghie St WS12 .... 210 A3
McGough St ST6 .... 41 E2
Mckellin Cl ST7 .... 39 F1
McKie Way WS15 .... 196 C3
McKinley St ST6 .... 41 E2
Mclean Rd WV10 .... 240 B1
Mead Ave ST7 .... 25 F4
Mead Cl WS9 .... 256 A3
Mead Cres DE15 .... 186 A3
Mead The Sedgley DY3 .... 271 D4
  Trentham ST4 .... 88 A4
Mead Wlk DE15 .... 186 A4
Meadfoot Dr ST6 .... 275 D4
Meadlands The WV5 .... 269 F3
Meadow Ave
  Cheddleton ST9 .... 60 A3
  6 Longton ST3 .... 73 E1
  Newcastle-u-L ST5 .... 56 A2
  Weston CW2 .... 37 D3
Meadow Bank Wlk ST16 .. 155 E4

Meadow Cl Aldridge B74 ...... **256** C1
Blythe Bridge ST11 .... **90** C3
Eccleshall ST21 .... **133** F4
Forsbrook ST11 .... **91** D4
Gnosall ST20 .... **171** F4
Market Drayton TF9 .... **97** D1
Wheaton Aston ST19 .... **205** D3
Meadow Croft
Hagley DY9 .... **281** F2
Huntington WS12 .... **209** E2
Perton WV6 .... **254** B2
Streethay WS13 .... **215** D1
Meadow Ct Barlaston ST12 .. **88** B1
Burton u T DE14 .... **166** C2
Stafford ST17 .... **175** D4
Meadow Dr Cheadle ST10 .... **76** B2
Haughton ST18 .... **172** C3
Longton ST3 .... **89** D4
Meadow Glade ST18 .... **158** B4
Meadow Gr WS6 .... **227** D1
Meadow Hill Dr WS11 .... **210** A2
Meadow La
Acton Trussell ST17 .... **193** D4
Blythe Bridge ST11 .... **106** C4
Burton u T DE13 .... **167** A4
Colwich ST18 .... **177** E4
Millmeece ST21 .... **117** F4
Newcastle-u-L ST5 .... **56** A2
Roston DE6 .... **96** B4
Seighford ST18 .... **154** C1
Swadlincote DE11 .... **186** C3
Trentham ST4 .... **88** B4
Wombourne WV5 .... **270** A4
Yoxall DE13 .... **200** A4
Meadow Lark Cl WS12 ...... **210** A2
Meadow Pk B79 .... **249** F3
Meadow Pl ST3 .... **74** A1
Meadow Rd
Albrighton WV7 .... **237** D3
Aldridge WS9 .... **256** A2
Barlaston ST12 .... **88** B1
Burton u T DE14 .... **166** C2
Chell Heath ST6 .... **42** B3
Endon ST6 .... **43** D3
Newport TF10 .... **169** D2
Stafford ST17 .... **174** C4
Wolv WV3 .... **265** E4
Meadow Ridge ST17 .... **175** E4
Meadow Rise DE13 .... **183** F1
Meadow Side ST8 .... **27** D3
Meadow St
Newcastle-u-L ST5 .... **55** F3
Norton-in-t-M ST2 .... **43** D1
Tamworth B77 .... **250** B2
Meadow The ST9 .... **43** F4
Meadow Vale WV8 .... **239** D1
Meadow View
Burntwood WS7 .... **229** E3
Doveridge DE6 .... **127** E4
Rolleston DE13 .... **147** E4
Sedgley DY3 .... **266** B1
Meadow View Cl TF10 ...... **169** D2
Meadow View Rd
Newport TF10 .... **169** D2
Swadlincote DE11 .... **186** C3
Meadow View Terr WV6 .... **255** F2
Meadow Way
Armitage WS15 .... **198** A2
Cannock WS12 .... **210** B1
Kingswinford DY8 .... **275** E1
Lawton-gate ST7 .... **25** D3
Stone ST15 .... **119** F3
Upper Tean ST10 .... **92** B2
Whitmore ST5 .... **85** E3
Meadow Wlk WV8 .... **238** C1
Meadowbank Ave ST18 ...... **138** B1
Meadowbrook Ct ST15 ...... **120** B3
Meadowbrook Rd WS13 ...... **214** A2
Meadowcroft Ave ST3 .... **90** B4
Meadowcroft Gdns ST19 .... **205** E3
Meadowfields Cl DY8 .... **275** F1
Meadowhill Dr DY8 .... **275** F1
Meadowlands Dr WS4 .... **244** B1
Meadowpark Rd DY8 .... **279** E4
Meadows Prim Sch The
CW3 .... **69** D4
Meadows Rd ST7 .... **25** F1
Meadows Sch The ST8 .... **27** E3
Meadows The Endon ST9 .... **44** A4
Hilderstone ST15 .... **106** B1
Kingstone ST14 .... **141** E4
Rugeley WS15 .... **197** D3
Uttoxeter ST14 .... **111** D1
Meadowside Ashley TF9 ...... **99** E3
Blythe Bridge ST11 .... **91** D1
Mayfield DE6 .... **81** E3
Trentham ST4 .... **88** A4
Meadowside Ave ST3 .... **39** E1
Meadowside Dr DE14 .... **166** C2
Meadowside L Ctr DE14 .... **166** C2
Meadowside Rd B74 .... **257** F2
Meadowview ST15 .... **118** C3
Meadway WS12 .... **210** B2
Meadway Dr ST17 .... **175** E3
Meadway WS7 .... **229** D3
Meadway The WV6 .... **255** D3
Meaford Ave ST15 .... **104** C1
Meaford Dr ST5 .... **72** C2
Meaford Rd
Barlaston ST15 .... **104** B3
Stone ST15 .... **104** B3
Meakin Ave ST5 .... **71** D2
Meakin Cl Cheadle ST10 ...... **76** B1
Congleton CW12 .... **6** A1
Stone ST15 .... **120** B3

Meakin Gr ST16 .... **155** D3
Meakin Ho ST15 .... **104** C1
Mear Greaves La DE15 ...... **167** D2
Mear's La WS15 .... **198** C4
Mease Ave WS7 .... **229** E3
Mease La B79 .... **218** A1
Meddins Cl DY7 .... **278** A2
Meddins La DY7 .... **277** F2
Meddins Rise DY7 .... **277** F2
Medina B77 .... **250** C1
Medina Cl WV10 .... **240** C2
Medina Way
Kidsgrove ST7 .... **26** A1
Kingswinford DY6 .... **275** E3
Medway B77 .... **250** B1
Medway Dr ST6 .... **16** B1
Medway Pl ST7 .... **71** D2
Medway Rd WS8 .... **228** B1
Medway Wlk
Brownhills WS8 .... **228** B1
Chell Heath ST6 .... **42** A2
Meece Rd Millmeece ST15 .... **118** B3
Swynnerton ST15 .... **118** C3
Meerash La WS7 .... **229** E2
Meerbrook Cl ST4 .... **88** A3
Meerbrook Rd ST13 .... **19** E1
Meere Cl ST5 .... **42** C2
Meeson Cl WV7 .... **237** D3
Meg La WS7 .... **212** A1
Megacre ST7 .... **40** A1
Meigh Rd ST9 .... **59** D2
Meigh St ST1 .... **282** C3
Meiklejohn Pl ST6 .... **42** A3
Meir Heath Prim Sch ST3 .... **90** A2
Meir Prim Sch ST3 .... **74** A1
Meir Rd ST3 .... **73** F1
Meir St ST6 .... **41** F2
Meir View ST3 .... **74** A1
Meirhay Rd ST3 .... **73** F1
Melbourne Ave DE15 .... **167** E2
Melbourne Cl DY6 .... **275** F2
Melbourne Cres
Cannock WS12 .... **210** C1
Stafford ST16 .... **156** A3
Melbourne Rd WS12 .... **210** C1
Melbourne St ST3 .... **73** C3
Melbury Way WS11 .... **209** F1
Melchester Gr ST3 .... **73** F1
Melchester Wlk WS11 .... **209** F1
Melfont St ST6 .... **41** F2
Melford B79 .... **249** F3
Melford Cl DY3 .... **266** B1
Melford Grange WS7 .... **211** F1
Melford Rise WS7 .... **211** F1
Meliden Way ST4 .... **71** F3
Mellard St
Audley ST7 .... **39** E1
Newcastle-u-L ST5 .... **284** A1
Mellor Dr
Sutton Coldfield B74 .... **257** F2
Uttoxeter ST14 .... **111** D1
Mellor Rd DE14 .... **185** D4
Mellor St ST7 .... **26** C1
Mellors Bank ST7 .... **26** B3
Mellow La ST10, ST13 .... **47** F2
Mellowdew Rd DY8 .... **275** E2
Mellwaters B77 .... **262** B4
Melmerby B77 .... **262** B4
Melrose Ave
Blythe Bridge ST3 .... **90** A3
Hanley ST1 .... **57** E4
Newcastle-u-L ST5 .... **71** D3
Stafford ST17 .... **174** A4
Stone ST15 .... **120** B3
Stourbridge DY8 .... **279** F1
Melrose Cres TF9 .... **112** A4
Melrose Dr
Cannock WS12 .... **209** F4
Perton WV6 .... **254** C2
Melrose Pl ST13 .... **30** A3
Melstone Ave ST6 .... **41** F2
Melville Ct ST5 .... **71** E1
Melville Rd ST3 .... **73** F1
Melville St ST1 .... **57** F2
Melvyn Cres ST6 .... **56** B4
Menai Dr ST8 .... **27** E3
Mendip Ave ST1 .... **175** F3
Mendip Cl Sedgley DY3 ...... **271** E2
Wolv WV2 .... **266** C4
Mendip Gr ST2 .... **43** D1
Mendip Pl ST5 .... **55** F2
Mendip Rd WS12 .... **195** D1
Mendip Way B77 .... **251** E1
Mentone Cres TF10 .... **168** A2
Meon Gr WV6 .... **254** C2
Mercer Ave ST15 .... **120** B4
Mercer St ST3 .... **73** D1
Merchant Cl WV6 .... **253** E2
Merchants Way WS9 .... **256** A4
Mercia Cl Hatton DE65 ...... **146** B4
Tamworth B79 .... **249** F4
Mercia Cres ST6 .... **57** D3
Mercia Dr WV6 .... **254** C3
Mercian Ct TF9 .... **97** E1
Mercian Way
Tamworth B77 .... **251** D2
Wheaton Aston ST19 .... **206** A4
Mercury Ct B77 .... **251** D2
Mercury Pl ST7 .... **42** B1
Mercury Rd WS11 .... **210** A3
Mere Cl TF10 .... **168** C2
Mere Dr B75 .... **258** A1
Mere Green Cl B75 .... **258** A1
Mere Green Comb Sch
B75 .... **258** A1
Mere Green Rd B75 .... **258** A1
Mere La DY7 .... **273** E3
Mere Pool Rd B75 .... **258** C1

Mere Rd Stourbridge DY8 .... **279** F2
Weston CW2 .... **37** D3
Mere Rd ST21 .... **132** B4
Meredith Cl DE14 .... **166** B3
Meredith Rd DY3 .... **271** D3
Merelake Rd Alsager ST7 .... **40** A4
Kidsgrove ST7 .... **40** A4
Meremore Dr ST5 .... **40** B1
Merevale Ave ST2 .... **58** A1
Merganser B77 .... **262** A3
Meriden Ave DY8 .... **279** E3
Meriden Cl
Cannock WS11 .... **226** A4
Stourbridge DY8 .... **279** E3
Meriden Rd
Newcastle-u-L ST5 .... **71** E1
Wolv WV10 .... **240** A1
Merlin Cl Cannock WS11 ...... **209** E1
Chell Heath ST6 .... **42** A4
Uttoxeter ST14 .... **126** B3
Merlin Cres DE14 .... **184** C4
Merlin Gn CW3 .... **68** C3
Merlin Way WS14 .... **232** C3
Merrial St ST5 .... **284** B3
Merrick St ST1 .... **282** C4
Merridale Ave WV3 .... **255** F1
Merridale Cl WV3 .... **255** F1
Merridale Gr WV3 .... **255** F1
Merridale Rd WV3 .... **255** F1
Merridale St W WV3 .... **266** A4
Merrill Cl WS6 .... **226** C1
Merrion Dr ST6 .... **42** A2
Merrivale Rd ST17 .... **174** C4
Merry Rd ST17 .... **174** C4
Merrydale Rd DE15 .... **186** A4
Merryfield Rd DY1 .... **271** F1
Merryfields Sch ST5 .... **56** A2
Mersey Cl WS15 .... **178** C2
Mersey Rd
Newcastle-u-L ST5 .... **71** D2
Walsall WS3 .... **243** F1
Mersey St ST1 .... **282** A2
Merton Ct WS7 .... **228** C3
Merton St ST3 .... **283** C4
Mervyn Rd ST5 .... **167** D2
Mesnes Gn WS14 .... **231** E4
Metcalf Cl WS7 .... **229** E4
Metcalfe Cl WS12 .... **210** B3
Metcalfe Rd ST6 .... **42** A2
Metfield Cl B79 .... **250** B4
Mewies Cl DE12 .... **184** B1
Mews Cl ST2 .... **58** A1
Mews The ST5 .... **56** B2
Meynall Ingram Hospl
DE13 .... **182** A1
Meynell Cl DE15 .... **167** D1
Meyrick Rd ST17 .... **155** F1
Mica Cl ST7 .... **251** D1
Michael Cl ST3 .... **74** A2
Michael's La DE6 .... **80** B3
Michaels Cl ST5 .... **56** B4
Michigan Cl WS11 .... **210** A4
Michigan Gr ST4 .... **88** A4
Micklea La ST9 .... **29** F1
Mickleby Way ST3 .... **90** B4
Micklegate ST19 .... **223** E4
Micklehome Dr DE13 .... **201** D2
Micklewood Cl ST19 .... **207** F4
Micklewood La ST19 .... **208** A2
Middle Cross St ST3 .... **283** C4
Middle Entry B79 .... **250** A4
Middle Friars ST17 .... **155** F1
Middle La Brewood WV9 .... **240** A3
Codsall, Coven Heath WV9 .... **240** A3
Codsall, Oaken WV8 .... **238** B1
Congleton CW12 .... **6** B2
Gnosall TF10 .... **188** B4
Middlefield Gnosall ST20 .... **171** F4
Wolv WV6 .... **239** F1
Middlefield Rd ST2 .... **73** E4
Middlehurst Specl Sch
ST7 .... **41** F4
Middlemore La WS9 .... **256** A3
Middlepark Rd DY1 .... **271** F1
Middleport Inf Sch ST6 ...... **56** C4
Middlesmoor B77 .... **262** B4
Middleton Cl ST16 .... **42** C2
Middleton Rd
Aldridge B74 .... **257** D1
Brownhills WS8 .... **229** D1
Whittington WS14 .... **232** C3
Middleway WS12 .... **211** D3
Middleway Ave DY8 .... **275** E2
Midfield Cl ST6 .... **16** B1
Midgley Dr B74 .... **258** A1
Midhurst Cl ST7 .... **41** F4
Midhurst Dr WS12 .... **210** B4
Midhurst Gr WV6 .... **255** E3
Midland Rd WS12 .... **209** E3
Midway Dr ST11 .... **90** C3
Midway The ST5 .... **284** B2
Milan Dr ST5 .... **70** C3
Milborne Dr ST5 .... **71** E3
Milburn B77 .... **262** B4
Mildon Rd ST6 .... **57** D3
Milcote Way DY6 .... **275** D4
Mildenhall B79 .... **250** B4
Mile Ct ST5 .... **55** F2
Mile Flat Kinver DY6 .... **274** C4
Swindon DY6 .... **274** C4
Mile Oak Cross Roads
B78 .... **249** E1
Milehouse La ST5 .... **56** A2
Miles Bank ST1 .... **282** B3
Miles Green ST7 .... **54** C4
Milestone Dr DY9 .... **281** F2
Milford Ave ST9 .... **59** D2

Milford Cl DY8 .... **275** F2
Weston CW2 .... **37** D3
Milford Rd
Newcastle-u-L ST5 .... **284** A1
Stafford ST17 .... **175** F4
Wolv WV2 .... **266** B4
Milford St ST4 .... **72** C3
Milgreen Ave ST1 .... **57** E4
Milk St ST13 .... **30** C4
Milking Bank DY5 .... **271** E1
Milking Bank Prim Sch
DY1 .... **271** F1
Mill Bank DY3 .... **271** E4
Mill Cl Blakedown DY10 ...... **281** D1
Caverswall ST11 .... **74** B2
Newton Solney DE15 .... **167** F4
Sedgley DY3 .... **271** E3
Mill Cotts ST18 .... **139** E3
Mill Cres
Barton-u-N DE13 .... **201** F4
Cannock WS11 .... **210** A1
Mill Croft ST18 .... **158** A1
Mill End La DE21 .... **200** C2
Mill Farm Ct ST21 .... **134** B3
Mill Fields DY7 .... **278** A2
Mill Gn WV10 .... **240** B2
Mill Gr Cheadle ST10 .... **76** C1
Codsall WV8 .... **239** E2
Kidsgrove ST7 .... **25** E1
Mill Hayes Rd
Biddulph ST8 .... **27** E2
Burslem ST6 .... **41** F1
Mill Hill Cres ST6 .... **42** A2
Mill Hill Dr DE15 .... **167** D2
Mill Hill La DE15 .... **167** D2
Mill Hill Prim Sch ST6 ...... **41** F2
Mill La
Acton Trussell ST17 .... **175** D1
Albrighton WV7 .... **220** C1
Aldridge WS9 .... **256** C4
Barthomley CW2 .... **38** B4
Barton-u-N DE13 .... **201** F4
Blakedown DY10 .... **281** D1
Blakenhall CW5 .... **52** A2
Burntwood WS7 .... **229** E2
Cheddleton ST9 .... **59** F4
Cheslyn Hay WS11 .... **226** B3
Codsall WV8 .... **238** C3
Colwich ST18 .... **158** A1
Congleton CW12 .... **16** B4
Doveridge DE6 .... **127** D4
Fazeley B78 .... **261** D4
Foston DE6 .... **129** E4
Gnosall ST20 .... **171** E3
Hartington SK17 .... **24** B3
Kingstone ST14 .... **124** C2
Kinver DY7 .... **278** A2
Kinver, Blundies DY7 .... **274** A2
Little Aston WS9 .... **257** D3
Madeley CW3 .... **68** C4
Milwich ST18 .... **122** B2
Oakamoor ST10 .... **78** A3
Roston DE6 .... **96** B4
Rugeley WS15 .... **178** C1
Scropton DE6 .... **129** F1
Shenstone WS14 .... **247** D3
Shenstone, Lower Stonnall
WS9, WS14 .... **246** A2
Standon ST21 .... **102** B2
Stone ST15 .... **105** F3
Tamworth B79 .... **250** B3
The Bank ST7 .... **26** A4
Tong TF11 .... **220** B4
Upper Tean ST10 .... **92** C1
Weston CW2 .... **37** D3
Weston-u-L TF11 .... **220** B4
Wheaton Aston ST19 .... **205** E3
Wolv WV6 .... **255** D2
Wombourne WV5 .... **270** A3
Mill Park Ind Est WS11 ...... **210** A1
Mill Pk WS11 .... **210** A1
Mill Pond The WS13 .... **214** B1
Mill Pool Rd WS12 .... **210** A3
Mill Rd
Brownhills, Catshill WS8 ...... **245** D4
Brownhills, Shelfield WS4 ...... **244** B1
Mill Rise ST7 .... **26** A1
Mill St Brierley Hill DY8 ...... **275** F1
Cannock WS11 .... **209** F1
Kingswinford DY8 .... **275** F1
Leek ST13 .... **30** B3
Newcastle-u-L ST5 .... **55** E1
Penkridge ST19 .... **192** C1
Rocester ST14 .... **96** A2
Stafford ST16 .... **155** F2
Stone ST15 .... **120** A4
Mill Stream Cl WV8 .... **239** D2
Mill View ST6 .... **42** B3
Mill Waters ST10 .... **76** C1
Mill Way WS15 .... **198** A1
Mill Way The ST15 .... **103** D2
Millbank ST10 .... **155** F2
Millbank Dr ST14 .... **96** A2
Millbank Pl ST5 .... **55** F1
Millbank St
Essington WV11 .... **241** F1
Longton ST3 .... **283** C3
Millbeck Cl CW2 .... **37** D3
Millbridge Cl ST3 .... **90** A3
Millbrook Cl WS11 .... **209** F1
Millbrook Dr WS14 .... **246** C3
Millbrook Gr ST2 .... **43** D1
Millbrook Way ST10 .... **76** C1
Millcroft Way WS15 .... **198** B2
Milldale Cres WV10 .... **240** B2
Milldale Rd WV10 .... **240** B2
Millend La ST7 .... **39** E3
Millenium Cl WS3 .... **244** A2
Miller Cres WV14 .... **266** C4

Miller St ST5 .... **284** C3
Millers Gn WV7 .... **237** D2
Millers Green Dr DY6 .... **275** D4
Millers Vale
Cannock WS12 .... **210** B1
Wombourne WV5 .... **269** E3
Millers View Cheadle ST10 .. **76** C1
Kidsgrove ST7 .... **26** A1
Millersdale Cl DE15 .... **167** D3
Millet St ST2 .... **58** A2
Milley's Hospital WS13 ...... **231** E4
Millfield Ave
Brownhills WS4 .... **244** A1
Walsall WS3 .... **243** E2
Millfield Cres ST2 .... **43** D1
Millfield Dr TF9 .... **97** F1
Millfield Jun Mix Inf Sch
WS8 .... **245** D4
Millfield Prim Sch B78 ...... **261** D4
Millfield Rd WS8 .... **245** D4
Millfields Way WV5 .... **269** F3
Millhouse Dr ST10 .... **76** C1
Millhouse Gdns ST19 .... **192** C1
Millicent Cl WS12 .... **210** A3
Millicent St ST4 .... **72** C3
Millington St WS15 .... **178** C1
Millmoor Ave WS15 .... **198** A2
Millpool The WV5 .... **263** F1
Millrise Rd ST2 .... **43** D1
Mills Cres WV2 .... **266** C4
Mills Rd WV2 .... **266** C4
Millstone Ave ST7 .... **25** F1
Millstone Edge ST13 .... **45** D1
Millstream Cl ST10 .... **76** C1
Millwalk Ave WS15 .... **120** B4
Millwalk Dr WV9 .... **240** A2
Millward Rd ST2 .... **58** B2
Millway La DE6 .... **35** F2
Milner Dr B79 .... **251** F4
Milner Terr ST13 .... **31** D4
Milnes St ST13 .... **73** D1
Milo Cres B78 .... **250** A1
Milton Ave B79 .... **250** A4
Milton Cres Kidsgrove ST7 .. **40** B4
Sedgley DY3 .... **271** D3
Milton Ct WV6 .... **254** C2
Milton Dr TF9 .... **97** E1
Milton Gr ST17 .... **174** A4
Milton Ho DE14 .... **166** B2
Milton Prim Sch ST2 .... **43** D1
Milton Rd Cannock WS11 .... **209** F2
Hanley ST2 .... **57** F4
Milton St Burton u T DE14 .. **166** B2
Hanley ST1 .... **282** A1
Milvale St ST6 .... **56** C4
Milverton Dr ST14 .... **110** C3
Milverton Pl ☒ ST3 .... **73** D2
Milward Gr ST3 .... **89** F3
Mimosa Wlk DY6 .... **275** F4
Minard Gr ST3 .... **74** A2
Minden Gr ST6 .... **57** E4
Minehead Rd Dudley DY1 .... **271** F1
Wolv WV10 .... **240** A1
Miners Wlk B78 .... **251** F1
Minerva Cl Biddulph ST8 .... **27** D3
Tamworth B77 .... **250** B3
Minerva Rd ST4 .... **72** C3
Minewood Cl WS3 .... **242** C2
Minfield Cl ST7 .... **41** D4
Minn-End-La Bosley SK11 .. **8** A3
Wincle SK11 .... **8** A3
Minors Hill WS14 .... **231** F4
Minshall St ST4 .... **72** B3
Minster St ST6 .... **42** A1
Minster The WV3 .... **266** A4
Minsterley Cl WV3 .... **265** F4
Minsterpool Wlk WS13 ...... **231** D4
Minton Cl Cheadle ST10 .... **76** B1
Congleton CW12 .... **6** A1
Minton Pl ST5 .... **56** B3
Minton St
Newcastle-u-L ST5 .... **56** B3
Stoke-on-T ST4 .... **71** E4
Miranda Gr ST6 .... **42** B1
Mires Brook La WS15 .... **160** C3
Mires The DE6 .... **35** D2
Mirfield Cl WV9 .... **240** A2
Miss Pickerings Field
ST17 .... **175** D1
Mistley Wlk ST6 .... **41** E4
Mitcham Cl WS12 .... **209** F4
Mitchel Rd DY6 .... **275** F2
Mitchell Ave ST5 .... **25** E1
Mitchell Cl ST5 .... **25** E1
Mitchell High Sch The
ST2 .... **58** B2
Mitchell Rise ST15 .... **118** C3
Mitchell St ST6 .... **41** F1
Mitre Cl WV11 .... **242** A2
Mitre Rd WS6 .... **226** B1
Mitton Rd ST18 .... **191** E4
Moat Bank DE15 .... **167** E1
Moat Brook Ave WV8 .... **238** C2
Moat Dr B78 .... **260** C3
Moat Farm Way WS3 .... **244** A3
Moat Hall Prim Sch
WS6 .... **226** C2
Moat House Dr ST18 .... **172** C3
Moat La Audley ST7 .... **39** D2
Great Wyrley WS6 .... **227** D1
Newborough ST14 .... **162** C3
Moat The ST3 .... **74** A2
Moat Way WS15 .... **198** A2
Moatbrook La WV8 .... **238** B3
Moathouse ST17 .... **193** D4
Moatside Cl WS3 .... **244** A3
Mob La WS4 .... **244** B2
Mobberley Rd ST6 .... **41** E4

Moden Cl DY3 271 E3
Moden Hill DY3 271 E3
Moffat Gr ST2 73 F4
Moffat Way ST5 55 D1
Moises Hall Rd WV5 270 A4
Moisty La
Marchington ST14 127 E2
Uttoxeter ST14 126 C2
Mollatts Cl ST13 30 A1
Mollatts Wood Rd ST13 30 A1
Mollison Rd ST3 90 A4
Mona Rd DE13 166 A3
Monaco Pl ST5 70 C4
Monarch Cl DE13 166 C4
Monk St DE13 146 B4
Monkhouse ST10 76 B2
Monkleigh Cl ST4 88 A3
Monks Cl
Newcastle-u-L ST5 71 E3
Wombourne WV5 269 F3
Monks Way
Swynnerton ST15 103 D2
Tamworth B77 250 C3
Monks Wlk ST20 171 E3
Monkton Cl ST3 73 D1
Monkton Recn Ctr
ST19 192 B1
Monmouth Pl ST5 71 E2
Monpelier Cl DE14 185 D4
Monsal Gr ST1 57 F3
Monsaldale Cl
Brownhills WS8 244 C3
Burton u T DE15 167 D2
Monteagle Dr DY6 270 B1
Montford Gr DY3 271 E4
Montfort Pl ST5 71 D3
Montgomery Pl ST3 74 A1
Montley B77 262 B4
Montpellier Gdns DY1 271 F1
Montrose Cl WS11 209 F3
Montrose St ST4 72 C3
Montville Dr ST17 155 D1
Monty Pl ST4 73 D3
Monument Dr WV10 241 E4
Monument La Sedgley DY3 266 C1
Tittensor ST12 88 A1
Monument Rd ST7 40 B3
Monument View ST7 39 F1
Monyash Cl ST3 90 B4
Monyash Dr ST13 31 D3
Moon's La WS6 226 B1
Moor Cl
Acton Trussell ST17 175 D1
Biddulph ST6 16 C1
Perton WV6 254 C2
Moor Croft WS15 179 D3
Moor Fst Sch ST8 17 D1
Moor Gr ST14 126 A4
Moor Hall Dr B75 258 B1
Moor Hall La ST19 208 A4
Moor Hill Jun & Inf Sch
B75 258 B1
Moor La Cheadle ST10 76 C2
Church Leigh ST10 108 C3
Colton WS15 179 D4
Pattingham WV6 253 E1
Seighford ST18 154 B4
Shenstone WS14 246 C1
Tamworth, Amington B79 251 D3
Tamworth, Bolehall B77 250 B3
Moor Pk Perton WV6 254 B3
Walsall WS3 243 D2
Moor St Burton u T DE14 166 B1
Tamworth B79 250 A3
Moor St S WV2 266 B4
Moor The WS13 215 E4
Moor View WS7 212 A1
Moorcroft Ave ST5 71 D2
Moorcroft Cl ST10 76 B1
Moore Cl B74 257 F3
Moore St Burslem ST6 57 D4
Cannock WS12 210 B4
Moores Cl DE13 166 A3
Moores Croft B79 217 E3
Moorfield Ave ST8 27 E4
Moorfield Ct TF10 168 C1
Moorfield Cty Prim Sch
TF10 168 C1
Moorfield La TF10 168 B1
Moorfield Rd WV2 266 B4
Moorfields Leek ST13 30 C3
Stafford ST16 155 E4
Moorfields Cl ST10 63 F2
Moorfields Ind Est ST15 102 C2
Moorgate B79 250 A3
Moorgate Cty Prim Sch
B79 250 A3
Moorhead Dr ST9 43 F2
Moorhill Prim Sch WS11 209 F3
Moorhouse Ct ST15 119 D3
Moorhouse St ST13 30 C3
Moorings The
Alrewas DE13 200 C2
Colwich ST17 177 F4
Wolv WV9 239 F1
Moorland Ave ST9 59 E2
Moorland Cl
Caverswall ST9 59 D2
Rugeley WS15 178 B1
Moorland Rd Biddulph ST8 27 E4
Burslem ST6 57 D4
Cannock WS11 209 F3
Cheddleton ST13 45 E3
Chell Heath ST6 42 A1
Kidsgrove ST7 26 B4
Leek ST13 31 D3
Newport TF10 168 C1
Moorland View ST6 42 B2
Moorlands Farm Pk The
ST10 47 E2
Moorleys La ST18 139 D3
Moorpark Jun Sch ST6 42 A1
Moors Dr WV9 224 A1
Moorside High Sch ST9 59 F2
Moorside Rd ST9 59 E2
Moorson Ave ST7 25 F4
Moorsyde Rd ST4 71 F3
Moorthorne Cres ST5 56 A3
Moorview Gdns ST7 26 B3
Moran Gr ST6 56 C4
Moran Rd ST5 55 F1
Mordaunt Dr B75 258 C1
Moresby Cl ST2 43 D1
Moreton Ave
Kingsley ST10 61 E1
Tittensor ST5 87 E4
Wolv WV4 266 C2
Moreton Cl Caverswall ST9 59 D1
Kidsgrove ST7 41 D4
Moreton Com Sch
WV10 240 C1
Moreton La Colwich ST18 158 C2
Draycott in t C DE6 144 B4
Moreton Par ST5 56 B2
Moreton Rd WV10 240 B1
Moreton St WS11 209 F2
Morfe La DY7 273 E2
Morford Rd WS9 256 A4
Morgan Rd B78 250 A1
Morgan Way ST6 42 A3
Morland Cl ST15 120 A3
Morley Dr CW12 6 A1
Morley Rd WS7 229 D4
Morley Road Sh Ctr
WS7 229 D4
Morley St Hanley ST1 282 A2
Leek ST13 30 B3
Morley's Hill DE13 166 A4
Morlings Dr WS7 229 D4
Morning Pines DY8 279 F2
Morningside CW3 68 C3
Mornington Rd ST1 57 F4
Morpeth B77 261 E4
Morpeth St ST3 283 C3
Morridge View ST13 45 E2
Morris Dr ST16 156 B2
Morris Sq ST5 56 B3
Morston B77 261 E2
Morston Dr ST5 71 D1
Mortimer Pl ST3 73 F2
Morton Rd ST17 174 B3
Morton St ST6 56 C4
Morville Cl ST4 72 C4
Mosedale Ave ST3 89 F4
Moseley Ct WV11 241 F2
Moseley Old Hall La
WV10 241 D3
Moseley Rd
Essington WV10 241 D2
Wolv WV10 241 D2
Mosley Cty Prim Sch
DE13 165 E4
Mosley Dr ST14 111 D1
Mosley St DE14 166 B2
Moss Cl Aldridge WS9 256 A3
Caverswall ST9 59 D2
Huntington WS12 209 E3
Moss Gn WS15 178 B1
Moss Gr DY6 275 E4
Moss Hill ST9 43 E3
Moss La
Blythe Bridge ST15 106 C3
Cheadle ST10 77 D1
Cheswardine TF9 114 B2
Gnosall ST20 151 F4
Lawton-gate ST7 25 F2
Madeley CW3 68 B3
Maer ST5 84 C1
Norton in H TF9 97 F3
Whitmore ST5 85 E3
Moss Park Ave ST9 59 D2
Moss Pl ST7 26 A2
Moss Rd Astbury CW12 15 F4
Cannock WS11 210 A2
Congleton CW12 15 F4
Moss Rise ST5 71 E1
Moss Side ST1 57 F4
Moss St Cannock WS11 210 A2
Norton-in-t-M ST6 42 C3
Mossbank Ave WS7 229 D3
Mossdale B77 262 B4
Mossdale Way DY3 271 F4
Mossfield TF9 130 A3
Mossfield Rd Fenton ST3 73 E3
Longton ST3 73 E3
Mossland Rd ST3 73 E3
Mossley CE Prim Sch
CW12 16 A4
Mossley Cl WS3 242 C1
Mossley Ct CW12 15 F4
Mossley La WS3 242 C1
Mossley Prim Sch WS3 242 C1
Mosspit ST17 174 C3
Mossvale Gr ST16 155 D3
Mosswood St WS11 226 B4
Moston St ST1 57 E3
Mott Pl ST6 56 B4
Moulton Rd ST3 283 B4
Mount Ave
Cannock WS12 210 A4
Stoke-on-T ST4 71 F4
Stone ST15 104 C1
Mount Cl Caverswall ST9 59 E2
Cheslyn Hay WS6 226 C1
Sedgley DY5 271 E1
Wombourne WV5 270 A4
Mount Cres ST15 104 C1
Mount Dr WV5 270 A4
Mount Edge ST18 137 D1
Mount Gdns WV8 238 C2
Mount Ind Est ST15 104 C1
Mount La
Market Drayton TF9 112 B4
Sedgley DY5 271 E1
Mount Pl ST11 91 D4
Mount Pleasant
Ashley TF9 99 E3
Cheslyn Hay WS6 226 C1
Hanley ST1 282 A2
Kidsgrove ST7 26 A1
Kingswinford DY6 275 E2
Leek ST13 30 C3
Newcastle-u-L ST5 284 C2
Newcastle-u-L, Chesterton
ST5 55 F3
Seighford ST18 154 C1
Tamworth B77 261 E4
Mount Pleasant Ave
WV5 269 F4
Mount Pleasant CE
Prim Sch ST4 72 B3
Mount Pleasant Cl ST15 120 B3
Mount Pleasant Rd ST7 26 A4
Mount Rd
Brownhills WS3 244 A2
Burntwood WS7 229 D3
Forsbrook ST11 91 D4
Kidsgrove ST7 26 A1
Kingswinford DY8 275 F1
Leek ST13 31 D3
Linton DE11 186 B1
Rugeley WS15 178 A1
Stone ST15 104 C1
Wolv, Cinder Hill
WV4, WV14 266 C1
Wolv, Colton Hills WV4 266 A2
Wolv, Tettenhall Wood WV6 255 D2
Wombourne WV5 270 A4
Mount Road Ind Est
WS7 229 D3
Mount Row ST16 155 F2
Mount Sch for Deaf The
ST4 71 F4
Mount Side Rd WS12 210 B4
Mount St Burton u T DE15 167 D2
Cannock WS12 210 A4
Hanley ST1 57 F3
Newcastle-u-L ST5 55 F3
3 Stafford ST16 155 F2
Stone ST15 105 D1
Mount The Kidsgrove ST7 26 A1
Newcastle-u-L ST5 55 F3
Scholar Green ST7 25 F4
Mountain Ash Rd WS8 244 C3
Mountain Pine Cl WS12 210 A4
Mountbatten Cl
Burntwood WS7 211 F1
Burton u T DE13 166 B4
Mountfield Pl ST4 72 B3
Mountford Cres WS9 256 B4
Mountford St ST6 41 F1
Mountside Gdns ST13 31 D3
Mountsorrel Cl ST4 88 B3
Mountwood Covert
WV6 255 D2
Mouse Hill WS3 243 F2
Mousley St ST6 56 C4
Mow Cop Rd ST7 26 B3
Mow La Biddulph ST6 16 A1
Mount Pleasant ST7 26 A3
Mowbray Croft WS7 211 F1
Mowbray Wlk ST2 57 F4
Moxhull Cl WV12 242 B1
Moxhull Gdns WV12 242 B1
Moxley Ave ST1 57 E4
Mozart Ct WS11 210 B1
Muchal Rd WV4 266 A3
Mucklestone Rd TF9 99 E3
Mucklestone Wood La
TF9 99 E3
Muirfield B77 251 E3
Muirfield Cl WS3 243 D2
Muirville Cl DY8 275 E2
Mulberry Cl TF10 168 C1
Mulberry Gn DY1 271 F3
Mulberry Pl
Newcastle-u-L ST5 55 F4
Walsall WS3 242 C1
Mulberry Rd
Cannock WS11 209 F2
Walsall WS3 243 D1
Mulberry St ST1 282 C2
Muldoon Cl WS11 210 A2
Mulgrave St ST1 282 A4
Mulliner Cl ST2 58 B2
Munro St ST4 72 A3
Munster Terr ST4 71 F3
Murhall St ST6 56 C4
Murray St ST6 41 E4
Murton B77 262 B4
Muse La DE65 129 D4
Musk La DY3 271 D2
Musk La W DY3 271 D2
Muxloe Cl WS3 243 D2
Myatt Ave
Burntwood WS7 229 D4
Wolv WV2 266 C3
Myatt Cl WV4 266 B3
Myatt St ST1 282 C4
Myatt Way WS15 196 C3
Mynors St Hanley ST1 282 C3
Stafford ST16 156 A2
Myott Ave ST5 284 A1
Myrtle Ave ST3 74 A2
Myrtle Gr Brewood ST19 223 E3
Wolv WV3 265 F3
Myrtle St WV2 266 C3
Nab Hill Ave ST13 30 B3
Nabb La Alton ST10 94 C4
Denstone ST14 95 D2
Nabbswood Rd ST7 26 A1
Naden Ho WS12 209 E3
Naesby Rd WV6 254 C2
Nag ington Dr ST19 207 F4
Nailers Dr WS7 229 E3
Nairn Rd WS3 243 D2
Nankirk La DE13 165 D3
Nanny Goat La ST15 105 D1
Nantwich Rd Audley ST7 39 D1
Betley ST7 38 C1
Woore CW3 67 D1
Naomi Way WS9 245 D2
Napier B77 250 C2
Napier Gdns ST7 26 A1
Napier Rd WV2 266 B4
Napier St Burton u T DE14 166 B1
Fenton ST4 72 B3
Naples Cl ST3 73 F2
Naples Dr ST5 70 C3
Napley Dr TF9 82 B1
Napley Rd
Mucklestone TF9 82 B1
Norton in H TF9 82 B1
Narlow La DE6 51 F1
Narrow La
Brownhills WS8 244 C4
Denstone ST14 95 E3
Milwich ST15 121 F4
Narvik Cres ST6 42 A1
Nash Ave Perton WV6 254 C2
Stafford ST16 155 D3
Nash La
Acton Trussell ST17 193 D4
Elmhurst WS13 214 A3
Nash Peake St ST6 41 E2
Nash St ST5 55 F1
Nashe Dr ST3 73 D1
Natham Cl ST11 74 B2
Navigation Rd ST6 56 C4
Navigation St ST6 56 C4
Navigation Way WS11 210 A1
Naylor St ST6 41 F3
Naylor Yd ST13 30 C3
Naylors Gr DY1 271 F2
Neachless Ave WV5 270 A3
Neachley La
Albrighton TF11 220 A1
Shifnal TF11 220 A1
Neal Croft WS14 232 C3
Neale Pl ST2 58 A3
Neander B79 249 F3
Near Ridding ST20 171 E3
Neath Cl ST3 73 E2
Neath Pl 8 ST3 73 E3
Neath Rd WS3 242 C1
Neath Way WS3 242 C1
Needwood CE Prim Sch
DE13 162 C4
Needwood Cl WV2 266 A3
Needwood Ct DE13 146 B3
Needwood Dr WV4 266 C2
Needwood Grange
WS15 161 D3
Needwood Hill WS13 214 A1
Needwood St DE14 166 A2
Nellan Cres ST6 42 B1
Nelson Bank ST7 41 D4
Nelson Cres ST21 102 C1
Nelson Dr WS12 210 C2
Nelson Ind Est ST7 25 E1
Nelson Pl ST1 282 C2
Nelson Rd ST4 71 F4
Nelson St
Burton u T DE15 167 E2
Fenton ST4 72 B3
Leek ST13 30 C4
Newcastle-u-L ST5 56 B3
Nelson Way ST17 174 C3
Nene Cl DE13 147 E1
Nephew St ST6 56 C4
Neptune Gr ST1 57 F3
Ness Gr ST10 76 C3
Nest Comm WS3 243 F3
Nether Beacon WS13 214 A1
Nether La WS7 229 E4
Netherbridge Ave WS14 231 F4
Netherby Rd DY3 271 E4
Nethercote Pl ST2 73 E4
Nethergate DY3 271 F3
Netherseal Rd
Chilcote DE12 219 F2
Clifton Campville B79 218 C1
Netherset Hey La CW3 68 C3
Netherstone Gr B74 257 F3
Netherstowe WS13 214 B1
Netherstowe High Sch
WS13 214 A1
Netherstowe La WS13 214 B1
Netherton Gr ST2 43 E1
Nethy Dr WV6 255 D3
Netley Pl ST3 88 C4
Netley Rd WS3 242 C1
Netley Way WS3 242 C1
Nevada La ST6 57 D4
Neve Ave WV10 240 C1
Nevill St B79 250 A3
Neville Ave WV4 266 B3
Neville Cl DE13 147 D2
Neville St
Stoke-on-T ST4 71 F2
Tamworth B77 250 C2
Nevin Ave ST8 27 E3
Nevis Ct WV6 255 F1
Nevis Gr WV12 242 A1
New Ave ST11 91 E3
New Barns La WS14 246 A2
New Bldgs ST8 27 D2
New Century St ST1 282 A3
New Chapel Ct ST6 41 E2
New Close Ave ST11 91 D4
New Cotts ST10 62 B3
New Council Hos TF9 98 B1
New Dudley Rd DY6 275 E4
New Ford Prim Sch ST6 42 B1
New Forest Ind Est ST1 282 C4
New Garden St ST17 155 F1
New Haden Rd ST10 76 A1
New Hall Rd ST3 73 F1
New Hall St ST1 282 B3
New Hampton Rd W
WV6 255 F2
New Hayes Rd
Cannock WS12 211 E2
Tunstall ST6 41 F2
New Homage Gdns WV9 224 A1
New Horse Rd WS6 226 C2
New Inn Bank ST21 131 E4
New Inn La ST4 88 A4
New King St ST7 39 E1
New Kingsway ST3 74 A2
New La ST6 28 A1
New Landywood La WS6 242 C4
New Mill La B78 261 D4
New Park Gdns ST4 88 B3
New Penkridge Rd WS11 209 E1
New Rd
Aldridge WS9 256 A3
Alton ST10 78 C1
Armitage WS15 198 A3
Astbury CW12 15 D2
Audley ST7 39 F2
Bobbington DY3 268 C2
Brownhills WS8 244 C4
Burntwood WS7 229 D3
Caverswall ST2 58 C2
Cookley, Caunsall DY11 280 A4
Cookley, Lea Castle Hospl
DY10 280 B2
Dilhorne ST10 75 E2
Featherstone WV10 224 C1
Hixon ST18 158 A4
Madeley CW3 68 C4
Penkridge ST19 192 C1
Shenstone WS14 246 C3
Shuttington B79 235 E1
Swadlincote DE12 186 C3
Swindon DY3 269 D2
Tamworth B77 261 F4
Thorpe Constantine B79 235 E1
Upper Tean ST10 92 B2
Upper Tean, Checkley ST10 109 D4
Uttoxeter ST14 111 D1
Wolv WV6 255 F2
New Rd Est ST18 139 D1
New Row
Drayton Bassett B78 260 C3
Stafford ST18 174 B3
New St Biddulph ST8 28 A4
Brownhills WS4 244 B1
Burntwood, Chase Terrace
WS7 228 C4
Burntwood, Chasetown
WS7 228 C3
Burslem ST6 56 C4
Burton u T DE14 166 B1
Cannock, Bridgtown WS11 226 B3
Cannock, Hill Top WS12 210 B2
Cannock, Mill Green WS11 226 C4
Chebsey ST15 135 D4
Essington WV11 242 A2
Fazeley B78 261 D4
Great Wyrley WS6 227 D1
Kingswinford, Cot Lane DY6 275 E2
Kingswinford, Wall Heath
DY6 275 E4
Kingswinford, Wordsley DY8 275 E1
Leek ST13 30 C3
Newcastle-u-L ST5 56 B3
Newport TF10 168 C2
Polesworth B78 262 C4
Sedgley DY3 271 E2
Stafford ST16 155 E3
Stourbridge DY8 279 F3
Tamworth, Glascote Heath
B77 250 C2
Tamworth, Mount Pleasant
B77 250 B1
Uttoxeter ST14 126 A4
Walsall WS3 243 D1
Wolv, Merry Hill WV3 265 E4
Wolv, Parkfield WV4 266 C3
New St Cotts CW12 6 A3
New Wood Cl DY7 279 E4
New Wood Gr WS9 245 D2
Newall Ave ST16 156 A3
Newark Gr ST6 41 E4
Newborough Cl ST1 57 F3
Newbridge Ave WV6 255 F2
Newbridge Cres WV6 255 F2
Newbridge Dr WV6 255 F2
Newbridge Gdns WV6 255 F2
Newbridge Prep Sch
WV6 255 F2
Newbridge Rd DY6 275 E4
Newbridge St WV6 255 F2
Newburn Gr ST4 88 A4

Newbury Cl
Great Wyrley WS6 .... 226 C1
Stafford ST17 .... 175 E4
Newbury Dr DE13 .... 147 E1
Newbury Gr ST3 .... 88 C4
Newbury Rd
Kingswinford DY8 .... 275 C1
Wolv WV10 .... 240 B1
Newcastle Coll ST5 .... 284 A3
Newcastle Ent Ctr ST5 ...... 55 F1
Newcastle La ST4 .... 71 F3
Newcastle Rd Ashley TF9 .. 100 A4
Astbury CW12 .... 15 D4
Eccleshall ST21 .... 133 F4
Keele CW3 .... 69 D4
Kidsgrove ST7 .... 40 C4
Leek ST13 .... 30 B2
Madeley CW3 .... 68 C4
Market Drayton TF9 .... 97 F1
Stoke-on-T ST4 .... 71 F3
Stone ST15 .... 104 C1
Tittensor ST5 .... 87 E4
Woore CW3 .... 67 F1
Newcastle St Burslem ST6 .. 56 C4
Newcastle-u-L ST5 .... 55 F1
Stone ST15 .... 104 C1
Newcastle-u-Lyme Schs
ST5 .... 284 C2
Newchapel Rd ST7 .... 26 B2
Newcomen Cl WS7 .... 229 E4
Newcott Cl WV9 .... 239 F1
Newcrofts Wlk ST6 .... 42 B3
Newport Cty High Sch
for Girls TF10 .... 168 C1
Newfield Dr DY6 .... 275 F2
Newfield Rd DE15 .... 167 D2
Newfield St ST6 .... 41 E2
Newfold Cres ST6 .... 43 D4
Newford Cres ST2 .... 42 C1
Newgate WV6 .... 253 E2
Newgate St WS7 .... 229 D3
Newhall Cres WS11 .... 210 A2
Newhall Gdns WS11 .... 209 F1
Newhall Inf Sch DE11 ...... 186 C4
Newhall Jun Sch DE11 ...... 186 C4
Newhall St
Cannock WS11 .... 209 E1
Kingsley ST10 .... 61 E2
Newhaven Gr ST4 .... 88 A3
Newhouse La WV7 .... 237 D2
Newhouse Rd ST2 .... 58 A2
Newick Ave B74 .... 257 D2
Newington Gr ST4 .... 88 B3
Newland Ave ST16 .... 155 E4
Newland Cl WS4 .... 244 B1
Newlands Cl
Newcastle-u-L ST5 .... 71 D3
Penkridge ST19 .... 207 F4
Stone ST15 .... 119 F3
Newlands Ct WS11 .... 227 F4
Newlands La
Colton WS15 .... 179 E4
Norton Canes WS11 .... 227 E4
Newlands St ST4 .... 57 D1
Newleigh St ST2 .... 43 D1
Newlyn Ave CW12 .... 15 F4
Newlyn Cl WS14 .... 231 E4
Newman Ave WV4 .... 266 C2
Newman Cl ST15 .... 120 B4
Newman Dr DE14 .... 185 D4
Newman Gr WS15 .... 196 C4
Newman Rd WV10 .... 241 D1
Newmarket Way ST10 ...... 76 C3
Newmill St ST2 .... 43 D1
Newmount Rd ST4 .... 73 D3
Newpool Cotts ST8 .... 27 D3
Newpool Rd ST8 .... 27 D3
Newpool Terr ST8 .... 27 D3
Newport B77 .... 250 C3
Newport CE Jun Sch
TF10 .... 168 C1
Newport Cl DE13 .... 166 C4
Newport Croft ST19 .... 223 E3
Newport Cty Inf Sch
TF10 .... 168 C1
Newport Gr ST5 .... 40 C1
Newport La ST6 .... 56 C4
Newport Rd
Albrighton TF11 .... 220 B1
Chetwynd TF10 .... 168 B2
Codsall WV7 .... 237 F1
Eccleshall ST21 .... 133 F3
Edgmond TF10 .... 168 B2
Gnosall ST20 .... 171 D3
Seighford ST18 .... 135 E1
Stafford ST16 .... 155 E1
Sutton TF9 .... 112 C3
Tong TF11 .... 220 B2
Newport St
Brewood ST19 .... 223 E3
Burslem ST6 .... 56 C4
Newquay Ave ST17 .... 175 E4
Newquay Ct CW12 .... 15 F4
Newshaw Wlk ST1 .... 282 C3
Newstead B79 .... 249 E3
Newstead Prim Sch ST3 .... 88 C3
Newstead Rd ST2 .... 58 A3
Newstead Trad Est ST4 .... 88 B4
Newton Cl DE15 .... 167 E4
Newton St ST19 .... 59 D2
Newton La
Newton Regis CV9 .... 236 C1
Newton Solney DE15 .... 167 A4
Seckington B79 .... 236 A2
Newton Leys DE15 .... 167 E2

Newton Mews DE15 .... 166 C2
Newton Rd
Burton u T DE15 .... 167 D3
Lichfield WS13 .... 213 F1
Newcastle-u-L ST5 .... 56 A3
Stafford ST16 .... 155 F3
Newton Regis CE
Prim Sch B79 .... 236 B2
Newton Solney CE
Inf Sch DE15 .... 167 F4
Newton St ST4 .... 56 C1
Newton's College WS13 .. 231 D4
Newtown Kidsgrove ST7 .. 26 C1
Market Drayton TF9 .... 112 B4
Newport TF10 .... 168 C1
Niall Rd ST4 .... 71 F1
Nicholas Gr ST13 .... 30 A2
Nicholas St [18] ST6 .... 56 C4
Nicholl's La ST15 .... 105 D2
Nicholls St ST4 .... 72 A3
Nicholls Way WS12 .... 210 C1
Nicholson Way
Burton u T DE14 .... 166 A1
Leek ST13 .... 30 B3
Nicklaus Cl DE14 .... 185 D4
Nidderdale Cl CW12 .... 6 A3
Nightingale B77 .... 262 A3
Nightingale Cl WS12 .... 209 E4
Nile St ST6 .... 57 D4
Nimbus B77 .... 261 E2
Ninefoot La B77 .... 261 F4
Ninian Way B77 .... 261 F3
Nirvana Cl WS11 .... 209 E1
No Man's Green La DY7 .. 276 C3
No Man's Heath Rd
DE12 .... 219 F2
No Name Rd WS7 .... 228 C4
Noblett Rd ST1 .... 57 F4
Nocke Rd WV11 .... 241 F1
Noddington Ave WS14 .... 232 C3
Noddington La WS14 ...... 232 C3
Noddy Park Rd WS9 .... 256 A4
Noddy Pk WS9 .... 256 A4
Nook The WS6 .... 226 B1
Norbroom Ct TF10 .... 169 D2
Norbroom Dr TF10 .... 169 D2
Norbury Ave
Brownhills WS3 .... 244 A2
Norton-in-t-M ST2 .... 43 D1
Norbury CE Prim Sch
DE6 .... 96 C4
Norbury Cl ST20 .... 171 E3
Norbury Cres WV4 .... 266 C2
Norbury Hollow DE6 .... 80 B1
Norbury Rd ST20 .... 170 C4
Norfolk Cl ST5 .... 71 D1
Norfolk Cres WS9 .... 256 A4
Norfolk Dr B78 .... 250 A1
Norfolk Gr
Biddulph ST6 .... 16 B1
Great Wyrley WS6 .... 226 C1
Norfolk Rd
Burton u T DE15 .... 185 E4
Kidsgrove ST7 .... 25 F1
Stourbridge DY8 .... 279 E4
Wolv WV3 .... 266 A4
Norfolk St ST1 .... 57 D1
Norfolk Way ST17 .... 174 B4
Normacot Grange Rd ST3 .. 90 A4
Normacot Rd ST3 .... 283 C3
Norman Ave ST6 .... 41 F2
Norman Cl B79 .... 249 F4
Norman Gr ST5 .... 56 B1
Norman Keep DE13 .... 146 B3
Norman Rd
Penkridge ST19 .... 208 A4
Tutbury DE13 .... 146 B3
Normanbrook Ct TF9 ...... 97 E1
Normandy Ct ST2 .... 43 D1
Normanton Gr ST3 .... 73 E3
Norris Cl TF9 .... 100 B3
Norris Rd ST6 .... 41 F2
North Ave Leek ST13 ...... 30 B3
Stafford ST16 .... 155 E4
North Castle St ST16 ...... 155 E2
North Cres WV10 .... 241 E4
North Dr ST20 .... 171 E3
North Gn WV4 .... 265 E3
North Pl Bucknall ST2 ...... 58 A3
Stafford ST16 .... 155 E3
North Rd Burslem ST6 ...... 57 D4
Hanley ST6 .... 57 D4
North Springfield DY3 .... 266 C1
North St
Burntwood WS7 .... 211 F1
Burton u T DE15 .... 167 D2
Cannock WS11 .... 226 C3
Leek ST13 .... 30 B3
Mount Pleasant ST7 .... 26 A4
Newcastle-u-L ST5 .... 284 C3
Stoke-on-T ST4 .... 72 A4
North Staffordshire Hospl
ST6 .... 42 A2
North Staffordshire
Hospl Ctr
(Outpatients Dept) ST4 .... 71 F4
North Staffordshire
Maternity Hospl ST4 .... 71 E4
North Staffordshire
Nuffield Hospl The ST5 .... 71 E2
North Staffordshire
Royal Infmy ST4 .... 71 F4
North Terr ST5 .... 56 A1
North Walls ST16 .... 155 F2
North Way DY3 .... 266 B1
North West Terr ST6 ...... 42 B1
North Wlk ST3 .... 74 A1

Northam Rd ST1 .... 57 E3
Northcliffe [1] ST13 .... 30 B3
Northcote Ave ST4 .... 72 A4
Northcote Cl ST18 .... 177 F4
Northcote Ct ST5 .... 284 C3
Northcote Pl ST5 .... 284 C3
Northcote St ST4 .... 57 D1
Northdale WV6 .... 255 D2
Northesk Pl ST5 .... 71 D3
Northesk St ST15 .... 105 D1
Northfield Ave ST14 .... 96 A2
Northfield Cl ST14 .... 111 D1
Northfield Dr ST6 .... 16 C1
Northfield Gr WV3 .... 265 E4
Northfield Rd DE13 .... 166 B4
Northfleet St ST2 .... 58 A2
Northgate Aldridge WS9 .. 256 A4
Brownhills WS9 .... 245 D1
Northgate St ST4 .... 71 F1
Northgate Way WS9 .... 256 A4
Northicote Recn Ctr
WV10 .... 240 C2
Northicote Sch The
WV10 .... 240 C2
Northlands CW3 .... 67 E1
Northover WV9 .... 240 A1
Northumberland Cl B78 .. 250 A1
Northumberland Rd
DE15 .... 185 E4
Denstone ST14 .... 95 E3
Eccleshall ST21 .... 133 E3
Newcastle-u-L ST5 .... 55 F1
Stone ST15 .... 120 A4
Northwood Ct ST5 .... 71 E1
Northwood Ct ST1 .... 282 C3
Northwood Gn ST1 .... 57 F2
Northwood Inf Sch ST1 .... 57 F2
Northwood La
Ellastone DE6 .... 80 B2
Newcastle-u-L ST5 .... 71 E1
Tittensor ST5 .... 71 E1
Northwood Park Cl
WV10 .... 240 C2
Northwood Park Rd
Hanley ST1 .... 57 F2
Wolv WV10 .... 240 C2
Northycote La WV10 ...... 240 C2
Norton Ave ST6 .... 42 A2
Norton Bridge Sta
ST15 .... 135 D4
Norton Canes High Sch
WS11 .... 228 A4
Norton Canes Prim Sch
WS11 .... 228 A3
Norton Cl Tamworth B79 .. 250 B4
Wolv WV4 .... 265 E2
Norton Cres ST6 .... 57 E4
Norton Dr ST6 .... 57 E4
Norton Grange WS11 ...... 227 F2
Norton Grange Cres
WS11 .... 227 F2
Norton Green La WS11 .... 227 F2
Norton Hales CE Sch TF9 .. 82 B1
Norton Hall Cl ST6 .... 42 C2
Norton Hall La WS11 ...... 227 F2
Norton La Burntwood WS7 .. 229 E3
Great Wyrley WS6 .... 227 D2
Norton Canes WS11 .... 227 D4
Norton-in-t-M ST4 .... 42 C2
Norton Prim Sch ST6 ...... 42 B1
Norton Rd
Brownhills WS3 .... 244 A3
Burton u T DE13 .... 166 A3
Norton Canes WS11 .... 227 F4
Stourbridge DY8 .... 279 F1
Norton Springs WS11 ...... 227 F3
Norton St ST3 .... 43 D1
Norton Terr WS11 .... 227 F4
Norwich ST13 .... 214 B2
Norwich Pl ST5 .... 71 E3
Norwich Rd ST2 .... 58 B1
Nottingham Rd WS14 ...... 232 B2
Novi La ST13 .... 31 D4
Nuffield Hospl WV6 .... 255 E2
Nunn St ST13 .... 30 B3
Nunn's Cl ST3 .... 74 B3
Nuns La WS15 .... 180 A3
Nurseries The WV9 .... 224 A1
Nursery Ave
Aldridge WS9 .... 256 A3
Norton-in-t-M ST9 .... 43 E2
Nursery Cl Bradley ST18 .. 191 E4
Cheadle ST10 .... 76 B2
Endon ST6 .... 43 D4
Kidsgrove ST7 .... 25 E1
Nursery Croft WS13 .... 213 F1
Nursery Dr Biddulph ST6 .. 16 B1
Penkridge ST19 .... 192 C3
Wombourne DY3 .... 269 F2
Nursery Fields Country
Prim Sch WS15 .... 197 D3
Nursery Gdns
Brierley Hill DY8 .... 275 F1
Codsall WV8 .... 238 C2
Nursery La Hopwas B78 .. 249 D3
Norton-in-t-M ST9 .... 43 E2
Nursery Rd Rugeley WS15 .. 197 D3
Scholar Green ST7 .... 25 F3
Nursery St ST4 .... 72 A3
Nursery View CI B74 .... 256 C1
Nursery Wlk WV6 .... 255 D2
Nurton Bk WV6 .... 254 A2
Nurton Hill Rd WV6 .... 253 F4
Nutbrook Ave ST4 .... 72 B2
Nuthurst Dr WS11 .... 209 E1
Nyewood Ave WS3 .... 73 D1
Nymet B77 .... 261 F4

O'Hare Pl ST13 .... 31 D4
Oadby Rise DE13 .... 166 A3

Oak Ave Cheddleton ST13 .. 45 E2
Great Wyrley WS6 .... 227 D1
Huntington WS12 .... 209 E4
Newport TF10 .... 168 C1
Stafford ST17 .... 175 F3
Oak Cl Church Eaton ST20 .. 190 A4
Colwich ST18 .... 158 B1
Kinver DY7 .... 278 B2
Uttoxeter ST14 .... 110 C1
Oak Dr Seisdon WV5 .... 263 F1
Wheaton Aston ST19 .... 205 E3
Oak Gdns ST18 .... 172 C3
Oak Gn WV6 .... 255 D2
Oak Hill WV3 .... 255 E1
Oak Ind Pk The DY6 .... 270 C1
Oak La Bradley ST18 .... 191 E4
Burntwood WS7 .... 212 A1
Cheslyn Hay WS11 .... 225 E4
Kingswinford DY6 .... 270 C1
Oak Lea ST13 .... 30 A2
Oak Leys WV3 .... 255 E1
Oak Mount Rd ST9 .... 59 E2
Oak Park Rd DY8 .... 275 F1
Oak Pl ST3 .... 73 F1
Oak Rd Barton-u-N DE13 .. 201 E4
Brewood ST19 .... 223 E3
Brownhills, Holly Bank WS9 .. 245 D2
Brownhills, Pelsall Wood
WS3 .... 243 F3
Brownhills, Shelfield WS4 .. 244 B1
Denstone ST14 .... 95 E3
Eccleshall ST21 .... 133 E3
Newcastle-u-L ST5 .... 55 F1
Stone ST15 .... 120 A4
Oak St Burton u T DE14 .... 166 B1
Cheadle ST10 .... 76 B2
Hanley ST1 .... 57 F3
Kingswinford DY6 .... 275 E3
Newcastle-u-L ST5 .... 56 B2
Oak Tree Cl ST17 .... 174 A4
Oak Tree Wlk B79 .... 249 F6
Oakamoor Rd
Cheadle ST10 .... 77 E2
Oakamoor ST10 .... 77 C2
Oakapple Cl ST19 .... 221 F4
Oakdale ST5 .... 71 E2
Oakdale Trad Est DY6 ...... 270 C1
Oakdene Ave ST5 .... 56 A3
Oakdene Cl
Forsbrook ST11 .... 91 D3
Newcastle-u-L ST5 .... 56 A3
Oakdene Gr ST5 .... 56 A3
Oakdene Rd WS7 .... 229 E3
Oakdene Way ST8 .... 27 E4
Oaken Covert WV8 .... 238 C1
Oaken Dr WV8 .... 238 C2
Oaken Gdns WS7 .... 229 D4
Oaken Gr WV8 .... 238 C1
Oaken La WV8 .... 238 B2
Oaken Lanes WV8 .... 238 C2
Oaken Pk WV8 .... 239 D1
Oakenfield WS13 .... 214 A1
Oakenhayes Cres WS8 .... 228 C1
Oakenhayes Dr WS8 ...... 228 C1
Oakfield Ave DY6 .... 275 F3
Oakfield Cl
Brierley Hill DY8 .... 275 F1
Rugeley WS15 .... 178 A1
Oakfield Dr WS3 .... 244 A3
Oakfield Rd
Alrewas DE13 .... 201 D1
Codsall WV8 .... 239 D1
Market Drayton TF9 .... 97 D1
Oakfields DE13 .... 145 D2
Oakham Way ST2 .... 58 B1
Oakhill Ave ST4 .... 71 F2
Oakhill Cl ST10 .... 92 B2
Oakhill Prim Sch ST4 ...... 71 F2
Oakhill Rd WS11 .... 209 F1
Oakhurst WS14 .... 231 E4
Oakhurst Cres ST3 .... 90 A3
Oakhurst Pk WS15 .... 196 C3
Oakland Dr DY5 .... 271 D1
Oaklands Ave ST5 .... 56 B3
Oaklands Cl
Alrewas WS13 .... 215 E4
Cheddleton ST9 .... 60 A3
Hill Ridware WS15 .... 198 A4
Huntington WS12 .... 209 E3
Oaklands Dr ST17 .... 155 E1
Oaklands Ind Est WS12 .... 210 A2
Oaklands Rd WV3 .... 266 A4
Oaklands The
Church Eaton ST20 .... 190 A4
Rugeley WS15 .... 178 A1
Oaklands Way WS3 .... 244 A2
Oakleigh Ave DE11 .... 186 C3
Oakleigh Ct ST15 .... 120 B3
Oakleigh Dr
Codsall WV8 .... 239 D2
Rugeley WS15 .... 197 D3
Sedgley DY3 .... 271 E4
Oakleigh Wlk DY6 .... 275 F4
Oakleighs DY8 .... 275 E1
Oakley Ave WS9 .... 256 A3
Oakley Cl Lichfield WS13 .. 214 A1
Penkridge ST19 .... 193 D1
Oakley Folly TF9 .... 99 D2
Oakley Gr WV4 .... 265 D3
Oakley Pl ST6 .... 42 A4
Oakley Rd WV4 .... 265 D3
Oakleys ST19 .... 223 E4
Oakmount Cl WS3 .... 243 F2
Oakridge Cl ST17 .... 175 F3
Oakridge Cty Prim Sch
ST17 .... 175 F3
Oakridge Dr WS6 .... 226 C1
Oakridge Way ST17 .... 175 F3

Oaks Dr Cannock WS11 .... 209 E1
Featherstone WV10 .... 240 C4
Wombourne WV5 .... 270 A3
Oakshaw Cl WV9 .... 224 C2
Oakshaw Gr ST4 .... 88 A4
Oaksmoor Cl ST19 .... 205 E3
Oaktree Rd Rugeley WS15 .. 196 C3
Trentham ST4 .... 88 A3
Oakville Ave ST6 .... 42 A1
Oakwell Cl ST3 .... 73 E1
Oakwell Gr ST3 .... 73 E1
Oakwood WS15 .... 178 A1
Oakwood
Brownhills WS9 .... 244 C2
Essington WV11 .... 242 A2
Shenstone WS14 .... 247 D3
Oakwood Pl ST5 .... 55 F4
Oakwood Rd Leek ST13 .... 30 B3
Longton ST3 .... 72 C1
Oakwood Sch WS9 .... 245 D2
Oakwoods WS11 .... 226 B4
Oasthouse Cl DY6 .... 275 D4
Oatfield Cl WS7 .... 229 D2
Oatlands Way WV6 .... 254 B2
Oban Cl ST5 .... 70 C2
Oberon Cl ST6 .... 42 B1
Occupation Rd WS9 .... 245 D2
Occupation St ST5 .... 284 C2
Octagon Ctr The DE14 .... 166 B1
Odell Gr ST3 .... 41 F1
Odger Cl ST3 .... 74 A1
Odiam Cl B79 .... 250 B4
Odin Cl WS11 .... 210 A3
Offa St B79 .... 250 A3
Offa's Dr WV6 .... 254 C3
Offadrive B79 .... 250 A3
Offoxey Rd ST19 .... 221 E3
Ogden Rd ST1 .... 282 C2
Ogley Cres WS8 .... 245 D4
Ogley Hay Inf Sch WS8 .... 244 C4
Ogley Hay Rd
Burntwood, Boney Hay
WS7 .... 212 A1
Burntwood, Triangle
WS7 .... 229 D2
Ogley Rd WS8 .... 245 D4
Ogmore Gr ST3 .... 90 A4
Ohio Gr ST6 .... 57 D4
Old Armoury The TF9 ...... 112 B4
Old Bank DE6 .... 81 E4
Old Barn Cl ST20 .... 171 E4
Old Butt La ST7 .... 25 E1
Old Cannock Rd WV10 .... 225 D1
Old Castle Gr WS8 .... 228 C1
Old Chancel Rd WS15 ...... 178 C1
Old Coach La ST17 .... 176 A2
Old Coach Rd ST19 .... 221 F4
Old Coalpit La SK17 .... 5 F4
Old Croft Rd ST17 .... 175 F3
Old Dalelands TF9 .... 112 A4
Old Eaton Rd WS15 .... 178 C2
Old Fallings La WV10 ...... 240 C1
Old Fallow Ave WS11 ...... 209 F2
Old Fallow Rd WS11 .... 209 F2
Old Falls Cl WS6 .... 226 B2
Old Farm Meadow WV3 .... 265 E4
Old Hall Dr Elford B79 .... 216 B1
Newcastle-u-L ST5 .... 56 A4
Old Hall Farm B79 .... 236 B2
Old Hall La
Alrewas WS13 .... 215 E4
Millmeece ST21 .... 117 F4
Norton Canes WS11 .... 227 D4
Old Hall Rd WV10 .... 241 E4
Old Hall St ST1 .... 282 B3
Old Hampton La WV11 .... 241 E2
Old Hedging La B77 .... 261 D2
Old Hednesford Rd
WS11, WS12 .... 210 A2
Old Hill WV6 .... 255 E3
Old Knotty Way ST14 ...... 126 B4
Old La Endon ST6 .... 28 A1
Swynnerton ST4 .... 87 D1
Upper Tean ST10 .... 109 E4
Wolv WV6 .... 254 C1
Old Landywood La WS6 .... 242 B4
Old London Rd WS14 ...... 231 E1
Old Man of Mow The ST7 .. 26 B4
Old Manor Cl B78 .... 260 C3
Old Mill Gdns WS4 .... 244 B1
Old Mill La
Bagnall, Bagnall ST9 .... 44 A2
Bagnall, Tompkin ST9 .... 44 B2
Old Oak Cl WS9 .... 256 A4
Old Park Rd
Cannock WS12 .... 211 D3
Crewe CW1 .... 37 E4
Dudley DY1 .... 271 F2
Old Penkridge Rd WS11 .. 209 E1
Old Quarry Dr DY3 .... 271 F2
Old Rd
Armitage WS15 .... 198 A3
Audley ST7 .... 39 F2
Barlaston ST12 .... 88 B2
Betley CW3 .... 53 D2
Branston DE14 .... 184 C4
Stone ST15 .... 105 D3
Trentham ST4 .... 88 B2
Upper Tean ST10 .... 92 B2
Weston-u-T ST18 .... 138 B1
Old Rd Ct ST15 .... 105 D1
Old Rectory Gdns WS9 .... 256 B3
Old Rectory Rd ST15 ...... 120 A4
Old Rickerscote La ST17 .. 175 D3
Old School Cl ST15 .... 138 B2
Old Shackerley La WV7 .... 221 D1
Old Smithy Cl WV6 .... 253 E2
Old Stafford Rd WV10 .... 224 B2

Old Stoke Rd ST4 .... 56 C1
Old Town La WS3 .... 243 F2
Old Town Rd ST1 .... 282 B4
Old Tramway ST4 .... 72 C3
Old Vicarage Cl
  Brownhills WS3 .... 244 A1
  Wombourne WV5 .... 270 A4
Old Warstone La WV11 ... 242 A4
Old Weston Rd ST19 .... 221 F4
Old Wharf Pl ST7 .... 57 F1
Old Wharf Rd DY8 .... 279 F3
Old Whieldon Rd ST4 .... 72 B3
Oldacre La ST17 .... 176 A2
Oldacres Rd ST4 .... 88 B3
Oldcastle Ave ST5 .... 56 A3
Oldcott Cres ST7 .... 41 E4
Oldcott Dr ST7 .... 41 E4
Oldcourt St ST6 .... 41 E2
Olde Hall La WS6 .... 226 C2
Oldershaws La ST20 .... 150 C4
Oldfield Ave ST6 .... 42 B3
Oldfield Dr ST15 .... 120 B3
Oldfield La
  Eggington DE65 .... 148 A4
  Hilton DE65 .... 148 A4
  Snelston DE6 .... 81 D2
Oldfield St ST4 .... 283 A5
Oldfields Cres ST18 .... 158 B2
Oldfields Hall Cty Mid Sch
  ST14 .... 126 A4
Oldfields Rd ST14 .... 126 A4
Oldford La ST18 .... 154 A2
Oldham Cotts WS15 .... 179 D3
Oldham St ST1 .... 282 C1
Oldhill Cl ST7 .... 40 C3
Oldhill La ST18 .... 157 E1
Oldicote La DE15 .... 167 F2
Oldmill St ST4 .... 72 B4
Oldway Pl ST3 .... 73 E3
Olive Ave WV4 .... 266 C3
Olive Gr ST5 .... 40 B1
Oliver Rd ST1 .... 71 F4
Ollison Dr B74 .... 256 C1
Olof Palme Gr ST3 .... 283 C4
Omega Way ST4 .... 88 A4
One Oak Rise ST17 .... 174 C3
Onneley La CW3 .... 67 F2
Ontario Cl ST4 .... 88 A4
Opal Rd ST4 .... 72 C3
Opal Way ST15 .... 120 A3
Oram's La ST19 .... 223 E4
Orange La WS15 .... 161 E1
Orb St ST1 .... 282 B2
Orbital Way WS11 .... 226 C3
Orchard Ave WS11 .... 209 E1
Orchard Cl Ashley TF9 ..... 100 B3
  Brewood WV9 .... 224 A1
  Cheslyn Hay WS6 .... 226 C2
  Claverley WV5 .... 267 E4
  Lichfield WS13 .... 213 F1
  Pattingham WV6 .... 253 E2
  Penkridge ST19 .... 192 C1
  Rugeley WS15 .... 178 C2
  Stone, Oulton ST15 ...... 105 E2
  Stone, Walton ST15 ...... 119 F4
  Tamworth B77 .... 261 E3
  Uttoxeter ST14 .... 111 D1
  Walton-on-T DE12 .... 184 B1
Orchard Cres
  Kidsgrove ST7 .... 25 E1
  Penkridge ST19 .... 192 C1
  Wolv WV3 .... 265 D4
Orchard Ct
  Kingswinford DY6 .... 275 E3
  Wolv WV3 .... 265 D4
Orchard Gdns ST13 .... 30 B3
Orchard Gr
  Aldridge WS9 .... 256 A2
  Cookley DY11 .... 280 A3
  Kinver DY7 .... 278 A2
  Sedgley DY3 .... 271 D2
  Sutton Coldfield B74 ..... 257 F2
  Wolv WV4 .... 266 A4
Orchard La Bradnop ST18 ... 174 B3
  Codsall WV8 .... 239 D2
  Shareshill WV10 .... 225 E2
Orchard Pk DE14 .... 166 B1
Orchard Pl ST12 .... 88 B3
Orchard Rise
  Blythe Bridge ST11 .... 90 C4
  Market Drayton TF9 ...... 112 A4
Orchard St
  Burton u T DE14 .... 166 B1
  Newcastle-u-L ST5 .... 56 B4
  Stafford ST17 .... 155 F1
  Swadlincote DE11 .... 186 C3
  Tamworth B79 .... 250 A4
  Tamworth, Kettlebrook B77 ... 250 B2
Orchard The
  Albrighton WV7 .... 237 D3
  Brewood ST19 .... 223 E3
  Colwich ST18 .... 177 E4
  Endon ST6 .... 43 D4
  Stramshall ST14 .... 111 D2
  Swynnerton ST15 .... 103 D2
  Walsall WS3 .... 243 F1
  Wolv WV6 .... 255 F3
Orchards The WS15 .... 198 B2
Orchid Cl DE15 .... 186 A4
Ordish Ct DE14 .... 166 B1
Ordish St DE14 .... 166 B1
Ordley La ST6 .... 65 F1
Oregon Cl DY6 .... 275 F3
Oregon Gdns WS7 .... 228 C4
Orford St ST3 .... 43 F4
Orford St ST5 .... 56 B4
Orford Way ST3 .... 88 C4
Orgreave St ST6 .... 57 D4

Orgreaves Cl ST5 .... 56 A4
Oriel Cl Cannock WS11 .... 226 C4
  Sedgley DY3 .... 271 F1
Oriel Dr WV10 .... 240 B2
Orion Cl WS6 .... 226 C1
Orion Ct ST5 .... 70 C4
Orion St ST6 .... 42 B1
Orion Way WS11 .... 209 F3
Orkney Ave ST7 .... 41 F4
Orlestone Pl ST6 .... 42 A4
Orme Cl Biddulph ST8 .... 27 E3
  Newcastle-u-L ST5 .... 284 A2
Orme St ST6 .... 56 C4
Ormes La WV6 .... 255 E2
Ormonde St ST4 .... 72 C3
Oroxden Ct ST10 .... 92 B4
Orpheus Gr ST1 .... 57 F3
Orwell Pl ST5 .... 71 D2
Orwell Cl DY8 .... 279 E2
Orwell Dr Longton ST3 .... 73 F3
  Stafford ST17 .... 174 A4
Osberton Dr DY1 .... 271 F1
Osborne B79 .... 249 E4
Osborne Cres ST17 .... 175 E4
Osborne Ct DE13 .... 166 A3
Osborne Rd
  Stoke-on-T ST4 .... 71 F4
  Wolv WV4 .... 265 F3
Osborne S
  Burton u T DE15 .... 167 D2
  Leek ST13 .... 31 D3
Oslo Gr ST1 .... 57 F3
Osmaston Rd DY8 .... 279 F1
Osprey B77 .... 262 A3
Osprey Ave ST3 .... 90 A4
Osprey Cl DE15 .... 167 E2
Osprey Dr DY1 .... 271 F1
Osprey Gr WS12 .... 210 B1
Osprey View WS17 .... 26 B2
Ostend Pl ST5 .... 70 C4
Ostler Cl DY6 .... 275 D4
Ostlers La ST13 .... 45 D2
Oswald Ave ST3 .... 74 A3
Otherton Cl ST19 .... 207 F4
Otherton La ST19 .... 207 F3
Otterburn Cl
  Cannock WS12 .... 210 C1
  Stafford ST17 .... 175 E3
Otterstone Cl DY3 .... 266 B1
Ottery B77 .... 262 A3
Oulton CE Fst Sch ST15 ... 105 E2
Oulton La ST20 .... 170 A4
Oulton Rd Cheadle ST10 ..... 76 C2
  Chell Heath ST6 .... 42 A4
  Stone ST15 .... 105 D1
Oulton Way ST16 .... 155 D3
Ounsdale Cres WV5 .... 270 A4
Ounsdale High Sch WV5 ... 269 F4
Ounsdale Rd WV5 .... 269 F4
Ounty John La DY8 .... 281 F4
Our Lady & St Benedict
  RC Prim Sch ST2 .... 58 A3
Our Lady & St Werburgh's
  RC Prim Sch WS5 .... 71 D2
Our Lady's RC
  Prim Sch ST4 .... 72 B3
Ousley La DE6 .... 80 B3
Outclough Rd ST8 .... 27 D1
Outfield Rd DE15 .... 185 F4
Outwoods Cl
  Burton u T DE13 .... 166 A3
  Weston-u-T ST18 .... 138 B1
Outwoods La
  Anslow DE13 .... 165 E4
  Burton u T DE13 .... 165 F4
Outwoods St DE14 .... 166 A3
Oval The Cheddleton ST9 ... 59 F2
  Longton ST3 .... 283 A4
  Market Drayton TF9 ...... 112 B4
  Stafford ST17 .... 155 F1
Over The Hill ST8 .... 17 D1
Overbrook Cl DY3 .... 271 E1
Overdale Pl ST17 .... 30 A3
Overhill Rd DY1 .... 271 F1
Overhill Rd
  Burntwood WS7 .... 229 D3
  Stafford ST17 .... 175 D4
Overhouse St ST6 .... 41 F1
Overland Cl WS15 .... 197 D3
Overland Dr ST6 .... 43 D4
Oversetts Ct DE11 .... 186 C3
Oversetts Rd DE11 .... 186 C3
Oversley St ST6 .... 42 A4
Overton Bank ◪ ST13 .... 30 C3
Overton La WS7 .... 229 E3
Overton Rd ST6 .... 16 B3
Overton Wlk WV4 .... 265 E3
Overwood Rd B77 .... 262 A4
Overwoods Rd B77 .... 261 F3
Owen Gr ◪ ST6 .... 57 D4
Owen Rd WV3 .... 266 A4
Owen Wlk ST17 .... 174 B4
Owens Cl WS15 .... 178 C1
Ox Pasture ST13 .... 45 E3
Ox St DY3 .... 271 E3
Ox-Hey Cres ST6 .... 16 B1
Ox-Hey Dr ST6 .... 16 B1
Oxbarn Ave WV3 .... 265 F4
Oxbarn Rd ST17 .... 174 B3
Oxclose La DE6 .... 36 B1
Oxford Ave ST1 .... 57 F4
Oxford Cl WS6 .... 226 C2

Oxford Cres ST4 .... 72 A4
Oxford Dr DY8 .... 279 F2
Oxford Gdns WS16 .... 155 F3
Oxford Gn WS11 .... 226 C4
Oxford Rd Cannock WS11 ... 226 C4
  Chell Heath ST6 .... 42 A4
  Newcastle-u-L ST5 .... 56 B2
Oxford St Burton u T DE14 ... 166 A1
  Stoke-on-T ST4 .... 72 A4
Oxhay Cl ST5 .... 56 B2
Oxhay View ST5 .... 56 B2
Oxhey Fst Sch ST8 .... 16 C1
Oxleathers Ct ST17 .... 174 A4
Oxley Cl WS6 .... 226 C1
Oxley Moor Rd
  Wolv, Blakeley Green
  WV10, WV9 .... 255 F4
  Wolv, Oxley WV10, WV9 ... 240 A1
Oxley Rd DE15 .... 167 D2
Oxmead DE6 .... 81 E4

Pacific Rd ST4 .... 88 A4
Pack Horse La ST6 .... 56 C4
Packett St ST4 .... 283 B4
Packington La B78 .... 248 C3
Padarn Cl DY3 .... 266 B1
Padbury WV9 .... 240 A2
Padbury La WS7 .... 212 B1
Paddock Cl ST16 .... 155 E4
Paddock La Aldridge WS9 ... 256 A3
  Great Wyrley WS6 .... 227 D2
Paddock Rise ST4 .... 88 A3
Paddock The
  Brewood WV9 .... 224 A1
  Burton u T DE15 .... 167 D2
  Cheadle ST10 .... 76 B1
  Claverley WV5 .... 267 E4
  Codsall WV8 .... 238 C1
  Lichfield WS14 .... 231 E3
  Perton WV6 .... 254 B1
  Rolleston DE13 .... 147 D2
  Sedgley DY3 .... 271 F3
  Seighford ST18 .... 154 B3
  Wombourne WV5 .... 269 F3
Paddocks Cl B78 .... 251 F1
Paddocks Gn CW12 .... 15 F4
Paddocks The
  Market Drayton TF9 .... 97 D1
  Swadlincote DE11 .... 186 C3
  Swynnerton ST15 .... 118 C3
Padget High Sch DE14 .... 185 D4
Padstow B77 .... 250 C3
Padstow Way ST4 .... 88 B3
Padworth St ST3 .... 74 A2
Paget Cl ST19 .... 208 A4
Paget Dr WS7 .... 211 F1
Paget Rd WV3, WV6 .... 255 F2
Paget Rise WS15 .... 160 C3
Paget St DE14 .... 166 B1
Pagham CW9 .... 239 F1
Painsley RC High Sch The
  ST10 .... 76 B1
Paisley Cl ST2 .... 73 F4
Paladin Ave ST3 .... 74 A2
Palatine Dr ST5 .... 55 E3
Pale St DY3 .... 271 F3
Palfrey Rd DY8 .... 279 E3
Pall Mall ST1 .... 282 B2
Palmbourne Ind Pk ST16 ... 155 E2
Palmer Cl
  Barton-u-N DE13 .... 183 E1
  Branston DE14 .... 185 D4
  Essington WV11 .... 241 F1
  Stafford ST15 .... 156 A2
Palmer St ST3 .... 283 D4
Palmers Cross Prim Sch
  WV6 .... 255 E4
Palmers Gn ST4 .... 71 E4
Palmers Way
  Codsall WV8 .... 239 C1
  Newcastle-u-L ST5 .... 71 E4
Palmerston St
  Hanley ST1 .... 282 C1
  Newcastle-u-L ST5 .... 56 B2
Palmerston Way ST6 .... 16 B1
Pandora Gr ST1 .... 57 F3
Panton Cl ST16 .... 156 A2
Pantulf Cl ST17 .... 155 D1
Parade The
  Brownhills WS8 .... 228 C1
  Kingswinford DY6 .... 275 D4
  Newcastle-u-L ST5 .... 55 E1
Parade View WS8 .... 244 C4
Paradise La
  Brownhills WS3 .... 243 F2
  Featherstone WV10 ...... 224 C1
Paradise St ST6 .... 41 E2
Paragon Ave ST5 .... 71 D2
Paragon Cl ST10 .... 76 B1
Paragon Rd ST3 .... 283 D3
Parbury B77 .... 261 E3
Parchments The WS13 .... 214 A1
Pargeter St DY8 .... 279 F2
Paris Ave ST5 .... 70 C3
Park Ave
  Burntwood WS7 .... 229 D3
  Cheadle ST10 .... 76 C1
  Kidsgrove ST7 .... 40 C4
  Meir ST3 .... 74 A3
  Newcastle-u-L ST5 .... 56 B3
  Norton Canes WS11 ...... 228 A3
  Stafford ST17 .... 174 B4
  Stone ST15 .... 119 C4
  Uttoxeter ST14 .... 111 D1
  Wolv WV4 .... 266 B3
  Wombourne WV5 .... 269 F3
Park Ave W ST5 .... 56 A3

Park Cl Barton-u-N DE13 ... 183 E1
  Brownhills WS8 .... 244 C4
  Cheslyn Hay WS6 .... 226 C2
  Madeley CW3 .... 68 C4
Park Cres ST17 .... 155 F1
Park Ct ST5 .... 55 F4
Park Dr Barlaston ST12 ..... 104 C3
  Caverswall ST9 .... 59 E2
  Cheadle ST10 .... 76 B2
  Little Aston B74 .... 257 E2
  Sutton Coldfield B74 ..... 257 F1
  Trentham ST4 .... 87 F4
Park End Lichfield WS14 ... 231 E4
  Newport TF10 .... 168 C3
Park Farm Rd B77 .... 250 B1
Park Farm View ST6 .... 41 E4
Park Gate R
  Cannock WS12 .... 211 F3
  Kidderminster DY10 ...... 280 A1
Park Hall Ave ST3 .... 74 A2
Park Hall Cl WS15 .... 178 B2
Park Hall Cres ST3 .... 74 A2
Park Hall Ind Est ST3 .... 73 F3
Park Hall Prim Sch ST3 .... 74 A2
Park Hall Rd
  Bucknall ST3 .... 73 F3
  Longton ST3 .... 73 F3
  Wolv WV4 .... 266 B3
Park Hall St ST3 .... 283 C4
Park House Dr ST15 .... 120 B4
Park La Ashley TF9 .... 100 A4
  Audley ST7 .... 39 D2
  Biddulph ST8 .... 27 E3
  Blore TF9 .... 99 D1
  Brocton ST17 .... 176 A2
  Cheadle ST10 .... 76 B2
  Cheddleton ST13 .... 45 D3
  Colton WS15 .... 179 D4
  Congleton CW12 .... 6 A1
  Endon ST9 .... 44 A4
  Fazeley B78 .... 249 F1
  Fenton ST4 .... 72 C3
  Great Wyrley WS6 .... 227 D2
  Haughton ST18 .... 172 C3
  Ipstones ST10 .... 47 D1
  Kingswinford DY6 .... 275 D4
  Shenstone WS14 .... 247 D2
  Tutbury DE13 .... 146 A3
  Wheaton Aston ST19 .... 206 A3
  Whittington WS14 .... 232 B4
  Woodseaves ST20 .... 132 A1
Park Lane Cl ST10 .... 76 B2
Park Mid Sch ST8 .... 27 E3
Park Pale The DE13 .... 146 B3
Park Pl Fenton ST4 .... 72 C3
  Uttoxeter ST14 .... 126 B4
Park Prim Sch WS7 .... 229 D3
Park Rd Alrewas DE13 ...... 201 D3
  Barton-u-N DE13 .... 183 E1
  Burntwood, Chase Terrace
  WS7 .... 228 C4
  Burntwood, Triangle WS7 ... 229 D1
  Cannock WS11 .... 209 E1
  Caverswall ST9 .... 59 E2
  Chell Heath ST6 .... 42 A1
  Featherstone WV10 ...... 241 E4
  Leek ST13 .... 30 C4
  Newcastle-u-L ST5 .... 55 E1
  Norton Canes WS11 ...... 228 A3
  Sedgley DY3 .... 271 D2
  Stourbridge DY8 .... 279 E3
  Swadlincote DE12 .... 186 B3
  Tamworth B77 .... 261 E3
  Walsall WS3 .... 243 D1
  Whitmore ST5 .... 70 C1
Park Rd W DY8 .... 279 E3
Park Rise WV3 .... 255 F1
Park Specl Sch B79 .... 250 A4
Park St
  Brierley Hill DY8 .... 279 F4
  Burton u T DE14 .... 166 B1
  Cannock WS11 .... 226 C3
  Cheslyn Hay WS6 .... 226 C2
  Fenton ST4 .... 72 C3
  Kingswinford DY6 .... 275 E3
  Stafford ST17 .... 155 F1
  Tamworth B79 .... 250 A3
  Uttoxeter ST14 .... 111 D1
Park St S WV2 .... 266 B3
Park Terr ST6 .... 41 F2
Park The DE6 .... 81 E4
Park Venture Ctr WS11 .... 226 C3
Park View
  Blythe Bridge ST11 .... 90 C3
  Swynnerton ST15 .... 103 D2
Park View Rd
  Kidsgrove ST7 .... 26 A2
  Sutton Coldfield B74 ..... 257 E2
Park View Terr ST5 .... 178 B1
Park Way Forsbrook ST11 ... 91 D4
  Wolv WV11 .... 242 A1
Park Wood Dr ST5 .... 85 D4
Parkdale DY3 .... 271 E4
Parkend ST11 .... 91 D4
Parker Bowles Dr TF9 ..... 112 A4
Parker Paul Ind Est WV2 ... 266 B4
Parker Rd WV11 .... 241 F1
Parker St
  Burton u T DE14 .... 166 B3
  Hanley ST1 .... 282 A3
  Leek ST13 .... 31 D3
  Walsall WS3 .... 243 D1
Parker's Croft Rd ST17 .... 155 F1
Parker-Jervis Rd ST3 .... 73 F2
Parkers Cl ST20 .... 190 A4
Parkers Ct WV9 .... 224 B1

Parkes Ave WV8 .... 239 D1
Parkes Hall Rd DY3 .... 271 F3
Parkfield Ave B77 .... 250 B1
Parkfield Cl
  Barlaston ST12 .... 88 B1
  Tamworth B77 .... 261 E4
Parkfield Cres
  Tamworth B77 .... 261 E4
  Wolv WV2 .... 266 C3
Parkfield Gr WV2 .... 266 C3
Parkfield High Sch WV4 ... 266 C3
Parkfield La DE6 .... 81 E2
Parkfield Prim Sch WV4 ... 266 C3
Parkfield Rd Longton ST3 ... 73 C1
  Wolv WV2, WV4 .... 266 C3
Parkfields Endon ST9 .... 43 F4
  Stafford ST17 .... 174 B4
Parkfields Cl ST5 .... 55 D1
Parkgate La DE6 .... 79 F3
Parkhall Cty Pk ST3 .... 73 F3
Parkhall St ST10 .... 109 D3
Parkhead Cres ST3 .... 74 A2
Parkhead Dr ST3 .... 74 A2
Parkhead Gr ST3 .... 74 A2
Parkhill Rd WS7 .... 229 D4
Parkhouse Gdns DY3 .... 271 E2
Parkhouse Ind Est ST5 ..... 41 D1
Parkhouse Ind Est E ST5 ... 55 F4
Parkhouse Ind Est (E) ST5 ... 56 A4
Parkhouse Ind Est W ST5 ... 55 F4
Parkhouse Rd E ST5 .... 40 C1
Parkhouse Rd W ST5 .... 40 C1
Parkhouse St ST1 .... 282 A1
Parklands Biddulph ST8 ..... 17 D1
  Kidsgrove ST7 .... 26 A1
  Wolv WV3 .... 255 E1
Parklands Rd ST10 .... 92 C2
Parklands The CW12 .... 6 A1
Parks Cres WV11 .... 242 A2
Parkside Tamworth B77 .... 250 C1
  Trentham ST4 .... 88 A4
Parkside Ave ST5 .... 155 E4
Parkside Cres ST9 .... 43 F4
Parkside Cty Prim Sch
  ST16 .... 155 E4
Parkside Dr ST5 .... 56 B2
Parkside Dr ST5 .... 56 B2
Parkside Ind Est WV1 ...... 266 C4
Parkside La Gayton ST18 ... 139 D4
  Huntington WS12 .... 209 D1
Parkside Way B74 .... 257 D1
Parkstone Ave ST5 .... 284 C2
Parkstone Cl WS4 .... 244 B1
Parkview Dr WS8 .... 228 C1
Parkway Branston DE14 ... 165 F1
  Stone ST15 .... 120 B4
Parkway The Hanley ST1 ... 282 B4
  Perton WV6 .... 254 C2
  Trentham ST4 .... 87 F4
Parkwood Ave ST4 .... 87 F4
Parkwood Cl WS8 .... 245 D3
Parkyn St WV2 .... 266 C3
Parliament Row ST1 .... 282 B3
Parliament Sq ST1 .... 282 B3
Parliament St DE11 .... 186 C3
Parnell Sq CW12 .... 6 A1
Parson St B77 .... 261 F4
Parson's Croft WV9 .... 224 A1
Parsonage St ST6 .... 41 E2
Parsons Cl SK17 .... 24 B3
Parsons Dr ST20 .... 171 F3
Parsons La
  Butterton ST13 .... 33 E2
  Grindon ST13 .... 33 E2
Parton Gr ST3 .... 74 A2
Partridge Cl
  Huntington WS12 .... 209 E4
  Meir ST3 .... 90 A4
Partridge Croft WS13 ...... 231 E4
Partridge Dr ST14 .... 126 B3
Partridge Rd DY8 .... 279 E2
Partridge Ride TF9 .... 99 E2
Parva Ct ST4 .... 110 C1
Paskin Cl WS13 .... 215 E4
Pass Ave WS14 .... 232 C3
Passfield Ave ST4 .... 210 B4
Pastoral Cl CW3 .... 68 C3
Pasture Cl ST5 .... 85 E3
Pasture Gate WS3 .... 209 E1
Pasture View WS3 .... 243 F1
Pasturefields Ind Pk
  ST18 .... 158 A3
Pasturefields La ST18 ...... 158 A3
Pastures The
  Perton WV6 .... 254 B2
  Swadlincote DE11 .... 186 C3
Patch Cl DE13 .... 166 A3
Patch Meadow Rd ST10 ... 76 A2
Paterson Ave ST21 .... 117 F2
Paterson Pl WS8 .... 245 D3
Patricia Ave WV4 .... 266 B3
Patrick Pl ST8 .... 27 D1
Patshull Ave WV10 .... 240 A2
Patshull Gr WV10 .... 240 A2
Patshull Rd WV6 .... 253 D2
Patterdale Rd WS11 .... 210 A2
Patterdale Rd ST6 .... 42 A2
Pattingham La WV7 .... 253 E4
Pattingham Rd WV6 .... 254 B1
Paul St ◪ WV2 .... 266 B4
Paulet High Sch DE15 ..... 185 F4
Pauls Coppice WS8 .... 245 D3
Pauls Wlk ST14 .... 214 A2
Pavement The ST19 .... 223 E3
Pavilion Cl WS9 .... 256 B4

Pavilion Dr ST1 .... 57 D3
Pavilion The B77 .... 251 D2
Pavior's Rd WS7 .... 228 C2
Paxton Ave WV6 .... 254 C2
Paxton St ST1 .... 282 C1
Paynter St ST4 .... 72 C3
Peace Cl WS6 .... 226 C2
Peacehaven Gr ST4 .... 88 B3
Peacock Hay Rd ST7 .... 40 C2
Peacock La
  Swynnerton ST4, ST5 .... 87 D4
  Whitmore ST4, ST5 .... 87 D4
Peacock Rd ST5 .... 55 F3
Peacock View ST4 .... 57 F1
Peak Cl WS15 .... 198 A2
Peak Dale Ave ST6 .... 41 E4
Peak Dr DY1 .... 271 F2
Peak View ST13 .... 31 D3
Peake Cres WS8 .... 244 C3
Peake Rd WS8 .... 245 D3
Peake St ST5 .... 55 F2
Peakes Rd WS15 .... 178 A1
Peaks L Ctr B78 .... 250 A2
Pear Tree Ave DE11 .... 186 C4
Pear Tree Cl
  Barlaston ST12 .... 88 B1
  Gnosall ST20 .... 171 F3
  Huntington WS12 .... 209 E4
  Shuttington B79 .... 251 F4
Pear Tree Cty Prim Sch WS15 .... 196 C4
Pear Tree Dr CW3 .... 68 B4
Pear Tree La
  Brownhills WS8 .... 228 B1
  Claverley WV5 .... 268 A2
  Essington WV11 .... 241 D1
  Newcastle-u-L ST5 .... 55 E4
Pear Tree Rd ST7 .... 39 F1
Pearl Gr ST3 .... 90 A4
Pearson Dr ST15 .... 120 B4
Pearsons St WV2 .... 266 B4
Peartree La 180 A3
Peascroft Rd ST6 .... 42 B2
Pebble Cl B77 .... 251 D2
Pebble Mill Cl WS11 .... 209 F1
Pebble Mill Dr WS11 .... 210 A1
Pebble Mill St ST1 .... 56 C2
Peck Hill La ST8 .... 27 E1
Peckforton View ST7 .... 41 D4
Pedley Gr ST6 .... 42 B1
Pedley La CW12 .... 6 C2
Peebles Rd ST5 .... 54 C1
Peel Cl B78 .... 260 C3
Peel Dr Astbury CW12 .... 15 E4
  Cannock WS12 .... 209 F4
Peel Hollow ST7 .... 39 D1
Peel La CW12 .... 15 D4
Peel St Burton u T DE14 .... 166 B1
  Longton ST3 .... 283 C4
  Newcastle-u-L ST5 .... 56 B3
  Stafford ST16 .... 155 E3
  Tunstall ST6 .... 56 B4
Peel Terr ST16 .... 155 F3
Peelers Way B77 .... 250 B1
Pegasus Gr ST6 .... 42 B1
Pegasus Wlk B79 .... 249 F4
Peggs La ST20 .... 150 C4
Peggy's Bank ST7 .... 54 C4
Pegroy Gr ST6 .... 42 B1
Pelham St ST1 .... 282 C1
Pellfield Ct ST18 .... 138 B1
Pelsall Jun Mix Inf Sch WS3 .... 243 F2
Pelsall La
  Brownhills WS3 .... 244 A1
  Walsall WS3 .... 243 E2
Pelsall Rd WS8 .... 244 B4
Pemberton Dr ST3 .... 90 A3
Pembridge Rd ST3 .... 88 C4
Pembroke Dr
  Newcastle-u-L ST5 .... 284 A2
  Stone ST15 .... 120 B4
Pembroke Gdns DY8 .... 275 E1
Pembroke Rd ST2 .... 43 D1
Pen-y-bryn Way TF10 .... 168 C1
Penarth Gr ST1 .... 282 B4
Penarth Pl ST5 .... 284 A1
Pencombe Dr WV4 .... 266 B3
Penda Gr WV6 .... 254 C3
Pendeford Ave ST5 .... 255 F4
Pendeford Bsns Pk WV9 .... 239 F2
Pendeford Cl WV6 .... 255 F4
Pendeford Hall La WV9 .... 239 E3
Pendeford High Sch WV10 .... 240 A1
Pendeford La WV10 .... 240 A2
Pendeford Mill La WV8 .... 239 E2
Penderel St WS3 .... 243 E1
Pendinas Dr WV8 .... 239 D2
Pendine Gr ST4 .... 73 D3
Pendle Hill ST10 .... 210 B2
Pendrel Cl WS6 .... 242 C4
Pendrell Cl Codsall WV8 .... 239 D2
  Featherstone WV10 .... 241 D1
Pendrell Hall Adult Coll WV8 .... 238 B3
Pendrill Rd WV10 .... 240 C2
Pendryl Ct ST19 .... 223 E4
Penfleet Ave ST5 .... 74 A1
Pengrove ST10 .... 41 F4
Penhallow Dr WV4 .... 266 C3
Penk Dr WS7 .... 229 E3
Penk Dr N WS15 .... 178 B1

Penk Dr S WS15 .... 178 B1
Penk Rd ST11 .... 91 D4
Penk Rise WV6 .... 255 D2
Penkhull Inf Sch ST4 .... 72 A4
Penkhull New Rd ST4 .... 72 A3
Penkhull Terr ST4 .... 72 A3
Penkridge Bank WS15 .... 195 E3
Penkridge Cty Mid Sch ST19 .... 193 D1
Penkridge Ind Est ST19 .... 207 F4
Penkridge L Ctr ST19 .... 208 A1
Penkridge Sta ST17 .... 193 D4
Penkridge Sta ST17 .... 207 F4
Penkvale Rd ST17 .... 174 C3
Penkville St ST4 .... 72 A3
Penleigh Gdns WV5 .... 269 F4
Penmark Gr ST3 .... 89 F4
Penmere Dr
  Caverswall ST9 .... 59 D2
  Newcastle-u-L ST5 .... 71 E1
Penn Cl WS3 .... 243 E1
Penn Croft ST18 .... 177 E4
Penn Croft La DY3 .... 266 A1
Penn Fields Sch WV4 .... 265 F4
Penn Hall Sch WV4 .... 265 F2
Penn Hospl WV4 .... 265 F2
Penn Rd Himley DY3 .... 270 C4
  Wolv WV2, WV3, WV4 .... 266 A3
Penn St WV3 .... 266 A4
Pennell St ST2 .... 58 A2
Pennhouse Ave WV4 .... 265 F3
Pennine Dr
  Cannock WS11 .... 209 F1
  Sedgley DY3 .... 271 D2
Pennine Way
  Biddulph ST6 .... 16 C1
  Newcastle-u-L ST5 .... 55 F2
  Tamworth B77 .... 262 A4
Pennington Cl ST3 .... 74 B1
Penns Wood Cl DY3 .... 266 B1
Pennwood La Wolv WV4 .... 265 F2
  Wombourne WV4 .... 265 F2
Penny Cress Gn WS11 .... 227 F2
Penny Gr WS6 .... 242 C4
Penny Farthing Arc DY3 .... 271 D1
Pennycress Gdns WV10 .... 241 E4
Pennycroft La ST14 .... 111 E1
Pennycroft Rd ST14 .... 111 D1
Pennycrofts ST16 .... 155 F2
Pennyfields Rd ST7 .... 26 B1
Pennymoor Rd B77 .... 262 A4
Pennymore Cl ST4 .... 88 A4
Pennys Croft WS13 .... 214 C1
Penport Gr ST3 .... 283 A2
Penrhyn Ave ST6 .... 42 A1
Penrith Cl ST4 .... 88 B3
Penrith Cl ST5 .... 71 D3
Pens Meadow Sch DY8 .... 275 F2
Pensford St ST1 .... 57 F3
Pensgreave Rd DE13 .... 166 A3
Penshaw Cl WV9 .... 240 A1
Pensnett Trad Est The DY6 .... 275 F4
Penstone La WV4 .... 264 C2
Pentire Rd WS14 .... 231 E3
Pentland Gdns WV6 .... 255 F1
Pentland Gr ST5 .... 55 F2
Penton Pl ST3 .... 88 C4
Penton Wlk ST3 .... 88 C4
Penzer St DY6 .... 275 E4
Peolsford Rd WS3 .... 244 A2
Peover La CW12 .... 6 B3
Pepper St Keele ST5 .... 54 C1
  Newcastle-u-L ST5 .... 284 B2
Perceval St ST1 .... 57 F3
Percival Dr ST9 .... 43 E2
Percy St ST1 .... 282 B3
Peregrine Cl
  Burton u T DE15 .... 167 E2
  Dudley DY1 .... 271 F1
Peregrine Gr ST3 .... 90 A3
Perivale Cl ST1 .... 58 A3
Periwinkle La WS8 .... 244 B3
Perkins St ST6 .... 41 E4
Perks Rd WV11 .... 242 A1
Perle Brook ST21 .... 133 E4
Perott Dr B75 .... 258 B1
Perrin Cl ST17 .... 174 C3
Perry Cl ST1 .... 282 C2
Perrycrofts Cres B79 .... 250 B4
Pershore Cl WS3 .... 242 C1
Pershore Rd WS3 .... 242 C1
Pershore Way WS3 .... 242 C1
Perth Cl DE15 .... 167 E1
Perth St ST4 .... 283 A5
Perthy Gr ST4 .... 87 F4
Perton Brook Vale WV6 .... 254 C2
Perton Cty Fst Sch WV6 .... 254 C3
Perton Cty Mid Sch WV6 .... 255 D3
Perton Gr WV6 .... 254 C1
Perton Rd WV6 .... 254 C1
Perton Wood View ST3 .... 72 C2
Pessall La B79 .... 217 E4
Peter James Ct ST16 .... 155 F3
Peter's La WS7 .... 230 A3
Peterborough Dr WS12 .... 210 B1
Peterdale Dr WV4 .... 265 F2
Peterhead B77 .... 250 C3
Peters Wlk WS13 .... 214 A1
Petersfield WS11 .... 209 F2
Petersfield Rd ST6 .... 42 A4
Petershouse Dr B74 .... 257 F3
Pethills La ST13 .... 48 B3
Petrel Gr ST3 .... 90 A4
Pevensey Gr ST3 .... 73 E3
Peverill Rd Perton WV6 .... 254 C2
  Wolv WV4 .... 266 C2
Pezenas Dr TF9 .... 97 D1

Pheasant Wlk TF9 .... 99 E2
Philip Gr WS11 .... 209 F3
Philip La ST19 .... 59 D2
Philip St ST4 .... 72 C3
Phillips Ave WV11 .... 241 F1
Phillips Ct ST15 .... 120 B4
Phillipson Way ST6 .... 57 E4
Phoenix Bank TF9 .... 97 E1
Phoenix Cl WS15 .... 178 C1
Phoenix Rd WS11 .... 210 A1
Phoenix St Tunstall ST6 .... 41 E2
  Wolv WV2 .... 266 B3
Picasso Cl WS11 .... 210 B1
Picasso Rise ST3 .... 90 A4
Piccadilly ST1 .... 282 B2
Piccadilly Arc ST1 .... 282 B3
Piccadilly La DE6 .... 66 B1
Piccadilly St ST6 .... 41 E2
Pickering Cl ST3 .... 283 A1
Pickford Pl ST3 .... 74 A1
Pickleys La DE6 .... 127 E4
Pickmere Cl ST3 .... 43 D2
Picknal St ST14 .... 126 A4
Picknalls ST14 .... 126 A4
Picknalls Cty Fst Sch ST14 .... 126 A4
Pickwick Pl ST7 .... 25 E1
Pickwood Ave ST13 .... 31 D3
Pickwood Cl ST13 .... 31 D3
Picton St Hanley ST1 .... 282 C2
  Leek ST13 .... 30 B3
Piddocks Rd DE15 .... 186 A3
Pidduck St ST6 .... 56 C4
Pier St WS8 .... 244 C4
Pierce St ST6 .... 41 E2
Pigeonhay La ST14 .... 110 B1
Piggott Gr ST2 .... 58 A2
Pike Cl ST16 .... 156 A3
Pike La WS15 .... 198 A2
Pikelow La ST10 .... 49 D2
Pilgrim Pl ST16 .... 155 F1
Pilgrim St ST16 .... 155 F1
Pilkington Ave ST5 .... 71 D3
Pillaton Cl ST19 .... 207 F4
Pillaton Dr WS12 .... 209 E3
Pilsbury St ST5 .... 56 B3
Pilsden Pl ST3 .... 90 B4
Pimlico Ct DY3 .... 271 E2
Pinch The DE6 .... 36 A1
Pine Cl Branston DE14 .... 185 D4
  Great Wyrley WS11 .... 226 C2
  Kingswinford DY6 .... 275 D4
  Kinver DY7 .... 278 B2
  Market Drayton TF9 .... 97 D1
  Tamworth B79 .... 250 A4
Pine Cres ST17 .... 175 F3
Pine Ct Ashley TF9 .... 99 E2
  Blythe Bridge ST11 .... 90 B4
Pine Gr Burntwood WS7 .... 228 C3
  Swadlincote DE11 .... 186 C3
Pine Leigh B74 .... 258 A4
Pine Rd ST4 .... 72 B2
Pine St WS3 .... 243 E1
Pine Tree Cl WS12 .... 195 D1
Pine View Rugeley WS15 .... 178 B2
  Swindon DY3 .... 269 E2
Pine Wlk Codsall WV8 .... 238 C1
  Uttoxeter ST14 .... 125 F4
Pinehurst Cl ST5 .... 71 D2
Pines Park Mobile Homes The ST19 .... 209 E3
Pines The Lichfield WS14 .... 231 F4
  Wolv WV3 .... 255 E1
Pineside Ave ST13 .... 211 F3
Pinetree Dr Aldridge B74 .... 256 B1
  Blythe Bridge ST11 .... 90 B4
Pinetrees La TF9 .... 99 E3
Pineways
  Kingswinford DY8 .... 275 E1
  Sutton Coldfield B74 .... 257 E2
Pineways Dr WV6 .... 255 F2
Pinewood Ave
  Cannock WS11 .... 209 E2
  Kingsbury CV9 .... 262 B1
Pinewood Cl
  Brownhills WS8 .... 228 C1
  Wolv WV3 .... 265 D4
  Wombourne WV5 .... 270 A3
Pinewood Cres ST3 .... 74 B1
Pinewood Dr Ashley TF9 .... 99 F2
  Colwich ST18 .... 177 E4
Pinewood Gr
  Forsbrook ST11 .... 91 D3
  Newcastle-u-L ST5 .... 40 C1
Pinewood Prim Sch ST3 .... 74 B1
Pinewood Rd DE15 .... 185 D3
Pinewood Wlk DY6 .... 275 F4
Pinewoods Cl ST10 .... 168 C1
Pinewoods Ave DY9 .... 281 E2
Pinewoods Cl DY9 .... 281 E2
Pinfold Ave ST6 .... 42 B2
Pinfold Cl Tutbury DE13 .... 146 B3
  Wheaton Aston ST19 .... 205 D3
Pinfold Cres WV4 .... 265 E3
Pinfold Dr WS15 .... 198 B3
Pinfold Gr WV4 .... 265 E3
Pinfold Hill WS14 .... 246 C3
Pinfold La
  Abbots Bromley WS15 .... 161 C2
  Blore TF9 .... 98 B1
  Cheslyn Hay WS6 .... 226 B1
  Norbury ST20 .... 151 D2
  Norton Canes WS11 .... 227 F2
  Penkridge ST19 .... 192 B1
  Wheaton Aston ST19 .... 205 D3
  Wolv WV4 .... 265 F3
Pinfold Rd WS13 .... 213 F1

Pinfold St ST14 .... 126 B4
Pingle Farm Rd DE11 .... 186 C3
Pingle La
  Burntwood WS7 .... 229 E3
  Stone ST15 .... 120 A4
Pingle The WS15 .... 196 A4
Pinhoe Pl ST3 .... 73 F2
Pinnox St ST6 .... 41 F1
Pintail Cl ST17 .... 175 D4
Pipe Hay La DE6 .... 144 B3
Pipe La WS15 .... 198 A4
Pipe Wood La WS15 .... 180 A2
Piper Cl WV6 .... 254 C2
Piper Pl DY8 .... 279 F4
Piper Rd WV3 .... 265 D4
Piper's La TF10 .... 168 A2
Piper's Lodge TF10 .... 168 A2
Pipers Croft WS13 .... 214 A1
Pippins The
  Newcastle-u-L ST5 .... 71 E2
  Stafford ST17 .... 174 C3
Pireford Pl ST3 .... 41 D1
Pirehill Fst Sch ST15 .... 119 F3
Pirehill La ST15 .... 119 F3
Pirehill Rd ST5 .... 41 D1
Pirie Cl ST17 .... 6 A2
Pirie Rd CW12 .... 6 A2
Pit La ST7 .... 40 B3
Pitcairn St ST6 .... 41 F2
Pitchcroft La TF10 .... 187 D3
Pitcher La ST13 .... 31 D3
Pitfield Ave ST5 .... 56 B2
Pitgreen La ST5 .... 56 B3
Pitlea Pl 7 ST3 .... 73 E3
Pitsford St ST3 .... 73 F1
Pitstone Cl ST16 .... 136 B1
Pitt St
  Kidderminster DY10 .... 280 A1
  Stafford ST17 .... 155 E3
Pitt St E ST6 .... 57 D4
Pitt St W ST6 .... 57 D4
Pitts Hill Bank ST6 .... 41 F3
Plainfield Gr ST2 .... 73 E4
Plainview Cl B74 .... 256 C1
Plaisaunce The ST5 .... 71 D3
Plane Gr ST5 .... 40 C1
Planks La WV5 .... 269 F3
Plant Cres ST17 .... 174 C4
Plant La WS7 .... 228 C4
Plant St Cheadle ST10 .... 76 C1
  Kingswinford DY8 .... 275 F1
  Longton ST3 .... 283 C4
Plant Way WS3 .... 243 F2
Plantation La
  Fazeley B78 .... 249 D2
  Hopwas B78 .... 249 D2
  Wombourne WV3 .... 270 A2
Plantation Rd
  Cannock WS12 .... 195 D1
  Longton ST4 .... 88 B4
Plants Cl WS6 .... 243 D4
Plardiwick Rd ST20 .... 171 D3
Platt St WS11 .... 210 A3
Platts Ave ST9 .... 43 F3
Platts Cres DY8 .... 279 F4
Platts Dr DY8 .... 279 F4
Platts Rd DY8 .... 279 F4
Playdale TF10 .... 168 A2
Pleasant Cl DY6 .... 275 E2
Pleasant St ST6 .... 56 C4
Pleasant View WV3 .... 271 E1
Plex St ST6 .... 41 E2
Pleydell St ST1 .... 57 F4
Plough Bank ST9 .... 60 A4
Plough La TF10 .... 168 C3
Plough St ST1 .... 282 C4
Ploughmans Wlk
  Kingswinford DY6 .... 275 D4
  Lichfield WS13 .... 214 B2
  Wolv WV8 .... 239 F1
Plover Cl
  Featherstone WV10 .... 241 D4
  Meir ST3 .... 90 A4
Plover Dr ST8 .... 27 F4
Plover Field WV3 .... 68 B3
Plovers Rise WS15 .... 178 B1
Plummer Rd DE11 .... 186 C3
Plumtree Gr ST1 .... 57 F3
Plymouth Gr ST5 .... 55 F4
Pochard Cl ST6 .... 42 B1
Podmore Ave ST7 .... 54 C3
Podmore La ST7 .... 54 C3
Podmore St ST6 .... 57 D4
Pointon Gr ST3 .... 43 D3
Polesworth High Sch B78 .... 262 C4
Polesworth Sports Ctr B78 .... 262 C4
Police Dr TF9 .... 112 B4
Polperro Way ST3 .... 90 A4
Pomona Rise ST1 .... 57 E4
Pond Cres WV2 .... 266 C4
Pond Gr WV2 .... 266 C4
Pond La WV2 .... 266 B4
Ponesfield Rd WS13 .... 214 A1
Ponesgreen WS13 .... 214 A1
Pool Ave
  Norton Canes WS11 .... 228 A3
  Norton-in-t-M ST2 .... 43 D1
Pool Cl WV10 .... 225 E1
Pool Cres WS8 .... 228 B1
Pool Dam ST5 .... 284 B2
Pool Gn WS9 .... 256 A3
Pool Hall Cres WV3 .... 265 D4
Pool Hall Rd WV3 .... 265 D4
Pool La Brocton ST17 .... 176 B2
  Burntwood WS7 .... 228 C2

Pool Meadow WS6 .... 226 B1
Pool Meadow Cl WS15 .... 196 B4
Pool Rd Brownhills WS8 .... 228 C1
  Burntwood WS7 .... 228 C2
Pool Side
  Newcastle-u-L ST5 .... 284 A3
  Scholar Green ST7 .... 25 D4
Pool St Fenton ST4 .... 73 D3
  Newcastle-u-L ST5 .... 284 A2
  Wolv WV2 .... 266 B4
Pool View WS11 .... 227 D2
Poole St DY8 .... 279 F2
Poole's Way WS7 .... 229 E4
Pooles Rd ST8 .... 17 D1
Pooley La Gnosall TF10 .... 188 B4
  Polesworth B78 .... 251 F1
Poolfield Ave ST5 .... 70 C4
Poolfields Ave N ST5 .... 71 D4
Poolfields Cl ST5 .... 70 C4
Poolside Longton ST3 .... 88 C4
  Madeley CW3 .... 68 C3
Pope Gdns ST17 .... 174 B4
Pope Gr WS12 .... 209 F3
Pope Rd WV10 .... 241 D1
Poplar Ave
  Brownhills WS8 .... 245 D4
  Burntwood WS7 .... 228 C3
  Cannock WS11 .... 209 F2
  Newcastle-u-L ST5 .... 56 A2
Poplar Cl Eccleshall ST21 .... 133 F3
  Forsbrook ST11 .... 91 D3
  Haughton ST18 .... 172 C3
  Newcastle-u-L ST5 .... 56 A2
  Stone ST15 .... 119 F4
  Uttoxeter ST14 .... 110 C1
  Wombourne WV5 .... 270 A3
Poplar Cres DY8 .... 279 F2
Poplar Ct ST5 .... 56 A2
Poplar Dr Kidsgrove ST7 .... 26 A1
  Longton ST3 .... 72 C1
Poplar Gr Longton ST3 .... 73 D1
  Newcastle-u-L ST5 .... 284 D3
Poplar La Cannock WS11 .... 209 D1
  Huntington WS11 .... 226 A4
  Woore TF9 .... 82 C3
Poplar Rd
  Brownhills WS8 .... 245 D4
  Great Wyrley WS6 .... 227 D1
  Kingswinford DY6 .... 275 F3
  Stourbridge DY8 .... 279 F2
  Wolv WV3 .... 266 A3
Poplar Rise B74 .... 257 E3
Poplars
  Norton Canes WS11 .... 228 A3
  Wolv WV2 .... 266 B3
Poplars Dr WV8 .... 238 C1
Poplars Farm Way WV9 .... 224 A1
Poplars Rd
  Armitage WS15 .... 198 B2
  Burton u T DE13 .... 166 B4
Poplars The
  Brierley Hill DY8 .... 275 F1
  Cannock WS11 .... 209 F2
  Kingswinford DY8 .... 275 F1
Poppit's La ST14 .... 110 C2
Porlock Ave ST17 .... 175 F4
Porlock Gr ST4 .... 88 A3
Port La
  Abbots Bromley WS15 .... 160 C3
  Brewood WV8 .... 223 D2
Port St ST6 .... 56 C4
Port Vale St ST6 .... 56 C4
Portal Rd ST16 .... 156 A3
Porters Farm ST14 .... 127 F1
Porters La ST13 .... 31 F2
Porthill ST5 .... 56 B4
Porthill Gn ST5 .... 56 B3
Porthill Rd ST6 .... 56 B4
Porthkerry Gr DY3 .... 271 D4
Portland Ave
  Aldridge WS9 .... 256 A3
  Branston DE14 .... 185 D4
  Tamworth B79 .... 249 E2
Portland Cl ST11 .... 90 B4
Portland Dr
  Biddulph ST6 .... 16 B1
  Forsbrook ST11 .... 91 D4
  Market Drayton TF9 .... 97 D1
  Scholar Green ST7 .... 25 F3
Portland Gr ST5 .... 71 D2
Portland Mews ST5 .... 56 A3
Portland Pl
  Barlaston ST12 .... 88 C2
  Cannock WS11 .... 226 B4
  Waterhouses ST10 .... 48 C1
Portland Rd
  Aldridge WS9 .... 256 A3
  Longton ST3 .... 283 B4
Portland St Hanley ST1 .... 282 A4
  Leek ST13 .... 30 C3
Portland St N ST13 .... 30 C3
Portland St S ST13 .... 30 C3
Portleven Cl ST17 .... 175 F4
Portleys La B78 .... 260 B2
Portobello ST5 .... 178 C1
Portrush Rd WV6 .... 254 B2
Portswood Cl WV9 .... 239 F1
Portway Cl DY6 .... 275 F3
Portway Dr DE13 .... 146 B3
Portway La B79 .... 234 B4
Portway Pl DY10 .... 280 A3
Portway The DY6 .... 275 F3
Post La ST9 .... 43 F3
Post Office La
  Betley CW2 .... 37 F1
  Gnosall TF10 .... 188 B4
  Rugeley WS15 .... 196 A4

Post Office Rd
Alrewas DE13 .... 201 D2
Seisdon WV5 .... 263 F2
Post Office Sq CW3 .... 68 C3
Postern Rd DE13 .... 165 D2
Pothooks La ST13 .... 33 F2
Potteries Sh Ctr ST1 .... 282 B3
Potteries Way ST1 .... 282 C3
Potters Ave ST15 .... 118 C3
Potters End ST6 .... 16 B1
Pouk La WS14 .... 245 F4
Poulson St ST4 .... 72 A4
Pound Gdns ST6 .... 42 B2
Pound St WV5 .... 267 E4
Poundsgate Gr ST4 .... 88 A4
Pountney St WV2 .... 266 B4
Povey Pl ST5 .... 41 D1
Powderham Cl ST7 .... 41 F4
Powell Pl TF10 .... 168 C2
Powell St ST1 .... 282 A4
Power Gr ST3 .... 283 A4
Power Station Rd WS15 .... 178 C1
Power Station Road
  Ind Est WS15 .... 178 C1
Powy Dr ST7 .... 26 A1
Poxon Rd WS9 .... 245 D2
Poynings The WV6 .... 255 E3
Precinct The B79 .... 250 A3
Preedys Cl WS15 .... 160 C3
Prescott Ave ST16 .... 156 A2
Prescott Dr ST1 .... 193 D1
Prestbury Ave ST5 .... 71 D1
Preston St ST6 .... 57 E4
Preston Vale La ST19 .... 192 B1
Prestwick Rd DY6 .... 275 E3
Prestwood Cl ST17 .... 155 F1
Prestwood Dr DY7 .... 279 D4
Prestwood La ST14 .... 79 F1
Prestwood Rd DY7 .... 278 F2
Pretoria Rd ST1 .... 57 D2
Priam Cl ST5 .... 41 D1
Priam Gr WS3 .... 244 A3
Price Ave B78 .... 249 E1
Price Cl TF9 .... 99 E3
Price Ct DE14 .... 166 A2
Price St Burslem ST6 .... 56 C4
  Cannock WS11 .... 209 F1
Prices Rd DY3 .... 271 E2
Priestley Dr ST3 .... 283 D4
Prime St ST1 .... 57 F3
Primitive St ST7 .... 26 B4
Primley Ave B77 .... 261 F3
Primrose Ave WV10 .... 240 B2
Primrose Cl
  Brownhills WS3 .... 244 A3
  Wheaton Aston ST19 .... 205 E4
Primrose Dell CW3 .... 68 B3
Primrose Dr TF10 .... 168 C1
Primrose Gdns
  Codsall WV8 .... 239 D2
  Featherstone WV10 .... 241 D4
Primrose Gr ST5 .... 284 C4
Primrose Hill
  Kingswinford DY8 .... 275 F1
  Trentham ST4 .... 72 A1
Primrose Meadow
  WS11 .... 210 B1
Primrose Way ST14 .... 126 A4
Prince Albert Terr ST15 .... 135 D4
Prince Ave ST18 .... 172 C3
Prince Charles Ave ST13 .... 31 D4
Prince George St ST10 ...... 76 B2
Prince Rupert's Way
  WS13 .... 231 D4
Prince St
  Brownhills WS9 .... 244 C1
  Cannock WS11 .... 209 F3
  Leek ST13 .... 31 D3
Prince's Rd ST4 .... 71 F4
Prince's St ST15 .... 105 D1
Princefield Ave ST19 .... 207 F4
Princefield Fst Sch ST19 ..... 207 F4
Princes Dr WV8 .... 239 D1
Princes Gdns WV8 .... 239 D1
Princes Rd DY8 .... 279 E2
Princes Sq ST6 .... 56 B4
Princes St ST16 .... 155 F2
Princess Ave Audley ST7 ... 39 E1
  Leek ST13 .... 31 D4
Princess Cl WS7 .... 228 C4
Princess Ct ST5 .... 40 B3
Princess Dr ST3 .... 74 A2
Princess Gdns TF10 .... 168 C1
Princess Pl ST15 .... 155 F3
Princess Rd ST14 .... 111 D1
Princess St Biddulph ST8 ... 27 E4
  Burntwood WS7 .... 228 C4
  Cannock WS11 .... 209 F3
  Kidsgrove ST7 .... 40 B3
  Newcastle-u-L ST5 .... 284 C3
Princess Way DE14 .... 166 C4
Princeton Gdns WV9 .... 239 F1
Priorfield Cl ST3 .... 283 B4
Priors Mill DY3 .... 271 F3
Priory Ave ST13 .... 31 D4
Priory CE Inf Sch ST4 .... 87 F4
Priory Cl
  Congleton CW12 .... 16 A4
  Tamworth B79 .... 249 E4
  Tutbury DE13 .... 146 A3
Priory Cty Inf Sch ST5 .... 284 B2
Priory Dr ST18 .... 177 E4
Priory Field Cl WV14 .... 266 C4
Priory Green Jun
  & Inf Schs WV6 .... 240 A1
Priory La DY3 .... 271 E4
Priory Lands DE13 .... 147 F1
Priory Pl ST7 .... 26 B2

Priory Rd Bucknall ST2 ...... 58 A3
  Cannock WS12 .... 210 B2
  Newcastle-u-L ST5 .... 284 B1
  Rugeley WS15 .... 197 D3
  Stone ST15 .... 120 A4
Priory The ST3 .... 271 E4
Pritchett Ave WV4 .... 266 C2
Probert Rd WV10 .... 240 A1
Probyn Ct ST3 .... 283 C2
Proctors Rd WS15 .... 198 B2
Progress Dr WS11 .... 226 C4
Prospect Dr WS13 .... 231 F4
Prospect Manor Ct
  WS12 .... 210 B2
Prospect Pk WS11 .... 226 B4
Prospect Pl ST13 .... 30 C3
Prospect Rd
  Burntwood WS7 .... 229 D3
  Leek ST13 .... 31 D3
  Market Drayton TF9 .... 97 D1
  Sedgley DY3 .... 271 E1
  Stafford ST16 .... 155 F3
Prospect St Burslem ST6 .... 56 C3
  Tamworth B79 .... 250 A3
Prospect Terr ST4 .... 284 A3
Prosper Meadow DY6 .... 275 F4
Providence St ST1 .... 282 C4
Provost Pl ST13 .... 31 D4
Pruden Ave WV4 .... 266 C2
Puddle Hill ST18 .... 139 E1
Puddy La ST9 .... 44 A3
Pudsey Dr B75 .... 258 B2
Pugh Rd WV14 .... 266 C1
Pugin Cl WV6 .... 254 B2
Pullman Cl B77 .... 251 D1
Pullman Ct ST10 .... 76 B1
Pulteney Dr ST16 .... 155 D3
Pump Bank ST5 .... 69 F4
Pump La Doveridge DE6 ..... 127 D4
  Rugeley WS15 .... 178 B2
Pump St Leek ST13 .... 31 D4
  Stoke-on-T ST4 .... 72 A4
Purbeck St ST6 .... 57 D4
Purbrook B77 .... 261 F4
Purbrook Rd WV1 .... 266 C4
Purcell Ave WS13 .... 214 B1
Pye Green Rd WS11 .... 209 F2
Pye Green Valley Prim Sch
  WS12 .... 210 A4
Pyebirch La ST21 .... 134 A3
Pyenest St ST1 .... 282 A1

Quadrangle The ST9 .... 43 F4
Quadrant Rd ST1 .... 282 B3
Quadrant The Hanley ST1 ... 282 B3
  Sedgley DY3 .... 266 C1
Quadrille Lawns WV9 .... 239 F1
Quail Gn WV6 .... 254 C1
Quail Gr ST3 .... 90 A4
Quale Gr DY8 .... 275 E2
Quarry Ave ST4 .... 71 F4
Quarry Bank Keele ST5 ...... 54 C1
  Upper Tean ST10 .... 94 A3
Quarry Bank Rd
  Keele ST5 .... 69 F4
  Market Drayton TF9 .... 112 A3
Quarry Berry La DE12 .... 236 C4
Quarry Brow DY3 .... 271 F3
Quarry Cl Caverswall ST9 ... 59 D2
  Cheslyn Hay WS6 .... 226 C2
  Norton-in-t-M ST9 .... 43 E2
  Rugeley WS15 .... 196 A4
Quarry Hills La WS14 .... 231 E3
Quarry House La TF9 .... 112 A4
Quarry La ST20 .... 171 E3
Quarry Rd Stoke-on-T ST4 ... 71 F4
  Upper Tean ST10 .... 94 A2
Quarry Terr ST7 .... 26 A1
Quee La ST14 .... 126 A1
Queen Anne St ST4 .... 72 A4
**Queen Elizabeth's
  Mercian High Sch** B79 ... 250 B3
Queen Margaret's Rd
  TF9 .... 99 E3
Queen Mary Rd ST4 .... 72 A1
Queen Mary's Dr ST12 ...... 88 C2
Queen St Audley ST7 .... 39 E1
  Brownhills WS9 .... 244 C1
  Burntwood WS7 .... 228 C4
  Burslem ST6 .... 56 C4
  Burton u T DE14 .... 166 B1
  Cannock WS11 .... 209 E1
  Cannock, High Town
    WS11 .... 210 A3
  Cheadle ST10 .... 76 C2
  Cheslyn Hay WS6 .... 226 B2
  Kidsgrove ST7 .... 26 A1
  Kingswinford, Moss Grove
    DY6 .... 275 D4
  Kingswinford, Wordsley
    DY8 .... 275 E2
  Leek ST13 .... 30 C3
  Lichfield WS13 .... 231 D4
  Longnor SK17 .... 13 D3
  Market Drayton TF9 .... 97 E1
  Newcastle-u-L ST5 .... 284 C1
  Newcastle-u-L, Chesterton
    ST5 .... 55 F4
  Newcastle-u-L, Porthill ST5 ... 56 A3
  Rugeley WS15 .... 196 C4
  Stourbridge DY8 .... 279 F3
  Uttoxeter ST14 .... 126 B4
Queen Victoria Sch DY3 ..... 271 E4
Queen's Ave ST15 .... 41 F2
Queen's Croft Specl Sch
  WS13 .... 231 D4
Queen's Dr ST8 .... 27 E3

Queen's Rd
  Stoke-on-T ST4 .... 71 F4
  Stourbridge DY8 .... 279 F3
Queen's Row ST12 .... 88 C1
Queen's Sq ST15 .... 105 D1
Queens Cotts ST19 .... 206 A4
Queens Ct ST5 .... 284 C1
Queens Cty Prim Sch ST4 ... 73 D3
Queens Dr
  Burntwood WS7 .... 228 C3
  Leek ST13 .... 31 D1
  Newport TF10 .... 168 C1
Queens Gdns
  Codsall WV8 .... 238 C2
  Kidsgrove ST7 .... 40 B3
Queens Par WS3 .... 243 D1
Queens Park Ave ST3 .... 73 D1
Queens Rd Sedgley DY3 ..... 271 F4
  Shareshill WV10 .... 225 D3
Queens Rise ST3 .... 146 B3
Queens Sq WS11 .... 209 E1
Queens Terr ST1 .... 57 F2
Queens Way B78 .... 262 C3
Queens Wlk ST3 .... 74 A2
Queensberry Rd ST1 .... 73 E1
Queensland Cres DE15 ...... 167 E1
Queensmead Rd ST3 .... 89 F4
Queensville ST17 .... 175 D4
Queensville Ave ST17 .... 156 A1
Queensville Bridge ST17 ... 156 A1
Queensway Meir ST3 .... 74 A1
  Newcastle-u-L ST5 .... 71 D3
  Rugeley WS15 .... 196 C4
  Stafford ST16 .... 155 F2
  Stoke-on-T ST4 .... 72 B3
  Tamworth B79 .... 250 A4
Queensway Ind Est ST6 ...... 56 B4
Queenswood Rd B75 .... 258 A1
Quendale WV5 .... 269 F3
Quillets Rd DY8 .... 275 E2
Quince B77 .... 251 D2
Quince Tree Specl Sch
  B77 .... 251 D2
Quinton Gr ST5 .... 56 A2
Quinton Wlk ST6 .... 42 B1
Quixall Bank ST14 .... 95 F4
Quixhill La ST14, DE6 .... 79 F1
Quorn Cl DE15 .... 167 D1
Quorn Cres DY8 .... 275 E2

Rabbit La WV10 .... 241 D4
Raby St WV2 .... 266 B4
Race Course ST5 .... 55 E1
Racecourse La DY8 .... 279 F1
Racecourse Rd ST4 .... 72 A2
Rachel Gr ST4 .... 73 D3
Raddle La B79 .... 217 F3
Radford Bk ST17 .... 175 E4
Radford Cl ST15 .... 105 D1
Radford Dr WS4 .... 244 B1
Radford La WV3 .... 264 C4
Radford Rd ST4 .... 56 C1
Radford Rise ST17 .... 175 E4
Radford St ST15 .... 105 D1
Radhurst Rise DE13 .... 183 E1
Radley Way ST4 .... 59 D2
Radmore Cl WS7 .... 228 B4
Radmore La
  Abbots Bromley WS15 .... 161 E4
  Forton ST20 .... 170 B4
  Gnosall ST20 .... 170 B4
Radnor Ct WS9 .... 244 C2
Radnor Rd DY3 .... 271 E4
Radnor Rise WS12 .... 210 A2
Radstock Cl ST17 .... 175 F3
Radstock Rd WV12 .... 242 B1
Radstone Rise ST5 .... 71 D2
Radway Green Rd CW2 ...... 38 C4
Ragees Rd DY6 .... 275 F2
Raglan Aldridge B74 .... 256 C2
  Burton u T DE13 .... 166 B4
  Sedgley DY3 .... 271 D4
Raglan Rd WV6 .... 254 C2
Raglan St ST4 .... 72 C3
Ragley WS3 .... 243 D1
Raikes La
  Shenstone WS14 .... 246 B4
  Wall WS14 .... 246 B4
Railswood Dr WS3 .... 244 A2
Railton Ave ST3 .... 73 D1
Railway Cotts
  Congleton CW12 .... 6 A1
  Leek ST13 .... 30 C1
  Rugeley WS15 .... 197 D3
Railway Ct ST9 .... 43 F4
Railway La WS7 .... 211 F1
Railway Pas ST3 .... 283 C4
Railway Rd ST3 .... 73 F1
Railway St
  Cannock WS11 .... 226 C4
  Norton Canes WS11 .... 228 A3
  Stafford ST16 .... 155 F2
  Tunstall ST6 .... 41 F1
Railway Terr
  Kingsley ST10 .... 62 A2
  Longton ST3 .... 283 D3
Rainbow St WV2 .... 266 B4
Rainford St ST7 .... 26 C1
Rainham Gr ST6 .... 42 A4
Rainscar B77 .... 262 A4
Rake End Ct WS15 .... 179 F1
Rake Hill WS7 .... 229 D4
Rakegate Jun & Inf Schs
  WV10 .... 240 A1
Rakeway Rd ST10 .... 76 C1
Ralph Ct ST17 .... 174 A4
Ralph Dr ST1 .... 57 F4
Ralston Cl WS3 .... 243 D2

Ramage Gr ST3 .... 73 E1
Rambleford Way ST16 .... 155 E4
Ramillies Cres WS6 .... 226 C1
Ramsey Cl ST12 .... 88 C2
Ramsey Rd ST5 .... 284 A4
Ramsey St ST4 .... 72 B3
Ramshaw Gr 5 ST3 .... 73 E3
Ramshaw View ST13 .... 31 D4
Ramshorn Rd ST10 .... 78 C4
Randall Cl DY6 .... 275 F2
Randle Dr B75 .... 258 B2
Randles La ST9 .... 60 A3
Ranelagh Rd WV2 .... 266 B3
Ranelagh St ST1 .... 282 B2
Rangemoor La DE6 .... 80 B3
Rangemore Hill
  Dunstall DE13 .... 183 D4
  Tatenhill DE13 .... 183 D4
Rangemore St DE14 .... 166 A2
Rangemore Terr ST5 .... 56 B2
Ranger's Wlk WS15 .... 178 A1
Rangeways Rd DY6 .... 275 F2
Rangifer Rd B78 .... 249 F1
Ranleigh Ave DY6 .... 275 F2
Ranscombe Dr DY5 .... 271 E1
Ransome Pl ST3 .... 73 F2
Ranton Park Area 3
  WS11 .... 210 A1
Ranworth Cl ST5 .... 71 D1
Ranworth Rise WV4 .... 266 A3
Ratcliffe Ave DE14 .... 185 D4
Ratcliffe Cl DY3 .... 271 F3
Rathbone Ave ST5 .... 56 B2
Rathlin Cl WV9 .... 240 A2
Rathmore Cl DY8 .... 279 F1
Rattigan Dr ST3 .... 73 F2
Ratton St ST1 .... 282 C3
Raven Cl Cannock WS12 ..... 210 C2
  Cheslyn Hay WS6 .... 226 B1
  Huntington WS12 .... 209 E4
Raven Ct TF9 .... 97 E1
Raven Rd DE13 .... 182 A1
Raven's La ST7 .... 39 F2
Ravenhill Cl WS15 .... 196 C3
Ravenhill Cty Prim Sch
  WS15 .... 196 C3
Ravenhill Dr WV8 .... 239 D2
Ravenhill Terr WS15 .... 196 C4
Ravens Cl ST7 .... 39 F2
Ravens Ct WS8 .... 244 C4
Ravens Way DE14 .... 166 A2
Ravenscliffe Rd ST7 .... 41 D4
Ravenscroft DY8 .... 279 F3
Ravensholme WV6 .... 254 C1
Ravenslea Rd WS15 .... 196 C3
Ravensmead Prim Sch
  ST7 .... 39 F2
Ravenstone B77 .... 262 A4
Ravenswood Cl ST5 .... 71 D2
Ravenswood Crest ST17 .... 175 E4
Rawle Cl ST10 .... 76 B2
Rawlett High Sch B79 .... 234 A1
Rawlett Sports Ctr B79 ...... 234 A1
Rawlins St ST1 .... 57 F3
Rawnsley Rd WS12 .... 210 C4
Raygill Rd ST7 .... 262 A4
Rayleigh Rd WV3 .... 266 A4
Rayleigh Way ST2 .... 58 B1
Raymond Ave ST1 .... 57 E4
Raymond St ST1 .... 282 B1
Reacliffe Rd Rudyard ST9 ... 18 A2
  Woodhouse Green ST9 .... 18 A2
Read Ave ST15 .... 155 F3
Reades La CW12 .... 16 B4
Reading Way ST2 .... 58 B1
Reads Rd ST4 .... 72 C4
Reapers Wlk WV8 .... 239 F1
Reason Rd ST17 .... 174 C3
Rebecca Gdns WV4 .... 265 F2
Rebecca St ST4 .... 72 A4
Recorder Gr ST6 .... 42 A3
Recreation Rd ST3 .... 73 F1
Rectory Cl
  Church Leigh ST10 .... 109 D3
  Drayton Bassett B78 .... 260 C3
Rectory Dr TF11 .... 203 F1
Rectory Fields DY8 .... 275 F1
Rectory Gdns WS15 .... 198 A2
Rectory La
  Armitage WS15 .... 197 D2
  Haughton ST18 .... 172 C3
Rectory Rd Hanley ST1 ...... 282 A1
  Upper Tean ST10 .... 94 B1
Rectory St Hanley ST1 .... 282 A1
  Kingswinford DY8 .... 275 D2
Rectory View ST7 .... 40 B3
Red Bank Longton ST3 ...... 283 C3
  Market Drayton TF9 .... 112 A4
Red Bank La TF9 .... 112 A4
Red Hall Jun Sch DY3 .... 271 E2
Red Hall La ST7 .... 54 B3
Red Hill DY7 .... 277 F2
Red House Cres ST3 .... 283 A3
Red House Ind Est WS9 ...... 256 A3
Red La Himley DY3 .... 271 D1
  Madeley CW3 .... 68 C3
  Norton-in-t-M ST2 .... 43 E1
Red Lion Ave WS11 .... 228 A2
Red Lion Cl ST7 .... 40 B3
Red Lion Cres WS11 .... 228 A2
Red Lion La WS11 .... 228 A2
Red Lion Pas ST1 .... 282 B2
Red Lion St ST16 .... 155 F2
Red Rd Alton ST10 .... 78 A2
  Oakamoor ST10 .... 78 B2
Red Rock Dr WV8 .... 238 C1
Redacres WV6 .... 255 F3
Redbourn Rd WS3 .... 243 D2

Redbridge Cl ST4 .... 71 F1
Redbrook Cl WS12 .... 210 B1
Redbrook La WS15 .... 196 C3
Redcar Rd Trentham ST4 .... 88 C4
  Wolv WV10 .... 240 B2
Redcliff Dr WS7 .... 250 C3
Redcliffe Dr WV5 .... 270 A3
Redfern Dr WS7 .... 229 D3
Redfern Rd Stone ST15 ...... 119 F3
  Uttoxeter ST14 .... 111 D1
Redford Dr WV7 .... 237 D3
Redgrave Dr ST16 .... 155 E1
Redhall Rd DY3 .... 271 E1
Redheath Cl ST5 .... 55 D1
Redhill ST16 .... 155 E4
Redhill Ave WV5 .... 270 A3
Redhill Cl B79 .... 250 A4
Redhill Gdns ST15 .... 120 A4
Redhill Gorse ST16 .... 155 E4
Redhill La DE13 .... 146 C3
Redhill Prim Sch WS11 .... 209 F2
Redhill Rd Cannock WS11 ... 209 F2
  Stone ST15 .... 105 E1
Redhills ST21 .... 133 F3
Redhills Rd ST2 .... 57 F4
Redhouse Rd WV6 .... 255 D3
Redhurst Dr WV10 .... 240 A4
Redlake B77 .... 261 F4
Redland Dr ST2 .... 58 B2
Redlands The ST15 .... 120 B4
Redlands Way B74 .... 257 D1
Redlock Field WS14 .... 231 D3
Redman Gr ST6 .... 57 E4
Redmine Cl ST5 .... 56 A2
Redmond Cl WS15 .... 178 B1
Redmoor Cl DE15 .... 167 D2
Redmoor Gdns WV4 .... 266 A3
Redmoor Rd WS15 .... 211 F2
Redruth Cl DY6 .... 275 E4
Redwell Cl B77 .... 250 B3
Redwing B77 .... 262 A4
Redwing Cl WS7 .... 229 E3
Redwing Dr Biddulph ST8 ... 27 F4
  Huntington WS12 .... 209 E4
Redwood Ave
  Dudley DY1 .... 271 F2
  Stone ST15 .... 120 B4
Redwood Cl B74 .... 256 C1
Redwood Dr
  Burntwood WS7 .... 228 C4
  Burton u T DE15 .... 186 A4
  Cannock WS11 .... 210 A2
Redwood Pl ST3 .... 73 F1
Redwood Rd DY7 .... 278 A2
Reedbed Cl ST6 .... 42 B2
Reedham Gdns WV4 .... 265 E3
Reedham Way ST2 .... 58 B1
Reedly Rd WV12 .... 242 B1
Reedmace B77 .... 250 B1
Rees Dr WV5 .... 270 A4
Reeve Cl WS15 .... 198 A2
Reeve La WS13 .... 231 D4
Reeves Ave
  Chell Heath ST6 .... 42 A2
  Newcastle-u-L ST5 .... 56 A2
Reeves Gdns WV8 .... 239 D2
Refinery St ST5 .... 284 C2
Regency Cl ST7 .... 40 B3
Regency Cres WS15 .... 197 D3
Regency Way DE13 .... 166 B4
Regency Wlk B74 .... 257 E3
Regent Ave ST6 .... 41 F2
Regent Cl DY6 .... 275 E3
Regent Ct Ipstones ST10 .... 62 A4
  Newcastle-u-L ST5 .... 56 A3
Regent Rd Hanley ST1 .... 282 B1
  Wolv WV4 .... 265 F3
Regent St Leek ST13 .... 30 C3
  Stoke-on-T ST4 .... 72 A4
  Stone ST15 .... 104 C1
Regina Cres WV6 .... 255 E2
Regina St ST6 .... 42 B1
Reginald Mitchell
  Prim Sch The ST7 .... 25 E1
Reginald Mitchell Way
  ST5 .... 41 E3
Reginald St 5 ST6 .... 57 D4
Regis Rd WV6 .... 255 E3
Regis Sch WV6 .... 255 D3
Registry St ST4 .... 72 A4
Reid St ST6 .... 56 C4
Reindeer Rd B78 .... 260 C4
Relay Dr B77 .... 262 B4
Rembrandt Cl WS11 .... 210 B1
Remer St ST6 .... 57 D3
Remington Dr WS11 .... 226 C4
Renard Way ST3 .... 90 A4
Rendermore Cl ST19 .... 207 F4
Rene Rd B77 .... 250 C3
Renfrew Cl
  Kingswinford DY8 .... 275 E2
  Newcastle-u-L ST5 .... 70 C4
Renfrew Pl ST4 .... 72 A1
Rennie Cres ST13 .... 45 E3
Rennison Dr WV5 .... 270 A3
Renown Cl ST2 .... 57 F1
Renshaw Dr DE11 .... 186 C3
Renshaw Wood La WV8 ..... 221 F1
Renton Ave WV10 .... 240 A1
Renton Gr WV10 .... 240 A1
Renton Rd WV10 .... 240 A1
Repton Ave WV6 .... 254 C2
Repington Rd N B77 .... 251 D3
Repington Rd S B77 .... 251 D3

Repton Cl Cannock WS11 .... 226 A4
Stafford ST17 .... 156 A1
Repton Dr ST5 .... 70 C3
Repton Rd DE15 .... 167 F4
Reservoir Rd
  Burton u T DE13 .... 165 F2
  Cannock WS12 .... 210 B2
  Longton ST3 .... 73 F1
Retreat Gdns DY3 .... 271 F4
Retreat Gdns The WV6 .... 253 E2
Retreat St WV3 .... 266 A4
Reva Rd ST17 .... 174 C4
Revival St WS3 .... 243 D1
Reynards La SK17 .... 24 C2
Reynards Rise TF9 .... 99 E3
Reynolds Ave ST5 .... 55 F3
Reynolds Cl DY3 .... 269 F1
Reynolds Gr WV6 .... 254 C2
Reynolds Rd ST6 .... 42 A2
Rhodes Cl DY3 .... 271 D2
Rhodes Ct ST5 .... 56 B4
Rhodes St ST1 .... 57 E3
Rhondda Ave ST6 .... 57 E4
Rialto Pl ST6 .... 41 E2
Ribble Cl ST5 .... 71 D2
Ribble Dr ST5 .... 16 C1
Ribblesdale B77 .... 262 A4
Ribblesdale Ave CW12 ...... 6 A3
Ricardo St ST3 .... 73 E1
Riceyman Rd ST5 .... 56 A4
Richard Cooper Rd
  WS14 .... 246 C3
Richard Crosse CE
  Prim Sch DE13 .... 199 E3
Richard Ct WS11 .... 227 F3
Richard Wakefield CE
  Prim Sch DE13 .... 146 B3
Richards Ave
  Stafford ST16 .... 156 A2
  Tunstall ST6 .... 41 F2
Richardson Dr DY8 .... 279 F4
Richardson Pl ST6 .... 42 A3
Richborough Dr DY1 .... 271 F2
Riches St WV6 .... 255 F2
Richfield La ST17 .... 193 F4
Richmond Ave
  Hanley ST1 .... 57 E4
  Wolv WV3 .... 255 F1
Richmond Cl
  Cannock WS11 .... 210 A3
  Newport TF10 .... 168 C1
  Stafford ST17 .... 174 C4
  Tamworth B79 .... 250 A3
Richmond Dr
  Lichfield WS14 .... 231 E4
  Perton WV6 .... 254 C2
  Wolv WV3 .... 255 F1
Richmond Gdns
  Brierley Hill DY8 .... 279 F4
  Wombourne WV5 .... 270 A4
Richmond Gr DY8 .... 279 F4
Richmond Pk DY6 .... 275 E4
Richmond Rd
  Sedgley DY3 .... 271 F4
  Trentham ST4 .... 72 A1
  Wolv WV3 .... 255 F1
Richmond St ST4 .... 72 A4
Richmond Terr ST1 .... 282 A1
Rickerscote Ave ST17 .... 175 D3
Rickerscote Hall La
  ST17 .... 175 D3
Rickerscote Rd ST17 ..... 174 C3
Ridding Bank ST4 .... 87 D4
Ridding La
  Denstone ST14 .... 79 F1
  Kingstone ST14 .... 124 B2
Riddings Cres WS3 .... 243 F2
Riddings La DE6 .... 144 C3
Riddings The B77 .... 250 C3
Rider's Way WS15 .... 178 A1
Ridge Cl ST12 .... 104 B4
Ridge Cres ST3 .... 89 F3
Ridge Croft ST15 .... 120 B4
Ridge Prim Sch DY8 ..... 279 E3
Ridge Rd
  Kingswinford DY6 ...... 275 E3
  Tunstall ST6 .... 41 E3
Ridge St DY8 .... 279 E3
Ridge Way WS9 .... 256 A2
Ridge Wlk ST3 .... 89 F4
Ridgefields ST8 .... 17 D1
Ridgehouse Dr ST1 .... 57 D2
Ridgemont Cl ST15 .... 120 B4
Ridget La DE13 .... 201 D1
Ridgeway Hixon ST18 .... 158 B4
  Sedgley DY3 .... 271 E3
Ridgeway Cl
  Bradnop ST18 .... 174 B3
  Hopton ST18 .... 156 A4
Ridgeway Dr WV4 .... 265 F2
Ridgeway Prim Sch
  WS7 .... 229 D3
Ridgeway Rd
  Brierley Hill DY8 ...... 275 F1
  Burton u T DE15 ...... 185 F4
Ridgeway The WS7 ...... 229 D2
Ridgewood Ave DY8 .... 279 E4
Ridgewood Dr ST5 ..... 258 A1
Ridgewood High Sch
  DY8 .... 279 E3
Ridgwood Rise B77 .... 251 D3
Ridgmont Rd ST5 .... 70 C2
Ridgway Dr ST11 .... 90 B4
Ridgway Pl ST5 .... 56 B3
Ridgway Rd ST1, ST4 .... 57 E1

Ridings Brook Dr WS11 .. 210 A1
Ridley St ST4 .... 72 B3
Ridley Wlk ST4 .... 72 B3
Rifle Range Cnr WS15 ... 195 D3
Rigby Dr WS11 .... 209 F2
Rigby Rd ST7 .... 26 A2
Riley Rd ST7 .... 250 C2
Riley Ave ST6 .... 42 A1
Riley Cres WV4 .... 266 A3
Riley La Gnosall ST20 ... 152 A3
  Woodseaves ST20 ..... 151 F4
Riley St N ST6 .... 56 C4
Riley St S ST6 .... 56 C4
Rileys Way ST7 .... 39 F1
Rill St ST4 .... 283 B4
Rimbach Dr ST18 .... 177 E4
Rindle The ST10 .... 76 A2
Rindleford Ave WV4 .... 265 E3
Ring Rd WS7 .... 228 B4
Ring The ST18 .... 158 B1
Ringhills Rd WV8 ...... 239 D1
Ringland Cl ST3 .... 282 C3
Ringway WS11 .... 209 F1
Ringway Ind Est WS13 ... 214 B2
Ringwood Ave WS9 .... 256 A3
Ringwood Rd WV10 .... 240 B1
Ripon Ave ST5 .... 55 F4
Ripon Dr ST17 .... 175 E4
Ripon Rd ST3 .... 88 C3
Rise The
  Kingswinford DY6 .... 275 F3
  Rugeley WS15 .... 196 C3
  Stafford ST17 .... 175 F4
  Swadlincote DE11 .... 186 C3
Riseley Rd ST4 .... 71 E4
Rishworth Ave WS15 ... 178 C1
Rising Brook
  Stafford ST17 .... 174 C4
  Wolv WV6 .... 255 D2
Riskin St ST4 .... 73 E3
Rivendell Gdns WV6 ... 255 D3
Rivendell La ST13 .... 30 C1
River Lea Mews CW3 ... 68 C3
River Way ST15 .... 120 A4
Riverdale Cl DE15 .... 167 D3
Riverdale Dr ST7 ..... 41 F4
Riverdrive B78 .... 250 A2
Riverfield Gr B77 .... 250 B3
Riverhead Cl ST6 .... 42 C3
Riversfield Dr ST14 .. 95 F2
Riverside DE12 .... 184 B1
Riverside Dr DE14 .... 184 C4
Riverside Ind Est
  Rugeley WS15 .... 178 C1
  Tamworth B78 .... 250 A1
Riverside L Ctr ST16 .. 155 F2
Riverside Rd
  Stoke-on-T ST4 ..... 71 F1
  Upper Tean ST10 .... 92 B2
Riverside Way WV9 ... 224 A1
Riversleigh Dr DY8 ... 279 F4
Riversmead ST5 ...... 71 D2
Riversmead Way ST16 . 155 D3
Riverway ST17 .... 155 F1
Rivington Cl DY8 ..... 279 F2
Rivington Cres ST6 ... 42 A3
Rixdale Cl ST1 .... 282 B4
Roach B77 .... 261 E3
Robert Cl B79 .... 249 F4
Robert Heath St ST6 .. 42 B1
Robert Sherborne Inf Sch
  The DE13 .... 147 E2
Robert St Sedgley DY3 . 271 E2
  Tunstall ST6 .... 41 E2
Robert Sutton High Sch
  DE15 .... 186 A4
Robert Wynd WV14 ... 266 C1
Roberts Ave ST6 .... 284 B4
Roberts Cl Audley ST7 . 54 C3
  Brownhills WS9 .... 244 C1
Roberts Green Rd DY3 . 271 F2
Roberts Prim Sch DY3 . 271 E2
Robertson Dr ST5 .... 55 F2
Robertson Sq ST4 .... 71 F2
Robertville Rd ST2 ... 58 A2
Robey's La B78 ...... 251 E2
Robin Cl
  Huntington WS12 ... 209 E4
  Uttoxeter ST14 ..... 126 A3
Robin Croft 1 ST6 .. 56 C4
Robin Hill ST8 .... 28 A4
Robin Hill Gr ST4 ... 73 D3
Robin La TF10 .... 168 A2
Robina Dr ST10 ...... 76 C2
Robins Cl WS6 ...... 226 B1
Robins Rd ST7 ...... 228 C4
Robins The TF9 ..... 99 E2
Robinson Ave ST6 ... 57 E4
Robinson Cl B79 .... 249 F4
Robinson Rd
  Burntwood WS7 .... 228 C4
  Swadlincote DE11 .. 186 C3
  Trentham ST4 ..... 87 F4
Robinswood ST17 ... 175 D4
Robson Cl WS8 ..... 244 C3
Robson St ST1 ..... 282 A2
Rocester La DE13 ... 49 D1
Roche Ave ST13 .... 31 D4
Roche Rd WS3 ..... 242 C1
Roche The
  Burntwood WS7 .... 230 A4
  Cheddleton ST13 .. 45 E2
Roche Way WS3 .... 242 C1
Rochester Ave WS7 . 229 D4
Rochester Rd ST3 .. 73 E4
Rochester Way WS12 . 210 B2
Rochford ST13 .... 30 B3

Rochford Gr WV4 ..... 265 E3
Rochford Way ST2 .... 58 B1
Rock Cres ST15 ...... 105 E2
Rock End Rd ST13 .... 45 D1
Rock Farm Rd WS14 .. 232 C3
Rock Hill B78, WS14 .. 248 B2
Rock House Dr ST12 . 88 B1
Rock La Ashley TF9 ... 100 B4
  Mucklestone TF9 ... 99 E4
Rock Rd WV14 ...... 271 F4
Rock St DY3 .... 271 F3
Rockeries The ST17 . 175 D3
Rockfield Ave ST2 ... 43 E1
Rockhouse Dr ST18 . 158 A1
Rockhouse La ST7 ... 40 B4
Rockingham Cl
  Sedgley DY3 ...... 271 D2
  Walsall WS3 ...... 243 D1
Rockingham Dr WV6 . 254 C2
Rocklands Cres ST13 . 214 B1
Rocklands Specl Sch
  WS13 .... 231 E4
Rockrose Gdns WV10 . 241 D4
Rocks The ST6 ...... 43 D4
Rockside ST7 .... 26 B3
Rocky Wall DY7 .... 277 F2
Rodbaston Coll
  Hopwas WS14 ..... 248 A3
  Penkridge ST19 ... 207 F2
Rodbaston Dr ST19 . 207 F3
Roddam Ct TF10 ... 168 C1
Roddige La WS13 .. 216 A4
Rodger Ave CW3 ... 53 D3
Rodgers St ST6 .... 41 E4
Rodway Cl DY3 .... 266 B2
Roe Deer Gn TF10 . 168 C3
Roe La ST5 .... 71 D2
Roe Pk CW12 ..... 15 F1
Roebuck St ST4 ... 72 B4
Roedean Ave ST17 . 175 D4
Roford Ct DY3 .... 271 F3
Rogate Cl ST14 ... 73 D3
Rogers Ave ST5 ... 55 F2
Rogers Cl WV11 .. 242 A1
Rogerstone Ave ST4 . 71 F3
Rokewood Cl DY6 . 270 B1
Rokholt Cres WS11 . 209 E1
Rolfe Cl ST4 ...... 72 A1
Rolleston La ST3 .. 146 B3
Rolleston Rd DE13 . 166 B4
Roman Cl WS8 .... 228 C1
Roman Dr ST5 .... 55 E3
Roman La B74 .... 257 D2
Roman Pk B74 .... 257 D2
Roman Rd
  Brewood WV9 ... 224 A2
  Little Aston B74 .. 257 D3
Roman Rd (Sandy La)
  DY8 .... 279 E2
Roman View WS11 . 226 C3
Roman Way
  Lichfield WS14 .. 231 E4
  Tamworth B77 .. 249 F4
Roman Wlk WS14 . 230 B1
Romany Way DY8 . 279 E2
Romer Side ST2 .. 73 E4
Romford Meadow ST21 . 133 E3
Romford Pl ST11 . 90 A4
Romford Rd ST16 . 155 F3
Romilly Cl
  Lichfield WS14 .. 231 F4
  Stourbridge DY8 . 279 F3
Romney B77 ..... 261 F4
Romney Ave ST5 . 55 F3
Romsey Cl ST2 .. 73 E4
Romsey Gr WV10 . 240 B2
Romsey Rd WV10 . 240 B2
Romsey Way WS3 . 242 C2
Romsley Cl WS4 . 244 B1
Romsley La WV15 . 276 A1
Ronald St ST3 .. 283 C2
Ronald Wlk ST3 . 283 C2
Ronaldsway Dr ST5 . 284 A4
Ronson Ave ST4 . 71 F2
Rook The WV6 .. 255 F2
Rooker Ave WV2 . 266 C3
Rooker Cres WV2 . 266 C3
Rookery Ave ST3 . 73 D1
Rookery Cl
  Armitage WS15 . 198 B3
  Yoxall DE13 .... 182 A1
Rookery Cres ST11 . 91 E1
Rookery La
  Aldridge WS9 .. 256 A3
  Hints WS14 .... 248 B1
  Stoke-on-T ST4 . 71 F2
  Wolv WV2 .... 266 A3
Rookery Par WS9 . 256 A3
Rookery Rd
  Kidsgrove ST7 .. 26 B2
  Wombourne WV5 . 270 A4
Rookery Rise WV5 . 270 A3
Rookery The ST5 . 55 E1
Rookswood Copse ST17 . 175 E3
Rookwood Dr WV6 . 254 C1
Rope St ST4 .... 56 B1
Roper Way DY3 . 271 F3
Roper Wlk DY3 . 271 F3
Ropewalk The DE14 . 166 B1
Rose Ave
  Burton u T DE13 . 148 A1
  Kingswinford DY6 . 275 F3
Rose Bank Cres ST10 . 78 A3
Rose Bank St ST13 . 30 C3
Rose Bank Terr ST13 . 30 C3
Rose Bay Meadow WS11 . 210 B1
Rose Cott La DE14 . 166 B1

Rose Dr WS8 .... 244 C3
Rose Hill ST16 ...... 155 E2
Rose La WS7 .... 229 E4
Rose Mill TF9 ...... 99 E3
Rose St ST1 .... 57 F3
Rose Tree Ave ST4 . 71 F1
Rose Tree La DE11 . 186 C4
Rose Way WS15 .. 178 B1
Roseacre ST5 .... 70 C4
Roseacre Gr ST3 . 89 F3
Roseacre La ST11 . 90 C3
Roseberry Dr CW3 . 68 C4
Roseberry Gdns DY10 . 280 B2
Rosebery Cl ST7 . 27 F4
Rosebery Rd B77 . 261 E2
Rosebery St
  Hanley ST1 ..... 41 F3
Rosebury Gr WV5 . 269 F3
Rosedale Wlk DY6 . 275 F4
Rosehill WS12 .... 209 F4
Rosehill Cl ST2 .. 43 D1
Roseland Cres ST2 . 43 D1
Roseleigh Cres DE11 . 186 C3
Rosemary Ave
  Cheslyn Hay WS6 . 226 B2
  Stafford ST17 .... 174 C3
  Wombourne WV4 . 266 B3
Rosemary Cl WS8 . 244 B3
Rosemary Cres
  Sedgley DY3 .... 271 F3
  Wolv WV4 ..... 266 B3
Rosemary Cres W WV4 . 266 A3
Rosemary Dr
  Huntington WS12 . 209 E3
  Little Aston B74 . 257 E2
  Uttoxeter ST14 .. 126 A3
Rosemary Hill Rd
  Little Aston B74 . 257 E2
  Sutton Coldfield B74 . 257 E2
Rosemary La ST4 . 72 B4
Rosemary Nook B74 . 257 E2
Rosemary Pl ST1 . 57 F4
Rosemary Rd
  Cheslyn Hay WS11 . 226 B2
  Tamworth B77 .. 250 C2
Rosemary St ST5 . 55 F1
Rosemount Rd DE15 . 166 C2
Rosendale Ave ST5 . 55 F3
Rosendale Rd ST5 . 56 A3
Roseneath Pl ST2 . 43 D1
Rosevale Ct ST5 . 55 F4
Rosevale Rd ST5 . 55 F4
Rosevale St ST5 . 43 D1
Roseville Dr CW12 . 16 A4
Roseville Gdns WV8 . 239 D2
Rosewood Ave ST9 . 43 E2
Rosewood Cl B77 . 250 B2
Rosewood Ct B77 . 250 B2
Rosewood Gdns WV11 . 242 A2
Rosewood Pk WS6 . 226 B1
Rosewood Rd DE15 . 185 F3
Rosewood Specl Sch
  DY1 .... 271 F1
Rosey Bk ST9 .... 43 E2
Rosliston Rd
  Burton u T DE15 . 185 F4
  Rosliston DE15 .. 185 E2
  Walton-on-T DE12 . 202 C4
Rosliston Rd S DE15 . 185 F3
Ross Cl Longton ST3 . 74 A2
  Wolv WV6 ..... 255 F1
Ross Dr DY6 .... 275 E4
Ross Rd ST10 ... 62 B1
Rossall Ave ST5 . 70 C3
Rossett Gr ST7 . 41 F4
Rosslyn Rd ST3 . 283 C2
Rosvean Cl ST3 . 282 B4
Rosy Cross B79 . 250 A3
Rothay B77 ..... 261 F4
Rothbury Gn WS12 . 210 C1
Rother Wlk ST5 . 42 A2
Rothesay Ave ST5 . 70 C4
Rothesay Dr DY8 . 275 E2
Rothesay Rd ST3 . 73 E1
Rothley Gn ST3 . 88 C4
Rothsay Ave ST1 . 57 E4
Rothwell St ST4 . 71 F3
Rotten Row WS14 . 231 E4
Rotterdam St ST5 . 55 F1
Rotterdam Rd ST5 . 55 F1
Rough Bank CW12 . 16 C4
Rough Close CE Prim Sch
  ST3 .... 89 F2
Rough Hills Cl WV2 . 266 C3
Rough Hills Rd WV2 . 266 C3
Roughcote La ST11 . 74 B3
Roughley Dr B75 . 258 A3
Round Hill DY3 . 266 B1
Round House Rd DY3 . 271 F2
Roundfields ST9 . 43 E2
Roundhill Way WS8 . 229 D1
Roundway ST3 . 72 B1
Roundway Down WV6 . 254 C2
Roundwell St ST6 . 41 E2
Rouse Cl ST4 .. 155 E1
Rowallan Rd B75 . 258 B1
Rowan Cl Biddulph ST8 . 28 A4
  Kidsgrove ST7 . 41 D4
  Lichfield WS14 . 231 E4
  Stone ST15 ... 120 A3
Rowan Cres WV3 . 265 F4
Rowan Dr
  Armitage WS15 . 198 B3
  Essington WV11 . 242 A2
  Newport TF10 . 168 C1
Rowan Gr ST17 . 175 E3
Rowan Gr Brewood ST19 . 223 E3
  Burntwood WS7 . 228 C4
  Fenton ST3 ... 72 C2

Rowan La TF9 ...... 99 E3
Rowan Pl ST5 ..... 55 F4
Rowan Rd
  Cannock WS11 . 209 E1
  Market Drayton TF9 . 97 F1
  Sedgley DY3 ... 266 C1
Rowan Rise DY6 . 275 F3
Rowanburn Cl ST3 . 73 E3
Rowbury Dr DE15 . 167 D1
Rowena Gdns DY3 . 266 B1
Rowhurst Ct ST5 . 55 E4
Rowhurst Pl ST6 . 42 B3
Rowland St ST3 . 73 D1
Rowley Ave
  Newcastle-u-L ST5 . 55 F4
  Stafford ST15 .. 155 E1
Rowley Bank ST17 . 174 C4
Rowley Bank Gdns ST17 . 174 C4
Rowley Cl Cannock WS12 . 210 A4
  Rugeley WS15 .. 197 D3
Rowley Gr ST17 . 174 C4
Rowley Hall Cl ST17 . 174 B4
Rowley Hall Dr ST17 . 155 E1
Rowley Hall Hospl ST17 . 174 B4
Rowley St ST16 . 155 E3
Rowleyhill Dr ST19 . 206 C2
Rownall Pl ST3 . 74 A1
Rownall Rd
  Cheddleton ST9 . 59 E3
  Meir ST3 .... 74 A1
Rownall View ST13 . 30 B2
Rowney Cl TF9 .. 99 E2
Rowton Ave WV6 . 254 C2
Rowton St DE13 . 166 B3
Roxall Cl DY10 . 281 E1
Roxburghe Ave ST3 . 283 C2
Royal Cl B74 .. 256 C1
Royal Oak Dr ST19 . 221 F4
Royal St ST4 .. 283 A5
Royal Wolverhampton
  Sch WV2, WV3 . 266 A4
Royce Ave ST8 . 27 D3
Roycroft Cl ST5 . 56 A4
Royden Ave ST1 . 57 F2
Royds Cl ST18 . 172 C3
Royds St ST18 . 57 D4
Roylance St ST6 . 41 E4
Royston Chase B74 . 257 D2
Royston Way DY3 . 271 E4
Royston Wlk ST3 . 283 C3
Royville Pl ST6 . 57 E4
Rozel Ave DY10 . 280 A1
Rubens Way ST3 . 90 A4
Rubian St ST4 . 72 C3
Rudge Dale Rd TF9 . 100 A2
Rudge Rd
  Pattingham WV6 . 253 D1
  Rudge WV6 ... 263 D4
Rudyard Cl WV10 . 240 C2
Rudyard Gr ST5 . 56 B2
Rudyard Ho ST17 . 174 C3
Rudyard Rd
  Biddulph ST8 . 17 E1
  Heaton ST13 . 19 D1
  Rudyard ST13 . 29 F4
Rudyard Way ST10 . 76 C2
Ruffin Ct ST15 . 120 B4
Rufford B79 ... 249 F3
Rugby Cl
  Burton u T DE14 . 185 E4
  Newcastle-u-L ST5 . 70 C2
Rugby Rd DY8 . 279 C2
Rugeley Rd
  Armitage WS15 . 197 E3
  Burntwood WS7 . 229 E4
  Cannock, Hazelslade
    WS12 .... 211 D4
  Cannock, Hednesford
    WS12 .... 210 B4
  King's Bromley DE13 . 199 D3
Rugeley Town Sta
  SW15 .... 196 C4
Rugeley Trent Valley Sta
  WS15 .... 178 C2
Ruiton St DY3 . 271 E2
Rumer Hill Bsns Est
  WS11 .... 226 C4
Rumer Hill Rd WS11 . 226 C4
Running Hills WS15 . 197 F2
Runnymede ST5 . 120 A3
Runnymede Cl ST2 . 58 A2
Rupert St ST4 . 27 E4
Rush La Kingsbury B77 . 261 E2
  Market Drayton TF9 . 97 D1
Rushall Cl DY8 . 279 F4
Rushall Rd WV10 . 240 C1
Rushbrook Cl WS8 . 244 C3
Rushcliffe Dr ST5 . 90 A4
Rushey La WV7 . 252 B4
Rushford Ave WV5 . 270 A3
Rushmoor Gr ST3 . 90 A4
Rushton Ave ST10 . 61 D4
Rushton CE Prim Sch
  SK11 .... 8 A1
Rushton Cl ST6 . 43 D4
Rushton Gr 18 ST6 . 57 D4
Rushton Rd ST6 . 57 D4
Rushton Way ST11 . 91 D4
Rushtons La ST15 . 105 E2
Rushwater Cl WV5 . 269 F3
Ruskin Ave
  Sedgley DY3 . 271 D3
  Wolv WV4 ... 266 C1
Ruskin Cl ST3 . 283 D5
Ruskin Gr ST18 . 154 C1
Ruskin Pl DE14 . 166 B3
Ruskin Rd WV10 . 241 D1
Rusper Cl ST1 . 57 F3

Russel St ST16 .... 155 E2
Russell Bank Rd B74 .... 257 F2
Russell Cl
  Congleton CW12 .... 16 A4
  Essington WV11 .... 241 F1
Russell Gr ST9 .... 59 D2
Russell Pl ST6 .... 41 E3
Russell Rd ST6 .... 41 E3
Russell St
  Burton u T DE14 .... 166 B1
  Leek ST13 .... 30 C3
  Longton ST3 .... 283 B1
  Newcastle-u-L ST5 .... 56 B3
Russell's Hall Rd DY1 .... 271 F1
Russells Hall Prim Sch
  DY1 .... 271 F1
Russet Cl ST3 .... 90 A4
Russet Wlk WV8 .... 239 F1
Russett Cl WS7 .... 229 D3
Russetts The ST17 .... 174 C3
Rustington Ave ST3 .... 73 F2
Ruston Ave ST6 .... 42 A3
Rutherford Ave ST5 .... 71 D2
Rutherford Pl ST4 .... 71 F4
Rutherglen Cl WS15 .... 178 B1
Ruthin Rd ST2 .... 58 B1
Rutland Ave
  Rugeley WS15 .... 196 B3
  Wolv WV4 .... 265 E2
Rutland Cl DE15 .... 185 E3
Rutland Cres WS9 .... 256 A4
Rutland Dr B78 .... 250 A1
Rutland Pl
  Newcastle-u-L ST5 .... 71 E2
  Stourbridge DY8 .... 279 E4
Rutland Rd Cannock WS12 .... 210 C1
  Kidsgrove ST7 .... 26 A1
  Longton ST3 .... 283 C4
Rutland St ST1 .... 282 A4
Ruxley Rd ST5 .... 58 A2
Rycroft CE Mid Sch ST14 .... 95 F2
Rydal Cl WV12 .... 210 A4
Rydal Dr WV6 .... 254 C2
Rydal Way ST5 .... 71 D2
Ryder Cl DE11 .... 186 C1
Ryder Rd ST3 .... 90 A4
Ryder St DY8 .... 275 E1
Ryders Hayes
  Jun Mix Inf Sch WS3 .... 244 A3
Ryders Hayes La WS3 .... 244 A2
Rye Bank ST5 .... 284 B3
Rye Bank Cres ST5 .... 284 B3
Rye Ct ST16 .... 155 D3
Ryebrook Dr ST6 .... 41 F3
Ryecroft ST5 .... 284 B3
Ryecroft Ave WS4 .... 266 A3
Ryecroft Cl Sedgley DY3 .... 271 E4
  Upper Tean ST10 .... 92 C2
Ryecroft Dr WS7 .... 229 D4
Ryecroft Rd ST6 .... 42 C3
Ryecroft Sh Ctr WS7 .... 229 D4
Ryefield WV8 .... 239 F1
Ryehills ST7 .... 39 F1
Ryhope Wlk WV9 .... 240 A2
Rykneld Prim Sch DE14 .... 184 C4
Rykneld Rd WS13 .... 215 F4
Rykneld Cl B74 .... 257 F3
Rykneld St Alrewas DE13 .... 201 D1
  Lichfield WS14 .... 231 F3
Rykneld Trad Est DE14 .... 166 C3
Rylands Dr WV4 .... 266 A2
Ryle St WS3 .... 243 E1
Rylestone Cl ST3 .... 90 A4
Ryton B77 .... 261 F4

Sabine St ST17 .... 155 F1
Sabrina Rd WV6 .... 254 C1
Sackville St ST4 .... 56 C1
Saddler Ave ST15 .... 120 B4
Saddlestones The WV6 .... 254 B2
Saddleworth Rd WS3 .... 243 D2
Sadler Rd WS12 .... 245 D4
Sadlers Mill WS8 .... 245 D4
Saffron B77 .... 251 D2
Saffron Cl
  Barton-u-N DE13 .... 183 E1
  Meir ST3 .... 90 A3
Saffron Gdns WV4 .... 266 A2
Sage Cl ST1 .... 282 B1
St Aidan's Cl DE13 .... 166 B4
St Aidan's Rd WS11 .... 209 F3
St Aidan's St ST6 .... 41 E2
St Albans CE Prim Sch
  WV11 .... 242 A1
St Albans Cl WV11 .... 242 A1
St Albans Cl ST3 .... 166 B4
St Albans Rd ST16 .... 155 F4
St Andrew Cl WS12 .... 211 D3
St Andrew's CE Sch B79 .... 218 C1
St Andrew's Cl
  Clifton Campville B79 .... 218 C1
  Sedgley DY3 .... 271 D2
St Andrew's Dr
  Burton u T DE13 .... 166 B4
  Newcastle-u-L ST5 .... 70 C4
St Andrews B77 .... 251 D2
St Andrews Ave WS3 .... 244 A3
St Andrews CE Jun & Inf
  Schs WV6 .... 255 F2
St Andrews CE Prim Sch
  ST18 .... 138 B1
St Andrews Cl DY8 .... 279 F1
St Andrews Cres ST1 .... 57 E4
St Andrews Dr
  Kidsgrove ST7 .... 26 B2
  Perton WV6 .... 254 B3
St Andrews Rd ST17 .... 174 B4
St Andrews Way TF10 .... 168 C1

St Ann St ST1 .... 282 C3
St Ann Wlk ST1 .... 282 C3
St Anne's CE Prim Sch
  ST6 .... 28 A1
St Anne's Cl WS7 .... 228 C2
St Anne's RC Prim Sch
  ST17 .... 175 E4
St Anne's Rd WV10 .... 240 E1
St Anne's Vale ST6 .... 43 D4
St Annes Rd WS13 .... 214 A2
St Anthony's Dr ST5 .... 71 D4
St Anthony's RC Sch
  WV10 .... 240 B2
St Anthonys Cl WS15 .... 196 C4
St Anthonys Dr WS3 .... 244 A3
St Augustine's Fst Sch
  DE6 .... 144 B3
St Augustine's Rd WS15 .... 196 C3
St Augustines RC Prim
  Sch ST3 .... 89 F4
St Austell Cl
  Stafford ST17 .... 175 E4
  Tamworth B79 .... 250 A3
St Austin's RC Prim Sch
  ST17 .... 155 F1
St Barbara's Rd WS15 .... 198 B3
St Bartholomew's CE
  Jun Mix Inf Sch SK17 .... 13 D4
St Bartholomew's CE
  Prim Sch WV4 .... 265 E2
St Bartholomews Cl ST6 .... 42 C2
St Bedes CE
  Prim Sch WV5 .... 270 A4
St Benedict Biscop
  Prim Sch WV5 .... 270 A4
St Benedict's Dr ST18 .... 177 E4
St Benedict's Rd WS7 .... 229 D3
St Benedicts Rd WV5 .... 270 A3
St Bernadette's RC Jun
  Mix Inf Sch WS8 .... 244 C1
St Bernadettes RC Prim
  Sch WV5 .... 269 F3
St Bernard Pl ST2 .... 58 A3
St Bernard's Rd ST5 .... 55 F1
St Bernards Cl WS12 .... 211 E2
St Blaise Rd B75 .... 258 B2
St Brides Cl Sedgley DY3 .... 271 E4
  Wombourne WV5 .... 269 F3
St Catherine's Cres WV4 .... 265 F2
St Catherine's Rd DE11 .... 186 C3
St Catherines Rd WS13 .... 214 A2
St Chad's CE Prim Sch
  Cheadle ST10 .... 92 C4
  Newcastle-u-L ST5 .... 40 B1
St Chad's Cl
  Burton u T DE13 .... 166 B4
  Cannock WS11 .... 210 A2
  Denstone ST14 .... 95 E3
  Lichfield WS13 .... 214 A1
  Sedgley DY3 .... 271 D2
  Stone ST15 .... 120 B4
St Chad's Pl ST16 .... 155 F2
St Chad's Rd WS13 .... 214 B1
St Chad's Stowe CE Prim
  Sch WS13 .... 231 E4
St Chads CE Prim Sch
  WV6 .... 253 E2
St Chads Cl
  Brewood ST19 .... 223 E3
  Colwich WS18 .... 177 A3
  Pattingham WV6 .... 253 E1
St Chads RC Sch DY3 .... 271 E4
St Chads Rd
  Eccleshall ST21 .... 133 E3
  Tunstall ST6 .... 41 F2
St Chads Way TF9 .... 82 B1
St Christopher Ave ST4 .... 71 F3
St Christopher Cl WS12 .... 211 D3
St Christopher's Dr B77 .... 250 B1
St Christophers RC Prim
  Sch WV8 .... 239 D2
St Clair St ST3 .... 283 C2
St David Cl WS12 .... 211 D3
St David's Dr DE13 .... 166 B4
St Davids Cl WS3 .... 244 A3
St Davids Pl WS3 .... 243 E1
St Davids Rd
  Clifton Campville B79 .... 218 C1
  Stafford ST17 .... 174 B4
St Dominic's RC Prim Sch
  ST17 .... 104 C1
St Dominic's Sch ST19 .... 223 E3
St Dominics Ind Jun Sch
  ST4 .... 71 F4
St Editha's Cl B79 .... 250 A3
St Editha's Hospl B79 .... 250 A4
St Edmund's Ave ST5 .... 56 B3
St Edmund's Cl WV6 .... 255 F2
St Edmunds RC Sch
  WV6 .... 255 F2
St Edward St ST13 .... 30 C3
St Edward's CE Prim Sch
  ST13 .... 45 D3
St Edward's Hospl ST13 .... 45 E4
St Edward's Rd ST13 .... 45 E2
St Edwards CE Mid Sch
  ST13 .... 30 B3
St Edwards Cl DE11 .... 186 C3
St Edwards Gn WS15 .... 196 A3
St Elizabeth's Prim Sch
  B79 .... 249 F4
St Filumena's RC Prim Sch
  ST11 .... 74 C1
St Francis Cl
  Brownhills WS3 .... 244 A3
  Burton u T DE13 .... 166 B4
  Cannock WS12 .... 211 D3
St Francis of Assisi RC
  Comp Sch WS9 .... 256 B3

St Francis RC Prim Sch
  WS4 .... 244 B1
St Gabriels RC Prim Sch
  B77 .... 250 C1
St George Dr WS12 .... 211 D3
St George St ST13 .... 30 C3
St George & St Martin RC
  Prim Sch ST1 .... 282 C4
St George's Ave N ST5 .... 56 A3
St George's Ave S ST5 .... 56 A3
St George's Ave W ST5 .... 56 A3
St George's Cres ST4 .... 72 A1
St George's Rd
  Burton u T DE13 .... 165 F3
  Newcastle-u-L ST5 .... 284 A2
  Stafford ST17 .... 156 A1
  Stone ST15 .... 120 A4
  Stourbridge DY8 .... 279 E1
St Georges Ave
  Chell Heath ST6 .... 42 A2
  Endon ST9 .... 43 F3
St Georges Ct B74 .... 257 F3
St Georges Hospl ST16 .... 155 F2
St Gile's Rd ST5 .... 55 F1
St Giles Gr ST18 .... 172 C3
St Giles' RC Prim Sch
  ST10 .... 76 B2
St Giles Rd WS7 .... 229 D3
St Gregory's RC
  Jun & Inf Schs ST3 .... 283 B2
St Gregory's Rd ST3 .... 283 A3
St Helens Rd WS13 .... 214 A2
St Hellier Cl ST5 .... 70 C2
St Hilda's Ave ST5 .... 45 E2
St Ives Cl Stafford ST17 .... 175 E4
  Tamworth B79 .... 250 A3
St James CE Prim Sch
  DY8 .... 279 E4
St James Cl
  Brownhills WS3 .... 244 A3
  Longdon WS15 .... 198 A1
St James Cres ST17 .... 193 D4
St James Ct DE13 .... 183 E1
St James Gn ST21 .... 102 C2
St James Pl ST4 .... 72 A1
St James' Rd DE13 .... 183 E1
St James Rd
  Cannock WS11 .... 209 E1
  Norton Canes WS11 .... 228 A3
  Sutton Coldfield B75 .... 258 B1
St James St ST1 .... 282 A2
St James' St DY3 .... 271 E2
St James Wlk WS8 .... 244 C4
St John Cl B75 .... 258 B2
St John Fisher RC
  High Sch ST5 .... 284 A4
St John St Hanley ST1 .... 282 C4
  Lichfield WS13 .... 231 D4
St John The Evangelist RC
  Prim Sch ST5 .... 26 A2
St John's Ave
  Newcastle-u-L ST5 .... 56 B2
  Stoke-on-T ST4 .... 71 F2
  Stone ST15 .... 105 E2
St John's CE Inf Sch ST6 .... 56 C4
St John's CE Prim Sch
  Brewood ST19 .... 221 F4
  Cheddleton ST9 .... 60 A4
  Essington WV11 .... 242 A2
  Keele ST5 .... 69 F4
  Stafford ST16 .... 156 A2
St John's Cl
  Brownhills WS9 .... 244 C2
  Cannock WS11 .... 226 B4
  Lichfield WS13 .... 231 D3
  Swindon DY3 .... 269 E1
St John's Ct WS12 .... 210 C1
St John's Dr
  Shenstone WS14 .... 246 C3
  Swadlincote DE11 .... 186 C3
St John's Hill WS14 .... 246 C3
St John's Pl
  Biddulph ST8 .... 27 E4
  Newcastle-u-L ST5 .... 55 F1
St John's RC Prim Sch
  ST10 .... 78 C1
St John's RC Prim Sch
  ST4 .... 158 A1
St John's Rd
  Biddulph ST8 .... 27 E4
  Burton u T DE13 .... 166 B4
  Cannock WS11 .... 226 C4
St John's Rd CW12 .... 6 A3
St John's Rd DY8 .... 279 F3
St John's Sq ST7 .... 25 F1
St John's St B79 .... 250 A3
St John's the Evangelist
  RC Prim Sch ST7 .... 25 F1
St John's Wlk ST16 .... 156 A2
St John's Wood ST7 .... 25 F1
St Johns CE Jun Mix Inf
  Sch WS9 .... 245 D2
St Johns Hixon ST18 .... 139 E2
  Rugeley WS15 .... 196 B4
St Johns Prep Sch WS13 .... 231 D4
St Johns Ret Pk WV2 .... 266 B4
St Johns Rd Ashley TF9 .... 100 B3
  Brownhills, Highbridge
  WS3 .... 244 A3
  Brownhills, Shire Oak
  WS8 .... 245 D3
  Essington WV11 .... 242 A2
  Stafford ST17 .... 174 B4
St Johns Way TF9 .... 100 B3
St Joseph St ST6 .... 41 E4
St Joseph's Coll ST4 .... 71 F2

St Joseph's Convent Prim
  Sch WV6 .... 255 F2
St Joseph's RC Prim Sch
  WS15 .... 196 C4
St Joseph's RC Prim Sch
  Cannock WS12 .... 210 B2
  Lichfield WS14 .... 231 E4
  Uttoxeter ST14 .... 126 A4
St Joseph's & St Theresa's
  RC Prim Sch WS7 .... 228 C3
St Josephs Cl WS3 .... 244 A2
St Josephs RC Prim Sch
  DY8 .... 279 E1
St Jude's CE Inf Sch
  WV6 .... 255 F2
St Jude's CE Jun Sch
  WV3 .... 255 F2
St Jude's Ct WV6 .... 255 F2
St Jude's Rd WS11 .... 255 F2
St Jude's Rd W WV6 .... 255 F2
St Jude's Way DE13 .... 166 B4
St Lawrence Dr WS11 .... 210 A1
St Lawrence Prim Sch
  ST20 .... 171 F3
St Lawrence Way ST20 .... 171 E4
St Leonard's Ave
  Ipstones ST10 .... 62 A4
  Stafford ST17 .... 156 A1
St Leonard's CE Fst Sch
  ST10 .... 62 A4
St Leonard's CE Prim Sch
  B79 .... 234 A1
St Leonard's Prim Sch
  ST17 .... 156 A1
St Leonard's Way CW3 .... 67 E1
St Leonards View
  Dordon B78 .... 262 C4
  Polesworth B78 .... 262 C4
St Lucy's Dr ST5 .... 56 B4
St Luke St ST4 .... 282 C2
St Luke's CE Jun Sch
  WV2 .... 266 A3
St Luke's CE Prim Sch
  Hanley ST1 .... 282 C2
  Newcastle-u-L ST5 .... 55 D1
St Luke's Cl
  Cannock WS11 .... 226 B4
  Newcastle-u-L ST5 .... 55 D1
St Luke's Inf Sch WV2 .... 266 B4
St Luke's Rd
  Barton-u-N DE13 .... 183 E1
  Burntwood WS7 .... 229 E3
  Burton u T DE13 .... 166 B4
St Luke's Wlk WS15 .... 198 B2
St Lukes CE Prim Sch
  ST9 .... 43 F4
St Lukes Cl ST15 .... 135 D4
St Lukes Prim Sch SK17 .... 24 C4
St Margaret Ward RC
  High Sch ST6 .... 41 F3
St Margaret's B74 .... 257 E2
St Margaret's CE Jun Sch
  ST5 .... 56 B2
St Margaret's Ct
  Betley CW3 .... 53 D3
  Newcastle-u-L ST5 .... 56 B3
St Margaret's Dr ST1 .... 57 F4
St Margaret's Rd B79 .... 250 A4
St Margarets DE13 .... 165 F3
St Margarets Gr ST3 .... 72 C2
St Margarets Rd
  Brownhills WS3 .... 244 A2
  Lichfield WS13 .... 214 A2
St Maria Goreti RC Prim
  Sch ST17 .... 58 B1
St Mark's CE Prim Sch
  ST1 .... 282 A2
St Mark's Cl ST1 .... 282 A2
St Mark's Rd
  Burntwood WS7 .... 229 E3
  Burton u T DE13 .... 166 B4
St Mark's St ST1 .... 282 A1
St Marks Cl WS6 .... 226 C2
St Marks Rd
  Brownhills, Pelsall WS3 ..... 244 A1
  Brownhills, Shire Oak
  WS8 .... 245 D3
St Martin's Cl
  Burton u T DE13 .... 166 B4
  Wolv WV2 .... 266 C3
St Martin's La ST3 .... 283 C4
St Martin's Pl ST16 .... 155 F2
St Martin's Rd
  Kidsgrove ST7 .... 40 C3
  Newcastle-u-L ST5 .... 70 C4
St Mary of the Angels RC
  Jun Mix Inf Sch WS9 .... 256 A4
St Mary & St Chad CE
  Prim Sch ST19 .... 223 E3
St Mary & St Chad's Cath
  WS13 .... 231 D4
St Mary's CE Fst Sch
  Uttoxeter ST14 .... 111 D1
  Wheaton Aston ST19 .... 205 D3
St Mary's CE Prim Sch
  WS15 .... 178 C3
St Mary's CE Sch SK11 .... 7 E4
St Mary's
  Albrighton WV7 .... 237 D3
  Newton Solney DE15 .... 167 F4
  Sedgley DY3 .... 271 F4
  Upper Tean ST10 .... 109 D3

St Mary's Cres ST14 .... 111 D1
St Mary's Dr
  Burton u T, Clay Mills DE13 .. 147 F1
  Burton u T, Horninglow
  DE13 .... 166 B4
  Newcastle-u-L ST5 .... 284 A2
St Mary's Gate ST16 .... 155 F2
St Mary's Gr ST16 .... 155 F2
St Mary's Pl ST16 .... 155 F2
St Mary's RC Prim Sch
  Cannock WS11 .... 226 C4
  Chell Heath ST6 .... 42 B4
  Leek ST13 .... 30 C3
St Mary's Rd Ashley TF9 .... 99 E3
  Colwich WS18 .... 177 E4
  Lichfield WS13 .... 214 A2
  Longton ST3 .... 73 E3
  Newcastle-u-L ST5 .... 56 B3
St Mary's St
  Market Drayton TF9 .... 97 E1
  Newport TF10 .... 168 C2
St Mary's Way
  Aldridge WS9 .... 256 A3
  Tamworth B77 .... 250 C2
St Marys Cl Bradley ST18 .... 173 E1
  Shareshill WV10 .... 225 E1
St Marys Gr B79 .... 236 B2
St Marys Prim Sch WV7 .... 237 D3
St Marys RC Prim Sch
  ST19 .... 223 D3
St Mathew Cl WS12 .... 211 D3
St Mathew St ST4 .... 72 C3
St Matthew's Ave WS7 .... 229 F4
St Matthew's Rd WS7 .... 229 F4
St Matthew's St ST14 .... 185 E4
St Matthews Cl WS3 .... 244 A1
St Matthews Dr ST18 .... 154 C1
St Mawes Cl ST17 .... 175 E4
St Mawes Rd WV6 .... 255 D2
St Michael CE Prim Sch
  WV6 .... 255 F3
St Michael Rd WS13 .... 231 E4
St Michael's CE Fst Sch
  Rudyard ST9 .... 18 B1
  Stone ST15 .... 120 B4
St Michael's CE Prim Sch
  WS14 .... 231 E4
St Michael's Cl
  Adbaston ST20 .... 131 E2
  Brownhills WS3 .... 244 A1
  Penkridge ST19 .... 207 F4
  Stafford ST17 .... 175 E4
St Michael's Ct WV6 .... 255 F3
St Michael's Dr WS15 .... 197 D3
St Michael's Hospl
  WS13 .... 231 E4
St Michael's RC Prim Sch
  WV3 .... 265 E4
St Michael's Rd
  Chell Heath ST6 .... 41 F3
  Newcastle-u-L ST5 .... 56 B3
  Penkridge ST19 .... 207 F4
  Rugeley WS15 .... 197 D3
  Uttoxeter ST14 .... 110 C3
St Michael's Sq ST19 .... 192 C1
St Michaels CE Fst Sch
  ST19 .... 192 C1
St Michaels CE Prim Sch
  WS3 .... 244 A2
St Michaels Cl
  Kingsbury CV9 .... 262 B1
  Stone ST15 .... 120 A4
St Michaels Dr WS12 .... 211 D3
St Michaels Mount ST15 .... 120 B3
St Michaels Rd
  Burton u T DE13 .... 166 B4
  Himley DY3 .... 270 C3
St Mildred's CE Prim Sch
  ST10 .... 62 B2
St Modwen's Cl DE13 .... 166 B4
St Modwen's RC Prim Sch
  DE13 .... 166 A3
St Modwen's Wlk DE14 .... 166 B1
St Modwena Way ST19 .... 207 F4
St Nicholas Ave ST6 .... 42 C2
St Nicholas CE Fst Sch
  WV8 .... 238 C2
St Nicholas Cl WS3 .... 244 A2
St Nicholas Way WS15 .... 160 C3
St Oswald's CE Fst Sch
  DY10 .... 280 A1
St Patrick Cl WS12 .... 211 D3
St Patrick's Dr ST5 .... 70 C4
St Patrick's Pl ST16 .... 155 F2
St Patrick's RC Prim Sch
  ST16 .... 155 F3
St Patrick's St ST16 .... 155 F2
St Patricks Rd DE13 .... 166 B4
St Paul St ST6 .... 56 C4
St Paul's CE Fst Sch
  WV9 .... 224 B2
St Paul's CE Prim Sch
  ST17 .... 155 F1
St Paul's Cl Brewood WV9 .... 224 B1
  Cannock WS11 .... 210 A1
St Paul's Ct
  Burton u T DE14 .... 166 A4
  Longton ST3 .... 72 C1
  Tamworth B77 .... 261 E2
St Paul's Rd
  Burntwood WS7 .... 229 E3
  Cannock WS11 .... 210 A2
  Newcastle-u-L ST5 .... 284 A2

St Paul's Sq DE14 .... 166 A2
St Paul's St W DE14 .... 166 A2
St Pauls CE Jun Sch ST6 ..... 41 F1
St Pauls CE Prim Sch
  WV9 .... 240 A1
St Pauls Cres WS3 .... 244 A3
St Pauls Rd WS15 .... 196 C4
St Peter & St Paul RC
  Prim Sch WS3 .... 214 A1
St Peter & St Paul RC Sch
  TF10 .... 168 C2
St Peter's Bridge DE14 ..... 166 C1
St Peter's CE Fst Sch
  Alton ST10 .... 78 C4
  Marchington ST14 .... 127 F1
St Peter's CE Prim Sch
  Caverswall ST11 .... 74 B1
  Edgmond TF10 .... 168 A2
  Netherseal DE12 .... 219 F3
  Stoke-on-T ST4 .... 72 A3
St Peter's Cl
  Shenstone WS9 .... 245 F2
  Tamworth B77 .... 250 B1
St Peter's Collegiate Sec
  Sch WV6 .... 255 F2
St Peter's Ct ST20 .... 151 D2
St Peter's Gdns ST17 .... 174 C3
St Peter's High St ST4 .... 71 F4
St Peter's Prim Sch
  DE13 .... 182 A2
St Peter's RC Prim Sch
  Hanley ST6 .... 57 D3
  Walsall WS3 .... 243 D1
St Peter's Rd
  Burntwood WS7 .... 229 E3
  Cannock WS12 .... 210 B2
St Peter's St DE15 .... 166 C1
St Peter's Wlk ST6 .... 57 D3
St Peters CE Fst Sch
  ST14 .... 142 C4
St Peters CE Prim Sch
  Hixon ST18 .... 158 A4
  Shenstone WS9 .... 245 F2
St Peters CE Sch ST18 ...... 138 B1
St Peters Cl Stafford ST17 .. 174 C3
  Stoke-on-T ST4 .... 72 A4
St Peters Ct
  Burton u T DE15 .... 166 C1
  Walsall WS3 .... 243 D1
St Peters Dr WS3 .... 244 A2
St Phillip's Ave WV3 .... 265 E4
St Phillip's Gr WV3 .... 265 E4
St Saviour's CE Prim Sch
  ST7 .... 25 E1
St Saviour's St ST7 .... 25 E1
St Saviours Cl WV2 .... 266 C3
St Stephen's Rd WS7 .... 229 E3
St Stephens Ct DE13 .... 166 B4
St Stephens Prim Sch
  WS13 .... 215 A4
St Teresa's RC Prim Sch
  ST4 .... 71 F1
St Theresa's RC Prim Sch
  WV4 .... 266 C3
St Thomas Aquinas RC
  Prim Sch ST4 .... 56 C1
St Thomas' CE Prim Sch
  ST7 .... 26 A1
St Thomas' Cl WS9 .... 245 D1
St Thomas Dr WS12 .... 211 D3
St Thomas La ST18 .... 156 B2
St Thomas More RC Coll
  ST3 .... 73 D2
St Thomas More RC Prim
  Sch WS11 .... 227 D2
St Thomas Pl ST4 .... 71 F3
St Thomas' RC Prim Sch
  ST10 .... 92 C2
St Thomas St
  Kidsgrove ST7 .... 26 C4
  Stafford ST16 .... 156 A2
St Thomas's Rd ST10 .... 92 C2
St Vincent Pl ST5 .... 55 F1
St Vincent Rd ST15 .... 119 F4
St Werburgh's CE
  Prim Sch
  Hanbury DE13 .... 145 D2
  Kingsley ST10 .... 61 F1
St Wilfrid RC Prim Sch
  ST6 .... 41 F2
St Wulstan's RC Prim Sch
  ST5 .... 56 B2
Salcombe Ave ST17 .... 175 E4
Salcombe Cl WS11 .... 226 A4
Salcombe Pl ST1 .... 57 E4
Sale La DE13 .... 200 B1
Salem St ST1 .... 56 C2
Sales La DE15 .... 167 E2
Salisbury Ave
  Burton u T DE15 .... 167 E2
  Hanley ST1 .... 282 B1
Salisbury Cl
  Lichfield WS13 .... 214 B2
  Madeley CW3 .... 68 C4
  Sedgley DY1 .... 271 F2
Salisbury Dr
  Cannock WS12 .... 210 A1
  Stafford ST16 .... 156 A2
Salisbury Hill View TF9 ..... 112 A4
Salisbury Rd
  Market Drayton TF9 .... 112 A4
  Stafford ST16 .... 156 A2
Salisbury St Leek ST13 .... 30 C3
  Tunstall ST6 .... 41 F2
Salkeld Pl ST6 .... 42 A3

Sally Ward Dr WS9 .... 245 D2
Sallyfield La DE6 .... 65 F1
Salmond Ave ST16 .... 156 A3
Salop Dr WS11 .... 226 C4
Salop Gr ST5 .... 71 E2
Salop Pl ST7 .... 26 A2
Salt Ave ST17 .... 155 F1
Salt Banks ST18 .... 137 E2
Salt La ST18 .... 137 E3
Salt Rd Salt ST18 .... 137 F2
  Stafford ST17 .... 155 F1
Salt Works La ST18 .... 138 B1
Saltbrook La DE6 .... 144 C4
Saltdean Cl ST3 .... 73 F1
Salter St ST16 .... 155 F1
Salter's Ct TF10 .... 168 C2
Salter's La TF10 .... 168 C2
Salters Cl ST9 .... 59 D2
Salters Grange WS15 .... 160 C3
Salters La Caverswall ST9 ... 59 D1
  Tamworth B79 .... 250 A3
Saltersford La ST10 .... 94 C4
Saltheath La ST18 .... 137 F2
Salts La B78 .... 260 C3
Sam Barber Ct WS12 .... 210 C1
Sambar Rd B78 .... 249 F1
Sambrook Cres TF9 .... 97 F1
Sampson St ST1 .... 282 A3
Samuel Cl WS13 .... 214 B1
Samuel St Chell Heath ST7 ... 26 C1
  Walsall WS3 .... 243 D1
Sancton Gn **25** ST6 ...... 56 C4
Sand Bank WS3 .... 243 D1
Sand Rd DE13 .... 164 B4
Sandalwood Rd DE15 .... 185 F3
Sandbach Rd ST6 .... 57 D4
Sandcrest Pl ST3 .... 73 F1
Sandcrest Wlk ST3 .... 73 F1
Sanderling Cl WV10 .... 241 D4
Sanderling Rise WS7 .... 229 D4
Sandfield Bridge DY5 .... 271 D1
Sandfield Gr DY5 .... 271 D1
Sandfield Rd DY8 .... 275 F1
Sandford Cl WS15 .... 198 A4
Sandford Hill Cty Prim Sch
  ST3 .... 73 E3
Sandford Rd DY1 .... 271 F1
Sandford Rise WV6 .... 255 F3
Sandford St
  Lichfield WS13 .... 231 D4
  9 Longton ST3 .... 73 E3
  Newcastle-u-L ST5 .... 55 F4
Sandgate St ST3 .... 73 E2
Sandhill St ST3 .... 243 D1
Sandhurst Ave **5** ST3 ... 73 F1
Sandhurst Cl ST5 .... 56 B2
Sandhurst Dr WV4 .... 266 A2
Sandhurst Dr DY8 .... 275 F4
Sandhurst Pl ST3 .... 89 F4
Sandhurst Rd B74 .... 257 F3
Sandiford Cres TF10 .... 168 C1
Sandiway DE13 .... 201 F4
Sandiway Pl ST1 .... 57 F3
Sandmere Rise WV10 .... 240 C1
Sandon Ave ST5 .... 71 D3
Sandon Cl ST11 .... 91 E1
Sandon La ST18 .... 122 B3
Sandon Mews ST16 .... 155 F3
Sandon Old Rd ST18 .... 89 F4
Sandon Rd
  Blythe Bridge ST3 .... 89 F4
  Draycott in t M ST11 .... 91 E2
  Hilderstone ST15 .... 106 B1
  Hopton ST18 .... 137 E1
  Meir ST3 .... 89 F4
  Salt ST18 .... 137 E1
  Stafford ST16 .... 155 F3
  Wolv WV10 .... 240 A1
Sandon St Hanley ST1 .... 57 D2
  Leek ST13 .... 30 C2
Sandown B77 .... 250 C3
Sandown Ave WS6 .... 226 C2
Sandown Cl
  Branston DE14 .... 185 D4
  Burntwood WS7 .... 211 F1
  Cannock WS12 .... 211 D3
  Kingsley ST10 .... 76 C3
Sandown Cty Fst Sch
  WV6 .... 254 C2
Sandown Dr WV6 .... 254 C2
Sandown Pl ST2 .... 43 E1
Sandpiper B77 .... 262 A4
Sandpiper Cl WS12 .... 210 B4
Sandpiper Dr ST14 .... 126 A3
Sandra Cl Aldridge WS9 .... 256 A4
  Chell Heath ST6 .... 42 A1
Sandringham Ave DE15 .... 167 D1
Sandringham Cl
  Burntwood WS7 .... 211 F1
  Market Drayton TF9 .... 97 F1
  Stafford ST17 .... 175 E4
Sandringham Dr WS9 .... 245 D1
Sandringham Pl DY8 .... 275 E1
Sandringham Rd
  Kingswinford DY8 .... 275 C1
  Pattingham WV6 .... 253 E1
  Stafford ST17 .... 175 E4
  Wolv WV4 .... 266 A2
  Wombourne WV5 .... 269 F3
Sands La ST6 .... 28 A1
Sands Rd ST7 .... 26 B3
Sandsdown Cl ST6 .... 16 B1
Sandstone Cl
  Sedgley DY3 .... 271 C2
  Walsall WS3 .... 243 E2
Sandstone Rd WS3 .... 243 E2
Sandwell Pl ST3 .... 89 F4
Sandwell Rd WV10 .... 240 A1

Sandwick Cres ST1 .... 57 F3
Sandwood Cres ST3 .... 73 E3
Sandy Bank ST21 .... 102 B2
Sandy Cres WV11 .... 242 A1
Sandy Hill ST9 .... 59 E2
Sandy Hollow WV6 .... 255 F1
Sandy La Ashley TF9 .... 100 A4
  Blore TF9 .... 98 B2
  Brewood ST19 .... 223 E3
  Cannock WS11 .... 209 D1
  Chapel Chorlton ST5 .... 85 E2
  Codsall WV8 .... 238 C2
  Eccleshall ST21 .... 132 B4
  Endon ST6 .... 43 D4
  Kinver DY7 .... 277 F1
  Linton DE11 .... 186 A1
  Longsdon ST9 .... 44 C4
  Millmeece ST21 .... 102 B2
  Newcastle-u-L ST5 .... 284 D4
  Newton Regis B79 .... 236 B3
  Norton-in-t-M ST2 .... 43 E1
  Rugeley WS15 .... 196 C4
  Standon ST21 .... 102 B2
  Stourbridge DY8 .... 279 E2
  Sutton TF9 .... 112 B3
  Upper Tean SE10 .... 93 F4
  Weston-u-T ST18 .... 138 B2
  Whittington WS14 .... 232 B2
  Wolv, Claregate WV6 .... 255 F3
  Wolv, Elston Hall WV10 ... 240 C1
Sandy Mount WV5 .... 270 A4
Sandy Rd Biddulph ST6 ...... 16 B1
  Stourbridge DY8 .... 279 E1
  Tunstall ST6 .... 41 E3
Sandy Way B77 .... 251 D2
Sandybrook Cl ST13 .... 30 C2
Sandybrook La ST13 .... 30 C1
Sandycroft TF10 .... 168 C2
Sandyfield Rd ST1 .... 57 F3
Sandyfields ST5 .... 85 E3
Sandyfields Rd DY3 .... 271 D3
Sandyford St ST16 .... 155 F3
Sangster La ST6 .... 42 B1
Sankey Cres WS15 .... 196 C4
Sankey Rd WS15 .... 196 C4
Sankey's Cnr WS7 .... 228 C4
Sant St ST6 .... 56 C2
Saplings Cl ST19 .... 192 C1
Saplings The
  Newcastle-u-L ST5 .... 71 E2
  Penkridge ST19 .... 192 C1
Sapperton La DE65 .... 129 F4
Sapphire Dr WS11 .... 210 B2
Sara Ct DY4 .... 258 A2
Saracen Way ST3 .... 74 A1
Sarah Challinor Cl WS15 ... 196 C4
Saredon Cl WS3 .... 244 A1
Saredon Rd
  Cheslyn Hay WS6 .... 226 A2
  Shareshill WV10 .... 225 E1
Sargeant Ave ST6 .... 42 A3
Sark Cl ST5 .... 70 C2
Sark Pl **1** ST3 .... 73 E3
Sarraine Ind Pk ST10 .... 76 A1
Sarver La ST10 .... 75 E2
Sash St ST16 .... 155 F2
Saturn Rd Cannock WS11 ... 210 A3
  Chell Heath ST6 .... 42 B1
Saunders Cl WS12 .... 211 D3
Saunders Rd ST5 .... 56 A2
Saverley Green Rd ST11 ... 106 C4
Savey La DE13 .... 181 F1
Savoy Rd CW1 .... 37 D4
Sawpit La ST17 .... 176 A2
Sawyer Dr ST6 .... 16 B1
Saxifrage Dr ST15 .... 120 B3
Saxon Cl
  Burton u T DE15 .... 185 F4
  Great Wyrley WS6 .... 227 D1
  Polesworth B78 .... 251 F1
  Tamworth B77 .... 261 F3
Saxon Hill Specl Sch
  WS14 .... 231 E3
Saxon Mill La B79 .... 250 B2
Saxon Rd ST19 .... 207 F4
Saxon St DE15 .... 185 F4
Saxon Wlk WS13 .... 230 C4
Saxoncourt WV6 .... 255 F4
Saxondrive ST1 .... 250 B3
Saxonfields WV6 .... 255 E3
Saxton Dr B74 .... 257 F3
Sayers Rd ST16 .... 155 E4
Scalpcliffe Cl DE15 .... 166 C2
Scalpcliffe Rd DE15 .... 166 C2
Scammerton B77 .... 262 A4
Scamnell La ST11 .... 134 C4
Scampton Cl WV6 .... 254 C3
Scampton Way B79 .... 250 B4
Scarlett St ST5 .... 284 B2
Scarratt Cl ST11 .... 91 D4
Scarratt Dr ST11 .... 91 D4
Sceptre St ST1 .... 282 B2
Schofield La B79 .... 217 E3
Scholar Green Cty Prim
  Sch ST7 .... 25 F3
School Ave WS8 .... 244 C4
School Cl
  Audley ST7 .... 40 A1
  Burntwood WS7 .... 228 B4
  Codsall WV8 .... 239 D2
  Leek ST13 .... 30 B2
  Norton Canes WS11 .... 228 A3
  Seisdon WV5 .... 269 E4
  Wolv WV5 .... 265 D4
School Cres WS11 .... 228 A3
School Dr DY8 .... 279 F4
School Ground La TF10 ..... 169 D2
School House La WS15 ..... 161 D3

School La
  Admaston WS15 .... 159 F2
  Ashley TF9 .... 100 A3
  Astbury CW12 .... 15 D4
  Biddulph ST8 .... 17 D1
  Blymhill TF11 .... 203 F3
  Bradnop ST13 .... 31 F2
  Brewood WV9 .... 224 A2
  Brownhills WS3 .... 243 F1
  Burntwood WS7 .... 228 B4
  Caverswall ST3 .... 74 B1
  Colton WS15 .... 178 C3
  Colwich ST18 .... 158 A1
  Coppenhall ST18 .... 192 B4
  Dilhorne ST10 .... 75 E2
  Edingale B79 .... 217 E3
  Hill Ridware WS15 .... 198 A4
  Hints B78 .... 248 B1
  Hopwas B78 .... 249 D4
  Longdon WS15 .... 212 A3
  Longsdon ST9 .... 30 A1
  Longton ST3 .... 89 D4
  Maer TF9 .... 84 A4
  Market Drayton TF9 .... 112 A4
  Norton Canes WS3 .... 227 F1
  Rolleston DE13 .... 147 E2
  Sandon ST18 .... 137 F4
  Shareshill WV10 .... 225 E1
  Shuttington B79 .... 251 F4
  Stafford, Hillcroft Park
    ST17 .... 175 F4
  Stafford, Rickerscote
    ST17 .... 174 C3
  Sudbury DE6 .... 128 C2
  Tamworth B77 .... 261 E3
  Wheaton Aston ST19 .... 206 B2
  Wolv WV10 .... 240 C1
School Lane Cl ST17 .... 174 C3
School Pl ST16 .... 155 F3
School Rd Brewood ST19 .. 223 E3
  Bucknall ST2 .... 58 A3
  Eccleshall ST21 .... 133 E3
  Edgmond TF10 .... 168 A2
  Himley DY3 .... 270 A2
  Norton Canes WS11 .... 228 A3
  Seisdon WV5 .... 264 B1
  Uttoxeter ST14 .... 110 C1
  Wheaton Aston ST19 .... 205 B3
  Wolv WV6 .... 255 D2
  Wombourne WV5 .... 270 A4
School St Brownhills WS4 ... 244 B1
  1 Leek ST13 .... 30 C3
  Newcastle-u-L ST5 .... 284 C3
  Newcastle-u-L,
    Broad Meadow ST5 .... 55 F3
  Sedgley DY3 .... 271 F4
  Stoke-on-T ST4 .... 71 F2
  Stourbridge DY8 .... 279 F3
  Tamworth B77 .... 250 C2
School View ST14 .... 141 E4
School Wlk WS7 .... 228 B4
Schoolacre Rise B74 .... 256 C1
Schoolbridge St ST3 .... 30 C3
Schoolfields Rd WS14 ...... 247 D3
Schoolgate Cl WS4 .... 244 B1
Scimitar Cl ST3 .... 73 E3
Scot Hay Rd Audley ST7 ..... 54 C3
  Keele ST5 .... 54 C2
  Newcastle-u-L ST5 .... 54 C2
Scotch Orch WS13 .... 214 B1
Scotch Orchard Prim Sch
  WS13 .... 214 B1
Scotia Bsns Pk ST4 .... 41 F1
Scotia Rd Cannock WS11 .. 209 E2
  Tunstall ST6 .... 41 F1
Scott Ave WV4 .... 265 F2
Scott Cl WS4 .... 231 D3
Scott Lidgett Ind Est 56 B4
Scott Lidgett Rd ST6 .... 56 B4
Scott Rd Chell Heath ST6 .... 41 F3
  Tamworth B77 .... 250 C2
Scott St Cannock WS12 ..... 210 C2
  Newcastle-u-L ST5 .... 284 C3
Scott Way WS7 .... 211 F1
Scott's Cl ST5 .... 279 F3
Scott's Rd DY8 .... 279 F3
Scragg St ST7 .... 41 F4
Scrimshaw Dr ST6 .... 42 B2
Scrivener Rd ST4 .... 56 C1
Scropton Old Rd DE65 ..... 146 B4
Scropton Rd Hatton DE65 .. 146 A4
  Scropton DE65 .... 129 F1
Seabridge Jun & Inf Schs
  ST5 .... 71 D2
Seabridge La ST5 .... 71 D2
Seabridge Rd ST5 .... 284 A1
Seabrook Rd WS15 .... 197 D3
Seafield B77 .... 250 C3
Seafield Cl DY6 .... 275 F2
Seaford St ST4 .... 57 D1
Seaforth Gr WV11 .... 242 A1
Seagrave Pl ST5 .... 71 D3
Seagrave St ST5 .... 284 C3
Searle Ave ST16 .... 155 E1
Seaton B77 .... 261 F4
Seaton Ave ST17 .... 175 E4
Seaton Cl ST3 .... 89 F4
Seaton Pl DY8 .... 275 F4
Sebring Ave ST3 .... 89 F4
Seckham Rd WS13 .... 231 D4
Seckington La B79 .... 236 B2
Second Ave
  Branston DE14 .... 165 F1
  Brownhills WS8 .... 229 D1
  Bucknall ST2 .... 58 B2
  Kidsgrove ST7 .... 25 F1
  Kingswinford DY6 .... 275 F4
  Newcastle-u-L ST5 .... 56 B4
  Stafford ST16 .... 155 E4

Sedbergh Cl ST5 .... 70 C2
Seddon Rd ST3 .... 89 F4
Sedgefield Cl DY1 .... 271 F2
Sedgefield Gr WV6 .... 254 C2
Sedgeley Rd WV4 .... 265 F1
Sedgemoor Ave WS7 .... 229 D3
Sedgley Hall Ave DY3 ...... 271 E4
Sedgley St WV2 .... 266 B4
Sedgley Wlk ST3 .... 283 C4
Seedcroft La WS15 .... 160 C2
Seedfields Rd ST3 .... 72 C2
Seeds La WS8 .... 244 C4
Seedymill La WS13 .... 213 F4
Seesall The ST20 .... 171 F4
Sefton Ave
  Congleton CW12 .... 6 A1
  Hanley ST1 .... 57 F4
Sefton Cl DE15 .... 167 D1
Sefton Rd Longton ST3 .... 73 F1
  Tamworth B77 .... 261 E2
Sefton St ST1 .... 57 D2
Seighford Rd ST18 .... 154 B3
Seisdon Rd WV5 .... 264 C3
Selborne Dr ST6 .... 41 F4
Selbourne Dr ST6 .... 41 F4
Selby Cl ST5 .... 71 D3
Selby St ST3 .... 74 A3
Selby Way WS3 .... 242 C1
Selby Wlk ST3 .... 88 C4
Selker Dr B77 .... 250 C3
Sellman St ST20 .... 171 F3
Selman's Hill WS3 .... 243 E1
Selsdon Rd WS3 .... 242 C2
Selwood Cl **5** ST3 .... 73 E1
Selworthey Dr ST17 .... 175 F3
Selworthy Rd ST6 .... 43 D3
Selwyn Cl Alrewas DE13 ... 201 D2
  Wolv WV2 .... 266 B4
Selwyn St ST4 .... 72 A3
Semper Cl CW12 .... 6 A2
Senior Cl WS14 .... 242 A4
Serin Cl ST14 .... 126 B3
Setterfield Way WS15 ...... 196 C3
Settle Gr ST3 .... 90 A4
Setton Dr DY3 .... 271 F4
Seven Acres WS9 .... 256 A3
Seven Arches Way ST4 .... 72 B4
Sevenoaks Gr ST3 .... 90 A3
Sevens Rd WS12 .... 211 E2
Severn Cl Biddulph ST6 ..... 16 C1
  Burton u T DE13 .... 147 E1
  Congleton CW12 .... 6 A1
  Uttoxeter ST14 .... 126 B3
Severn Dr
  Brownhills WS8 .... 228 B1
  Burntwood WS7 .... 229 E3
  Burton u T DE14 .... 166 C2
  Newcastle-u-L ST5 .... 71 D2
  Perton WV6 .... 254 C2
Severn Rd
  Stourbridge DY8 .... 279 F2
  Walsall WS3 .... 243 F1
Severn St ST1 .... 282 A4
Seward Cl WS14 .... 231 E3
Seymour Ave DE13 .... 166 C4
Seymour Cl WS6 .... 226 B1
Seymour Gdns B74 .... 257 F2
Seymour St ST1 .... 57 F2
Shackerley La
  Albrighton WV8 .... 221 E1
  Boscobel WV8 .... 221 E1
Shackleton Dr WV6 .... 254 C3
Shackleton Rd WS3 .... 243 E1
Shackson Cl ST1 .... 282 B1
Shadwell Dr DY3 .... 271 E2
Shaffalong La ST13 .... 45 D3
Shaftesbury Ave ST6 .... 42 A1
Shaftesbury Dr WS12 .... 210 B4
Shaftsbury Rd WS15 .... 196 C3
Shakespeare Ave WS14 .... 231 D3
Shakespeare Cl
  Kidsgrove ST7 .... 41 D4
  Norton-in-t-M ST2 .... 43 D1
  Tamworth B79 .... 250 A3
Shakespeare Gr WS11 ...... 209 E2
Shakespeare Rd
  Burntwood WS7 .... 228 C4
  Burton u T DE14 .... 166 B3
  Sedgley DY3 .... 271 D2
  Stafford ST17 .... 174 B4
Shaldon Ave ST9 .... 43 E2
Shales The WV5 .... 269 F3
Shallcross La DY3 .... 271 E2
Shallowford Ct ST1 .... 57 D2
Shallowford Mews ST16 ... 155 E3
Shanklin Cl WS6 .... 227 D2
Shannon B77 .... 261 F4
Shannon Dr
  Brownhills WS8 .... 228 B1
  Tunstall ST6 .... 41 E4
Shannon Rd ST17 .... 174 B3
Shannon Wlk WS3 .... 228 B1
Shardlow Cl Fenton ST4 ..... 73 D3
  Stone ST15 .... 120 B3
Sharman Cl ST4 .... 71 F4
Sharmon Way ST20 .... 171 F4
Sharnbrook Dr WS15 .... 178 B1
Sharnbrook Gr ST17 .... 175 E3
Sharon Cl WV4 .... 266 C3
Sharon Way WS12 .... 210 B2
Sharpe St B77 .... 251 D3
Sharplands TF9 .... 99 E3
Sharrat Field B75 .... 258 B1
Sharron Dr ST3 .... 31 D3
Shaver's La WS15 .... 197 D3
Shaw Cl WS13 .... 215 E4
Shaw Dr WS7 .... 212 A1

Shaw Gdns ST17 .... 174 B4
Shaw Hall La WV9 .... 240 A4
Shaw La Albrighton WV7 .. 237 D3
  King's Bromley WS15 .... 198 C1
  Lichfield WS13 .... 231 D4
  Longdon WS15 .... 212 A2
  Tong TF11 .... 220 B3
  Wolv WV6 .... 255 D2
Shaw Pl ST13 .... 31 D3
Shaw Rd WV4 .... 266 B3
Shaw St Biddulph ST8 ...... 27 E4
  Hanley ST1 .... 282 A4
  Newcastle-u-L ST5 .... 284 B3
Shaw's La WS6 .... 227 D1
Shaw-wall La
  Cotton ST10 .... 62 C4
  Ipstones ST10 .... 62 C4
Shawbury Gr WV6 .... 254 C3
Shawe Park Rd ST10 .... 76 C4
Shawmains La ST18 .... 172 C4
Shawms Crest ST17 .... 175 E4
Shawport Ave ST5 .... 56 A4
Shaws La ST21 .... 133 E3
Shay La Forton TF10 .... 150 A2
  Ipstones ST10 .... 62 B3
  Norbury TF10 .... 150 A2
  Woodseaves TF10 .... 150 A2
Shayler Gr WV2 .... 266 B4
Sheaf Pas ST3 .... 283 C3
Sheaf St ST1 .... 282 A1
Shearer St ST1 .... 282 A1
Shebdon Cl ST16 .... 155 D3
Sheep Fair WS15 .... 178 C1
Sheep Market ST13 .... 30 C3
Sheepcote La B77 .... 250 C2
Sheepwalks La
  Enville DY7 .... 277 D4
  Kinver DY7 .... 277 D4
Sheepwash La
  Cookley DY7 .... 277 D1
  Kinver DY7 .... 277 D1
Sheffield St DE14 .... 166 B1
Shefford Rd ST5 .... 70 C2
Shelburne St ST4 .... 72 A3
Sheldon Ave CW12 .... 6 A1
Sheldon Gr ST5 .... 55 F3
Sheldon Rd WV10 .... 240 A1
Sheldrake Gr ST1 .... 73 D3
Shelfield Com Sch WS4 .. 244 B1
Shelford Rd ST1 .... 41 E3
Shelley Ave DE14 .... 166 B3
Shelley Cl Armitage WS15 .. 198 A2
  Burton u T DE14 .... 166 B3
  Colwich ST18 .... 177 E4
  Kidsgrove ST7 .... 41 D4
  Sedgley DY3 .... 271 E3
  Stafford ST16 .... 156 A3
Shelley Dr Cheadle ST10 .. 76 B1
  Sutton Coldfield B74 ...... 257 F3
Shelley Rd Bucknall ST2 .. 58 A3
  Burntwood WS7 .... 212 A1
  Cannock WS11 .... 209 F3
  Tamworth B79 .... 250 A4
  Wolv WV10 .... 240 B1
Shelmore Cl ST16 .... 155 D4
Shelmore Way ST20 .... 171 E4
Shelsey Rd ST10 .... 76 C3
Shelsley St ST19 .... 193 D1
Shelton Farm Rd ST1 ...... 282 A1
Shelton New Rd ST4 .... 56 C1
Shelton Old Rd ST4 .... 72 A4
Shelton St B77 .... 261 F4
Shemilt Cres ST6 .... 42 B2
Shendon Ct ST5 .... 56 A4
Shenfield Gn ST2 .... 58 B1
Shenley Gr ST4 .... 174 B3
Shenstone Ave DY8 .... 279 E2
Shenstone Cl B74 .... 257 F3
Shenstone Ct WV3 .... 266 A3
Shenstone Dr WS9 .... 256 A4
Shenstone Lodge
  Specl Sch WS14 .... 247 D2
Shenstone Sta WS14 ...... 246 C3
Shenton St ST3 .... 283 D5
Shepherd Cl WS13 .... 214 B2
Shepherd St ST8 .... 27 E4
Shepherds Bush St ST16 .. 155 F3
Shepherds Ct TF10 .... 169 D2
Shepherds Fold WS17 ...... 175 E3
Shepherds Pool Rd B75 .. 258 C4
Shepherds Wlk WV8 .... 239 F1
Shepley Cl ST15 .... 120 B4
Shepley Gr ST3 .... 88 C4
Sheppard St ST4 .... 72 A3
Shepwell Gdns WV10 ...... 241 E4
Sheraton Cl
  Aldridge WS9 .... 256 A3
  Cannock WS12 .... 210 A4
Sheraton Grange DY8 ...... 279 F1
Sherborne Ct ST3 .... 88 C4
Sherborne Ct WV10 .... 240 C1
Sherborne Dr ST5 .... 71 D3
Sherborne Gdns WV8 ...... 239 D2
Sherborne Rd WV10 .... 240 B1
Sherbourne Ave WS12 .... 210 C2
Sherbourne Dr DE14 ...... 185 D4
Sherbrook Cl ST17 .... 176 A2
Sherbrook Rd WS11 .... 209 E1
Sherbrooke Ave B77 ...... 261 F3
Sheridan Gdns
  Himley DY3 .... 270 C3
  Longton ST3 .... 72 C1
Sheridan St ST16 .... 156 A2
Sheridan Way ST15 .... 120 B4
Sheriffs Cl WS14 .... 231 F3
Sheriffs Way ST21 .... 133 E4
Sherifoot La B75 .... 258 A2
Sheringham Covert ST16 .. 156 B2

Sheringham Dr WS15 ...... 178 A1
Sheringham Pl ST5 .... 56 B2
Sherracop La WS15 .... 160 A1
Sherrans Dell DY3 .... 266 B2
Sherratt St ST6 .... 42 B2
Sherringham Dr WV12 .... 242 B1
Shervale Cl WV4 .... 266 A3
Sherwin Rd ST6 .... 41 F2
Sherwood Ave ST17 .... 174 C4
Sherwood Cl CV9 .... 262 B1
Sherwood Dr WS11 .... 210 A2
Sherwood Rd Meir ST3 .... 89 F4
  Stourbridge DY8 .... 279 F4
Shetland St ST3 .... 72 C2
Shillingford Dr ST4 .... 88 A4
Shilton Cl ST4 .... 71 F3
Shinwell Gr ST3 .... 90 A4
Ship Pl ST6 .... 42 B1
Shipley Cl DE14 .... 185 D4
Shippy La ST18 .... 172 B4
Shipston Rd ST17 .... 156 B1
Shipton Dr ST14 .... 110 C1
Shirburn Rd ST13 .... 31 D3
Shire Oak Com Sch
  WS8 .... 245 D3
Shire Ridge WS9 .... 245 D2
Shirebrook Cl ST3 .... 88 C4
Shirehall Pl WS11 .... 210 A1
Shirelea Cl WS7 .... 229 D4
Shireoaks Dr ST17 .... 175 E3
Shireview Gdns WS3 ...... 244 A2
Shireview Rd WS3 .... 244 A2
Shirley Ave ST9 .... 59 D2
Shirley Dr ST10 .... 94 C4
Shirley Rd ST1 .... 282 B1
Shirley St Burslem ST6 .... 56 B4
  Leek ST13 .... 30 B3
Shirley Wlk B79 .... 249 E4
Shirral Dr B78 .... 260 A3
Shirrall Dr B78 .... 259 F2
Shoal Hill Cl WS11 .... 209 D1
Shobnall Cl DE14 .... 166 A2
Shobnall Ct DE14 .... 166 A2
Shobnall Cty Prim Sch
  DE13 .... 165 F2
Shobnall Rd DE14 .... 166 A2
Shobnall St DE14 .... 166 A2
Sholing Cl WV8 .... 239 F1
Shooting Butts Rd WS15 .. 196 A4
Shop La Brewood ST19 .... 223 E3
  Codsall WV8 .... 238 B1
  Perton WV6 .... 264 A4
Shops The DY6 .... 275 E2
Short Bambury St ST3 .... 73 E3
Short La Barton-u-N DE13 .. 183 E1
  Cheslyn Hay WS6 .... 226 C2
  Kingstone ST14 .... 124 B1
Short Rd WV10 .... 240 C1
Short St Brownhills WS8 .. 244 C4
  Burton u T DE15 .... 185 F4
  Cannock WS11 .... 209 F2
  Longton ST3 .... 283 D3
  Stourbridge DY8 .... 279 F3
  Uttoxeter ST14 .... 126 A4
Short Street Inf Sch
  DE15 .... 185 F4
Shortbutts La ST17 .... 231 D3
Shortlands La WS3 .... 243 F2
Shorwell Gr ST7 .... 41 F4
Shotsfield Pl ST2 .... 43 D1
Shotsfield St ST2 .... 43 D1
Shotwoodhill La DE13 .... 147 D3
Showan Ave ST5 .... 56 B2
Showell La WV4 .... 265 D2
Shraleybrook Rd ST7 ...... 54 A4
Shredicote La ST18 .... 191 D4
Shrewsbury Cl WS3 .... 242 C1
Shrewsbury Dr
  Newcastle-u-L ST5 .... 40 C1
  Weston-u-L TF11 .... 203 F3
Shrewsbury Rd
  Burton u T DE13 .... 147 F1
  Edgmond TF10 .... 168 A2
  Market Drayton TF9 ...... 112 A4
  Stafford ST17 .... 155 F1
Shrewsbury Way TF10 .... 168 C1
Shropshire Brook Rd
  WS15 .... 198 A2
Shropshire St TF9 .... 97 E1
Shrubbery Cl DY10 .... 280 A3
Shrubbery The
  Elford B79 .... 216 C1
  Rugeley WS15 .... 197 D3
Shruggs La ST18 .... 121 F1
Shugborough Cotts
  ST18 .... 177 E4
Shugborough Dr DY1 ...... 271 F1
Shugborough Farm Mus
  ST18 .... 177 D4
Shugborough House
  & Gardens ST18 .... 158 A1
Shugborough Rd WS15 .... 178 B2
Shugborough Way
  WS11 .... 210 B1
Shugborough Cl ST9 .... 59 D2
Shuker's Cl TF10 .... 169 D1
Shut La ST14 .... 116 A3
Shutt Green La ST19 ...... 223 D3
Shuttington Rd B79 .... 251 D3
Sich La DE13 .... 182 B2
Sidcot Pl ST1 .... 57 E4
Siddals St DE14 .... 167 D2
Siddons Cl WS13 .... 213 F1
Sideway ST4 .... 72 A3
Sidings Pl ST3, ST4 .... 283 B4
Sidings Rd ST15 .... 104 C1

Sidings The
  Cannock WS12 .... 210 B4
  Cheadle ST10 .... 76 B1
Sidmouth Ave
  Newcastle-u-L ST5 .... 284 C3
  Stafford ST17 .... 156 B1
Sidney Ave ST17 .... 174 C4
Sidney Dr ST10 .... 62 A1
Sidney St WV2 .... 266 B4
Sidon Hill Way WS11 ...... 210 B1
Siemens Rd ST17 .... 155 F1
Signal Gr WS3 .... 243 D1
Signal Wlk B77 .... 251 D1
Silica Rd B77 .... 251 D1
Silk Mill La DE13 .... 146 B3
Silk St ST13 .... 30 C3
Silkmore Cres ST17 .... 175 D4
Silkmore La ST17 .... 175 D4
Silkmore Prim Sch ST17 .. 174 C4
Sill Gn B79 .... 234 B1
Sillitoe Pl ST4 .... 72 A3
Silsden Gr ST3 .... 74 B1
Silva Ave DY6 .... 275 F2
Silver Birch Coppice
  B74 .... 257 E4
Silver Birch Dr
  Kinver DY7 .... 277 F3
  Uttoxeter ST14 .... 126 A3
Silver Birch Rd
  Aldridge B74 .... 256 C1
  Huntington WS12 .... 209 E4
  Norton Canes WS11 ...... 228 A3
  Wolv WV2 .... 266 C4
Silver Cl ST8 .... 27 E4
Silver Ct WS8 .... 244 C4
Silver Ct Gdns WS8 .... 244 C4
Silver Fir Cl WS12 .... 210 A4
Silver La ST14 .... 127 F1
Silver Link Rd B77 .... 250 C1
Silver Ridge ST12 .... 104 B4
Silver St Brownhills WS8 .. 244 C4
  Cheadle ST10 .... 76 C3
  Norton-in-M ST6 .... 42 C2
  Tamworth B79 .... 250 A3
  Uttoxeter ST14 .... 126 A4
Silverdale TF10 .... 168 A2
Silverdale Cl TF10 .... 168 C1
Silverdale Gdns DY8 ...... 275 E2
Silverdale Prim Sch ST5 .. 55 E1
Silverdale Rd ST5 .... 55 F1
Silverdale St ST5 .... 55 F2
Silvergate Ct CW12 .... 15 F4
Silverhill Cl DE13 .... 166 B4
Silvermine Ct ST7 .... 26 A1
Silverster St ST6 .... 57 D4
Silverstone Ave ST10 ...... 76 C2
Silverstone Cres ST7 ...... 41 F4
Silverthorn Way ST17 .... 175 E4
Silverton Cl ST5 .... 56 A4
Silverwood Ct ST6 .... 26 A1
Silvester Way ST17 .... 175 F3
Simcox St WS12 .... 210 B2
Simeon Way ST15 .... 120 B3
Simmonds Cl WS3 .... 243 E2
Simmonds Rd WS3 .... 243 E2
Simmonds Way WS8 ...... 245 D3
Simmons Cl B78 .... 260 A1
Simmons Rd WV11 .... 242 A1
Simon Pl ST1 .... 57 D1
Simonburn Ave ST4 .... 71 F4
Simons Rd TF9 .... 112 A4
Simpkins Cl WS9 .... 245 D2
Simpson Cl ST16 .... 155 D4
Simpson Rd WS13 .... 214 A1
Simpson St Hanley ST1 .... 282 C1
  Newcastle-u-L ST5 .... 56 A3
Sinai Cl DE13 .... 165 F2
Sion Ave ST7 .... 280 A1
Sion Hill Mid Sch DY10 .. 280 A1
Sir Graham Balfour
  High Sch ST16 .... 155 E4
Sir John Offley CE
  Prim Sch CW3 .... 68 C3
Sir Robert Peel Hospl
  B78 .... 249 E1
Sir Thomas Boughey
  High Sch ST7 .... 54 B4
Siskin Cl WS7 .... 229 E3
Siskin Pl ST3 .... 90 A4
Sitwell Gr ST3 .... 283 D4
Six Ashes Rd DY7 .... 272 B4
Six Roads End DE13 ...... 144 B2
Skeath La ST7 .... 137 E2
Skellern Ave ST6 .... 42 B2
Skellern St ST7 .... 25 E1
Skidmore Ave
  Tamworth B77 .... 261 E3
  Wolv WV4 .... 265 F4
Skipacre Ave ST6 .... 42 B1
Skipness B77 .... 250 C3
Skipton Pl WS11 .... 226 A4
Skye ST17 .... 73 F2
Skylark Cl
  Huntington WS12 .... 209 E4
  Sedgley DY5 .... 271 E4
  Uttoxeter ST14 .... 126 B3
Slab La ST20 .... 190 A1
Slack La DE6 .... 81 E4
Slacken La ST7 .... 25 E1
Slacky La WS3 .... 243 F1
Slade Ave WS7 .... 229 D4
Slade Fields ST11 .... 111 D1
Slade Gdns WV8 .... 239 D2
Slade La
  Sutton Coldfield B75 ...... 259 D2
  Tamworth B77 .... 261 E2
  Waterhouses ST13 .... 49 D3

Slade Rd Hints B75 .... 259 D2
  Sutton Coldfield B75 ...... 258 C2
  Wolv WV10 .... 240 B2
Slade View Rise WS12 .... 211 D3
Sladehollow La DE6 .... 65 E1
Sladiburn Gr Hanley ST1 .. 57 F3
  Stafford ST17 .... 175 E4
Slaney St ST5 .... 284 C1
Slang La WS15 .... 211 F3
Slapton Cl ST2 .... 57 F1
Slate La WV8 .... 238 B3
Slater St Biddulph ST8 .... 27 E4
  Burslem ST6 .... 56 C4
Sleeve The ST13 .... 30 B2
Sleigh Gr ST13 .... 30 C3
Slessor Rd ST16 .... 156 A3
Slindon Cl ST5 .... 40 B1
Sling La ST19 .... 206 A2
Slingsby B77 .... 261 E4
Slippery La ST1 .... 282 A2
Slitting Mill Rd WS15 ...... 196 A4
Sloane Way ST4 .... 73 D3
Small La ST21 .... 133 F4
Small Mdws DE13 .... 183 F1
Smallbrook La WV5 .... 270 A4
Smalley Cl WS11 .... 210 A3
Smallman St ST16 .... 155 F2
Smallridge WS13 .... 213 F1
Smallshire Way ST6 .... 279 E4
Smallthorne Prim Sch
  ST6 .... 42 B1
Smallwood Cl ST5 .... 40 B1
Smallwood Gr ST1 .... 57 F3
Smallwood Rd WV8 .... 239 F1
Smarts Ave WS14 .... 258 A4
Smedley Ct DE65 .... 148 A3
Smerston Sec Sch
  WV6 .... 255 D1
Smestow Bridge Ind Est
  WV5 .... 269 E3
Smestow La DY3 .... 269 E2
Smillie Pl WS11 .... 209 F2
Smith Child St ST6 .... 41 E2
Smith St Kingsbury CV9 .. 262 B1
  Longton ST3 .... 283 C5
Smith's Cl WS7 .... 228 B4
Smithfield 13 ST13 .... 30 C3
Smithfield Cl TF9 .... 97 E1
Smithfield Ct ST1 .... 282 B1
Smithfield Rd
  Market Drayton TF9 ...... 97 E1
  Uttoxeter ST14 .... 126 A4
  Walsall WS3 .... 243 E1
Smithfield Rise WS13 ...... 231 E4
Smithpool Rd ST4 .... 72 B3
Smiths Bldgs ST3 .... 74 A1
Smiths Pas ST3 .... 73 D3
Smithy Bank ST10 .... 78 C1
Smithy Dr WS3 .... 244 A2
Smithy La
  Barthomley CW2 .... 38 B3
  Barthomley CW2 .... 38 B4
  Biddulph ST6 .... 16 B1
  Bosley SK11 .... 7 F3
  Bradley ST18 .... 191 D4
  Cheadle ST10 .... 92 B4
  Clifton Campville B79 .... 218 C1
  Eccleshall ST21 .... 117 D1
  Hixon ST18 .... 158 B4
  Lichfield WS13 .... 214 A1
  Longdon WS15 .... 212 C4
  Longton ST3 .... 283 C3
  Sedgley DY5 .... 271 D1
  Seighford ST18 .... 154 A4
  Tamworth B77 .... 261 F4
  Weston CW2 .... 37 E3
  Whitmore ST5 .... 85 F3
  Woore TF9 .... 83 D3
Smithyfield Rd ST6 .... 42 B2
Smokies Way ST6 .... 16 B1
Smout Cres WV14 .... 266 C1
Snape Hall Cl ST5 .... 85 E3
Snape Hall Rd ST5 .... 85 E4
Snape Hollow CW2 .... 37 F2
Snape La CW2 .... 37 F2
Snape Rd WV11 .... 242 A1
Snapes La DE6 .... 81 D1
Snead Cl ST16 .... 156 B2
Sneyd Ave Leek ST13 ...... 30 C3
  Newcastle-u-L ST5 .... 70 C4
Sneyd Cl ST13 .... 45 E2
Sneyd Com Sch WS3 ...... 242 B1
Sneyd Cres ST5 .... 70 C4
Sneyd Green Prim Sch
  ST6 .... 57 E4
Sneyd Hall Rd WS3 .... 243 D1
Sneyd High Sch ST5 .... 70 C4
Sneyd Hill ST6 .... 57 D4
Sneyd Ind Est ST6 .... 57 D4
Sneyd La
  Essington WV11 .... 242 B1
  Walsall WS3 .... 242 C1
Sneyd St Hanley ST6, ST1 .. 57 E3
  Leek ST13 .... 30 C3
Sneyd Terr ST5 .... 55 D1
Sneyd Trad Est ST6 .... 57 D4
Sneydlands WS15 .... 178 C1
Snipe Cl WV10 .... 241 D1
Snow Hill Hanley ST1 ...... 282 A1
  Stafford ST16 .... 155 F2
Snowberry Dr DY5 .... 271 E1
Snowdon Way WV3 .... 74 A1
Snowdon Rd
  Cannock WS11 .... 209 F3
  Pattingham WV6 .... 252 A3
Snowdon Rise DY3 .... 271 E3
Snowdon Way WV12 ...... 242 A1

Snows Yd ST16 .... 155 E2
Snowshill Gdns DY1 .... 271 F2
Soames Cres ST4 .... 73 E3
Solent Cl WV9 .... 239 F1
Solney Cl DE11 .... 186 C2
Solway Gr ST3 .... 73 F2
Solway Gr ST3 .... 73 F2
Somerfield Cl WS4 .... 244 B1
Somerford Cl
  Brewood WV9 .... 224 A1
  Great Wyrley WS6 .... 226 C1
Somerford Rd WV10 ...... 240 C1
Somerford La ST19, WV9 .. 223 F3
Somerley Rd ST1 .... 57 F3
Somerset Ave
  Kidsgrove ST7 .... 25 F1
  Rugeley WS15 .... 196 B3
Somerset Cl B78 .... 250 A1
Somerset Dr DY8 .... 279 E4
Somerset Pl WS11 .... 209 F2
Somerset Rd
  Burton u T DE15 .... 185 E3
  Hanley ST1 .... 57 F2
  Stafford ST17 .... 174 B4
Somerton Rd ST9 .... 59 D2
Somerton Way ST3 .... 283 D5
Somervale ST17 .... 175 E3
Somerville Ave ST5 .... 56 B2
Somerville Rd DE13 .... 201 D1
Somerville Sq ST17 .... 174 C3
Sonning Dr WV9 .... 239 F1
Sopwith Cl ST15 .... 118 C3
Sorbus B77 .... 251 D2
Sorrel B77 .... 251 D3
Sorrel Ave ST10 .... 92 C2
Sorrel Cl Bucknall ST2 .... 58 A2
  Featherstone WV10 ...... 241 D4
  Uttoxeter ST14 .... 126 A3
Sorrento Gr ST3 .... 73 F2
Souldern Way ST3 .... 73 E2
Soulthorpe Rd DY10 ...... 281 D1
South Ave DY8 .... 279 F2
South Broadway St DE14 .. 185 E4
South Cl WS11 .... 226 B4
South Cres WV10 .... 241 E3
South Dr DE11 .... 186 C3
South Gn WV4 .... 265 E3
South Hill DE13 .... 147 E2
South Moorlands L Ctr
  ST10 .... 76 C1
South Oak St DE14 .... 185 D4
South Oval DY3 .... 271 D3
South Pl ST6 .... 42 B3
South Rd Bucknall ST2 .... 58 A3
  Millmeece ST21 .... 118 B3
  Stourbridge DY8 .... 279 F2
South St
  Mount Pleasant ST7 ...... 26 A3
  Norton-in-t-M ST6 .... 42 B3
  Stafford ST16 .... 155 E2
South Staffordshire
  Bsns Pk WS11 .... 226 B2
South Terr
  Newcastle-u-L ST5 .... 56 B3
  Stoke-on-T ST4 .... 72 A3
South Uxbridge St DE14 .. 185 D4
South View Biddulph ST8 .. 27 E4
  Mayfield DE6 .... 81 E3
South View Cl
  Codsall WV8 .... 239 D1
  Featherstone WV10 ...... 241 D3
South View Rd DY3 .... 271 E4
South View Wlk ST14 ...... 95 F2
South Walls ST16 .... 155 F2
South Wlk ST4 .... 74 A1
South Wolf St ST4 .... 72 A4
South Wood St ST4 .... 85 D4
Southall Way ST2 .... 58 A1
Southampton St ST1 ...... 282 C4
Southbank St ST13 .... 30 C3
Southbank View DY6 ...... 275 F2
Southborough Cres ST6 .. 42 B2
Southbourne Pl WS11 .... 209 E1
Southbourne Rd WV10 .... 240 B2
Southern Cl DY6 .... 275 F2
Southern Cross WS14 .... 231 E4
Southern Way ST6 .... 42 B1
Southerndown Rd DY3 .... 271 D4
Southfield Gr WV3 .... 265 E4
Southfield Way WS6 .... 226 C1
Southfields Cl ST17 .... 174 B3
Southfields Rd ST17 .... 174 B3
Southgate Brewood ST19 .. 223 E4
  Cannock WS11 .... 226 A4
Southgate Ave ST4 .... 88 B3
Southgate End WS11 ...... 226 A4
Southlands Ave
  Longton ST3 .... 283 B1
  Newcastle-u-L ST5 .... 56 B3
Southlands Cl ST13 .... 30 B3
Southlands Rd CW12 ...... 16 A4
Southlowe Ave ST9 .... 59 F2
Southlowe Rd ST9 .... 59 F2
Southwark Cl WS13 .... 214 B2
Southway Ct DY6 .... 275 F2
Southwell Est ST21 .... 133 F3
Southwood Cl DY3 .... 275 F3
Sovereign Dr DY1 .... 271 F1
Sovereign La TF9 .... 100 B3
Sovereign Works DY1 ...... 271 F2
Sowdley Gn ST19 .... 205 D3
Sowdley La ST19 .... 205 D2
Spa St ST6 .... 57 E4
Spalding Pl ST2 .... 73 F4
Sparch Ave ST5 .... 56 B2

Sparch Gr ST5 56 B2
Sparch Hollow ST5 56 B2
Spark St ST4 72 A4
Spark Terr ST4 72 A4
Sparrow Cl ST18 177 E4
Sparrow St ST6 42 B1
Sparrow Terr ST5 56 A3
Sparrowbutts Gr ST7 26 B1
Sparrows End La ST19 223 E3
Speakman St ST3 283 D2
Spearhill WS14 231 F4
Spedding Rd ST4 72 C4
Spedding Way ST8 27 F4
Speechley Dr WS15 178 B1
Speedwall St ST3 73 E3
Speedwell Cl WS9 256 A3
Speedwell Gdns WV10 241 D4
Speedwell Rd ST5 40 C1
Speedy Cl WS11 209 F3
Spencer Ave Endon ST9 43 F3
Leek ST13 30 C3
Perton WV6 254 C2
Spencer Cl
Burton u T DE13 147 E1
Sedgley DY3 271 D2
Weston-u-T ST18 138 B1
Spencer Pl ST5 55 F3
Spencer Rd
Lichfield WS14 231 D3
Stoke-on-T ST4 72 B4
Spencroft Rd ST5 56 A3
Spend Hill DE6 66 C4
Spens St ST6 56 C4
Spenser Cl Stafford ST17 174 B4
Tamworth B79 250 A3
Sperry Cl ST3 90 A4
Spey Dr ST7 26 B1
Spiceal Mews ST14 126 B4
Spicer's Cl WV5 267 E4
Spills Meadow DY3 271 F3
Spindlewood Cl WS11 210 B1
Spinney Cl
Brownhills WS3 244 A1
Burntwood WS7 212 A1
Endon ST9 43 F4
Kingswinford DY8 275 E2
Norton Canes WS11 227 F3
Spinney Dr CW2 37 D3
Spinney Farm Rd WS11 226 A4
Spinney La WS7 211 F1
Spinney Rd DE14 184 C4
Spinney The
Biddulph ST8 27 E3
Keele CW3 69 D4
Lawton-gate ST7 25 F2
Little Aston B74 257 D3
Newcastle-u-L ST5 71 E1
Sedgley DY5 271 E1
Wolv WV3 255 E1
Spinneyfields ST17 175 E3
Spinning School La B79 250 A3
Spire Cl ST6 42 C2
Spires Croft WV10 225 E1
Spires The WS14 231 F3
Splash La WS12 210 B2
Spode Ave
Armitage WS15 198 B2
Hopton ST18 156 A4
Spode Cl ST10 76 B1
Spode Gr ST5 71 D2
Spode Pl WS11 210 A1
Spode St ST4 72 A3
Spout La ST2 43 E1
Spoutfield Rd ST4 56 C1
Spragg House La ST6 42 C2
Spratslade Dr ST3 283 B2
Spreadoaks Dr ST17 175 E3
Sprengers Cl ST19 193 D1
Spring Bank ST7 26 A4
Spring Cl
Brownhills WS4 244 B1
Hagley DY9 281 F2
Kinver DY7 277 F3
Swadlincote DE11 186 C1
Spring Cres ST6 43 E4
Spring Garden Rd ST3 283 B2
Spring Gdns
Forsbrook ST11 91 D4
Leek ST13 30 B3
Stone ST15 120 A3
Spring La Brownhills WS4 244 B1
Whittington WS14 232 C3
Spring Meadow WS6 226 B1
Spring Rd
Brownhills WS4 244 B1
Lichfield WS13 214 B1
Longton ST3 73 F1
Spring St Cannock WS11 226 C4
Stoke-on-T ST5 56 B1
Spring Terr Rd DE15 166 C1
Spring Vale Prim Sch
WV4 266 C2
Springbank Ave ST9 43 F3
Springcroft ST11 90 C3
Springcroft Prim Sch
ST11 90 C4
Springdale Jun & Inf Schs
WV4 265 E3
Springfarm Rd DE15 167 D1
Springfield Ashley TF9 99 E3
Blythe Bridge ST11 90 C3
Springfield Ave
Newport TF10 168 C1
Rugeley WS15 196 C4
Sedgley DY3 266 C1
Springfield Cl
Biddulph ST8 27 E4
Leek ST13 31 D3
Newcastle-u-L ST5 55 F3
Springfield Cres ST3 283 B2
Springfield Ct Leek ST13 31 D3
Stafford ST17 174 C3
Springfield Dr
Forsbrook ST11 91 D4
Leek ST13 31 D3
Stafford ST17 174 C3
Wheaton Aston ST19 205 E3
Springfield Gr DY3 266 B1
Springfield La WV10 240 B2
Springfield Prim Sch
ST4 71 F3
Springfield Rd
Biddulph ST8 27 E4
Leek ST13 31 D3
Tamworth B77 261 E4
Uttoxeter ST14 126 A4
Springfield Rise WS12 210 B3
Springfield Sch The ST13 31 D3
Springfields Cty Fst Sch
ST15 118 C3
Springfields Ind Est
TF10 168 C1
Springfields Rd
Rugeley WS15 178 B2
Stoke-on-T ST4 71 F3
Springhead Cl ST7 40 B3
Springhead Prim Sch ST7 40 B3
Springhill Ave WV4 265 E2
Springhill Cl WS4 244 B1
Springhill Gr WV4 265 E2
Springhill La WV4 265 D2
Springhill Pk WV4 265 D2
Springhill Prim Sch WS7 229 D3
Springhill Rd
Brownhills WS8 245 D4
Burntwood WS7 229 D3
Springhill Terr WS15 196 C4
Springle Styche La WS7 212 B1
Springpool ST5 70 B3
Springs Bank ST9 44 A1
Springside Pl ST3 88 C4
Springvale Prim Sch
WS11 226 C4
Springvale Rise ST16 155 E4
Springwood Dr ST15 120 B4
Springwood Rd ST5 55 E4
Sprink Bank Rd ST6 42 A3
Sprink La CW12 6 B3
Sprinkswoods La DE6 81 F3
Sprinkwood Gr ST3 74 A2
Sproston Rd ST6 41 F2
Spruce B77 251 D2
Spruce Rd WS12 195 D1
Spruce Way WV3 255 E1
Spruce Wlk WS15 178 B2
Spur Lea ST18 173 E1
Spur St ST1 282 C1
Spur Tree Ave WV3 255 D1
Square The
Aldridge WS9 256 A3
Caverswall ST11 74 C1
Codsall WV8 238 C2
Colwich ST18 158 A1
Elford B79 216 B1
Fazeley B78 261 D4
Marchington ST14 127 F1
Meir ST3 74 A1
Newcastle-u-L ST5 71 D3
Newport TF10 168 C2
Oakamoor ST10 78 A3
Pattingham WV6 253 E1
Wolv WV2 266 B4
Woore CW3 67 E1
Squiers View ST4 72 B4
Squirel's Hollow WS7 212 A1
Squires Gate WS7 229 E4
Squirrel Cl
Cannock WS12 210 B1
Huntington WS12 209 E3
Squirrel Hayes Ave ST8 27 F3
Squirrel Hayes Fst Sch
ST8 27 E4
Squirrel Wlk
Little Aston B74 257 E3
Stafford ST17 174 C2
Wolv WV4 266 A3
Squirrels The ST5 71 E2
Stable Ct DY3 271 F3
Stable La Alstonefield DE6 35 D1
Market Drayton TF9 97 D1
Shareshill WV10 225 D4
Stableford Bank ST5 86 A1
Stables The ST18 158 A1
Stacey Cl SK17 23 D1
Stackhouse Cl WS9 245 D2
Stackhouse Dr WS3 244 A2
Stackyard La TF10 168 A2
Stadium Ct ST1 57 D3
Stadmorslow La ST7 26 C2
Stafford Ave ST5 71 E3
Stafford Brook Rd WS15 195 F4
Stafford Castle ST16 155 D1
Stafford Cl Stone ST15 120 A4
Walsall WS3 243 D1
Stafford Coll ST16 155 E2
Stafford Coll
(The Oval Annexe)
ST17 155 F1
Stafford Cres
Newcastle-u-L ST5 71 E2
Whittington WS14 232 B2
Stafford Ct WV10 240 B3
Stafford Gram Sch ST18 174 B3
Stafford La
Cannock WS12 210 A3
Codsall WV8 238 C1
Hanley ST1 282 B3
Weston-u-T ST18 138 B2
Stafford North
Service Area ST15 119 E2
Stafford Rd
Brewood WV10 224 B3
Cannock WS11 209 E1
Cannock, Huntington WS12 209 E3
Eccleshall ST21 133 F3
Gnosall ST20 171 F3
Great Wyrley WS3 243 D2
Huntington WS12 209 E3
Lichfield WS13 213 F1
Newport TF10 169 D2
Stone ST15 120 A3
Uttoxeter ST14 125 F3
Walsall WS3 243 D2
Wolv WV10 240 B2
Stafford St
Brewood ST19 223 E3
Burton u T DE14 166 B3
Cannock WS12 210 C1
Eccleshall ST21 133 F4
Hanley ST1 282 B3
Market Drayton TF9 97 E1
Newcastle-u-L ST5 284 C2
Newport TF10 168 C2
Stafford ST16 155 F2
Stone ST15 120 A4
Stafford Sta ST16 155 E1
Staffordshire General
Hospl ST16 156 A2
Staffordshire General
Infmy ST16 155 E2
Staffordshire Univ
Hopton ST18 156 B3
Stoke-on-T ST4 72 B4
Stag Cl WS15 178 A1
Stag Cres WS11 228 A3
Stag Dr WS12 209 E3
Stagborough Way WS12 210 A2
Staines Ct ST15 120 B4
Staite Dr DY10 280 A3
Stakenbridge La
Blakedown DY10 281 E2
Hagley DY10 281 E2
Staley Croft WS12 209 E2
Stalling's La DY6 275 E4
Stallings La DY6 271 D1
Stallington Cl ST11 90 B2
Stallington Gdns ST11 90 C3
Stallington Hospl ST11 90 B2
Stallington Rd ST11 90 B2
Stamer St ST4 72 A3
Stamford Cres WS7 229 D4
Stamford St DY8 279 F4
Stamford Way WS9 245 E1
Stamps Cl DE15 167 E2
Standard St ST4 72 B3
Standedge B77 262 A4
Standersfoot Pl ST6 42 A3
Standhills Rd DY6 275 F3
Standing Butts Cl DE12 202 B4
Stanfield Cres ST10 76 B1
Stanfield Rd ST6 42 A1
Stanfield St 4 ST3 73 E3
Stanford Cl ST19 192 C1
Stanford Rd WV2 266 B4
Stanhope St
Burton u T DE15 167 D2
Hanley ST1 282 A1
Stanier St Fenton ST4 72 C3
Newcastle-u-L ST5 284 B3
Stanley Bank ST9 44 A3
Stanley Cl DE12 219 F4
Stanley Cres ST14 111 D1
Stanley Ct WV6 254 C2
Stanley Dr
Newcastle-u-L ST5 40 B1
Swindon DY3 269 F1
Stanley Gr
Newcastle-u-L ST5 56 B1
Norton-in-t-M ST2 43 D1
Stanley Head Outdoor
Education Ctr ST9 44 A2
Stanley Matthews Sports
Ctr ST4 72 B4
Stanley Moss La ST9 43 F3
Stanley Moss Rd ST9 43 F3
Stanley Rd Bagnall ST9 43 F2
Biddulph ST6 16 B1
Cannock WS12 210 A3
Newcastle-u-L ST5 56 C1
Stoke-on-T ST4 71 F4
Stourbridge DY8 279 F2
Wolv WV10 240 B1
Stanley St Biddulph ST8 27 E4
Burton u T DE14 166 B1
Leek ST13 30 C3
Tunstall ST6 41 F2
Walsall WS3 243 E1
Stansgate Pl ST1 282 A4
Stanshope La DE6 35 E1
Stansmore Rd ST3 74 A1
Stanton Ave DY3 271 F3
Stanton Cl ST5 55 F1
Stanton La DE6 65 F1
Stanton Prim Sch DE15 186 A3
Stanton Rd
Burton u T DE15 185 F4
Meir ST3 74 A1
Stanway Ave ST6 57 E4
Stanways La ST8 17 D1
Stapenhill Rd DE15 166 C1
Stapleford Gdns WS7 229 E3
Stapleford Gr DY8 275 F1
Stapleton Cres ST3 73 D1
Star And Garter Rd ST3 89 F4
Star Bank Cotton ST10 78 B4
Oakamoor ST10 78 B4
Star St WV3 265 F4
Starkey's La ST19 205 E4
Startley La
Longdon WS15 196 C1
Rugeley WS15 196 C1
Starwood Rd ST3 89 F4
Starwood Terr ST10 78 A3
Statfold La Alrewas, DE13 200 C2
Alrewas, Fradley WS13 215 E4
Statham St ST1 282 A2
Station App Stone ST15 104 C1
Sutton Coldfield B74 257 F3
Station Bridge Rd ST4 72 C3
Station Cl WV8 238 C2
Station Cotts ST5 85 E3
Station Cres ST6 42 B1
Station Ct TF10 169 D1
Station Dr
Armitage WS15 198 A2
Blakedown DY10 281 E1
Keele ST5 69 E4
Penkridge WV10 224 B3
Station Gr ST2 43 D1
Station La DE12 184 B1
Station Rd
Albrighton WV7 237 D3
Aldridge WS9 256 A3
Alton ST10 78 C1
Astbury ST7 15 D1
Audley ST7 54 B4
Barlaston ST12 88 B1
Barton-u-N DE13 183 F1
Biddulph ST6 16 B1
Brownhills WS3 244 A2
Burntwood WS7 229 F2
Cannock WS12 210 B3
Cheadle ST10 76 B1
Chebsey ST15 118 C1
Cheddleton ST13 45 E3
Codsall WV8 238 C2
Endon ST9 43 F4
Gnosall ST20 171 E3
Great Wyrley WS6 226 C2
Haughton ST18 172 C4
Hixon ST18 139 E2
Keele ST5 69 F4
Kidsgrove ST7 25 F1
Kidsgrove, Newchapel ST7 26 C1
Lichfield WS13 231 D4
Madeley, CW3 68 C3
Madeley, Onneley CW3 68 A1
Millmeece ST15 118 B3
Mow Cop ST7 26 B4
Newcastle-u-L ST5 55 D1
Newport TF10 168 C1
Penkridge ST19 192 C1
Penkridge, Four Ashes ST19 224 B3
Rolleston DE13 147 E2
Rugeley WS15 178 C1
Scholar Green ST7 26 A4
Shenstone WS14 246 C3
Stafford ST16 155 E1
Stoke-on-T ST4 72 A4
Stone ST15 104 C1
Uttoxeter ST14 126 B4
Wombourne WV5 270 A4
Station St Burslem ST6 56 B4
Burton u T DE14 166 B2
Cheslyn Hay WS6 226 C2
Leek ST13 30 B3
Station View ST3 74 A1
Station Wlks ST7 54 B4
Staunton Rd WS3 243 D2
Staveley Cl ST2 58 A2
Staveley Pl ST5 55 D1
Steadman Cres ST17 174 C3
Stedman St ST1 282 C4
Steel St ST4 71 F4
Steele Ave ST6 42 A1
Steele Cl ST13 45 E3
Steelhouse La WV2 266 C4
Steenwood La WS15 160 A1
Steere Ave B79 250 B4
Stellar St ST6 42 B1
Stenbury Cl WV10 240 C2
Step Row 6 ST13 30 C3
Stephen Ave ST10 61 E1
Stephens Rd DE14 185 D4
Stephens Way ST7 39 F1
Stephens Wlk WS13 214 A1
Stephenson Cl B77 251 D1
Sterndale Dr Fenton ST4 73 D3
Newcastle-u-L ST5 71 D2
Sterndale Moor SK17 5 F3
Sterrymere Gdns DY7 278 A2
Stevens Dr WS12 210 B3
Stevens Gate 8 WV2 266 B4
Stevenson Dr ST17 174 B4
Stevenson Rd
Bucknall ST2 58 A2
Doveridge DE6 127 D4
Tamworth B79 250 A3
Stevenson Wlk WS14 231 D3
Steventon Pl ST6 56 C4
Stewart Cl DE14 185 D3
Stewart Ct ST2 58 B1
Stewart Rd
Brownhills WS9 245 D2
Kingswinford DY6 275 E2
Stewart St Fenton ST4 72 B3
Wolv WV2 266 B4
Stewkins DY8 279 F4
Stickley La DY3 271 E2
Stile Cl Biddulph ST8 27 D3
Rugeley WS15 196 C3
Stile Cop Rd WS15 196 B2
Stile House La ST13 31 F3
Stirling Cl ST2 73 F4
Stirling Pl WS11 226 A4
Stirling Rise DE13 166 B4
Stirling St 8 ST6 57 D4
Stitchings The DE6 65 E1
Stock La ST14 143 D4
Stockbridge Cl WV6 254 C1
Stockfield Rd ST3 89 F4
Stockford La WS13 216 A2
Stockhay La WS7 229 E3
Stockholm Gr ST1 57 F4
Stocking La ST18 153 D3
Stocking-gate La ST18 153 F1
Stockings La Longdon WS15 197 E1
Wheaton Aston ST19 205 E3
Stocks La ST14 125 E4
Stockton La ST17 175 F4
Stockwell End WV6 255 E3
Stockwell Gr ST3 73 E2
Stockwell Rd WV6 255 E3
Stockwell St ST13 30 C3
Stockwood Rd ST5 71 D2
Stoke Rd Hanley ST4 57 D1
Stoke-on-T ST1 57 D1
Stoke Recn Ctr ST4 72 A3
Stoke Ski Ctr ST6 56 C3
Stoke's La WS11 227 F4
Stoke-on-Trent Coll ST1 57 D1
Stoke-on-Trent Sixth Form
Coll ST4 72 B4
Stoke-on-Trent Sta ST4 72 A4
Stokesay Ave WV6 254 C2
Stokesay Gr ST6 57 D4
Stone Bank Rd ST7 41 D4
Stone Bsns Pk ST15 120 A2
Stone Chair La ST7 25 F4
Stone Cross ST19 192 C1
Stone Ent Ctr ST15 120 B3
Stone La DY7 278 A2
Stone Pine Cl WS12 209 F4
Stone Rd Chebsey ST21 134 A4
Eccleshall ST21 133 F4
Stafford ST16 155 E3
Stoke-on-T ST4 71 F1
Tittensor ST12 88 A1
Trentham ST4 87 F4
Uttoxeter ST14 126 A4
Stone St ST4 72 A4
Stone Station ST15 104 C1
Stoneacre Cl WV3 255 D1
Stonefield Sq ST15 105 D1
Stonehaven B77 250 C3
Stonehaven Gr ST1 282 C1
Stonehill Wlk B77 261 F3
Stonehouse Cres ST9 59 D2
Stonehouse Dr B74 257 E2
Stonehouse Rd
Caverswall ST9 59 D2
Rugeley WS15 178 A1
Stonelea WS9 256 A3
Stoneleigh Ct ST18 174 B3
Stoneleigh Gdns WV8 238 C2
Stoneleigh Rd ST6 42 A3
Stoneleigh Way DY3 271 E3
Stonepine Cl ST17 175 E4
Stonepit B77 250 B1
Stonewall Pl ST5 55 E1
Stonewell La SK17 24 B3
Stonewood Cl ST4 71 F2
Stoney Brook Leys WV5 269 F3
Stoney Croft WS11 209 F1
Stoney Dale ST10 77 F2
Stoney La Endon ST9 43 F4
Hagley DY9 281 F2
Walsall WS3 243 E2
Waterhouses ST13 63 E3
Wheaton Aston ST19 206 B2
Wolv WV4 266 A3
Stoney Lea Rd WS11 209 F1
Stoneycroft ST2 43 D1
Stoneydale Cl DE11 186 C3
Stoneyfields ST8 28 A4
Stoneyfields Ave ST2 43 D1
Stoneyfields Cl WS11 209 F1
Stoneyfields Ct ST5 284 D4
Stoneyford Terr ST14 126 B3
Stoneywell La WS15 213 D3
Stonier Dr ST14 141 E4
Stonnall Gate WS9 256 B4
Stonnall Rd WS9 256 B4
Stonor Rd ST6 57 D3
Stony La ST10 49 E1
Stonydelph Jun & Inf Schs
B77 251 D1
Stonydelph La B77 262 A4
Stonyford La Colton WS15 179 F2
Hill Ridware WS15 179 F2
Stormont Cl ST6 42 B1
Stour B77 262 A3
Stour Cl WS7 229 E3
Stourbridge Coll DY8 279 F3
Stourbridge Rd
Blakedown DY9 281 F1
Cookley DY10 280 B1
Himley WV5, DY3 270 A3
Kidderminster DY10 280 B1
Wombourne WV5, DY3 270 A3
Stourton Cres DY7 278 C4
Stouton Dr WV4 265 E3
Stowe Hill Gdns WS13 214 B1
Stowe La ST18 139 E1
Stowe Rd WS13 231 E4
Stowe St WS13 231 E4
Stowecroft WS13 214 B1

Stowford Gr ST4 .... 88 A4
Stradbroke Dr ST3 .... 73 D1
Straight Mile WV10 .... 225 D3
Straits Gn DY3 .... 271 D2
Straits Prim Sch DY3 .... 271 D3
Straits Cl DY3 .... 271 D2
Straits The DY3 .... 271 D2
Strand Cl ST2 .... 58 A1
Strand Pas ST3 .... 283 B4
Strand The ST3 .... 283 B3
Strangman St ST13 .... 30 C3
Stranraer Cl ST3 .... 74 A2
Stratford Ave ST5 .... 56 C2
Stratford Cl
  Forsbrook ST11 .... 91 D4
  Norton-in-t-M ST6 .... 42 C1
  Sedgley DY1 .... 271 F1
Stratford Dr WS9 .... 256 B4
Stratford Way WS11 .... 209 F3
Stratheden Rd ST6 .... 42 A1
Strathfield Wlk WV4 .... 265 E3
Strathmore Cres WV5 .... 265 D1
Strathmore Pl WS11 .... 209 F1
Strawmoor La WV8 .... 238 B2
Stream Meadow WS4 .... 244 B1
Stream Pk DY6 .... 275 F2
Stream Rd DY6, DY8 .... 275 E2
Streamside Cl ST19 .... 207 F4
Streather Rd B75 .... 258 B1
Street The ST20 .... 150 C3
Streetly Cres B74 .... 257 E2
Streetly Dr B74 .... 257 E2
Streetly La B74 .... 257 E1
Streetly Wood B74 .... 257 D1
Streets Corner Gdns
  WS9 .... 245 D2
Streets La WS6 .... 226 C1
Streetway Rd WS14 .... 247 D4
Stretton Ave
  Newport TF10 .... 168 C1
  Stafford ST16 .... 155 D3
Stretton Gdns WV8 .... 238 C2
Stretton Rd
  Newcastle-u-L ST5 .... 54 C1
  Walsall WV12 .... 242 B1
  Wheaton Aston ST19 .... 206 A3
Stretton St B77 .... 250 C2
Strine Way TF10 .... 168 C2
Stringer Cl B75 .... 258 A2
Stringer's St ST8 .... 27 E4
Stringers Hill WS12 .... 210 B4
Strode Rd WV2 .... 266 B3
Stroma Cl **15** ST6 .... 56 C4
Stross Ave ST6 .... 41 F3
Stroud Cl ST3 .... 90 A4
Stuart Ave
  Draycott in t M ST11 .... 91 E4
  Trentham ST4 .... 88 A4
Stuart Cl ST15 .... 119 F3
Stuart Cl N ST15 .... 119 F3
Stuart Gr ST5 .... 56 B2
Stuart Rd ST1 .... 57 F1
Stubbers Green Rd
  Aldridge WS9 .... 256 A4
  Brownhills WS4 .... 244 B1
Stubbs Dr ST15 .... 120 B4
Stubbs' Gate ST5 .... 284 C2
Stubbs La ST1 .... 282 C2
Stubbs Rd WV3 .... 266 A3
Stubbs St ST6 .... 56 C4
Stubbs' St ST5 .... 284 C2
Stubbsfield Rd ST5 .... 284 C1
Stubby La DE6 .... 144 A3
Stubwood Hollow ST14 .... 95 E3
Stud Farm Cotts B78 .... 249 F1
Studley Gate DY8 .... 279 E3
Studley Rd WV3 .... 265 E4
Sturgeon's Hill WS14 .... 231 E4
Sturgess St ST4 .... 72 A4
Stychbrook Gdns WS13 .... 214 A1
Stychfields ST17 .... 155 F1
Suckling Green La WV8 .... 238 C1
Sudbourne Cl ST7 .... 41 F4
Sudbury Hall & Mus DE6 .... 128 B3
Sudbury Pk DE6 .... 128 B4
Sudbury Pl ST5 .... 71 D1
Sudbury Prim Sch DE6 .... 128 C2
Sudbury Rd DE13 .... 182 A2
Sudeley B77 .... 261 E4
Sudgrove Pl ST3 .... 90 A4
Sudlow St ST6 .... 57 D4
Suffolk Cl ST5 .... 71 E2
Suffolk Gr WS9 .... 256 A4
Suffolk Rd DE15 .... 185 E4
Sugar Loaf La
  Blakedown DY10 .... 281 D4
  Kinver DY10 .... 281 D4
Sullivan Way WS13 .... 214 B1
Sullivan Wlk WS13 .... 214 B1
Sumbeam Dr WS6 .... 226 C2
Summer Dr DY3 .... 271 E2
Summer Gr WS13 .... 214 B1
Summer Hill DY6 .... 275 E3
Summer La
  Brownhills WS4 .... 244 B1
  Sedgley DY3 .... 271 E2
Summer Row ST3 .... 283 C2
Summer St
  Kingswinford DY6 .... 275 E3
  Stoke-on-T ST4 .... 72 A3
  Stourbridge DY8 .... 279 F3
Summerbank Central Prim
  Sch ST6 .... 41 E2
Summerbank Rd ST6 .... 41 E2
Summercourt Dr DY6 .... 275 E3
Summercourt Sq DY6 .... 275 E3
Summerfield ST7 .... 26 A1
Summerfield Ave DY6 .... 275 E4

Summerfield Dr ST14 .... 126 A4
Summerfield Rd
  Burntwood WS7 .... 229 D3
  Tamworth B77 .... 250 B2
Summerfields ST15 .... 118 C3
Summergate DY3 .... 271 E2
Summerhill Dr ST5 .... 40 B1
Summerhill Gdns TF9 .... 112 B4
Summerhill La ST18 .... 135 F3
Summerhill Sch ST5 .... 275 D3
Summerhouse Gr TF10 .... 168 C2
Summerside Ave WS12 .... 211 E2
Summervale Rd DY9 .... 281 F3
Summerville Rd ST4 .... 71 F2
Summit Pl DY3 .... 271 D1
Sun St Cheadle ST10 .... 76 C2
  Hanley ST1 .... 282 A2
Sunbeam B77 .... 250 B2
Sunbeam St WV2 .... 266 B4
Sunbury Ave WS14 .... 231 F4
Sunbury Cl ST4 .... 88 B3
Sundorne Pl ST2 .... 58 A1
Sundour Cres WV11 .... 241 D1
Sundown Dr ST17 .... 174 A4
Sundridge Wlk WV4 .... 265 E3
Sunfield Rd WS11 .... 209 D1
Suningdale Cl DE13 .... 147 E1
Sunley Dr WS12 .... 210 B4
Sunningdale Stone ST15 .... 120 A4
  Tamworth B77 .... 251 E3
Sunningdale Ave WV6 .... 254 B3
Sunningdale Cl
  Chell Heath ST6 .... 42 A2
  Stourbridge DY8 .... 279 F1
Sunningdale Dr ST16 .... 156 B2
Sunningdale Gr ST5 .... 55 E4
Sunningdale Rd DY3 .... 266 A1
Sunningdale Way WS3 .... 243 D2
Sunny Bank ST6 .... 56 C3
Sunny Hill Cl WV5 .... 270 A3
Sunny Hollow ST5 .... 56 B2
Sunny Side ST10 .... 61 E3
Sunnybank Cl B74 .... 256 C1
Sunnycroft Ave ST3 .... 283 A1
Sunnyfield Oval ST3 .... 43 E1
Sunnyhills Rd ST13 .... 30 B2
Sunnymead Rd WS7 .... 212 A1
Sunnymeade Rd DY6 .... 275 F2
Sunnyside
  Brownhills WS9 .... 245 D1
  Swadlincote DE11 .... 186 C4
Sunnyside Ave ST6 .... 41 F2
Sunnyside Rd ST14 .... 111 D1
Sunridge Ave WV5 .... 270 A4
Sunridge Cl ST2 .... 43 D1
Sunrise Hill WS12 .... 210 A3
Sunset Cl Brewood WV9 .... 224 A2
  Great Wyrley WS6 .... 226 C2
  Tamworth B79 .... 250 A3
Sunset Pl WV4 .... 266 C2
Surrey Cl
  Cannock WS11 .... 226 C4
  Rugeley WS15 .... 196 B3
Surrey Dr
  Kingswinford DY6 .... 275 F2
  Tamworth B78 .... 250 A1
  Wolv WV3 .... 255 F1
Surrey Cl Kidsgrove ST7 .... 26 A1
  Stafford ST17 .... 174 B4
Surrey Wlk WS9 .... 245 D1
Surtees Gr ST4 .... 73 D3
Sussex Ave WS9 .... 256 A4
Sussex Dr
  Cannock WS12 .... 210 A3
  Kidsgrove ST7 .... 25 F1
  Wolv WV3 .... 255 F1
Sussex Rd DE15 .... 185 F3
Sutherland Ave
  Longton ST3 .... 283 B1
  Wolv WV1 .... 266 C4
Sutherland Cres ST11 .... 90 C3
Sutherland Dr
  Newcastle-u-L ST5 .... 70 C3
  Wombourne WV5 .... 265 D1
Sutherland Gr WV6 .... 254 C2
Sutherland Prim Sch ST3 .... 72 C1
Sutherland Rd
  Cheslyn Hay WS6 .... 226 C1
  Longsdon ST9 .... 30 A1
  Longton ST3 .... 283 C1
  Stone ST15 .... 120 B4
  Tittensor ST12 .... 88 A1
  Wolv WV4 .... 266 A3
Sutherland St ST4 .... 72 B3
Sutton Ave B78 .... 250 A1
Sutton Cl WS15 .... 196 C3
Sutton Ct DY3 .... 266 C1
Sutton Dr Stafford ST16 .... 155 D2
  Stoke-on-T ST4 .... 71 F2
Sutton Pl ST6 .... 42 A2
Sutton Rd Aldridge WS9 .... 256 A1
  Drayton Bassett B78 .... 260 A4
  Fazeley B78 .... 249 E1
  Hints B78 .... 259 F3
Sutton St Brierley Hill DY8 .... 275 F1
  Newcastle-u-L ST5 .... 55 F3
Sutton Way TF9 .... 112 A4
Swadlincote La DE11 .... 186 C4
Swaffham Way ST2 .... 58 B1
Swainsfield Rd DE13 .... 182 A1
Swainsley Cl **12** ST6 .... 57 D4
Swaledale Ave CW12 .... 6 A3
Swallow Cl
  Huntington WS12 .... 209 E4
  Kidsgrove ST7 .... 26 A1
  Meir ST3 .... 90 A4
  Rugeley WS15 .... 178 B1
  Uttoxeter ST14 .... 126 A3

Swallow Croft Leek ST13 .... 30 B2
  Lichfield WS13 .... 214 A1
Swallow Wlk ST8 .... 27 E4
Swallowdale
  Brownhills WS9 .... 245 D2
  Stafford ST17 .... 175 E3
  Wolv WV6 .... 254 C1
Swallowfall Ave DY8 .... 279 E2
Swallowfield B79 .... 249 F3
Swallowfields Dr WS12 .... 210 A2
Swallowfields Rd DY3 .... 266 B1
Swallows Cl WS3 .... 244 A3
Swan Bank Kidsgrove ST7 .... 40 B4
  Wolv WV4 .... 265 F2
Swan Cl Blakedown DY10 .... 281 D1
  Cheslyn Hay WS6 .... 226 B1
  Kidsgrove ST7 .... 40 B4
  Longdon WS15 .... 197 F1
  Rugeley WS15 .... 197 D3
  Stafford ST17 .... 155 E1
Swan Corner Sh Ctr
  WS7 .... 229 D3
Swan Cotts WS14 .... 232 C3
Swan Farm La CW3 .... 67 D1
Swan La
  Abbots Bromley WS15 .... 161 D3
  Brierley Hill DY8 .... 275 F1
  Kingswinford DY8 .... 275 F1
  Penkridge ST18 .... 192 C3
  Shareshill WV10 .... 225 E1
  Stoke-on-T ST4 .... 71 F2
Swan Mews WS13 .... 231 D4
Swan Pas ST11 .... 90 C4
Swan Pool Gr WS4 .... 244 B1
Swan Rd
  Draycott in t C DE6 .... 144 B3
  Lichfield WS13 .... 231 D4
  Whittington WS14 .... 232 C3
Swan Sq ST6 .... 56 C4
Swan St Stoke-on-T ST4 .... 72 A4
  Stourbridge DY8 .... 279 F3
Swan Wlk DE14 .... 166 B1
Swanage Cl ST3 .... 90 A4
Swancote Dr WV4 .... 265 E3
Swanfield Rd DY8 .... 275 F1
Swanfields WS7 .... 229 D3
Swanholme Way ST5 .... 85 E2
Swanland Gr ST3 .... 73 E2
Swanmere TF10 .... 168 C3
Swanmore Cl WV3 .... 265 F4
Swanmote B79 .... 249 F3
Swannington St DE13 .... 166 A3
Swanton Pl ST4 .... 87 F4
Swarbourn Cl DE13 .... 182 A1
Swaythling Gr ST2 .... 58 B1
Sweetbriar Way ST17 .... 175 E1
Sweetbrier Dr **3** ST5 .... 275 F1
Sweetman St WV6 .... 255 F4
Sweetplace La ST20 .... 189 F1
Sweetpool La DY8 .... 281 F3
Swift B77 .... 250 C2
Swift Cl WS7 .... 26 A1
Swift Pl ST3 .... 73 F3
Swin Forge Way DY3 .... 269 F1
Swinburne Cl
  Longton ST3 .... 72 C1
  Stafford ST17 .... 174 B4
Swindale B77 .... 262 A4
Swindon Dr DY6 .... 275 D4
Swinfen Broun Rd
  WS13 .... 231 D4
Swinford Leys WV5 .... 269 E3
Swingle Hill Rd ST3 .... 72 C2
Swinscoe Hill DE6 .... 66 A1
Swinson Cl ST14 .... 96 A2
Swiss Dr DY8 .... 275 F1
Swiss Lodge Dr B78 .... 260 C4
Swithin Dr ST4 .... 73 D3
Swynnerton Dr WV11 .... 241 F2
Swynnerton RC Fst Sch
  ST15 .... 103 D2
Sycamore B77 .... 261 F4
Sycamore Cl Biddulph ST6 .... 16 C1
  Blythe Bridge ST3 .... 90 A3
  Kidsgrove ST7 .... 40 C4
  Stourbridge DY8 .... 279 E1
  Uttoxeter ST14 .... 125 F4
Sycamore Cres WS15 .... 197 D3
Sycamore Dr Hixon ST18 .... 158 B4
  Wolv WV3 .... 255 E1
Sycamore Gn
  Cannock WS11 .... 209 F3
  Dudley DY1 .... 271 F3
Sycamore Gr Fenton ST3 .... 72 C2
  Newcastle-u-L ST5 .... 56 B2
Sycamore Green Prim Sch
  DY1 .... 271 F3
Sycamore Hill WS15 .... 211 F3
Sycamore La ST17 .... 174 A4
Sycamore Rd
  Burntwood WS7 .... 228 C4
  Burton u T DE15 .... 185 F3
  Cannock WS12 .... 210 C2
  Kingswinford DY6 .... 275 D1
  Mayfield DE6 .... 81 E4
  Stone ST15 .... 120 A4
Sycamore Way
  Huntington WS12 .... 209 E4
  Market Drayton TF9 .... 97 C2
Sycamores The WS14 .... 231 D3
Sydenham Pl ST3 .... 73 E4
Sydnall La TF9 .... 112 C1
Sydney St
  Burton u T DE14 .... 166 B3
  Newcastle-u-L ST5 .... 56 B1
Syerscote La
  Clifton Campville B79 .... 218 A1
  Wigginton B79 .... 234 B1

Sykesmoor B77 .... 262 A4
Sylvan Gr ST4 .... 71 F2
Sylvan Way ST17 .... 175 E3
Sytch La WV5 .... 270 A2
Sytch Rd ST6 .... 43 D4

T.P. Riley Com Sch WS3 .... 243 E1
Tack Farm Rd DY8 .... 275 E1
Tadgedale Ave TF9 .... 99 E3
Tag La TF9 .... 113 F2
Tagg La DE45 .... 14 C4
Talaton Cl WV9 .... 240 A1
Talbot B77 .... 250 C2
Talbot Ave B74 .... 257 E3
Talbot Cl TF10 .... 168 B1
Talbot Cty Fst Sch ST14 .... 141 E4
Talbot Rd Rugeley WS15 .... 196 C3
  Stafford ST17 .... 155 F1
  Wolv WV2 .... 266 B3
Talbot St Hanley ST1 .... 282 C1
  Rugeley WS15 .... 196 C4
Talbot Way TF9 .... 97 C3
Talke Rd ST5 .... 40 C1
Tall Ash Ave CW12 .... 6 A2
Tall Trees Cl B74 .... 257 E3
Talland Ave B77 .... 250 C3
Tallis Gr ST1 .... 57 F3
Tallpines ST17 .... 175 E4
Talsarn Gr ST4 .... 88 B3
Tamar Cl WS8 .... 228 B1
Tamar Dr DY3 .... 271 E3
Tamar Gr Cheadle ST10 .... 76 C1
  Perton WV6 .... 254 C2
  Stafford ST17 .... 174 A4
Tamar Rd Kidsgrove ST7 .... 26 A1
  Tamworth B77 .... 262 A3
Tame Ave WS7 .... 229 E3
Tame Cl ST6 .... 16 B1
Tame Ct B79 .... 250 A3
Tame Dr WS3 .... 244 A1
Tame Gr WS11 .... 226 B4
Tame Rd ST8 .... 250 B2
Tame Valley Ind Est B77 .... 261 E4
Tame Wlk ST3 .... 74 A2
Tamedrive B78 .... 250 A2
Tameside Prim Sch
  B79 .... 250 A3
Tamworth
  Allen End B75 .... 259 D1
  Elford B79 .... 233 F4
  Fazeley B79 .... 261 D4
  Kingsbury CV9 .... 262 B1
  Lichfield WS14 .... 231 F3
  Polesworth B78 .... 251 F1
  Sutton Coldfield B75 .... 259 D1
  Tamworth B77 .... 250 B2
  Whittington WS14 .... 232 A2
Tamworth Bsns Ctr B77 .... 251 D2
Tamworth Bsns Pk B77 .... 251 D2
Tamworth Cl WS8 .... 228 C1
Tamworth Coll of F Ed
  B79 .... 250 A3
Tamworth Rd (Amington)
  B77 .... 250 C3
Tamworth Rd (Dosthill)
  B77 .... 261 E3
Tamworth Service Area
  B77 .... 262 B3
Tamworth St WS13 .... 231 D4
Tamworth Sta B79 .... 250 B3
Tan Bank TF10 .... 168 C2
Tanfield Cl WV6 .... 255 D2
Tanglewood Gr DY3 .... 266 B1
Tangmere Cl WV6 .... 254 C3
Tanhill B77 .... 262 A4
Tanners Rd ST2 .... 58 A4
Tannery Cl WS15 .... 178 C1
Tansey Cl ST2 .... 58 A2
Tansley Green Rd DY6 .... 271 D1
Tansley View WV2 .... 266 B4
Tansy B77 .... 250 B2
Tanyard WS13 .... 231 E4
Tape St ST10 .... 76 C2
Taplin Cl ST6 .... 155 E4
Taplow Pl WS11 .... 209 F2
Tapton Cl WS3 .... 243 E2
Targate Ct WS15 .... 198 A3
Target Cl ST7 .... 40 C3
Tarleton Rd ST1 .... 57 F2
Tarporley Gr ST4 .... 71 F3
Tarragon Dr ST3 .... 90 A3
Tarrant B77 .... 261 F4
Tarvin Gr ST6 .... 41 F3
Tasman Dr ST16 .... 156 A3
Tasman Gr WV6 .... 254 C3
Tasman Sq ST1 .... 57 F3
Taurus Gr ST6 .... 41 F3
Taverners Cl WV12 .... 242 B1
Tavistock Rd ST17 .... 156 B1
Tavistock Cl B79 .... 250 B4
Tavistock Cres ST5 .... 71 D3
Tavistock Pl ST7 .... 56 C1
Tawney Cl ST7 .... 26 A1
Tawney Cres ST3 .... 74 A1
Tay Cl Biddulph ST6 .... 16 C1
  Kingsley ST10 .... 76 C3
Taylor Ave ST5 .... 56 B2

Taylor Rd Bucknall ST2 .... 58 A3
  Wolv WV4 .... 266 C3
Taylor St
  Newcastle-u-L ST5 .... 56 B2
  Tunstall ST6 .... 41 E4
Taylor Wlk ST17 .... 174 B4
Taylor's La WS15 .... 178 C1
Taynton Cl ST6 .... 42 A4
Teal Cl ST5 .... 85 E3
Tean Cl Burntwood WS7 .... 229 E3
  Burton u T DE15 .... 167 D1
Tean Rd ST10 .... 76 B1
Teanhurst Cl ST10 .... 92 C1
Teanhurst Rd ST10 .... 92 C1
Teasel Gr WV10 .... 241 D4
Tebworth Cl WV9 .... 239 F1
Tedder Rd ST16 .... 156 A3
Teddesley Ct WS11 .... 209 F2
Teddesley Rd
  Acton Trussell ST17, ST19 .... 193 D3
  Penkridge ST18 .... 192 C1
Teddesley Way WS12 .... 209 E3
Teign B77 .... 262 A3
Telegraph St ST17 .... 155 F1
Telford Ave
  Albrighton WV7 .... 237 D3
  Great Wyrley WS6 .... 226 C2
Telford Cl
  Burntwood WS7 .... 229 D4
  Congleton CW12 .... 6 A1
  Kidsgrove ST7 .... 40 C4
Telford Dr ST16 .... 155 F4
Telford Gdns
  Brewood ST19 .... 223 E4
  Wolv WV3 .... 265 E4
Telford Gr WS12 .... 210 A4
Telford La ST20 .... 171 E3
Telford Rd B79 .... 249 F4
Telford Way ST6 .... 42 A2
Tellwright Gr ST5 .... 56 A4
Tellwright St ST6 .... 42 A1
Telmah ST10 .... 147 E1
Teme Rd DY8 .... 279 F2
Temperence Pl ST6 .... 41 E4
Tempest St B79 .... 250 A3
Templar Cres ST5 .... 56 A3
Templar Terr ST5 .... 56 A3
Templars Way ST19 .... 207 F4
Temple Cl DE13 .... 166 C4
Temple St Fenton ST4 .... 72 B3
  Sedgley DY3 .... 271 E2
Templeton Ave ST17 .... 174 C4
Ten Butts Cres ST17 .... 174 C3
Tenacre La DY3 .... 271 F3
Tenbury Ct WV4 .... 265 E3
Tenbury Dr WV9 .... 256 B4
Tenbury Gdns WV4 .... 265 E3
Tenbury Gn ST2 .... 58 B1
Tenby Dr ST16 .... 155 F3
Tenby Gr ST5 .... 55 F4
Tenford La ST10 .... 92 B3
Tennant Pl ST5 .... 56 A4
Tennscore Ave WS6 .... 226 C2
Tennyson Ave
  Burntwood WS7 .... 212 A1
  Kidsgrove ST7 .... 41 D4
  Sutton Coldfield B74 .... 257 F3
  Tamworth B79 .... 250 A3
Tennyson Cl Cheadle ST10 .... 76 A1
  Market Drayton TF9 .... 112 A4
Tennyson Gdns ST3 .... 72 C1
Tennyson Rd
  Burton u T DE14 .... 166 B4
  Essington WV10 .... 241 D1
  Sedgley DY3 .... 271 D2
  Stafford ST17 .... 174 B4
Tenterbanks ST16 .... 155 E2
Tercel Br ST3 .... 90 A4
Terence Wlk ST8 .... 27 D1
Tern Ave ST7 .... 26 B1
Tern Cl Biddulph ST8 .... 27 F4
  Wolv WV3 .... 266 B2
Tern Gr TF9 .... 99 E3
Tern View TF9 .... 112 A4
Terrace The Cheadle ST10 .... 76 B2
  Wolv WV3 .... 255 E1
Terrington Dr ST5 .... 71 D1
Terry Cl Lichfield WS13 .... 213 F1
  Meir ST3 .... 74 A2
Terson Way ST3 .... 73 F2
Tettenhall Coll WV6 .... 255 E1
Tettenhall Comm DE13 .... 164 C1
Tettenhall Rd
  WV1, WV3, WV6 .... 255 F2
Tettenhall Wood Sch
  WV6 .... 255 D2
Teveray Dr ST19 .... 207 F4
Tewkesbury Gr ST2 .... 58 A2
Tewkesbury Rd WS3 .... 242 C1
Tewnals La WS13 .... 213 F3
Tewson Gn ST6 .... 57 E4
Thackeray Dr Longton ST3 .... 73 D1
  Tamworth B79 .... 250 A4
Thackeray Wlk ST17 .... 174 B4
Thames Dr Biddulph ST8 .... 27 F4
  Cheadle ST10 .... 76 C1
Thames Rd
  Newcastle-u-L ST5 .... 71 D2
  Walsall WS3 .... 243 D1
Thames Way ST17 .... 174 A4
Thanet Cl DY6 .... 275 E4
Thanet Gr ST3 .... 283 A3
Thatcham Gr ST3 .... 88 C4
Thatcher Gr ST8 .... 27 D4
Thatchmoor La DE13 .... 182 B4
Thelma Ave ST6 .... 43 D4

Theodore Rd ST2 .... 58 A2
Threaas Cl ST4 .... 72 A1
Thicknall La DY9 .... 281 F2
Third Ave Branston DE14 ... 165 F1
  Brownhills WS8 .... 229 D1
  Bucknall ST2 .... 58 B2
  Kidsgrove ST7 .... 25 F1
  Kingswinford DY6 .... 275 F4
Thirlmere Cl
  Cannock WS11 .... 209 F1
  Wolv WS11 .... 255 E4
Thirlmere Dr WV11 .... 242 A1
Thirlmere Gr Longton ST3 ... 73 F2
  Perton WV6 .... 254 C2
Thirlmere Pl ST5 .... 71 D3
Thirlmere Rd WV6 .... 255 E4
Thirlmere Way ST17 .... 174 C4
Thirsk Pl ST5 .... 55 D1
Thistle Cl WS15 .... 178 B1
Thistle Down Cl B74 .... 257 F1
Thistleberry Ave ST5 .... 70 C4
Thistledown Ave WS7 ...... 229 D3
Thistledown Dr WS11 ...... 210 B1
Thistledown Rd ST10 .... 241 D4
Thistledown Wlk DY3 ...... 266 B1
Thistles The ST5 .... 70 C4
Thistley Hough ST4 .... 71 F3
Thistley Hough High Sch
  ST4 .... 71 F3
Thistley Nook WS13 .... 214 A1
Thomas Alleynes High Sch
  ST14 .... 126 B4
Thomas Ave
  Newcastle-u-L ST5 .... 56 A2
  Stafford ST16 .... 155 D2
  Stone ST15 .... 120 B3
Thomas Barnes Cty Prim
  Sch B78 .... 249 D4
Thomas Greenway WS13 .. 214 A1
Thomas Russell Inf Sch
  DE13 .... 183 F1
Thomas Russell Jun Sch
  DE13 .... 183 F1
Thomas St Biddulph ST6 .... 16 B1
  Chell Heath ST7 .... 26 C1
  Kidsgrove ST7 .... 40 B4
  Leek ST13 .... 30 B3
  Tamworth B77 .... 250 B2
  Wolv WV2 .... 266 B4
Thompson Ave WV2 .... 266 C3
Thompson Cl ST17 .... 174 B4
Thompson Rd WS15 .... 197 D3
Thompstone Ave ST5 .... 55 F2
Thor Cl WS11 .... 210 A3
Thoresby B79 .... 249 F3
Thorn Cl WS15 .... 197 D4
Thorn Tree La
  Bretby DE15 .... 186 C4
  Swadlincote DE15 .... 186 C4
Thornburrow Dr ST4 .... 71 F4
Thornbury Ct WV6 .... 255 D2
Thornby Ave B77 .... 261 F4
Thorncliff Gr ST1 .... 57 F3
Thorncliff Rd ST13 .... 31 E4
Thorncliffe View ST13 .... 31 D4
Thorndyke St ST1 .... 282 A1
Thorne Pl ST3 .... 74 A2
Thornes Croft WS9 .... 245 F2
Thornescroft Gdns DE14 .. 185 D4
Thornewill Dr DE13 .... 147 F1
Thorney Cl WV11 .... 241 F1
Thorney Lanes ST14 .... 142 C3
Thorney Rd B74 .... 256 C1
Thorneycroft Ave ST6 .... 42 C4
Thorneyfields La ST17 ..... 174 A4
Thornfield Ave ST13 .... 31 D3
Thornfield Cres WS7 .... 229 D4
Thornfield Croft DY3 .... 271 F4
Thornham Cl ST5 .... 71 D1
Thornham Gn ST2 .... 58 B1
Thornhill Cl DE13 .... 183 E1
Thornhill Dr CW3 .... 68 C4
Thornhill Rd
  Aldridge B74 .... 257 D1
  Bucknall ST2 .... 73 F4
  Cannock WS12 .... 209 F4
  Leek ST13 .... 30 B2
  Little Aston B74 .... 257 D1
Thornleigh DY3 .... 271 E3
Thornley Dr ST10 .... 76 C1
Thornley Rd
  Chell Heath ST6 .... 42 A2
  Essington WV11 .... 241 F1
Thornley St DE14 .... 166 B3
Thornton Rd ST4 .... 72 B4
Thorny Lanes WS15 .... 143 D1
Thornyedge Rd
  Bagnall ST9 .... 44 A1
  Bagnall, Thorneyedge ST9 .. 44 B1
Thornyfields La ST17 .... 174 A4
Thornyhurst La WS14 ...... 246 A3
Thorpe Ave WS7 .... 228 B4
Thorpe Cl WS7 .... 228 B4
Thorpe Gn ST3 .... 88 C4
Thorpe Rise ST10 .... 76 C3
Thorpe St WS7 .... 228 B4
Thorswood La DE6 .... 65 D1
Three Mile La ST5 .... 69 F2
Three Spires Sh Ctr
  WS13 .... 231 D4
Three Tuns La WV10 .... 240 B1
Three Tuns Par WV10 ..... 240 B1
Thurlstone Dr WV4 .... 265 F2
Thurlstone Rd WS3 .... 243 D2
Thurlwood Dr ST6 .... 42 C1

Thurne B77 .... 261 F4
Thursfield Ave ST7 .... 26 A2
Thursfield Pl ST6 .... 42 B2
Thursfield Prim Sch ST7 ... 26 C2
Thursfield Wlk ST6 .... 42 B3
Thurso B77 .... 250 C3
Thurston Way ST2 .... 73 E4
Thurvaston Rd DE6 .... 96 C1
Thyme Gr ST3 .... 90 A3
Tibb St ST7 .... 39 F1
Tibberton Cl WV3 .... 265 E4
Tiber Dr ST5 .... 55 E3
Tickhill La ST10 .... 75 D4
Tidebrook Pl ST7 .... 41 F4
Tideswell Gn DE11 .... 186 C3
Tideswell Rd ST3 .... 283 C5
Tierney St ST1 .... 282 C4
Tiffany La WV9 .... 239 F1
Tilbrook Cl ST2 .... 73 E4
Tilbury Cl WV3 .... 265 D4
Tilcon Ave ST17 .... 156 B1
Tildesley Cl ST19 .... 207 F4
Tilehurst Pl ST3 .... 72 C1
Tilery La ST3 .... 88 B4
Tilewright Cl ST7 .... 26 A1
Tilia Rd B77 .... 251 D3
Till Wlk ST3 .... 73 E3
Tillet Gn ST3 .... 74 A2
Tilling Dr ST15 .... 120 A3
Tillington Manor Cty Prim
  Sch ST16 .... 155 E3
Tillington St ST16 .... 155 E3
Tilson Ave ST4 .... 71 F4
Tilstone Cl ST7 .... 41 D4
Timber Gr ST19 .... 223 E3
Timber La ST14 .... 126 A3
Timber Pit La ST19 .... 205 D2
Timberfields ST15 .... 118 C3
Timble Cl ST2 .... 73 E4
Times Sq ST3 .... 283 B4
Timmis St ST1 .... 57 D1
Timor Gr ST4 .... 88 A4
Timothy Cl ST3 .... 73 E3
Tinacre Hill WV6 .... 254 C1
Tinker's Castle Rd WV5 ... 263 E1
Tinker's La ST14 .... 143 D4
Tinkers Green Rd B77 ..... 262 A3
Tinkers La Ashley TF9 ..... 100 A2
  Brewood ST19 .... 223 F3
Tintagel Cl
  Burton u T DE13 .... 147 F1
  Perton WV6 .... 254 C2
Tintagel Dr DY1 .... 271 F1
Tintagel Pl ST2 .... 73 E4
Tintern Cres WS3 .... 242 C1
Tintern Ct WV6 .... 254 C2
Tintern Pl ST5 .... 55 F4
Tintern St ST1 .... 57 F2
Tintern Way WS3 .... 242 C1
Tipping Ave ST3 .... 74 A1
Tipping St ST16 .... 155 F2
Tipton Rd DY3 .... 271 F4
Tipton St DY3 .... 271 F4
Tirley St ST4 .... 72 C3
Tissington Pl ST3 .... 90 B4
Titan Way WS13 .... 231 F4
Titchfield Cl WV10 .... 240 C2
Tithe Barn Ct ST16 .... 156 A2
Tithe Barn Rd ST16 .... 156 A2
Tithebarn Rd WS15 .... 178 C1
Tittensor CE Fst Sch
  ST12 .... 88 A1
Tittensor Rd
  Barlaston ST12 .... 104 A4
  Newcastle-u-L ST5 .... 71 E3
Titterton La ST13 .... 33 D2
Titterton St ST4 .... 72 B3
Tittesworth Ave ST13 .... 31 D4
Tittesworth Est ST13 .... 20 C1
Tiverton Ave ST17 .... 175 E4
Tiverton Cl DY6 .... 275 F2
Tiverton Rd ST2 .... 73 E4
Tixall Ct ST18 .... 157 F2
Tixall Mews ST18 .... 157 E2
Tixall Rd
  Hopton ST16, ST18 .... 156 B2
  Stafford ST16, ST18 .... 156 B2
  Tixall ST18 .... 157 D1
Toby's Hill DE6 .... 144 B3
Toft End Rd ST5 .... 41 D1
Tolkien Way ST4 .... 72 A4
Toll Bar Rd ST19 .... 59 E2
Toll Gate La B79 .... 233 F2
Tolldish La ST18 .... 158 B2
Tollgate Ave ST5 .... 85 E3
Tollgate Cl ST7 .... 40 B4
Tollgate Dr ST6 .... 155 F4
Tollgate Ind Est ST16 ...... 155 F4
Tollgate Rd ST9 .... 29 E3
Tolman Dr B77 .... 250 B2
Tolson Ave B78 .... 261 D4
Tolson Cl B77 .... 261 E3
Tolworth Gdns WV2 .... 266 C4
Tom Fields ST7 .... 39 F1
Tom La DY7 .... 268 C3
Tomkin Rd Bagnall ST9 .... 44 A2
  Endon ST9 .... 44 A2
Tomlinson St ST6 .... 56 B4
Tommy's La CW12 .... 6 A2
Tonadine Cl WV11 .... 242 A1
Tonbridge Ave ST6 .... 42 A2
Toney Pl ST7 .... 57 F2
Tong Cl ST19 .... 221 F4
Tong Rd ST19 .... 221 F4
Tongue La ST7 .... 27 F1
Tontine Sq ST1 .... 282 B3
Tontine St ST1 .... 282 B3
Tontines Sh Ctr The ST1 .. 282 B3

Toothill Rd ST14 .... 126 B2
Top Chapel La ST6 .... 28 A1
Top Heath Row ST6 .... 43 D4
Top La ST14 .... 87 E1
Top Rd
  Acton Trussell ST17 .... 175 D1
  Biddulph ST8 .... 17 E2
Top Station Rd ST7 .... 26 B4
Topham Pl ST2 .... 57 F2
Tor St ST1 .... 57 E4
Tor Way WS3 .... 243 F2
Torbay B77 .... 250 C3
Torc Ave B77 .... 250 C2
Torc High Sch B77 .... 250 C1
Torfield WV8 .... 239 F1
Torrance Cl DE14 .... 185 D3
Torrance Gr ST14 .... 110 C1
Torres Wlk ST1 .... 57 F3
Torridge B77 .... 262 A3
Torridge Dr ST11 .... 174 A4
Torridon Cl ST4 .... 88 B3
Torridon Rd WV11 .... 242 A1
Torrington Ave ST17 .... 175 F4
Torside B77 .... 262 A4
Torvale Rd WV6 .... 255 D1
Torville Dr ST8 .... 27 F4
Totnes Cl ST13 .... 166 B4
Tower Cl Biddulph ST8 ...... 27 D3
  Market Drayton TF9 .... 97 D1
Tower Hill Rd ST7 .... 26 C4
Tower Rd Burton u T DE15 .. 167 D1
  Cannock WS12 .... 194 C1
  Sutton Coldfield B75 .... 258 A2
Tower Sq ST4 .... 41 E2
Tower St DY3 .... 266 B1
Tower View Prim Sch
  DE15 .... 167 E2
Tower View Rd WS6 .... 242 C4
Town End ST10 .... 76 B2
Town Head ST10 .... 78 C1
Town Hill DE13 .... 182 A1
Town Meadows Way
  ST14 .... 126 A4
Town Rd ST1 .... 282 B4
Townend Cl ST7 .... 25 E1
Townend La Swinscoe DE6 .. 65 F3
  Waterhouses ST10 .... 48 C2
Townfields ST7 .... 25 E1
Townfields WS13 .... 231 D4
Townfold WS3 .... 244 A2
Townsend Ave DY3 .... 271 E4
Townsend Cl B79 .... 236 B2
Townsend La ST7 .... 25 D4
Townsend Pl Bucknall ST2 .. 58 A2
  Kingswinford DY6 .... 275 E3
Townsend Prim Sch ST2 .... 58 B2
Toy Cl WS15 .... 178 B1
Trade St ST4 .... 72 A4
Trafalgar Cl WS12 .... 210 C2
Trafalgar Rd ST4 .... 71 F4
Trafalgar St ST1 .... 282 B4
Trafford Cl ST13 .... 31 D3
Transport La ST13 .... 283 B3
Tranter Cres WS11 .... 210 A2
Tranter Rd ST2 .... 58 A3
Tranwell Cl WV9 .... 239 F1
Travellers Cl WS7 .... 229 D3
Travers St ST6 .... 56 C4
Treasure Cl B77 .... 250 C2
Trecastle Gr ST3 .... 73 F1
Treetops ST17 .... 175 E4
Trefoil B77 .... 251 D3
Tregaron St ST9 .... 59 D2
Tregenna Cl ST3 .... 90 A4
Tregew Pl ST5 .... 55 E1
Tregony Rise WS14 .... 231 E1
Tregowan Cl ST5 .... 42 A2
Trenance Cl WS14 .... 231 E4
Trenchard Ave ST16 .... 156 A3
Trent Cl Burntwood WS7 .. 229 E3
  Cheadle ST10 .... 76 C1
  Colwich ST18 .... 158 A1
  Perton WV6 .... 254 C2
  Stafford ST17 .... 174 C3
Trent Gr Biddulph ST8 .... 27 E3
  Newcastle-u-L ST5 .... 71 D2
Trent Hospl (Geriatric)
  ST15 .... 119 F4
Trent Ind Est DE14 .... 166 C2
Trent La Colwich ST18 ..... 158 A1
  Hixon ST18 .... 157 F4
  Newton Solney DE15 .... 167 F4
Trent Rd Brownhills WS3 .. 244 A1
  Cannock WS11 .... 209 F3
  Forsbrook ST11 .... 91 D4
  Stone ST15 .... 104 C1
Trent St Bucknall ST2 .... 57 F2
  Burton u T DE14 .... 166 B1
Trent Terr
  Burton u T DE14 .... 166 C2
  Norton-in-t-M ST6 .... 43 D3
Trent Vale CE Prim Sch
  ST4 .... 71 F2
Trent Valley Cotts WS13 .. 214 C1
Trent Valley Rd
  Lichfield WS13, WS14 ..... 231 D4
  Stoke-on-T ST4 .... 71 F3
Trent Valley Trad Est
  WS15 .... 178 C2
Trent View Cl WS15 .... 197 D4
Trent Wlk Hanley ST1 ..... 282 C4
  Ingestre ST18 .... 157 F4
Trentfield La ST18 .... 137 E3
Trentfields Rd ST2 .... 43 D1
Trentham Cl WS11 .... 210 A1
Trentham Ct ST4 .... 87 F4
Trentham Gardens Cl ST4 .. 87 F4

Trentham Gr ST5 .... 56 B2
Trentham High Sch ST4 .... 87 F4
Trentham Rd Longton ST3 .. 88 C4
  Whitmore ST4, ST5 .... 86 C4
Trentham Rise WV2 .... 266 C4
Trentley Dr ST8 .... 28 A4
Trentley Rd ST4 .... 88 A4
Trentmill Rd ST1 .... 57 F1
Trentside Rd ST6 .... 43 D3
Trentway Cl ST2 .... 58 A2
Tresham Rd DY6 .... 275 D4
Trevelyan's Gn ST16 ...... 155 E4
Trevelyn Cl DE15 .... 167 E1
Trevithick Cl WS7 .... 229 E4
Trevitt Pl ST19 .... 205 E3
Trevor Ave WS6 .... 227 D2
Trevor Dr ST11 .... 74 B2
Trevor Rd WS3 .... 243 F2
Trevose Cl WS3 .... 242 C2
Trimley Way ST2 .... 58 A1
Trimpley Gdns WV4 .... 265 F2
Trimpos ST10 .... 76 A2
Triner Pl ST6 .... 42 C2
Tring Cl ST2 .... 73 E4
Tring Ct WV6 .... 255 F2
Trinity Cl Cannock WS11 .. 226 C4
  Kingswinford DY8 .... 275 E1
  Shenstone WS14 .... 246 C3
Trinity Ct ST5 .... 55 F4
Trinity Gorse ST16 .... 155 E4
Trinity Pl Bucknall ST2 ...... 58 A2
  Congleton CW12 .... 16 A4
Trinity Rd Eccleshall ST21 .. 133 E3
  Sutton Coldfield B75 .... 258 B1
  Uttoxeter ST14 .... 126 B4
Trinity Rise ST16 .... 155 D4
Trinity Sq ST14 .... 126 B4
Trinity St ST1 .... 282 B3
Trinity Wlk ST14 .... 126 B4
Tristram Gr DE13 .... 147 F1
Triton Cl WS6 .... 226 C1
Triton Wlk ST6 .... 42 B1
Triumph B77 .... 250 C2
Trojan B77 .... 250 C2
Troon B77 .... 251 E2
Troon Cl Burton u T DE13 .. 147 E1
  Walsall WS3 .... 243 D2
Troon Ct WV6 .... 254 B3
Troon Pl DY8 .... 275 E2
Troutdale Cl ST4 .... 73 D3
Trowbridge Cres ST2 .... 58 B2
Trubshaw Cl ST18 .... 177 F4
Trubshaw Cross ST6 .... 56 B4
Trubshaw Ct ST7 .... 26 B2
Trubshaw Pl ST7 .... 26 A2
Trubshaw St ST6 .... 56 B4
Truro Cl Congleton CW12 .. 15 F4
  Lichfield WS13 .... 214 A2
Truro Pl Bucknall ST2 .... 58 A1
  Cannock WS11 .... 227 E4
Trussell Cl ST17 .... 175 D1
Trustley Cl ST4 .... 185 D4
Trysull Gdns WV3 .... 265 E4
Trysull Holloway WV5 .... 264 B2
Trysull Rd Wolv WV3 ...... 265 E4
  Wombourne WV5 .... 269 F4
Tudor Cl Burntwood WS7 .. 229 D3
  Cheslyn Hay WS6 .... 226 C2
  Lichfield WS14 .... 231 F3
  Newport TF10 .... 169 D2
  Stoke-on-T ST4 .... 72 A3
  Stone ST15 .... 119 C3
Tudor Cres
  Tamworth B77 .... 250 C2
  Wolv WV2 .... 266 A3
Tudor Ct Essington WV11 .. 241 F2
  Newcastle-u-L ST5 .... 56 A3
Tudor Gdns DY8 .... 279 F3
Tudor Gr ST5 .... 56 B2
Tudor Hollow
  Blythe Bridge ST11 .... 90 C1
  Burton u T DE13 .... 166 B4
Tudor Pl DY3 .... 271 F3
Tudor Rd Burntwood WS7 .. 229 E3
  Cannock WS12 .... 209 F4
  Dudley DY3 .... 271 F3
Tudor Rise
  Clifton Campville B79 ..... 218 C1
  Stafford ST16 .... 155 E4
Tudor Vale DY3 .... 271 F3
Tudor Way
  Cheslyn Hay WS6 .... 226 B1
  Stafford ST17 .... 155 D1
Tudors The ST6 .... 41 F2
Tulip Gr ST5 .... 284 C4
Tulley Pl ST2 .... 58 A2
Tullis St ST16 .... 155 E1
Tulsa Cl ST2 .... 58 A1
Tunbridge Dr ST5 .... 54 C1
Tunley St ST15 .... 104 C1
Tunnicliffe Cl ST3 .... 73 F2
Tunnicliffe Dr WS15 .... 178 B1
Tunnicliffe Way ST14 ...... 110 C1
Tunstall La ST20 .... 131 F1
Tunstall Rd Biddulph ST8 ... 27 E3
  Bosley SK11 .... 7 E4
  Congleton CW12 .... 6 C1
  Woodhouse Green
  SK11, CW12 .... 7 E4
Tunstall Road Ind Est
  ST8 .... 27 D2
Tuppenhurst La
  Armitage WS15 .... 198 B2
  King's Bromley WS15 ..... 198 B2
Turf Cotts WV5 .... 265 F1
Turf Pitts La B75 .... 258 C2
Turin Dr ST5 .... 70 C3
Turls Hill Rd DY3 .... 271 F4

Turls St DY3 .... 271 F4
Turnberry B77 .... 251 E3
Turnberry Dr ST4 .... 88 A4
Turnberry Gr WV6 .... 254 B3
Turnberry Rd WS3 .... 243 D2
Turnbury Cl DE14 .... 185 D4
Turner Ave Audley ST7 .... 40 A1
  Wolv WV4 .... 266 C1
Turner Cl WS11 .... 210 B1
Turner Cres ST5 .... 55 F3
Turner Croft WS13 .... 215 E4
Turner Gr WV6 .... 255 D2
Turner St Hanley ST1 .... 57 F3
  Sedgley DY3 .... 271 E2
Turner's Gr DY3 .... 271 E2
Turner's Hill Rd DY3 ...... 271 E2
Turners La TF10 .... 168 A2
Turney Gr ST17 .... 174 B4
Turney Rd DY8 .... 279 F3
Turnham Gn WV6 .... 254 C2
Turnhill Cl ST17 .... 174 B3
Turnhill Gr ST5 .... 56 A4
Turnhurst Rd ST7 .... 41 F4
Turnlea Cl ST18 .... 27 D3
Turnock St ST2 .... 58 B2
Turnstone Dr WV10 .... 241 D4
Turquoise Gr WS11 .... 210 B2
Turton Cl
  Alrewas DE13 .... 201 D1
  Walsall WS3 .... 243 D2
Tuscan Cl ST10 .... 76 B1
Tuscan St ST3 .... 283 C4
Tuscan Way ST5 .... 55 E3
Tutbury B77 .... 261 E4
Tutbury Ave WV6 .... 255 D2
Tutbury Cl WS11 .... 210 B2
Tutbury Gr ST3 .... 73 E2
Tutbury & Hatton Sta
  DE65 .... 146 B4
Tutbury Rd DE13 .... 166 A4
Tutehill B77 .... 262 A4
Tweed Gr ST5 .... 71 D2
Tweed St ST4 .... 72 C2
Twemlow Cl ST18 .... 154 B1
Twemlow St ST1 .... 57 D2
Twentylands DE13 .... 147 E2
Twickenham Ct DY8 .... 279 E4
Twigg St ST2 .... 58 A1
Two Gates Cty Prim Sch
  B77 .... 250 B1
Two Gates Prim Sch
  B77 .... 261 E4
Twyford Cl
  Aldridge WS9 .... 256 A3
  Swadlincote DE11 .... 186 C1
Twyning Gn ST3 .... 88 C4
Tylecote Cres ST18 .... 158 A1
Tyler Gr 21 Burslem ST6 ... 56 C4
  Stone ST15 .... 119 F4
Tyndall Pl ST4 .... 71 F4
Tyne Cl WS8 .... 228 B1
Tyne Way ST5 .... 71 D2
Tynedale Cres WV4 .... 266 C2
Tyneham Gr ST2 .... 43 D1
Tyning Cl WV9 .... 240 A1
Tyninghame Ave WV6 .... 255 E3
Tynings La WS9 .... 256 A3
Tynsel Parkes CE Fst Sch
  ST14 .... 111 D1
Tynsel Parkes Fst Sch
  ST14 .... 110 C1
Tynwald Grange ST5 .... 56 A2
Tyrell Gr ST2 .... 57 F4
Tyrley Cl WV6 .... 255 D1
Tyrley Rd TF9 .... 112 C3
Tyrol Cl DY8 .... 279 E3
Tyson Gn ST2 .... 73 E4
Tythebarn Dr DY6 .... 275 D4

Ubberley Gn ST2 .... 58 B1
Ubberley Rd ST2 .... 58 B1
Uffington Par ST2 .... 73 E4
Ufton Cres ST3 .... 88 C4
Ullswater B77 .... 262 A4
Ullswater Ave ST6 .... 56 C4
Ullswater Dr
  Cheadle ST10 .... 76 C2
  Stone ST15 .... 120 B4
Ullswater Gdns DY6 .... 275 E3
Ullswater Ho ST17 .... 174 C3
Ullswater Pl WS11 .... 209 F1
Ullswater Rd WV11 .... 242 A1
Ulster Cl WS11 .... 210 A2
Ulster Dr DY6 .... 275 F2
Ulster Terr ST4 .... 72 A3
Ulverston Rd ST3 .... 88 C4
Umberleigh Rd ST3 .... 88 C4
Under Rainow Rd CW12 ..... 6 C1
Underhill Cl TF10 .... 168 C2
Underhill Jun & Inf Sch
  WV10 .... 241 D1
Underhill La WV10 .... 241 D1
Underhill Wlk DE14 .... 166 B1
Underley Cl DY6 .... 275 D4
Undertown La DE6 .... 96 B3
Underwood Cl ST16 .... 155 E4
Underwood Rd ST5 .... 55 D1
Unicorn Pl ST6 .... 41 F3
Union Cl ST1 .... 282 B4
Union St Wolv WV5 .... 264 B1
Union St
  Burntwood WS7 .... 228 C3
  Burton u T DE14 .... 166 B1
  Cannock WS11 .... 226 C3
  Hanley ST1 .... 282 B4
  Leek ST13 .... 30 C3
Unity Ave ST1 .... 57 E4
Univ of Keele ST5 .... 70 A4

Univ of Sheffield SK17 ...... 4 A4
Univ of Wolverhampton
Compton Park Campus
  WV6 .... 255 F1
Unwin Cres DY8 .... 279 F3
Unwin St ST6 .... 42 A2
Upfield Way WS15 .... 178 B1
Uplands Ave
  Caverswall ST9 .... 59 D2
  Chell Heath ST6 .... 41 F3
  Wolv WV3 .... 265 E4
Uplands Cl
  Cannock WS15 .... 211 F3
  Penkridge ST19 .... 192 C1
Uplands Croft ST9 .... 59 D2
Uplands Dr
  Caverswall ST9 .... 59 D2
  Sedgley DY3 .... 271 E4
  Wolv WV3 .... 265 F4
  Wombourne WV5 .... 270 A3
Uplands Gn WS15 .... 196 B3
Uplands Jun & Inf Sch
  WV3 .... 265 E4
Uplands Rd Bucknall ST2 ... 58 A4
  Stafford ST17 .... 174 B3
Uplands The
  Biddulph ST6 .... 16 C1
  Colwich ST18 .... 158 A1
  Newcastle-u-L ST5 .... 284 C4
Upmeadows Dr ST16 .... 155 D1
Upper Bar TF10 .... 168 C1
Upper Belgrave Rd ST3 ...... 73 E1
Upper Brook St WS15 ...... 196 C4
Upper Cres ST4 .... 71 F4
Upper Cross Rd WS15 ...... 196 C4
Upper Cross St ST3 .... 283 C4
Upper Furlong St ST4 .... 72 B3
Upper Gn WV6 .... 255 E3
Upper Gungate B79 .... 250 A3
Upper Hillchurch St ST1 .... 282 C3
Upper Huntbach St ST1 ..... 282 C3
Upper Landywood La
  WS6 .... 226 B1
Upper Lodge Rd WS15 ...... 197 F2
Upper Market Sq ST1 .... 282 B3
Upper Marsh ST5 .... 56 B2
Upper Normacot Rd
  [1] Longton, Longton ST3 .. 73 E1
  Longton, Normacot ST3 ..... 73 F1
Upper Sneyd Rd WV11 ...... 242 A1
Upper St WV6 .... 255 E3
Upper St John St WS14 ..... 231 D3
Upper Villiers St WV2 .... 266 B3
Upper Way WS15 .... 197 D1
Upper Zoar St WV3 .... 266 A4
Upton Ct TF9 .... 97 E1
Upton Pl WS15 .... 178 B1
Urmston Pl ST3 .... 88 C4
Usam Trad Est WV10 .... 240 B1
Usulwall Cl ST21 .... 133 E3
Utterby Side ST2 .... 73 E4
Uttoxeter L Ctr ST14 .... 126 A4
Uttoxeter Race Course
  ST14 .... 126 C3
Uttoxeter Rd
  Abbots Bromley WS15 ...... 160 C3
  Alton ST10 .... 94 C4
  Armitage WS15 .... 198 B2
  Blythe Bridge ST11 .... 90 C4
  Draycott in t M ST11 .... 91 E3
  Forsbrook ST11 .... 90 C4
  Foston DE65 .... 129 F2
  Foston, HM Detention Ctr
    DE65 .... 129 E2
  Hill Ridware, Blithbury
    WS15 .... 180 A3
  Hill Ridware, Hill Ridware
    WS15 .... 198 A4
  Longton ST3 .... 283 C3
  Meir ST3 .... 74 A1
  Milwich ST18 .... 122 B3
  Sandon ST15 .... 121 E4
  Stone ST15 .... 120 C4
  Upper Tean ST10, ST14 ... 109 E4
Uttoxeter Sta ST14 .... 126 B4
Uxbridge Cl DY3 .... 271 E1
Uxbridge Ct Burntwood WS7 228 C3
  Cannock WS2 .... 210 B3
Uxbridge St Burton u T DE14 166 B1
  Cannock WS2 .... 210 B2

Vale Ave Aldridge WS9 ..... 256 B2
  Sedgley DY3 .... 271 E3
Vale Cl WS13 .... 214 A1
Vale Gdns ST19 .... 207 F4
Vale Head Dr WV6 .... 255 D1
Vale Park (Port Vale FC)
  ST6 .... 42 A1
Vale Pleasant ST5 .... 55 E1
Vale Rise ST19 .... 207 F4
Vale Row DY3 .... 271 E3
Vale St
  Newcastle-u-L, Chesterton
    ST5 .... 55 F4
  Newcastle-u-L, Silverdale
    ST5 .... 55 D1
  Sedgley DY3 .... 271 E3
  Stoke-on-T ST4 .... 72 A4
Vale View Aldridge WS9 .... 256 A2
  Newcastle-u-L ST5 .... 56 B4
Valentine Rd ST7 .... 26 A1
Valerian Way ST3 .... 90 A3
Valley Cty Prim Sch The
  ST10 .... 78 A4
Valley Dr ST13 .... 30 A3
Valley Gn WS6 .... 226 C1
Valley La Lichfield WS13 ... 231 E4
  Tamworth B77 .... 261 F4

Valley Park Sch WV6 .... 255 F3
Valley Park Way ST3 .... 72 C2
Valley Rd
  Cannock, Hazelslade
    WS12 .... 211 D3
  Cannock, Hednesford
    WS12 .... 210 B3
  Meir ST3 .... 74 A2
  Sedgley DY3 .... 271 F4
  Stone ST15 .... 120 A3
  Walsall WS3 .... 243 E1
Valley Side WS3 .... 243 F1
Valley View
  Brownhills WS8 .... 245 D4
  Market Drayton TF9 .... 112 A4
Van Diemans Rd WV5 .... 269 F3
Van Gogh Cl WS11 .... 210 B1
Vanbrugh Ct WV6 .... 254 C2
Vanguard B77 .... 261 E3
Vanity Cl ST15 .... 105 E2
Vanity La ST15 .... 105 E2
Varden Ct WS15 .... 178 C1
Vardon Cl ST16 .... 156 B2
Vaudrey Cres CW12 .... 6 A2
Vaughan Cl B74 .... 257 F3
Vaughan Gdns WV8 .... 238 C2
Vaughan Way ST17 .... 155 E1
Vaughan's La WS15 .... 159 E3
Vauxhall Cres TF10 .... 168 C1
Vauxhall Terr TF10 .... 168 C2
Velvet St [4] ST6 .... 56 C4
Venery Cl ST14 .... 125 E4
Venice Ct ST5 .... 70 C4
Venn Pl ST1 .... 57 F1
Ventnor Gr ST3 .... 88 C3
Venton Cl ST6 .... 42 C2
Ventura Park Rd B78 .... 250 A2
Vercourt B74 .... 257 D2
Verdi Ct WS19 .... 214 B1
Verdon Cl ST19 .... 208 A4
Verity Wlk DY8 .... 275 F1
Vermont Gn WS11 .... 210 A2
Verney Way ST3 .... 88 C3
Vernon Ave Audley ST7 ...... 39 E1
  Brownhills WS8 .... 245 D4
  Congleton CW12 .... 15 F4
Vernon Cl Audley ST7 .... 39 E1
  Essington WV11 .... 241 F2
  Sutton Coldfield B74 .... 257 F3
Vernon Lodge Prep Sch
  ST19 .... 206 B2
Vernon Rd ST4 .... 72 A4
Vernon Terr DE14 .... 166 B2
Vernon Way WS3 .... 242 B1
Vernons Pl WV10 .... 225 D1
Veronica Ave WV4 .... 266 C3
Verulam Rd ST16 .... 155 F4
Verwood Cl ST16 .... 156 B2
Vesey Cl B74 .... 257 F1
Vessey Terr ST5 .... 284 C2
Vestry Cl ST4 .... 72 A3
Vicar St DY3 .... 271 E4
Vicar's Cl Lichfield WS13 ... 231 D4
  Stone ST15 .... 105 E2
Vicarage Bank ST18 .... 138 C3
Vicarage Cl Brownhills WS8 245 D4
  Burton u T DE15 .... 167 D2
  Dordon B78 .... 262 C3
  Eccleshall ST21 .... 133 C4
Vicarage Cres
  Newcastle-u-L ST5 .... 284 C1
  Tittensor ST12 .... 88 A1
  Upper Tean ST10 .... 92 C2
Vicarage Croft DE13 .... 199 E3
Vicarage Ct DY7 .... 278 A2
Vicarage Dr
  Caverswall ST11 .... 74 B2
  Kinver DY7 .... 278 A2
  Uttoxeter ST14 .... 110 C2
Vicarage Field DE15 .... 166 C1
Vicarage Hill B78 .... 260 A1
Vicarage La
  Barlaston ST12 .... 88 C1
  King's Bromley DE13 ...... 199 E3
  Madeley CW3 .... 68 C3
  Stoke-on-T ST4 .... 71 F2
Vicarage Rd
  Brewood ST19 .... 223 E3
  Brierley Hill DY8 .... 279 F4
  Brownhills, Ogley Rd WS8 245 D4
  Brownhills, Pelsall WS3 ... 244 A1
  Cheslyn Hay WV10 .... 225 D4
  Leek ST13 .... 30 C3
  Penkridge WV10 .... 224 D1
  Sedgley DY3 .... 271 F3
  Stoke-on-T ST4 .... 71 F4
  Stourbridge DY8 .... 279 E4
  Upper Tean ST10 .... 92 C2
  Wolv WV2 .... 266 B4
  Wolv, Penn WV4 .... 265 F2
Vicarage Way ST17 .... 155 E1
Vicars Croft WS15 .... 178 C1
Vichy Cl ST5 .... 70 C4
Vickers Rd ST6 .... 42 A3
Victor St Brownhills WS3 ... 244 A1
  Stone ST15 .... 104 C1
Victoria Ave Audley ST7 .... 54 C4
  Hanley ST1 .... 282 B4
  Kidsgrove ST7 .... 25 F1
  Walsall WS3 .... 243 E1
Victoria Cl ST5 .... 55 E1
Victoria Cres DE14 .... 166 B3
Victoria Ct Fenton ST4 .... 72 C3
  Newcastle-u-L ST5 .... 56 B2
Victoria Dr B78 .... 261 D4
Victoria Gdns WS13 .... 230 C4
Victoria Rd WV5 .... 270 A4

Victoria Hospl WS13 .... 231 D3
Victoria Meadow DE13 .... 199 E3
Victoria Park Rd ST6 .... 41 F2
Victoria Pk TF10 .... 168 C2
Victoria Pl Fenton ST4 ...... 72 C3
  Newcastle-u-L, Chesterton
    ST5 .... 55 F4
  Newcastle-u-L, Wolstanton
    ST5 .... 56 B3
Victoria Prim Sch DE14 ... 166 B2
Victoria Rd
  Brownhills WS3 .... 244 A2
  Burton u T DE14 .... 166 B2
  Fenton ST4 .... 72 C4
  Market Drayton TF9 .... 97 D1
  Newcastle-u-L ST5 .... 284 C2
  Sedgley DY3 .... 271 F4
  Stafford ST16 .... 155 E2
  Tamworth B79 .... 250 B3
  Wolv, Oxbarn WV3 .... 265 F4
  Wolv, Stockwell End WV6 255 F3
Victoria Row ST8 .... 27 E2
Victoria Sq ST1 .... 282 A2
Victoria St
  Cannock WS11 .... 226 B4
  Cannock, Chadsmoor
    WS11 .... 209 F2
  Cannock, Hednesford
    WS12 .... 210 B3
  Cheadle ST10 .... 76 C2
  Kingswinford DY6 .... 270 A1
  Leek ST13 .... 31 D3
  Newcastle-u-L ST4 .... 284 C2
  Newcastle-u-L, Chesterton
    ST5 .... 55 F4
  Newcastle-u-L, Silverdale
    ST5 .... 55 E1
  Stafford ST16 .... 155 F2
  Stoke-on-T ST5 .... 56 B1
  Stone ST15 .... 105 D1
  Yoxall DE13 .... 182 A2
Victoria Terr ST16 .... 155 F3
Victoria Way ST17 .... 175 F3
Victory Ave WS7 .... 228 C4
Victory Cl WS12 .... 210 C2
Victory Cres ST10 .... 76 C2
Victory Terr B78 .... 261 D4
Vienna Cl WS7 .... 70 C3
Vienna Way ST3 .... 73 F3
View St WS12 .... 209 F3
Viewfield Ave WS12 .... 209 F4
Viewfield Cres WS12 .... 271 E3
Viewlands Dr WV6 .... 255 D1
Viggars Pl ST5 .... 55 F1
Vigo Cl WS9 .... 244 C1
Vigo Pl WS9 .... 256 A4
Vigo Rd WS9 .... 244 C1
Vigo Terr WS9 .... 244 C1
Villa Cl Biddulph ST8 .... 27 E4
  Shareshill WV10 .... 225 E1
Villa Rd ST13 .... 45 E4
Villa St ST4 .... 72 A3
Village Gdns ST17 .... 175 F4
Village The
  Astbury CW12 .... 15 D4
  Endon ST9 .... 29 D1
  Kingswinford DY6 .... 275 F4
  Stafford ST17 .... 175 F3
Villas The Ipstones ST10 .... 62 B3
  Stoke-on-T ST4 .... 72 A3
Villiers Ind Est WV2 .... 266 A4
Villiers St ST3 .... 283 B1
Vincent St ST1 .... 57 F3
Vine Bank Rd ST7 .... 26 A1
Vine Cl ST18 .... 158 A4
Vine La WS11 .... 226 B3
Vine Row ST4 .... 72 A3
Vine St DY8 .... 275 F1
Vinebank St ST4 .... 72 A3
Vineyard Dr TF10 .... 168 C2
Vineyard Rd TF10 .... 168 C2
Violet La DE6 .... 81 E1
Violet Lane Sch DE15 ...... 185 F4
Violet Way DE15 .... 186 A4
Virginia Dr WV4 .... 265 F2
Virginsalley La DE6 .... 81 E1
Viscount Rd WS7 .... 211 F1
Viscount Wlk ST3 .... 90 A4
Vista The DY3 .... 266 B1
Vivian Rd ST4 .... 72 C3
Vowchurch Way ST2 .... 58 B1
Voyager Dr WS11 .... 226 C3
Vulcan Rd WS13 .... 214 C1

Waddell Cl WV14 .... 266 C1
Wadden St ST18 .... 138 C2
Wade Ave ST5 .... 56 B3
Wade Cl Cheadle ST10 .... 76 B1
  Hill Ridware WS15 .... 197 F4
Wade La WS15 .... 197 F4
Wade St Chell Heath ST6 .... 42 A1
  Lichfield WS13 .... 231 D4
Wadebridge Rd ST2 .... 58 A1
Wadesmill Lawns WV10 ... 240 C2
Wadham St ST4 .... 72 A4
Waggon La DY6 .... 280 C2
Waggoner's La B78 .... 259 F4
Wain Ave
  Newcastle-u-L ST5 .... 70 C4
  Norton-in-t-M ST6 .... 42 C3
Wain Dr WS4 .... 71 F3
Wain St ST6 .... 41 F1
Wainrigg B77 .... 262 A4
Wainwood Rise ST4 .... 71 F3
Wainwright Wlk ST1 .... 282 C3
Wakefield Ave DE13 .... 146 A3
Wakefield Rd ST4 .... 71 F2

Wakeley Hill Wolv WV4 .... 265 F2
  Wombourne DY3 .... 266 B2
Walcot St ST5 .... 258 A2
Walcot Gr ST2 .... 58 A1
Walcote Cl WV12 .... 242 B1
Walden Ave WS15 .... 155 E3
Walden Gdns WV4 .... 265 F3
Wales La DE13 .... 183 E1
Walford Ave WV3 .... 265 F4
Walford Rd DE13 .... 147 E2
Walhouse CE Jun Sch
  WS11 .... 209 E1
Walhouse Dr ST19 .... 207 F4
Walhouse St WS11 .... 226 C4
Walk La WS9 .... 270 A3
Walk The DY3 .... 266 B1
Walker Dr DY10 .... 280 A1
Walker Rd ST6 .... 41 F2
Walker St
  Burton u T DE14 .... 166 A1
  Tunstall ST6 .... 41 E1
Walkers Croft WS13 .... 214 B1
Walkers Rise WS12 .... 210 B4
Walkersgreen Rd ST5 .... 40 B1
Walkfield Rd DE13 .... 200 C1
Walklate Ave ST5 .... 56 B2
Walkley Bank TF10 .... 169 E2
Walkmill Bsns Pk WS11 ... 226 B3
Walkmill La WS11 .... 226 B3
Walkmill Rd TF9 .... 112 B4
Walkmill Way WS11 .... 226 B3
Walks The ST13 .... 30 B3
Wall Croft WS9 .... 256 A4
Wall Ditch DE6 .... 35 D1
Wall Heath La WS14 .... 245 F3
Wall La WS14 .... 230 B2
Wall La Terr ST13 .... 45 E3
Wall Rd DE14 .... 185 D4
Wallace Cl WS11 .... 227 F3
Wallace Ct WS6 .... 226 B1
Wallace Rd WS8 .... 244 C4
Wallbridge Cl ST13 .... 30 B2
Wallbridge Dr ST13 .... 30 B2
Wallbridge Prec ST13 .... 30 B2
Wallbrook Rd ST18 .... 122 C2
Walley Dr ST6 .... 41 E3
Walley Pl ST6 .... 57 D4
Walley St Biddulph ST8 ..... 27 E4
  Burslem ST6 .... 41 F4
Walley's Dr ST5 .... 56 B1
Wallfield Cl ST10 .... 92 B2
Wallheath Cres WS14 .... 245 F3
Wallington Cl WS3 .... 243 D1
Wallington Heath WS3 ..... 243 D1
Wallis Pl ST2 .... 58 A3
Wallis St ST4 .... 72 C3
Wallis Way ST2 .... 43 D1
Wallows Wood DY3 .... 271 D2
Walls Wood ST5 .... 85 D2
Wallshead Way TF10 .... 168 C4
Walmer Meadow WS9 ...... 256 A4
Walmer Pl ST4 .... 283 B5
Walmers The WS9 .... 256 A4
Walney Gr ST1 .... 282 B4
Walnut Ave WS8 .... 239 D2
Walnut Cl Cannock WS11 .. 209 F2
  Newport TF10 .... 168 C1
Walnut Cres ST18 .... 158 B4
Walnut Ct WS15 .... 197 D3
Walnut Dr Cannock WS11 .. 209 F2
  Wolv WV3 .... 255 E1
Walnut Gr Lichfield WS14 . 231 F4
  Newcastle-u-L ST5 .... 55 E4
Walnut Tree La TF10 .... 188 A4
Walpole St ST3 .... 283 D5
Walrand Cl B79 .... 234 A1
Walsall Rd Aldridge WS9 ... 256 A3
  Brownhills, Heath End
    WS3 .... 244 A1
  Brownhills, Vigo WS9 ..... 244 C1
  Cannock WS11 .... 226 C4
  Great Wyrley WS6 .... 227 D1
  Lichfield WS13 .... 230 B3
  Little Aston B74 .... 257 E2
  Norton Canes WS11 .... 227 E2
  Shenstone WS14 .... 245 F4
  Sutton Coldfield B74 .... 257 E2
  Wall WS13 .... 230 B3
Walsall Wood Jun Mix Inf
  Sch WS9 .... 245 D2
Walsall Wood Rd WS9 ...... 256 A4
Walsingham Gdns ST5 ...... 71 C1
Walter St WS3 .... 244 A1
Walton Cres Fenton ST4 .... 72 B3
  Wolv WV2 .... 266 C3
Walton Gdns WV8 .... 238 C2
Walton Gr ST7 .... 40 B4
Walton Grange ST14 .... 120 C4
Walton Hall Specl Sch
  ST21 .... 134 A2
Walton Heath WS3 .... 242 C2
Walton High Sch ST17 ...... 175 F3
Walton Ind Est ST15 .... 120 A3
Walton La ST17 .... 176 A3
Walton Lodge ST17 .... 175 F3
Walton Mead Cl ST17 ...... 175 F4
Walton Pl ST5 .... 55 F3
Walton Priory Cty Mid Sch
  ST15 .... 119 F3
Walton Rd Aldridge WS9 ... 245 D1
  Stoke-on-T ST4 .... 71 F2
  Walton-on-t DE15 .... 185 E3
  Wolv WV2 .... 266 C3
Walton Way Kidsgrove ST7 . 40 B4
  Stone ST15 .... 119 F2
Walton-on-Trent CE
  Prim Sch DE12 .... 202 B4

Waltonbury Cl ST17 .... 175 F3
Waltonhurst La ST21 .... 134 B2
Wanderers La WV2 .... 266 B3
Wandsbeck B77 .... 261 F4
Wannerton Rd DY10 .... 281 D1
Wansbeck Wlk DY3 .... 271 F3
Warburton St [2] ST6 .... 57 D4
Ward Gr WV4 .... 266 C2
Ward Pl ST6 .... 42 A3
Ward Rd Codsall WV8 ...... 238 C2
  Wolv WV4 .... 266 B3
Ward St WS12 .... 209 F3
Wardel Cres WS13 .... 30 C2
Wardel La ST2 .... 43 E1
Wardle Cl B75 .... 258 A2
Wardle Pl WS11 .... 209 F3
Wardle St
  Tamworth B79 .... 250 A3
  Tunstall ST6 .... 41 F2
Wardles La WS6 .... 226 C1
Wardlow Cl WV4 .... 266 A3
Wards La CW12 .... 16 B4
Warings The WV5 .... 269 F2
Warm Croft ST15 .... 120 B4
Warminster Pl ST3 .... 283 C3
Warmson Cl ST3 .... 73 E3
Warner Rd WV8 .... 238 C2
Warner St ST1 .... 282 B2
Warnford Wlk WV4 .... 265 E3
Warren Cl
  Burton u T DE13 .... 147 F1
  Cannock WS12 .... 211 D3
  Lichfield WS13 .... 231 F4
Warren Croft WS15 .... 198 B2
Warren Ct TF9 .... 97 E1
Warren Dr DY3 .... 266 B1
Warren Gdns DY6 .... 275 E3
Warren La DE14 .... 184 C4
Warren Pl
  Brownhills WS8 .... 245 D4
  Longton ST3 .... 283 D2
Warren Rd
  Burntwood WS7 .... 229 D3
  Chell Heath ST6 .... 42 A3
Warren St ST3 .... 283 D2
Warrens La ST16 .... 155 D3
Warrilow Heath Rd ST5 ..... 40 B1
Warrington Dr ST13 .... 30 B3
Warrington Rd ST4 .... 57 E1
Warrington St ST4 .... 72 C3
Warsill Gr ST3 .... 73 E2
Warstone Hill Rd WV6 ..... 253 F2
Warstone Rd WS6 .... 242 B4
Warstones Cres WV4 .... 265 E3
Warstones Dr WV4 .... 265 E3
Warstones Gdns WV4 ...... 265 E3
Warstones Prim Sch
  WV4 .... 265 F3
Warstones Rd WV4 .... 265 E3
Wartell Bank DY6 .... 275 E4
Wartell Bank Ind Est
  DY6 .... 275 E4
Warwick Ave Meir ST3 ...... 73 F1
  Newcastle-u-L ST5 .... 71 E4
  Perton WV6 .... 254 C2
Warwick Cl
  Branston DE14 .... 184 C4
  Cannock WS11 .... 226 C4
  Kidsgrove ST7 .... 26 A2
  Market Drayton TF9 .... 97 F1
Warwick Dr WV8 .... 238 C2
Warwick Gr ST5 .... 56 C2
Warwick Rd
  Kingswinford DY8 .... 275 E1
  Stafford ST17 .... 175 D4
  Tamworth B77 .... 250 C2
Warwick St Biddulph ST8 ... 27 E4
  Burton u T DE13 .... 166 B3
  Hanley ST1 .... 57 D2
  Newcastle-u-L ST5 .... 55 F4
Warwick Way WS9 .... 245 D1
Wasdale Dr DY6 .... 275 F3
Wasdale Rd WS8 .... 244 B3
Wash Dale La ST15 .... 105 D3
Washbrook La
  Norton Canes WS11 .... 227 E3
  Tissington DE6 .... 51 F2
Washerwall La ST9 .... 59 D2
Washerwall St ST2 .... 73 E4
Washington Cl ST6 .... 16 B1
Washington St ST6 .... 41 F1
Waste La DE6 .... 79 C2
Wastwater Ct WV6 .... 254 C2
Wat Tyler Cl WS15 .... 178 B2
Watchfield Cl ST3 .... 73 F1
Water Dale WV3 .... 255 F1
Water Eaton La ST19 .... 207 F4
Water La Enville DY7 .... 268 B1
  Newport TF10 .... 168 C2
Water Rd DY3 .... 271 E1
Water St Burntwood WS7 .. 228 C4
  Kingswinford DY6 .... 275 F4
  Newcastle-u-L ST5 .... 284 C3
  Newcastle-u-L, Red Street
    ST5 .... 40 B1
  Stafford ST16 .... 155 F2
  Stoke-on-T ST4 .... 72 A3
Waterbeck Gr ST4 .... 88 B3
Waterbrook Cl ST19 .... 207 F4
Waterdale WV5 .... 269 F3
Waterdale Gr ST3 .... 73 F2
Waterford Cl WS11 .... 178 C1
Waterford Dr TF10 .... 168 C1
Waterford Rd DY6 .... 275 E4
Watergate St ST6 .... 41 E2

Waterhead Cl WV10 .... 241 D1
Waterhead Dr WV10 .... 241 D1
Waterhead Rd ST3 .... 73 F1
Waterhouses CE Prim Sch
ST10 .... 48 C1
Watering Trough Bank
CW3 .... 69 D4
Waterloo Bvd WS12 .... 210 C2
Waterloo Gr ST7 .... 26 A1
Waterloo Rd
Burslem ST6, ST1 .... 57 D3
Edgmond TF10 .... 168 A3
Hanley ST6, ST1 .... 57 D3
Waterloo St
Burton u T DE14 .... 166 B2
Hanley ST1 .... 282 C2
Leek ST13 .... 30 B3
Watermeadow Dr WS4 ...... 244 B1
Watermint Cl WS12 .... 210 C2
Waterpark Rd DE6 .... 127 D4
Waters Dr B74 .... 257 E2
Waters Rd WS15 .... 160 C2
Waters View WS3 .... 244 A3
Waterside
Burton u T DE15 .... 185 F4
Rugeley WS15 .... 196 C3
Waterside Cl CW3 .... 68 C3
Waterside Ct ST20 .... 171 E3
Waterside Dr Longton ST3 ... 88 C4
Market Drayton TF9 .... 97 F1
Waterside Jun Sch DE15 ... 185 F4
Waterside Mews TF10 .... 168 C2
Waterside Rd
Burton u T DE15 .... 185 E4
Walton-on-T DE15 .... 185 E4
Waterside Way
Brownhills WS8 .... 228 B1
Wolv WV9 .... 240 A2
Watersmead Cl WS12 .... 210 C2
Watersmeet Ct ST15 .... 120 B3
Waterways Gdns DY8 .... 275 F1
Watery La
Abbots Bromley WS15 .... 160 B2
Ashbourne DE6 .... 81 F4
Astbury CW12 .... 15 E3
Codsall WV8 .... 239 D3
Ellastone DE6 .... 80 A2
Haughton ST18 .... 172 C3
Kingswinford DY8 .... 275 F1
Lichfield WS13 .... 214 B2
Meir ST3 .... 73 E1
Scropton DE65 .... 129 F1
Swadlincote DE11 .... 186 B3
Watford Gap Rd B75 .... 258 A4
Watford St ST4 .... 72 B4
Wathan Ave WV14 .... 266 C1
Watkin St ST4 .... 72 B3
Watkiss Dr WS15 .... 178 B1
Watlands Ave ST5 .... 56 B3
Watlands Rd ST7 .... 39 F1
Watlands View ST5 .... 56 B3
Watling St
Brownhills WS8 .... 228 B1
Cannock WS11 .... 226 B3
Dordon B78 .... 262 B3
Fazeley B78 .... 249 F1
Gre B78 .... 262 B3
Great Wyrley WS11 .... 226 B3
Hints B78 .... 248 B2
Norton Canes WS11 .... 227 E2
Tamworth B78 .... 262 B3
Watling Street Jun Mix Inf
Sch WS8 .... 228 C1
Watson Cl WS15 .... 178 B2
Watson Rd
Stoke-on-T ST4 .... 71 F2
Wolv, Cinder Hill WV14 ..... 266 C1
Wolv, Pendeford WV10 ...... 240 A1
Watson St
Burton u T DE14 .... 166 B1
Stoke-on-T ST4 .... 72 A4
Watt Pl ST10 .... 76 B2
Wattfield Cl WS15 .... 197 D3
Wattles La ST17 .... 175 D1
Waveney B77 .... 261 F4
Waveney Ave WV6 .... 254 C2
Waveney Gr
Cannock WS11 .... 209 D1
Newcastle-u-L ST5 .... 71 D2
Waveney Wlk N ST6 .... 42 A2
Waveney Wlk S ST6 .... 42 A2
Wavenham Cl B74 .... 257 F3
Waverley Cres
Wolv, Cinder Hill WV4 .... 266 C2
Wolv, Goldthorn Hill WV4 ... 266 A3
Waverley Gdns
Rugeley WS15 .... 178 A1
Wombourne WV5 .... 270 A4
Waverley La DE14 .... 166 A2
Waverley Pl ST5 .... 71 D3
Waverley Rd WS3 .... 242 C1
Waverton Rd ST2 .... 73 F4
Wavertree Ave ST7 .... 25 F4
Waybutt La Betley CW2 ...... 52 B4
Hough Common CW2 .... 52 B4
Wayfield Dr ST16 .... 155 E4
Wayfield Gr ST4 .... 71 E4
Wayside WV8 .... 239 F1
Wayside Acres WV8 .... 238 C1
Wayside Ave ST5 .... 56 B2
Wayside Dr B74 .... 257 E2
Wayte St ST4 .... 72 B3
Wealden Hatch WV10 .... 240 C2
Wealdstone Dr DY3 .... 271 E1
Weathercock La CW12 .... 6 C2

Weatheroaks WS9 .... 245 D2
Weaver Cl Biddulph ST6 ...... 16 B1
Cheadle ST10 .... 76 C3
Weaver Dr ST17 .... 174 A4
Weaver Pl ST5 .... 71 D2
Weaver Rd ST14 .... 111 D1
Weaver St ST1 .... 282 B3
Weavers La ST15 .... 120 B4
Weavers The ST14 .... 95 E3
Weavers Wlk ST15 .... 103 E2
Weaving Gdns WS11 .... 209 F1
Webb St ST3 .... 74 A2
Webberley La ST3 .... 283 C3
Webley Rise WV10 .... 240 C2
Webster Ave ST3 .... 73 F3
Webster St ST5 .... 284 C2
Webster Wlk WS11 .... 210 A2
Wedgwood Cl
Burntwood WS7 .... 229 E4
Burton u T DE15 .... 167 D1
Wedgwood Meml Coll
ST12 .... 88 C1
Wedgwood Rd ST18 .... 156 A4
Wedgwood Ave
Audley ST7 .... 40 A1
Newcastle-u-L ST5 .... 284 A1
Wedgwood Cl WV5 .... 269 F4
Wedgwood Ct ST1 .... 57 D2
Wedgwood Dr ST12 .... 88 C2
Wedgwood Halt ST12 .... 88 B2
Wedgwood La
Barlaston ST12 .... 88 C2
Biddulph ST6 .... 16 B1
Wedgwood Pl 18 ST6 .... 56 C4
Wedgwood Rd
Cheadle ST10 .... 76 B1
Fenton ST4 .... 72 C3
Kidsgrove ST7 .... 40 B4
Wedgwood St
17 Burslem ST6 .... 56 C4
Newcastle-u-L ST5 .... 56 B3
Wedgwood Visitor Ctr
& Mus ST12 .... 88 B2
Weeford Rd B75 .... 258 C2
Weeping Cross ST17 .... 175 E4
Weetman St ST6 .... 41 E4
Weighton Gr ST2 .... 58 C1
Weir Bank DE15 .... 185 F3
Weir Gr ST7 .... 26 A1
Weirside DE6 .... 81 E4
Welbeck Pl ST2 .... 58 B3
Welbury Gdns WV6 .... 255 F3
Welby St ST4 .... 72 B3
Welch St ST4 .... 72 A4
Weldon Ave ST4 .... 74 A2
Welford Gr B74 .... 257 F2
Welford Rd B77 .... 261 E3
Welford Rise DE13 .... 166 A3
Well La Biddulph ST6 .... 16 B2
Great Wyrley WS6 .... 227 D1
Norbury TF10 .... 150 B2
Walsall WS3 .... 243 F1
Warslow SK17 .... 22 A1
Well St Biddulph ST8 .... 27 E4
Cheadle ST10 .... 76 C2
Forsbrook ST11 .... 91 D4
Hanley ST1 .... 282 C2
Leek ST13 .... 30 C3
Mow Cop ST7 .... 26 B4
Newcastle-u-L ST5 .... 284 C2
Welland Cl DE15 .... 167 D3
Welland Gr ST1 .... 71 D2
Wellbury Cl ST4 .... 88 B3
Weller St ST4 .... 71 F4
Wellesbourne B79 .... 250 B4
Wellesbourne Cl WV3 .... 265 D4
Wellesley St ST1 .... 282 A1
Wellfield Cl WS11 .... 226 A4
Wellfield Rd
Aldridge WS9 .... 256 A4
Alrewas DE13 .... 201 D1
Bucknall ST2 .... 58 B1
Wellington Ave WV3 .... 265 F4
Wellington Cl DY6 .... 275 F2
Wellington Cres WS13 ...... 215 D2
Wellington Ct ST1 .... 282 C3
Wellington Dr
Cannock WS11 .... 226 A1
Rugeley WS15 .... 196 C4
Wellington Rd
Albrighton WV7 .... 220 C1
Branston DE14 .... 166 A1
Burton u T DE14 .... 166 A1
Hanley ST1 .... 282 C2
Kidsgrove ST7 .... 26 A1
Newport TF10 .... 168 C1
Wellington St
Burton u T DE14 .... 166 A2
Hanley ST1 .... 282 C2
Leek ST13 .... 30 C3
Newcastle-u-L ST5 .... 56 B3
Wellington St W DE14 ...... 166 A2
Wellington Terr ST1 .... 282 C2
Wells Cl Biddulph ST8 .... 27 E4
Cannock WS11 .... 209 F3
Perton WV6 .... 254 B2
Wells Dr ST17 .... 175 F4
Wells La ST18 .... 191 E4
Wells Rd WV4 .... 265 F3
Wellyards Cl ST18 .... 138 B1
Welney Gdns WV9 .... 240 A1
Wendell Crest WV10 .... 240 C2
Wendling Cl ST2 .... 58 B1
Wendover Gr ST2 .... 58 B1
Wendover Rd WV4 .... 266 C1
Wendy Cl ST2 .... 58 A1
Wenger Cres ST4 .... 88 A4
Wenham Dr ST3 .... 90 A4

Wenlock B77 .... 250 B2
Wenlock Ave WV3 .... 265 F4
Wenlock Cl
Chell Heath ST6 .... 42 A4
Newcastle-u-L ST5 .... 40 C1
Sedgley DY3 .... 271 E4
Wenlock Dr TF10 .... 168 C1
Wensleydale Ave CW12 .... 6 A3
Wensleydale Cl ST1 .... 57 E4
Wentlows Ave ST10 .... 92 B3
Wentlows Rd ST10 .... 92 B3
Wentworth Cl WS7 .... 229 E4
Wentworth Ct B75 .... 258 A1
Wentworth Dr
Burton u T DE13 .... 147 E1
Kidsgrove ST7 .... 26 B2
Lichfield WS14 .... 231 E3
Stafford ST16 .... 156 B2
Wentworth Gr Hanley ST1 ... 57 F4
Perton WV6 .... 254 B3
Wentworth Rd
Stourbridge DY8 .... 279 F4
Walsall WS3 .... 242 C2
Wolv WV10 .... 240 C2
Werburgh Dr ST4 .... 88 A4
Wereton Rd ST7 .... 39 E1
Wergs Dr WV8 .... 255 D4
Wergs Hall Rd
Codsall WV8 .... 254 C4
Wolv WV8 .... 255 D4
Wergs Rd Codsall WV8 ...... 254 C4
Wolv WV6 .... 255 D3
Werneth Gr WS3 .... 243 D2
Werrington Prim Sch
ST9 .... 59 D2
Werrington Rd ST2 .... 58 A2
Wesker Pl ST3 .... 73 F2
Wesley Ave
Cheslyn Hay WS6 .... 226 B2
Codsall WV8 .... 239 D1
Wesley Cl WS7 .... 211 F1
Wesley Dr ST15 .... 120 B3
Wesley Pl Audley ST7 .... 54 B4
Cannock WS11 .... 210 B4
Newcastle-u-L ST5 .... 70 C4
Wesley Rd WV8 .... 239 D1
Wesley St Audley ST7 .... 40 A1
Forsbrook ST11 .... 91 D4
Tunstall ST6 .... 41 E2
Wesley Way B77 .... 250 C2
Wesleyan Rd TF9 .... 100 A3
Wessenden B77 .... 262 A4
Wessex Cl WS8 .... 244 C4
Wessex Dr
Cannock WS11 .... 209 F1
Trentham ST4 .... 88 A4
Wessex Rd WV2 .... 266 C3
West Ave
Kidsgrove ST7 .... 25 E1
Newcastle-u-L ST5 .... 56 B1
Stoke-on-T ST4 .... 71 F4
Weston CW2 .... 37 D3
West Bank ST4 .... 72 A3
West Beeches WV9 .... 224 A1
West Brampton ST5 .... 284 B3
West Butts Rd WS15 .... 178 A1
West Cl Stafford ST16 .... 156 A2
Stone ST15 .... 119 F4
West Coppice Rd WS8 ...... 244 B4
West Cres ST1 .... 57 F4
West Dr Cheddleton ST13 ... 45 E4
Fazeley B78 .... 249 F1
West End Ave ST13 .... 30 B3
West Gn WV4 .... 265 E3
West Hill ST14 .... 126 B3
West Hill Ave WS12 .... 210 A3
West Hill Prim Sch
WS12 .... 210 A3
West Par ST1 .... 72 B3
West Prec ST1 .... 282 B2
West St Biddulph ST8 .... 27 E4
Burton u T DE15 .... 167 D2
Cannock WS11 .... 226 C3
Leek ST13 .... 30 C3
Meir ST3 .... 74 A3
Mount Pleasant ST7 .... 26 A3
Newcastle-u-L ST5 .... 284 C2
Newcastle-u-L, Porthill ST5 ... 56 B4
Newcastle-u-L, Silverdale
ST5 .... 55 D1
Stourbridge DY8 .... 279 F3
Tamworth B79 .... 250 B3
Tamworth, Kettlebrook
B77 .... 250 B2
West Terr ST1 .... 42 A3
West View Mayfield DE6 .... 81 E3
Newcastle-u-L ST5 .... 56 A3
Rocester ST14 .... 96 A2
Stone ST3 .... 89 F2
Uttoxeter ST14 .... 125 D4
West View Dr DY6 .... 275 F3
West Way
Brownhills WS3 .... 244 A1
Stafford ST17 .... 174 B4
Uttoxeter ST14 .... 110 C1
West Way Gn ST17 .... 155 E1
Westacre ST1 .... 57 F2
Westacre Cres WV3 .... 255 E1
Westacre Dr DE11 .... 186 C1
Westacre Inf Sch WV3 ..... 255 E1
Westbeech Rd WV6 .... 253 E3
Westbolly Way WV5 .... 269 F3
Westbourne Ave
Cannock WS11 .... 209 E2
Cheslyn Hay WS6 .... 226 C1
Westbourne Cl ST13 .... 30 B3
Westbourne Cres WS7 ...... 229 D4

Westbourne Dr ST6 .... 41 F3
Westbourne Rd WV4 .... 266 A3
Westbridge Park
Sports Ctr ST15 .... 120 A4
Westbrook Ave WS9 .... 256 A3
Westbury Cl ST1 .... 57 F3
Westbury Hayes ST17 .... 174 A4
Westbury Rd ST5 .... 71 D2
Westcliffe Ave ST5 .... 71 D2
Westcliffe Hospl ST6 .... 41 F4
Westcott Cl DY6 .... 275 F2
Westcott La TF9 .... 130 A4
Westcroft Ave WV10 .... 241 D1
Westcroft Rd
Pattingham WV6 .... 254 C3
Sedgley DY3 .... 266 A1
Westcroft Specl Sch
WV10 .... 241 D1
Westerby Dr ST9 .... 59 D2
Westerham ST14 .... 87 F4
Westering Parkway
WV10 .... 240 C2
Western Ave DY3 .... 271 D4
Western By Pass WS13 ..... 213 F1
Western Rd
Cannock WS12 .... 210 A3
Stourbridge DY8 .... 279 F2
Western Springs Prim Sch
WS15 .... 178 B1
Western Springs Rd
WS15 .... 178 B1
Westfield Cty Prim Sch
WV5 .... 269 F4
Westfield Dr WV5 .... 269 F4
Westfield Gr WV3 .... 265 E4
Westfield Manor B75 .... 258 A2
Westfield Rd
Bucknall ST2 .... 58 A2
Burton u T DE13 .... 166 A3
Mow Cop ST7 .... 26 B4
Sedgley DY3 .... 266 C1
Westfields Cotton ST10 ...... 63 F2
Leek ST13 .... 30 C4
Westfields Rd WS15 .... 197 F2
Westfields Rise CW3 .... 67 E1
Westgate Brewood ST19 ... 223 E4
Cannock WS11 .... 211 D3
Westgate Cl DY3 .... 271 E4
Westhall St ST19 .... 223 E3
Westhead Ave ST16 .... 156 A2
Westhead Rd DY10 .... 280 A2
Westhead Rd N DY10 .... 280 A2
Westhead Wlk ST1 .... 282 A2
Westhill ST3 .... 255 E1
Westhouse La DE6 .... 79 F2
Westland Ave WV3 .... 255 F1
Westland Gdns
Brierley Hill DY8 .... 279 F4
Wolv WV6 .... 255 F1
Westland Rd
Market Drayton TF9 .... 97 D1
Wolv WV6 .... 255 F1
Westland St ST4 .... 72 A4
Westlands Audley ST7 .... 39 F1
Woore TF9 .... 83 D4
Westlands Ave ST5 .... 70 C4
Westlands Prim Sch ST5 ... 70 C3
Westlands Rd ST14 .... 126 A3
Westleigh Rd WV5 .... 269 F3
Westmarsh Gr ST6 .... 42 A2
Westmead Rd DE13 .... 183 E1
Westmere Cl CW2 .... 37 D3
Westmill St ST1 .... 282 C1
Westminster Ave WV4 ...... 266 A3
Westminster Cl ST17 .... 175 E4
Westminster Dr DE13 .... 166 B4
Westminster Pl ST4 .... 72 A1
Westminster Rd
Cannock WS11 .... 209 F3
Kingswinford DY8 .... 275 F1
Leek ST13 .... 31 D4
Westmorland Ave ST7 .... 40 C4
Westmorland Cl
Chell Heath ST6 .... 42 A4
Tamworth B78 .... 250 A1
Weston Bank ST18 .... 138 A1
Weston Cl Brewood ST19 ... 221 F4
Cannock WS11 .... 210 B1
Caverswall ST9 .... 59 D2
Newcastle-u-L ST5 .... 55 F2
Weston Coney Rd ST3 .... 74 A2
Weston Coyney Inf Sch
ST3 .... 74 A2
Weston Coyney Jun Sch
ST3 .... 74 A2
Weston Coyney Rd ST3 ...... 73 F2
Weston Cres WS9 .... 256 A4
Weston Cty Prim Sch
CW2 .... 37 E3
Weston Dr
Great Wyrley WS6 .... 226 C1
Meir ST3 .... 74 A2
Weston La
Shavington CW2 .... 37 D3
Standon ST21 .... 102 A2
Weston Park Ave DE13 .... 166 C4
Weston Rd
Albrighton WV7 .... 237 D3
Hopton ST16 .... 156 B2
Lichfield WS13 .... 214 A1
Meir ST3 .... 74 A2
Stafford ST16, ST18 .... 156 B2
Weston CW1 .... 37 D4
Weston Rd High Sch
ST18 .... 156 B3
Weston St Leek ST13 .... 31 D3
Longton ST3 .... 73 E3

Westonfields Dr ST3 .... 73 F2
Westonview Ave ST3 .... 73 E3
Westport Greenway ST6 .... 41 E1
Westport Rd ST6 .... 41 F3
Westridge DY3 .... 271 D4
Westsprink Cres ST3 .... 73 F1
Westview Cl ST13 .... 30 B3
Westward Cl ST14 .... 111 D1
Westwick Cl WS9 .... 245 D3
Westwood Ave ST3 .... 279 E2
Westwood Cl ST13 .... 45 E2
Westwood Ct ST1 .... 282 C3
Westwood Fst Sch ST13 ..... 30 B3
Westwood Gr ST13 .... 30 B3
Westwood Heath Rd ST13 ... 30 B3
Westwood High Sch The
ST13 .... 30 A3
Westwood Manor (Cicely
Haughton Sch) ST13 .... 44 C1
Westwood Park Ave ST13 ... 30 A3
Westwood Park Dr ST13 .... 30 A3
Westwood Pk DE11 .... 186 C3
Westwood Rd Leek ST13 .... 30 B3
Meir ST3 .... 74 A1
Newcastle-u-L ST5 .... 56 B3
Westwood Sch WS15 .... 180 A2
Westwood Terr 4 ST13 .... 30 B3
Westwoods Hollow
WS7 .... 229 D4
Wetherall Cl WS15 .... 178 B1
Wetherby Cl
Kingsley ST10 .... 76 C3
Newcastle-u-L ST5 .... 55 F4
Wolv WV10 .... 240 B3
Wetherby Gr WS3 .... 243 D2
Wetherby Rd ST4 .... 88 A4
Wetherel Rd DE15 .... 167 E1
Wetley Ave ST9 .... 59 F2
Wetley La ST13 .... 33 D1
Wetmore La DE14 .... 166 C3
Wetmore Rd DE14 .... 166 C3
Wettenhall Dr ST13 .... 30 A2
Wetton Rd ST13 .... 34 A3
Wexford Cl DY1 .... 271 F1
Weybourne Ave ST2 .... 43 D2
Weyhill Cl WV9 .... 239 F1
Weymouth Dr B74 .... 257 F2
Whalley Ave ST5 .... 71 F3
Wharf Cl WS14 .... 231 E4
Wharf La Astbury CW12 ...... 15 D2
Brownhills WS7 .... 228 C2
Burntwood WS7 .... 228 C2
Wharf Pl ST4 .... 72 B4
Wharf Rd Biddulph ST8 .... 27 E4
Burton u T DE14 .... 166 C3
Gnosall ST20 .... 171 E3
Rugeley WS15 .... 196 C4
Wharf St ST5 .... 284 C2
Wharf Terr CW3 .... 69 D4
Wharfdale Cl DY6 .... 275 D4
Wharfdale Rd CW12 .... 6 A3
Wharfedale Wlk ST3 .... 283 A3
Wharmadine La
Ashley ST21 .... 100 C4
Maer ST5 .... 84 C1
Wharwell La WS6 .... 227 D1
Whateley La B77 .... 261 F2
Whatmore St ST6 .... 42 B1
Wheat Breach Cl DE13 ..... 166 A3
Wheatcroft Cl
Burntwood WS7 .... 229 D3
Penkridge ST19 .... 207 F4
Wheatfields ST6 .... 42 B2
Wheathill Cl WV4 .... 265 F2
Wheatlands Cl WS11 .... 210 B1
Wheatlands Rd DE15 .... 185 F4
Wheatlands The WV6 .... 254 B2
Wheatley Ave ST4 .... 71 F3
Wheatley Cl B75 .... 258 B2
Wheatley La DE15 .... 167 E2
Wheatley St WV2 .... 266 C3
Wheatmill Cl DY10 .... 281 D1
Wheatridge Cl DY6 .... 275 D4
Wheatsheaf Rd WV8 .... 239 F1
Wheatstone Cl DY3 .... 271 F3
Wheel Ave WV8 .... 238 C2
Wheel La WS13 .... 213 F1
Wheeler Cl WV8 .... 238 C2
Wheeler St DY8 .... 279 F3
Wheelfield WV8 .... 238 C2
Wheelock Way ST7 .... 26 A1
Whetstone Field Jun Mix
Inf Sch WS2 .... 256 A2
Whetstone Gn WV10 .... 240 B1
Whetstone La WS9 .... 256 A2
Whetstone Rd ST6 .... 16 B1
Whieldon Cres ST4 .... 72 B3
Whieldon Rd ST4 .... 72 B3
Whilmot Cl WV10 .... 241 D3
Whimple Side ST2 .... 58 A1
Whimster Sq ST17 .... 174 A4
Whinberry Rise DY5 .... 271 E1
Whinyates Rise WS11 ...... 226 C4
Whisper La ST4, ST5 .... 86 C4
Whiston Cl WV7 .... 237 D3
Whiston Eaves La ST10 ...... 62 B1
Whitacre La WS14 .... 245 F4
Whitaker Rd ST3 .... 72 C2
Whitbread Dr ST8 .... 27 F4
Whitburn Cl WV9 .... 240 A1
Whitby Cl Stafford ST17 .... 174 B4
Walsall WS3 .... 242 C2
Whitby Way WS11 .... 226 B4
Whitchurch Gr ST5 .... 40 C1
Whitcliffe Pl ST3 .... 72 C2
Whitcombe Rd ST3 .... 74 A1
White Bark Cl WS12 .... 210 A4
White Farm Rd B74 .... 257 F2

White Hall Rd ST7 ..... 25 F1
White Hill DY7 ..... 277 F3
White Horse Rd WS8 ..... 228 C1
White House La DY7 ..... 268 C1
White Lion St ST17 ..... 155 F1
White Oak Dr
  Kingswinford DY6 ..... 275 E3
  Wolv WV3 ..... 255 F5
White Oaks ST17 ..... 175 E3
White Row WV5 ..... 264 B1
White's Dr DY3 ..... 271 F4
White's Meadow ST18 ..... 153 E2
Whitebeam Cl
  Brownhills WS8 ..... 244 C3
  Newcastle-u-L ST5 ..... 40 B1
Whitebridge La ST15 ..... 104 C1
Whitebridge Lane Ind Est
  ST15 ..... 104 C1
Whitefield Cl WV8 ..... 239 D1
Whitefields La ST10 ..... 49 D1
Whitehall Ave ST7 ..... 25 F1
Whitehall Cl ST14 ..... 141 E4
Whitehall Rd
  Kingswinford DY6 ..... 275 E3
  Wolv WV4 ..... 266 A2
Whitehaven Dr ST1 ..... 282 B4
Whitehead Rd ST6 ..... 42 A3
Whitehill Rd ST7 ..... 26 A1
Whitehorn Cres B74 ..... 256 B1
Whitehouse Ave WV3 ..... 265 E4
Whitehouse Cres
  Burntwood WS7 ..... 229 D4
  Essington WV11 ..... 241 F1
Whitehouse La
  Codsall WV8 ..... 238 B4
  Sandon ST15 ..... 121 D4
  Swindon DY7, DY3 ..... 269 D1
Whitehouse Rd
  Bucknall ST2 ..... 58 A3
  Newcastle-u-L ST5 ..... 56 A2
Whitehouse Rd N ST5 ..... 56 A2
Whitehurst La ST10 ..... 75 E3
Whitemill La ST15 ..... 119 F4
Whiteoaks Dr ST19 ..... 221 F4
Whiteridge Rd ST7 ..... 26 A1
Whites La CW2 ..... 37 D3
Whites Wood WV5 ..... 270 A3
Whitesands Gr ST3 ..... 90 A4
Whitesmith Cl DY3 ..... 271 E4
Whitestone Rd ST3 ..... 90 A3
Whitesytch La ST15 ..... 106 B1
Whitethorn Ave ST12 ..... 88 B1
Whitethorn Cl ST17 ..... 210 A4
Whitethorn Rd DY8 ..... 275 F1
Whitethorn Way ST5 ..... 40 C1
Whitfield Ave ST5 ..... 284 A1
Whitfield Rd
  Cannock WS12 ..... 210 B4
  Kidsgrove ST7 ..... 26 A1
  Norton-in-t-M ST6 ..... 42 B3
Whitfield St ST13 ..... 30 C2
Whitfield Valley Prim Sch
  ST6 ..... 42 A4
Whitgreave Ave WV10 ..... 241 D4
Whitgreave Ct ST16 ..... 155 E3
Whitgreave La
  Rugeley WS15 ..... 196 C3
  Seighford ST18 ..... 135 E2
  Whitgreave ST18 ..... 136 A2
Whitgreave Prim Sch
  WV10 ..... 241 D4
Whiting B77 ..... 261 E4
Whitley Ave B77 ..... 250 C3
Whitley Cl WV6 ..... 255 D1
Whitley Rd ST6 ..... 42 B3
Whitmore Ave ST9 ..... 59 D2
Whitmore Rd Keele ST5 ..... 69 F2
  Newcastle-u-L ST5 ..... 70 C2
  Stourbridge DY8 ..... 279 E3
  Swynnerton ST4, ST5 ..... 87 E4
  Tittensor ST4, ST5 ..... 87 E4
  Trentham ST4, ST5 ..... 87 E4
  Whitmore ST5 ..... 70 C2
Whitmore St ST1 ..... 57 D2
Whitney Ave DY8 ..... 279 E3
Whitridge Gr ST2 ..... 73 E4
Whittaker St WV2 ..... 266 C3
Whittingham Dr ST17 ..... 174 A4
Whittington Common Rd
  WS14 ..... 232 A3
Whittington Hall La DY7 ..... 279 D2
Whittington Prim Sch
  WS14 ..... 232 C2
Whittington Rd DY8 ..... 279 E2
Whitty La ST13 ..... 20 B3
Whitworth La WS15 ..... 178 A1
Whygate Gr ST1 ..... 57 F3
Wickets The DE15 ..... 185 F4
Widecombe Ave ST17 ..... 175 F4
Widecombe Rd ST1 ..... 57 F3
Widney Ave WS9 ..... 245 D1
Wigeon Gr WV10 ..... 241 D4
Wigford Rd B77 ..... 261 E3
Wiggington Rd B79 ..... 250 A4
Wightman Cl WS14 ..... 231 F3
Wightwick Bank WV6 ..... 255 D1
Wightwick Cl WS3 ..... 243 D1
Wightwick Ct WV6 ..... 255 D1
Wightwick Gr WV6 ..... 255 D1
Wightwick Hall Rd
  WV6 ..... 254 C1
Wightwick Hall Sch
  WV6 ..... 254 C1
Wigley Bank Rd DY7 ..... 277 E3
Wigmore Pl ST3 ..... 73 E3
Wignall Rd ST6 ..... 41 E3
Wilbraham's Wlk ST7 ..... 39 E1

Wilcox Ave WS12 ..... 210 A4
Wild Goose Ave ST7 ..... 26 B2
Wildacres DY8 ..... 279 E3
Wildfowl Wlk ST5 ..... 85 E2
Wildhay La DE6 ..... 80 B4
Wilding Rd ST6 ..... 42 B3
Wildtree Ave WV10 ..... 241 D1
Wildwood Dr ST17 ..... 175 F4
Wildwood Lawns ST17 ..... 175 E4
Wileman Pl ST4 ..... 72 C3
Wileman St ST4 ..... 72 C3
Wilfred Pl ST4 ..... 71 F4
Wilke's Rd ST18 ..... 154 C4
Wilkes Cl WS3 ..... 243 F2
Wilkes Croft DY3 ..... 271 E4
Wilkes Rd WV8 ..... 238 C2
Wilkin Rd WS8 ..... 228 B1
Wilkins Croft DE13 ..... 200 C1
Wilkinson Cl WS7 ..... 229 D4
Wilkinson St ST6 ..... 41 E1
Wilks St ST6 ..... 41 F2
Willatt Pl ST2 ..... 43 D1
Willcock Rd
  Branston DE14 ..... 185 D4
  Wolv WV2 ..... 266 C3
Willdale Gr ST1 ..... 57 F3
Willerby Fold WV10 ..... 240 C2
Willeton St ST2 ..... 58 A2
Willett Ave
  Brownhills WS7 ..... 228 C3
  Burntwood WS7 ..... 228 C3
Willey La ST20 ..... 171 E3
Willfield La ST6 ..... 43 E3
William Allitt Sch DE11 ..... 186 C4
William Ave
  Biddulph ST8 ..... 27 E4
  Meir ST3 ..... 90 B4
William Baxter Specl Sch
  WS12 ..... 210 A3
William Birch Rd ST2 ..... 58 A1
William Cl ST11 ..... 91 D4
William Clowes St ST6 ..... 56 C4
William Fiske Ct ST4 ..... 71 F2
William Hutson Jun Sch
  DE13 ..... 166 A4
William IV Rd DE13 ..... 201 D2
William MacGregor
  Prim Sch B77 ..... 250 B2
William Morris Ct WS15 ..... 178 B2
William Morris Gr WV11 ..... 209 F2
William Nadins Way
  DE11 ..... 186 C2
William Newton Cl
  DE65 ..... 148 A3
William Rd ST7 ..... 26 A1
William Ruston Rd ST6 ..... 42 B1
William Shrewsbury
  Prim Sch DE13 ..... 147 F1
William St
  Burton u T DE14 ..... 166 B3
  Congleton CW12 ..... 6 A2
  Fenton ST4 ..... 72 C3
William Terr ST6 ..... 42 A3
Williams Cl ST16 ..... 155 D2
Williams St ST16 ..... 155 F4
Williams Wlk WS15 ..... 103 E2
Williamson Ave
  Cannock WS12 ..... 211 E2
  Norton-in-t-M ST6 ..... 42 C3
Williamson St
  Tunstall ST6 ..... 41 E1
  Wolv WV3 ..... 266 A4
Willington Rd B79 ..... 250 A4
Williscroft Pl WS15 ..... 179 D3
Willmer Cres ST7 ..... 26 A3
Willmott Cl B75 ..... 258 B2
Willmott Rd B75 ..... 258 B2
Willoughby Cl ST19 ..... 207 F4
Willoughby Ct ST14 ..... 125 E4
Willoughby Rd B79 ..... 249 F4
Willoughby St ST6 ..... 41 E4
Willow Ave WS7 ..... 229 E3
Willow Bank WV3 ..... 255 E1
Willow Brook ST18 ..... 154 C1
Willow Cl
  Brewood WV9 ..... 224 A1
  Hagley DY9 ..... 281 F3
  Kidsgrove ST7 ..... 41 D4
  Newcastle-u-L ST5 ..... 40 B1
  Stafford ST17 ..... 175 F3
  Upper Tean ST10 ..... 92 B3
Willow Dale ST15 ..... 120 B2
Willow Dr Codsall WV8 ..... 239 D2
  Swadlincote DE11 ..... 186 C4
Willow Gr
  Essington WV11 ..... 242 A2
  Fenton ST3 ..... 72 C1
Willow La ST3 ..... 90 A2
Willow Pl Biddulph ST8 ..... 17 D1
  Burton u T DE15 ..... 185 F4
Willow Rd
  Barton-u-N DE13 ..... 183 E1
  Kinver DY7 ..... 278 A2
  Stone ST15 ..... 120 A4
  Wolv WV8 ..... 265 E4
Willow Row ST3 ..... 283 B4
Willow Way WS11 ..... 91 D4
Willow Wlk WS12 ..... 209 E4
Willowbank B78 ..... 250 A1
Willowcroft ST20 ..... 151 F4
Willowdale Ave ST4 ..... 72 B3
Willowdale Grange WV6 ..... 255 F3
Willowherb Cl WS11 ..... 210 B1
Willowmoor ST17 ..... 174 C2
Willowood Gr ST3 ..... 74 B1
Willows Dr ST3 ..... 90 A2
Willows Prim Sch WS13 ..... 214 A1

Willows The
  Burton u T DE14 ..... 166 B1
  Cannock WS11 ..... 209 E1
  Leek ST13 ..... 30 B3
  Rugeley WS15 ..... 197 D3
  Stone ST15 ..... 120 A3
  Swynnerton ST15 ..... 118 C3
  Wombourne WV5 ..... 269 F3
Willowsmere Dr WS14 ..... 231 F4
Willowtree Cl WS13 ..... 214 A1
Willridding La DE6 ..... 80 B4
Wilmcote Dr B75 ..... 258 B2
Wilmore Ct ST18 ..... 137 E1
Wilmorehill La ST18 ..... 137 E1
Wilmot Cl ST5 ..... 55 F2
Wilmot Dr ST5 ..... 55 F2
Wilmot St ST3 ..... 73 E3
Wilmott Cl WS13 ..... 231 D4
Wilncote High Sch
  B77 ..... 261 F3
Wilncote Jun Sch
  B77 ..... 261 F4
Wilncote L Ctr B77 ..... 261 F3
Wilncote St WS3 ..... 243 F3
Wilncote Sta B77 ..... 261 E4
Wilner's View WS3 ..... 243 F3
Wilson Gr ST4 ..... 210 B3
Wilson Rd ST4 ..... 71 F1
Wilson St
  Chell Heath ST6 ..... 42 A1
  Newcastle-u-L ST5 ..... 284 B3
Wilson Way ST6 ..... 41 E3
Wiltell Rd WS14 ..... 231 D3
Wilton Ave ST9 ..... 59 F2
Wilton Cl DY3 ..... 271 F4
Wilton St ST5 ..... 284 A4
Wiltshire Gr ST5 ..... 71 E2
Wimberry Dr ST5 ..... 40 B1
Wimblebury Rd WS12 ..... 210 C1
Wimborne Ave ST3 ..... 88 C4
Wimhurst Meadow
  WV10 ..... 240 C2
Winceby Rd WV6 ..... 254 C2
Winchcombe Cl DY1 ..... 271 F2
Winchcombe Dr DE15 ..... 167 D1
Winchester Ave ST2 ..... 58 B1
Winchester Cl
  Armitage WS15 ..... 198 A2
  Lichfield WS13 ..... 214 B2
Winchester Ct ST17 ..... 175 E3
Winchester Dr
  Burton u T ST14 ..... 185 E4
  Newcastle-u-L ST5 ..... 70 C2
Winchester Rd
  Cannock WS11 ..... 210 A2
  Wolv WV10 ..... 240 B2
Wincote Dr WV6 ..... 255 E2
Wincote La ST21 ..... 133 E2
Windermere Dr
  Aldridge B74 ..... 256 C2
  Kingswinford DY6 ..... 275 E3
Windermere Pl WS11 ..... 209 F1
Windermere Rd
  Newcastle-u-L ST5 ..... 71 D2
  Wolv WV6 ..... 255 E4
Windermere St ST1 ..... 282 A4
Windermere Way ST10 ..... 76 C2
Windings The WS13 ..... 214 A1
Windmill Ave ST7 ..... 41 D4
Windmill Bank
  Longdon WS15 ..... 212 A3
  Wombourne WV5 ..... 270 A4
Windmill Cl
  Farewell WS13 ..... 213 F1
  Stone ST15 ..... 89 F2
  Tamworth B79 ..... 250 A4
Windmill Cres WV3 ..... 255 D1
Windmill Dr ST14 ..... 127 F2
Windmill Gr DY6 ..... 275 D4
Windmill Hill ST5 ..... 89 F2
Windmill La
  Ecclesall ST21 ..... 116 A2
  Lichfield WS13 ..... 214 A1
  Longdon WS15 ..... 212 A2
  Snelston DE6 ..... 81 F1
  Wolv WV3, WV7 ..... 255 D1
Windmill St
  Hanley ST1 ..... 282 C3
  Sedgley DY3 ..... 271 E3
Windmill View ST9 ..... 59 E2
Windmillhill La WS14 ..... 232 C3
Windrow The WV6 ..... 254 B2
Windrush Cl ST4 ..... 88 B3
Windrush Rd WS11 ..... 209 F3
Windsmoor St ST4 ..... 72 A3
Windsor Ave
  Longton ST3 ..... 283 D2
  Wolv WV4 ..... 265 F3
Windsor Cl
  Burntwood WS7 ..... 211 F1
  Sedgley DY5 ..... 271 D1
  Stone ST15 ..... 119 F3
  Tamworth B79 ..... 250 B4
Windsor Cres DY7 ..... 277 F2
Windsor Dr
  Burton u T DE15 ..... 166 C1
  Leek ST13 ..... 31 D4
  Market Drayton TF9 ..... 97 C1
Windsor Gdns
  Codsall WV8 ..... 238 C2
  Wolv WV4 ..... 265 D4
Windsor Gr
  Brownhills WS4 ..... 244 B1
  Kingswinford DY8 ..... 275 F1
Windsor Holloway DY7 ..... 278 B1
Windsor Ind Est DE14 ..... 166 C2
Windsor Park CE Mid Sch
  ST14 ..... 126 A4

Windsor Rd
  Albrighton WV7 ..... 237 D3
  Cheslyn Hay WS11 ..... 226 C2
  Pattingham WV6 ..... 253 F1
  Stafford ST17 ..... 175 D4
  Stourbridge DY8 ..... 279 F2
  Trentham ST4 ..... 72 A1
  Uttoxeter ST14 ..... 111 D1
  Wolv WV4 ..... 266 C3
  Wombourne WV5 ..... 269 F3
Windsor St ST5 ..... 284 C3
Windy Arbour ST10 ..... 76 C2
Windycote La ST9 ..... 60 A1
Windyridge SK17 ..... 13 D3
Winford Ave DY6 ..... 275 F2
Wingate Wlk ST3 ..... 88 C3
Winghay Cl ST5 ..... 56 B4
Winghay Pl ST6 ..... 42 A3
Winghay Rd ST7 ..... 26 B2
Winghouse La ST12 ..... 103 F4
Wingrove Ave [4] ST3 ..... 73 E1
Winifred Gdns ST3 ..... 88 C4
Winifred St ST1 ..... 282 A4
Winnipeg Cl ST4 ..... 88 A4
Winpenny Rd ST5 ..... 55 F4
Winscar Croft DY3 ..... 271 E2
Winsford Ave ST3 ..... 73 F1
Winsford Cres ST17 ..... 175 F3
Winshill Inf Sch DE15 ..... 167 D3
Winslow Dr WV6 ..... 255 F2
Winslow Gn ST2 ..... 58 B1
Winsor Ave WS12 ..... 210 A3
Winstanley Pl WS15 ..... 178 B1
Winster Gn DE11 ..... 186 C3
Winston Pl ST2 ..... 58 A2
Winston Rd
  Cookley DY11 ..... 280 A3
  Swindon DY3 ..... 269 F1
Winston Terr ST5 ..... 56 B3
Winter Cl WS3 ..... 214 B1
Winterbourne Gr ST3 ..... 73 F2
Wintercroft La DE6 ..... 51 F1
Winterfield La ST3 ..... 74 A4
Winterley Gdns DY3 ..... 271 F3
Winterside Cl ST5 ..... 40 B1
Winton Sq ST4 ..... 72 A4
Wintonfield St ST4 ..... 72 B4
Wiscombe Ave ST19 ..... 193 F4
Wise St ST3 ..... 283 C1
Wissage Ct WS13 ..... 231 E4
Wissage La WS13 ..... 214 B1
Wissage Rd WS13 ..... 231 E4
Wistmans Cl DY1 ..... 271 F1
Wistwood Hayes WV10 ..... 240 C2
Witchford Cres ST3 ..... 88 C4
Witham Way ST6 ..... 16 C1
Withern Way ST2 ..... 58 A1
Withers Rd WV8 ..... 239 D2
Withies Rd ST4 ..... 71 F2
Within La ST18 ..... 137 E1
Withington Rd ST6 ..... 42 A3
Withnell Gn ST6 ..... 42 A3
Withymere La WV5 ..... 270 B4
Withystakes Rd ST9 ..... 59 E2
Withywood Cl WV12 ..... 242 B1
Witney Cl ST4 ..... 249 F4
Witney Gr WV10 ..... 240 A2
Witney Rd ST16, ST18 ..... 156 B1
Witney Wlk ST3 ..... 88 C3
Witton Rd WV4 ..... 266 A3
Witton St DY8 ..... 279 F2
Wobaston Rd
  Codsall WV9 ..... 239 F2
  Wolv WV9 ..... 240 A2
Woburn B77 ..... 250 B2
Woburn Cl ST4 ..... 88 B3
Wodehouse Cl WV5 ..... 269 F3
Wodehouse La
  Himley WV5, DY3 ..... 270 B4
  Wombourne WV5, DY3 ..... 270 B4
Woden Cl WV5 ..... 269 F4
Wogan St ST16 ..... 155 F3
Wold The WV5 ..... 267 E4
Wolfe St ST4 ..... 72 A3
Wolfscote Dale DE11 ..... 186 C1
Wolgarston High Sch
  ST19 ..... 208 A4
Wolgarston Way ST19 ..... 207 F4
Wollaston Ct DY8 ..... 279 E3
Wollaston Rd
  Brierley Hill DY8 ..... 279 F4
  Kinver DY7 ..... 279 E4
Wolmer Rd WV11 ..... 242 A1
Wolmore La WV5 ..... 263 D1
Wolseley B77 ..... 250 C2
Wolseley Ct ST17 ..... 177 F4
Wolseley Rd
  Newcastle-u-L ST5 ..... 56 A3
  Rugeley WS15 ..... 178 C2
  Rugeley,
    Sand & Gravel Quarry
    WS15 ..... 177 F1
  Stafford ST16 ..... 156 B2
  Stoke-on-T ST4 ..... 71 F2
Wolsey Rd WS13 ..... 213 F1
Wolstanton High Sch
  ST5 ..... 56 B2
Wolstanton Ret Pk ST5 ..... 56 C2
Wolstern Rd ST3 ..... 73 E3
Wolverhampton,
  Dudley & District
  Inst for the Blind The
  WV4 ..... 266 B2
Wolverhampton Girls
  High Sch WV6 ..... 255 F2
Wolverhampton
  Gram Sch WV3 ..... 255 F1

Wolverhampton Rd WS3
  Brownhills WS3 ..... 243 F2
  Cheslyn Hay WS6 ..... 226 B1
Cheslyn Hay, Wedge's Mills
  WS11 ..... 226 A4
  Codsall WV8 ..... 239 D2
  Cookley DY10 ..... 280 A2
  Essington WV11 ..... 242 A2
  Kidderminster DY10 ..... 280 A2
  Kingswinford DY6 ..... 270 B1
  Pattingham WV6 ..... 253 F2
  Penkridge ST19 ..... 207 F4
  Sedgley DY3 ..... 266 B1
  Stafford ST17 ..... 155 F1
  Walsall WS3 ..... 243 D1
Wolverhampton Rd E
  WV4 ..... 266 B3
Wolverhamton Rd
  WS11 ..... 226 A4
Wolverley Ave
  Stourbridge DY8 ..... 279 E3
  Wolv WV4 ..... 265 E3
Wolverley Ct WV7 ..... 237 D3
Wolverley Rd DY10 ..... 280 A1
Wolverson Rd WS9 ..... 245 D2
Wombourne Cl DY3 ..... 271 F1
Wombourne Ent Pk DY3 ..... 269 E2
Wombourne L Ctr WV5 ..... 269 F4
Wombourne Pk WV5 ..... 269 F2
Wombourne Rd
  Swindon DY3 ..... 269 F2
  Wombourne DY3 ..... 269 F2
Wombrook Dale WV5 ..... 269 E3
Wood Ave Brewood WV9 ..... 224 A2
  Kingsley ST10 ..... 61 E1
  Sedgley DY3 ..... 271 E2
Wood Bank La ST19 ..... 193 D1
Wood Bank Rd WV3 ..... 265 D4
Wood Cres Stafford ST16 ..... 155 D3
  Stone ST15 ..... 119 F3
Wood Ct DE14 ..... 166 B1
Wood Eaton Rd ST20 ..... 190 A4
Wood End Fst Sch CV9 ..... 262 B1
Wood End La
  Alrewas WS13 ..... 215 D3
  King's Bromley WS13 ..... 214 A4
Wood End Rd WV11 ..... 241 E1
Wood End Way WS9 ..... 245 D1
Wood Hayes Rd WV11 ..... 241 E1
Wood Hill Dr WV5 ..... 269 F3
Wood La Aldridge B74 ..... 256 C1
  Brownhills WS3 ..... 243 F2
  Cannock WS12 ..... 210 B2
  Cheslyn Hay WS11 ..... 225 F3
  Hanbury DE13 ..... 144 C2
  Kingstone ST14 ..... 124 B1
  Shenstone WS14 ..... 246 A1
  Stone ST15 ..... 119 F3
  Swadlincote DE11 ..... 186 C4
  Uttoxeter ST14 ..... 126 C3
  Wheaton Aston ST19 ..... 206 B2
  Wolv WV10 ..... 240 B1
  Yoxall DE13 ..... 182 A3
Wood Lane Prim Sch
  ST7 ..... 40 A1
Wood Pl ST3 ..... 74 A1
Wood Rd Codsall WV8 ..... 238 C2
  Longsdon ST13 ..... 45 D4
  Sedgley DY3 ..... 271 E2
  Wolv WV6 ..... 255 E2
  Wombourne WV5 ..... 270 A4
Wood Ridings WS13 ..... 214 A1
Wood St Audley ST7 ..... 39 F2
  Burton u T DE14 ..... 166 B3
  Kingsbury CV9 ..... 262 B1
  Leek ST13 ..... 30 C3
  Longton ST3 ..... 283 C4
  Mow Cop ST7 ..... 26 B4
  Stourbridge DY8 ..... 279 E3
Wood Terr ST1 ..... 282 A1
Wood The ST3 ..... 74 B1
Wood View Audley ST7 ..... 40 A1
  Rugeley WS15 ..... 196 C3
Woodall St ST1 ..... 57 D2
Woodbank Rd DY3 ..... 271 E4
Woodbank St ST6 ..... 56 C4
Woodberry Ave ST4 ..... 71 F3
Woodberry Cl
  Stafford ST17 ..... 174 C2
  Stoke-on-T ST4 ..... 71 F3
Woodbridge Cl
  Brownhills WS4 ..... 244 B1
  Walsall WS3 ..... 243 D2
Woodbridge Rd ST5 ..... 71 D1
Woodcock Gdns WV10 ..... 241 D4
Woodcock La ST7 ..... 26 B3
Woodcock Rd WS15 ..... 178 B1
Woodcocks' Well CE
  Prim Sch ST7 ..... 26 B3
Woodcote Rd WV6 ..... 255 E2
Woodcote The ST17 ..... 175 E4
Woodcroft WV7 ..... 40 A1
Woodcroft Ave
  Leek ST13 ..... 30 B2
  Tamworth B79 ..... 250 A3
Woodcroft Fst Sch ST13 ..... 30 B2
Woodcroft Rd ST13 ..... 30 B2
Woodcross La WV14 ..... 266 C1
Woodcross St WV14 ..... 266 C1
Wooddisse La ST13 ..... 33 F1
Woodedge La ST14 ..... 143 F3
Woodend Pl WV6 ..... 255 D2
Woodend St ST4 ..... 72 C3
Woodfield Ave WV4 ..... 265 F3
Woodfield Cl WS11 ..... 227 F4

Woodfield Ct ST13 .... 31 D3
Woodfield Dr WS11 .... 227 F4
Woodfield Hts WV6 .... 255 E2
Woodfield Jun & Inf Schs
WV4 .... 265 F3
Woodfield Rd DY3 .... 271 E2
Woodfields Dr WS14 .... 231 F3
Woodfold Croft WS9 .... 256 A4
Woodford Cl WV9 .... 239 F1
Woodford Cres WS7 .... 229 D4
Woodford End WS11 .... 209 F2
Woodford La WV5 .... 269 E4
Woodford Way
  Cannock WS12 .... 210 B1
  Wombourne WV5 .... 269 E3
Woodgate Ave ST7 .... 25 D3
Woodgate St ST3 .... 74 A1
Woodhall Pl ST5 .... 54 C1
Woodhall Rd
  Kidsgrove ST7 .... 26 B2
  Wolv WV4 .... 265 F3
Woodhaven
  Brownhills WS4 .... 244 B1
  Cheslyn Hay WS11 .... 226 A3
Woodhead Rd
  Bagnall ST2 .... 58 B4
  Bucknall ST2 .... 58 B4
Woodhead Yd ST10 .... 76 C3
Woodheyes Lawns
  WS15 .... 178 B1
Woodhill Cl WV5 .... 269 F3
Woodhouse High Sch
  B77 .... 250 C2
Woodhouse Jun Sch
  ST3 .... 283 C5
Woodhouse La
  Albrighton WV7 .... 237 E2
  Biddulph ST6 .... 16 C1
  Buerton TF9 .... 82 A4
  Endon ST6 .... 42 C3
  Scropton DE65 .... 129 F4
  Tamworth B77 .... 251 D3
Woodhouse Mid Sch
  ST8 .... 16 C1
Woodhouse Rd WV6 .... 255 D2
Woodhouse Rd N WV6 .... 255 D2
Woodhouse Sports Ctr
  B77 .... 251 D2
Woodhouse St ST4 .... 72 A3
Woodhouses La WS7 .... 229 F3
Woodhouses Rd WS7 .... 230 A4
Woodhurst Cl B77 .... 250 C3
Woodingdean Cl 12 ST3 ...... 73 E3
Woodkirk Cl ST6 .... 42 A4
Woodland Ave
  Hagley DY8 .... 281 F3
  Newcastle-u-L ST5 .... 56 B3
  Norton-in-t-M ST6 .... 42 C2
  Wolv WV6 .... 255 D2
Woodland Cl
  Albrighton WV7 .... 237 D3
  Cannock WS12 .... 210 A4
Woodland Cres
  Brownhills WS3 .... 243 F4
  Wolv WV3 .... 265 E4
Woodland Ct WS14 .... 258 A4
Woodland Dr
  Cheslyn Hay WS11 .... 226 C2
  Foston DE6 .... 129 E2
Woodland Gr
  Chell Heath ST6 .... 42 A1
  Cookley DY10 .... 280 B2
  Sedgley DY3 .... 271 D2
Woodland Hills CW3 .... 68 C4
Woodland Rd
  Swadlincote DE15 .... 186 A2
  Tamworth B77 .... 251 D2
  Wolv WV3 .... 265 E4
Woodland St
  Biddulph ST8 .... 27 E3
  Tunstall ST6 .... 41 F2

Woodland View DY3 .... 269 E2
Woodland Views ST14 ...... 127 F1
Woodland Way
  Burntwood WS7 .... 229 D3
  Polesworth B78 .... 262 C4
Woodland Wlk WS12 .... 209 E2
Woodlands Ave
  Cheddleton ST13 .... 45 D1
  Kidsgrove ST7 .... 25 E1
  Stone ST15 .... 119 F4
Woodlands Cl
  Stafford ST16 .... 155 E4
  Stone ST15 .... 119 F4
Woodlands Cotts WV4 .... 265 F2
Woodlands Dr WV9 .... 224 A2
Woodlands Gr ST3 .... 90 A2
Woodlands La WS11 .... 225 D4
Woodlands Paddock
  WV4 .... 265 F2
Woodlands Prim Sch
  B77 .... 250 C2
Woodlands Rd
  Cookley DY10 .... 280 A2
  Stafford ST16 .... 155 D4
  Stoke-on-T ST4 .... 71 F2
  Wombourne WV5 .... 270 A3
Woodlands The WS13 ...... 231 E4
Woodlands Way WS15 ...... 198 B2
Woodlawn Gr DY6 .... 275 E3
Woodleighton Gr ST14 .... 126 B3
Woodleighton Rd ST14 .... 126 B3
Woodleyes Cres ST17 ...... 175 F4
Woodman La WS11 .... 226 C2
Woodman St ST2 .... 43 D1
Woodmill La WS15 .... 161 D4
Woodpark La ST3 .... 89 E4
Woodpecker View TF9 ...... 99 E2
Woodpecker Way WS11 .... 210 B2
Woodridge Cl TF10 .... 168 A2
Woodroffe's Cliff ST14 .... 143 E3
Woodrow Way TF9 .... 100 B3
Woodruff Cl ST8 .... 27 D1
Woods Croft WS13 .... 214 A1
Woods La DE15 .... 167 D1
Woodseaves CE Prim Sch
  ST20 .... 151 F4
Woodsetton Specl Sch
  DY3 .... 271 F3
Woodshot Ave WS15 ...... 198 B2
Woodshutt's St ST7 .... 25 F1
Woodside
  Chapel Chorlton ST5 .... 85 E2
  Lawton-gate ST7 .... 25 F2
  Madeley CW3 .... 68 C4
  Sutton Coldfield B74 ...... 257 F1
Woodside Ave
  Endon ST6 .... 43 D3
  Kidsgrove ST7 .... 26 A1
Woodside Cl ST18 .... 177 E4
Woodside Cres ST5 .... 71 E1
Woodside Dr
  Blythe Bridge ST3 .... 90 A2
  Little Aston B74 .... 257 E3
Woodside Gr WV8 .... 239 D1
Woodside La ST13 .... 30 B1
Woodside Pl
  Cannock WS11 .... 209 F3
  Norton-in-t-M ST2 .... 43 D1
Woodside Villas ST3 ...... 283 D4
Woodside Way WS9 .... 256 A3
Woodsorrel Rd DY1 .... 271 F2
Woodstile Cl B75 .... 258 B2
Woodstock Cl
  Kingswinford DY8 .... 275 D1
  Newcastle-u-L ST5 .... 56 B2
Woodstock Dr
  Huntington WS12 .... 209 E4
  Kingswinford DY8 .... 275 E1
  Sutton Coldfield B74 ...... 257 E2
Woodstock Rd
  Kidsgrove ST6 .... 41 D4
  Stafford ST16 .... 156 B1
Woodstock St ST6 .... 41 E4
Woodstone Ave ST9 .... 43 F3
Woodtherne Cl ST19 ...... 207 F4

Woodthorne Cl
  Rugeley WS15 .... 178 B1
  Sedgley DY1 .... 271 E1
Woodthorne Jun &
  Inf Schs WV6 .... 255 D2
Woodthorne Rd WV6 ...... 255 D3
Woodthorne Rd S WV6 .... 255 D3
Woodthorne Wlk DY6 ...... 275 F4
Woodvale Cres ST9 .... 43 F4
Woodview Rd DE11 .... 186 C3
Woodville Gdns DY3 ...... 266 C1
Woodville Pl ST3 .... 74 A1
Woodville Rd ST3 .... 74 A1
Woodville Terr ST3 .... 74 A1
Woodward St ST1 .... 57 E3
Woody Bank WS6 .... 226 C1
Woodyard Dr B79 .... 217 E3
Woodyard La DE65 .... 129 F3
Woolands Rise DE6 .... 144 A4
Woolliscroft Ave ST5 .... 56 B2
Woolliscroft Rd ST2 .... 58 A2
Woolrich St ST6 .... 56 C4
Woolston Ave CW12 .... 6 A1
Woore Cty Prim Sch
  CW3 .... 67 D1
Woosnam Cl DE14 .... 185 D3
Wootton Cl WS11 .... 210 A1
Wootton Dr ST16 .... 155 D4
Wootton La ST10 .... 78 C2
Wootton Rd WV3 .... 265 E4
Woottons St WS11 .... 209 F1
Worcester Cl
  Cannock WS11 .... 226 C4
  Kidsgrove ST7 .... 40 B4
  Lichfield WS13 .... 214 B2
  Sutton Coldfield B75 ...... 258 B2
Worcester Ct WV3 .... 266 A3
Worcester Gr WV6 .... 254 B2
Worcester La B75 .... 258 B2
Worcester Pl ST2 .... 58 B1
Worcester Rd
  Burton u T DE15 .... 185 F3
  Hagley DY9 .... 281 F2
  Whittington WS14 .... 232 B2
Worcester St DY8 .... 279 F2
Wordsley Green Sh Ctr
  DY8 .... 275 E1
Wordsley Hospl DY6 ...... 275 F2
Wordsworth Ave
  Stafford ST17 .... 174 B4
  Tamworth B79 .... 250 A3
  Wolv WV4 .... 266 C2
Wordsworth Cl
  Armitage WS15 .... 198 A2
  Burton u T DE14 .... 166 B3
  Cannock WS11 .... 209 E2
  Cheadle ST10 .... 76 B1
  Lichfield WS14 .... 231 D3
Wordsworth Dr TF9 .... 112 A4
Wordsworth Rd
  Burntwood WS7 .... 229 D4
  Sedgley DY3 .... 271 D3
Worfield Gdns WV3 .... 265 F3
Works Dr CW3 .... 69 D4
Worsley Dr CW12 .... 6 A1
Worston La
  Chebsey ST15, ST18 ...... 135 D3
  Seighford ST15, ST18 .... 135 D3
Worth Cl ST3 .... 73 E2
Worthing Pl ST3 .... 283 B3
Worthington Rd WS13 .... 215 B3
Worthington Way DE14 .. 166 C2
Wragby Cl WV9 .... 240 A2
Wragg's La ST8 .... 17 D1
Wrekin Ave TF10 .... 168 C1
Wrekin Dr
  Wolv, Bradmore WV3 ...... 265 F4
  Wolv, Wergs WV6 .... 255 D3
Wrekin La WV6 .... 255 D3
Wrekin View
  Brownhills WS8 .... 245 D3
  Huntington WS12 .... 209 E4
Wrekin View Rd DY3 ...... 271 E4
Wren Ave WV6 .... 254 B2

Wren Cl ST8 .... 27 F4
Wren View Ashley TF9 ...... 99 E2
  Longton ST3 .... 283 D2
Wrenbury Cl ST5 .... 40 B1
Wrenbury Cres ST2 .... 58 A1
Wrenswood ST17 .... 175 E3
Wrexham Cl ST6 .... 16 B1
Wright Ave ST5 .... 55 F4
Wright St
  Kidsgrove ST7 .... 25 E1
  Stafford ST16 .... 155 F3
Wright's Ave WS11 .... 209 F3
Wrighton Cl ST2 .... 57 F1
Wrighton Dr DY5 .... 271 E1
Wrinehill Rd CW2 .... 52 B4
Wrottesley Park Rd
  WV6 .... 254 B3
Wrottesley Rd WV6 .... 255 D3
Wrottesley Rd W
  Perton WV6 .... 254 C3
  Wolv WV6 .... 255 D3
Wroxham Way ST5 .... 71 D1
Wulfad Ct ST15 .... 120 B4
Wulfric Cl ST19 .... 208 A4
Wulfrun Coll WV6 .... 255 F2
Wulfruna Gdns WV3 ...... 255 F1
Wulstan Dr ST5 .... 56 B2
Wulstan Rd ST6 .... 57 D3
Wyatt St ST6 .... 41 E4
Wych Elm Rd WS8 .... 244 C3
Wychall Dr WV10 .... 240 C2
Wychbold Cl WV12 .... 242 B1
Wychbold Way WV12 .... 242 B1
Wychbury Rd WV3 .... 265 E4
Wycherwood Gdns
  ST17 .... 175 E3
Wycliffe Rd ST6 .... 56 C4
Wye Cl
  Cheadle ST10 .... 76 C1
  Perton WV6 .... 254 C2
Wye Dale DE11 .... 186 C1
Wye Rd
  Newcastle-u-L ST5 .... 71 D3
  Walsall WS3 .... 243 F1
Wyggeston St DE13 ...... 166 B3
Wykeham Gr WV6 .... 254 B2
Wymondley Gr ST4 .... 88 A3
Wynbank Cl ST7 .... 54 C4
Wynchcombe Ave WV4 .. 265 E2
Wynd The DY3 .... 266 B1
Wyndham Cres DE15 ...... 167 E2
Wyndham Rd ST3 .... 88 C4
Wynford Pl ST2 .... 58 A1
Wynn Rd WV4 .... 265 F3
Wynne Cres WV3 .... 265 E2
Wynstay Ave ST9 .... 59 D2
Wynstay Ct ST5 .... 71 E1
Wynyates B79 .... 249 F3
Wyre Cl WS9 .... 244 C2
Wyre Rd DY8 .... 279 F4
Wyrley Brook Pk WS11 .. 226 B3
Wyrley Cl
  Brownhills WS8 .... 228 C2
  Lichfield WS13 .... 231 D3
Wyrley La WS3 .... 243 F4
Wyrley Rd B75 .... 258 B1
Wyvern B77 .... 250 C2
Wyvern Gr WS12 .... 210 A3
Wyvis Cl WV6 .... 255 F1

Yale St ST6 .... 56 C4
Yardley Pl ST3 .... 88 C3
Yardley St ST6 .... 42 C3
Yardley Wlk ST3 .... 88 C3
Yarlet Croft ST16 .... 155 C3
Yarlet Hall Prep Sch
  ST18 .... 136 B4
Yarlet La ST18 .... 136 B3
Yarmouth Wlk ST3 .... 283 D5
Yarnbrook Gr ST6 .... 42 B2
Yarner Cl DY1 .... 271 F1
Yarnfield Cl ST3 .... 74 A1
Yarnfield La Stone ST15 .. 119 D4
  Swynnerton ST15 .... 118 C3
Yarrow Cl WS3 .... 244 A3

Yateley Cl ST2 .... 58 A1
Yates Cft B74 .... 257 F3
Yates St ST1 .... 282 A2
Yaxley Ct ST5 .... 71 D1
Yaxley Pl ST3 .... 88 C3
Yeadon Gdns WV3 .... 265 E4
Yeaman St ST4 .... 72 A3
Yeatsall Rd WS15 .... 160 C3
Yeldham Pl ST3 .... 88 C3
Yelt La DE6 .... 127 E4
Yelverton Ave ST17 ...... 175 E4
Yelverton Cl WS3 .... 243 D2
Yenton Cl B78 .... 250 A1
Yeoman Ind Est DE14 .... 166 C3
Yeoman Way WS15 .... 198 A2
Yeovil Pl ST3 .... 88 C3
Yeovilton B79 .... 250 B4
Yerley Hill DE6 .... 66 B3
Yew Cl WS15 .... 198 A2
Yew Pl ST5 .... 55 E4
Yew Tree Ave
  Lichfield WS14 .... 231 F4
  Longton ST3 .... 72 C1
Yew Tree Cl
  Norton Canes WS11 ...... 228 A3
  Norton-in-t-M ST2 .... 43 E1
  Seighford ST18 .... 154 C1
Yew Tree Ct ST17 .... 174 C2
Yew Tree Dr ST19 .... 205 E3
Yew Tree Gdns WV8 ...... 239 D2
Yew Tree La
  Astbury CW12 .... 15 E2
  Wolv WV6 .... 255 D3
Yew Tree Pl WS3 .... 243 E2
Yew Tree Rd
  Brownhills WS4 .... 244 B1
  Pattingham WV6 .... 253 E1
  Rugeley WS15 .... 196 C3
  Swadlincote DE12 .... 186 C4
Yew Tree Terr ST7 .... 41 D4
Yewtree Cres DE15 .... 185 F4
York Ave
  Blythe Bridge ST11 .... 90 C1
  Wolv WV3 .... 255 F1
York Cl Biddulph ST6 .... 16 B1
  Forsbrook ST11 .... 91 D4
  Lichfield WS13 .... 214 B2
York Cres
  Stourbridge DY8 .... 279 E4
  Wolv WV3 .... 255 F1
York Gdns WV3 .... 255 F1
York Pl ST5 .... 284 B3
York Rd
  Cannock WS11 .... 226 C4
  Meir ST3 .... 74 A2
  Stafford ST17 .... 175 D4
  Wolv WV3 .... 265 D4
York St
  Burton u T DE14 .... 166 B2
  Hanley ST1 .... 282 B3
  Leek ST13 .... 30 C3
  Newcastle-u-L ST5 .... 284 B3
  Stone ST15 .... 105 D1
Yorkdale Cl ST19 .... 271 E2
Yorksand Rd B78 .... 260 C4
Youlgreave Ave ST2 .... 58 A1
Youlton Pl ST2 .... 58 A1
Young Ave ST16 .... 155 E3
Young St Cheadle ST10 .... 76 C2
  Chell Heath ST6 .... 41 F3
Younger St ST4 .... 72 B3
Yoxall Ave ST4 .... 71 F4
Yoxall Rd
  King's Bromley DE13 ...... 199 E4
  Newborough DE13 .... 162 C4

Zamenhof Gr ST6 .... 42 B1
Zennor Gr ST2 .... 58 A1
Zetland Pl ST3 .... 88 C3
Zetland Wlk ST3 .... 88 C3
Zion Cl WS6 .... 226 B2
Zion St ST6 .... 57 D4
Zoar St DY3 .... 271 E2
Zodiac Dr ST6 .... 41 F3
Zouche Cl DY8 .... 279 F4

The Street Atlases are available from all good bookshops or by mail order direct from the publisher. Orders can be made in the following ways.

By phone Ring our special Credit Card Hotline on **01933 443863** during office hours (9am to 5pm) or leave a message on the answering machine, quoting your full credit card number plus expiry date and your full name and address.

By post or fax Fill out the order form below (you may photocopy it) and post it to: **Philip's Direct, 27 Sanders Road, Wellingborough, Northants NN8 4NL** or fax it to: **01933 443849.** Before placing an order by post, by fax or on the answering machine, please telephone to check availability and prices.

STREET ATLASES ORDER FORM

COLOUR LOCAL ATLASES	PAPERBACK	Quantity @ £3.50 each	£ Total
CANNOCK, LICHFIELD, RUGELEY		☐ 0 540 07625 2 ➤	
DERBY AND BELPER		☐ 0 540 07608 2 ➤	
NORTHWICH, WINSFORD, MIDDLEWICH		☐ 0 540 07589 2 ➤	
PEAK DISTRICT TOWNS		☐ 0 540 07609 0 ➤	
STAFFORD, STONE, UTTOXETER		☐ 0 540 07626 0 ➤	
WARRINGTON, WIDNES, RUNCORN		☐ 0 540 07588 4 ➤	

COLOUR REGIONAL ATLASES				
	HARDBACK	SPIRAL	POCKET	
	Quantity @ £10.99 each	Quantity @ £8.99 each	Quantity @ £4.99 each	£ Total
MERSEYSIDE	☐ 0 540 06480 7	☐ 0 540 06481 5	☐ 0 540 06482 3 ➤	
	Quantity @ £12.99 each	Quantity @ £8.99 each	Quantity @ £5.99 each	£ Total
BERKSHIRE	☐ 0 540 06170 0	☐ 0 540 06172 7	☐ 0 540 06173 5 ➤	
	Quantity @ £12.99 each	Quantity @ £9.99 each	Quantity @ £4.99 each	£ Total
DURHAM	☐ 0 540 06365 7	☐ 0 540 06366 5	☐ 0 540 06367 3 ➤	
	Quantity @ £12.99 each	Quantity @ £9.99 each	Quantity @ £5.50 each	£ Total
GREATER MANCHESTER	☐ 0 540 06485 8	☐ 0 540 06486 6	☐ 0 540 06487 4 ➤	
TYNE AND WEAR	☐ 0 540 06370 3	☐ 0 540 06371 1	☐ 0 540 06372 X ➤	
	Quantity @ £12.99 each	Quantity @ £9.99 each	Quantity @ £5.99 each	£ Total
BIRMINGHAM & WEST MIDLANDS	☐ 0 540 07603 1	☐ 0 540 07604 X	☐ 0 540 07605 8 ➤	
BUCKINGHAMSHIRE	☐ 0 540 07466 7	☐ 0 540 07467 5	☐ 0 540 07468 3 ➤	
CHESHIRE	☐ 0 540 07507 8	☐ 0 540 07508 6	☐ 0 540 07509 4 ➤	
DERBYSHIRE	☐ 0 540 07531 0	☐ 0 540 07532 9	☐ 0 540 07533 7 ➤	
EDINBURGH & East Central Scotland	☐ 0 540 07653 8	☐ 0 540 07654 6	☐ 0 540 07656 2 ➤	
NORTH ESSEX	☐ 0 540 07289 3	☐ 0 540 07290 7	☐ 0 540 07292 3 ➤	
SOUTH ESSEX	☐ 0 540 07294 X	☐ 0 540 07295 8	☐ 0 540 07297 4 ➤	
GLASGOW & West Central Scotland	☐ 0 540 07648 1	☐ 0 540 07649 X	☐ 0 540 07651 1 ➤	
NORTH HAMPSHIRE	☐ 0 540 07471 3	☐ 0 540 07472 1	☐ 0 540 07473 X ➤	

STREET ATLASES
ORDER FORM

COLOUR REGIONAL ATLASES

	HARDBACK	SPIRAL	POCKET	
	Quantity @ £12.99 each	Quantity @ £9.99 each	Quantity @ £5.99 each	£ Total
SOUTH HAMPSHIRE	☐ 0 540 07476 4	☐ 0 540 07477 2	☐ 0 540 07478 0	➤
HERTFORDSHIRE	☐ 0 540 06174 3	☐ 0 540 06175 1	☐ 0 540 06176 X	➤
EAST KENT	☐ 0 540 07483 7	☐ 0 540 07276 1	☐ 0 540 07287 7	➤
WEST KENT	☐ 0 540 07366 0	☐ 0 540 07367 9	☐ 0 540 07369 5	➤
NORTHAMPTONSHIRE	☐ 0 540 07745 3	☐ 0 540 07746 1	☐ 0 540 07748 8	➤
OXFORDSHIRE	☐ 0 540 07512 4	☐ 0 540 07513 2	☐ 0 540 07514 0	➤
SURREY	☐ 0 540 07794 1	☐ 0 540 07795 X	☐ 0 540 07796 8	➤
EAST SUSSEX	☐ 0 540 07306 7	☐ 0 540 07307 5	☐ 0 540 07312 1	➤
WEST SUSSEX	☐ 0 540 07319 9	☐ 0 540 07323 7	☐ 0 540 07327 X	➤
WARWICKSHIRE	☐ 0 540 07560 4	☐ 0 540 07561 2	☐ 0 540 07562 0	➤
SOUTH YORKSHIRE	—	☐ 0 540 07667 8	☐ 0 540 07669 4	➤
WEST YORKSHIRE	☐ 0 540 07671 6	☐ 0 540 07672 4	☐ 0 540 07674 0	➤
	Quantity @ £14.99 each	Quantity @ £9.99 each	Quantity @ £5.99 each	£ Total
LANCASHIRE	☐ 0 540 06440 8	☐ 0 540 06441 6	☐ 0 540 06443 2	➤
NOTTINGHAMSHIRE	☐ 0 540 07541 8	☐ 0 540 07542 6	☐ 0 540 07543 4	➤
	Quantity @ £14.99 each	Quantity @ £10.99 each	Quantity @ £5.99 each	£ Total
STAFFORDSHIRE	☐ 0 540 07549 3	☐ 0 540 07550 7	☐ 0 540 07551 5	➤

BLACK AND WHITE REGIONAL ATLASES

	HARDBACK	SOFTBACK	POCKET	
	Quantity @ £11.99 each	Quantity @ £8.99 each	Quantity @ £3.99 each	£ Total
BRISTOL & AVON	☐ 0 540 06140 9	☐ 0 540 06141 7	☐ 0 540 06142 5	➤
	Quantity @ £12.99 each	Quantity @ £9.99 each	Quantity @ £4.99 each	£ Total
CARDIFF, SWANSEA & GLAMORGAN	☐ 0 540 06186 7	☐ 0 540 06187 5	☐ 0 540 06207 3	➤

Name..

Address..

....

....

....

..........................Postcode.......................

◆ **Add £2 postage and packing per order**

◆ All available titles will normally be dispatched within 5 working days of receipt of order but please allow up to 28 days for delivery

☐ Please tick this box if you do not wish your name to be used by other carefully selected organisations that may wish to send you information about other products and services

Registered Office: 2-4 Heron Quays, London E14 4JP
Registered in England number: 3597451

Total price of order £ [ ]

(including postage and packing at £2 per order)

I enclose a cheque/postal order, for £ [ ]

made payable to *Octopus Publishing Group Ltd,*

or please debit my ☐ Mastercard ☐ American Express

☐ Visa   account by £ [ ]

Account no

☐☐☐☐ ☐☐☐☐ ☐☐☐☐ ☐☐☐☐

Expiry date ☐☐ ☐☐

Signature..

Post to: Philip's Direct, 27 Sanders Road, Wellingborough, Northants NN8 4NL